D1625785

C334101674

Wellington's Brigade Commanders

Wellington's Brigade Commanders

Peninsula and Waterloo

Ron McGuigan and Robert Burnham

Pen & Sword
MILITARY

First published in Great Britain in 2017 by
Pen & Sword Military
an imprint of
Pen & Sword Books Ltd
47 Church Street
Barnsley
South Yorkshire
S70 2AS

ISBN 978 1 47385 079 8

A CIP catalogue record for this book is available from the British Library

Typeset in Ehrhardt by
Mac Style Ltd, Bridlington, East Yorkshire
Printed and bound in the Malta by Gutenberg Press Ltd.

Pen & Sword Books Ltd incorporates the imprints of Pen & Sword
Archaeology, Atlas, Aviation, Battleground, Discovery, Family History,
History, Maritime, Military, Naval, Politics, Railways, Select, Transport,
True Crime, and Fiction, Frontline Books, Leo Cooper, Praetorian Press,
Seaforth Publishing and Wharncliffe.

For a complete list of Pen & Sword titles please contact
PEN & SWORD BOOKS LIMITED
47 Church Street, Barnsley, South Yorkshire, S70 2AS, England
E-mail: enquiries@pen-and-sword.co.uk
Website: www.pen-and-sword.co.uk

Contents

Acknowledgements	vii
Introduction	ix
Abbreviations	xiii

Acland, Wroth Palmer	1
Adam, Frederick William	4
Alten, Victor Baron	8
Anson, George	13
Anson, William	19
Anstruther, Robert	23
Aylmer, Matthew, 5th Baron Aylmer	29
Barnes, Edward	34
Bayly, Henry	40
Beresford, Lord George Thomas	43
Bernewitz, John de	46
Bock, George Baron	49
Bowes, Barnard Foord	54
Bradford, Thomas	57
Brisbane, Thomas	61
Brooke, William	67
Burne, Robert	69
Byng, John	74
Cameron, Alan	79
Campbell, Henry Frederick	84
Craufurd, James Catlin	87
de Grey, Hon. George	91
Dornberg, William de	94
Drieberg, George de	98
Drummond, George Duncan	100
Dunlop, James	102
Erskine, James	106
Fane, Henry	108
Ferguson, Ronald Craufurd	116
Grant, Colquhoun	120
Halkett, Colin	125
Hay, Andrew	130
Hinuber, Henry de	136
Hoghton, Daniel	140
Hulse, Richard	144
Inglis, William	147
Johnstone, George	151

Keane, John 153
Kemmis, James 157
Lambert, John 161
Langwerth, Ernest Baron 166
Le Marchant, John Gaspard 168
Lightburne, Stafford 172
Long, Robert Ballard 176
Low, Sigismund Baron 184
Lumley, Hon. William 187
Mackenzie, John Randoll 192
Mackenzie, Kenneth 196
Mackinnon, Henry 199
Maitland, Peregrine 203
Nightingall, Miles 207
O'Callaghan, Hon. Robert William 212
O'Loghlin, Terence O'Bryan 215
Pack, Denis 218
Peacocke, Warren Marmaduke 226
Ponsonby, Hon. William 231
Power, Manley 236
Pringle, William Henry 240
Rebow, Francis Slater 244
Robinson, Frederick Philipse 246
Ross, Robert 251
Skerrett, John Byne 257
Slade, John 261
Somerset, Lord Robert Edward Henry 267
Sontag, John 272
Stewart, Richard 276
Stopford, Hon. Edward 280
Vandeleur, John Ormsby 284
Vivian, Richard Hussey 293
Walker, George Townshend 300
Wheatley, William 308

Appendix 312
Bibliography 314

Acknowledgements

This book could not have been written without the encouragement and generous assistance of a number of people.

A thank you to both Dr Rory Muir and Howie Muir for suggesting the idea for the book. Dr Muir kindly provided his research on filling in the blanks of the names suppressed in Wellington's dispatches and correspondence as well as providing many of the unpublished letters of Henry Torrens, the Military Secretary to the Commander-in-Chief. Without this generous assistance, the book would be the poorer. A simple thank you is just not enough, Dr Muir. A further thank you to Howie Muir for providing a translation of a letter in French and also for readily answering any questions on different subjects concerning the generals, especially checking General Orders. We must also thank several individuals who were so helpful in our research, including Michael-Andreas Tänzer, the Director of the Arbeitskreis Hannoversche Militärgeschichte, who was a fount of knowledge on the King's German Legion; Gareth Glover, the foremost expert on British memoirs; Mark Thompson for information on General Robert Long; John Gill for helping locate and translate obscure German regimental histories; Andrew Bamford for his help in finding long out-of-print primary sources; and Jenn Scott, Secretary of the Stewart Society, Edinburgh. Hopefully we have not forgotten anyone!

Several people and institutions generously opened their collections to provide us with portraits of the generals. We must thank Tony Broughton, who provided many of the images in this book. Tony has been very helpful in writing all of our books over the years. We would also like to thank: the National Portrait Gallery of London; the National Portrait Gallery of Australia, Canberra; Lord Balniel and the Balcarres Heritage Trust who gave us permission to use the only known image of James Craufurd and the Van Reebeck Society who provided us with their copy of it; Sir Charles Keane Bart of Cappoquin House for allowing us to use the portrait of John Keane; Lucy Bamford for help in tracking down a portrait of Francis Rebow; and Peter Herrington of the Anne S.K. Brown Military Collection, Brown University Library. We are also indebted to several museums who also provided images: the Arbeitskreis Hannoversche Militärgeschichte, the Queen's Own Highlanders Museum, the Fusilier Museum, Colchester & Ipswich Museum, and the Staffordshire Regiment Museum.

We could not have written this book fifteen years ago, because too many of our sources were only available in specialized libraries. However, now there is Google Books and the London Gazette Online which have given us access to hundreds of rare books, official documents, and contemporary newspapers. Then there is the Napoleon Series, a website that has tens of thousands of articles, images, and maps. It has superb research on the British Army by many different authors, but we drew heavily on that of Andrew Bamford, Steve Brown, and Ray Foster.

A very special thank you to my wife Debbie McGuigan for her encouragement, patience and understanding, and to my children, Shannon and Ian, for their usual support. I too need to thank my wife, Denah Burnham, for maintaining her sense of humor and for listening patiently to the many anecdotes I told her about these generals. When I told her we had finished the draft, her first question was when were we starting on the next book? I think she may be worried I will not have enough to do in my retirement!

We close with a thank you to Rupert Harding, our publisher, who quickly gave approval to go ahead with the book.

Introduction

The Duke of Wellington is regarded as Great Britain's best general of the Napoleonic era. Numerous books have been written on his life, his battles and his campaigns. Books have also been written on his principal subordinates, well-known senior generals commanding divisions such as Rowland Hill, Thomas Picton and Robert Craufurd. These senior subordinates were those on whom Wellington relied upon to carry out his plans and orders.

But what of the junior generals commanding brigades who were in turn relied upon to put into action these plans and orders? Few if any books have been written about them or on their service during the Napoleonic Wars. Many of these generals went on to greater things after the Napoleonic Wars. They were Members of Parliament, governors of colonies, and commanders of armies in India. As generals they ran the gamut of competency. Most were good commanders and some extremely so; others were promoted beyond their abilities. Most wanted to be there, although for some the longer they served in the Peninsula, the less enthused they were about the war or serving under Wellington. The single characteristic that most displayed, however, was that they were brave as lions. They repeatedly showed this by leading their men from the front. As brigade commanders, twenty-five were wounded and eight were killed in action. Nine of those who had been wounded were wounded multiple times and three of them would eventually be killed in action. They also shared the same hardships as their men and were not immune to disease, exhaustion, or accidents. Ten had to return to England from the Peninsula broken in health, while six died from non-combat causes. This was a 63 per cent casualty rate!

Among the seventy-one generals covered in this book, there was a small group that caused Wellington immense frustration. This was especially true in the early days of the Peninsular War, when he had to take whatever generals that were sent out to him. He expressed his feelings to Lieutenant Colonel Henry Torrens in a letter dated 29 August 1810:

> Really when I reflect upon the characters and attainments of some of the General officers of this army, and consider that these are the persons on whom I am to rely to lead columns against the French Generals, and who are to carry my instructions into execution, I tremble; and, as Lord Chesterfield said of the Generals of his day, 'I only hope that when the enemy reads the list of their names he trembles as I do.'[1]

But even with the incompetents, these were the men that led the British Army to victory after victory in the Peninsular War and at Waterloo.

This book, 'a who was who', takes a concise look investigating the lives and careers of those men who performed a vital role in Wellington's Army serving as brigadier or major

---

1. *WSD;* Vol. 6, page 582.

generals during the Peninsular War and the campaign in 1815. All but one commanded a brigade and none ever became a permanent division commander.

Each biography features a table covering essential information on the individual, his birth and death dates, dates of his promotions, and details of his major commands under Wellington. This is followed by a concise account of his life and service. Their careers are traced from the first time they joined the army until their death. You will be able to trace their promotions, whether by purchase or not, look at their level of experience before joining Wellington and their service after the wars ended. Any rewards for service are noted. Their biographies give us a fascinating insight into their individual backgrounds, their strengths and weaknesses, and the makeup of the society they came from. In addition we add some personal details and look at their parents, brothers who also served, spouses, and children. Because of space limitations, however, each entry mainly focuses on the general's service under Wellington and his relationship with him. In many cases Wellington left candid assessments of their abilities and character: mostly positive, but sometimes not.

During the course of the Peninsular War, Wellington's command was extended to include Cadiz, Cartagena, and the East Coast of Spain. Due to space limitations, those generals who only served in these locations are excluded. Also excluded are one or two generals placed upon Wellington's staff but who were not given a brigade command, as they either left after a short stay or never went to the Peninsula; as well as a number of generals who came out and were assigned temporary command of a division due to the absence of the permanent commander and never commanded a brigade during their service. The generals of the King's German Legion are covered, because the Legion was part of the British Army. Those who served only in either the Portuguese or the Hanoverian Service and never commanded as a British general are also excluded.

For many of those who survived the rigors of campaigning, their service was the highlight of their career. For others they would rise to the highest ranks of the British Army. Here you will find the competent and the incompetent; those whom Wellington wished to keep and those whom he wanted to have recalled home. Whomever they were, this book will rescue them from obscurity and restore them to their rightful place in history.

As this is a concise look, comprehensive details of their actions during the wars cannot be recorded and we can only provide an overview. For further details of their actions in battle, we recommend the old standbys of Sir John Fortescue's *History of the British Army*, Sir Charles Oman's *A History of the Peninsular War* and William Siborne's *History of the War in France and Belgium 1815*. There are also available many modern histories of the wars in general or for specific campaigns.

The dates provided, for promotions and commands, are mostly taken from the General Orders, *Army Lists*, and the *London Gazette*. They may not in all cases reflect when the officer was notified of his promotion, his assignment to a command or when he actually joined. We arbitrarily chose April 1814 as the cut-off date for the period of command under Wellington for the Peninsular War. It is difficult to determine the changes in the command structure after Toulouse, Bayonne and the peace, as officers went on leave, were sent to America, etc. in April, May and June as Wellington disbanded the remainder of the army.

Instead of an index, there is an appendix where the generals are grouped by period of service. There you can see at a glance which generals served under Wellington at different periods. The periods are 1808, which covers the force that Wellington commanded in Portugal for a few months until he was superseded in command. Then 1809 from when Wellington returned as Commander-in-Chief of the Peninsular Army in April 1809 until the peace of April 1814. Next is the Campaign of 1815 from when Wellington formed his army in April 1815 until the end of November 1815. The last is the Army of Occupation in France from November 1815 until November 1818.

During this period, in the British Army, it was usual practice for a division to be commanded by a lieutenant general while a brigade was commanded by either a major general, brigadier general on the staff or colonel on the staff depending upon the size of the force. It should be noted that in the British Army of the time the rank of brigadier general was an appointment and not a substantive rank.[2] He would receive the pay and allowances that went with the appointment, but only as long as he held it. Once he was no longer in the position, his pay reverted back to that of his substantive rank.

Regardless of actual rank, an officer commanding a brigade was often referred to as its brigadier. We use the generic term 'General' throughout the text regardless if the officer was a lieutenant general, major general or brigadier general.

An officer's seniority in a unit was determined by the date on which he either joined it or was promoted in it. An officer's overall seniority in army rank was determined by the date he was promoted to the rank.

In a Royal Warrant of 25 May 1772, senior lieutenants holding the regimental rank of captain-lieutenant obtained the rank of captain in the army with the same date-of-rank as when they were promoted to captain-lieutenant. They were shown in the *Army Lists* as captain-lieutenant and captain. In an order of 6 June 1803, the regimental rank of captain-lieutenant was abolished and the officers who held that rank were then simply shown as captains in their regiment.

Brevet rank was not regimental, but was overall a higher army rank, and therefore did not entitle the holder to receive either the pay or responsibility of that rank in his unit. An officer could not exchange units using his brevet rank. It was usually awarded for long service or in some cases for merit and did place the officer on the path for promotion by patronage of the Commander-in-Chief. Local rank was basically the granting of higher army rank only in a particular location. It was usually granted to award pay and allowances to officers equal to the command they exercised. For example, an officer might be made a local brigadier general commanding a brigade while only a brevet colonel. If the officer left the location he would revert to his substantive rank. Army tradition, however, allowed the individual to be referred to by his highest rank held. For example, John Smith may have been promoted to brevet colonel and be in a position that is traditionally only held by a lieutenant colonel, such as a commander of an infantry battalion. Even though he was in a substantive billet, he was still called Colonel Smith.

Half pay was a system of semi-retirement for an officer. He received half the pay of his last substantive rank as a retainer, making him available to be placed back on full pay and active duty with a unit. While upon half-pay the officer had no regimental duties, but was available to serve in staff appointments.

A regimental colonel was an appointment and a sinecure usually granted to general officers as a reward for merit or long service. They did not command the regiment in the

---

2. Substantive rank was a rank for which an officer received pay and could not be reduced to lower rank except by a court-martial.

field, which was left to the regiment's senior lieutenant colonel. The regimental colonel's duties were generally administrative, such as providing uniforms and equipment to their regiment. For some multi-battalion regiments or individual battalions, such as the 60th Foot or the King's German Legion (KGL), colonels of the battalions were called colonel commandant as the regimental colonel for the entire regiment was called colonel-in-chief.

The rank structure in the Foot Guards Regiments was different from the line. The officers held 'dual rank'. Regimental ensigns were substantive lieutenants,[3] regimental lieutenants were substantive captains, and regimental captains were substantive lieutenant colonels in the army. They were promoted in the army and exchanged regiments based upon their army rank.

The Life Guards had dual rank for regimental cornets as substantive sub-lieutenants, regimental majors as substantive lieutenant colonels, and regimental lieutenant colonels as substantive colonels in the army.

At this time, due to the privilege of the Guards, only a Guards officer could be appointed to the command of a Guards Brigade; whereas, a Guards officer could be appointed to the command of a line brigade. Similarly, KGL brigades were commanded by KGL officers.

During the Peninsular War there was no official method of referring to the brigades in the divisions. Most often they were called by the name of the brigade commander. There was a practice within some divisions to refer to their brigades as 1st, 2nd, 3rd, etc. based upon the seniority of the brigade commander. Another practice was to use the designation of Right Brigade, Left Brigade and Centre Brigade to designate the seniority of the brigades. To simplify this, we have used the name of its commander when we write about a brigade.

Wellington's cavalry was formed in two divisions between 19 June 1811 and 21 April 1813. The 1st Division served with the main field army while the 2nd Division served attached to General Rowland Hill's Corps. The cavalry brigades were transferred between the divisions as needed for operations. On 21 April 1813 the divisions were broken up and the individual cavalry brigades were once again placed under one overall commander as they had been before 19 June 1811. The assignment of brigades to the divisions is not recorded in the Tables.

During this time, the Commanders-in-Chief of the British Army were Prince Frederick Duke of York from 10 February 1795 to 25 March 1809 and again from 29 May 1811, and David Dundas from 25 March 1809 to 29 May 1811. Their Military Secretaries were James Gordon from 4 August 1804 to 2 October 1809 and Henry Torrens from 2 October 1809. Mention of Horse Guards refers to the Headquarters of the Commander-in-Chief of the British Army, so called as it was located in Horse Guards Parade in Whitehall, London.

The Duke of Wellington was known as Arthur Wellesley until 4 September 1809, when he was granted a peerage. To simplify things, we always refer to him as Wellington in the text. Nor do we note his rank or title. He was a lieutenant general 25 April 1808–31 July 1811, a local general 31 July 1811–21 June 1813, and a field marshal from 21 June 1813.

Because the spelling of the names of the battles have changed over the past 200 years, we use the modern spelling of them, for example Vimeiro for Vimiera.

Ron McGuigan and Robert Burnham

---

3. Granted in 1815.

Abbreviations

AAG:	Assistant Adjutant General
ADC:	Aide-de-Camp
AG:	Adjutant General
AGC:	Army Gold Cross
AGM:	Army Gold Medal
AOOF:	Army of Occupation in France
AQMG:	Assistant Quartermaster General
c:	Circa
CB:	Companion of the Most Honourable Order of the Bath from 1815
CTS:	Knight Commander of the Portuguese Order of the Tower and Sword
d:	Pence
DAAG:	Deputy Assistant Adjutant General
DAG:	Deputy Adjutant General
DAQMG:	Deputy Assistant Quartermaster General
DQMG:	Deputy Quartermaster General
GCB:	Knight Grand Cross of the Most Honourable Order of the Bath from 1815
GCH:	Knight Grand Cross of the Royal Hanoverian Guelphic Order
GCMG:	Knight Grand Cross of the Most Distinguished Order of St Michael and St George
G.O.:	General Order
HEGL:	Hessian Order of the Golden Lion
HEIC:	Honourable East India Company
HEIH:	Hessian Order of the Iron Helmet
HM:	Hanseatic Medal for the Campaign of 1813–1814
Hon.:	Honourable
HQ:	Headquarters
KB:	Knight of the Most Honourable Order of the Bath to 1815
KC:	Knight of the Crescent
KCB:	Knight Commander of the Most Honourable Order of the Bath from 1815
KCH:	Knight Commander of the Royal Hanoverian Guelphic Order
KCMJ:	Knight Commander of the Bavarian Order of Maximilian Joseph
KG:	Knight of the Most Noble Order of the Garter
KGL:	The King's German Legion
KMT:	Knight of the Austrian Order of Maria Theresa
KP:	Knight of the Most Illustrious Order of St Patrick
KSA:	Russian Order of St Anne, First Class
KSG:	Russian Order of St George
KSI:	Knight of the Most Exulted Order of the Star of India to 1866
KSW:	Russian Order of Saint Vladimir
Kt:	Knight
KT:	Knight of the Most Ancient and Most Noble Order of the Thistle

KTS: Knight of the Portuguese Order of the Tower and Sword
KW: Dutch Military Order of William
£:   Pounds
MGSM: Military General Service Medal
MP: Member of Parliament
POM: Prussian Order of Military Merit
QMG: Quartermaster General
RA: Royal Artillery
RANO: Russian Order of Alexander Nevsky
RM: Russian Medal for Campaigns
RN: Royal Navy
RPM: Russian Medal for the Capture of Paris
RTM: Russian Medal for the Turkish Campaign
s: Shillings

Acland, Wroth Palmer

Date of Birth:	16 March 1770
Date Commissioned:	Ensign 17th Foot: 25 April 1787 by purchase
Promotions:	Lieutenant 17th Foot: 4 June 1790 by purchase
	Captain Independent Company: 24 January 1791 without purchase[1]
	Captain 3rd Foot: 2 March 1793 by exchange
	Major 19th Foot: 18 March 1795 by purchase
	Lieutenant Colonel 19th Foot: 1 September 1795 without purchase
	Captain & Lieutenant Colonel Coldstream Foot Guards: 10 May 1800 by exchange[2]
	Brevet Colonel: 25 September 1803
	Brigadier General on the Staff: 25 July 1804
	Major General: 25 July 1810
	Lieutenant General: 4 June 1814
Regimental Colonel:	1st Battalion[3] 60th Foot: 9 August 1815–8 March 1816
Major Commands under Wellington:	Brigade: 15 July–5 September 1808[4]
Awards:	AGM with clasp: Maida & Vimeiro
Thanks of Parliament:	Maida, Roliça & Vimeiro
	KCB: 2 January 1815
Date of Death:	8 March 1816 in Bath, England

Name is also spelled Ackland, Acklin, Wrothe and William in various official documents.

Wroth Acland was born on 16 March 1770, the twelfth child of Arthur Acland and Elizabeth Oxenham, at Fairfield Somersetshire. His father died when he was 1.[5]

Wroth Acland was commissioned as an ensign in the 17th Foot in 1787 and except for two years he was on half-pay, he would spend much of the next twelve years on active service.[6] In 1790 he served as a marine in the Channel Fleet and in 1793 he was in the West Indies. The following year he was in Flanders with the Duke of York and by March 1795 he was on his way to the West Indies. Wroth Acland would be sent to the Far East in 1796 where he was stationed in India and Ceylon. In 1799 he was struck by an unspecified illness, which forced him to return to England. This illness would plague him over the next ten years. During those twelve years he rose to lieutenant colonel and command of a battalion. Upon returning to England, Lieutenant Colonel Acland exchanged into the Coldstream Guards. In 1805 he was appointed a brigadier on the staff in the Eastern District.

---

1. Promoted in exchange for recruiting men for the army. His company was disbanded in 1791 and the men were drafted into other regiments.
2. Removed from the regiment as a general officer receiving unattached pay, 25 July 1814.
3. The battalions of the 60th Foot had a colonel commandant in addition to its regimental colonel-in-chief.
4. The brigade was numbered the 8th Brigade in a General Order dated 21 August 1808.
5. Kingsley; '(16) Palmer-Acland'.
6. He was on half-pay from 1791 to 1793, only coming off it when he exchanged into the 3rd Foot in 1793.

In 1805 General Acland joined the staff of General Sir James Craig and sailed to the Mediterranean. He was part of the expeditions to Malta and Naples. In 1806 he commanded the 2nd Brigade at the battle of Maida, where he and his brigade distinguished themselves. He was recalled to England in late 1806 and in February 1807 was to command the light brigade in the expedition to the River Plate. General Acland arrived too late to take command and by December he was back in Ireland. In February 1808 he took command of a brigade in Harwich and was placed in Wellington's force that was headed to Portugal.

General Acland and his brigade landed in Portugal on 20 August,[7] too late to fight at Roliça. The brigade was present the next day at Vimeiro, but was not engaged. After the battle, command of the British forces was taken over by a senior general, Sir Hew Dalrymple. He re-organised the army on 5 September and General Acland was appointed to command a new brigade in General Sir John Hope's 2nd Division. The government then decided to form two forces, one under General John Moore to serve in Spain, and a garrison for Portugal. Acland was chosen to serve under General Moore. On 8 October Moore re-organised his force and General Acland continued to serve as a brigade commander in General Hope's Division, but with different battalions in his brigade. Before the newly organised army could advance into Spain, General Acland became incapacitated once again due to sickness and was sent home. On 21 November he had arrived in Portsmouth and was still extremely ill.[8] Despite being sick, General Acland was called upon to testify at the Convention of Cintra Court of Inquiry the next month.[9]

On 22 June 1809, General Acland was appointed to command a brigade in the 3rd Division of the Right Wing in what became known as the Walcheren Expedition. He and his brigade would fight at the siege of Flushing. He would remain as part of the garrison on Walcheren until September 1809.[10] Upon his return to England General Acland served on the Home Staff in the Eastern District until he was promoted to major general on 25 July 1810. He served in the South West District in 1811 and the North West District in 1812. In 1813 he was once again in the Eastern District and would remain there until 1814, when he was removed from the staff upon his promotion to lieutenant general.

Between 1806 and 1809, General Acland had fought in four different theatres of war and sailed over 25,000 kilometers. The effects of his illness in Portugal, followed within eight months by the rigors of the Walcheren Expedition, was too much for General Acland. He was unable to fully restore his health and never had another active assignment. In the winter of 1816 he had a relapse of the fever that he caught in Portugal and died on 8 March 1816. General Acland never married.

Wroth Acland is mentioned in very few memoirs so it is difficult to ascertain his personality. Ensign Robert Parker of the 76th Foot did not think very highly of him. In a letter to his father in April 1809, Ensign Parker complained that 'Genl. Acklin of the Guards who had threaten'd to put me with some other officers in a blanket and piss on

---

7. Brown, Steve; 'All Bound for Lisbon'.
8. Glover, Gareth (ed.); *Wellington's Voice*, page 12.
9. Oman; *A History of the Peninsular War*, Vol. 1, page 294.
10. Burnham; 'The British Expeditionary Force to Walcheren: 1809'.

us if we did not go out of the Town of Ipswitch immediately'.[11] Unfortunately the young officer did not say what he had done to deserve this treatment!

General Acland served under Wellington for less than two months. They appeared to have gotten along well. When Wellington was recalled from Portugal because of the Treaty of Cintra, General Acland was one of the officers who contributed over 1,000 guineas to present him with a piece of plate.[12]

---

11. French; page 121.
12. Muir, Rory; *Wellington: The Path to Victory, 1769–1814*, page 262.

Adam, Frederick William

Date of Birth:	17 June 1784
Date Commissioned:	Ensign 26th Foot: 4 November 1795
Promotions:	Lieutenant 26th Foot: 2 February 1796
	Captain-Lieutenant 9th Foot: 30 August 1799
	Lieutenant & Captain Coldstream Foot Guards:
	8 December 1799
	Major 5th Reserve Battalion:[1] 9 July 1803
	Lieutenant Colonel 5th Reserve Battalion:
	18 August 1804
	Lieutenant Colonel 21st Foot: 5 January 1805[2] by exchange[3]
	Brevet Colonel: 20 February 1812
	Major General: 4 June 1814
	Local Lieutenant General Ionian Islands:
	10 February 1824
	Lieutenant General: 22 July 1830
	General: 9 November 1846.
Regimental Colonel:	73rd Foot: 22 May 1829–4 December 1835
	57th Foot: 4 December 1835–31 May 1843
	21st Foot: 31 May 1843–17 August 1853
Major Commands under Wellington:	Brigade on the East Coast of Spain: 1812–1813
	3rd Brigade: 11 April–30 November 1815
Awards:	KCB: 22 June 1815
	GCMG: 27 December 1821
	GCB: 20 June 1840
	MGSM with clasp for Egypt
	Waterloo Medal
	KMT
	KSA
Thanks of Parliament:	Waterloo
Date of Death:	17 August 1853 in London

Name is sometimes spelled Adams.

Frederick Adam was born in 1784, the fourth son of the Right Hon. William Adam and Hon. Eleanora Elphinstone of County Kinross, Scotland. His mother was the daughter of the 10th Lord Elphinstone. He was the younger brother of Admiral Sir Charles Adam. His father was a Member of Parliament for twenty-six years, the Solicitor General for Scotland, Attorney General to the Prince of Wales, and the Lord Lieutenant of Kinross. He was also a 'close personal friend of the Prince of Wales'.[4] These political connections would serve Frederick Adam well.

---

1. Renamed 5th Garrison Battalion 30 October 1804 and disbanded 24 February 1805.
2. He was removed from the 21st Foot as a general officer receiving unattached pay in 1814.
3. All other promotions were by appointment.
4. 'Adam, William (1751–1839)'.

Frederick Adam was commissioned at the age of 11 as an ensign in the 26th Foot, which was stationed in Canada. Because of his age, he was sent to study at Woolwich for two years prior to joining his regiment. Lieutenant Adam never served with his regiment and did not see active service until he was 14. In 1799, he was attached to the 27th Foot and fought with them in Holland. In August of that year, he became a captain-lieutenant in the 9th Foot. Four months later he was a lieutenant and captain in the Coldstream Guards and went with them to Egypt. In 1802 he took a leave of absence and studied German in Dresden.[5] By 1803 he was back in England and was appointed a major in the 5th Garrison Battalion. The following year, at the age of 20, he was appointed lieutenant colonel of the battalion. Five months later he exchanged into the 21st Foot. Someone was looking after his interests for there is no record of him purchasing any promotion. All appear to have been appointments.

Lieutenant Colonel Adam sailed with his battalion in 1806 to the Mediterranean, where he would serve much of the next six years. Some sources state that he fought at Maida, however, the battle was over before he arrived. He fought in Calabria and at the siege of Scylla; during the battle of Mili he commanded a brigade. In 1809 he participated in the British expedition to the Ionian Islands. Lieutenant Colonel Adam went on home leave in 1811 and while there he was appointed an ADC to the Prince Regent. His duties to the Prince were cut short when he went back to Sicily that autumn in anticipation of future operations.

In February 1812 Lieutenant Colonel Adam was promoted to colonel and was appointed the DAG for the British forces in Sicily. He arrived on the east coast of Spain in July as part of the British expedition under General Frederick Maitland. He would remain in Alicante, Spain through the winter and was appointed a brigade commander. His brigade fought in the Castalla Campaign and Colonel Adam commanded the rearguard when the French counter-attacked at Biar on 12 April 1813. His performance at the combat of Biar was observed by the British general commanding the Spanish troops in the campaign, who wrote that it was 'a beautiful field-day, by alternate battalions: the volleys were admirable, and the successive passage of several ravines conducted with perfect order and steadiness. From the heights occupied by my troops it was one of the most delightful panoramas that I ever beheld.'[6] Colonel Adam was wounded in the left shoulder, but continued to command throughout the action.

On 12 September 1813 Colonel Adam and his brigade were once again in the van of the army and had orders to defend the pass at Ordal. He was very careless with his troop dispositions and did not take basic precautions, including neglecting to send a cavalry vidette to provide early warning and not fortifying a bridge leading into his position. He was caught by surprise by a French attack and forced from the pass with heavy casualties. Colonel Adam was severely wounded in the left arm, which was broken, and the left hand, which was mutilated. He never regained the use of his hand again.[7]

Colonel Adam returned to Great Britain to recover from his wounds and on 4 June 1814 he was promoted to major general. He was 29 years old and the youngest general in the British Army.[8]

---

5. Von Reumont; page 12.

6. Whittingham; page 216.

7. *RMC*; Vol. 3, page 386. Von Reumont; page 20.

8. To put this in perspective, the Duke of Wellington was 32 years old when he was promoted to major general in 1802.

On 28 March 1815, he was appointed to the staff of the British Army forming in the Netherlands. He was assigned to command the 3rd Brigade on 11 April.[9] His brigade was also known as the Light Brigade. At Waterloo his brigade saw little action through much of the day, however, it made its reputation for its actions against the French Imperial Guard that evening. During the attack by the French, the 3rd Brigade swung around so it could fire into the column's right flank. This, along with the attack on the left flank of the column by the British Guards, was enough to cause the final French assault to fail. General Adam and his brigade pursued the defeated French until they came across three battalions of the Imperial Guard formed in squares. They engaged in a sharp fight with the French and eventually forced them to retire.

General Adam's brigade was instrumental in the defeat of the French Imperial Guard, but there is considerable evidence that he personally had little to do with it. It was Lieutenant Colonel John Colborne, the commander of the 52nd Light Infantry, who took the initiative to wheel his battalion to the left to catch the French column in its flank without waiting for orders from General Adam to do so. Wellington saw what the 52nd Light Infantry was doing and ordered the 2nd Battalion 95th Rifles up to support it. As this was going on, General Adam was on the far right ordering the 71st Foot and the 3rd Battalion 95th Rifles to move to support the rest of the brigade. Before long, the French began to waiver and Lieutenant Colonel Colborne, once again on his own initiative, ordered his battalion to charge the French.[10]

General Adam was badly wounded in the leg at Waterloo.[11] When it occurred is unknown. It was most likely in the late evening during the fight with the French Imperial Guard. His wound was severe enough to keep him from participating in the pursuit of the defeated French. He initially remained in Brussels and since he was the least wounded of all the British generals, he served as the commander of the numerous British wounded left there. While he was in Brussels, his brigade would be the first British unit to enter Paris. General Adam returned to England to recuperate and by September had recovered from his wounds and rejoined his brigade. On 30 November 1815, the British Army in France was re-organised and General Adam's brigade was disbanded. He was not given another command. By the winter of 1816 he had returned to his home in Scotland.

In 1817, General Adam returned to the Mediterranean. He commanded the British forces in the Ionian Islands and in 1824 became the Lord High Commissioner there. He served there until 1831. As governor he supported the Greek revolution against the Ottoman Empire and made many charitable contributions to the welfare of the people of Corfu. He is honoured by a statue that was erected on the Greek island.[12] While he was in Greece, General Adam was appointed to the Consolidated Board of General Officers in 1819. Although he served on the Board for several years, his duties in Greece prevented him from taking an active part in its proceedings. On 25 October 1832 he became governor of Madras, India, and served there until 4 March 1837. Upon returning to England he retired from public office due to poor health.

General Adam was married three times. The first was to Amelia Thompson on 19 July 1811. He brought her back to Sicily, but she died shortly after arriving there. He married Diamantina Pallatiano of Corfu on 23 June 1820: she died in 1844. He remarried on 24

---

9. General Order, 11 April 1815.
10. Siborne; pages 272–295. Glover, Gareth; *Letters from the Battle of Waterloo*; pages 178–97.
11. Glover, Gareth; *Waterloo*, page 168.
12. Bromley; Vol. 1, page 3.

July 1851 to Ann Lindsay Maberly and in 1853 his only heir, a son, was born. General Adam died from a heart attack in the Greenwich Railroad Station on 17 August 1853.[13]

Frederick Adam's meteoric rise in rank was due to his father's political connections rather than his own merit. His father, a Member of Parliament and friend of the Royal Family, used his influence to ensure his son had a successful career. Frederick Adam received his commission as an ensign and his lieutenancy in the 26th Foot because his father was a friend of General Sir Charles Stuart, who was also a Member of Parliament. In 1799 he was appointed as a lieutenant and captain in the Coldstream Guards by the Duke of York, whom his father knew. In late 1804, his father heard that there was to be a vacancy in the 21st Foot, which he mentioned to the Duke of York who arranged his exchange to fill it. His father did not just limit his requests to his friends in England. In late 1812 he even contacted Wellington, asking him to find a position for his son should the army on the East Coast of Spain join the main field army![14] In 1815, the Duke of York promised General Adam a brigade in the army being formed in the Netherlands and thus he commanded the 3rd Brigade of the 2nd Division during the Waterloo Campaign.[15] After Waterloo, the Duke of York proposed that General Adam be placed upon the staff of the Army of Occupation in France. However, he was not appointed to a brigade command in the General Order of 30 November 1815.

There is very little evidence that Wellington had ever met Frederick Adam prior to the Waterloo Campaign. In a letter dated 31 March 1815 that announced General Adam's appointment to the British Army in the Netherlands, General Torrens, the Military Secretary to the Horse Guards, wrote to Wellington that 'He is a very distinguished and intelligent officer, and I have not the least doubt but that he will give you satisfaction.'[16] William Napier crucified General Adam's performance at Ordal, stating that 'whoever relies upon the capacity of Sir Frederick Adam either in peace or war will be disappointed.'[17] Charles Oman is a bit more generous in his appraisal of Colonel Adam. He believed that the combat of Biar 'was one of the most creditable rearguard actions fought during the whole Peninsular War.'[18] Yet Oman was scathing of Adam's performance at Ordal, claiming that 'he and his whole force went to sleep ... he neither kept a cavalry vidette a mile or two out along the road, nor placed a picket at the bridge.'[19] John Fortescue is kinder with his evaluation. Rather than criticising his poor tactics he blames Colonel Adam's superiors for leaving him in such an exposed position at Ordal.[20] He further tries to exonerate him by saying that Frederick Adam's 'fortunes, unluckily for him, had been linked to John Murray and William Bentinck.'[21] Neither Generals John Murray nor Lord William Bentinck were overly successful commanding on the East Coast of Spain.

13. Von Reumont; page 54.
14. *WD*; Vol. 6, page 226.
15. *RMC* 1820; Vol. 3, pages 385–78.
16. *WSD*; Vol. 10, page 10.
17. Napier; Vol. 6, page 61. John Fortescue (Vol. 9, page 81) claims that Napier's criticism '... was plainly dictated by personal animosity arising out of a matter utterly unconnected with the campaigns in the Peninsula.'
18. Oman; *History of the Peninsular War*, Vol. 6, page 288.
19. Oman; *History of the Peninsular War*, Vol. 7, page 100.
20. Fortescue; Vol. 9, page 81.
21. Fortescue; Vol. 10, page 240.

Alten, Victor Baron

Date of Birth:	2 November 1755 in Burgwedel, Hanover
Date Commissioned:	Ensign 2nd Regiment: 1 May 1770
Hanoverian Service:	Lieutenant Life Guards: 5 August 1774
	Captain Life Guards: 15 November 1785
	Captain 8th Cavalry Regiment: 1791
	Brevet Major: 23 July 1794
	Major 4th Cavalry Regiment: 1799
	Brevet Lieutenant Colonel: 13 December 1802
	Major General: 25 July 1810[1]
	Lieutenant General: 16 April 1818
British Service:	Lieutenant Colonel of Cavalry, KGL 15 November 1803[2]
	Lieutenant Colonel 1st Light Dragoons, KGL: 1804
	Colonel: 19 December 1804
	Major General: 25 July 1810[3]
Regimental Colonel:	2nd Light Dragoons,[4] KGL: 19 December 1804–24 February 1816
	2nd Osnabruck Hussar Regiment Hanoverian Army: 1816
Major Commands under Wellington:	Cavalry Brigade: 18 July 1811–28 December 1813
	Superintended Hanoverian Cavalry: 31 May–30 November 1815
Awards:	AGM with clasp: Salamanca & Vitoria
	Waterloo Medal[5]
	KCH: 1816
Thanks of Parliament:	Salamanca
Date of Death:	23 August 1820 in Osnabruck, Hanover

His real name was Adolph Viktor Christian Jobst von Alten. While in Hanoverian service he was known as Viktor von Alten. While in British Service he was known as Victor Baron Alten.

Victor Baron Alten was born at his family home, Willenburg, near Burgwedel, on 2 November 1755 to August Eberhard Alten and Henriette Philippine Marie Hedwig von Vincke. He was the older brother of Major General Charles Baron Alten (Karl von Alten).

Victor Alten was commissioned as an ensign in the Hanoverian Army at the age of 15 in 1770. Promotion was slow and it was not until 1802 that he received a brevet to lieutenant colonel. After the annexation of Hanover by Napoleon and the subsequent disbanding of the Hanoverian Army in 1803, Lieutenant Colonel Alten fled to England and joined the

---

1. British Army rank recognised when KGL officers entered new Hanoverian Army.
2. Temporary rank in British Army.
3. Permanent rank in British Army, 18 August 1812.
4. The 2nd Light Dragoons were renamed the 2nd Hussars on 25 December 1813. A regimental colonel in the KGL was called a colonel commandant.
5. There is some confusion on whether or not General Alten was present at Waterloo. Although he is shown as receiving the Waterloo Medal in the British Army lists, he is not recorded as receiving it in Hanoverian sources. He may have been on the frontier with the 2nd Hussars KGL during the battle. [*Hannoverscher und Churfürstlich-Braunschweigisch-Lüneburgischer Staatskalender* 1819.]

newly formed King's German Legion (KGL) as a lieutenant colonel. In 1804 he helped form the 1st KGL Light Dragoons and by the end of the year he was a colonel and the commander of the 2nd KGL Light Dragoons. His first active service with the British Army came when he and his regiment participated in the Baltic Expedition and the siege of Copenhagen in 1807. By the end of the year they had returned to England. In 1809 Colonel Alten and his regiment were part of the Walcheren Expedition and like the rest of the force took heavy losses to disease.[6]

Colonel Alten was promoted to major general in July 1810, but it was not until the following year that he was sent to Wellington's Army in the Peninsula. His appointment was announced to Wellington in a letter dated 9 April, from Lieutenant Colonel Torrens. 'The Prince has directed that Baron Alten should be placed upon the Staff as a M. General in Portugal to command the Cavalry of the Legion ... Alten is an excellent Officer!'[7] The initial announcement of his orders placing him on the staff was made in a General Order dated 27 July 1811, but backdated to 16 April 1811. To add further confusion, in the General Orders of 12 September 1811, the date he was placed on the staff was changed to 13 April 1811.[8]

When General Alten arrived in Portugal is unknown, however, on 18 July 1811 he took command of a cavalry brigade in the 1st Cavalry Division. The regiments in his brigade would change several times and occasionally he would be on detached duty; however, during the thirty months he spent in command his brigade was always assigned to the 1st Cavalry Division.

In early August 1811, General Alten and his brigade moved towards the Spanish border and began screening Ciudad Rodrigo. On 25 September, the brigade and General Charles Colville's brigade of the 3rd Division were surprised in a forward position at El Boden by a large French force under Marshal Marmont. The French forces included almost 2,000 cavalry. Despite being outnumbered four to one, General Alten was able to hold off the French cavalry, allowing the British infantry to retreat to safety. It was General Alten's finest hour.

During the autumn of 1811, General Alten's forces were deployed along the Agueda River, a disease-ridden area that caused the death and hospitalisation of thousands of British troops.[9] By late October, his brigade would be down to less than 520 effectives, only 55 per cent of its actual strength. The rest were either sick or on detached duty. By early October, General Alten was stricken with Agueda Fever and had to relinquish command to his senior regimental commander. He would not return until 8 January 1812.[10]

After successfully taking the border city of Ciudad Rodrigo in January, Wellington began shifting his army south to Badajoz. While the bulk of the army was gone, the 5th Infantry Division and General Alten's brigade were to protect the newly captured city. His brigade had been reduced to the 1st KGL Hussars which had an effective strength of less than 400 men. They were deployed 16 kilometers east of Ciudad Rodrigo and ordered to screen the city from the French forces in Salamanca, about 80 kilometers away.

6. The August 1809 monthly strength report showed over 30 per cent of the regiment listed as sick or in the hospital.
7. Unpublished letter provided by Dr Rory Muir.
8. *General Orders*; Vol. 3, pages 187–8.
9. This disease was known as Agueda Fever and was either typhus, malaria, or a combination of both.
10. Beamish; Vol. 2, page 19; Oman, *Wellington's Army*, page 359.

In late March, the French moved out of Salamanca towards Ciudad Rodrigo. General Alten immediately pulled his forces back to the west of Ciudad Rodrigo along the Agueda River. On 1 April, when two squadrons of French cavalry approached the only passable ford on the river, he again pulled his troops back and continued to retreat. Five days later he was in Castello Branco, 160 kilometers away from the area he was supposed to protect. He did not stop there. Even though the enemy was 80 kilometers away, he continued to retreat until he reached Vila Velha, a strategic crossing site of the Tagus River. He began preparations to destroy the bridge, but was stopped by orders from Wellington.

General Alten's panicky withdrawal endangered the other forces covering Ciudad Rodrigo. They had to retreat and soon the French had the city under blockade. Before long the French moved back into Portugal, threatening Almeida and the British logistical points at Celorico and Guarda. They also began to move on Castello Branco. When he received word of what General Alten had done, Wellington was furious. He had just captured Badajoz and instead of moving into southern Spain as he had planned, he had to order the army back north to relieve Ciudad Rodrigo. Fortunately for the British, poor logistics forced the French to retreat back to Salamanca before they could do serious harm.

On 11 April Wellington wrote to General Alten that

> in case the enemy followed your march to Ciudad Rodrigo, you were to move gradually, and you were not directed to proceed farther than Castello Branco without further orders. I cannot consider movements to be gradual which brought you from Val de Lobos to Castello Branco in two days. You have now crossed the Tagus at Villa Velha without orders ... If upon receipt of this letter you have no positive intelligence that the enemy are actually in Castello Branco, you will march there, and act according to the orders contained in the letter from the Quarter Master General ...[11]

Wellington did not let the matter drop. He forwarded the correspondence between him and General Alten to the Earl of Liverpool, the Secretary of State, on 24 April.[12] However, Wellington did not take steps to remove him from command.

On 13 June Wellington set his army in motion and headed into central Spain. General Alten's brigade formed the advance guard of the centre column. They distinguished themselves at Castrillo on 18 July where they mauled a French dragoon brigade and then pursued a broken infantry regiment. The brigade was credited with capturing 350 prisoners including the commander of the French dragoons.

At the Battle of Salamanca on 22 July 1812, General Alten's brigade was deployed on the right flank of the army. Early in the day he could see the movements of French columns to his front, but could not determine what exactly they were doing because they were obscured by a skirmish screen and woods. About 8 a.m. he rode forward for a better view and was promptly shot. The bullet hit him in the thigh, grazed the bone, and started to bleed heavily. He was evacuated to the rear where his wound was dressed. Before he left he told his ADC, Captain Ernest Baron Linsingen, to stay with his replacement and if the situation began to deteriorate to send word. General Alten was adamant that he

11. *WD*; Vol. 9, pages 53–4.
12. Ibid; pages 87–8.

did not want to become a prisoner of the French. About 3 p.m. a message arrived from Captain Linsingen that the outcome of the battle was in doubt. General Alten, despite the protests of his surgeon who was worried that General Alten would re-open his wound and possibly bleed to death, called for his horse, and rode away towards Ciudad Rodrigo. He was about 2 kilometers down the road when another messenger caught up to him and told him that the army was about to attack the French and there was no doubt in anyone's mind that they would win. The general, however, refused to believe the messenger. General Alten returned to his quarters in Salamanca only after he heard the firing of the 3rd Division, which convinced him that the army was indeed attacking. He had spent almost two hours on his horse before getting back to his sickbed.[13] Dr James McGrigor, the senior surgeon in the army, personally checked on him a few days later and reported back to the Duke of Wellington that General Alten had 'some unpleasant symptoms … but I still do not conceive [him] to be in danger.'[14]

Two months later General Alten had still not returned to his brigade. Wellington, possibly influenced by Dr McGregor's report, might have thought General Alten was shirking his duties. On 21 September, Wellington wrote to General Charles Alten, to tell his brother that 'He desired his brother to take command of his brigade.'[15] General Victor Alten took the hint and was back with his brigade by the end of the month. During the retreat to the Portuguese border that began in October, he and his brigade would serve in the rearguard. Despite six months of ceaseless campaigning, his brigade still had two-thirds of its men fit for duty by the time they reached the Portuguese border.

By 2 December Wellington had had enough of General Alten. He wrote to Colonel Torrens at the Horse Guards that 'I should wish, if possible, to get rid of Sir Wm. Erskine, General Slade & General Long, particularly the first and the last … I think also that it would be an advantage to the army to get rid of Victor Alten.'[16] On 30 December, Colonel Torrens notified Wellington that General Alten would be recalled. Wellington was not pleased with the news for he realised that he had made a mistake. On 22 January 1813 Wellington wrote back to Colonel Torrens that he was concerned that he forgot to request that General Alten be employed on the home staff. Thus he did not want to have any of his officers removed unless they were given a job elsewhere.[17] Since Colonel Torrens could not guarantee further employment for him, General Alten was left in command of his brigade.

By late April 1813 General Alten had still not been recalled. Wellington sought General Stapleton Cotton's advice on re-organising the cavalry and in a letter dated 7 April he told him, 'I have received discretionary orders to send to England Slade, Alten and Long … I have not sent home any of these officers, because I am not quite certain what your wishes and opinions are, and because I doubt whether you would mend matters very materially by their removal.'[18] Wellington also asked him which of the three generals he wished to have recalled in order to make room for General Henry Fane, who was coming out. General Alten was not selected to go home.

---

13. Beamish; Vol. 2, page 70.
14. Muir; *Salamanca*, page 74.
15. *WD*; Vol. 9, page 424.
16. *WSD*; Vol. 7, page 485. General Alten's name was suppressed in the published *Dispatches*.
17. *WD*; Vol. 10, page 33.
18. *WD* (enlarged ed.); Vol. 6, page 406.

In April 1813, General Alten was in trouble with Wellington once again. A Staff Corps of Cavalry was being formed and commanders were told to allow their soldiers to volunteer. The commander of the 1st KGL Hussars complained and General Alten supported him in a letter to Wellington, who dismissed his protests. In the same letter, Wellington took General Alten to task for sympathising with the 2nd KGL Hussars for being ordered to leave their horses with the army when the regiment returned to England the following month. The regiment were quite vocal in their dissatisfaction of losing their mounts and General Alten had to intervene. He advised the regiment to 'bear their fate quietly, and as good disciplined and brave soldiers ought to do …'[19] Wellington's response was quite terse. 'I had believed the 2nd Hussars would certainly behave in such a manner on all occasions and under all circumstances; and that, if there should be any doubt on the subject, something more forcible than advice would have been given to ensure their good behavior.'[20]

The Vitoria Campaign of 1813 would see General Alten in the advance guard once again. However, they saw little action and took no casualties at the Battle of Vitoria on 21 June. After the battle, the brigade led the pursuit of the retreating French Army and was part of the force blockading the French in Pamplona. By November the brigade was in France.

Soon after his arrival in France, General Alten requested to be allowed to return to England. He turned over command on 28 December to Colonel Richard Vivian. There is some question on whether he was expected to return, because the general orders announcing his departure stated that Colonel Vivian would command in his absence, implying that he would be back.[21] This was his last command under Wellington. In April 1814 he was appointed to the staff of the British Forces in Holland; however, hostilities had ceased by the time he arrived. By the summer, the KGL cavalry in Wellington's Army were sent to Holland. The two brigades were formed into a division and General Alten was placed in command of it. Despite this, a year later, during the Waterloo Campaign, General Alten was not given a command under Wellington. Instead he was given the responsibility for all of the Hanoverian cavalry in the army, but in a staff role only.[22]

In December 1815, General Alten returned to Hanover. He went on half-pay from the British Army in February 1816 and took command of the 3rd Cavalry Brigade of the Hanoverian Army. He commanded it until his death in 1820.

Victor Alten married Charlotte Louise Wilhelmine Freiin Kinsky von Wchinitz und Tettau in 1796. They had two sons and two daughters. He probably spoke fluent English. A review of his letters show that he was fluent in writing English.

---

19. *WD*; Vol. 10, page 257.
20. Ibid.
21. *General Orders*; Vol. 5, page 412. The General Order was dated 28 December 1813.
22. General Order, 31 May 1815.

Anson, George

Date of Birth:	12 August 1769[1]
Date Commissioned:	Cornet 16th Light Dragoons: 3 May 1786
Promotions:	Lieutenant 16th Light Dragoons: 16 March 1791
	Lieutenant 20th Light Dragoons: 20 January 1792
	Captain 20th Light Dragoons: 9 September 1792
	Major 20th Light Dragoons: 25 December 1794
	Major 16th Light Dragoons: 15 June 1797 by exchange
	Lieutenant Colonel 20th Light Dragoons: 21 December 1797
	Lieutenant Colonel 15th Light Dragoons: 6 September 1798 by exchange
	Lieutenant Colonel 16th Light Dragoons: 12 December 1805 by exchange
	Brevet Colonel: 1 January 1805
	Brigadier General on Staff: 1809–1810
	Major General: 25 July 1810
	Lieutenant General: 12 August 1819
	General: 10 January 1837
Regimental Colonel:	23rd Light Dragoons: 3 August 1814–25 January 1818[2]
	4th Dragoon Guards: 24 February 1827–4 November 1849
Major Commands under Wellington:	Brigade 4th Division: 22 June–16 July 1809
	Cavalry Brigade: 16 July 1809–2 July 1813
Awards:	AGM with two clasps: Talavera, Salamanca & Vitoria
	CTS: 12 October 1812
	KCB: 2 January 1815
	GCB: 29 July 1833
Thanks of Parliament:	Talavera, Salamanca & Vitoria
Member of Parliament:	Lichfield: 24 February 1806–8 September 1841
Date of Death:	4 November 1849 at Chelsea Hospital

Until 1773 the family name was Adams.

George Anson was the second son of George Anson and Mary Vernon. His mother was the daughter of 1st Lord Vernon. He was brother of General Sir William Anson 1st Baronet, Lieutenant Colonel Sambrooke Anson, and Captain Edward Anson. He was named after his uncle, Admiral George Lord Anson, who had circumnavigated the globe and became the 1st Lord of the Admiralty in 1751. George's father inherited two estates and his family was quite wealthy, which enabled him to purchase all of his promotions. He grew up in Shugborough Hall, Staffordshire and attended Eton from 1779 to 1785.

George Anson was commissioned as a cornet in the 16th Light Dragoons in 1786 but exchanged into the 20th Light Dragoons six years later. He went with his regiment to Jamaica in 1792 and over the next two years was able to purchase first a captaincy and then the rank of major. He returned to England in 1797 after exchanging back into the 16th Light Dragoons. He was not long in England before he purchased his lieutenant

---

1. Massue; Vol. 1, page 544.
2. The regiment was disbanded on 25 January 1818.

colonelcy in the 20th Light Dragoons. He did not, however, return to Jamaica to serve with them. Nine months later he exchanged into the 15th Light Dragoons and served with them in the 1799 expedition to Holland. While there, he served as the regiment's 2nd lieutenant colonel and did not command it. He was with the regiment until 1805, when exchanged back into the 16th Light Dragoons, where he served as its commander. That same year he was appointed an ADC to the King and was promoted to colonel.

In early April 1809, Colonel Anson and the 16th Light Dragoons embarked at Falmouth for Portugal. They sailed on 7 April and arrived in Lisbon on the 15th.[3] They were the advance guard of the army during the Oporto Campaign and, after the French were ejected from the city, were part of the pursuit of the fleeing French. This would be the last time Colonel Anson commanded the regiment in action.

Colonel Anson was the senior colonel in the Peninsula and Wellington offered to appoint him a colonel on the staff so that he could command an infantry brigade, the only vacancy available. Colonel Anson declined the offer, preferring to stay in command of his cavalry regiment. Unbeknownst to either of them, on 25 May, His Majesty appointed George Anson a brigadier general on the staff. Word reached the army within a few weeks and in a General Order dated 22 June, Wellington appointed him brigade commander of the infantry brigade. The new general would not command his infantry brigade long. On 16 July, Wellington gave General Anson command of General James Erskine's Cavalry Brigade[4] while General Erskine was sick. Although the composition of the brigade would change over the years, he would command it until 1813.

General Anson had less than twelve days to get to know his brigade and to meld it into a cohesive fighting force. He was not up to the task. On 28 July he was positioned on a large plain on the left flank of the British Army at Talavera. No reconnaissance of the area was made by him or his subordinate commanders. A French infantry division and cavalry brigade approached about a kilometer away. Wellington sent a staff officer, Lieutenant Colonel John Elley, with orders for General Anson to charge the French. The two regiments were formed with the 23rd Light Dragoons on the right and the 1st KGL Light Dragoons on the left. As soon as they were formed, the 23rd Light Dragoons began their charge and were at a gallop shortly after that. Lieutenant Colonel Elley led them in their headlong charge. The 1st KGL Light Dragoons followed but at a slower pace. Neither General Anson or Lieutenant Colonel Elley, nor either of the regimental commanders, knew there was a wide ditch less than 150 metres from the French infantry, who had formed themselves into squares. By the time they saw, it was too late to stop the charge. The first line of the 23rd Light Dragoons tumbled into it and the second line landed on top of them. Many men and horses were killed or seriously injured. About one third of the 23rd Light Dragoons were able to make it across the ditch, reform, and charge the waiting French squares. Unable to break the squares, they soon found themselves surrounded by the French cavalry. Less than ten of the men who continued the charge after the disaster at the ditch made it back to the British lines.

The 1st KGL Light Dragoons, who were on the left and moving at a slower speed, were able to navigate the ditch without much mishap. But they too were repelled by

---

3. Tomkinson; page 1.

4. *WD* (enlarged ed.); Vol. 3, page 338. This brigade was formed on 25 May 1809 but General Erskine fell ill and could not continue to command it. He left the Peninsula in September 1809.

fire from the French squares. Their casualties were significantly lighter than the other regiment's.

The charge at Talavera was a disaster for General Anson's brigade. He lost control almost as soon as he gave the orders for them to charge. Instead of moving in unison the two regiments charged separately and the results were dire. In less than an hour the brigade had suffered 25 per cent casualties with the 23rd Light Dragoons losing 40 per cent of its strength. The regiment was so badly cut up that it was sent back to England three months later. There is also a question about what did General Anson did once the charge began: he did not lead it, for all the accounts state that it was led by Lieutenant Colonel Elley, the staff officer who had brought the orders. Furthermore none of the accounts left by the survivors of the charge mentioned him going forward or trying to bring the 23rd Light Dragoons back under control.

After the retreat back to Portugal, General Anson's brigade was stationed in the vicinity of Ciudad Rodrigo, along the River Agueda. It would work closely with the Light Division during June and July 1810 and would cover the British Army as it retreated deeper into Portugal. The brigade was not engaged at Busaco on 27 September.

After the Battle of Busaco, General Anson's Brigade formed part of the rearguard of the army as it retreated to the Lines of Torres Vedras. For ten days the brigade was in constant contact with the French cavalry, fighting to delay their advance. The brigade took heavy casualties before it reached the safety of the Lines. Although the individual regiments of the brigade performed admirably, the retreat was marked by poor coordination between the overall cavalry commander and his subordinate brigade commanders, including General Anson. The staff work at the brigade level was not much better. In one of the more memorable incidents of the retreat, Captain Bull's Royal Horse Artillery troop attached to the brigade was billeted in a village between the advancing French and the rest of the brigade. The duty squadron had to ride over a kilometer to its rescue.[5]

In late May 1811 General Anson led the vanguard of the British Army as it marched south from Ciudad Rodrigo. By early June they were in the vicinity of Badajoz screening the besieging forces. Two months later they returned to the vicinity of Ciudad Rodrigo. The brigade was engaged at Caprio on 25 September and a few days later went into winter quarters at Freixadas. In 1812, the brigade was part of the advance guard of the British Army that was moving into central Spain. However, General Anson had been on home leave in England and did not reunite with his command until 1 July. They fought at Castrejon on 18 July, but was in reserve at Salamanca on 22 July. After the defeat of the French, the brigade was part of the pursuit and was present at Garcia Hernandez the next day. During the epic retreat back to the Portuguese border in the fall, the brigade would be part of the rearguard of the army. It was in daily contact with the pursuing French cavalry. On 23 October the French caught up with the rearguard at Venta Del Poza. The two brigades of British cavalry were outnumbered four to one. A British diplomat saw the desperate fight:

I twice thought that Anson's brigade (which is weak in numbers and much exhausted by constant service) would have been annihilated and I believe we owed the preservation of that and of the German heavy brigade to the admirable steadiness

5. Tomkinson; page 85.

of Hackett's [sic] two light German battalions.[6] In talking of brigades, however, it is necessary to state that Anson's brigade had only 460 swords in the field, which is not more than one strong regiment, and that the German heavy brigade consists of two weak squadrons. On the other hand the French had from 1600 to 2000 swords against them. We literally had to fight our way for four miles; retiring, halting, charging, and again retiring ... notwithstanding all our difficulties we made some prisoners, and destroyed at least three times as many as we lost.[7]

The French eventually broke off their pursuit and the British Army made it back to the Portuguese border. General Anson spent the winter of 1813 with his brigade in central Portugal. In late May, the British Army was on the move again. General Anson's brigade was assigned to the northern column, which was commanded by General Thomas Graham. On 27 May it crossed into Spain. The brigade fought at Vitoria on 21 June and led the pursuit of the French convoy that was trying to escape via the road to Bayonne. It was General Anson's last battle. On 2 July he turned over command of the brigade to General John Vandeleur.

George Anson returned to England from the Peninsula several times between January 1810 and July 1812 to take up his duties in Parliament. He was absent from his command over 25 per cent of the time he commanded it. These absences totaled over twelve months and caused him to miss key battles and campaigns. They included February through April 1810, where he missed the opening moves of the French invasion of Portugal; four months in early 1811, by the time he returned it was too late to lead his brigade at the battle of Fuentes d'Oñoro; and the first six months of 1812, during which he missed the opening stages of the Salamanca Campaign. Although there were valid reasons for him to return to England, his absences were noted by his subordinates.[8] This could not have been good for morale.

By December 1812, Wellington was tired of General Anson spending so much time in England. In a letter to Colonel Torrens of the Horse Guards, he wrote that, 'I think also that it would be an advantage to the army to get rid of ... *Anson*, who spends the greatest part of his time in England, and is not very energetic when he is here.'[9] On 3 February 1813, General Anson requested in a letter to Wellington that he be sent back to England to serve on the Home Staff. Wellington forwarded his request while noting that he was sorry that General Anson was thinking of leaving.[10] It was not until 2 July that permission was granted for him to return home. The next day Wellington requested passage for him to sail home on the first warship returning to England.[11]

Upon his return to England in 1813, General Anson was assigned to the Home Staff of the Kent and then Sussex Districts until 1814. George Anson was a Member of Parliament from 1806 to 1841 and included the time he served in the army. He was Whig.

---

6. 'Hackett' is correct in the published quote. However, this refers to Lieutenant Colonel Colin Halkett.
7. *WSD*; Vol. 7, pages 464–5.
8. Tomkinson; pages 65, 120, 262.
9. *WSD*; Vol. 7, page 485.
10. *WD*; Vol. 10, page 92.
11. *WD*; Vol. 10, pages 494–5, and 498.

His official biography described him as a 'very lax attender, who was "no orator" and seldom spoke …'[12] He retired from Parliament in 1841.

In addition to his military awards, George Anson received numerous other honours. These included ADC to King George III on 1 January 1805, Groom of the Bedchamber to the Duke of Kent in 1800, Equerry to the Duke and Duchess of Kent from 1810–20, and Groom of the Bedchamber to Prince Albert, the Royal Consort, from 1840 to 1841.[13] On 23 February 1846, he was appointed the Lieutenant Governor of the Royal Hospital at Chelsea and its Governor on 18 May 1849. He died a few months later.

George Anson married Frances Hamilton on 27 May 1800. They had eight sons and six daughters. One son went into the army, one into the RN, and one into the military service of the HEIC.[14]

In 1812, Wellington referred to George Anson as a friend in a letter to Colonel Torrens.[15] They were the same age and both attended Eton at the same time as teenagers, although Wellington was a year behind him. Since this is the only time in their life prior to the Peninsular War that their paths crossed, it is likely that this was where their friendship was formed. Wellington did not let their friendship prevent him from requesting that General Anson be recalled to England in late 1812. However, when General Anson went back to England for the last time, Wellington took steps to ensure he received a berth on the next ship home.[16] Wellington continued to look after George Anson in the post-war years. In 1827 he interceded with King George IV on his behalf to ensure that Anson was appointed the regimental colonel of the 4th Dragoon Guards. The King was considering giving it to Lord George Beresford, who, despite being a major general, had never seen active service. Wellington also pointed out in the letter that he was doing this for the good of the army, even though George Anson was a Whig and opposed his government.[17]

In addition to being friends, there was a strong possibility that Wellington kept George Anson in command for as long as he did for political reasons. The Anson family was politically well connected, having virtually their own seat in Parliament from 1761 to 1868.[18] George Anson held that seat while he was Wellington's subordinate. Although he was a Whig and rarely supported the Tory Government, Wellington might have kept George Anson in command to demonstrate that as the army commander he was above politics, and to give the army a supporter in Parliament. Not to be discounted was the fact the Ansons were a noble family. George Anson had earls and lords on both his father's and mother's side, while his oldest brother was a viscount. He also had strong connections to the royal family. In addition to being an ADC to King George III, he was also the Equerry to the Duke and Duchess of Kent, Prince Edward Augustus and Princess Victoria of Saxe-Coburg-Saalfeld, the parents of Queen Victoria.

The four years General Anson served as a brigade commander was the longest that any individual commanded a brigade under Wellington. No other general came close. During those four years General Anson tried to be both a commander and a Member of

12. 'Anson, Sir George (1769–1849)'.
13. Ibid.
14. Few sources agree on the number of children they had. The number varies from a low of two to a high of fifteen. We have been able to identify fourteen by name.
15. *WSD*; Vol. 7, page 485.
16. *WD*; Vol. 10, pages 494–5, and 498.
17. *WND*; Vol. 3, pages 597–600.
18. In the span of 117 years, an Anson held the seat for 107 of them.

Parliament, which prevented him from doing either job well. Although his initial period as a commander was marked by the worse defeat of a British cavalry in the Peninsular War, he grew to be a competent commander. His biggest weakness was his lack of aggressiveness and drive that was expected of a light cavalry leader. Wellington realised this and as a result never considered giving him a division to command. Wellington's comment that he 'is not very energetic when he is here'[19] was supported by one of General Anson's subordinate officers, who served under him for the forty-eight months he commanded the brigade. He wrote that,

> General Anson here missed a good opportunity of doing something with their rear. It is always the case. When we come near the enemy, the body of the brigade is halted, and three squadrons sent forward under the field officer of the day. The same in retiring, three squadrons are always left unsupported.[20]

---

19. *WSD*; Vol. 7, page 485.
20. Tomkinson; page 191.

Anson, William

Date of Birth:	13 August 1772
Date Commissioned:	Ensign 1st Foot Guards: 13 June 1789 by purchase
Promotions:	Lieutenant & Captain 1st Foot Guards: 25 April 1793 without purchase
	Captain & Lieutenant Colonel 1st Foot Guards: 28 September 1797 by purchase[1]
	Brevet Colonel: 30 October 1805
	Major General: 4 June 1811
	Lieutenant General: 12 August 1819
	General: 10 January 1837
Regimental Colonel:	66th Foot: 7 December 1829–25 March 1835
	47th Foot: 25 March 1835–13 January 1847
Major Commands under Wellington:	Brigade 4th Division 9 April 1812–April 1814
	Temporarily commanded 4th Division: 9 April–c. 4 July and 22 July–October 1812
Awards:	AGC with three clasps: Corunna, Salamanca, Vitoria, Pyrenees, Nivelle, Orthes & Toulouse
	Mentioned in Dispatches: Castrejon, Salamanca, the Pyrenees, Nivelle & Orthes[2]
	KCB: 2 January 1815
Thanks of Parliament:	Salamanca, Pyrenees & Orthes
Date of Death:	13 January 1847, Brockhall near Weedon, Northamptonshire

Until 1773 the family name was Adams.

William Anson was the third son of George Anson and Mary Vernon. His mother was the daughter of 1st Lord Vernon. He was the brother of General Sir George Anson, Lieutenant Colonel Sambrooke Anson, and Captain Edward Anson. William's father inherited two estates and his family was quite wealthy. He grew up in Shugborough Hall, Staffordshire.

William Anson was commissioned as an ensign in the 1st Foot Guards in 1789. It was his family's regiment. Many of his relatives had served in the regiment over the past 100 years; several would serve with him; and others would continue to serve in it long after him. It would be his home for the next twenty-two years. In February 1793 he went with the 1st Battalion to Flanders, but two months later he returned to England when he was promoted to lieutenant and captain. He went to Flanders again in 1794 and stayed there until the army returned in 1795. He was promoted to captain and lieutenant colonel in 1797 and became a company commander. In 1805 he was promoted to colonel and deployed with the 1st Battalion to Sicily in 1806 as the commander of the Grenadier Company.[3] Colonel Anson returned to England with his battalion in December 1807.[4]

1. Removed from the regiment as a general officer receiving unattached pay, 25 July 1814.
2. Bromley; Vol. 1, page 15.
3. Hamilton; Vol. 2, page 376.
4. Ibid; page 375.

In October 1808, the 1st Battalion 1st Foot Guards, commanded by Colonel Anson, sailed for Spain as part of General David Baird's Division. After landing at Corunna on 28 October, the division marched east to link up with General John Moore's army. On 19 November, General Baird divided his division into two temporary divisions and gave command of one to General Henry Warde. This left the Guards Brigade with no commander and Colonel Anson was given command of it. After General Baird's force joined General Moore, the army was reorganised on 20 December. General Warde resumed command of his brigade and Colonel Anson returned to command his battalion. Before long the army was given orders to withdraw back to Corunna and thus began one of the epic retreats of the British Army. At times, Colonel Anson and his battalion would fight as part of the rearguard and the discipline and the bearing of his troops were noted several times by the army commander. At the end of the retreat, as they marched into Corunna, an eyewitness wrote that he was watching them come in

> when Sir John called his attention, saying: – 'Arbuthnot, look at that body of men in the distance; they are the Guards, by the way they are marching.' They watched them and saw them march into Corunna by sections, their drums beating, the drum-major in front flourishing his stick, the sergeant-major at the head, and the drill-sergeants on the flanks keeping the men in step, exactly as if they were on their own drill-ground at home. Sir Robert said: 'It was a fine sight, and one he would never forget.'[5]

Colonel Anson and his battalion fought at Corunna on 16 January 1809 but were not heavily engaged. After the battle the army embarked for England.[6]

Less than six months after Colonel Anson returned to England, he and the 1st Battalion 1st Foot Guards joined the Walcheren Expedition. They stayed in the disease-ridden area less than two months before they went back to England. The 1st Battalion saw little combat in the sixty days they were there, however, 'Walcheren Fever' took a terrible toll on it. The battalion left England with a strength of 1,524 officers and men.[7] By February 1810, the battalion had three officers and over 100 other ranks die from the fever since leaving Walcheren five months earlier.[8] Another 10 per cent would be too incapacitated for active service. Colonel Anson stayed with his battalion until 4 June 1811, when he was promoted to major general. Within a month he was assigned to the military staff in Ireland.

In a letter dated 3 November 1811, Lieutenant Colonel Torrens of the Horse Guards informed Wellington that General Anson had been appointed to his staff. He arrived in Portugal in early April and on 9 April 1812 he replaced General James Kemmis as a brigade commander in the 4th Division. Paperwork was a bit slow reaching the Peninsula, for it was not until 13 May that was he officially appointed to the staff of the army in the Peninsula. However, his appointment was backdated to 25 November 1811 in the same general orders.

General Anson took command of his brigade on 9 April 1812, three days after Badajoz had fallen. He assumed temporary command of the 4th Division as soon as he arrived and led it on 13 June when it advanced into Spain. Three weeks later, General Lowry

---

5. Ibid; page 392.
6. Ibid; pages 394–7.
7. Ibid; page 400.
8. Ibid; page 405.

Cole returned from sick leave to take command of it. General Anson and his brigade would distinguish themselves at the Battle of Castrillo on 18 July.[9] During the Battle of Salamanca on 22 July, they were on the left flank of the division and had the mission of holding the Lesser Arapiles. It was instrumental in defeating the main French attack on the centre of the British line in mid-afternoon.

The Battle of Salamanca shattered the command structure of the 4th Division. General Cole was seriously wounded as were the other two brigade commanders. By the end of the day General Anson was in command of the division. A few days later the division marched on Madrid and spent the next three months in its vicinity. In October General Cole was back and commanded the division during the retreat to the Portuguese border.

General Anson commanded at Vitoria and in the desperate fighting at the First and Second Battles of Sorauren in late July 1813. The brigade crossed the Pyrenees into France in mid-October and was part of the assault on the Lesser Rhune at the Battle of Nivelle on 10 November. After the battle they went into winter quarters. In late December 1813, rumors were spreading that General Anson would be leaving the brigade. General Sir John Hope had arrived in Spain two months before as the replacement for General Thomas Graham, who was heading home due to poor health. In addition to commanding the 1st Division, he was to command the Left Wing of the army. The rumors had General Hope being appointed the permanent commander of the Left Wing and General Kenneth Howard, the commander of the Guards Brigade, taking permanent command of the 1st Division. General Anson would then take command of the vacant Guards Brigade.[10] It was not to happen. General Howard did assume temporary command of the 1st Division, but Colonel Peregrine Maitland was given temporary command of the Guards Brigade.[11]

In February 1814, Wellington went on the offensive. General Anson led his brigade at Orthes on 27 February. Its final battle was at Toulouse on 10 April. Two days later, the war was over.

With the army breaking up starting in May, General Anson was placed in command of the 2nd Division.[12] He commanded until the army was completely disbanded in June and he returned to England. Despite being a senior major general, he was not given command during the Waterloo Campaign. He would never have an active command again. Other than being a regimental colonel from 1829 to 1847, his only military duties was as one of the members of the Consolidated Board of General Officers, of which he was a member from 1816 until his death.[13]

William Anson did not receive the numerous honours that his older brother George did. He was made a KCB in 1815. In 1831 his service to his country was finally recognised and he was created the Baronet of Birch Hall, Lancashire by King William IV.

William Anson married Louisa Dickenson on 26 January 1815. They had seven children. One son went into the army. He died in 1847 and was interred in the family catacombs in Kensal Green Cemetery in London. His brother, George Anson, would also be interred there upon his death in 1849.[14]

---

9. This battle was a running combat that began in Castrejon and lasted for several hours. The two are often treated as separate combats. Wellington wrote one dispatch for both.
10. Glover, Gareth; *Wellington's Lieutenant*; page 233.
11. Oman; *History*, Vol. 7, pages 169–170. Oman; *Wellington's Army*; page 371.
12. General Order, 25 May 1814.
13. *RMC*; Vol. 3, page 59. *New Companion*; page 149.
14. Bromley; Vol. 1, pages 14–15.

General Anson was a tough but fair disciplinarian. Very few results of court-martials he presided over still exist. Those that do show a variety of verdicts, ranging from not guilty, guilty, and not guilty of one charge but guilty of others. When a soldier was found guilty, sentences range from 100 to 1,000 lashes, while 800 or more lashes were common.[15] In early 1813, General Anson was ordered to Lamego, Portugal, where he presided over a sitting court-martial and heard a number of cases.[16] In the one case that the verdict and sentence is known three privates from the 1st Battalion 27th Foot were accused of robbing Portuguese shepherds. The evidence against them was overwhelming. They were found guilty and sentenced to 1,000 lashes each. Lieutenant Charles Crowe of the 27th Foot left a vivid account of the punishment:

> The 48th Regiment was ordered to attend the punishment, with our own, which from the appalling number of lashes occupied a long time, but as most of our drummers were boys did not prove so severe as I dreaded. The first culprit received 875, the second 925 and Gallagher 975. When he was taken from the halberds, the audacious villain turned round and said 'Thank-you colonel! The next battle we are in we will settle this affair!'[17]

General Anson looked out for his subordinates, whether they were in his brigade or in his former regiment. His ADC was Ensign Henry Vernon, 1st Foot Guards.[18] In 1813 he twice had to select a temporary brigade major. Each time his initial selection was an officer from within his brigade. However, both times the division commander overruled him and appointed someone else. The first time it happened, the officer was told by his battalion commander that,

> You know that our brigade major is killed; as our regiment has borne the brunt of the battle, our brigadier, Major General Anson, requested me to name an officer to fill the post, until someone was officially appointed. I recommended and General Anson readily accepted you, but General Cole overheard our conversation and asserted his claim to make the appointment. A very warm altercation ensued between the lieutenant [general] and major general and I am fearful you will not be called upon.[19]

Unlike his brother George, William Anson had few political or royal connections to further his career. It does not appear that he had any ambition to advance himself by his own initiative. He did his duty accepting what was given, but did not expect more. He was a competent brigade commander and his performance as the temporary commander of the 4th Division showed that he was capable of commanding a division. It was likely he would have eventually risen to division command if the war had lasted longer.

---

15. General Order, 12 July 1812.
16. Glover, Gareth; *Wellington's Lieutenant*; page 173. General Anson turned over command to his senior battalion commander, Lieutenant Colonel George Bingham, because he was over 70 kilometers away from the command for about six weeks.
17. Glover, Gareth; *An Eloquent Soldier*; page 58.
18. Ensign Vernon was also his first cousin.
19. Glover; *An Eloquent Soldier*; pages 145 & 293.

Anstruther, Robert

Date of Birth:	3 March 1768
Date Commissioned:	Ensign 3rd Foot Guards: 21 September 1785 by purchase
Promotions:	Lieutenant & Captain 3rd Foot Guards: 16 May 1792 by purchase
	Brevet Major: 30 March 1797
	Major 66th Foot: 17 August 1797 without purchase
	Lieutenant Colonel 68th Foot: 31 August 1797 by purchase
	Captain & Lieutenant Colonel 3rd Foot Guards: 16 August 1799 by exchange
	Brevet Colonel: 1 January 1805
	Brigadier General on the Staff: 1808–1809
Major Commands under Wellington:	Brigade: 15 July–5 September 1808[1]
Awards:	Sultan's Gold Medal for Egypt
	AGM: Vimeiro
Mentioned in Dispatches:	Den Helder, Egypt & Vimeiro
Date of Death:	14 January 1809 from pneumonia and exhaustion in Corunna, Spain

Robert Anstruther was born in 1768, the eldest son of Sir Robert Anstruther, 3rd Baronet of Balcaskie, Fifeshire in Scotland and Janet Erskine. His mother was the daughter of the 5th Earl of Kellie. He was educated at the Westminster School in London and as a teenager attended military schools in Strasburg, France and Berlin. He was fluent in French and could speak German.[2]

In 1785, Robert Anstruther was commissioned in the 3rd Foot Guards and fought with the regiment in the Flanders Expedition from 1793 to1795. In early 1796 he was attached to the headquarters of the Austrian Army in south-west Germany as an observer. He served for about a year and was wounded in the side.[3] In 1799 Lieutenant Colonel Anstruther was appointed DQMG on the staff of the British Expeditionary Force to Den Helder. While there he worked closely with both General Ralph Abercromby and General John Moore. His outstanding performance on the staff was recognised by the Duke of York, the overall commander of the force. The following year he became the QMG to General Abercromby when he assumed command of the British forces in the Mediterranean. During the two years he was the QMG for the British forces in the Mediterranean, he also served as the QMG of the army that General Abercromby took to Egypt to oust the French Army there. While in Egypt he became close friends with General Sir John Moore. Lieutenant Colonel Anstruther was mentioned in dispatches for his stellar work as a staff officer in both the Den Helder and the Egypt Campaigns.[4]

After the capitulation of the French Army in Egypt in 1801, Lieutenant Colonel Anstruther returned to England. In early 1802 he was appointed DQMG to the Army, but in May he was sent to Ireland where he became the AG. He would hold that position until his death in Spain in 1809. On 1 January 1805, he was promoted to colonel and made an ADC to the King. While in Ireland, Colonel Anstruther worked closely with

---

1. The brigade was numbered the 7th Brigade on 19 August 1808.
2. *RMP* 1811; Vol. 4, page 306.
3. Anderson; Vol. 1, page 142.
4. *RMP* 1811; Vol. 4, pages 306–7.

Wellington, who was the Chief Secretary of Ireland.[5] Three years later he was promoted to brigadier general on the home staff in Ireland.

In 1808 the British Government decided to send an expeditionary force to Portugal. General Anstruther received command of a brigade that was located in Ramsgate, England. The initial plan was for them to go to Cadiz, but at the last minute it was assigned to Wellington's command. The brigade sailed on 16 July and landed at Mondego Bay on 19 August.[6] The brigade was renamed the 7th Brigade when it linked up with the army. Two days later they fought the French at Vimeiro.

General Anstruther's brigade was deployed on a hill just south of Vimeiro. They were in the front line and met the first assault by the French. He described the fight in his journal:

Went out in front of a small wood, about three-quarters of a mile from the left of Fane's[7] brigade, from whence I saw distinctly the advance of the enemy. His force appeared to consist of a large corps of cavalry, and six or seven brigades of infantry, marching on a wide front, and advancing rapidly towards our centre. A large column seemed also pointing towards our left – but being distant, and partly concealed by the heights, could not see them distinctly. Sent Gordon to report to Sir Arthur these particulars, and that there was every appearance of a general attack. On returning to my brigade, received orders to march to the left; but the enemy by this time was so close that there was no possibility of leaving my ground. Drew up my brigade, amounting to two thousand four hundred men, as follows: 97th in Front, in prolongation of the front of General Fane's brigade; 52nd in line, in echelon to the left flank of 97th: 9th in open column behind, on the left flank of the 52nd; 43d in open column behind right flank 97th. The enemy came down rapidly along the road, directly in front of the 50th, and when within about nine hundred yards deployed to their left, so as to bring their front parallel to ours: heavy cannonade from our guns, which caused the enemy much loss but did not check his advance. Brigadier-General Fane sent out nearly all the 60th and companies 95th to skirmish with their sharpshooters; after a good deal of firing our people were driven in. Sent the light company 97th and three companies 52d to cover their retreat; the latter made a gallant stand, but were at length driven in almost to the position, and the enemy advanced to the edge of the copse, about one hundred and fifty yards from us. Ordered the 97th, who were concealed behind a dip of the ground, to rise and fire; after two or three rounds, they began to advance from the position, and finding it impossible to stop them without great risk, ordered the 52d to support them on their right, and, if possible, to turn the left of the enemy. This they did very dexterously; whilst the 97th made a vigorous attack in front. The enemy soon gave way, and was pursued to the skirts of the wood, beyond which his superiority in cavalry made it imprudent to advance. Rallied the 97th and 52d, and leaving strong piquets in the wood, brought them back to the position: the 9th remained in reserve and was but little engaged. In the mean time Brigadier-General Fane, on my left, was very warmly engaged ... Sent the 43d and all the cavalry to Fane's assistance

5. Muir; *Wellington: The Path to Victory*, page 228.
6. Moorsom; page 84.
7. General Henry Fane.

– the former being obliged to put two companies in the front houses of the village, the enemy being very near it. The 50th regiment, however, by a very bold attack, defeated the enemy opposed to them, taking all their guns, tumbrils, &c.; and the 43d, with equal gallantry, came to the bayonet with the corps on the left, and drove them completely back.[8]

After defeating the 1st French assault, General Anstruther's Brigade did not see any other action that day. Within seven months of Vimeiro, a legend had grown about General Anstruther's calm demeanour during the battle. His brigade was about to receive the brunt of the French assault and Wellington had sent one of his aides-de-camp to say that reinforcements were on the way should he need assistance. General Anstruther replied, 'Sir, I want no assistance: I am beating the French and am able to beat them whenever I meet them.'[9]

On 5 September 1808, General Hew Dalyrmple reorganised the army and General Anstruther was appointed to command a new brigade in General Edward Paget's Advance Corps. That same day he received orders to go to Almeida to oversee the evacuation of the French garrison there. However, he was to go via Oporto, where he was to 'confer with the Bishop; endeavor to prevail on him to come to Lisbon, and place himself at the head of the government.'[10] He left Lisbon on 7 September and arrived in Oporto on 15 September. He met with the bishop that night.[11]

While in Oporto, General Anstruther took time to write to Wellington on 16 September to inform him that the bishop had consented to serve as the president of the Regency if asked. He also reminded Wellington 'that you will recollect my anxious wish to be employed under your command, and that you will endeavour to manage that for me should you have a separate command, which I conclude will be the case.'[12]

General Anstruther succeeded in his mission to have the bishop join the new government and in the middle of the following week he headed to Almeida. In addition to arranging for the turnover of Almeida and the evacuation of the French garrison to Lisbon, he had been told to 'obtain every necessary information, should the army eventually enter Spain by that route.'[13] This included meeting with Portuguese and Spanish officials to ensure the smooth passage of the army.[14] Over the next two months, General Anstruther organised billets, arranged for supplies, and coordinated the movement of the different divisions as the army passed through the area on its way into Spain. To help in this he had the assistance of Lieutenant Colonel Benjamin D'Urban (AQMG), who spoke Portuguese, and Major Mark de Montalembert (AQMG).

In September the government decided to form a force to operate in Spain, under General John Moore, and a garrison for Portugal. General Anstruther was chosen to serve with General Moore. On 8 October he reorganised the army and General Anstruther was appointed to command a new brigade in General Edward Paget's Division. By

---

8. Anstruther; pages 108–9.
9. *Universal Magazine*; Vol. 11, January–June 1809; page 350.
10. Anstruther; page 117.
11. Dalrymple; page 97.
12. *WSD*; Vol. 6, page 138.
13. Dalrymple; page 105.
14. Anstruther; page 241.

21 November he was still in Almeida awaiting orders to rejoin his brigade in Spain.[15] Around 1 December he received a letter dated 29 November from Lieutenant Colonel George Murray, the army's QMG. It did not contain the orders he wished for. Instead Lieutenant Colonel Murray was passing on news of the Spanish defeat at Tudela and that General Anstruther needed to make arrangements for the army returning to Portugal if the situation in Spain deteriorated.[16] General Anstruther had anticipated this and had ordered Lieutenant Colonel D'Urban to do a reconnaissance of the area that Lieutenant Colonel Murray proposed as the fallback position for the army.[17] Lieutenant Colonel D'Urban noted in his diary on 3 December that:

> Here let me pay tribute of respect to the firm and comprehensive mind of General Anstruther. When no human being thought of the possibility of a retreat, when the conquest and success were in every mouth, he alone looked forward to a reverse, he provided for falling back, though it was a thing almost out of the question, and when he sent me to reconnoiter [*sic*] the Frontier Line of the Coa, he said to me 'No one can say how soon this knowledge may be necessary. A Retreat into Portugal may yet be upon the Cards, and as we have leisure, we will be prepared.' Now, although evidently loathing the measure of retiring, and condemning the doing so without a Battle as a loss of National Honour, he has so effectually exerted himself that in a few hours every preparation is made, the Convoys all turned back, orders for provisions given, and all this with so much finesse that whatever the Spaniards may imagine from the unguarded steps nearer to Head Quarters, the Portuguese at least believe that these measures are in a part a feint to deceive the Enemy, in part a provision for reinforcements from Lisbon and Oporto, to countenance which the Garrison of the latter place in March for Lamega.[18]

Shortly after hearing from Lieutenant Colonel Murray, General Anstruther received orders to join the main army. After riding over 220 kilometers in less than a week, he linked up with the army in the vicinity of Toro by 14 December. On 20 December, General Moore reorganised the army again. General Anstruther was kept in command of his brigade and was augmented with nine companies from the 1st Battalion 95th Rifles. General Paget continued to command the division, but it was renamed the Reserve Division.

On 23 December General Moore received word at his headquarters in Astorga that Napoleon had gathered forces together to destroy the British Army. General Moore recognised that his army was too small to defeat Napoleon and ordered it to retreat. Instead of returning to Portugal via Almeida, he decided to head north-west and evacuate his army from Corunna. The route the army took was about 275 kilometers long, through the most mountainous region of Spain. The road was poor and the weather terrible, with bitterly cold temperatures, snow, sleet and ice every day. The initial stages of the retreat were covered by Colonel Robert Craufurd's Light Brigade and General Charles Stewart's Cavalry Brigade. Despite the horrible weather and little food, the army was able to make Lugo (about 175 kilometers from Astorga) in eight days. On 31 December,

---

15. Dalrymple; pages 314–15.
16. Anstruther; page 254.
17. D'Urban; page 11.
18. Ibid; pages 14–15.

General Moore sent Colonel Craufurd's Brigade to Vigo and continued with the rest of the army to Corunna. General Anstruther and his brigade, which were still at Bembibre, became the rearguard until they reached Corunna eleven days later. Those eleven days saw numerous skirmishes and combats, including on 3 January 1809, when the brigade turned to face the pursuing French cavalry. The 95th Rifles were bringing up the rear that day and in the bitter fight that followed, the French commander, General Auguste Colbert, was killed. By the time the brigade reached Corunna on 11 January, they had marched and fought over 130 kilometers.

During the retreat, General Anstruther bivouacked in the open with his troops.[19] The hardship of the retreat, combined with the stress of commanding the rearguard during horrible weather over an extended period, was too much. His health began to decline a few days before the brigade reached Corunna. On 10 January 1809, Dr Adam Neale, a physician assigned to his brigade, examined him at Betanzos, a town about 30 kilometers from Corunna.

He was evidently laboring under inflammation of the lungs; but was relieved by losing blood. On visiting him early on the following morning, he was no better, and I was a good deal alarmed to find that he had hardly any recollection of what had passed the preceding evening. He had been advised to travel in a carriage to Corunna. That conveyance, however, could not be procured, and he was obliged to ride on horseback – a circumstance which was to be lamented, as the morning was cold, and he was inclined to perspire. He informed the gentlemen about him, that he had been for twenty-two hours on horseback, during which time he had tasted nothing, except a bit of sea biscuit and a drop of rum; and that at length, quite worn out with fatigue, he had thrown himself down in a field, and slept for about an hour in the rain. To this circumstance he attributed his illness. On the 11th, after his ride to Corunna, he was much worse. He was again bled, without his symptoms being alleviated. The disease ran its course very speedily, uninterrupted by any of the remedies employed. The delirium, apparently almost from the first attack, speedily increased, and on the night of 14th he was no more.[20]

Dr Neale wrote that during his delirium, General Anstruther often spoke of the military situation in the Asturias and Montana and conversed with his friends who were not present.[21]

General Anstruther was buried on the north-east bastion of the citadel of Corunna. Because of the seriousness of the military situation, only Major de Montalembert and Captain Gordon attended his burial.[22]

---

19. *RMC* 1811; Vol. 2, page 332.
20. Neale; pages 343–4.
21. Ibid; page 344.
22. *Universal Magazine*; Vol. XI, January–June 1809; pages 349–51. Unfortunately we have not been able to determine the identity of Captain Gordon. General Anstruther's ADC was Captain George St Leger Gordon, however, he was promoted to major in August 1808 and by the time of the funeral commanded the 6th Foot. Another possibility was the ADC to General Mackenzie Fraser, who commanded the 3rd Division. He was Captain Orford Gordon. Despite the mix-up in the ranks, it was likely George St Leger Gordon who attended the funeral out of respect for his former commander.

Robert Anstruther excelled as both a commander and a staff officer. During the campaign in Portugal and Spain in 1808 and 1809 he performed brilliantly at Vimeiro and during the retreat to Corunna. Over the years his talents were recognised by the three greatest British generals of the Napoleonic era: Sir Ralph Abercromby, Sir John Moore, and Wellington. He was close to all three and named his eldest son Ralph Abercromby. General Sir John Moore, who was mortally wounded at the Battle of Corunna two days after Robert Anstruther died from pneumonia, requested that they be buried together. When Wellington heard of his death, he wrote to Colonel Hugh Mackay Gordon, Military Secretary to General Charles Stanhope Earl of Harrington, the commander of the forces in Ireland:

> You will have heard of the death of poor Anstruther, which I doubt not will have grieved you and Lord Harrington as much as it has me. He is a great loss to us in Ireland, and it will be very difficult to replace him.[23]

In the same letter, Wellington took steps to ensure that General Anstruther's family was taken care of. He was successful and Charlotte Lucy Anstruther received a pension from the government of £300 per year.[24] She also received a pension from the Hereditary Revenue of Scotland of £276 10s per year. Robert Anstruther married Charlotte Lucy Hamilton on 16 March 1799. She was the daughter of Colonel James Hamilton. They had five children.

General Anstruther was well thought of by his peers. General Charles William Stewart, who commanded the rearguard cavalry during the retreat to Corunna, testified in Parliament on 25 January 1809 that 'General Anstruther, an officer for whom I entertained the sincerest love and affection, who had promised to become one of the brightest ornaments of the British army, but who, unfortunately for his country, died in consequence of the fatigue of the late retreat.'[25]

In addition to being an outstanding brigade commander, General Anstruther was a superb staff officer. He knew this and was concerned that he would be removed from command and placed on the staff. Upon learning he was to go to Almeida, he wrote:

> I beg permission to state, that my great object in coming on service on this occasion, was to be placed in command of troops; that I avoided or declined all proposals that seemed likely to interfere with that view. Now I cannot divest myself of some apprehension that this Almeida business may eventually throw me back into pen and ink, and defeat a purpose which, the more I consider it, the more I feel it to be advantageous and necessary to my future progression in the service.[26]

Had General Anstruther survived the retreat to Corunna, Wellington may have been able to arrange another brigade command for him. However, he was too junior to be considered for command of a division. Because of his reputation as a staff officer it is more likely that Wellington would have made him his AG.

23. *WSD*; Vol. 5, pages 537–8.
24. *Estimates and Accounts*; page 279.
25. Elliot; page 248.
26. *Universal Magazine*; Vol. XI, January–June 1809; page 105.

Aylmer, Matthew, 5th Baron Aylmer

Date of Birth:	24 May 1775
Date Commissioned:	Ensign 49th Foot: 19 October 1787 by purchase
Promotions:	Lieutenant 49th Foot: 26 October 1791 by purchase
	Captain 49th Foot: 8 August 1794 by purchase
	Major 85th Foot: 9 October 1800 without purchase
	Lieutenant Colonel 85th Foot: 25 March 1802 by purchase
	Captain & Lieutenant Colonel Coldstream Foot Guards: 9 June 1803 by exchange[1]
	Brevet Colonel: 25 July 1810
	Major General: 4 June 1813
	Lieutenant General: 27 May 1825
	General: 23 November 1841
Regimental Colonel:	56th Foot: 29 October 1827– 23 July 1832
	18th Foot: 23 July 1832– 23 February 1850
Major Commands under Wellington:	Deputy Adjutant General: 1 January 1812–April 1814
	Acting Adjutant General:[2] December 1812–July 1813
	Independent brigade:[3] July 1813–April 1814
Awards:	AGC with clasp: Talavera, Busaco, Fuentes de Oñoro, Vitoria & Nive
	Kt: 6 June 1815
	KCB: 2 January 1815
	GCB: 10 September 1836
Thanks of Parliament:	Vitoria
Date of Death:	23 February 1850 in London from a heart aneurysm

Name was originally Matthew Aylmer, however, he was known as Matthew, Lord Aylmer from 22 October 1785 to 23 February 1850. He changed his last name to Whitworth-Aylmer on 4 July 1825.

Matthew Lord Aylmer was born in 1775, the eldest son of Henry 4th Baron Aylmer of Balrath, Meath, Ireland and Catherine Whitworth. He was the older brother of Admiral Sir Frederick (who later became the 6th Baron Aylmer). He was fluent in French and spoke 'with the greatest ease and elegance.'[4] His family was Irish nobility and when his father died in 1785, he succeeded him both as the 8th Baronet of Balrath, Meath and as the 5th Baron Aylmer of Balrath, Meath.

Matthew Aylmer was commissioned as an ensign in the 49th Foot in 1787 at the age of twelve. He immediately went to the West Indies where, after nine months, he became very sick and had to return to England. In 1789 he was back with his regiment, which was in Santo Domingo, and would remain with them for the next five years. While there, he purchased his lieutenancy and captaincy. In late September 1794, he departed for England on sick leave. In 1797, Captain Aylmer was appointed the ADC to General John Leland who was serving in the Eastern District. A year later, in May 1798, he commanded the

---

1. Removed from the regiment as a general officer receiving unattached pay, 25 July 1814.
2. He was the DAG at the time.
3. Despite being a brigade commander, he was never officially removed from his duties as the DAG.
4. Buckner.

Grenadier Company of the 49th Foot and went with them to Flanders on a raid to destroy the locks of the Ostend-Bruges Canal. He and his company were taken prisoner near Ostend and he remained in captivity until November. The following summer he returned to Flanders as part of the Den Helder Expedition. He fought at Den Helder, Alkmaar, and Bergen. He was back in England by the end of November and was appointed the ADC to General Lord Charles Somerset. Ten months later he was promoted to major in the 85th Foot. In 1801, he and his regiment were sent to Jamaica.[5]

In March 1802, Major Aylmer purchased a lieutenant colonelcy in the 85th Foot, however, he was placed on half-pay when his battalion was disbanded ten months later. In June 1803, he exchanged in to the Coldstream Guards. In 1805 he attended the Royal Military College, a school for training officers to serve on the staff. Lieutenant Colonel Aylmer rejoined his regiment in time to go with them in General Edward Finch's Guards Brigade both to Hanover – from November 1805 to February 1806 – and to Copenhagen from August to October 1807. Upon his return from Denmark in 1807, he was appointed to his first staff position and became an AAG in the Kent District. He served there until late 1808.[6]

In December 1808, Lieutenant Colonel Aylmer was appointed the DAG of General John Sherbrooke's force that was being sent to secure Cadiz in southern Spain. They sailed on 15 January 1809 but encountered contrary winds and a gale. The force eventually reached Cadiz on 8 March, but the Spanish government refused to allow it to land. General Sherbrooke turned his force around and sailed for Lisbon, arriving on 13 March 1809. Its four battalions joined the British Garrison in Portugal. Lieutenant Colonel Aylmer was appointed as an AAG to the army in April 1809 and attached to the 1st Division on 18 June.

In June 1810, Lieutenant Colonel Aylmer requested permission to resign as the AAG of the 1st Division and to rejoin his battalion, the 1st Battalion Coldstream Guards, which was in Portugal. General Charles Stewart, the AG, responded that Wellington considered it 'impossible ... to permit you to retire from the Adjutant General's department, especially at a juncture like the present, when the division is passing into new hands, and when your efficient services will be so much required.'[7] The next month saw him promoted to Colonel and appointed an ADC to the King.

Seven months later, Colonel Aylmer asked to be appointed the DAG at Cadiz, since the officer filling the positon wished to return to England. Wellington took up his case and wrote to General Graham on 13 January 1811: 'I assure you that you could not have an Officer...more fit for the situation, and better calculated to give you satisfaction, than Lord Aylmer...you will find him a most useful Staff Officer.'[8] However, when a vacancy did occur, another officer was appointed in his place by General Sir Thomas Graham. During the summer of 1811, Colonel Aylmer became seriously ill and went home. Wellington was concerned that his poor health would keep him from returning, and his fears were not misplaced, for Colonel Aylmer would not be back with the army for another fifteen months.[9]

5. *RMC*; Vol. 3, pages 330–1.

6. *RMC*; Vol. 3, page 331. Ward; pages 24–6, and 170.

7. *WSD*; Vol. 13, page 411.

8. *WD*; Vol. 7, page 141.

9. *WD*; Vol. 8, pages 189–190 & 534. Fremantle; page 117.

When it was decided in late 1811 that General Edward Pakenham had to relinquish his staff appointment as DAG, since he was commanding a brigade, discussion centred on Colonel Aylmer being appointed to the position. Lieutenant Colonel Henry Torrens of the Horse Guards wrote to Wellington on 17 November 1811 that the Duke of York favoured him for the position, but wanted Wellington's opinion on it.[10] Not much later, in January 1812, Lieutenant Colonel Torrens wrote that he had talked to General Pakenham about Colonel Aylmer being appointed. General Pakenham replied 'that no person is better calculated to succeed him.'[11] Colonel Aylmer was appointed as the DAG in a General Order dated 29 January 1812, with the appointment to date from 1 January. It would be many months before he actually reported for duty.

While Colonel Aylmer was in England, gossip spread among the officers of his regiment (the Coldstream Guards) that he was under pressure from the regimental colonel, the Duke of Cambridge,[12] to resign his appointment as the DAG. At first the speculation was that despite the Duke of Cambridge being 'exceedingly angry at his accepting the situation [to be the DAG]'[13] part of the rumor was that Aylmer would not give up his appointment and would transfer out of the regiment. By May 1812, the rumors had changed to speculating when he would return to Portugal. At least one had him not coming back to the Peninsula because he was still very sick, while another stated that he would not until he received a promotion to major general. In July the gossip had changed to not whether he would return, but whether he would come back as the commander of the 1st Battalion.[14] By November 1812, Colonel Aylmer had returned to Portugal and had taken up his duties as the DAG of the army. However, by then the AG, Charles Stewart, had left the Peninsula in April 1812 and never returned. Colonel Aylmer became the acting AG.

In December 1812 a discussion took place on a possible replacement for his missing AG, Charles Stewart. Colonel Torrens wrote to Wellington on 23 December 1812 that, 'HRH will be totally guided by your wishes. If you should not fix upon Pakenham…the only eligible Candidates I know of …and Lord Aylmer…I merely throw out these names for your consideration.'[15] Colonel Aylmer was well thought of by his subordinates in the Adjutant General Department. In the spring of 1813, one DAAG wrote: 'Ld. Aylmer was at this time the head of the Adjutant General's department an excellent Officer much respected & beloved. He was exceedingly methodical in all his arrangements & appeared fully to enjoy the confidence of Ld. Wellington.'[16]

By mid-April a replacement for General Stewart had still not been found. On 14 April 1813, Wellington wrote a series of letters to General Pakenham, Colonel Torrens and Earl Bathurst proposing that General Pakenham be the new AG. He also stated that he would recommend Aylmer for the position should General Pakenham decline to accept it.[17] General Pakenham agreed to the appointment, but it was not until July 1813 that he actually began to serve in the position.

---

10. Unpublished letter from Torrens to Wellington, dated 17 November 1811.
11. Unpublished letter from Torrens to Wellington, dated 4 January 1812.
12. Prince Adolphus Duke of Cambridge, a son of King George III.
13. Fremantle; page 103.
14. Ibid; pages 101, 103, 111, 113 and 117.
15. Unpublished letter from Torrens to Wellington, dated 23 December 1812.
16. Buckley; page 204.
17. *WD*; Vol. 10, pages 293–4.

Promoting Colonel Aylmer to brigadier general was not an option, since he was only the DAG and junior to nine colonels in Wellington's army. Convention at the time prevented Wellington from promoting a deserving officer over the heads of other officers in his army who were senior, but possibly not as deserving. If he had promoted Colonel Aylmer to brigadier general, he would have had to promote the others or send them back to England. The promotions to major general of 4 June 1813, in honour of King George III's birthday, included all colonels who were promoted in July 1810, not just for the eleven colonels in Wellington's army. Colonel Aylmer was one of the colonels promoted to major general. Wellington was able to give brigade command to six of these newly promoted major generals, but sent home four others. Despite being junior to the others, Major General Aylmer was retained on the staff by Wellington.[18]

On 20 July 1813, Major General Aylmer was ordered to Pasajes to take command of a brigade that was being formed by battalions new to the army. This independent brigade was never assigned to a division, but was attached to the 1st Division throughout the rest of the war.

General Alymer's new brigade was not filled with veterans. One battalion was part of the British garrison in Cadiz, while another was so devastated by Walcheren Fever in 1809 that it took four years before it was considered fit for active duty. The third had left Portugal two years before and had so many discipline problems among its officers, the Duke of York had replaced all but one of them the previous year. Many of the men in the battalions were new recruits and not ready for active campaigning. The brigade was initially deployed in support of the siege of San Sebastian. They were at San Murcial in late August, and stormed the village of Urrogne at the Battle of Nivelle. At the Battle of Nive, General Lord Aylmer's brigade led the assault on Barrouillet. Shortly afterwards it went into winter cantonments and did not see any action for three months. In February 1814, they were part of the British force that invested Bayonne and would remain there until April when Napoleon abdicated.

By late May 1814, General Aylmer's brigade was disbanded and he returned to England. He was placed on the staff of first the Centre District and then the Eastern District, both in Ireland. On 22 December 1814 he was appointed the AG of Ireland until July 1815, when the position was abolished. General Aylmer spent the next seven years traveling through Italy and Switzerland. While on the continent, he was promoted to lieutenant general in 1825. That same year he changed his name to Whitworth-Aylmer, after his uncle, the Earl of Whitworth, died.[19] In early 1825 he was one of the general officers whom Wellington put forward to Charles W. Wynn, the President of the HEIC, to command in India. Wellington thought he was 'very fit'.[20] Despite Wellington's recommendation, he was not selected for the position.

On 30 July 1830, General Aylmer was appointed the Governor-General and Commander-in-Chief of British North America.[21] This included Upper and Lower Canada,[22] Nova Scotia, Cape Breton, New Brunswick, Prince Edward Island, and

---

18. General Order, 2 July 1813.
19. Buckner.
20. *WND*; Vol. 2, page 425. Duke of Buckingham; Vol. 2, page 231.
21. Sources vary on the date of his appointment. Some give it as 11 August 1830 and others 24 November 1830.
22. Modern-day Ontario and Quebec.

Newfoundland.[23] He would rule from Quebec, which would be his downfall. He became intimately involved in the politics of Lower Canada and many of his decisions were controversial. He was a supporter of French and Catholic rights, which alienated the British members of the colony. Yet he also backed the Colonial Office in London on fiscal matters, which, over time, angered the French members of the Legislative Assembly of Lower Canada. By the summer of 1835 the situation had become so untenable that he was dismissed as governor and recalled to London.[24]

General Aylmer was offered an appointment as the Commander of the Forces in Ireland, but he refused to take it unless the government exonerated him. The government would not do so, but awarded him a GCB the following year. He would never have another military or governmental positon again. Matthew, Lord Aylmer married Louisa Call on 4 August 1801. His wife was the sister of General Henry Mackinnon's wife. They had no children. He died from a heart aneurysm on 25 February 1850.[25]

Unfortunately General Aylmer's reputation has been tarnished because of his time as governor of Canada. Yet Wellington considered him a superb staff officer. When he was promoted to major general in 1813, this created a problem for Wellington. In the Peninsula there were fifteen other officers who were promoted with him. Six of them were not commanding a brigade at the time. General Aylmer was junior to all of them. Based solely on seniority, he could not be offered a brigade, because there were only two brigades available that summer and he was too junior to be given one. It was likely that he would return to England, rather than continuing to serve as the DAG. Although it was possible Wellington might have been able to convince him to continue to serve as the DAG, Wellington did not want to take a chance that he would return home. His new AG, Edward Pakenham, had health issues and he was not sure how long General Pakenham would be able to serve. General Aylmer was an acceptable replacement should that occur. However, if he returned to England he would not be available to fill the position if need be. Wellington's solution to the problem was to send home the four officers who were not offered a brigade and then create a brigade for General Aylmer to command. That way, if something happened to General Pakenham, he could be appointed in his place. General Pakenham stayed healthy and General Aylmer was able to command his brigade to the end of the war.

---

23. British forces in Bermuda were part of the Nova Scotia command.
24. Buckner.
25. Buckner.

Barnes, Edward

Date of Birth:	1776
Date Commissioned:	Ensign 47th Foot: c. November 1792[1]
Promotions:	Lieutenant Independent Company: 27 March 1793
	Lieutenant 86th Foot: 30 October 1793 appointed
	Captain 99th Foot:[2] 11 February 1794
	Major 99th Foot: 16 November 1794
	Major 79th Foot: 17 February 1800 by exchange
	Brevet Lieutenant Colonel: 1 January 1800
	Lieutenant Colonel 46th Foot:[3] 23 April 1807
	Brevet Colonel: 25 July 1810
	Brigadier General on the Staff: 7 October 1812
	Major General: 4 June 1813
	Local Lieutenant General Ceylon: 20 March 1823
	Lieutenant General: 27 May 1825
	Local General India: 7 June 1831
Regimental Colonel:	2nd Garrison Battalion: 27 November 1815–24 October 1816
	99th Foot 24 October 1816–25 November 1818[4]
	2nd Battalion Rifle Brigade:[5] 13 May 1820–25 August 1822
	78th Foot: 25 August 1822–10 October 1834
	31st Foot: 10 October 1834–19 March 1838
Major Commands under Wellington:	Brigade 5th Division: 28 October–6 December 1812
	Brigade 7th Division: 6 December 1812–20 November 1813
	Brigade 2nd Division: 20 November 1813–April 1814
	Adjutant General: April–30 November 1815
	Adjutant General AOOF: 30 November 1815–November 1818
Awards:	KCB: 2 January 1815
	GCB: 24 February 1831
	Sultan's Gold Medal for Egypt
	AGC with three clasps: Martinique, Guadeloupe, Vitoria, Pyrenees, Nivelle, Nive & Orthes
	Waterloo Medal
	KMT
	KSA
Mentioned in Dispatches:	Pyrenees
Thanks of Parliament:	Pyrenees, Orthes & Waterloo
Member of Parliament:	Sudbury: 1834–1835, 1837–1838
Date of Death:	19 March 1838 in Piccadilly, London

Edward Barnes was born in 1776, the son of John Barnes, a former governor of Senegal from 1763 to 1765, and Mary Park. After he left the colonial service, John Barnes became

---

1. *London Gazette*; War Office Announcement dated 10 November 1792.
2. The regiment was disbanded in 1797.
3. Removed from the regiment as a general officer receiving unattached pay 1814.
4. The regiment was disbanded in 1818.
5. Colonels of the Battalions were called Colonel Commandant and the Regimental Colonel for the entire regiment was called Colonel-in-Chief.

a wine merchant in London. The exact date of Edward Barnes's birth, his place of birth, or where he grew up, is unknown.

Unlike most of his contemporaries, little is known about Edward Barnes's military career before 1807. He was commissioned at the age of 16 as an ensign in the 47th Regiment and served in several different regiments until 1797 when his regiment, the 99th Foot, was disbanded. He was on half-pay until 1799, when he exchanged into the 79th Foot as a major. There is no evidence that he purchased any of his promotions. It is most likely he served in Great Britain all those years. In 1800 he received a brevet lieutenant colonelcy and went on active service with his regiment. Much of the year was spent in Spain and Gibraltar and in 1801 he fought with them in the Egypt Campaign. By 1802 he was back in Spain, but in June the regiment returned to Great Britain and would spend the next five years on garrison duty in Ireland.

Lieutenant Colonel Barnes exchanged into the 46th Foot and took command of the 1st Battalion. In 1808 they were sent to the West Indies and he would serve occasionally as the Lieutenant Governor and acting Governor of Dominica during the next four years. Lieutenant Colonel Barnes was a brigade commander during the expedition to capture Martinique during January and February 1809. A year later, during January and February, he commanded his battalion in the expedition to capture Guadeloupe. Lieutenant Colonel Barnes remained with his regiment in Dominica and was promoted to colonel in July 1810. In the autumn of 1811, he and his regiment returned to England.

In a letter dated 6 August 1812, Wellington was informed that the Duke of York had proposed that Colonel Barnes be sent out to him.[6] Colonel Torrens of the Horse Guards also wrote to Wellington on the same day, telling him that 'a Colonel Barnes was going out to him as a Brigadier ... spoken of as sensible ... young and active ...'[7] He was appointed a brigadier on Wellington's staff in a General Order dated 7 October 1812. He was given command of a brigade in the 5th Division on 28 October but only commanded it until 6 December, when he took command of a brigade in the 7th Division.[8]

When Wellington went on the offensive in 1813, General Barnes initially saw little action. Although he and his brigade were at Vitoria on 21 June, they took no casualties. In early July he found out that he had been promoted to major general and was retained in command.[9] The brigade participated in the blockade of Pamplona, but continued to see little action until the French attacked through the Pyrenees passes on 25 July. At the Maya Pass, the British forces under General William Stewart were overwhelmed and being pushed out of the pass, when General Barnes arrived with his brigade and immediately counter-attacked. The shock of the attack caused the French to fall back in disorder and the situation was restored. General Stewart wrote of the attack 'the opportune arrival of Major General Barnes's brigade enabled us not only to retain, but even to recover, by a general charge upon the enemy, the whole of the ground ... A very spirited charge by the 6th regiment led on by Major General Barnes in the most animated stile [*sic*] upon the enemy's corps which had gained our left, preceded this success ...'[10]

The army had begun to take notice of General Barnes. But it was not until the combat of Echalar on 2 August that his reputation made. The British Army was pursuing the retreating French through the Pyrenees mountains when it came across two French

---

6. *WSD*; Vol. 7, page 375.
7. Unpublished letter dated 6 August 1812.
8. *General Orders*, Vol. 4, pages 198 and 235.
9. General Order, 2 July 1813.
10. *RMC* 1815; Vol. 1, page 245.

infantry divisions deployed on the heights behind the village of Echalar. Wellington's plan was to have the 4th and 7th Divisions attack the centre while the Light Division turned the enemy's right flank. The 4th and Light Divisions were delayed in their attack, as well as two of the three brigades in the 7th Division. This did not deter the division commander who ordered General Barnes to attack the 6,000 French on the hill. He deployed his three battalions in line and up the steep hill they went. One eyewitness described the attack: 'Barnes set at the French as if every man had been a bull-dog, and himself the best bred of all.'[11] They advanced under heavy fire and after delivering their first volley, despite outnumbering the British four-to-one, the two French divisions broke. Wellington described the charge in his dispatch:

> Major-General Barnes' brigade was formed for the attack and advanced before the 4th and Light Division could co-operate, with a regularity and gallantry I have seldom seen equaled, and actually drove the two divisions of the enemy, notwithstanding the resistance opposed to them, from those formidable heights. It is impossible that I can extol too highly the conduct of Major-General Barnes and these brave troops which was the admiration of all who were witnesses of it.[12]

An officer in the Light Division who saw the attack wrote, 'It was asserted that General Barnes had twenty musket-shots through his clothes, hat, and saddle, without one of them touching his body.'[13]

General Barnes's reputation also made it back to the Horse Guards in London. On 19 August 1813, Colonel Torrens wrote to Wellington in a bit of an 'I told you so' voice that 'I am a little proud of General Barnes whom I selected for your staff, and who...formed part of the batch of Generals that alarmed you so much.'[14] General Barnes continued to command his brigade in the 7th Division until 20 November 1813, when General George Walker was given temporary command of the division while its commander was absent. General Barnes assumed command of General Walker's old brigade in the 2nd Division. In February 1814, word was received that the 7th Division commander was returning and General Walker informed Wellington that he wished to resume command of his old brigade in the 2nd Division. This in turn would displace General Barnes. The AG wrote on 12 February to him on Wellington's instructions, to explain this and to inform him that it was Wellington's intention to give him a vacant brigade in the 3rd Division, 'where your services will be not less valuable or less appreciated than in the appointment you now hold.'[15] He was asked to reply and state if he concurred with the arrangement. However, General Walker was wounded in February and went home, so General Barnes remained in the 2nd Division through to the end of the war.[16] While with the 2nd Division he was seriously wounded at the Battle of Saint Pierre on 13 December 1813, defending a critical hill, and wounded a second time at the Battle of Aire on 2 March 1814, when he led the main assault against the French line.

---

11. Cannon; *Historical Records of the British Army: The Sixth or Royal First Warwickshire Regiment*, page 84.
12. *WD*; Vol. 10, page 598.
13. Leach; page 334.
14. Unpublished letter dated 19 August 1813.
15. *WSD*; Vol. 14, page 384.
16. Muir et al.; *Inside Wellington's Peninsular Army*; page 190.

After the abdication of Napoleon in April, the army began to disband. On 14 April, the Duke of York wrote to Wellington that the government intended to reinforce North America with two divisions drawn from Wellington's army. Selected to command brigades in this force were Generals Barnes and Robert Ross. Colonel Torrens also wrote on the same day, informing Wellington that if any of the proposed brigade commanders were not available or did not wish to go, then he could name their replacements. On 18 May another letter was sent to him by Earl Bathurst, stating that a special corps would be formed for independent duty to work with Admiral Cochrane[17] along the coasts of the United States. Wellington was left with the decision as to who would command it, either General Barnes or General Ross. On 29 May, Wellington appointed General Ross to its command. Eight days later, on 6 June, General Barnes was reported to have left for England.[18]

There is some speculation on why General Ross was selected to command the force and not General Barnes. One theory described him as 'even-tempered but energetic, and having had some experience of cooperation with the navy, he could be relied upon to work in partnership with Cochrane.'[19] Yet General Barnes was the more experienced commander and had worked with the navy in the West Indies in 1809 and 1810. The most likely reason is that he expressed a desire to return to England when he was informed of the opportunity to command the force.

General Barnes did not stay in England for long. By August he was appointed the AG of the Anglo-Allied Army in the Netherlands.[20] He was left in the position when Wellington took command of the army on 11 April 1815. Although he was the senior staff officer in the army, General Barnes never let it prevent him from getting in the thick of a fight. At a critical moment during the Battle of Quatre Bras on 16 June, he rode up to the 92nd Highlanders, a regiment that was in his brigade in 1814, and, 'observing this second column of the enemy's marching towards these houses, said "What have we got here?" When we informed him they were enemy infantry, and that they had got another body who had possessed themselves of the houses and ground immediately about them, he then took off his hat and said "92nd follow me"; when we instantly charged down the road and received a very destructive fire from the enemy at the houses, we, however, drove them out …'.[21] During the charge, General Barnes's horse was killed.[22]

At Waterloo, he continued to expose himself and was with Wellington watching the action near Hougoumont in the late afternoon. General Adam's brigade was sent to drive back the French. Wellington and General Barnes went with them. They were 'exposed to a shower of leaden hailstones', one of which severely wounded General Barnes in the shoulder.[23] He was evacuated from the battlefield by his ADC, Major Andrew Hamilton, who 'got him mounted on a horse and had led him (himself on foot slightly wounded in 2 places) the whole way from the field of battle, and having had his wound dressed

---

17. Admiral Alexander Cochrane, who commanded the North American Station.
18. *WSD*; Vol. 9, pages 82–8, 118–19, and 135.
19. Reilly; page 141.
20. When General Barnes became the AG it was known as the Subsidiary Army in the Netherlands. By Waterloo, it was commonly referred to as the Anglo-Allied Army.
21. Glover, Gareth; *Letters from the Battle of Waterloo*; pages 279–80.
22. Glover, Gareth; *Waterloo Archive*, Vol. 1, page 226.
23. Cotton; page 93.

& put him to bed'[24] by 10 p.m. that night. The next morning a visitor came and 'found him propped up in bed, covered with blood with a very dangerous wound through the shoulder, grinning from ear to ear at the news, & as composed & indifferent about himself as if he had done or suffered nothing.'[25] It would be his third wound in eighteen months. It was not surprising that he was somewhat of a bullet magnet, for during the campaign he was wearing a 'gold embroidered scarlet coat; most of our staff officers wore blue frock coats in the field.'[26]

General Barnes would spend a month in Brussels recovering from his wound. He rejoined the army in Paris in August and served as the AG of the Army of Occupation in France until November 1818. In early 1819 he was appointed to the Staff in Ceylon and would officially hold the position until 1824. However, on 1 February 1820 he became the lieutenant governor of the colony and served in that position until 2 February 1822. On 22 April 1823 he was appointed governor of the colony, but did not assume the office until January 1824. His tenure as governor was noted for his civil works and he oversaw the building of the first modern roads on the island. His governorship ended on 23 April 1831, when word reached him that he had been appointed the Commander-in-Chief of India. Although he was appointed on 17 October 1830, he did not assume office until 10 June 1832. He resigned on 16 October 1833 and returned to England.

On 7 March 1835, General Barnes was appointed to a commission formed to investigate the 'several modes of punishment now authorized and in use for the maintenance of discipline … in His Majesty's land forces …'[27] Specifically the commission was to determine if 'it may be practicable to dispense with the power of inflicting corporal punishment.'[28] In 1834, General Barnes was elected to the Parliament as a Conservative from Sudbury in a by-election. He was not re-elected the following year, but won the election in 1837.

Edward Barnes was initially unlucky in love. He proposed to Maria Capel, but she rejected his offer. He then started courting her older sister Harriet, but failed in that also. While in Paris during the occupation, he met John Fremantle's sister Albinia, but soon loss interest.[29] He married Maria Fawkes on 31 July 1824. She was twenty-two years younger than him. They had a daughter and a son, who joined the army. Edward Barnes was known for the greyhounds he bred[30] and was one of the founders of the Army Navy Club in London. He died on 19 March 1838 in Piccadilly, London.

General Barnes was a superb brigade commander. He led from the front and was aggressive whether on the attack or defense. His courage was legendary throughout the army. At Waterloo he earned the nickname of 'Our Fire-eating Adjutant General'.[31] Yet he had his detractors. General Barnes's finest moment was when he attacked two divisions of French infantry at Echalar, despite being outnumbered four-to-one. An eyewitness to the attack wrote that it was 'one of the boldest and most successful attacks on five time his number, but one in which bravery and success far exceeded judgment or utility.'[32]

---

24. Glover, Gareth; *Waterloo Archive*, Vol. 1, page 228.
25. Ibid; page 229.
26. Cotton; page 93SS.
27. *United Services Magazine*; 1835, Part 1, page 554.
28. Ibid.
29. Fremantle; pages 230–8.
30. Smith; page 302.
31. Cotton; page 93.
32. Smith; page 115.

General Barnes had little staff experience when he became the AG. His work was adequate, but not exceptional. Less than a month after assuming command of the Anglo-Allied Army in 1815, Wellington had a visit from Captain Thomas Browne, who had served in the Adjutant General Department in the Peninsula. Captain Browne was on his way to Vienna and Wellington wished for him to carry letters to the British mission there. While he was preparing his correspondence, Wellington asked Captain Browne to 'see Genl. Barnes (the Adjt Genl. At Brussels) tell him I sent you to him to talk over with him the arrangements for the Adjt Genl. Department, which were adopted in Spain, & which I wish to be continued here. I went to Sir E. Barnes, dined with him, told him all the regulations of the Adjt. Genl. Department which had been adopted in the Peninsular, & left him about ten at night.'[33]

The real mystery is why General Barnes was not offered a brigade when Wellington took command of the army in April 1815. Seniority was not an issue, since eighteen of the brigade commanders were junior to him. Furthermore, General Matthew Lord Aylmer, an officer with considerable experience in the Adjutant General Department in the Peninsula, was available to become the AG. Yet General Barnes was kept on instead.

---

33. Browne; page 281.

Bayly, Henry

Date of Birth:	Unknown
Date Commissioned:	Ensign 85th Foot:[1] 12 April 1783 without purchase
Promotions:	Ensign Coldstream Foot Guards: 27 October 1790 appointed
	Lieutenant & Captain Coldstream Foot Guards: 28 August 1793 without purchase
	Captain & Lieutenant Colonel Coldstream Foot Guards:[2] 5 September 1799
	Brevet Colonel: 25 October 1809
	Major General: 1 January 1812
	Lieutenant General: 27 May 1825
	General: 23 November 1841
Regimental Colonel:	8th Foot: 13 September 1825–20 April 1846
Major Commands under Wellington:	Independent Provisional Militia Brigade: 25 February–April 1814
Awards:	Kt: 17 January 1834
	GCH: 1834
Date of Death:	20 April 1846 at Dover Street, Piccadilly, London

Henry Bayly was the second son of Colonel Nicholas Bayly and Frances Nettlefold. His father was a colonel in West Middlesex Militia, a former captain and lieutenant colonel in the 1st Foot Guards, and a Member of Parliament for Anglesey from 1784 to 1790. The family home was Plas Newydd in Anglesey, Wales.[3] His brother was Colonel Edward Bayly and his first cousin was Henry Paget, the Marquess of Anglesey, who commanded the British cavalry at Waterloo.

Henry Bayly was commissioned as an ensign in the 85th Foot in 1783 and almost immediately went on half-pay when the regiment was disbanded the same year. Seven years later he was able to exchange into the Coldstream Guards and would stay in the regiment for the next twenty-four years. In April 1793, he went to Flanders and joined the 1st Battalion at Tournay. Ensign Bayly fought at Famars on 23 May, the siege of Valenciennes in July, and Lincelles on 17 August, where he was severely wounded in his right hand while he carried the battalion's colours. At Valenciennes, he won a promotion to lieutenant and captain for his bravery. He returned to England after his promotion and stayed there until 1798, when he was sent to Ireland to help put down the rebellion. In August 1799, he went with the British Expedition to Den Helder and served as the orderly officer to General Ralph Abercromby during the amphibious landings. He was promoted to captain and lieutenant colonel in his regiment shortly after he arrived in Den Helder. Captain Bayly fought at Krabbendam on 10 September and returned to England shortly after the battle.[4]

Lieutenant Colonel Bayly served with the Coldstream Guards in England until November 1808 when he became the private secretary to Mr John Villiers, the British Minister to the Portuguese Court in Lisbon. He left Portugal in April 1809 and carried

---

1. Disbanded 1783.
2. Removed from the regiment as a general officer receiving unattached pay 25 July 1814.
3. Williams; page 7.
4. *RMC*; Vol. 3, page 201. *United Service Magazine*; Vol. 51, page 319. *Gentleman's Magazine*; Vol. 180, page 94.

dispatches back to England from Wellington and Minister Villiers. In October 1809 he was promoted to colonel and on 8 February 1811 was appointed an ADC to the Prince Regent.[5] Colonel Bayly was promoted to major general in 1812 and was made an Equerry to the Prince Regent. In June 1813, he was placed on the staff of the Home District in England.

In November 1813, a bill was introduced in Parliament that would allow militia regiments to volunteer to serve outside the British Isles. The goal was to raise 30,000 new recruits. The hopes of Parliament were unrealistic and fewer than 8,000 militia volunteered. Colonel Nicholas Bayly, the father of General Bayly, was instrumental in convincing many of them to volunteer. The plan to send out individual regiments was scrapped and instead three provisional militia battalions were formed and brigaded together.[6] Initially the plan was to reinforce Wellington's army with the brigade, however, after General Thomas Graham's defeat at Bergen-op-Zoom in the Netherlands, it was decided to reinforce his army instead. This decision changed and the brigade joined Wellington's army as originally planned.[7] In a General Order dated 30 April 1814, General Bayly was placed on the staff of Wellington's army to command this brigade.[8]

Wellington was less than enthusiastic about having General Bayly's brigade in his army. The previous year he had written to Earl Bathhurst when the subject was first broached:

> I found that, however, to be so entirely divested of interior economy, and real discipline and subordination, that, however well the soldiers may be disciplined, as far as regards their exercise and movements, I should very much doubt that a large militia army would be very useful in the field for more than a momentary exertion. My notion of them is, that the officers have all the faults of those of the line to an aggravated degree, and some peculiarly their own.[9]

Colonel Torrens, of the Horse Guards, only re-enforced Wellington's reservations when he wrote to him: 'I hope that when the three provisional battalions of militia now forming reach you, they will fight well; but at present they are more troublesome than the whole army put together.'[10]

Despite Wellington's reluctance, the brigade embarked in mid-March and landed at Bordeaux, France on 12 April. It was placed under the command of the 7th Division. The brigade arrived the day after word had been received that Napoleon had abdicated and the war was over. The officers of the brigade had a high opinion of their troops and thought 'we should have the honour of the occupation of Paris.'[11]

An officer in the 1st Foot Guards left a different portrait of their time in France:

> The militia regiments appeared but a sorry sight in comparison with British veterans who had marched through Portugal and Spain, fighting a hundred battles,

---

5. The future King George IV.
6. *United Service Magazine*; Part 2, 1830, page 75. Muir; *Inside Wellington's Peninsular Army*, pages 221–223.
7. *WSD*; Vol. 8 pages 636 and 649. *WSD*; Vol. 14, page 437. *WD* (enlarged ed.); Vol. 7, page 419.
8. The orders were backdated to 25 February 1814.
9. Letter dated 24 September 1813, *WD*; Vol. 11, page 140.
10. Letter dated 26 January 1814, *WSD*; Vol. 3, page 544.
11. *United Service Magazine*; Part 2, 1830, page 75.

and afterwards remained some time at Bordeaux, where they gained the respect of the inhabitants by their orderly conduct and manly bearing. Unfortunately, too, our militiamen did not conduct themselves in a becoming manner; for, delighted at the cheapness of the wine and brandy, and happening to be officered by men incapable of looking after them properly, when off duty they were constantly tipsy, and getting into all sorts of scrapes and broils with the inhabitants ...[12]

Wellington had little patience for General Bayly's brigade and sent them home on 6 June, less than eight weeks after arriving in France.

In March 1816, General Bayly was appointed the Lieutenant Governor of Guernsey and commanded the forces there and in Alderney until June 1821. He was appointed Colonel of the 8th Foot in 1825 and served as its regimental commander until he died. Although he never had an active command after 1821, he did receive a yearly salary and pension of £2,420.[13] General Bayly never married and died in 1846.

---

12. Gronow; *Captain Gronow's Last Recollections*, pages 44–5.
13. He received £1,154 as the Regimental Colonel; £350 pension for the wound he received in 1793; and £750 for being the Equerry to the King. *Parliamentary Papers, House of Commons and Command*; Vol. VII, page 38.

Beresford, Lord George Thomas

Date of Birth:	12 February 1781
Date Commissioned:	Cornet 14th Light Dragoons: 30 April 1794
Promotions:	Lieutenant 107th Foot:[1] 31 May 1794 appointed
	Captain 124th Foot:[2] 24 September 1794 appointed
	Captain 88th Foot: 29 July 1796 by exchange
	Major 6th Dragoon Guards: 3 December 1800 appointed
	Lieutenant Colonel Dillon's Regiment: 24 September 1803 appointed
	Lieutenant Colonel 71st Foot: 16 August 1804 appointed
	Lieutenant Colonel 2nd Dragoon Guards:[3] 30 July 1807 by exchange
	Brevet Colonel: 1 January 1812
	Major General: 4 June 1814
	Lieutenant General: 22 July 1830
Regimental Colonel:	3rd Light Dragoons: 16 September 1829–26 October 1839
Major Commands	
under Wellington:	8th Cavalry Brigade: 22 June–30 November 1815
Awards:	GCH: 1827
Member of Parliament:	County Londonderry: 1802–July 1812
	Coleraine: 1812–14 May 1814
	County Waterford: 25 May 1814–1826
	County Waterford: 2 March 1830–1831
Date of Death:	26 October 1839 at the Palace, Armagh, Ireland

Between 19 August 1789 and October 1839 he went by the name Lord George Beresford.

George Beresford was born in 1781, the fourth son of George Beresford, 1st Marquess of Waterford and Elizabeth Monck. He was the half-brother of General William Viscount Beresford and Admiral Sir John Beresford, Baronet. He attended Eton from 1791 to 1793.

The year after he left Eton, Lord George was commissioned as a cornet in the 14th Light Dragoons. A month after being commissioned he was appointed a lieutenant in the 107th Foot. Within four months he was promoted to captain in the 124th Foot, a regiment his brother, William Beresford, was raising. When he received his captaincy he was only 13 years old, which made him one of the youngest captains in the army. Shortly after he transferred to the 124th Foot, the regiment was disbanded, and Captain Beresford was unemployed. According to the *Army Lists*, despite the disbanding of his regiment he was still carried on the regimental rolls and received his full pay despite having no regimental duties. In July 1796 he joined the 88th Foot, where his brother was now a lieutenant colonel. On Christmas Day 1798, Captain Beresford sailed with his regiment for India. He was stationed in Bombay until December 1800,[4] when he was appointed a major in the 6th Dragoon Guards.

Major Beresford stayed with the regiment until September 1803, when he was promoted to lieutenant colonel in Dillon's Regiment. A year later he was appointed as a lieutenant colonel in the 71st Foot. Lieutenant Colonel Beresford was in the 71st Foot

---

1. Disbanded 1795.
2. Disbanded 1795.
3. Removed from the regiment as a general officer receiving unattached pay 1814.
4. Jourdain; Vol. 1, page 9.

for three years when he exchanged into the 2nd Dragoon Guards, which was stationed in England. He and his regiment remained in England during the Peninsular War, although in 1813 they received orders to go to Spain. They were at Ramsgate preparing to embark when the orders were rescinded.

Lieutenant Colonel Beresford was promoted to colonel in January 1812 and appointed Comptroller of the King's Household the following August. He was the comptroller until 1830. In June 1814, he was promoted to major general. In the twenty years he had been in the army, General Beresford only served on garrison duty and had never seen combat. He had missed the Napoleonic Wars.

In 1815, four days after the Battle of Waterloo, the Duke of York wrote to Wellington that he was, 'obliged to appoint Lord George Beresford to go out with the heavy regiments now under orders.'[5] General Torrens also wrote to Wellington the same day that he was to be reinforced by a brigade of heavy cavalry. This brigade would be commanded by General Beresford with the understanding that 'it is left to your Grace to continue them as a brigade or not, as you may consider expedient.'[6]

General Beresford was appointed on the staff of Wellington's army in a General Order of 18 August, but his appointment was to date from 22 June 1815. His command was designated the 8th Cavalry Brigade, but by the time it was organised the major fighting had all but ended in France. He was not retained on the staff when the Amy of Occupation was formed in November 1815.

In 1802, at the age of 21, Lord George Beresford was elected to Parliament. Except for a four-year period between 1826 and 1830, he would hold one of the Irish seats in the Parliament until 1831. He was a Conservative and despite being from Ireland, opposed Catholic Emancipation. His opponents often accused him of only representing the landed class. He did not run for re-election in 1831.

In early 1827, the colonelcy of the 4th Dragoon Guards became vacant. Based on seniority, General George Anson was supposed to receive it. However, in February King George IV recommended General Beresford for the Colonelcy of the 4th Dragoon Guards. He asked Wellington what he thought. Wellington was adamant in his support for General Anson and outlined his reasons in a lengthy letter to the King on 20 February. He stated that Anson was senior by 175 places over Beresford. Wellington also implied that it would be perceived that General Beresford would be receiving the appointment for political reasons, since he was a strong supporter of the government, while General Anson was in opposition. Wellington pointed out that his predecessor, the Duke of York, had established the tradition that the colonelcies were meant to honour and reward an individual for his military service regardless of his politics. He closed his letter with a summary of General Anson's service in the Peninsular War, while General Beresford had none.[7] The King listened to Wellington and General Anson was appointed Colonel of the 4th Dragoon Guards four days later.

In 1829, the King proposed that General Beresford be appointed Colonel of the 3rd Light Dragoons. Even this appointment was controversial. General Rowland Lord Hill, the Commander-in-Chief of the British Army, did not feel he could object a second time 'even though he "would not have selected" him for command of a regiment of cavalry'.[8]

---

5. *WSD*; Vol. 10, pages 534–5.
6. Ibid; page 557.
7. *WND*; Vol. 3, pages 597–600.
8. Beresford.

Wellington was never asked and after he heard that the appointment had been made 'he wrote immediately to the king expressing his astonishment ... at the selection of a man who had never seen a shot fired to the exclusion of many a true and valuable veteran.'[9]

After losing his seat in Parliament in 1826, General Beresford was appointed the Governor and Custos Rotulorum (the principle justice of the peace) of County Waterford. The same year, he became the colonel of the Waterford militia and would hold the position until his death in 1839.

Lord George Beresford married Harriet Schutz on 22 November 1808. They had four daughters. He died on 26 October 1839 and was buried in the family burial place at Clonegam, County Waterford on 4 November 1839.

---

9. Ibid.

Bernewitz, John de

Date of Birth:	27 December 1760, Dresden, Saxony[1]
Date Commissioned:	Ensign in Specht's Regiment: 26 June 1775
Brunswick Service:[2]	Lieutenant in Riedesel's Regiment: 1783
	Staff Captain in Prinz Friedrich's Regiment: 17 April 1793
	Company Commander in Prinz Friedrich's Regiment: 15 July 1798
	Major in von Griesheim's Regiment: 11 April 1805[3]
	Lieutenant Colonel Brunswick Light Battalion: 26 April 1809
	Colonel: 28 April 1809
	Brigadier: 28 April 1809[4]
	Major General: 1813
	Lieutenant General: 16 January 1815
British Service:[5]	Lieutenant Colonel Brunswick-Oels Corps: 14 February 1811
	Brevet Colonel: 1811[6]
	Local Major General in the Peninsula: 23 November 1811
	Major General: 1 January 1812
Major Commands	
under Wellington:	Brigade 7th Division: 23 December 1811–March 1813
	Temporarily commanded 7th Division: September–October 1812
Awards:	AGM: Salamanca
	KCH: 1818
Mentioned in Dispatches:	Salamanca
Thanks of Parliament:	Salamanca
Date of Death:	12 December 1821 in Brunswick

His real name was Johann Heinrich Karl von Bernewitz, however, when he was in British service he went by John de Bernewitz.

John de Bernewitz was the son of Karl and Elisabeth von Bernewitz and the oldest of seven children. He entered the army as a cadet in the Lieb Regiment in 1774 and was commissioned as an ensign in 1775 in Sprecht's Regiment. In 1776, Ensign de Bernewitz and his regiment were sent to North America in support of British efforts to crush the American Revolution. They arrived in Quebec in September too late to participate in that year's fighting and went into winter quarters. In June 1777, Ensign de Bernewitz fought in the Saratoga Campaign and became a prisoner-of-war when the British Army surrendered at Saratoga on 17 October 1777. He was a prisoner for three years, when the Brunswick officers were allowed to rejoin the army in Canada at the end of October 1780. He remained in Canada until 1783.

In 1806, the Duchy of Brunswick joined Prussia in its war with France. Major de Bernewitz commanded a battalion in the Brunswick contingent at the Battle of Jena on

---

1. Some sources give his date of birth as 27 December 1754.
2. Information on dates of rank for his Brunswick service is from Kortzfleisch; Vol. 1, page 335.
3. Became a battalion in the regiment on 8 May 1805.
4. Backdated to 1 April 1809.
5. All ranks were temporary in the British Army.
6. *London Gazette*; War Office Announcement dated 6 August 1811. Rank was antedated to 24 September 1809.

14 October, when the Prussian Army was destroyed by Napoleon. He again became a prisoner-of-war on 26 October. In 1807, Napoleon created the Kingdom of Westphalia out of Brunswick, Hesse and Magdeburg. Major de Bernewitz chose to retire rather than serve in the new Westphalian Army. In April 1809, the dispossessed Duke of Brunswick created the Brunswick Black Legion in Austria. Major de Bernewitz was promoted to lieutenant colonel and given command of a light infantry battalion on 26 April. Three days later he was promoted to colonel and then brigadier on the same day and given command of the Black Legion. This force consisted of about 2,000 soldiers. During the Franco-Austrian War of 1809, they fought in Austria, Saxony, and eventually returned to Westphalia, where they liberated the city of Brunswick. Shortly after taking the city, his force was in danger of being surrounded and overwhelmed by troops loyal to Napoleon. Rather than surrender, Colonel de Bernewitz retreated north. On 9 August he and what was left of the Legion were evacuated from Bremerhaven by the British Royal Navy.

The Black Legion landed on the Isle of Wright and was incorporated into the British Army in September 1809. They were officially named the Duke of Brunswick Oels Corps. The officers received temporary rank in the British Army, but only while serving in the Corps. Although Colonel de Bernewitz had commanded the Black Legion he was not given command of the Brunswick Oels Infantry. Instead he was appointed a lieutenant colonel but was unattached with no duties. On 14 February 1811, Lieutenant Colonel de Bernewitz was given command of the Brunswick Oels Infantry,[7] after its commander, Lieutenant Colonel Georg de Korfuss, died in Portugal.[8]

Lieutenant Colonel de Bernewitz arrived in Portugal in May 1811, too late to fight at Fuentes de Oñoro. In August he was promoted to colonel, but with his date of rank backdated to September 1809, when the Black Legion was incorporated into the British Army. This promotion made him the senior colonel in Wellington's Army. This created a problem for Wellington. Several colonels who were junior to him had been promoted to brigadier general ahead of him. Since promotion to general officer was based on seniority, tradition within the army could not have someone junior commanding a brigade when there was someone who was senior was available. Wellington had three options: he could send Colonel de Bernewitz home; he could convince him to stay in command of his regiment; or he could promote him as soon as possible. Wellington chose to promote him, but would later regret this decision.

Colonel de Bernewitz commanded the Brunswick Oels until 23 December, when he was appointed a local major general on the staff of Wellington's army. His date of rank was backdated to 23 November 1811.[9] His notification that he had been promoted to major general arrived rather awkwardly. On 25 December 1811 he received an order sent to Major General de Bernewitz, but did not believe it meant a promotion as the letter's contents had nothing to do with promotion! It was only on 27 December 1811 that the General Order announcing his promotion reached him.[10] Upon his promotion to local major general, he was given a brigade in the 7th Division. Over a month later he was promoted to major general in the British Army in the general brevet of 1 January 1812. He commanded his brigade at Salamanca on 22 July 1812 and was part of the force that besieged the Retiro in Madrid in mid-August.

---

7. *London Gazette*, 19 February 1811. The appointment was backdated to 14 February 1811.
8. Lieutenant Colonel de Korfuss died in December 1810.
9. General Order, 23 December 1811.
10. Kortzfleisch; Vol. 1, page 192.

On 23 September 1812, General de Bernewitz took temporary command of the 7th Division after its commander fell ill and had to return to England. He led it during the siege of Burgos and during the initial stages of the retreat back to the Portuguese border, until General George Ramsay Lord Dalhousie took command on 28 October. On 6 December 1812, Wellington wrote to Colonel Torrens at the Horse Guards that, 'I should wish to get rid of General de Bernewitz … General de Bernewitz ought not to be a General Officer in this army'.[11] On 14 January 1813, Colonel Torrens wrote to Wellington, 'Your wishes in regard to the infantry Generals have been acceded to, as you will perceive by the Duke's letter recalling … Bernewitz.'[12]

On 27 February 1813, General de Bernewitz was relieved of his command, the stated reason being that the Duke of Brunswick had requested his services. On 24 March 1813, General de Bernewitz sailed from Lisbon and arrived in England on 19 April.[13] The Duke wished him to help form the Brunswick contingent that would be part of the British Expeditionary Force that was being sent to northern Germany. This never came about. Instead, in the autumn, the Duchy of Brunswick was reformed when the Kingdom of Westphalia, an ally of the French, was overrun by the Allies. On 6 November 1813, the Duke of Brunswick ordered a Brunswick Army to be raised in the Duchy. On 8 December 1813, he and General de Bernewitz left England for Brunswick. They arrived home on 22 December. He would spend the next eighteen months rebuilding the Brunswick Army. Between January and April 1814 units were raised and the recently disbanded Brunswick Oels, which General de Bernewitz commanded in Portugal and Spain, joined it. On 16 January 1815, General de Bernewitz was promoted to lieutenant general and commandant of the city of Brunswick. Despite being the most experienced general officer in the Brunswick Army, he did not lead it at Waterloo.[14]

John de Bernewitz married Franziska von Bodenstaff on 28 January 1798. They had four sons, three of whom served in the military. General de Bernewitz's service to the British did not go unrecognised. He was placed on half-pay in 1814 and received it until his death in the city of Brunswick in 1821.

There are very few clues why Wellington requested General de Bernewitz be sent home. Perhaps it was his age. By the end of 1812, General de Bernewitz was 52 years old, several years older than his contemporaries and the years of campaigning might have begun to take its toll.[15] Wellington most likely recognised this and realised that he had made a mistake when he requested that General de Bernewitz be promoted the previous year. In the same letter that Colonel Torrens wrote telling him that General de Bernewitz had been recalled, he also said, 'I am only surprised that you should never have expressed a wish for his recall before. He was originally sent out to command the Brunswick corps and it was in consequence of your own recommendation … that he was placed upon the Staff as a General Officer. His high rank at that time would have been an excellent plea for sending him to England if he objected to act in his regimental capacity.'[16]

---

11. *WSD*; Vol. 7 pages 494–5.
12. *WSD*; Vol. 7 page 527.
13. Kortzfleisch; Vol. 1, page 256.
14. 'Bernewitz'. Nafziger; pages 72–80.
15. Fortescue; Vol. 9, page 87.
16. *WSD*; Vol. 7, page 527.

Bock, George Baron

Date of Birth:	1755
Date Commissioned:	2nd Lieutenant 5th Infantry Regiment: 1774
Hanoverian Service:	2nd Lieutenant 13th Infantry Regiment: 1774
	2nd Lieutenant Life Guard Regiment: 29 November 1779
	Captain Life Guard Regiment: 9 December 1783
	Major Life Guard Regiment: 13 February 1794
	Lieutenant Colonel Life Guard Regiment: 24 July 1799
British Service:[1]	Lieutenant Colonel of Cavalry KGL: 21 April 1804
	Brevet Colonel KGL: 21 April 1804
	Colonel 1st Dragoons KGL: 18 August 1804
	Brigadier General on the Staff: 1810
	Major General: 25 July 1810[2]
Regimental Colonel:	1st Regiment of Dragoons KGL[3]: 18 August 1804–21 January 1814
Major Commands under Wellington:	Cavalry Brigade KGL: 11 January 1812–January 1814
	Temporarily commanded the 1st Cavalry Division: July–October 1812 and December 1812–April 1813
	Temporarily commanded the Cavalry: 21 April 1813–25 June 1813
Awards:	AGM with clasp: Salamanca & Vitoria
Mentioned in Dispatches:	Salamanca & Vitoria
Thanks of Parliament:	Salamanca & Vitoria
Date of Death:	21 January 1814 by shipwreck

Real name was Eberhard Otto George von Bock, however, while in British service he went by George Baron Bock.

George Baron Bock was commissioned as a 2nd lieutenant in the 5th Infantry Regiment in 1774, but transferred to the 13th Infantry the same year. Five years later he transferred to the Life Guard Cavalry Regiment in which he served for the next twenty-four years. In May 1803, the French were poised to invade Hanover. Lieutenant Colonel Bock was part of the delegation sent to negotiate with them. On 2 June they returned with the news that the French were requiring the Hanoverian Army to surrender. The delegation was sent back to the French with instructions to obtain the best terms for the country. The convention they negotiated dismantled the Hanoverian Army, but the troops would not be taken as prisoners-of-war as long as they refrained from taking up arms against the French or their allies. King George III, the sovereign of Hanover, refused to ratify the convention and negotiations started again, with Lieutenant Colonel Bock as one of the negotiators. Eventually a treaty was agreed upon to disband the Hanoverian Army and allow its members to return to their homes.

With the disbanding of the Hanoverian Army and the French occupation of Hanover, King George III considered the officers and men free to serve in the British Army and authorised British ships to take aboard any Hanoverian officer or soldier who wished to

---

1. All ranks were temporary in the British Army until 1812.
2. Permanent rank in British Army: 18 August 1812.
3. Renamed the 1st Regiment of Light Dragoons KGL on 25 December 1813. In the KGL, regimental colonels were called colonel commandants.

go to England. This was an area of dispute with the French that lasted throughout the wars.

Lieutenant Colonel Bock arrived in England in the early autumn. Since the King's German Legion was just beginning to be formed, he was not offered immediate employment. On 21 April 1804 he received a temporary commission as a lieutenant colonel in the British Army and on the same day was promoted to colonel. He took command of the 1st Dragoons KGL four months later.

Colonel Bock commanded his regiment in the expedition to Hanover from November 1805 to February 1806. Upon their return to the British Isles they were stationed in Ireland. Colonel Bock was promoted to brigadier general on the staff of the South West District in 1810 and then the Western District, both in Ireland. He was promoted to major general during the summer of 1810. He took command of the newly formed Heavy Dragoon Brigade KGL in the summer of 1811. In December, the brigade received orders to prepare for service in the Peninsula and embarked from Cork, Ireland. General Bock was placed on the staff of Wellington's army in a General Order dated 11 January 1812, but his appointment was to date from 25 December 1811.

General Bock's brigade landed at Lisbon on 1 January 1812 and remained near there until March when it joined the 2nd Cavalry Division; on 14 April it was assigned to the 1st Cavalry Division. It was at the Battle of Salamanca on 22 July, but was in reserve and took no casualties. The brigade was part of the force that was pursuing the retreating French Army the next day when it caught up with its rearguard at Garcia Hernandez. The French were deployed just north of the village with its cavalry on the left and its infantry on the right. Opposite them were the cavalry brigades of General Bock and General George Anson. Wellington ordered them to charge the French cavalry and what happened next made General Bock's reputation. His ADC, Captain Charles Baron Hodenberg, wrote a few days later:

we broke three solid squares of French infantry, in which no cavalry have ever succeeded before. General Bock led us in noble style: Decken's squadron was the first, Reizenstein's the second, and to both their unparalleled bravery is in a measure owing our great exploit; but indeed every one, without exception, was conspicuous in gallantry, or we could never, never, have succeeded. We dashed in like madmen, and our blades carried with them the bloody revenge that we have so long owed them. In less than half an hour we had 1500 prisoners, and 200 more towards evening ... Our loss – my heart bleeds to tell you – is great, 150 men either dead or so badly wounded that we are burying them every minute. Reizenstein is perfectly well, so are the general and I, and we survivors glory in our achievement.[4]

Wellington wrote to Earl Bathurst the next day that:

I have never witnessed a more gallant charge than was made on the enemy's infantry by the heavy brigade of the King's German Legion, under Major General Bock,

---

4. Oman, Charles; 'A Dragoon of the Legion', pages 298–9. Captain Baron Hodenberg's account of the charge is the only one known by a participant of the charge. The charge only destroyed two infantry battalions in square and a third that was in column. An impressive feat that rarely occurred in the Napoleonic Wars.

which was completely successful; and the whole body of infantry, consisting of three battalions of the enemy's 1st division, were made prisoners.[5]

After Salamanca, General Bock took temporary command of the 1st Cavalry Division, while General Stapleton Cotton recovered from his wounds. He commanded it until October, when General Cotton returned. Despite the successes of Wellington's army in the summer, the British were forced to retreat to the Portuguese border in October. General Bock's Brigade was part of the rearguard. It was greatly reduced, with about 450 men, less than half with which they had begun with at the start of the campaign. On 23 October, at Venta del Pozo, the rearguard turned to face the French, which was following closely. Once again the brigade was working with General Anson's brigade, which had about 600 men. Captain Baron Hodenberg was by General Bock's side and wrote shortly afterwards:

> Our brigade was formed in line on the left of the road, with a little river about 400 yards to our front. This river ran across the whole plain, and crossed the road under a bridge. Upon the road, and on our left flank, was Major Bull's troop of horse artillery ... General Anson's brigade was intended, after having retreated over the bridge, to form line on the right of the guns. Unfortunately ... they formed in our rear, not on our flank, and when ordered to take up the ground intended for them, they crossed in front of our artillery. This prevented the battery from opening in time, and a considerable body of the French passed over to our side before the guns could commence ... The enemy filed over nineteen squadrons at a gallop, without being once hit ... Scarce over the bridge, they formed a line with incredible celerity ... They were hardly in line when they rode up the hill, at the same moment that our charge commenced. Our two squadrons on the right, met them with such vigor that we were in an instant completely mixed ... The contest, man to man, lasted perhaps a long minute, during which the ground was strewed with French, and our own loss was severe in the extreme ... General Bock, who always charges at the head of his brigade had a narrow escape: he was at one time surrounded by six French dragoons, all cutting and stabbing at him, but he defended himself well, and got out safe. General Anson's brigade, whose horses were tired, did not come up level in the charge, and out-numbered and outflanked on all sides, we were obliged to give way, particularly when a second line of French cavalry, composed entirely of heavy dragoons ... was brought up against us. We made several attempts to reform and charge, but being reduced to a mere nothing – half of our men were put hors de combat – we were unable to re-establish ourselves until the enemy's vigorous advance was checked by the destructive fire of our Light Infantry battalions ...[6]

The brigade lost about 100 men in the fight. Within a few weeks, General Bock and his brigade were back across the Portuguese border. He assumed temporary command of the 1st Cavalry Division in December and commanded it until April 1813. When Wellington merged the two cavalry divisions into one division on 21 April 1813, as the senior officer General Bock commanded in the absence of General Cotton. General Bock would

---

5. *WD*; Vol. 9, page 305.
6. Oman, Charles; 'A Dragoon of the Legion', pages 300–1.

command all of the cavalry in Wellington's army until 25 June, when General Cotton returned.

General Bock was not able to replace the casualties that his brigade had the previous year. On 25 May 1813, it had a strength of less than 650 men, about half its strength of the previous year. Fortunately for them, the brigade saw little action in 1813. It was at Vitoria on 21 June, but was in reserve for most of it, having only one man killed. For the next four months they were part of the force that blockaded Pamplona.

In December 1813, after the liberation of Hanover, General Bock applied for a leave of absence to go home. He had been away for almost ten years. In January he, his son Captain Lewis Baron Bock[7], and Captain Charles Baron Hodenberg[8] embarked on the transport *Bellona*. On 21 January, a storm came up in the Bay of Biscay. *Bellona* was driven onto rocks off the coast of Brittany and all aboard perished. General Bock's body was washed ashore near Pleubian, France and he was buried by the villagers.

One of the legends that appeared after his death is that General Bock had poor eyesight. According to N. Ludlow Breamish's *History of the King's German Legion*, at Garcia Hernandez 'Bock was near-sighted, and not being aware of the proximity of the enemy, when colonel May[9] brought him the order to charge, added, after expressing his readiness to comply; – "but you will be good enough to shew us the enemy." To this request colonel May readily assented, and gallantly accompanied the first squadron in the charge, where he was severely wounded.'[10] Beamish's account has been re-told many times over the past 200 years and has been used to verify that General Bock could not see very well. Unfortunately there are several problems with this. We can find no contemporary sources that state he was near-sighted. Furthermore, the one source that was with him daily during 1812 and 1813 was Captain Baron Hodenberg, General Bock's ADC. He wrote a series of letters during that time, eleven of which still survive today. He never mentions General Bock's eyesight in any of them.

Wellington had a keen interest in his generals's health, especially if it impacted their ability to command in the field. Two cavalry generals, Sir William Erskine and Sir Charles Stewart, were known to have poor eyesight. On 24 April 1811, Wellington wrote to Marshal Beresford that General Erskine had ask for command of his cavalry. Wellington stated, 'You will find him more intelligent and useful than any body you have.'[11] But he then went on to warn Marshal Beresford that 'He is very blind, which is against him at the head of the cavalry, be very cautious.'[12] Wellington left the decision on whether General Erskine would command the brigade to Marshal Beresford. In a letter dated 25 June 1811 to the Duke of York, Wellington expressed his concerns about giving General Stewart a cavalry command. He stated that General Stewart 'labours, however, under two bodily defects, the want of sight and of hearing, which must ever prevent him from forming an immediate judgment of what is going on in the field, and from acting on that judgment with the promptitude which is necessary in an officer in the command of a large body of cavalry; and the defect in his sight having been occasioned by a wound, it

7. Was in the 2nd Hussars KGL but was serving as General Bock's extra ADC.
8. Was in the 1st Dragoons KGL, but was serving as General Bock's ADC.
9. Lieutenant Colonel John May AAG.
10. Beamish; Vol. 2, page 82.
11. *WD* (enlarged ed.); Vol. 4, pages 771–2.
12. Ibid; page 772.

cannot be remedied by the assistance of glasses.'[13] In the same letter Wellington pointed out that while General Stewart's eyes were irreparable, General Erskine eyes could 'receive the assistance of glasses'.[14] General Stewart never received a cavalry command in Wellington's army.

When we posed the question of General Bock's eyesight to Michael-Andreas Tänzer, Director of the Arbeitskreis Hannoversche Militärgeschichte and the foremost modern authority on the King's German Legion, he responded that, 'As Beamish was sanctioned by the then still living members of the KGL, and the new Bock family history by the now living Bocks, I believe the story to be true.'[15] It is possible that General Bock was near-sighted, but despite what Beamish wrote, it would not have been so severe that it had an impact on his ability to perform his duties. If it did, Wellington would have considered relieving him of command. The legend of his poor eyesight probably came from a misinterpretation of what Beamish wrote. General Bock's ADC was with him when Colonel May arrived with the orders to charge. It is improbable that both he and Captain Baron Hodenberg were unable to see the enemy troops formed on a hill less than a kilometer away. Instead of asking Colonel May where the enemy was because he could not see them, General Bock was most likely asking him for clarification on where Wellington wanted him to charge. Since both General Bock and Captain Baron Hodenberg died in 1814, they could not dispute Colonel May's version of what was said. And thus the legend was born.

---

13. *WSD*; Vol. 7, pages 165–6.
14. Ibid; page 166.
15. E-mail to Robert Burnham, dated 22 January 2015.

Bowes, Barnard Foord

Date of Birth:	c. 1769
Date Commissioned:	Ensign 26th Foot; 25 October 1781
Promotions:	Lieutenant 26th Foot: 8 August 1783
	Captain Independent Company:[1] 24 January 1791
	Captain 26th Foot: 2 February 1791 by exchange
	Major 85th Foot: 15 June 1796
	Lieutenant Colonel 6th Foot: 1 December 1796
	Brevet Colonel: 1 January 1805
	Brigadier General on the Staff: 1808–1810
	Major General: 25 July 1810
Major Commands	
under Wellington:	4th Brigade: 7 August–5 September 1808[2]
	On Staff at Cadiz: 1811
	Brigade 4th Division: 9 February–2 May 1812
	Brigade 6th Division: 2 May–23 June 1812
Awards:	AGM with clasp: Roliça and Vimeiro & Badajoz
Thanks of Parliament:	Roliça, Vimeiro & Badajoz
Date of Death:	23 June 1812 at Salamanca, Spain

Known as Barnard Bowes Foord until name changed to Barnard Foord Bowes 17 May 1791.

The exact date of birth for Barnard Foord Bowes is unknown, however, he was baptized on 7 July 1769 at Saint Saviour's Church in York. He was the oldest son of Dr Barnard Foord and Ann Bowes. He changed his name in 1791 in order to inherit from his mother's family.[3]

Barnard Bowes's family purchased him a commission in the 26th Foot in 1781. He was 12 years old. Except for a month when he commanded an independent company in 1791, he served with the regiment for the next fifteen years[4] when he purchased a majority in the 85th Foot. Six months later he purchased a lieutenant colonelcy in the 6th Foot and joined them in Ireland. He would take command of the 1st Battalion 6th Foot in 1798 and led them during the Irish Rebellion. In 1799, Lieutenant Colonel Bowes and the 6th Foot was sent to Canada. He was promoted to colonel in January 1805 and succeeded to the command of all British troops in Canada upon the death of General Peter Hunter in August. On 27 September 1806 Colonel Bowes resigned the command and left for England, where he rejoined his regiment.

In 1807, Colonel Bowes and the 6th Foot were transferred to the British forces at Gibraltar. They were part of General Brent Spencer's Corps that were sent from Gibraltar to support the British expedition to Portugal under Wellington. General Hew Dalrymple, the Governor of Gibraltar, had written to General Spencer on 17 July that the Horse Guards had not placed Colonel Bowes as a brigadier general on the staff of Gibraltar, therefore he could not be put in orders to be one by General Dalrymple.

---

1. The company was disbanded or drafted into another battalion.
2. General Order, 7 August 1808.
3. Sarginson.
4. He was on half-pay for a short period in early 1791.

'urthermore, he wrote that Colonel Bowes should return to Gibraltar and not remain
ıs a colonel in an army to which he was not regularly attached. That being said, General
Dalrymple did give his permission for Colonel Bowes to stay with Wellington's force.[5]

Wellington apparently thought Colonel Bowes was on the staff of Gibraltar. Since
Colonel Bowes was senior to the officers commanding brigades as brigadier generals,
Wellington assigned him to the command of the 4th Brigade in Portugal with the rank
ıf brigadier general. General Bowes served at the Battles of Roliça on 17 August and
Vimeiro on 21 August 1808. When General Dalrymple took command in Portugal, he
reorganised his army on 5 September. General Bowes was not appointed to command
ı brigade, as he was never officially placed upon the staff and he returned to Gibraltar.[6]

On 7 February 1810, General Bowes was sent with reinforcements from Gibraltar to
ıelp secure Cadiz. He was retained there by General William Stewart, the commander
ıf the British forces there. On 27 February, Wellington wrote to General Stewart that
'I approve of your detaining Brig. Gen. Bowes, he is an officer of whom I am well
ıcquainted, and is highly deserving of the confidence which you are disposed to place in
ıim.'[7] He did not remain long in Cadiz. By 23 March he was back in Gibraltar. In June,
ıe was commanding a small force sent from Gibraltar to Málaga, where they were to land
ınd take post at Casares in support of a Spanish force under General Lacey, which was
operating nearby. He never landed and was back at Gibraltar by 2 July. Later that month
ıe was promoted to major general.[8]

In late 1811, General Bowes was placed on the staff of Wellington's army. The exact
date of his appointment is unknown, perhaps in November, but certainly before 27
January 1812. By February he was in Portugal and took command of the Fusilier Brigade
of the 4th Division. He led them during the siege of Badajoz and on 6 April during the
assault on the breach near the bastion of La Trinidad, where he was severely wounded,
being shot in the thigh and stabbed with a bayonet.[9] General Bowes's ADC, Captain
James Johnson (who was his brother-in-law), was killed at the same time. Lieutenant
Robert Blakeney, who helped move General Bowes back to his tent, wrote, 'He enquired
anxiously about poor Johnson, his relative, not being aware that this gallant officer
received his death-shot while he was being carried to the rear in consequence of a wound
which he had received when cheering on a column to one of the breaches.'[10]

General Bowes spent the next six weeks recovering from his wounds and returned to
duty sometime before 28 May 1812. While he was convalescing he was transferred from
command of the Fusilier Brigade to the command of a brigade in the 6th Division on
2 May. By June 1812, the army had advanced into Spain and General Bowes's brigade was
part of the force besieging three French fortresses in Salamanca. A decision was made to
assault Fort Cayetano on the night of 23 June with six companies from the 6th Division.
General Bowes was the commander of the attacking force. He was slightly wounded at
the beginning of the attack and when he heard that the assault was faltering at the foot
of the walls, he rushed forward to rally the troops for a second attempt. He was at the
bottom of the ladder when he was shot and killed. This proved the breaking point for

5. Dalrymple; pages 271–2.
6. Muir et al.; *Inside Wellington's Peninsular Army*, pages 48–50.
7. *WD* (enlarged ed.); Vol. 3, page 748.
8. Delavoye; page 382.
9. Hall; page 69.
10. Blakeney; page 266.

the troops and they retreated. The British requested a flag of truce to 'bury the dead and remove the wounded, but it was not received.'[11] It is unknown when Bowes' body was recovered, possibly not until the fort surrendered on 27 July.

Barnard Bowes married Maria Johnson on 15 April 1805, while he was stationed in Canada. Her father was Sir John Johnson, a wealthy landowner and Superintendent of Indian Affairs. They had no children. Their home was in Beverley, Yorkshire and there is a monument to him in the Beverley Minster.

General Bowes saw little combat until 1812. Without a doubt he was brave and led from the front, regardless of the danger. Wellington wrote after his death that General Bowes 'was so eager for the success of the enterprise, that he had gone forward with the storming party'.[12] He was criticised for unnecessarily exposing himself to danger when he should have delegated the duty to a subordinate. The assault force at Fort Cayetano probably numbered less than 400 men and each brigade's three light companies were commanded by a lieutenant colonel,[13] including Lieutenant Colonel Bingham who wrote three days after his death, 'General Bowes, poor man, who was killed, and who had no business there in person, chose to neglect the advice of the engineer, and would take the troops straight across the glacis, when by a detour he might have got within fifty yards of the place, or less under cover.'[14] Sir Charles Oman also pointed out that 'General Bowes ... had insisted on going forward with his light companies – though this was evidently not brigadier's work.'[15]

An early biographer of Wellington's generals perhaps summed up his leadership style the best:

> Major-General Bowes, a rising officer, who had never been engaged without distinguishing himself, lost his life in the first attempt to carry the forts by escalade. He was wounded early, but hearing that the troops were giving way, he returned to head them a second time, and fell. There was no occasion for his leading so small a force, which duty belonged more properly to a lieutenant colonel or major; but British generals are ever prone to sacrifice themselves by unnecessary daring.[16]

---

11. Ross-Lewin; page 171.
12. *WD* (enlarged edition); Vol. 9, page 253.
13. Lieutenant Colonels Samuel Hinde and George Bingham.
14. Glover, Gareth; *Wellington's Lieutenant*, page 131.
15. Oman; *History of the Peninsular War*. Vol. 5, page 371.
16. Cole; Vol. 2, page 176.

Bradford, Thomas

Date of Birth:	1 December 1777
Date Commissioned:	Ensign 1st West Regiment of Yorkshire Militia: 30 October 1792 without purchase
British Service:	Ensign Independent Company: 20 October 1793 without purchase
	Lieutenant Independent Company: 9 December 1793 by purchase
	Captain Independent Officers: 15 April 1794 without purchase[1]
	Major[2] Loyal Nottinghamshire Fencibles:[3] 9 September 1795 without purchase
	Major 3rd Battalion of Reserve:[4] c.25 September 1804 by appointment
	Major 3rd Garrison Battalion:[5] 25 February 1805 by appointment
	Major 87th Foot: 30 May 1805 by appointment
	Brevet Lieutenant Colonel: 1 January 1801
	Lieutenant Colonel 34th Foot: 18 May 1809 without purchase
	Lieutenant Colonel 82nd Foot:[6] 21 December 1809 by exchange
	Brevet Colonel: 25 July 1810
	Major General: 4 June 1813
	Lieutenant General: 27 May 1825
	General: 23 November 1841
Portuguese Service:	Brigadier: 19 December 1811–4 June 1813
	Major General: 4 June 1813–October 1814
Regimental Colonel:	94th Foot: 1 December 1823–18 April 1829
	30th Foot: 18 April 1829–7 February 1846
	4th Foot: 7 February 1846–28 November 1853
Major Commands under Wellington:	Independent Brigade[7] Portuguese Army: 20 January 1812–April 1814
	Temporarily commanded the 3rd Division: 18 July–30 November 1815
	6th Brigade AOOF: 30 November 1815–30 March 1817
	5th Brigade AOOF: 30 March 1817–November 1818
Awards:	AGC with clasp: Corunna, Salamanca, Vitoria, San Sebastian & Nive
	KCB: 2 January 1815
	GCB: 15 February 1838
	GCH: 1831
	CTS: 13 May 1813
	Portuguese Cruz de Condecoração da Guerra Peninsular: 28 May 1820[8]
	Portuguese Medalha De Distinção De Comando: 1 December 1820[9]
Thanks of Parliament:	Salamanca
Date of Death:	28 November 1853 at Eaton Square, London

1. Was promoted for convincing men to enlist.
2. With permanent rank in the army.
3. Disbanded 28 February 1803.
4. The 3rd Battalion was renamed the 3rd Garrison Battalion on 30 October 1804. It was disbanded in February 1805.
5. A new 3rd Garrison Battalion was raised in February 1805.
6. Removed from the regiment as a general officer receiving unattached pay in 1814.
7. Numbered as the 10th Brigade in a General Order dated 13 August 1813.
8. Commonly known as the Peninsular Cross.
9. Commonly known as the Commander's Medal for the Peninsular War.

Thomas Bradford was born in 1777, the eldest son of Thomas Bradford and Elizabeth Otter of Ashdown Park, Sussex. He was the brother of Lieutenant Colonel Sir Henry Hollis Bradford and Captain Keating Bradford. His initial military career was vastly different than his contemporaries. Instead of purchasing a commission in a regular army regiment, he was appointed an ensign in the 1st West Regiment of Yorkshire Militia in 1792 and then served in a variety of militia, independent and fencible units. He was promoted captain a year later for convincing a large number of men to enlist.[10] In 1797 he became a major in the Loyal Nottinghamshire Fencibles and was given permanent rank in the army. He went with them to Ireland and helped suppress the rebellion in 1798.

Upon appointment as an AAG on the Home Staff in Scotland in 1801, Major Bradford received a brevet lieutenant colonelcy. In February 1803, Lieutenant Colonel Bradford was placed on half-pay until September 1804. While on half-pay he was appointed an Inspecting Field Officer of Yeomanry and Volunteer Corps on 7 February 1804.[11] Seven months later he was appointed as a major in the 3rd Battalion of Reserve, which was renamed the 3rd Garrison Battalion the following month. It was disbanded in February 1805 and a new 3rd Garrison Battalion was raised the same month. Major Bradford was assigned to this newly formed battalion. In 1805 he was appointed a major in the 87th Foot, but by late autumn he was an AAG with the expedition to Hanover. Upon the return of the expedition he was made an AAG at the Horse Guards. In the autumn of 1806 he returned to his regiment when it was ordered to take part in the British expedition to the River Plate in South America. Shortly after he joined the expedition, he was a DAG to the force and was at the siege of Montevideo and the assault on Buenos Aires.[12]

Lieutenant Colonel Bradford continued to serve outside his regiment on the army staff and in 1808 went to Portugal as an AAG under General Hew Dalrymple. He arrived in Portugal too late to fight at Roliça on 17 August, but was at the Battle of Vimeiro four days later as an observer with no responsibilities. In October he was sent to Corunna to meet with the force coming from England under the command of General David Baird. He would serve as the AG for General Baird until after the Battle of Corunna when the army was evacuated to Great Britain. In May 1809 he was assigned as an AAG on the Home Staff in the Kent District. That same month he was promoted to lieutenant colonel in the 34th Foot, but was only in the regiment for seven months when he exchanged into the 82nd Foot in December. The 82nd Foot would be his regiment until 1814.[13] He commanded the 2nd Battalion 82nd Foot and was promoted to colonel in July 1810.

In the autumn of 1811, Colonel Bradford was offered the opportunity to command a brigade in the Portuguese Army. On 2 December he was officially assigned to the Portuguese Army and on 19 December promoted to brigadier general by the Portuguese.[14] He was given command of an independent brigade until the end of the Peninsular War. In 1812, the brigade distinguished itself at Salamanca and was part of the force that besieged

---

10. It was common at the time for an officer to be promoted to captain if he enlisted enough men to form a company.
11. An officer could serve on the staff and receive pay for his army rank while being on half-pay from his regiment.
12. *United Service Magazine*; January 1854, page 157.
13. Until 1814, unless a general was assigned to a specific staff, they were paid at whatever rank they had in their regiment. After July 1814 they were removed from the regiment and paid as general officers, regardless of their duties.
14. General Order, 2 December 1811.

Burgos. During the retreat to the Portuguese border in that autumn, Bradford would lose a third of his soldiers due to hardship and fatigue. In June 1813 he was promoted to major general in the British Army but was retained on the staff of the Portuguese Army.[15] His brigade was in reserve at the Battle of Vitoria on 21 June, but was part of the force that pursued the retreating French Army back to France. It was then assigned to the force besieging San Sebastian and took heavy casualties in the assault on 31 August. They saw little action until December, when the brigade was heavily engaged at the Battle of Nive. After the battle the brigade went into winter quarters.

By January 1814, General Bradford's brigade was down to 1,600 effectives, having lost a third of its strength in the previous eight months. In February it was part of the force that crossed the Adour and besieged Bayonne. It would stay in the vicinity of the city until the end of the war two months later.

General Bradford was well thought of by the officers who served under him, however, Captain Thomas Bunbury of the 5th Caçadores described him during the investment of Bayonne in 1814, as 'a terrible fire-eater, and always anxious to get the regiments of his brigade engaged.'[16] He also wrote that he did not think General Bradford had 'orders to take any part in this last operation, beyond supporting the troops engaged in the duty, and the 5th Caçadores were originally posted in the rear'.[17] At the Battle of Nive on 11 December 1813, Captain John Dobbs, who also commanded a company in the 5th Caçadores, said that General Bradford's orders were 'to get my company into fire wherever I could.'[18] General Bradford did lead from the front and rode a large white horse in combat. At the Battle of Nive, Captain Dobbs wrote that General Bradford 'ordered me to move forward and ascertain what they were about – the General riding with us on a large white horse … I at once told General Bradford that they would pick him off, but he continued to expose himself till his horse was shot under him.'[19]

General Bradford continued to take chances and on 14 April, when the French sortied from Bayonne, he was seriously wounded. Captain Dobbs was also wounded and when he returned to his quarters he found that they were turned into a makeshift hospital. General Andrew Hay, a brigade commander in the 5th Division, lay dead in his room. General Bradford was being attended to by a surgeon, but when he saw the wounded Captain Dobbs, he insisted the surgeon stop working on him and look after Captain Dobbs's wound.[20]

After the disbanding of Wellington's army, General Bradford stayed with his brigade until they returned to Portugal. In October 1814, he left Portuguese service and returned to England. He was placed on the Home Staff of the Northern District. He was not at Waterloo; however, on 24 June 1815, General Henry Torrens of the Horse Guards informed Wellington that General Bradford was ordered to join his army without delay.[21] On 2 July he was placed upon the staff of Wellington's army in France and given temporary command of the 3rd Division, whose commander[22] was severely wounded

15. General Order, 2 July 1813.
16. Bunbury; Vol. 1, pages 231–2.
17. Ibid; page 231.
18. Dobbs; page 53.
19. Ibid; page 57.
20. Ibid; page 59.
21. *WSD*; Vol. 10, page 572.
22. Lieutenant General Carl Baron Alten.

at Waterloo. He commanded the division until the British Army was reorganised as the AOOF in November 1815. He was kept on the staff and given command of the 6th Brigade.[23] In March 1817 he took command of the 5th Brigade and commanded it until November 1818.

General Bradford returned to Great Britain in late 1818 and was appointed the Commander-in-Chief Scotland in 1819. In early 1825 he was one of the general officers whom Wellington put forward to Charles W. Wynn, the President of the HEIC, to command in India. Wellington thought he was 'very good'.[24] On 20 July 1825, he was appointed the Commander-in-Chief Bombay Presidency. When he left England for India is not known, however, he arrived in Bombay on 3 May 1826. He continued the reforms of the previous Commander-in-Chief, General Charles Colville, but was often at odds with his counterpart in the army of the HEIC. On 3 December 1829 he resigned his position and returned to Great Britain.[25]

Upon his return to England, General Bradford had no military duties other than that of the regimental colonel of the 30th Foot. He held the position until 1846, when he became the regimental colonel of the 4th Foot. In 1841 he was promoted to general. General Bradford received a £350 pension for the wound he received at Bayonne in 1814.

On 1 June 1818, Thomas Bradford married Mary Anne Ainslie, the widow of Lieutenant Colonel Charles Ainslie who died in 1811. Thomas and Mary Anne had five children. While in India, she and her children were sick much of the time. She died at the Cape of Good Hope, on the passage home from Bombay in February 1830. Ten years later, on 13 July 1840, Thomas married Anne Goad. He died in 1853 in London.

---

23. General Order, 30 November 1815.
24. *WND*; Vol. 2, page 425. Duke of Buckingham; Vol. 2, page 231.
25. *United Service Magazine*; Vol. 59, March 1848, pages 348–9.

Brisbane, Thomas

Date of Birth:	23 July 1773 at Brisbane House, Largs, Scotland
Date Commissioned:	Ensign 71st Foot:[1] 10 January 1782[2]
Promotions:	Ensign 38th Foot: 9 April 1789 by exchange[3]
	Lieutenant 38th Foot: 30 July 1791 without purchase
	Captain Independent Company: 12 April 1793 without purchase
	Captain 53rd Foot: 1 January 1794 by exchange
	Major 53rd Foot 5 August 1795 by purchase
	Lieutenant Colonel 69th Foot: 4 April 1800 by purchase
	Brevet Colonel: 25 July 1810
	Brigadier General on the Staff: 25 November 1812
	Major General: 4 June 1813
	Lieutenant General: 27 May 1825
	General: 23 November 1841
Regimental Colonel:	34th Foot: 16 December 1826–27 January 1860
Major Commands under Wellington:	Brigade 3rd Division 25 March 1813–April 1814
	14th Brigade: 24 August–30 November 1815
	Temporarily commanded 7th Division: 24 August–30 November 1815
	5th Brigade AOOF: 30 November 1815–30 March 1817
	3rd Brigade AOOF: 30 March 1817–November 1818
Awards:	AGC with clasp: Vitoria, Pyrenees, Nivelle, Orthes & Toulouse
	KCB: 2 January 1815
	GCB: 6 February 1837
	GCH: 1831
	MGSM with clasp: Nive
Thanks of Parliament:	Orthes
Date of Death:	27 January 1860 at Brisbane House, Largs, Scotland

Changed his name to Makdougall-Brisbane in 1826.

Thomas Brisbane was born in 1773, the oldest child of Thomas Brisbane and Eleonora Bruce of Stenhouse. His father served under the Duke of Cumberland at Culloden and his mother was a direct descendant of King Robert the Bruce. He was educated by tutors and attended both the University of Edinburgh and the English Academy, Kensington. He had a strong interest in mathematics and astronomy.

Thomas Brisbane was commissioned an ensign in the 71st Foot in 1782, at the age of 8. He was on half-pay until 1789, when he exchanged into the 38th Foot. He went to Ireland and was stationed in Cork and then in Galway, where he struck up a friendship with Wellington. They spent much of their time hunting on the estate of the Earl of Westmeath. In 1790, both men went to Dublin and spent their free time together for the next two years. Ensign Brisbane was promoted to lieutenant in 1791 and returned to Scotland in 1793 to raise an independent company that was attached to the 53rd Foot.

---

1. Disbanded 1783.
2. *Army List*; 1845, page 185.
3. *London Gazette*; 11 April 1789, page 270.

This earned him a promotion to captain. He and his company went with the 53rd Foot to Flanders in the spring of 1793. He was wounded in May, but over the next two years took part in every battle and siege the expeditionary force fought in, including the sieges of Valenciennes, Dunkirk, Nieuport, Landrecies and Nijmegan.[4] In January 1794 he officially joined the 53rd Foot when he exchanged into the regiment.

Captain Brisbane returned to England in the spring of 1795, when the British Expeditionary Force evacuated the continent. He was promoted to major in August and went with the 53rd Foot to the West Indies. He served there until 1799, when word reached him that he was promoted to lieutenant colonel in the 69th Foot. When he returned to England he found out that the regiment had sailed to Jamaica. He delayed joining the regiment due to his poor health. He took command of the regiment in Kingston in 1801 and two years later they returned to England. In the autumn of 1804, the regiment was ordered to India. Lieutenant Colonel Brisbane had never fully recovered from a severe liver complaint and on the recommendation of his doctor went on half-pay instead of going to India with his regiment. In February 1805 he exchanged into the disbanded York Rangers.[5] He remained on half-pay with the disbanded York Rangers until he was removed from half-pay as a general officer receiving unattached pay in 1814.

While on half-pay, Lieutenant Colonel Brisbane continued his studies in astronomy and in 1808 built the second observatory in Scotland on his family estate in Largs. In 1810 he was accepted as a Fellow of the Royal Society of London. He was promoted to colonel in July 1810 and was appointed AAG on the Home Staff at Canterbury.

By 1812 Colonel Brisbane was healthy enough to join Wellington's army in Portugal. He wrote to both Wellington and General Picton of his desires.[6] Colonel Torrens, of the Horse Guards, wrote to Wellington in late November that Colonel Brisbane was an excellent officer[7] and a discussion took place on where he could best be used. He was considered a possible replacement for General Charles Stewart, Wellington's AG. Colonel Torrens wrote to Wellington that 'HRH[8] will be totally guided by your wishes. If you should not fix upon Pakenham … the only eligible Candidates I know of Brigr Generals Brisbane … I merely throw out … for your consideration'.[9] It is possible that Wellington was not in favour of having Colonel Brisbane as his AG, for Colonel Torrens wrote back to him that, 'I have been led to believe that you formerly knew him and that you had a favorable opinion of him.'[10] Regardless of the misunderstanding between the two, Colonel Brisbane was placed on the staff of Wellington's army as a brigadier general on 7 January 1813 to date from 25 November 1812.

General Brisbane arrived in Portugal in the winter of 1813, but did not know what he would be doing. He wrote:

> I proceeded immediately thereafter to Lisbon, and from thence to Coimbra and Frenada, the head-quarters of the Duke, who received me with the utmost kindness, and said he was glad to see me, as he had two brigades vacant for me, one in the third

---

4. Brisbane; pages 8–12. *RMC*; Vol. 3, page 262.
5. Brisbane; pages 19–22. *RMC*; Vol. 3, page 262.
6. Brisbane; page 22.
7. Unpublished letter dated 26 November 1812.
8. The Duke of York, the Commander-in-Chief of the British Army.
9. Unpublished letter dated 23 December 1812.
10. Unpublished letter dated 17 February 1813.

and the other in the seventh division; the former commanded by my old friend Sir Thomas Picton, under whom I served in the West Indies, and the other under the Earl of Dalhousie.[11] I selected accordingly the third division …[12]

The nickname of General Picton's 3rd Division was the Fighting Division. During the seventeen months that General Brisbane commanded one of its brigades, its nickname was re-affirmed. General Picton often exceeded the scope of his orders to get his division into the fight and General Brisbane's brigade was heavily engaged many times. It fought in four major battles and took heavy casualties in three of them. At Vitoria on 21 June 1813 the brigade lost 16 per cent of its men. In the final two battles it took the heaviest casualties of any brigade engaged. At Orthes on 27 February 1814, its 477 casualties were 30 per cent of all British casualties for the day. Six weeks later at Toulouse, the brigade lost another 354 men, 17 per cent of the British casualties.[13]

General Brisbane described being wounded at Toulouse:

While standing on the banks of the canal, exposed to a heavy fire from the enemy's artillery and musketry, a cannon-shot took off the cock of my hat, spun me round with irresistible force, and knocked me flat on the ground. I was so confused with the violence of the concussion, that I deemed it prudent to send for the officer next in command to be near me, and to take the command of the brigade in case of necessity. While in this state of confusion I was shot through the left arm by a musket-ball, when the blood, flowing profusely from the wound, immediately relieved my head, and restore me to my senses.[14]

General Brisbane was promoted to major general on 4 June 1813. Wellington could have used this as an excuse to send him home, but chose to retain him on the staff.[15] In October 1813, General Picton returned to England due to ill health. This caused a problem about who would temporarily command the 3rd Division in his absence. General Manley Power, who was serving in the Portuguese Army, took temporary command of the division as the senior brigade commander. He did so as he held superior rank in the Allied Army over General Brisbane, who was General Power's senior in British Army rank. General Brisbane challenged his right to do so. The AG responded on behalf of Wellington, who had decided in General Power's favour. There the matter ended.[16]

With the war won in Europe, in April 1814 the British Government decided to send a large force to fight in North America against the United States. Most of the officers and men were to be taken from Wellington's army. In June 1814, General Brisbane was selected to go as a brigade commander. Wellington praised him and the other generals sent to Canada to serve in the war of 1812 in a letter to Earl Bathurst on 30 October 1814: 'the general officers I sent him, which are certainly the best of their rank in the army'[17] Brisbane and his brigade arrived in Montreal in late July and he was given command of

---

11. General George Ramsay Earl of Dalhousie.
12. Brisbane; page 22.
13. Oman; *A History of the Peninsular War*. Vol. 6, pages 751 and 758 ; Vol. 7, pages 541, 553, 558–9.
14. Ibid; page 44.
15. General Order, 2 July 1813.
16. A.G. to General Brisbane 18 October 1813; *WD* (enlarged ed.), Vol. 7, page 72.
17. Hitsman; page 267. Wellington was referring to Generals Power, Kempt, Brisbane and Robinson.

the Advance Guard during the Plattsburg Campaign. Upon returning to Montreal the army went into winter quarters. In February 1815, word had reached Montreal that the war was over. By June, General Brisbane and his brigade were headed back to Europe to reinforce the British Army in the Netherlands. His ship was off of France when he received word of the defeat of Napoleon at Waterloo. On 18 July, Earl Bathurst informed Wellington that General Brisbane was accompanying the regiments returned from Canada and was being sent to reinforce his army.[18]

General Brisbane was placed on the staff of Wellington's army on 31 August 1815. His appointment was to date from 16 July.[19] He was appointed to command the 14th Brigade 7th Division on 24 August, however, in the absence of a senior officer to command the division, he took temporary command of it the same day. General Brisbane was placed on the staff of the AOOF and given command of the 5th Brigade on 30 November 1815. On 30 March 1817 he became the commander of the 3rd Brigade until November 1818, when the army was disbanded and he returned to England.

In 1820 General Brisbane was on the staff of the Southern District in Munster, Ireland. In 1815 he had applied to be the governor of New South Wales, but the position had already been filled. In November 1820, based on the recommendation of Wellington, General Brisbane received the appointment. His tenure as governor was marked by expansion and growth of the colony. His goal was to make the colony economically independent of Great Britain. His policies were opposed by some, especially the entrenched bureaucracy and those with a vested interest in keeping things the way they were before he arrived. Four years after his appointment he was recalled. Brisbane, the third largest city in Australia, is named after him.[20]

General Brisbane was promoted to lieutenant general in 1825. Upon his return from Australia in 1826, he was appointed the colonel of the 34th Foot and commanded them until his death in 1860. While he was in Australia, in early 1825 he was one of the general officers whom Wellington put forward to Charles W. Wynn, the President of the HEIC, to command in India. Although General Brisbane was still in Australia, Wellington knew that he had been recalled. Wellington thought he was 'a very respectable officer and very fit for the situation'.[21] He was not selected for the position, possibly because he was not immediately available. General Brisbane spent the rest of his years pursuing his studies in astronomy and built Scotland's third observatory in Makerstoun. In 1827 he became the vice president of the Royal Astronomical Society and over the years received honourary degrees from Edinburgh, Oxford and Cambridge. On 8 March 1836, he was created a baronet[22] and in 1841 he was promoted to general.

Thomas Brisbane married Anna Maria Makdougall, the heiress of Sir Henry Hay Makdougall, on 15 November 1819.[23] They had two daughters and two sons. He outlived all of his children. In 1826 he formally changed his name to Makdougall-Brisbane in order to receive his wife's inheritance. In the later years of his life he was plagued with rheumatic gout. Sir Thomas died on the morning of Friday, 27 January 1860, at 3.16 a.m.

---

18. Brisbane; pages 29–30. *WSD*; Vol. 11, page 34.
19. General Order, 31 August 1815.
20. Brisbane; pages 43–60. Heydon.
21. *WND*; Vol. 2, page 425. Duke of Buckingham; Vol. 2, page 231.
22. *London Gazette*; 21 February 1836.
23. *Scots Magazine*; Vol. 84, page 581.

in the same bed he was born in at Brisbane, Scotland.[24] He had been a soldier for seventy-eight years. His home, Brisbane House, was destroyed during a training exercise in the Second World War. In 1961, his collection of medals were stolen from an auction house in London and have never been recovered.[25]

Thomas Brisbane was a friend of Wellington and while they were in Paris they grew closer. However, this friendship had its limits. Wellington would help General Brisbane if his assistance was not detrimental to the army or violated established customs in regards to seniority. For example, Wellington let General Brisbane choose which brigade he wanted to command in 1813. Additionally, according to General Brisbane if he had had returned from Canada in time for the Waterloo Campaign, he might have been given a division command by Wellington. When he returned from Canada in the summer of 1815:

> Major-General Sir Manby [*sic*] Power[26] and the late Lord Kean [sic][27] informed me that they had written to the Duke of Wellington at Brussels, offering themselves for employment in the army which he was forming for Waterloo. His Grace replied that he should be very happy to comply with their request, but he could hold out no promise to them until Sir Thomas Brisbane had received the Division he preferred. This I learned from the above-named Generals, but the Duke never mentioned it to me himself.[28]

Whether there is truth in this cannot be ascertained. However, had he returned in time, General Brisbane would have been one of the senior major generals in the Waterloo Army and thus possibly could have been in line to receive command of a division.[29] All of these considerations were extended to him because they fell within the boundaries of the established customs concerning seniority. Yet when General Brisbane asked for the temporary command of the 3rd Division in 1813, Wellington refused to give it to him because, despite being senior to General Power in the British Army, General Power was senior to him based on his rank in the Portuguese Army.

General Brisbane was an aggressive leader and demanded much of his troops. Yet at the same time he looked after their welfare. When he took command of the 69th Foot in Jamaica, he found it in poor shape. Many of its soldiers were in the hospital. Although the climate caused some of the problems, many were directly related to poor leadership on the part of the regiment's officers. Instead of ensuring the troops were being fed properly, they were allowing the soldiers to spend their daily allowance for fruit and vegetables on alcohol. By the time the regiment returned to England, its health had improved so dramatically the garrison was able to close two hospitals that housed the sick soldiers.[30]

During the Peninsular War, General Brisbane also took a keen interest in the welfare of his troops. An example of this can be found in the memoirs of his brigade major, Major James Campbell, who wrote that General Brisbane's policy was:

---

24. Brisbane; page 129.
25. 'Brisbane Observatory'.
26. Manley Power.
27. John Lord Keane.
28. Brisbane; page 34.
29. Burnham and McGuigan; *British Army against Napoleon*, page 55.
30. Ibid; pages 19–20.

No officer commanding a corps was allowed, under any pretence, to keep his men unnecessarily under arms, especially after a march. As soon as the soldiers reached their cantonments, or ground of encampment, they were ordered to be instantly dismissed, and allowed to go into their quarters or tents to take off their accoutrements, knapsacks, &c, so that they might as soon as possible recover from the fatigues of the march; for keeping men standing, after being heated, till they became chilled, was always found to be injurious to their health.[31]

General Brisbane also looked after his soldiers in other ways. After the Battle of Vitoria, where treasures stolen from Spain by the French fell to the victorious British, General Brisbane stated:

So signal was the defeat that King Joseph's carriages, plate, and wines, and everything belonging to him fell into our hands ... Had I allowed my men to follow and pick up the boxes of money which could have been gathered, they might have enriched themselves to a very great extent. As it was, I waylaid the stragglers and made them disgorge their plunder, and next morning I had three such piles of dollars as enabled me to divide five dollars to every soldier belonging to the brigade.[32]

This division of the spoils did not keep him from dining on King Joseph's plate and drinking his wine![33]

On a more practical matter that concerned the safety of his men, during the war of 1812, when General Brisbane commanded the advance guard of the British Army in the Plattsburg Campaign, he was appalled by the atrocities committed by both sides. This was especially true against the outposts and picquets, who were often attacked and killed for no other reason than that their enemy could do so. He saw little military value in this and considered this against the customs that the British and the French practiced in the Peninsula. He contacted the opposing American commander and they reached an agreement that the outposts of both sides would stop shooting at each other.[34]

Very few of Thomas Brisbane's contemporaries in the British Army shared his interest in science and mathematics. While on campaign, he would carry with him a pocket sextant chronometer and an artificial horizon. He would take readings on the altitude of the sun to determine the time of day whenever he could. Wellington became aware of this and he became the army's time-keeper. In 1818, Wellington had the army publish a pamphlet written by General Brisbane on his method for determining accurate time. During his three-year stay in Paris after Waterloo, he continued his studies. In 1816 word reached him that allied troops were planning to destroy the buildings of the Institute of France, which included the Académie Française. He rushed over to the Institute and ordered the soldiers back to their barracks. He was unanimously elected a corresponding member of the Institute for his actions. In 1817, Wellington tasked him to draw up a table that compared British weights and measurements to their French equivalent, since the army was being supplied using the French system.[35]

---

31. Campbell; page 192.
32. Brisbane; page 22.
33. Ibid; page 23.
34. Ibid; page 29.
35. Ibid; pages 34–5, 43, and 61. *Dictionary of National Biography*; Vol. 2, page 1263.

Brooke, William

Date of Birth:	1770 at Madras, India
Date Commissioned:	Cornet 8th Light Dragoons: 29 June 1793
Promotions:	Lieutenant 83rd Foot: 7 October 1793 without purchase
	Captain Independent Company: 14 December 1793
	Captain 96th Foot:[1] 25 March 1794 appointed
	Major 96th Foot: 13 December 1794 by purchase
	Major 56th Foot: 4 January 1805 by exchange
	Major 5th Dragoon Guards: 25 July 1805 by exchange[2]
	Brevet Lieutenant Colonel: 1 January 1800
	Brevet Colonel: 25 July 1810
	Brigadier General on the Staff: 14 January 1813
	Major General: 4 June 1813
	Lieutenant General: 27 May 1825
	General: 23 November 1841
Major Commands under Wellington:	On the staff at Lisbon: 26 September 1812–April 1814
Date of Death:	9 September 1843 at Alfred Place, Bath

William Brooke was the son of Henry Brooke and Mary Allbeary, who was allegedly the illegitimate daughter of Frederick Louis, the Prince of Wales. William's father was a former governor of Fort St George in Madras, India. By 1786 the family had returned to the British Isles and was living in Ireland. William was commissioned as a cornet in the 8th Light Dragoons in June 1793 and was promoted as a lieutenant in the newly formed 83rd Foot four months later. Two months later he was promoted to captain of an independent company. In March 1794 he was appointed a captain in the 96th Foot, which was being formed. He went with the regiment to the West Indies in September 1794, where he was promoted to major in December. Major Brooke commanded the garrison of St Marc on the island of Santo Domingo from March 1795 until August 1796, when his regiment was disbanded and he returned to England. Despite the disbanding of his regiment, Major Brooke was still carried on the regimental rolls and thus received his full pay. He had no regimental duties.

Major Brooke went on half-pay on 1 March 1798. Despite being on half-pay he was promoted to brevet lieutenant colonel in January 1800. He tried to come off half-pay in 1804 by arranging an exchange into the 48th Foot on 24 May. However, the exchange was cancelled on 9 June with no reason given.[3] He did successfully exchanged into the 56th Foot in January 1805, but this was just a stepping stone until he was able to exchange into the 5th Dragoon Guards six months later.

Lieutenant Colonel Brooke's efforts to come back on active duty, in particular as an officer in the 5th Dragoon Guards, came under scrutiny in 1809. The Parliament was investigating allegations that the Duke of York's mistress, Mary Clarke, was selling her influence with the Duke to expedite promotions and exchanges. During the inquiry it came out that Mrs Clarke received £200 to ensure the exchange between Lieutenant

---

1. Disbanded in 1795.
2. Removed from the regiment as a general officer receiving unattached pay 1814.
3. *London Gazette*; War Office Announcements dated 2 June and 16 June 1804.

Colonel Brooke and Lieutenant Colonel Henry Knight of the 5th Dragoon Guards happened. Lieutenant Colonel Knight had been trying to exchange out of the regiment for some time and a previous application had been disapproved, because the officer he wished to exchange with had no cavalry experience. It was only after he paid Mrs Clarke the £200 bribe that his request was approved.[4] No witness testified that Lieutenant Colonel Brooke was involved with the bribery.

In July 1810, William Brooke was promoted to colonel. The following summer, the 5th Dragoon Guards received orders to join Wellington's army in Portugal and left Portsmouth in August with six troops. Colonel Brooke stayed in Canterbury with the other four troops. Eleven months later, Colonel William Ponsonby, the commander of the regiment, was given command of the cavalry brigade in which the 5th Dragoon Guards was part of.

Colonel Brooke arrived in Portugal in September 1812 to take command of the 5th Dragoon Guards. This posed a problem for Wellington. Colonel Brooke was senior to Colonel Ponsonby in army rank. By army custom, Colonel Brooke should have been offered the command of the brigade. Colonel Torrens of the Horse Guards realised there might be a problem and belatedly wrote to Wellington on 4 October:

> As you have given Ponsonby a Brigade he will be a Brigr according to your desire: you will observe that Colonel Brooke... is senior in the Army to Ponsonby. If you can, or chuse [sic] to give him a Command he may of course be a Brigadier also. If not, the Com. in Chief wishes you should leave it to his option, either to remain in Command of the 5th Dragoon Guards, or to return to England.[5]

In addition to the seniority problem that Colonel Brooke brought with him to Lisbon, he also brought a lack of experience commanding cavalry in the field. General Brooke had been in the army for twenty years, but for nine of those years he was on half-pay, while another seven years were spent on garrison duty in the British Isles. His only field experience was in a small garrison in Santo Domingo. He was too inexperienced to be given a command.

Wellington solved the problem by appointing Colonel Brooke on the staff as a colonel on 26 September. He was assigned to Lisbon where his primary duty was to serve as the president of court-martials. Brooke was appointed a brigadier general on the staff on 5 February 1813 with the appointment to date from 14 January 1813. As late as 1 May 1813, Wellington noted that General Brooke was without a brigade command.[6] Despite this he was not given a brigade when vacancies occurred. In July 1813, General Brooke was retained on the staff when he was promoted to major general.[7] He would stay in Lisbon until the end of the Peninsular War.

When General Brooke returned to England he was never appointed to another position in the army. He appeared to have been forgotten when so many of his contemporaries were awarded as KCBs or CBs in 1815. However, because promotion was based on seniority, he continued to be promoted and was promoted to lieutenant general in 1825 and general in 1841. He was never made a regimental colonel.

William Brooke married Mary Nicholls, daughter of General Oliver Nicholls, in June 1815. There is no record of them having children.

---

4. Cobbett; pages 268 and 700.
5. Unpublished letter from Colonel Torrens to the Duke of Wellington, dated 4 October 1812.
6. *WD* (enlarged ed.); Vol. 6, page 457.
7. General Order, 2 July 1813.

Burne, Robert

Date of Birth:	c. 1753
Date Commissioned:	Ensign 36th Foot: 28 September 1773 by purchase
Promotions:	Lieutenant: 36th Foot 13 January 1777 by purchase
	Captain-Lieutenant: 36th Foot 7 May 1784 without purchase
	Captain 36th Foot: 28 October 1784 without purchase[1]
	Brevet Major: 1 March 1794
	Major 36th Foot: 15 April 1796 by purchase
	Brevet Lieutenant Colonel: 1 January 1798
	Lieutenant Colonel 36th Foot:[2] 13 November 1799 without purchase
	Brevet Colonel: 25 April 1808
	Brigadier General on the Staff: 21 January 1811
	Major General: 4 June 1811
	Lieutenant General: 19 July 1821
Major Commands under Wellington:	Brigade 6th Division: 5 March 1811–24 April 1812
	Temporarily commanded 6th Division: 5 November 1811– 9 February 1812
Awards:	AGM with clasp: Roliça & Vimeiro & Corunna
Mentioned in Dispatches:	Vimeiro
Date of Death:	9 June 1825 at Berkeley Cottage, Stanmore, Hertfordshire

Family name was occasionally spelled Byrne.

Little is known about Robert Burne prior to him being commissioned. The exact date and place of his birth is unknown. It is likely he came from an affluent family because he purchased his commission and several other ranks. Robert Burne was commissioned in 1773 in the 36th Foot and would serve with them for the next thirty-eight years. He never took a position outside of the regiment until he was promoted to brigadier general in 1811.

In 1775, Ensign Burne went to Ireland with his regiment and served there until 1780, when it returned to England. While in Ireland he was promoted to lieutenant. In March 1783 the regiment was sent to India, arriving at Madras four months later. In October 1784 he was promoted to captain and commanded the regiment's Grenadier Company. The regiment served in General Lord Cornwallis's campaigns against Tipu Sultan[3] of Mysore in a number of actions including the siege of Bangalore in March 1791 and at the capture of Seringapatam in February 1792. Legend has it that during the battle, Captain Burne personally killed Hajah Aftab Khan, the leader of the Sultan's cavalry.[4] Captain Burne and his regiment were at the surrender of French-held Pondicherry on 23 August 1793. They would remain in India until October 1798, when they sailed for England. Due to poor weather, it took the regiment ten months to complete the voyage, landing in Portsmouth in July 1799. While in India, Captain Burne was able to purchase

---

1. *London Gazette*; War Office Announcement, dated 22 October 1785.
2. Removed from the regiment as a general officer receiving unattached pay in 1814.
3. Also known as Tippoo Sultan.
4. Gleig; page 107.

his majority in 1796 and was promoted to brevet lieutenant colonel two years later. He was promoted to lieutenant colonel in the regiment and took command of it in November 1799. He would command it for the next twelve years.

Lieutenant Colonel Burne and the regiment were back in Ireland by January 1800 and were soon embarked for a series of raids on the French coast. By the autumn they were in the Mediterranean and garrisoned in Minorca. Lieutenant Colonel Burne was forced to return to England in 1801 due to poor health. He rejoined the regiment when it returned to Ireland in 1802. They would remain in Ireland until October 1805, when they joined Wellington's brigade in the expedition to Hanover. They returned to England in February 1806 and in October they embarked for South America.

The 36th Foot was part of General Robert Craufurd's force that joined with General Samuel Auchmuty's for the attack on and capture of Montevideo, Uruguay in February 1807. Six months later, they were part of General William Lumley's brigade at the failed assault on Buenos Aires. Lieutenant Colonel Burne distinguished himself during the attack on the city. The assaulting force, including the 36th Foot, was trapped in the narrow streets of the city and the Spanish commander brought up guns to force them to surrender:

> Colonel Burne seeing that his old grenadier company was near the rear of the column then all compressed in a road, wheeled it about and thus addressed them. 'Now my lads I've come to lead you once more to an assault – you see those guns – if we don't take and spike them our regiment will be swept away – there is just room in the road for my old grenadiers' – then plucking a flower from the adjacent garden hedge, he coolly adjusted it in his button hole and drawing his sword he and his grenadiers had in 15 minutes sent all the Spaniards back into the town and spiked every gun![5]

Despite the bravery of Lieutenant Colonel Burne, the British were forced to surrender and were released only after the British commander agreed to evacuate the city and never return.

Lieutenant Colonel Burne and the 36th Foot returned to Ireland in December 1807. In April 1808 he was promoted to colonel. Three months later they were notified that they would be part of the British force going to Portugal. They were assigned to General Ronald Ferguson's 2nd Brigade and landed in Mondego Bay in early August. They fought at Roliça on 17 August and at Vimeiro on 21 August 1808. During the Battle of Vimeiro, while waiting for the French column that was about to assault his position, a soldier fired without permission 'old Burne, our Colonel, crying out as he shook his yellow cane, that "by God" he would "knock down any who fired a shot".'[6] It was not long before the French arrived and 'Colonel Burne now dashed in amongst them with the 7 Companies, and after keeping up a hot fire for a Quarter of an hour, charged, scattering them with dreadful slaughter.'[7] Colonel Burne was mentioned in dispatches for his actions that day.

In the reorganisation of the army on 5 September, Colonel Burne's regiment was placed in General Ferguson's brigade in the 2nd Division. When an army for service

---

5. Murchison; page 99.
6. Murchison; page 172.
7. *Blackwell*; July 1933, pages 161–2.

n Spain under General John Moore was formed on 8 October, Colonel Burne and his regiment were selected to serve with it, but were placed in General Catlin Craufurd's brigade. It remained in the brigade during the advance into Spain and the retreat to Corunna. They were at the Battle of Corunna on 16 January 1809 but did not see much action. After the battle, the regiment returned to southern England.

The regiment was not in England for long. In July it was assigned to the British Expedition to Walcheren and was part of General Thomas Picton's brigade in the 4th Division. In September it was re-assigned to General Henry Montressor's brigade and selected to garrison Walcheren. Over the next three months the regiment lost over 200 men to Walcheren Fever. It was finally evacuated from the island and returned to England in December.[8]

Colonel Burne and the regiment were stationed in southern England for a year. In January 1811 they were sent to Portugal and on 25 March he was placed on the staff of Wellington's army as a brigadier general.[9] He took command of a brigade in the 6th Division and commanded them at the Battle of Fuentes de Oñoro on 3–5 May. The brigade was on the far left of the British Army and saw no action during the battle. After the battle, they were part of the covering force that was masking the French garrison in Almeida. General Burne's brigade was responsible for screening the approaches to Barba del Puerco, the nearest bridge across the Agueda River. On the night of 10 May, the French commander of Almeida blew up the fortress. A series of miscommunications on the part of the British permitted the French to go through the area General Burne's brigade was supposed to be guarding, and escape across the bridge. Wellington was furious at the commanders who allowed the garrison to escape. Despite this setback, General Burne was retained on the staff when he was promoted to major general in June.[10] He temporarily commanded the 6th Division from 5 November 1811 to 9 February 1812.

In late 1811, Wellington decided that General Burne needed to return to England. He wrote to Colonel Torrens of the Horse Guards on 2 December 'there are two whom we could dispense with advantage Burne and Kemmis. They are both respectable Officers as commanders of regiments, but they are neither of them very fit to take charge of a large body.'[11]

Colonel Torrens responded a month later that 'The Duke[12] will relieve you from the burthen of Burne and Kemmis, if possible, yet to be recalled without some object might appear harsh to the old veterans who have done their best.'[13] Wellington replied that 'It will be very desirable to get rid of Burne and Kemmis, but not in a manner to mortify them'.[14] Colonel Torrens wrote back that 'HRH also means to relieve you from the burthen of Burne ...'[15]

---

8. Cannon, Richard; *Historical Record of the Thirty-Sixth*, page 77.

9. General Order, 25 March 1811. His promotion was backdated to 21 January.

10. General Order, 26 June 1811.

11. *WD* (enlarged ed.); Vol. 5, page 387. The names were suppressed in the published letter but other unpublished correspondence provides evidence that Burne and Kemmis are the two referred to.

12. The Duke of York, the Commander-in-Chief of the British Army.

13. Unpublished letter dated 4 January 1812.

14. Wellington to Torrens dated 28 January 1812. *WD* (enlarged ed.); Vol. 5, page 487. Names were suppressed in published letter.

15. Unpublished letter dated 6 February 1812.

By 24 April 1812, General Burne had returned to England and was appointed to the Home Staff serving in the Inland District. His duties included command of the camp at Lichfield until 1813 and then at Nottingham until 1814. He was promoted to lieutenant general in 1821 and died four years later.[16]

General Burne received little recognition for his many years of service. He was appointed Governor of Carlisle on 8 September 1808 and would serve as the governor until his death. Yet when Wellington was asked to recommend deserving officers who had served in the Peninsula to receive the Most Honourable Order of the Bath, General Burne's name was not on the list. He was one of the few general officers who served in the Peninsula who was not inducted into the Order on 2 January 1815.

Possibly tainting General Burne's reputation was the minor scandal of his infatuation with one of the Adams sisters, who were professional dancers. It was apparently widely known and Wellington felt that it might be affecting his duties. In the same letter that he requested General Burne be recalled, he also mentioned that, 'I understand that Burne wishes to return home to unite himself with a lady of easy virtue … I shall try if I can get them away in this manner, as I would not on any account hurt the feelings of either.'[17] Colonel Torrens also knew of it and voiced his opinion on General Burne's obsession and identified the object of his affection with 'One of the dancing Miss Adams's[18] is the Chere Amie I believe of old Burne – what a blockhead!!'[19]

Wellington's issues with General Burne stem from his time as a brigade commander, for Wellington thought highly of him as a regimental commander. The day after the Battle of Vimeiro, he wrote to Viscount Castlereagh, 'I have mentioned Col. Burne of the 36th regt., in a very particular manner; and I assure you that there is nothing that will give me so much satisfaction as to learn that something has been done for this old and meritorious soldier.'[20] The result of Wellington's letter was that Colonel Burne was appointed Governor of Carlisle. In early 1809, Wellington happened across Colonel Burne on Bond Street in London. He greeted him with, 'Ah my dear Burne, glad to see you once more – one of your youngsters eh! Well things won't do as they are. I shall soon be at it again and then I can't do without the 36th!'[21]

Why Wellington sought the relief of General Burne is a bit of a mystery. Although he was never publicly rebuked for his part in the escape of the French garrison at Almeida in May 1811, Wellington would not have forgotten his negligence. Another problem was his age. By the time he reported to the Peninsula in 1811, General Burne was 58 years old and had been a soldier for thirty-eight of them. The rigors of decades of campaigning had probably taken its toll on his health. He had problems in 1801 that forced him to give up his command and return to England to recover. Furthermore, there was a possibility that like so many of his regiment, he may have caught Walcheren Fever. Those who did survive the fever took years to recover. General Burne had about a year to convalesce before he was back in Portugal.

---

16. Leslie; Vol. 3, page 384.
17. See footnote 11.
18. There were four Adams sisters who were professional dancers in Ireland. Three only went by their first initial E., H. and S. The fourth and youngest sister was Anna Mathilda Adams.
19. Unpublished letter dated 4 January 1812.
20. *WD* (enlarged ed.); Vol. 3, page 96.
21. Murchison; page 335.

Despite Wellington's opinion of him, Robert Burne was well thought of by the officers of the 36th Foot. In many ways he was the regiment. He never served in another regiment and had been with it for twenty-six years before he assumed its command. A young lieutenant recorded in his diary on 19 June 1809, that the regiment formed up and Fired three vollies [*sic*], and afterwards presented Colonel Burne with a sword value 120 guineas. His reply to the address was gratifying and impressive – I cd. not help shedding tears, but they did not proceed from sorrow's Channel – I wd. not have exchanged my feelings at the time for Millions.'[22]

Another young lieutenant named Roderick Murchison kept a diary of his years in the 36th Foot and left some vivid descriptions of Robert Burne. According to Murchison, he was a heavy drinker who,

> loved to sit [in the regimental mess] habitually from five to ten o'clock swallowing glass after glass of port and never being himself the slightest degree affected except that his nose was then assuming the purple colour and bottle shape which rendered him so conspicuous in the Peninsular War! Indeed he could not tolerate a drunken man and he perfectly despised what he called a spewing ensign, who could not stand his two or three bottles of bad port.[23]

Lieutenant Murchison also stated that Colonel Burne was an exacting drillmaster. 'In field work and drill he was most methodical and such a crack regiment had been the 36th at the camp on the Carragh [*sic*] of Kildare that Lord Cathcart[24] admiring the steadiness of its movement once called out "Bravo Colonel Burne—Humphrey Bland himself could not have done better."'[25]

Both in garrison or on campaign, Colonel Burne always carried a large bamboo cane with a golden head. Furthermore, he expected his officers and men to keep up the highest standards of dress, regardless if they were in garrison or on campaign. Lieutenant Murchison stated that,

> the end of my pigtail had its regular three turns given to it every morning by the regimental barber, Francis, whilst my glazed Cock'd hat then worn square to the front, so as almost blind me in a sunny day, was never turned fore and aft except in some lane remote from the barracks and the colonel's piercing dark brown eye. We wore long white pipe clayed gloves coming up to our elbows whilst the poor soldier had a broad queue which when unplastered fell 'en nape' down his sacrum like a woman's hair and the preparing plating and adjusting of which together with the black balling of its cover was half a mornings work ... laugh at these features of the old school; for I presently narrate how we drubbed the French in their loose attire, whilst we of Roliça and Vimeiro had pig tails, long gloves, glazed cock'hats and above all bright shining muskets.[26]

Perhaps the most revealing comment about Robert Burne was made by the same lieutenant. 'It was of course my glory to follow every move and idea of my gallant old Colonel.'[27]

---

22. *Blackwell*; April 1934, page 13.
23. Murchison; pages 100–1.
24. General William Lord Cathcart was the commander of the forces in Ireland.
25. Murchison; page 100. General Humphrey Bland wrote a *Treatise of Military Discipline* in 1727. Its 9th edition was published in 1762. It included forming troops and drill.
26. Ibid; page 101.
27. Ibid; page 99.

Byng, John

Date of Birth:	1772
Date Commissioned:	Ensign 33rd Foot: 30 September 1793 without purchase
Promotions:	Lieutenant 33rd Foot: 1 December 1793 without purchase
	Captain 33rd Foot: 24 May 1794 without purchase
	Major 60th Foot: 28 December 1799 by purchase
	Lieutenant Colonel 29th Foot: 14 March 1800 by purchase
	Captain & Lieutenant Colonel 3rd Foot Guards:[1] 4 August 1804 appointed
	Brevet Colonel: 25 July 1810
	Brigadier General on the Staff: 25 November 1812
	Major General: 4 June 1813
	Lieutenant General: 27 May 1825
	General: 23 November 1841
	Field Marshal: 2 October 1855
Regimental Colonel:	York Light Infantry Volunteers: 26 December 1815–1816[2]
	4th West India Regiment: 12 December 1816–1819[3]
	2nd West India Regiment: 26 July 1822–23 January 1828
	29th Foot: 23 January 1828–15 August 1850
	Coldstream Foot Guards: 15 August 1850–3 June 1860
Major Commands under Wellington:	Brigade 2nd Division: 21 September 1811–April 1814
	2nd British Brigade: 3 May–October 1815
	Temporarily commanded 1st Division 18 June, July, August–October 1815
	Temporarily commanded I Corps: 18 June–July 1815
Awards:	AGC with clasp: Vitoria, Pyrenees, Nivelle, Nive & Orthes
	Waterloo Medal
	MGSM with clasp: Toulouse
	KCB: 2 January 1815
	GCB: 6 June 1831
	GCH: 1826
	KMT
	KSG
Thanks of Parliament:	Peninsula, Orthes and Waterloo
Member of Parliament:	Poole: 1831–1835
Date of Death:	3 June 1860 in London

John Byng was born in 1772, the fourth son of Major George Byng and Anne Conolly of Wrotham Park, Middlesex. His grandfather was Admiral Sir George Byng, the 1st Viscount Torrington. He was named for his uncle, Admiral John Byng, who was executed for dereliction of duty after the Battle of Minorca in 1757. He attended the Westminster School. John Byng was commissioned as an ensign in the 33rd Foot in 1793.

---

1. Removed from the regiment as a general officer receiving unattached pay on 25 July 1814.
2. The regiment was disbanded in 1816.
3. The regiment was disbanded in 1819.

Ensign Byng entered the regiment the same month Wellington took command of it. He was initially stationed in Cork, Ireland but in 1794 went with it to Flanders. He was promoted to captain in May 1794 and commanded a company during the campaign. He was wounded on 5 January 1795 at Geldermalsen during the retreat to Bremen. By April he was back in England. In 1797 he was appointed the ADC to General Richard Vyse, the commander of the Southern District in Ireland. He was wounded during the Irish Rebellion of 1798 but continued to serve as the ADC until December 1799, when he purchased a majority in the 60th Foot. He was not with them long, for in March 1800 he purchased a lieutenant colonelcy in the 29th Foot. In June 1802 he and the 29th Foot went to Halifax, Nova Scotia. He remained there until August 1804, when he was appointed a captain and lieutenant colonel in the 3rd Foot Guards.

Lieutenant Colonel Byng served as company commander in the 1st Battalion 3rd Foot Guards in General Finch's Guards Brigade during the expedition to Hanover from November 1805 to February 1806. After returning to England he was appointed an AAG on the Home Staff. In 1807 he returned to the 1st Battalion and was part of General Edward Finch's Guards Brigade during the siege of Copenhagen from August to October 1807. In 1808 he was an AAG in the Severn District. During the summer of 1809, Lieutenant Colonel Byng took command of the Grenadier Company of the 2nd Battalion and commanded them during the Walcheren Expedition. In July 1810 he was promoted to colonel.

Colonel Byng continued to command the Grenadier Company until the summer of 1811, when he was sent to the Peninsula to join the 1st Battalion. The Duke of York wrote to Wellington on 7 July that Colonel Byng was going to join his regiment and was put in command of reinforcements being sent out. The Duke recommended him to Wellington as an 'intelligent and excellent officer, in whom you may place full confidence for any command you may have to entrust to an officer of his rank, I cannot do less than recommend him to your attention and good office.'[4] Wellington followed the Duke's recommendation and Colonel Byng was appointed a colonel on the staff and given command of a brigade in General Rowland Hill's 2nd Division.[5]

In the autumn of 1811 and through much of 1812, Colonel Byng and his brigade were in Estremadura, guarding the approaches to Badajoz. After the French abandoned southern Spain, General Hill's division rejoined the main part of Wellington's army in central Spain. They saw little action and unlike most of the army endured the retreat to Portugal in the late autumn with little hardship. Assistant Surgeon Walter Henry, of the 66th Foot, wrote that:

General Byng's Brigade were resting after the fatigues and privations of the Burgos retreat, although the indifferent rations, muddy streets and wretched hovels of this village afforded but slender facilities for recovering health and efficiency. However, our Brigade had suffered little, comparatively – the men having been well taken care of and well fed on the retreat, whilst others were starving, under the watchful eye of the best Brigadier, assisted by Mr. Edwards, one of the best Commissaries in the service.[6]

---

4. *WSD*; Vol. 7, page 177.
5. General Order, 21 September 1811.
6. Henry; page 60.

Colonel Byng was well regarded by General Rowland Hill, who did not want to lose him. When it seemed likely that Colonel Byng would have to give up command of his brigade to a senior officer, Wellington wrote twice to General Hill. The first time, on 5 December 1811, to let him know, 'I shall not move Byng from his brigade if I can help it; but we have many General Officers coming out, all of whom will require commands.'[7] Two months later, on 7 February 1812, Wellington wrote that Colonel William Inglis was on the staff and senior to Colonel Byng. 'I must employ him to command the brigade in which the 57th are, but when the Major Generals all join, I shall be able to make an arrangement which will suit Byng equally well, and will be equally suitable to you.'[8] Wellington did make other arrangements and Colonel Byng retained his brigade in the 2nd Division.[9] On 26 November 1812, Colonel Henry Torrens of the Horse Guards wrote to Wellington that Colonel Thomas Brisbane was being sent out to the army as a brigadier. This was a problem since Colonel Byng was senior to Colonel Brisbane. Wellington's solution was to promote Colonel Byng to brigadier general on the staff.[10]

In June 1813, General Byng was promoted to major general. His brigade was part of the southern wing of the British Army. At Vitoria on 21 June, it was part of the force that attacked and cleared the heights of Puebla at the start of the battle. It took part in the general attack on the French left but was not heavily engaged. Its total casualties for the day were 7 per cent of its effectives. In late July they were part of the force blockading Pamplona and were covering the pass through the Pyrenees at Roncesvalles. The French attacked on 25 July, but were unable to break through to lift the siege. The French tried again at Sorauren on 29 and 30 July. During the two days, General Byng's brigade took about 10 per cent casualties.

By November the British Army was in France and General Byng led his brigade at the Nivelle on 10 November and at Saint Pierre on 13 December, where he was wounded. Late in the battle, General Hill ordered him to take his brigade and drive the French off the Croix de Mouguerre heights. General Byng and two battalions charged.[11] In an effort to inspire his men, he took the King's Colours of the 31st Foot from Lieutenant James Elwyn and raced up the hill. His only protection was two grenadiers from the regiment. He planted the colours on the top of the ridge. The two battalions hurried up the ridge after their general and forced the French from it.[12] Despite the heroics of the brigade, Wellington relieved one of its battalion commanders for cowardice.[13] General Byng and his brigade fought through to the end of the war, seeing action at Garris on 15 February and Orthes on 27 February. They were at Toulouse on 10 April. Shortly after the battle, on 17 April, an armistice was declared and the war was over.

---

7. *WD* (enlarged ed.); Vol. 5, page 392.
8. *WD*; Vol. 8, page 565.
9. Colonel William Inglis was seriously wounded at Albuera on 16 May 1811. He had not fully recovered by February 1812 and was unable to command a brigade in the field. He was retained on the staff, but became the permanent President of Court-Martials in Lisbon until appointed to command a brigade in the 7th Division in 1813.
10. General Order dated 7 January 1813 with the promotion to date from 25 November 1812.
11. 1st Provisional Battalion, which was made up of companies from the 2nd Battalion 31st Foot and the 2nd Battalion 66th Foot, and the 1st Battalion 57th Foot.
12. L'Estrange; page 147. *RMC*; Vol. 3, page 280.
13. Lieutenant Colonel William Bunbury of the 1st Battalion 3rd Foot.

General Byng's brigade was disbanded in June 1814 and he returned to England by way of Paris.[14] After Napoleon escaped from exile on Elba in March 1815, the British began to reinforce their army in the Netherlands that would be commanded by Wellington. On 15 April 1815 General Torrens wrote to Wellington, informing him that General Byng had been placed upon the staff of his army.[15] The next day, he wrote again to Wellington that the Commander-in-Chief had decided that General Byng would command a brigade of the Guards Division in Flanders.[16] He was placed on staff of Wellington's army in Flanders to command the 2nd British Brigade of General George Cooke's 1st Division.[17]

At Waterloo General Byng and his brigade were on the right flank of the army and had the mission of defending Hougomount. About 4 p.m. General Cooke was seriously wounded and General Byng assumed command of the 1st Division.[18] Later in the day he succeeded to the command of the 1st Corps after the Prince of Orange was wounded. General Byng continued to command the corps during the advance to Paris. After the Prince of Orange returned to the 1st Corps in July, General Byng resumed command of the 1st Division. By 23 July, General Kenneth Howard came out to command the 1st Division and General Byng again reverted to command of his brigade. However, General Howard assumed command of the 1st Corps around 22 August and so once again General Byng commanded the division, this time until he went on leave at the beginning of October.

The Duke of York was quite content with leaving General Byng as the commander of the 1st Division, but could not ignore the claims of more senior generals to be appointed to such a command.[19] General Byng was offered command of the Eastern District instead. He wrote to Wellington on 22 October regarding his accepting command of the Eastern District. Wellington replied on 27 October that, 'I see no reason whatever why you should not accept the command offered you in Essex'.[20] He commanded the Eastern District until 1816 and then the Northern District for twelve years. His tenure as commander of these districts was marked by political unrest and violence. Although he was reluctant to do so, he did call out the troops to put down violent protests when necessary. In early 1825, the Directors of the HEIC considered him for a high command in India. They felt that he might be chosen as the government owed him a good command for his past services. Charles W. Wynn, the President of the HEIC, thought that Byng 'would be very proper and I should like much to know whether [he] would be disposed to take it.'[21] Wellington was asked for a list of a suitable candidates and General Byng was one of those he recommended.[22] He did not get the job. He was promoted to lieutenant general on 27 May 1825 while commanding the Northern District in England. In 1828, General Byng was appointed the Commander of the Forces in Ireland and held that post until 1831.

In the spring of 1831, General Byng ran for Parliament as a reform candidate for County Londonderry. Despite spending £2,000 of his own money on the election, he only took third place. In October he was convinced to run for a vacant seat in Poole and

---

14. L'Estrange; page 188.
15. *WSD*; Vol. 10, page 78.
16. *WSD*; Vol. 10, page 85.
17. General Order, 3 May 1815.
18. Glover, Gareth; *Waterloo Archive*, Vol. 4, pages 143–4.
19. *WSD*; Vol. 10, page 573.
20. *WD* (enlarged ed.); Vol. 8, page 287.
21. Duke of Buckingham; Vol. 2, pages 215 & 218.
22. *WND*; Vol. 2, page 425.

won the seat as a Whig.[23] He was the chairman of the military subcommittee but was largely ineffective. He voted against setting up an inquiry on military punishments and also voted against ending flogging in the army. He opposed any motion to reduce the military. He was an ardent reformist and was one of the few generals in Parliament who supported the Reform Act of 1832. While in Parliament he was appointed the Governor of Londonderry and Culmore on 15 June 1832. This was an honourary position that provided him a sinecure of £1,200 per year. This appointment, as well as his support of the Reform Act, did not sit well with his constituents, but despite their complaints he was re-elected in 1832. Lord Melbourne, the Prime Minister, rewarded his support by creating him Baron Strafford of Harmondsworth on 12 May 1835. Upon becoming a baron, General Byng was elevated to the House of Lords.[24]

General Byng had no military duties other than that of the regimental colonel of the 29th Foot after 1831. He was promoted to general in 1841 and was created Earl of Strafford and Viscount Enfield on 28 August 1847. In 1850 he was made the regimental colonel of the Coldstream Guards and would serve in that position until his death. In 1855 he was promoted to field marshal. He died in his home at 6 Portman Square, London in 1860. At the time of his death he was 88 years old and the second oldest member of the House of Lords.

John Byng married Mary Mackenzie on 14 June 1804. She died in 1806. They had one son. He married Marianne James on 9 May 1808. They had three daughters and a son, who joined the army.

Many of those who served under him in the Peninsula and at Waterloo mention General Byng in their letters and memoirs. The recurring comments were about his coolness under fire. Captain Rees Gronow wrote:

> No individual officer more distinguished himself than did General Byng at the battle of Waterloo. In the early part of the day he was seen at Huguemont [*sic*] leading his men in the thick of the fight; later he was with the battalion in square, where his presence animated to the utmost enthusiasm both officers and men. It is difficult to imagine how this courageous man passed through such innumerable dangers from shot and shell without receiving a single wound.[25]

Surgeon Henry wrote that General Byng was 'a first-rate officer – clear-headed and cool in action, and brave as a lion'.[26]

It was not only his subordinates who recognised General Byng's bravery. On 7 July 1815, because of his bravery at the Battle of Nive, His Royal Highness the Prince Regent granted General Byng and his descendants a license to augment their coat-of-arms, 'Over the arms of the family Byng, in bend sinister, a representation of the color of the 31st regiment, and the following crest of honourable augmentation viz. Out of a mural crown an arm embowed, grasping the color of the aforesaid 31st regiment, and pendent from the wrist by a ribband, the gold cross presented to him by His Majesty's command, as a mark of his royal approbation of his distinguished services, and in an escrol above "Monguerre".'[27]

---

23. Very few of Wellington's generals who were Members of Parliaments were Whigs.
24. 'Byng, Sir John (1772–1860)'. Also, *Dictionary of National Biography*; Vol. VII, page 122. Mosse; page XIII.
25. Gronow; *Reminiscences of Captain Gronow*, page 105.
26. Henry; page 198.
27. *RMC*; Vol. 3, page 260.

Cameron, Alan

Date of Birth:	1750 at Erracht Inverness-shire, Scotland
Date Commissioned:	Lieutenant Queen's Royal Regiment of Rangers:[1] 1775
Promotions:	Major Commandant 79th Foot: 17 August 1793
	Lieutenant Colonel Commandant[2] 79th Foot: 30 January 1794
	Brevet Lieutenant Colonel: 3 May 1796
	Brevet Colonel:[3] 26 January 1797
	Brevet Colonel: 1 January 1805
	Brigadier General on the Staff: 1808–1810
	Major General: 25 July 1810
	Lieutenant General: 12 August 1819
Regimental Colonel:	79th Foot: 1 January 1805–9 March 1828
Major Commands under Wellington:	7th Brigade: 27 April–18 June 1809
	Brigade 1st Division: 18 June 1809–November 1810
Awards:	Sultan's Gold Medal for Egypt
	AGM: Talavera
	KCB: 2 January 1815
Mentioned in Dispatches:	Talavera
Thanks of Parliament:	Talavera
Date of Death:	9 March 1828 at Fulham, London

His given name was also spelled Allan. He was known as the 9th Cameron of Erracht.

Alan Cameron was born in 1750 the oldest child of Donald Cameron and Marsali MacLean.[4] Alan was educated at home by tutors from Aberdeen and St Andrew's Universities, but when he was older he attended Saint Andrews. When he was 22, Alan fought a duel and accidentally killed his opponent. He was forced to flee to avoid the angry relatives of the man he killed. His father's lawyer advised him that while he would probably not be prosecuted, he would still be in danger from the family of the man he killed. Alan decided to leave Scotland and in the spring of 1773 he emigrated to Jamaica, where he took a job as a bookkeeper on a plantation.[5]

Alan Cameron did not like Jamaica and within a year went to South Carolina where he worked for John Stuart, the Superintendent General in charge of Indian Affairs for the Department of the South. He was offered a commission in the colony's Regiment of Rangers in June 1775, but declined it. The colonists let their displeasure be known and Alan Cameron decided to head to Boston, where a regiment of Highland emigrants was being raised. On his way north, he carried letters to Governor Dunmore of Virginia from the governor of South Carolina and was offered a commission as a lieutenant in the Queen's Royal Regiment of Rangers that Lieutenant Colonel John Connolly was

---

1. A local Virginia Provincial Corps that was disbanded c. 1775/6. Maclean; page 17.
2. Temporary rank backdated from 10 February 1794.
3. Temporary rank.
4. His exact date of birth, including the year he was born, is unknown. Sources have given it as 1745, 1750 and 1753. Loraine Maclean's biography of him provides evidence that he was born in 1750, but did not give a firm date.
5. Maclean; pages 9–11.

planning to raise in Detroit. The regiment would be recruited among westerners loyal to the Crown and Indians.

Not long after Lieutenant Cameron and Lieutenant Colonel John Connolly left Virginia, they were arrested in Hagerstown, Maryland for being loyalists. In late December they were sent under armed guard to Philadelphia. The city's Committee of Safety charged Cameron with treason against America and he was kept in the city jail. In December 1776, the British were approaching the city and orders came to send the prisoners to Baltimore. Lieutenant Cameron and his companions decided to try and escape rather than be moved. The plan was to climb out a third storey window and lower themselves to the ground using ropes made out of old bedding. Cameron went first, but the rope could not hold his weight and he fell 15 metres to the pavement below, breaking both of his ankles. Lieutenant Cameron hobbled away and went into hiding with local loyalists. In June 1777, he was arrested in New Jersey while trying to contact the British navy. He was eventually exchanged for American prisoners in 1778.[6]

Lieutenant Cameron returned to Great Britain after his release. While on board his transport he became friends with Colonel Mostyn, who invited him to spent time in London. While there he met Ann Philips, the only child of Nathaniel Philips, a wealthy merchant involved in the sugar trade. Despite her being only 13 years old, Alan and Ann eloped to Scotland. Eventually they reconciled with her father. In 1793 he was granted a letter of service to raise a regiment of Highlanders. For doing so, he was promoted to major. He did not have the money to cover the expenses of raising the regiment, but his father-in-law provided the necessary funds. Within two months 750 men were enlisted.[7]

In January 1794, Major Cameron was promoted to lieutenant colonel commandant and in June the regiment was sent to Flanders. They would fight there until the British forces were evacuated back to Great Britain in May 1795. Two months later they embarked for the West Indies. In less than two years the regiment was decimated by disease. Lieutenant Colonel Cameron and the officers, NCOS and musicians were ordered back to England. The 229 surviving other ranks were drafted into other regiments. While in the West Indies, he was promoted to colonel. Once in Great Britain, he returned to Scotland to bring his regiment back up to strength. This time it took Colonel Cameron longer to find recruits, but by June 1798 the regiment was ready for active service.[8]

In June 1799, the regiment went to Flanders. It distinguished itself in its first battle at Egmont-op-Zee on 2 October. Early in the battle, Colonel Cameron was shot in the arm and later in the wrist. The army evacuated Flanders shortly after the battle and was back in England by 1 November. In June 1800, the regiment joined the British expedition sent to destroy the Spanish shipping and arsenals in Ferrol and Cadiz. In November they sailed to Egypt. They fought there until the French surrendered in 1802 and at the Battle of Alexandria on 28 March 1801. After the defeat of the French in Egypt, the 79th Foot was sent to Minorca until the summer of 1802, when it returned to England. In 1803, the regiment was sent to Ireland. While there, in April 1804, Colonel Cameron was requested to raise the 2nd Battalion for the 79th Foot. He returned to Scotland and within a year had recruited 1,000 men for it.[9] Upon the 79th Foot becoming a two battalion regiment, Colonel Cameron was appointed its regimental colonel.

---

6. Johnson, William; pages 29–46.
7. MacKenzie, Alexander; pages 330–2. MacKenzie, Thomas; pages 7–8.
8. MacKenzie, Thomas; pages 10–12.
9. Ibid; pages 20–3.

The 1st Battalion remained in Ireland for three years and in November 1805 it returned to England. In July 1807, it joined the British Expedition to Denmark. After the Danes surrendered, Colonel Cameron was appointed the commandant of Copenhagen. He held the position until the British returned to England in November. In May 1808, he was appointed a brigadier general on the staff of General John Moore's force that was being sent to Sweden. General Cameron was given command of the Highland Brigade of the 1st Division. No agreement could be reached with the Swedish Government and they returned to England in July. They were only there for a short time when they were ordered to Portugal.

General Cameron landed with his brigade at Maceira Bay on 25 August. On 5 September the army was reorganised and he was given command of a brigade in the Reserve under General Brent Spencer. Later that month he was appointed the Commandant of Lisbon. In September, a field army was formed for service in Spain under General Moore. A force was left to garrison Portugal and supply the field army. In a General Order of 26 September 1808 the garrison of Portugal was formed and Brigadier Cameron was selected to join the garrison. He was again given command of a brigade. In December, he was sent to try and reinforce General Moore's army, but could not get through to them due to poor weather. In early January 1809, General Cameron was in Almeida. On 5 January he tried again to unite with General Moore's army, but he turned his brigade around when news that the British Army was retreating reached him on 9 January. In January and February he organised two Battalions of Detachments from soldiers left behind by the army due to their poor health. He increased their numbers by including stragglers from General Moore's army that evaded the French after the British Army evacuated Spain.

General Cameron remained as part of the garrison of Lisbon until April 1809, when Wellington returned to Portugal and took command of the British Army there. He was given command of the 7th Brigade on 27 April.[10] He led the brigade in the Oporto Campaign but on 18 June the army was reformed and General Cameron took command of a brigade in the 1st Division. At Talavera on 26–27 July, his brigade was on the right flank of the British Army. On the last day of the battle, the 1st Division charged across the Portina Stream in pursuit of the retreating French. General Cameron halted his brigade on the far side of the stream, but the brigades on either side of him continued to charge forward. They were soon strung out in a long line and were hit by the French reserve. In the chaos that ensued, the two brigades broke and ran back towards the British lines on the other side of the stream, taking General Cameron's brigade with them in their panic. Fortunately the French stopped at the stream and did not pursue them.

In March 1810, General Cameron was too sick to command his brigade. While he was recuperating, he was promoted to major general in July and retained on the staff of the army.[11] On 4 August, Robert Stewart Lord Blantyre was appointed to command it in his absence. By 1 October he was back in command but while leading his men towards Lisbon, his horse stumbled and threw him to the ground. He suffered a severe contusion to his chest. It healed very slowly. In November, he requested that he be allowed to return to England. On 24 November Wellington forwarded a letter to Lord Liverpool from General Cameron along with a request that some mark of the government's favour, a

---

10. Confirmed in a General Order on 4 May 1809.
11. General Order, 8 September 1810.

baronetcy or at least a government, be granted the old soldier. Wellington noted that General Cameron was worn out from service and was being granted leave to go home. He also praised him, writing, 'He has served His Majesty with zeal and ability, as far as line of service has gone, till at last he is quite worn out …'[12]

At the time of his resignation, General Cameron was 60 years old and his more than thirty years of campaigning had caught up with him. He had difficulty walking due to his broken ankles never properly healing. Compounding his problems was the wound to his wrist received eleven years before. It was so severe that he had lost all use of his arm. On 26 November, General Cameron was given a leave of absence to return to England.[13] He took his time leaving Portugal and did not arrive in England until the following February.[14]

After the Battle of Fuentes de Oñoro in 1811, Wellington took the time to write him a letter informing him that his son, Lieutenant Colonel Philips Cameron, had been seriously wounded. On 15 May he wrote again to let him know that his son had died from his wounds. Wellington's words were heartfelt. 'You will always regret and lament this loss, I am convinced; but I hope that you will derive some consolation from the reflection that he fell in the performance of his duty, at the head of your brave regiment, loved and respected by all that knew him …'[15]

Cameron would continue to serve as the 79th Foot's regimental colonel and took great interest in its affairs. In late June 1815, he received a letter from Lieutenant Colonel Duncan Cameron, the acting commander of the regiment, with news of the regiment's casualties from the Waterloo Campaign. The 79th Foot started the campaign with forty-one officers and 735 enlisted soldiers. They fought at Quatre Bras on 16 June and Waterloo on 18 June. In the two battles six officers were killed and another nine wounded. The regiment also saw fifty-seven sergeants and other ranks killed and 386 wounded. At the close of the battle the 79th Foot was down to less than 300 officers and men fit for duty.[16] Upon hearing the news, General Cameron rushed to Brussels with his daughter to ensure his men were being taken care of. In 1819 he was promoted to lieutenant general.

Alan Cameron married Ann Philips on 16 September 1779. They had four sons and three daughters. Three of his sons were officers in the 79th Foot. Ann went with the regiment when it was sent to the West Indies. On 1 September 1795, while on passage to Martinique, she fell overboard and drowned.[17] He never re-married. Lieutenant General Cameron died at Fulham, London on 9 March 1828. He was buried in the Saint Marylebone churchyard in London.

In many ways, the 79th Foot was the Cameron family business. In addition to Alan Cameron, his younger brother Ewan and his oldest son Philips were among the first officers appointed to the regiment. Lieutenant Colonel Philips Cameron would become the 1st Battalion's commander after his father became a brigade commander. His second son, Lieutenant Colonel Nathaniel Cameron, was the 2nd Battalion's commander in 1813, while his youngest son, Captain Ewan Cameron, served as his ADC during the 1809 Talavera Campaign. Four of his nephews also served in the regiment.

---

12. *WD*; Vol. 7, page 5.
13. General Order, 26 November 1810.
14. Maclean; page 229.
15. *WD*; Vol. 7, page 544.
16. MacKenzie, Thomas; page 59.
17. Maclean; pages X and 137.

The Cameron family paid a steep price for having so many members in the regiment. Two of Alan Cameron's sons died during the Peninsular War: Lieutenant Colonel Philips Cameron was killed leading his battalion at Fuentes de Oñoro in 1811; while Captain Ewan Cameron died from a fever in Lisbon in 1810. Two of his nephews, Captain John Cameron and Lieutenant Ewan Cameron, were killed at Toulouse in 1814. Two other nephews were at Waterloo, and by the time night had fallen, Lieutenant Alexander Cameron was the senior unwounded officer and commanded the regiment. Alexander's younger brother, Ensign Archibald Cameron, survived the battle unscathed.

Although numerous members of General Cameron's family were in the 79th Foot, there is no indication that any nepotism was involved after the regiment was raised. Promotions within a regiment were based on seniority or purchase, although as regiments were expanded as the wars went on, officers were also appointed. Furthermore, all promotions, purchase or otherwise, were researched by the Military Secretary and given to the Commander-in-Chief for his approval. General Cameron could not promote of his own accord, but as the regimental colonel he could let his preferences to fill vacancies be known. As the regimental colonel he could, however, approve or deny exchanges to his regiment.

General Cameron was very popular with his men. They called him 'Old Cia Mar Tha' because he greeted them with 'Cia mar tha thu?' which was Gaelic for 'How are you?'[18] He also took great interest in their health and welfare. A biographer described him as,

> a firm friend of the soldier, and considered every man in his regiment committed to his personal charge. In health he advised them; in sickness he saw that all their wants were supplied; and when any of them became disabled, he was incessant in his efforts until he managed to secure a pension for them. Numerous stories are told of the many encounters between him and Sir Harry Torrens, Military Secretary to the Commander-in-Chief, and his persistent applications for pensions and promotions. The poor fellows, for whom he was never tired of interceding, were naturally grateful for his fatherly feelings and actions towards them.[19]

Colonel William Napier, author of *The History of the War in the Peninsula*, wrote General Alan Cameron's obituary. He summed up his character in twenty words: 'By birth a Highlander; in heart and soul a true one; in form and frame the bold and manly mountaineer.'[20]

---

18. Mackenzie, Alexander; page 320.
19. Ibid; page 321.
20. *Gentleman's Magazine*; April 1828, page 367.

Campbell, Henry Frederick

Date of Birth:	10 July 1769
Date Commissioned:	Ensign 1st Foot Guards: 20 September 1786 without purchase
Promotions:	Lieutenant & Captain 1st Foot Guards: 25 April 1793 by purchase
	Captain-Lieutenant & Lieutenant Colonel 1st Foot Guards: 6 April 1796 by purchase
	Captain & Lieutenant Colonel: 1st Foot Guards 5 September 1796 without purchase
	3rd Major 1st Foot Guards: 21 October 1813 without purchase
	2nd Major 1st Foot Guards:[1] 28 April 1814 without purchase
	Brevet Colonel: 25 September 1803
	Brigadier General on the Staff: 1808–1810
	Major General: 25 July 1810
	Lieutenant General: 4 June 1814
	General: 10 January 1837
Regimental Colonel:	88th Foot: 16 January 1824–20 October 1831
	25th Foot 20 October 1831–3 September 1856
Major Commands under Wellington:	Guards Brigade: 27 April–18 June 1809
	Guards Brigade 1st Division: 18 June–28 July 1809, June–July 1811 and August 1811–July 1812
	Temporarily commanded 1st Division: July–August 1811 and c. May–11 October 1812
Awards:	AGM with clasp: Talavera & Salamanca
	KCB: 2 January 1815
	GCH: 1818
Thanks of Parliament:	Talavera & Salamanca
Member of Parliament:	Nairnshire: 1796–1802, 1806–1807
Date of Death:	3 September 1856

Henry Frederick Campbell was the son of Lieutenant Colonel Alexander Campbell and Frances Meadows. His family were part of the Campbells of Cawdor Clan. His grandfather, John Campbell, was a Lord of the Treasury and a Lord of the Admiralty. Henry studied at Greenwich from 1778 to 1780 and was commissioned as an ensign in the 1st Foot Guards in 1786 at the age of 17.

For the first six years after he was commissioned. Ensign Campbell was on garrison duty in southern England. In February 1793 he went with the 1st Battalion to Flanders, but he was not there for long. In April a decision was made to include two light companies in each of the 1st Foot Guards's battalions. Captain Campbell was selected as one of the new light companies's officers and he returned to England in May to assist in their formation. In June 1794, his light company rejoined the army in Flanders and saw combat at Boxtel on 14 September 1793. A decision was made to evacuate the British Army from Flanders and three months later he was back in England. In April 1796, Captain Campbell was promoted to captain-lieutenant and lieutenant colonel and took command of a company. In September 1799, he commanded the Light Company of the 3rd Battalion and led them in the expedition to Den Helder. He saw little action and by the end of October he was back in England. In September 1803, he was promoted to colonel.

---

1. Removed from the regiment as a general officer receiving unattached pay, 25 July 1814.

In September 1806, Colonel Campbell was still in the 3rd Battalion of the 1st Foot Guards and commanded its 2nd Company. He was part of the force that sailed for Sicily, which they garrisoned until they returned to England in January 1808. In May 1808 Colonel Campbell was appointed a brigadier on the staff and was given temporary command of the 2nd Guards Brigade in England.[2] By December, General Campbell was permanently in command of the brigade and it was assigned to General John Sherbrooke's force sent to secure Cadiz. They sailed on 15 January 1809 and upon arrival the Spanish Government refused to allow them to disembark. They sailed to Lisbon and joined the British garrison in Portugal. General Campbell was retained on the staff when Wellington was appointed commander of the British forces in Portugal in April 1809.[3] He led the Guards Brigade during the Oporto Campaign in May. Wellington reorganised his army after the Oporto Campaign and on 18 June, the 2nd Guards Brigade was assigned to the newly formed 1st Division.

In the summer of 1809, the Guards Brigade participated in the Talavera Campaign. General Campbell and his brigade were on the right flank of the British Army at Talavera on 27 and 28 July. It saw little action on the first day of the battle, however, late on 28 July after the 1st Division had successfully repulsed the attack of the French 4th Corps, General Sherbrooke ordered it to attack the retreating French. The 1st Division crossed the Portina Creek in hot pursuit. Instead of halting, three of its brigades, including the Guards Brigade, continued to charge the fleeing French until they came up against the French reserves. The disorganised British were cut down in droves. The three brigades broke and fled back across the creek. General Campbell's brigade took over 30 per cent casualties, with twenty of its officers killed or wounded.

Among the casualties was General Campbell who was wounded in the face.[4] His wound was so severe that he could not command his brigade. On 1 August he turned over command while he recovered.[5] His wound was slow to heal and by 26 September he returned to England to recuperate. Rumors abounded in his brigade that there were other reasons for him going. 'Brigadier General Campbell ... has sailed to England after being quite recovered – he was much in confidence of Sir Arthur and it is believed by many that he has been sent home confidentially for the purpose of representing to Ministers the state of affairs, the same as General Stewart[6] was sent from Sir John Moore ...'[7] There is no evidence, however, to support this camp gossip that Wellington had sent him home as his personal emissary. While in England General Campbell was on the Home District Staff and in 1810 temporarily commanded a portion of the 3rd Guards Brigade that was stationed in England. In July 1810, he was promoted to major general.

In June 1811, General Campbell returned to the Peninsula and resumed command of his brigade.[8] Shortly after arriving in the country he was placed in temporary command of the 1st Division on 25 July, because General Brent Spencer had returned to England. General

---

2. Since 26 June 1803, the seven battalions of Foot Guards had been continuously brigaded with the 1st Brigade composed of the 1st and 3rd Battalions 1st Foot Guards, the 2nd Brigade composed of the 1st Battalions of the Coldstream and 3rd Foot Guards and the 3rd Brigade composed of the 2nd Battalions of all three regiments.
3. General Order, 27 April 1809.
4. *RMC*; Vol. 2, page 410. Aitchison; page 61 has him severely wounded in the thigh.
5. General Order, 1 August 1809.
6. Charles Stewart.
7. Aitchison; pages 61–2.
8. General Order, 21 June to date from 25 May 1811.

Campbell's command of the 1st Division did not last long. On 9 August General Thomas Graham assumed command of the division and General Campbell returned to his brigade.[9] He led it at the sieges of Ciudad Rodrigo in January 1812 and Badajoz in April 1812.

In May, General Graham was given command of the Right Column of Wellington's army as it moved into Spain. This consisted of three divisions, so General Campbell succeeded, by seniority, to the temporary command of the 1st Division. In early July General Graham was forced to return to England due to health problems, so General Campbell continued in temporary command of the 1st Division.[10] He led the division at Salamanca on 22 July, where it was on the left flank of the army and lightly engaged. Late in the battle, the disorganised French Army began to retreat and Wellington ordered him forward to prevent them from escaping. General Campbell's pursuit was half-hearted and the beaten French were able to avoid being surrounded. Three months later, a Guards officer wrote as he visited the battlefield, 'When the French were defeated, the 1st & Light Divisions which had not been engaged were on their flank. Lord Wellington sent to General Campbell to support the attack, which he did with the light infantry companies. Had a man like General Graham been there who would not have been cowed by the fear of responsibility & who possessed a coup d'oeil, by moving both divisions, few of the enemy would have escaped ...'[11]

Wellington possibly felt the same way, for on 7 September 1812 he wrote to Colonel Henry Torrens of the Horse Guards that, 'I think also that General Campbell will not last long.'[12] Wellington's prediction was correct, for on 11 October Campbell relinquished command of the 1st Division and returned to England. He would not have a combat command again. General Campbell was promoted to lieutenant general in June 1814. He was appointed the regimental colonel of the 88th Foot in January 1824 and of the 25th Foot in October 1831. In 1837 he was promoted to general.

Henry Campbell was a Member of Parliament, representing Nairnshire from 1796 to 1802 and 1806 to 1807. His seat was the family seat and he was the 5th generation of Campbells of Cawdor to hold it. His period as an MP was so unremarkable that there is no record of him ever making a speech before the House. He likely voted with the government on most issues. Yet the only notable vote that he made was with the minority opposing the use of militia during the 1798 Irish Rebellion. He did not run in 1802, but in 1806 he was elected again, despite the fact he was serving in Sicily. He did not run in 1807.[13]

General Campbell was well connected to the royal family. In 1792 he succeeded his uncle, Charles Pierrepont, 1st Earl Manvers, as the Prothonotary of the Palace of the Court of Westminster. This was a sinecure and he held it until 1849. On 25 September 1803, he was appointed an ADC to the King and in 1809 a Groom of the Bedchamber. In 1812, he was appointed a Groom of the Bedchamber for Windsor Castle. He held the position until 1820. Henry Campbell also served as the Secretary and Comptroller to the Queen from 1817 to 1818. He was not re-appointed when Queen Charlotte died in November 1818.[14]

Henry Campbell married Emma Knox (*née* Williams) on 10 April 1808. She was the sister of General William Wheatley's wife. They had a son and two daughters. His son was a colonel in the Grenadier Guards. Henry Campbell died in 1856.

---

9. Oman; *Wellington's Army*, page 353.
10. General Order dated 6 July 1812 stated that this appointment was 'til further orders'.
11. Stanhope; pages 88–9.
12. *WD* (enlarged ed.); Vol. 6, page 55.
13. Fisher, David R.; 'Campbell, Henry Frederick (1769–1856)'.
14. Ibid.

Craufurd, James Catlin

Date of Birth:	23 January 1776
Date Commissioned:	Ensign 24th Foot: 28 December 1791[1] by purchase
Promotions:	Lieutenant Independent Company: 7 March 1793 by purchase
	Captain Independent Company: 10 September 1793 by purchase
	Captain 30th Foot: 22 October 1793 appointed
	Major Unattached: 15 April 1795 by purchase
	Major 98th Foot: 18 May 1796[2] appointed
	Lieutenant Colonel 98th Foot: 25 April 1797 by purchase
	Brevet Colonel: 30 October 1805
	Brigadier General on the Staff: 14 June 1808
	Brigadier General on the Staff: 26 July 1809
Major Commands under Wellington:	Highland Brigade: 23 June–7 August 1808[3]
	5th Brigade: 7 August–5 September 1808
	Independent Brigade: 26 July–13 September 1809
	Brigade 2nd Division: 14 September 1809–12 September 1810
Mentioned in Dispatches:	Corunna, 18 January 1809[4]
Thanks of Parliament:	Roliça & Vimeiro
Awards:	AGM with clasp: Roliça & Vimeiro & Corunna
Date of Death:	25 September 1810 at Abrantes in Portugal from malaria

Name is frequently spelled Crauford, Crawfurd, and Crawford. Although his first name was James, he was most often referred to by his middle name Catlin, even in official correspondence. Misspelling of his name was not just confined to his last name: his obituary in the 25 October 1810 edition of the *Morning Chronicle* spelled his name as Catlen.[5]

James Catlin Craufurd was born on 23 January 1776, the illegitimate son of Lieutenant Colonel James Craufurd, who was the governor of Bermuda and an equerry to Queen Charlotte. His family was part of the Craufurd of Auchinames in the County of Ayr.[6] His father had a serious gambling problem and was heavily in debt.[7] Catlin's uncle, John 'Fish' Craufurd, a Member of Parliament, looked after his nephew's interests. Catlin often referred to him as his guardian.[8]

In 1791, while living in New York City, Catlin purchased a commission as an ensign in the 24th Foot, which was stationed in Canada. He did not remain with the regiment long. Fourteen months later he purchased a lieutenancy in an independent company and by October 1793 he was a captain in the 30th Foot, which was stationed in the Mediterranean as fleet marines.[9] In 1795 he purchased the rank of major of foot. This was an unattached army rank receiving full pay, however, he had no regimental duties.

1. McGuigan, Ron. 'Craufurd, James Catlin'. Reid; Vol 1. page 274.
2. The 98th Foot was renumbered as the 91st Foot in 1798.
3. Numbered 5th Brigade in a General Order dated 7 August 1808.
4. *Universal Magazine*; Vol. 11, January–June 1809; page 84.
5. *Morning Chronicle*; 25 October 1810.
6. Burke; pages 384–387.
7. Namier; page 268.
8. Barnard; page 24.
9. Brown.

He remained unemployed until he was appointed major in the 98th Foot in 1796. In 1797 at the age of 21, he purchased his lieutenant colonelcy in the same regiment. Since his father was heavily in debt, his most likely source of income to purchase these ranks was his Uncle John.

In 1796, Lieutenant Colonel Craufurd went to the Cape Colony with his regiment, where it served as part of the occupation force. He was the regiment's second lieutenant colonel and did not command it initially. For much of the time in South Africa he served as the ADC to the governor, the Earl of Macartney.[10] As the ADC, Lieutenant Colonel Craufurd became part of the inner circle of the local society and was introduced to Anne Elizabeth Barnard, the sister of Sir Andrew Barnard[11] and a cousin of Lady Anne Barnard, who served as 'the first lady of the colony.'[12] In February 1799, Lieutenant Colonel Craufurd married Anne Elizabeth. He had mixed motives for doing so. She was two years older than him[13] and he confided in Lady Anne that:

> I do not pretend, said he to tell you that I am in love with Miss Barnard, I am not, I am not unhappy at a distance from her, & if she had said that we were posatively [sic] too poor for her to have me, I do not say I shoud [sic] have broke [sic] my heart, nor have been very sorry, because unless she loves me & can make up her mind thoroughly to be a poor mans [sic] wife I woud [sic] not wish her to marry me. No – my feeling [?] to her is founded on thinking her jus that most amiable girl I ever saw, good tempered with good principles & good conduct, such a one who if I was to leave for half a year or a year would not disgrace me in my absence ...[14]

Despite his misgivings, his marriage was solid and over the next ten years they would have four daughters and two sons. One of their daughters died while they were still in South Africa.[15] The Craufurds returned to England with the regiment in 1803 and were stationed in Lewes. On 30 October 1805, Lieutenant Colonel Craufurd was promoted to colonel. The regiment stayed in southern England until December 1805, when it embarked as part of the expeditionary force to Hanover. It had spent less than two months in northern Germany when it was ordered back to England. In January 1807 the regiment was sent to Ireland and remained in a variety of locations throughout the island. On 13 June 1808 it embarked for service in Portugal.[16]

On 14 June 1808, Colonel Craufurd was appointed as a brigadier general on the staff of Wellington's corps and given command of a brigade. His brigade would fight at Roliça on 17 August and Vimeiro on 21 August. The army was reorganised by General Hew Dalrymple on 5 September and General Craufurd lost his brigade command. He became supernumerary to the army. He remained so until a new reorganisation of the army took place. On 8 October General John Moore took command of the British Army organised for service in Spain. In the same general order that announced General

10. *Morning Chronicle*; 25 October 1810.
11. Hurl-Eamon; page 143. Sir Andrew Barnard would serve with the 95th Rifles for most of the Peninsular War and at Waterloo. He would eventual become a lieutenant general.
12. Barnard; page xi.
13. *Gentleman's Magazine*; Vol. 133, page 284.
14. Barnard; pages 23–4.
15. Ibid; page 292.
16. Goff; pages 19–20; 25–6.

Moore's assumption of command, General Craufurd was appointed only a colonel on the staff and given a command of a brigade. He was not allowed to keep his appointment as a brigadier general. His brigade was assigned to General John Hope's 2nd Division. He commanded it throughout the British advance into Spain and its subsequence retreat to Corunna. Colonel Craufurd was mentioned in dispatches for his performance at the Battle of Corunna on 16 January 1809.[17]

In May 1809 Craufurd was appointed a colonel on the staff in Kent District. In the summer of 1809, Colonel Craufurd returned to Portugal and was appointed a brigadier general on the staff on 26 July 1809. He was given command of an infantry brigade comprised of three battalions that had just arrived in the Peninsula.

In August 1809, Wellington was anticipating having to pull back from the Spanish border, deeper into Portugal. General Craufurd was ordered to Abrantes where he was to defend the area until the rest of the British Army could extricate itself from Spanish Estremadura. His orders were very specific and gave him little latitude. If pressed hard, he was to 'throw himself into Abrantes, which place he will maintain at all events as long as possible'.[18] General Craufurd obeyed his orders but grew impatient, abandoned Abrantes, crossed the Tagus River and moved his brigade to Zarza la Mayor to support Marshal William Beresford. Wellington was furious when he heard what he had done, for this left the army's northern flank undefended. He ordered General Craufurd back to Abrantes.[19] His comments to Marshal Beresford, whom General Craufurd was supporting, were quite scathing:

> Gen. Craufurd's disobedience of orders, although well intended, was positive, and committed with his eyes open; and as his corps was useless at Zarza la Mayor, and in your retreat might have embarrassed you, I was not sorry, by ordering him back to the position which he had quitted, to show him and the army that I must command and they must obey.[20]

On 14 September 1809, General Craufurd and his brigade were assigned to the 2nd Division.[21] The 2nd Division would spend the next year guarding the right flank of the British Army, much of the time along the Guadiana River. This area was notoriously unhealthy due to marshy ground and stagnant pools of water and gave its name to what was known as Guadiana Fever. This fever was most likely a very virulent form of malaria. Between September 1809 and August 1810, General Craufurd's brigade averaged 25 per cent of its strength too sick to fight. During the same time period another 621 men died from various causes, most from disease. Within twelve months General Craufurd lost 25 per cent of his force without fighting one battle.[22] In September, General Craufurd was stricken with Guadiana Fever. On 18 September, Major Alexander Dickson saw him at Villa de Rei and noted in his diary that, 'General Craufurd is at the Captain *Mors* very

17. *Gentleman's Magazine*; Vol. 133, page 284.
18. *WD* (enlarged edition); Vol. 3, page 413.
19. Ibid; pages 420–1; 429.
20. Ibid; page 429.
21. General Order, 14 September 1809.
22. Bamford, Andrew; 'The Guadiana Fever Epidemic' and 'British Army Individual Unit Strengths: 1808–1815'.

ill. He was on his way to Abrantes but unable to proceed any further.'[23] Catlin Craufurd made the 30 kilometer journey to Abrantes, but died there on 25 September 1810.

After his death, General Craufurd's wife and five children moved in with his uncle 'Fish' Craufurd. They had no income. Wellington interceded on their behalf in a letter to the Secretary of State, the Earl of Liverpool, on 30 November 1810:

> Captain Churchill, the aide de camp of the late Brigadier General Catlin Craufurd, has informed me that it is intended by his friends to apply to Government for some provision for his widow, who has been left with a large family in very bad circumstances. Although General Craufurd was not killed in action, he certainly died of a fever which he caught in the performance of his duty in this country; and as he was a respectable officer, who had served in the Peninsula with distinction, and I believe that his widow is a person of excellent character, I beg leave to recommend her case to the favorable consideration of Government.[24]

Wellington's effort was effective and Anne Craufurd received an annual pension of £300 beginning on 25 September 1811.[25]

James Catlin Craufurd might have gone far if he had not died so young. Had General Craufurd survived he would have been promoted a major general in the army, along with a number of other officers, in a general brevet of 4 June 1811, celebrating King George III's birthday. Surprisingly he is mentioned in very few memoirs. Captain John Patterson, 50th Foot, described him as 'a tall fine-looking man, with a fair complexion and sandy hair'[26] while Captain Charles Cadell, 28th Foot, referred to him as 'that excellent officer Brigadier-general Catlin Crawford.'[27]

---

23. Dickson; Vol. 1, page 285.
24. *WD*; Vol. 7, page 14.
25. *Estimate and Accounts*; page 15.
26. Patterson; page 34.
27. Cadell; page 272.

de Grey, Hon. George

Date of Birth:	11 June 1776
Date Commissioned:	Cornet 1st Dragoons:[1] 1794 by purchase
Promotions:	Lieutenant 1st Dragoons:[2] 1794 by purchase
	Captain 25th Light Dragoons: 13 March 1794 without purchase
	Major 25th Light Dragoons: 25 May 1795 by purchase
	Lieutenant Colonel 26th Light Dragoons: 3 May1799 without purchase
	Lieutenant Colonel 1st Dragoons: 6 June 1799 appointed
	Brevet Colonel: 25 April 1808
	Major General: 4 June 1811
	Lieutenant General: 19 July 1821
Major Commands under Wellington:	Cavalry brigade: 13 May 1810–July 1811
Awards:	AGM: Albuera
Date of Death:	26 April 1831 in London

After 16 January 1818, he was known as George, Lord Walsingham.

George de Grey was born on 11 June 1776, the oldest son of Thomas 2nd Baron Walsingham and Augusta Irby. His father was an MP and inherited from his uncle the family estates at Merton, Norfolk. His mother was the daughter of 1st Baron Boston. He attended Eton and was commissioned as a cornet in the 1st Dragoons in 1794.

The exact date of Cornet de Grey's commission is unknown, but it is very likely at the beginning of the year. Almost immediately after he was commissioned Cornet de Grey purchased a lieutenancy in his regiment, the date of which is also unknown. However, on 13 March 1794 he was appointed a captain in the newly raised 25th Light Dragoons. Fourteen months later he purchased a majority in the same regiment. He was still only 18 years old at the time. Major de Grey's commanding officer in the 25th Light Dragoons was Stapleton Cotton, later Lord Combermere, who commanded the British cavalry in the Peninsula.

A year after Major de Grey joined the 25th Light Dragoons, they sailed to India. By August 1796 he was at the Cape Colony and witnessed the capture of the Dutch fleet at Saldanha Bay. In India the regiment was part of the garrison at Madras. He participated in the 4th Mysore War in 1799 and fought at the Battle of Mallavelly and during the siege of Seringapatam. By the end of the year, word reached him that he had been promoted to lieutenant colonel in the 26th Light Dragoons. He never served with the regiment, for by the time he returned to England he had been appointed as a lieutenant colonel in the 1st Dragoons.

Lieutenant Colonel de Grey joined the 1st Dragoons in Kent and was there for two years. In 1803 he was appointed an AAG on the staff of the Home District until 1805, when he rejoined his regiment as its commander. Over the next three years, Lieutenant Colonel de Grey and his regiment would march the length of Great Britain, from the south to Scotland and then to Ireland in 1807. In April 1808, he was promoted to colonel

---

1. *London Gazette*; War Office Announcement dated 12 April 1794.
2. *London Gazette*; War Office Announcement dated 5 August 1794.

and with the promotion came an appointment as an ADC to the King. By late 1808, the regiment received word that it would be going to Portugal; however, the orders were cancelled when word of the evacuation of the British Army from Corunna was reached in England. In August 1809, they were ordered to Portugal once again and they arrived in Lisbon in mid-September.[3]

Colonel de Grey and the 1st Dragoons spent the rest of 1809 in the vicinity of Lisbon. In early 1810 they moved towards the Spanish border near Ciudad Rodrigo. On 13 May, Colonel de Grey was given command of a cavalry brigade.[4] They were at Busaco on 27 September and were in the rearguard as the British retreated to the Lines of Torres Vedras that protected Lisbon. The brigade was part of the force that pursued the French as they retreated away from Lisbon in November 1810 and the subsequent retreat back to Spain in early March 1811.

After the French had left Portugal, Colonel de Grey and his brigade were assigned to Marshal William Beresford's force that was moving into Estremadura to besiege Badajoz. They were in reserve at Campo Mayor on 25 March, heavily engaged at Los Santos on 16 April, and at Albuera on 16 May. The brigade's greatest achievement was the destruction of a French dragoon brigade at Usagre on 25 May. In a short fight, they inflicted 250 casualties on the French, to only twenty of their own.

On 4 June 1811, Colonel de Grey was promoted to major general. Before the promotion was announced, Lieutenant Colonel Henry Torrens wrote to Wellington asking if he wished to have Colonel de Grey on his staff as a major general as he was to be promoted in the 4 June General Brevet.[5] Wellington agreed to keep him and the announcement was made in a General Order on 26 June. In late June, the British Army was reorganised and General de Grey's brigade was assigned to the newly formed 2nd Cavalry Division.[6] By August the brigade was heading north to the vicinity of Ciudad Rodrigo, where it would spend the rest of the year. In October it was re-assigned to the 1st Cavalry Division.[7]

During the summer of 1811, General de Grey had health problems caused by throwing his shoulder out. He wrote to Wellington requesting that he be allowed to return to England. Wellington responded that he would have to get a medical certificate before he would release him.[8] In August Colonel Granby Calcraft, 3rd Dragoon Guards, was commanding the brigade. There are references to General de Grey's brigade in September and October, but no commanding officer is given. Permission was eventually given for him to leave, but the exact date of his departure is unknown.[9] However, he was gone from the Peninsula by the end of the year and his brigade was broken up in late January 1812.[10]

After he returned to England, General de Grey was placed on the Home Staff in the Kent District. He served there until 1814. It was the last military duties he would have. Upon the death of his father on 16 January 1818, he became the 3rd Baron Walsingham.

3. de Ainslie; pages 108–10.
4. General Order, 13 May 1810.
5. Unpublished letter dated 3 June 1811.
6. General Order, 19 June 1811.
7. General Order, 3 October 1811.
8. *WD* (enlarged ed.); Vol. 5, pages 185 and 176.
9. His biography in the *RMC*, which was based on input from him, does not mention any Peninsula service after Usagre.
10. General Order, 29 January 1812.

He also inherited his sinecure position of Comptroller of the First Fruits. In 1821, he was promoted to lieutenant general. Unlike many of his Peninsular War contemporaries, he was never created a KCB or appointed a regimental colonel.

George de Grey married Matilda Methuen on 16 May 1804. They had no children. On 26 April 1831, he and his wife were living in their home on Harley Street in London. His bed caught fire and he was unable to escape. The fire was so intense it burned through the floor and his corpse was found in the drawing room below. Only his head and part of his body remained. Lady Matilda escaped the fire but panicked and jumped out of the window, breaking both of her thighs. She died four hours later. They were buried in Merton, Norfolk.[11]

Nothing in General de Grey's performance as a brigade commander stands out, either good or bad. Unfortunately for him, his name is often linked with Major General Robert Long and the combat at Campo Mayor, where the other British cavalry regiment, which was under General Long, charged out of control. Wellington appeared not to hold this association against General de Grey when he approved his staying with the army after he was promoted in June 1811. General de Grey possibly might have changed Wellington's feelings, however, with his ill-timed request to Wellington to be allowed to return to England in July 1811. General de Grey was one of many senior officers who had made the request and Wellington was not pleased. He wrote to Lieutenant Colonel Torrens that 'as usual, all the Officers of the army want to go home, some for their health, others on account of business, and others, I believe, for their pleasure … Till we can get the minds of the Officers of the army settled to their duty we shall not get on as we ought.'[12]

Many years later, General de Grey has been all but forgotten. The three great historians of the Peninsular War, William Napier, Charles Oman and John Fortescue, ignored his contributions during the war. Although they did write that he kept his brigade under control at Campo Major, none of them mentioned his name when they told the story of Usagre. In all three accounts, it was General Lumley who gave the orders to the regiments of his brigade, not Colonel de Grey.

---

11. *Gentleman's Magazine*; June 1831, pages 558–9.
12. *WD* (enlarged ed.); Vol. 5, page 185.

Dornberg, William de

Date of Birth:	14 April 1768 in Schloss Hausen near Bad Hersfeld, Hesse-Kassel
Date Commissioned:	2nd Lieutenant 1st Guards Battalion Hesse-Kassel Service: January 1783[1]
Early German Service:	1st Lieutenant 1st Guards Battalion Hesse-Kassel Service: 22 January 1785[2]
	Staff Captain 1st Guards Battalion Hesse-Kassel Service: 17 December 1792[3]
	Captain Light Infantry Battalion Prussian Service: 1796–1807
	Colonel Guard Jaeger Battalion Westphalian Service: 28 February 1809
	Colonel Duke of Brunswick's Cavalry: 1809
British Service:	Colonel Brunswick Oels Hussars:[4] 25 September 1809
	Major General:[5] 1 January 1812
Hanoverian Service:	Major General:[6] 1816
	Lieutenant General 18 April 1818
Regimental Colonel:	Brunswick Oels Hussars:[7] 25 September 1809
	1st Light Dragoons KGL:[8] 15 June 1815–25 February 1816
	Guard Cuirassier Regiment Hanoverian Army: 1816–1850
Major Commands under Wellington:	1st Cavalry Brigade KGL: 11 April–31 May 1815
	3rd Cavalry Brigade:[9] 31 May–30 November 1815
Awards:	Honourary KCB: 2 January 1815
	GCH: 1815
	Waterloo Medal
	HEGL 1st Class
	HEIH
	HM
	KSA 1st Class
	KSG 3rd Class
	KW
	POM
	RANO
	RM
	RPM
Date of Death:	19 March 1850, Munster, Prussia

Full name was Wilhelm Caspar Ferdinand von Dörnberg, however, he went by William de Dornberg while in British Service. He was sometimes called Baron Dornberg or Sir William Dörnberg. Some sources identify him as a Freiherr but he is not recorded as such in either British or Hanoverian Service.

1. 'Wilhelm von Dörnberg'.
2. Ibid.
3. Ibid.
4. Temporary rank.
5. Temporary rank.
6. Backdated to 1 January 1812. British Army rank was recognised when KGL officers entered new Hanoverian Army.
7. Its regimental colonel was called a colonel commandant.
8. A regimental colonel in the KGL was called a colonel commandant.
9. The cavalry brigades were reorganised and renumbered in a General Order dated 31 May 1815.

William de Dornberg was born in 1768 in Hesse-Kassel, the son of Karl Sigismund von Dörnberg and Henriette von und zu Mansbach. His family was an old military family. His great-grandfather was Prussian General Johann Sigismund von Heiden, while his uncle, Johann Friedrich von und zu Mansbach, was a general in the Danish Army.[10]

William de Dornberg was commissioned in the 1st Guards Battalion of Hesse-Kassel in 1783. Over the next thirty-three years he would serve in seven different armies, including those of Hesse-Kassel, Prussia, Westphalia, Brunswick, Russia, Great Britain and Hanover. He fought in France in 1792 and was promoted to staff captain at the end of the year. In 1794 he was part of the Hessian contingent fighting in the Netherlands. The following year the Hesse-Kassel army was reduced after the Treaty of Basel was signed with France. Captain de Dornberg resigned his commission on 22 January 1796 and joined the Prussian Army. He was assigned to Fusilier Battalion #2, also known as Fusilier Battalion Bila.[11] Captain de Dornberg fought with the battalion during the 1806 Campaign that saw the Prussian Army destroyed by the French in less than a month. His arrived too late in the evening to participate in the Battle of Jena on 14 October and retreated to Lübeck. There he surrendered with the remnants of the Prussian Army under General Blücher.

After the Treaty of Tilsit in July 1807, Hesse-Kassel was dissolved and the Kingdom of Westphalia was created from its territories. Captain de Dornberg resigned his commission in the Prussian Army and returned to his family estates in Bad Hersfeld. In early 1809, Captain de Dornberg was offered the command of the Westphalian Guard Jaeger Battalion. He accepted the command and the promotion to colonel that came with it. He took the commission in order to be in a position to plot the overthrow of the government. The uprising began on 22 April, but it received little support from the people or the army. It was quickly suppressed and Colonel de Dornberg fled to Austria and joined the Black Legion under General John de Bernewitz. He was given command of the cavalry of the Black Legion and led them during the unsuccessful campaign to liberate northern Germany. He was evacuated to England with the survivors of the Legion on 9 August.[12]

In September the officers of the Black Legion were taken on the strength of the British Army as the Duke of Brunswick Oels's. Their rank was temporary and only valid while serving. Colonel de Dornberg was included in the initial promotion of officers in the British Army and was appointed the commander of the Brunswick Oels Hussars. He was promoted to major general in early 1812 and given permission to serve in the Russian Army later that year. In 1813 General de Dornberg was appointed the commander of the Russo-German Legion and led them into northern Germany. The Legion was incorporated into the Corps of General Count Ludwig von Wallmoden-Gimborn and General de Dornberg became the commander of the cavalry. They fought against Marshal Davout at Hamburg and at the Battle of Göhrde on 16 September 1813. During the campaign in Holstein in December 1813 he commanded the Advance Guard of the Corps.

After Napoleon abdicated in April 1814, the KGL was sent to Flanders. General de Dornberg joined them there and took command of the Light Cavalry Brigade KGL[13] in

---

10. Mühlhan.
11. 'Wilhelm von Dörnberg'.
12. Fisher, Herbert; pages 250–5.
13. General de Dornberg joined the KGL when he was appointed the Colonel Commandant of the 1st Light Dragoons KGL on 15 June 1815.

the British Subsidiary Army in early 1815. It was stationed in Mons. In April, Wellington took command of the army and reorganised it. General de Dornberg was kept in command of his brigade, which was renamed the 1st Cavalry Brigade, but it was sent to Mechelen.[14] Instead of going with his brigade, General de Dornberg was kept in Mons to oversee the gathering of intelligence on the French Army that was amassing along the border. His job was not to manage intelligence assets, but to collate the information that was collected and forward it to Wellington's headquarters in Brussels.

The French crossed the border on 15 June and General de Dornberg,

> learned that the Prussian advance posts had been attacked, and I sent this information to Brussels. I then rode towards Binch and saw that the Prussians were retreating. Towards evening, I rode from Mons to Brussels in accordance with my orders to only stay until the start of hostilities, and not to become surrounded. I arrived at Brussels in the morning between 4 and 5 o'clock and immediately went to the Duke, who was still in bed. He jumped up right away, told me that this day we would probably be fighting at Quatre Bras, and ordered me to ride at once to Waterloo with the order for General Picton[15] to have his division march to Quatre Bras without delay. My own brigade, cantonned [*sic*] at Mechelen, had already received the order also to march there.[16]

General de Dornberg rejoined his brigade[17] on the night of 16 June. The following day they covered the retreat of the army from Quatre Bras through Genappe to Waterloo. During the Battle of Waterloo on 18 June, General de Dornberg's brigade was on the right flank of the army, in the vicinity of Hougoumont. It saw little action until around 5 p.m. when the French cavalry charged. He wrote that:

> Since both of my regiments were light cavalry, I ordered them to stay in column. As soon as I sounded the signal to attack, the 23rd Regiment was to thrust vigorously into the enemy's right flank, and the 1st to do the same against the enemy's right flank. The three rear squadrons were to halt and deploy as soon as the enemy had been repulsed, while only the No. 1 squadrons were to pursue the enemy. This attack fully succeeded, and the cuirassier regiment[18] was completely overthrown. Unfortunately, our rear squadrons could not be held back and they all rushed after the enemy, only to be stopped by his reserve, which then turned us back again. But because this reserve followed only at the trot, I had time to more or less reform the two regiments and to repulse that reserve, which had come up to the plateau. Order had hardly been restored after this attack, when another cuirassier regiment came trotting up to the plateau. We advanced against it in line and at the gallop, whereupon the enemy regiment halted and pointed its swords at us. Our men beat at them with their curved sabres, but without much success … With some of our men, I attacked that regiment on its right flank and rear. But even then we were unable to accomplish much against

---

14. Mechelen is known as Malines in French.
15. Thomas Picton.
16. Glover, Gareth; *Waterloo Archive*, Vol. V, pages 11–12.
17. It had been renumbered the 3rd Cavalry Brigade on 31 May.
18. The French cuirassiers were either the 2nd or 3rd Cuirassier Regiments of the 1st Brigade of the 12th Cavalry Division.

the well armoured cuirassiers. They, however, started to move at first to the left, but then retreated in fairly good order. On this occasion I received a stab in my left chest, which penetrated my lung. As blood was coming out of my mouth and my speaking was much impaired, I had to ride off to the rear.[19]

General de Dornberg was too badly wounded to return to his brigade and eventually made it to Brussels. Despite the seriousness of his wounds, he was not bedridden for long. By 25 July he was back with his brigade in the vicinity of Paris. He would spend the autumn in Amiens and Doullens. In December the British Government ordered the KGL to return to Hanover and on 24 February 1816, its regiments were incorporated into the Hanoverian Army. With the disbandment of the KGL, General de Dornberg went on half-pay from the British Army and would continue to receive it until 1827. In March 1816, he was appointed the commander of the 1st Cavalry Brigade of the Hanoverian Army and was confirmed in the rank of major general. About the same time he was made the regimental colonel of the Guard Cuirassier Regiment, in which he served until his death in 1850. He was promoted to lieutenant general in 1818 and retired from the Hanoverian Army on 23 September 1831. After his retirement from military service he was made the ambassador to Russia.

William de Dornberg married Julie von Münster-Meinhövel in 1796. They had five sons and three daughters.[20] He died in 1850 in Munster, Prussia.

Several sources state that General de Dornberg was fluent in both French and English. The reports he sent from Mons to Wellington's headquarters in the spring of 1815 were in clear concise English. His spoken English appeared to be just as good. Lieutenant Standish O'Grady of the 7th Hussars served briefly under him at Genappe on 17 June and wrote that,

> Whilst I was so employed Sir William Dörnberg joined me. Thus we continued to dispute every inch of ground until we came within a short distance of the town of Genappe. Here Sir William Dörnberg told me that he must leave me; that it was of the utmost importance to face the Enemy boldly at this spot, as the bridge in the town of Genappe was so narrow we must pass it in file; that I should endeavour if possible to obtain time for the skirmishers to come in, but that I was not to compromise my Troop too much. Sir William had been riding with me some hours, and when he bid me farewell he shook my hand, and I saw plainly he never expected to see me again … When I arrived at the opposite entrance of the town I found the 7th drawn up on the road in a column of divisions, and having re-formed our Squadron we took our place between those already formed and the town. Here I met Sir William Dörnberg, who appeared surprised to see me, and asked me how we had effected [*sic*] our retreat, and if we had saved any of the skirmishers, and when I told him we had not lost a man or a horse, he exclaimed, 'Then Buonaparte is not with them; if he were, not a man of you could have escaped.'[21]

---

19. Glover, Gareth; *Waterloo Archive*, Vol. II, pages 29–30.
20. 'Wilhelm von Dörnberg'.
21. Siborne; pages 132–3.

Drieberg, George de

Date of Birth:	1747 in Hastedt, Hanover
Date Commissioned:	10th Regiment:[1] 1766
Hanover Service:	Captain 10th Regiment: 25 April 1783
	Major 2nd Grenadier Battalion: 6 April 1794
	Lieutenant Colonel 10th Infantry Regiment:[2] 6 May 1797
British Service:	Colonel 5th Line Battalion KGL: 1 April 1804[3]
	Brigadier General on the Staff: 26 September 1808[4]
Regimental Colonel:	5th Line Battalion KGL: 1 April 1804–2 June 1810[5]
Major Commands	
under Wellington:	Infantry Brigade KGL: 4 May–June 1809
Date of Death:	3 January 1832 in Celle, Hanover

His full name was Ernst Georg von Drieberg, however, he went by George de Drieberg while in British Service.

Little is known about the life of George de Drieberg other than his service with the British King's German Legion. He was born in 1747 in Hastedt, near the city of Stade. He was commissioned in the 10th Regiment of the Hanoverian Army in 1766 and would serve in the regiment for the next eighteen years. He went with his regiment on the expedition to Flanders in 1793. In 1794 he was promoted to major in the 2nd Grenadier Battalion, but returned to his original regiment three years later when he was promoted to lieutenant colonel. He remained with the regiment until the Hanoverian Army was disbanded in 1803.

Many of the officers and men of the former Hanoverian Army fled to England, because the King of Great Britain was also the ruler of Hanover. They formed the King's German Legion. The officers were given temporary rank in the British Army while they served. Lieutenant Colonel de Drieberg was not one of the initial officers who joined. In December 1805, he was appointed a colonel and given command of the 5th Line Battalion of the KGL, which was not organised until the following month. Colonel de Drieberg's commission was backdated to April 1804, when the initial infantry of the KGL was officially formed.

In April 1806, Colonel de Drieberg was appointed the commander of one of its brigades. It was stationed in Winchester until the summer of 1807 when it was selected for the expedition to Copenhagen in August 1807. They returned to England in late October, having successfully avoided being shipwrecked like so many of their fellow soldiers in the 3rd KGL Brigade.

In April 1808, Colonel de Drieberg was appointed the commander of a KGL brigade in the 2nd Division of General John Moore's Expeditionary Force that was sent to Sweden. No agreement could be reached with the Swedish Government that would have

---

1. Was also known as the Prince Carl von Mecklenburg-Strelitz Regiment.
2. Renamed the 9th Regiment in 1802.
3. Temporary rank only. *London Gazette*; War Office Announcement dated 10 December 1805. His date of rank was backdated.
4. Temporary rank in the British Army.
5. A regimental colonel in the KGL was called a colonel commandant.

allowed the force to land and it was sent to reinforce the British Army in Portugal on 31 July. He landed with his brigade at Maceira Bay on 25 August, too late to fight at Roliça or Vimeiro. On 5 September, the army was reorganised and Colonel de Drieberg was not listed on the staff nor given a brigade command. It is not clear if he served under General John Murray who commanded the four KGL battalions with the army. In September, a field army was formed to campaign in Spain under General Moore. The plan called for an additional force to be left to garrison Portugal and supply the field army. In a General Order of 26 September the garrison of Portugal was formed. Colonel de Drieberg was selected to join the garrison as a brigadier general and was given command of a KGL brigade. He was originally stationed in Lisbon, however, by 6 January 1809 he was in Santarem.

After Wellington returned to Portugal in April, he reorganised the army and General de Drieberg was retained on the staff[6] and given command of a KGL brigade.[7] This brigade was one of two brigades of KGL infantry that were under the command of General Murray. General de Drieberg commanded his brigade during the Oporto Campaign but in June 1809 his health began to decline and he returned to England.[8] He retired from British service on 2 June 1810 and received a pension of 7 shillings 6 pence per day beginning on 9 June. His temporary rank in the British Army ended when he took a pension.[9]

George de Drieberg married Catharina Margaretha Von Uffell on 11 January 1789.[10] He died at Celle, Hanover on 3 January 1832 at the age of 84.

6. General Order, 27 April 1809.
7. General Order, 4 May 1809.
8. *WD* (enlarged ed.); Vol. 3, page 388.
9. Beamish; Vol. 2, page 651.
10. 'Ernst Georg Von Drieberg'.

Drummond, George Duncan

Date of Birth:	Unknown
Date Commissioned:	Ensign 33rd Foot: 13 October 1781
Promotions:	Ensign 1st Foot Guards: 2 June 1786 appointed
	Lieutenant & Captain 1st Foot Guards: 1 February 1793
	Captain-Lieutenant & Lieutenant Colonel 1st Foot Guards: 19 April 1799
	Captain & Lieutenant Colonel 1st Foot Guards: 19 April 1799
	Lieutenant Colonel 24th Foot: 11 February 1808 by exchange
	Brevet Colonel: 25 October 1809
	Brigadier General on the Staff: 23 July 1811
Major Commands under Wellington:	Brigade Light Division: 7 February–8 September 1811
	Temporarily commanded Light Division: February–March 1811
Awards:	AGM: Talavera
Date of Death:	8 September 1811 in Fuenteguinaldo, Spain

George Drummond was the oldest child of Lieutenant General Duncan Drummond, RA and Miss Forbes.[1] His grandfather was George Drummond, the Lord Provost of Edinburgh. His younger brother was Major General Percy Drummond, RA. He was commissioned as an ensign in the 33rd Foot in 1781 and was appointed to the 1st Foot Guards in 1786. He would spend the next twenty-two years with the 1st Foot Guards.

In 1793, Ensign Drummond was promoted to lieutenant and captain and went to Flanders with the 1st Battalion of his regiment. Little is known about his subsequent service other than he was promoted to captain and lieutenant colonel in 1799. He commanded a company when the 1st Battalion went to Sicily in the summer of 1806 and returned with it to England in December 1807. Two months later, Lieutenant Colonel Drummond exchanged into the 24th Foot.

On 11 February 1808, Lieutenant Colonel Drummond took command of the 2nd Battalion of the 24th Foot. They were stationed on Guernsey until 1 April 1809 when they embarked for Portugal. They arrived in Lisbon on 28 April and marched east to Castelo Branco where they joined General John Mackenzie's brigade, which was watching the frontier with Spain.[2] The brigade led the army during the advance into central Spain in the summer of 1809. At Talavera the 24th Foot was in the second line, almost immediately behind the Guards Brigade of the 1st Division on both days of the battle. On the second day (28 July), after the poorly executed charge by the Guards Brigade on the French line, it was the 24th Foot that stood firm after the Guards broke and raced to the rear. The battalion stood in line for about thirty minutes under intense fire while the Guards rallied and reorganised their men. By nightfall, the 24th Foot had taken 50 per cent casualties. Among the wounded was Lieutenant Colonel Drummond.

The severity of his wounds forced Lieutenant Colonel Drummond to return to England. In October he was promoted to colonel and he remained in England until

---

1. It is difficult to determine who exactly Miss Forbes was, but she was likely a member of the Forbes-Drummond Clan.
2. General Order, 1 May 1809.

early 1811. By February he was back with the army in Portugal. On 7 February 1811 he was appointed a colonel on the staff to command a brigade in the Light Division. It is not clear why Colonel Drummond was chosen to command the brigade after Colonel James Wynch died in January.[3] Colonel Drummond's appointment was unusual since his regiment was not in the Light Division nor did he have any experience commanding light troops. Wellington might have had initial misgivings about the appointment; however, two months later after the Battle of Sabugal, he wrote in a dispatch on his operations in pursuit of Marshal Massena that, 'I had also great reason to be satisfied with the conduct of Col. Drummond …'[4]

Almost immediately after assuming command of his brigade, Colonel Drummond was given temporary command of the Light Division. He led it until 7 March when General William Erskine was appointed as its temporary commander. Colonel Drummond commanded his brigade at Sabugal on 1 April and at Fuentes d'Onoro in early May, where his brigade was lightly engaged. After the battle his brigade remained along the Portuguese-Spanish border. He was promoted to brigadier on the staff in August.[5]

A month after his promotion General Drummond became ill. On 8 September he died in the arms of his brigade major, Captain Harry Smith, in the village of Fuenteguinaldo, Spain. Captain Smith described the cause of his death as 'a putrid sore throat',[6] which was the contemporary name for trench mouth or acute necrotising ulcerative gingivitis.[7] It was usually fatal. General Drummond never married and had no children.

General Drummond had a hands-off approach to commanding his brigade. His style was eccentric. When Captain Harry Smith reported to duty as his brigade major, he asked the general, '"Have you any orders for the picquets sir?" He was an old Guardsman the kindest though oddest fellow possible. "Pray, Mr. Smith, are you my Brigade Major?" "I believe so, sir." "Then let me tell you, it is your duty to post the picquets, and mine to have a d—d good dinner for you every day." We soon understood each other. He cooked the dinner often himself, and I *commanded* the Brigade.'[8]

Despite his unusual approach to command, George Drummond was not afraid to take the initiative or disobey orders if the tactical situation warranted it. At Sabugal on 2 April 1811, Colonel Thomas Beckwith's brigade of the Light Division was in danger of being overwhelmed by the French 2nd Corps. Captain John Bell, the DQMG assigned to the division, wrote, 'Just as the 2nd Brigade [Colonel Drummond's Brigade] changed its direction, the General [William Erskine], being at some distance, sent an order for it not to engage. But the staff officer who carried it, and Drummond, seeing how matters stood, took the liberty of forgetting the message, so that Beckwith should have the full benefit at hand. No question was ever asked to the non-delivery of the order.'[9] Colonel Drummond's timely intervention not only saved the other brigade, but led to a victory that Wellington described as 'one of the most glorious that British troops were ever engaged in'.[10]

---

3. Colonel Wynch replaced Lieutenant Colonel Robert Barclay who had been severely wounded at Busaco.
4. *WD* (enlarged ed.); Vol. 4, page 734.
5. General Order, 6 August 1811, with the promotion backdated to 23 July 1811.
6. Smith; page 50.
7. 'Trench Mouth'. Mackenzie, Morell; pages 30–2.
8. Smith; page 45.
9. Unpublished manuscript quoted in Oman; *History of the Peninsular War*, Vol. 4, page 194.
10. *WD*; Vol. 7, page 445.

Dunlop, James

Date of Birth:	19 June 1759
Date Commissioned:	Lieutenant 82nd Foot:[1] 1 January 1778
Promotions:	Captain 82nd Foot: 6 May 1782 by purchase
	Captain 76th Foot: 1787 appointed[2]
	Captain 77th Foot: 25 September 1787 by exchange
	Brevet Major: 1 March 1794
	Major 77th Foot: 1 September 1795
	Lieutenant Colonel 77th Foot: 12 November 1795
	Lieutenant Colonel 59th Foot:[3] 31 March 1804 by exchange
	Brevet Colonel: 25 September 1803
	Brigadier General on the Staff: 25 July 1804–1808
	Major General: 25 July 1810
	Lieutenant General: 4 June 1814
Regimental Colonel:	75th Foot: 10 November 1827–30 March 1832
Major Commands under Wellington:	Brigade 5th Division: 5 November 1810–3 October 1811.
	Temporarily commanded 5th Division: February–22 April 1811 and 11 May–October 1811
Member of Parliament:	Kirkcudbright: 1812–1826
Date of Death:	30 March 1832 at Southwick, Hampshire

Was also known as Dunlop of that ilk.[4]

James Dunlop was born in 1759 to John Dunlop of that ilk and Frances Wallace, who was the heir of Sir Thomas Wallace of Craigie and a close friend and patron of Robert Burns. James inherited the family estate in Dunlop in 1804 when his older brother, General Andrew Dunlop, died with no heirs.

In January 1778, James Dunlop was commissioned as a lieutenant in the 82nd Foot. He went with his regiment to Halifax, Nova Scotia in March, where they joined the garrison. The next spring the garrison's grenadier and light companies were ordered to New York City. Unfortunately for Lieutenant Dunlop, his transport ran aground on the coast of New Jersey and he was taken prisoner. He remained in captivity for twenty months until he was exchanged and released to the British garrison in New York City. Lieutenant Dunlop's regiment was not part of the garrison, so he volunteered to go with the 80th Foot to Virginia. In April 1781 he was able to rejoin a detachment of his regiment in Wilmington. While there he took command of a troop of dragoons that the detachment was forming. He led this troop until May 1782 when he was promoted to captain and given command of a company. He joined his company in Halifax and remained there until the autumn of 1783, when they returned to England. They arrived there in late spring and the regiment was disbanded in June 1784.[5]

---

1. Disbanded 1784.
2. *London Gazette*; War Office Announcement dated 26 January 1788.
3. Removed from the regiment as a general officer receiving unattached pay 1814.
4. 'That ilk' is a Scottish term used to show that individual was from the same place as his family name. For example, instead of James Dunlop of Dunlop, he went by James Dunlop of that ilk.
5. *RMC*; Vol. 2, pages 402–3.

Captain Dunlop was on half-pay until 1787 when he was appointed into the 76th Foot. In September he exchanged into the 77th Foot and in April 1788 went with them to India. While there, he fought in the 3rd and 4th Mysore Wars against Tipu Sultan. In 1794 he was promoted to brevet major and initially served as the Deputy Paymaster General of the British forces in the Bombay Presidency. He served in that position for a short time and was appointed the Military Secretary to the Governor of Bombay. In 1795 he was promoted to major in September and to lieutenant colonel in November. At the siege of Seringapatam from March to May 1799, Lieutenant Colonel Dunlop commanded the Centre Brigade of the Bombay Army serving with General George Harris's army. During the assault on the breach of the city, he was seriously wounded in the right arm by a sabre blow which left him incapacitated for several months. He never fully recovered from this wound and returned to England in 1800.[6]

In June 1803, Lieutenant Colonel Dunlop was given command of the newly raised 2nd Battalion 77th Foot. He commanded them for only three months, when he was promoted to colonel. In March 1804, he exchanged into the 59th Foot and in July was appointed a brigadier on the staff of the Western District. In January 1806 he was given command of a Highland Brigade in the Eastern District. It appears that General Dunlop's tenure on the staff ended in 1808 and he returned to duty with his regiment. In July 1810, General Dunlop was promoted to major general but had no official duties outside his regiment.

It is highly likely that Wellington knew General Dunlop from their time in India. In September, Colonel Henry Torrens of the Horse Guards wrote to him that, 'Lord Wellington having some time since expressed a desire of Availing himself of your Services in The Field under his command, I have the pleasure to acquaint you that The Comdr in Chief will be glad…of submitting your name to the King for the purpose of proceeding to join the Staff of the Army in Portugal, and I hope to hear…that your health will enable you to go upon this service without delay.'[7] The following day, Colonel Torrens wrote to Wellington that as per his request, General Dunlop would be appointed to his staff.[8]

General Dunlop accepted the appointment and arrived in Portugal in early November. He was officially placed on the staff of Wellington's army on 5 November[9] and given a brigade in the newly formed 5th Division. When the division commander returned to England in February 1811, General Dunlop was placed in temporary command of the division. He led it at Sabugal on 3 April, but it was in reserve and saw no action. He was replaced in command of the division by General William Erskine on 22 April. General Dunlop's brigade was on the far left of the army at Fuentes de Oñoro and once again saw no action. On 11 May, General Dunlop was re-appointed the temporary commander of the 5th Division. During this time he was known to wear green spectacles, which were probably sunglasses.[10]

Despite having the temporary command of a division, General Dunlop was having second thoughts about serving in the Peninsula. As early as 9 July 1811, he was considering whether to go home on leave. He wrote to Wellington to ask for his opinion and received a reply that it was up to the general officers themselves to decide and to fix the period of leave. Wellington, however, made it clear that he did not like officers going home that

---

6. Ibid; pages 403–4.

7. Unpublished letter from Henry Torrens to James Dunlop dated 18 September 1810.

8. Unpublished letter from Henry Torrens to Wellington dated 19 September 1810.

9. General Order, 5 November 1810. His appointment was backdated to 19 September.

10. Hunter; page 128.

were not unwell, a position also taken by the Commander-in-Chief and the government. Wellington informed General Dunlop that he would consult the Commander-in-Chief before granting leave except for health reasons.[11]

On 25 July, Wellington notified the Horse Guards that General Dunlop had requested leave to go home and settle his affairs.[12] Permission to leave was slow in coming. By late September he was still commanding the 5th Division, but by mid-October General Dunlop had left the army to go to England. Wellington did not expect him to return,[13] however, shortly after General Dunlop arrived home, Colonel Torrens of the Horse Guards wrote to Wellington that, 'General Dunlop will certainly return, but not for some weeks to come.'[14]

Wellington's prediction was correct and General Dunlop never came back. Upon returning to England, General Dunlop had no official duties. In 1814 he was promoted to lieutenant general and in 1827 he was appointed the regimental colonel of the 75th Foot. He served as its colonel until his death.

The reason why General Dunlop did not return to the Peninsula was that he planned to run for Parliament. In 1812 he was elected to represent Kirkcudbright. General Dunlop was a Tory, but was accused of really being a Whig. He generally voted with the government, and in 1825 voted for both the Irish Unlawful Societies Bill and the Catholic Relief Bill. He was defeated for re-election in 1826. His time as an MP was low key and his official parliamentary biographer noted that, 'He is not known to have contributed to debate in 14 years as a Member ...'.[15]

James Dunlop married Julia Baillie in 1802. They had two daughters and three sons, one of whom was an army officer and another a Royal Navy officer. James Dunlop died in 1832 after a long illness.[16]

After Sabugal in April 1811, there were rumors about General Dunlop's conduct during the battle. These rumors included an accusation of cowardice against him that was made by General Andrew Hay who commanded the other brigade in the 5th Division. Sergeant John Douglas, who served in the 1st Foot, wrote:

> It is my firm belief that had we been allowed to have attacked the enemy at that time, the army of Masséna would have been easily annihilated. General Hay rode up in rage to General Dunlop, who commanded the Division, and demanded why he did not attack the enemy. His reply was, 'I am waiting for a guide.' 'There's the enemy, there's your guide,' exclaimed Hay. He then wanted his own Brigade to lead the attack, but 'No'; on which sheathing his sword with madness, he exclaimed in front of the Division, 'I shall report your cowardice to Lord Wellington this night,' and I believe he was as good as his word, as the General went off to England in a few days and did not make his appearance for several months.[17]

---

11. *WD* (enlarged ed.); Vol. 5, page 144.
12. Ibid; Vol. 5, page 185.
13. *WD* (enlarged ed.); Vol. 5, pages 324–5.
14. Unpublished letter from Henry Torrens to Wellington dated 13 November 1811.
15. 'Dunlop, James (1759–1832), of Dunlop, Ayr and Southwick, Kirkcudbright'.
16. Ibid.
17. Douglas; page 28.

here are problems with Sergeant Douglas's account. It is possible that the two generals
nay have had a heated conversation about the deployment of the 5th Division, but it is
unlikely that it would have been made in front of the whole division. Furthermore, if
General Hay had made such a public accusation of cowardice, he would have been court-
nartialed for conduct unbecoming of an officer. If General Hay did go to Wellington
nd made the accusation in private, Wellington chose not to act on it. Nor is there any
indication that he had lost confidence in General Dunlop. Wellington not only kept
him in temporary command of the division for several weeks after Sabugal, but also re-
ppointed him the temporary commander in May. General Dunlop kept the command
until October 1811, when he returned to England. Upon his departure, Wellington wrote
to Colonel Torrens of the Horse Guards, 'I was obliged to give General Dunlop leave to
go home, and I doubt his coming out again; and he is really a loss.'[18] Further on in the
ame letter he wrote about the problems of finding suitable commanders for his division
and stated, 'I wish I could get back Dunlop'.[19]

18. *WD* (enlarged ed.); Vol. 5, pages 324–5.
19. Ibid; page 325.

Erskine, James

Date of Birth:	30 September 1772
Date Commissioned:	Ensign 26th Foot: 26 February 1788 by purchase
Promotions:	Lieutenant 7th Foot: 9 January 1793 by purchase
	Captain Independent Company: 8 March 1793 by purchase
	Captain 37th Foot: 1 November 1793 appointed
	Brevet Major: 19 May 1794
	Lieutenant Colonel 133rd Foot:[1] 22 August 1794 by purchase
	Lieutenant Colonel 15th Light Dragoons: 27 February 1796 by exchange
	Lieutenant Colonel 2nd Dragoon Guards:[2] 10 February 1803 by exchange
	Brevet Colonel: 1 January 1800
	Brigadier General on the Staff: 3 March 1804
	Major General: 25 April 1808
	Lieutenant General: 4 June 1813
Major Commands under Wellington:	Cavalry Brigade: 25 May–16 July 1809
Date of Death:	3 March 1825, Dover Street, Piccadilly, London

James Erskine was born in 1772 at Torrie House in Fife, Scotland. He was the second son of General Sir William Erskine, 1st Baronet of Torrie, and Frances Moray. His older brother, General William Erskine, commanded the 2nd Cavalry Division in Wellington's army in the Peninsula. James was commissioned an ensign in the 26th Foot in 1788 and sailed to Canada with his regiment in 1789. In January 1793, he purchased a lieutenancy in the 7th Foot and two months later a captaincy in an independent company. With his promotions came a new duty station and in July Captain Erskine returned to England. While in England he was appointed a captain in the 37th Foot.

After he returned to England, Captain Erskine went to Flanders in late 1793. He fought at the Battles of Le Cateau on 26 April 1794, Cysoing on 10 May 1794, Tournai on 22 May 1794, and of Boxtel on 14 September 1794. Captain Erskine was promoted to brevet major in May 1794 and in August of the same year he purchased a lieutenant colonelcy in the 133rd Foot. In April 1795 he returned to England but in 1796 his regiment was disbanded and he became unemployed. However, Lieutenant Colonel Erskine was still carried on the regimental rolls and received his full pay, but had no regimental duties.

Lieutenant Colonel Erskine was unemployed until late February 1796, when he exchanged with his brother William into the 15th Light Dragoons. On 25 September 1799, Lieutenant Colonel Erskine went with three troops to Holland, where they distinguished themselves at the Battle of Egmont-op-Zee on 2 October. He was wounded during the battle but remained in command. Shortly after the battle, Lieutenant Colonel George Anson arrived with two additional troops. Despite their gallantry, the situation in Holland was untenable for the British and they withdrew to England in November.

Lieutenant Colonel Erskine's actions in Holland were noticed. On 1 January 1800, he was promoted to colonel and on Christmas Day he was made an ADC to King

1. Disbanded 1796.
2. Removed from the regiment as a general officer receiving unattached pay 1814.

George III. Colonel Erskine commanded the 15th Light Dragoons until 1803, when he exchanged into the 2nd Dragoon Guards. He joined his regiment in Ireland and in 1804 was promoted to brigadier on the staff. He stayed in Ireland until 1806 when he joined the staff in Scotland. In 1808 he was promoted to major general.

General Erskine remained in Scotland until 18 April 1809 when he was sent to Portugal. Shortly after arriving there he was appointed on the staff of Wellington's army.[3] Initially Wellington intended to give him a heavy cavalry brigade, which was to serve with General John Mackenzie on the frontier with Spain. However, General Erskine was senior to him and Wellington did not want to supersede General Mackenzie in the command. Wellington also noted General Erskine's lack of experience in the region in a letter to John Villiers: 'I really believe that I should have every reason to place confidence in Gen. Erskine, if he had been a little longer in Portugal.'[4]

It was not until late May, when the 1st KGL Hussars arrived, that General Erskine received a command.[5] The other regiment, the 23rd Light Dragoons, did not arrive until June. He would not command the brigade for long. By 1 July General Erskine's health was in question and Wellington wrote him a warm letter suggesting that he go home to recover before it became worse. He even sent a carriage to convey General Erskine to the army's headquarters at Castelo Branco, so that General Erskine could make his way to Lisbon.[6] The exact nature of his illness is listed as severe indisposition, which was a catchall phrase to describe a variety of ailments that were incapacitating but usually not life threatening. Furthermore they were not classified as a disease.[7] Whatever his problem was, Wellington wrote to General Erskine that, 'I cannot conclude without expressing my concern to lose your assistance; I am convinced that, if you were to stay, you would be unable to afford me any, and that you will become worse instead of better.'[8]

General Erskine made his way to Lisbon and was invalided home on 20 September 1809. General Erskine was on the Home Staff commanding in the Sussex and Western Districts from 1811 to 1813. He was promoted to lieutenant general in June 1813, but had no military duties after his promotion.

James Erskine married Lady Louisa Paget, the sister of Field Marshal Marquess of Anglesey,[9] on 5 March 1801. They had no children. In 1813 his brother, General William Erskine, the 2nd Baronet of Torrie, died. Since the baronet had no heirs, James Erskine inherited the title and became the 3rd Baronet of Torrie. He died in 1825.

James Erskine's military career is often overshadowed by his hobby. He and his wife were avid art collectors and had an extensive collection of Dutch and Flemish landscapes, Italian paintings and Renaissance bronzes. He left the collection to Edinburgh University in his will.[10]

---

3. General Order, 27 April 1809.
4. *WD* (enlarged ed.); Vol. 3, pages 208–9.
5. General Order, 25 May 1809.
6. *WD* (enlarged ed.); Vol. 3, page 336.
7. Nineteenth-century Parliamentary documents listed such complaints as diarrhoea, jaundice, pneumonia, broken bones, bronchitis, and ringworm as forms of severe disposition. *Parliamentary Papers*; 1846. Vol. 20, page 23.
8. Ibid.
9. Also known as General Henry William Paget, the Earl of Uxbridge. Louisa's other brother was General Edward Paget.
10. 'The Torrie Collection'.

Fane, Henry

Date of Birth:	26 November 1778
Date Commissioned:	Cornet 7th Dragoon Guards: 31 May 1792 without purchase
Promotions:	Lieutenant 55th Foot: 29 September 1792 without purchase
	Captain Independent Company: 3 April 1793 without purchase
	Captain-Lieutenant 4th Dragoons Guards: 31 August 1793 appointed
	Captain 4th Dragoons Guards: 30 September 1793 without purchase
	Major 4th Dragoons Guards: 24 August 1795 purchase
	Lieutenant Colonel 4th Dragoon Guards: 1 August 1797 without purchase
	Lieutenant Colonel 1st Dragoon Guards: 25 December 1804 appointed
	Brevet Colonel: 1 January 1805
	Brigadier General on the Staff: 1808–1810
	Major General: 25 July 1810
	Lieutenant General on the Continent: 17 January 1817
	Lieutenant General: 12 August 1819
	General India: 30 January 1835
	General: 10 January 1837
Regimental Colonel:	23rd Light Dragoons: 13 July–3 August 1814
	4th Dragoon Guards: 3 August 1814–24 February 1827
	1st Dragoon Guards: 24 February 1827–24 March 1840
Major Commands under Wellington:	Light Brigade: 23 June–7 August 1808
	6th (Light) Brigade: 7 August–5 September 1808[1]
	Cavalry Brigade: 7 May 1809–13 May 1810
	Cavalry with Hill's Detached Corps: 13 May–December 1810
	Cavalry Brigade: 20 May–December 1813
	Cavalry with Hill's Detached Corps: December 1813–April 1814
	Cavalry with AOOF: January 1817–November 1818
Awards:	AGC with clasp: Roliça & Vimeiro, Corunna, Talavera, Vitoria & Orthes
	KCB 2 January 1815
	GCB 24 January 1826
Thanks of Parliament:	Roliça & Vimeiro, Corunna, Talavera & Orthes
Member of Parliament:	Lyme Regis: 1802–1818
	Sandwich: 1829–1830
	Hastings: 1830–1831
Date of Death:	24 March 1840 at sea while returning to England from India

Henry Fane was born in 1778, the oldest son of Hon. Henry Fane of Fullbeck, Lincolnshire and Anne Batson. Among his brothers were Lieutenant Colonel Charles Fane and General Milday Fane. His father was an MP for Lyme Regis. His grandfather was the 8th Earl of Westmorland.[2]

---

1. General Order, 7 August 1808.
2. 'The Fanes', page 14.

Henry Fane was commissioned as a cornet in the 7th Dragoon Guards in 1792 and in September he was promoted to lieutenant in the 55th Foot. The next year he was appointed an ADC to his cousin, John Fane, the 10th Earl of Westmorland and Lord Lieutenant of Ireland. While there, he met and worked with Wellington who was also an ADC to the Earl of Westmorland. Lieutenant Fane served as the ADC until 1794, when his cousin was appointed the Master of the Horse. During the two years he was his cousin's ADC, Henry Fane was promoted to captain-lieutenant and then captain in the 4th Dragoon Guards. In 1795, he purchased a majority in the regiment and in 1797, at the age of 18, he was promoted to lieutenant colonel in it. Lieutenant Colonel Fane's promotion was by appointment and was most likely due to his family's political connections. He fought in the Irish Rebellion of 1798 and went with the regiment to England in 1799.

Lieutenant Colonel Fane was never the senior lieutenant colonel in the 4th Dragoon Guards and thus never commanded the regiment. On Christmas Day 1804, he was transferred to the 1st Dragoon Guards, and as the senior lieutenant colonel he became its commander. A week later, he was promoted to colonel and made an ADC to King George III.

Colonel Fane's political connections continued to serve him well. He was placed upon the staff of Wellington's Corps for service in Spain or Portugal on 14 June 1808 as a brigadier general. Despite having no experience commanding as an infantry officer, he was given command of the Light Brigade. He landed in Portugal on 1 August and commanded it at Roliça on 17 August. His brigade was re-designated the 6th Brigade the next day and he led it at Vimeiro on 21 August. The army was reorganised by General Hew Dalrymple on 5 September and General Fane was appointed to command a brigade in General Alexander Mackenzie-Fraser's 3rd Division. When it was decided to form a field army for service in Spain under General John Moore, the army was reorganised on 8 October and General Fane was selected to join the field army.[3] He commanded an independent brigade. On 1 December, his brigade was assigned again to General Mackenzie-Fraser's Division. General Fane led the brigade during the retreat to Corunna and at the battle there on 16 January 1809. After the battle, he and his brigade boarded ships and returned to England. General Fane was not destined to remain in England long.

On 27 April 1809, General Fane was placed upon the staff of Wellington's army in Portugal.[4] He arrived there in early May and was given command of a cavalry brigade.[5] This brigade was attached to General John Mackenzie's force watching the frontier with Spain. It was with the army when it entered Spain in the summer and fought at Talavera on 17–18 July. His brigade helped cover the retreat of the army back to Portugal and spent the next ten months along the border with Spain.

Wellington wrote to General Rowland Hill on 11 May 1810 that he had chosen General Fane to command the English and Portuguese cavalry serving under him, 'which arrangement, I hope, will be agreeable to you.'[6] General Hill commanded a detached corps in the vicinity of Badajoz and General Fane had five regiments of cavalry under his

---

3. General Order, 8 October 1808.

4. General Order, 27 April 1809.

5. General Order, 7 May 1809.

6. *WD* (enlarged ed.); Vol. 4, page 58.

command.[7] General Fane was promoted to major general in July and was retained on the staff of the army.[8]

The stress of eighteen months of campaigning began to take its toll. On 22 December 1810, General Fane wrote to Wellington that he was suffering from ill health. Wellington responded the next day that he was 'exceedingly concerned that you have suffered and are still suffering so much'.[9] Wellington granted him three months leave to go to England to recuperate and also arranged for passage in a ship of war for him (something he was not doing for others). Wellington ended by writing, 'I don't know what I shall do with your command during your absence.'[10]

General Fane arrived in England in January and there was some doubt that he would return to the Peninsula. His friend, General Robert Long, wrote on 25 January that Fane had 'no apparent intention of going back'[11] to Portugal. By 13 April 1811, Wellington was aware that General Fane was not returning, writing to Marshal William Beresford, 'Gen. Fane will, I fear, not be able to come out again this summer'.[12] After convalescing in England for the rest of the year, General Fane was placed on the Home Staff in South West and Kent Districts in 1812.

By the spring of 1813, word reached the army in Portugal that General Fane would be returning. Wellington had written to Colonel Torrens at the Horse Guards in December 1812 requesting that General Fane be sent out and that if he did come he would command the cavalry that would be attached to General Hill's Corps.[13] One bit of gossip gave a more selfish reason for his returning. Rumors had it that deserving officers would soon be invested into the Order of the Bath and that General Fane 'seeing the red ribbon flying about in all directions is of course anxious to be a candidate for such a favor'.[14] Regardless of his reasons for coming, General Fane arrived in Portugal in late April and was appointed on the staff of the army to date from 25 December 1812.[15]

Wellington's intention to place him in command of the cavalry in General Hill's corps did not happen initially. Instead General Fane was given command of a cavalry brigade assigned to the Cavalry Division.[16] In May he was attached to General Hill's corps and as the army moved into Spain, he led his brigade in pursuit of the retreating French, catching a detachment of them trying to ford the Tormes River at Santa Marta. A large number of prisoners were taken during the action; however, because the British had no infantry available, the French were able to form square and march away. His brigade was at Vitoria on 21 June, but saw limited action. They were part of the pursuit of the defeated French Army, but stopped to plunder the French baggage train. Unfortunately for General Fane, his brother Charles was seriously wounded at Vitoria and died on 27

---

7. The British 13th Light Dragoons and four regiments of Portuguese cavalry.
8. General Order, 8 September 1810.
9. *WD* (enlarged ed.); Vol. 4, page 472.
10. Ibid.
11. Long; page 48.
12. *WD* (enlarged ed.); Vol. 4, page 745.
13. *WSD*; Vol. 7, page 485.
14. Long; page 262.
15. General Order, 24 April 1813.
16. General Order, 20 May 1813.

une. He took the loss badly and it appeared 'to affect him deeply, and he is gone to the rear to give vent to his feelings'.[17]

General Fane rejoined his brigade and spent the summer helping blockade the French garrison in Pamplona. After the garrison surrendered on 31 October, the brigade went into winter quarters. In December Wellington fulfilled his promise to place General Fane in command of the cavalry of General Hill's corps. Although he still kept command of his brigade, as the senior cavalry officer in the corps he was responsible for all its cavalry. Most of the time he would have control of two cavalry brigades, but depending on the operation his command could be as small as one brigade and as large as three. He led them through the winter campaign of 1814 in southern France. His final battle was at Orthes on 27 February.

After the abdication of Napoleon in April 1814, General Fane was left to organise the movement of the cavalry and horse artillery from southern France back to England. The 900 kilometer march to Calais took three months. There they were placed aboard transports. He finally reached England in August and was appointed the Inspecting General of Cavalry. In March 1815, Napoleon escaped from Elba and returned to France. In April General Fane was offered the command of the Household Cavalry Brigade, which had been ordered to Wellington's army in the Netherlands. General Fane declined the appointment and was placed on the Home Staff in the Sussex and Inland Districts. He missed the Waterloo Campaign, but replaced Lord Combermere[18] in command of the British cavalry in the Army of Occupation of France in 1817. Upon assuming command in the AOOF, he was promoted to lieutenant general on the continent[19] and remained in France until the army was broken up in 1818.

General Fane returned to England and had few military duties. In early 1825, he was considered for a high command in India. However, his service – believed to be mostly in the cavalry – excluded him by a decision of the Directors of the HEIC.[20] At the same time, his name was included in the list of general officers submitted by Wellington to Charles W. Wynn, the President of the HEIC, to command in India. Wellington considered him one of the best of the general officers submitted, but doubted that General Fane would go to India then.[21] General Fane continued as the regimental colonel of the 4th Dragoon Guards until 1827, when he became the colonel of the 1st Dragoon Guards. He was their colonel until his death in 1840. He was an original member of the Consolidated Board of General Officers, which was set up in November 1816, and served on it until his death.[22]

Henry Fane was a Member of Parliament and a Tory. Despite serving eighteen years in Parliament little is known about his time as a MP. He represented Lyme Regis from 1802 to 1818, but since it was a closed borough he never had to run for election. During that time he spent over four years outside of the country on active service with the army. In 1829 he was appointed the Surveyor General of Ordnance[23] by Wellington and ran

---

17. Long; page 280.
18. Lord Combermere was Stapleton Cotton, who had been raised in the peerage.
19. His date of rank was 17 January 1817. However, this was local rank only and when he returned to England in late 1818 he reverted back to his old rank of major general.
20. Duke of Buckingham; Vol. 2, page 214.
21. *WND*; Vol. 2, page 425.
22. Unless a member was on the Board's Acting Committee he had few if any duties. General Fane was never on the Acting Committee.
23. He held the position from 21 March 1829 to 12 January 1831.

for election in Sandwich, which he won. He voted against Jewish emancipation and the abolition of capital punishment for forgery. The following year he was up for re-election and rather than taking a chance of losing his seat, he was offered the Treasury Interest of Hastings. This seat was controlled by the Crown. He was declared the winner of the election when his opponent, who won 90 per cent of the vote, was disqualified. Henry Fane decided against running again in 1831. Perhaps his political career is best known for his comment on the rumor that the government was going to ban flogging in the army 'the army is gone if the power is taken away.'[24]

In 1831 Henry Fane was considered a candidate to become the Viceroy of Ireland. He was not given the appointment because the new government felt he was too close to Wellington. In 1832, he applied for the governorship of the Cape Colony, but was denied that also. It was only after the Tories returned to power in 1835 that Wellington, in his capacity as the acting Prime Minister, appoint General Fane the Commander-in-Chief of India.[25]

The trip to India and the change of climate badly affected General Fane's health. His nephew, Ensign Henry Edward Fane, who served as his ADC, wrote after he arrived in India in August that 'he looks very thin and ill, and much altered for the worse, since I last saw him in England.'[26] General Fane assumed command on 5 September 1835. It was peaceful for the first several years he was there and he spent it inspecting every garrison in his command. In late 1838 he organised the Army of the Indus for the invasion of Afghanistan. A change in the objective of the campaign and a downsizing of the force to be used led General Fane to resign his command of the Army of the Indus in protest. His resignation was rejected by the government and he led the army in the initial stages of the war. In late 1839, he handed over command of the Army of the Indus to General John Keane, thus avoiding the debacle of the First Anglo–Afghan War.

In December 1839, General Fane's health declined further. He left India on 1 January 1840. He became weaker on the trip home and died on 24 March. The cause of death was water on the chest, another name for pleural effusion, which is an abnormal amount of fluid in the membrane around the lungs. It is often caused by heart disease or cancer.[27] He was buried at sea off São Miguel Island in the Azores.

Henry Fane was romantically involved with Isabella Gorges Cooke, the wife of Edward Cooke, who was an Under-Secretary of the Colonial and Foreign Offices. She eventually separated from her husband. Henry and she had six children, four of whom survived to reach adulthood. The eldest son was an army officer. There is a question on whether they ever married. Some sources state that they married privately, while others say that she was Henry's common-law wife. She did not accompany him to India.[28]

As an infantry brigade commander during the initial months of the Peninsular War, General Fane was a charismatic leader who led from the front. He was energetic and was known to patrol the outposts to ensure they were alert,[29] and at Roliça he was often with the skirmishers. During the pursuit of the French after Vimeiro, he and his staff

24. 'Fane, Sir Henry (1778–1840), of Fulbeck, nr. Grantham, Lincs. and Avon Tyrell, Hants.'
25. Date of appointment was 4 February 1834.
26. Fane, Henry Edward; Vol. 1, page 28.
27. 'Pleural Effusion'.
28. 'Fane, Sir Henry (1778–1840), of Fulbeck, nr. Grantham, Lincs. and Avon Tyrell, Hants.'
29. Harris; page 13.

aptured an artillery piece that the French were attempting to move off the field.[30] Yet his personality changed by 1813. Before General Fane returned to Portugal, General Long had received a letter from London stating that 'he is very violent in his authority'.[31] A modern history of the Royal Dragoons, which was based on the regimental journals described him as 'a strong and stern disciplinarian.'[32] Yet when word reached the army that he was replacing General Slade,[33] one cavalry officer wrote in his diary, 'Major-General Slade is at length gone to England, and is succeeded by Major General Fane. The change I consider a good one, and so do most others.'[34]

Wellington appeared to be very close to General Fane both as a military commander and in the political arena. Their friendship was probably formed back when they were both ADCs in Ireland. It was possible that Wellington served as a mentor for the young lieutenant and Henry Fane's political connections probably did not hurt their relationship. The fact that he was a very competent commander also helped and his abilities were highly thought of by Wellington. His correspondence reflects this, for there is neither a reproach nor any expression of disappointment on General Fane's performance in command of the de facto cavalry division that General Fane commanded in 1810.

In late 1812, Wellington was looking to replace cavalry commanders who were not working out. On 2 December he wrote to Colonel Torrens and specifically requested that General Fane be sent out as one of their replacements. He stated that except for 'Fane, however, I do not desire to have any General officers from England'.[35] Furthermore, in the same letter, Wellington wrote that he intended to give General Fane command of the cavalry of General Hill's corps.

Although General Fane was among the best cavalry commanders in Wellington's army, he had a major weakness. He was very cognizant of his seniority and took offense if a general who was junior to him was given responsibilities that he felt he should have. In late November 1813, General Fane submitted his resignation to General Cotton, the commander of the British cavalry. It was forwarded to Wellington who responded with a lengthy letter on 24 November, stating that General Fane had not corresponded with him on the subject of his resignation. Wellington initially thought it was due to the inactivity of the cavalry at the time, but found out it was because officers junior to General Fane were being placed in command of infantry divisions.[36]

Wellington told General Fane that should he change his mind about resigning he wanted him to take command of the cavalry on the right of the army and to join General Hill's corps. Wellington then went on to explain in regard to the divisional commands, the junior officers were only in temporary command until the division commanders returned. Wellington was honest and stated that he never thought of assigning General Fane to the infantry. Wellington ended by asking that if his resignation was due to either circumstance and whether what he had written would induce him to withdraw his resignation.[37]

---

30. Landman; Vol. 2, pages 222–3.
31. Long; page 266.
32. Clark-Kennedy; page 70.
33. John Slade.
34. Tomkinson; page 235.
35. *WSD*; Vol. 7, page 485.
36. *WD* (enlarged ed.); Vol. 7, pages 159–60.
37. Ibid.

Wellington wrote to General Fane on 8 December that, 'I am very happy to find that you have determined to remain with the army. I shall appoint you to command of a division of infantry as soon as one may be vacant, and it shall come to your turn'.[38] At the time of his writing the letter, Wellington had yet to receive word that General Fane had joined General Hill to command his cavalry and asked him if he had. Yet Wellington was also straightforward in the same letter, telling General Fane that part of the blame was his own. 'You must not blame me if your situation is not what you like. It is exactly what it was in 1810, only that there has been less scope lately for the use of the cavalry.'[39]

True to his word, on 21 January 1814 Wellington offered General Fane the temporary command of the 7th Division until the return of its commander. Wellington told him that if he declined it would be offered to a junior officer.[40] General Fane turned down the appointment, choosing to stay with General Hill's corps, because at the time his command consisted of two brigades of cavalry and was a small ad hoc division.

General Fane's prickliness about being slighted in seniority carried into 1815. After Napoleon escaped from Elba and the British began assembling an army in the Netherlands, General Torrens wrote to Wellington that it was proposed that General Fane should command the Household Brigade, going out to join his army. General Torrens probably anticipated General Fane's position on seniority and noted that the brigade was small and that General Fane 'looked higher than a brigade.'[41]

On 21 April, General Torrens wrote to General Fane that his appointment was not put in orders,

> from a knowledge that considering your standing as a M General, and your general Claims, you would look for a higher course of employment, than could be arranged for you until the ultimate organisation of the Cavalry should be effected. When the Household Brigade was proposed to be formed, The Prince Regent was graciously and spontaneously pleased to select you for its Command! It would thus be a difficult & perhaps an injurious proceeding towards yourself to give the Prince an impression that you thought such a distinction beneath you, or that you were going on Service dissatisfied with the arrangements proposed by H.R.H. I should therefore humbly recommend that you should acquiesce, and your Rank as being next in Seniority to Lord Uxbridge[42] will undoubtedly bring you into a command & employment suitable to your views & pretensions. I shall explain the whole to the D. of Wn …[43]

On the same day that he wrote to General Fane, General Torrens wrote to Wellington that the Household Cavalry Brigade was to be reinforced by the 1st Dragoon Guards and that the Prince Regent had selected General Fane for the command of the brigade. However, General Fane was not pleased with only commanding a brigade and that his appointment was not put in orders sooner than other commanders. General Torrens wrote to Wellington that he had advised General Fane 'to make no difficulties on this subject in consideration of the manner in which he has been named by the Regent; and as

---

38. Ibid; pages 187–8.
39. Ibid.
40. Ibid; page 279.
41. Unpublished letter from Henry Torrens to Wellington, dated 21 April 1815.
42. General Henry Paget, Earl of Uxbridge.
43. Unpublished letter from Henry Torrens to Henry Fane, dated 21 April 1815.

e will be next in seniority to Lord Uxbridge, he will have the benefit of any organization ou may think proper to make eventually in the cavalry.'[44]

General Torrens was correct in how he thought Wellington would employ General ane. Wellington wrote to Colonel Torrens on 21 April that, 'I shall be most happy to ave Fane; and as soon as Lord Uxbridge arrives, I hope to make an arrangement for him, vhich will be more agreeable to him and advantageous to the service than to leave him in ommand of a brigade.'[45] But General Fane was still insulted by these perceived slights nd on 25 April 1815 General Torrens notified Wellington that, 'Fane has been excused rom going with the Household Brigade ...'[46]

It turns out General Fane did not communicate his wishes to General Torrens very clearly. In 1824, he wrote a puzzling letter to Wellington and enclosed a copy of the letter e sent to General Torrens in 1815. He explained to Wellington that he believed that he vas being offered a choice about the command and did not see his declining the offer as efusing the offer of command. He thought because the army would have many foreign roops, his inability to speak either German or French would hurt his ability to command hem. He felt that this would damage his reputation and implied that he thought he vould be offered a different command if he declined the original offer.[47]

General Fane never joined the army in the Netherlands and missed the Waterloo Campaign, along with the awards that the senior officers received. He believed that his absence at Waterloo caused him to be treated badly when GCBs were being awarded. He was unhappy in 1820, when Lieutenant General Kenneth Howard received a GCB and he did not. Not only was General Howard junior to him but he too was not at Waterloo. Things came to a head in 1824, when Lieutenant General John Oswald also received a GCB and once again Fane did not. Like General Howard, General Oswald was junior to General Fane, had less than a year's service in the Peninsula, and was not at Waterloo. Twice he wrote to Wellington soliciting his help. Wellington wrote back to General Fane that he had talked with Lord Bathurst, but he was not willing to promise the next GCB would go to him. He also pointed out that only a limited number of individuals could serve as a GCB at any given time and there were currently no vacancies.[48]

In early 1826, Wellington wrote to Earl Bathurst in support of General Fane receiving a GCB, saying, 'his services in the field were far superior to those of many even of those, some his juniors, who have obtained the order'; that it would be unjust 'to remember only his mistake', and that, 'with a view to the public interest', it was 'important that a man so capable of serving the public well should not feel himself disgraced, and in a manner under the necessity of keeping himself in the background.'[49] Lord Bathurst finally agreed to forward General Fane's name to the King, but only after admitting that he had deliberately not nominated him because of his refusal to serve during a time of crisis and felt he needed to be made an example of.[50] General Fane was invested as a GCB a few weeks later.

---

44. *WSD*; Vol. 10, page 130.
45. *WD* (enlarged ed.); Vol. 8, page 38.
46. Unpublished letter from Henry Torrens to Wellington, dated 25 April 1815.
47. Unpublished letter from Henry Fane to Wellington, dated 21 April 1824. In the Wellington Papers Database, Southampton University. (#Docref=WP1/790/27).
48. Unpublished letter from Wellington to Henry Fane, dated 4 March 1824. In the Wellington Papers Database, Southampton University. (#Docref=WP1/789/1).
49. 'Fane, Sir Henry (1778–1840), of Fulbeck, nr. Grantham, Lincs. and Avon Tyrell, Hants.'
50. Unpublished letter from Lord Bathurst to Wellington, dated 6 January 1826. In the Wellington Papers Database, Southampton University. (#Docref=WP1/846/4).

Ferguson, Ronald Craufurd

Date of Birth:	8 February 1773 in Edinburgh, Scotland
Date Commissioned:	Ensign 53rd Foot: 3 April 1790 by purchase
Promotions:	Lieutenant Independent Company: 24 January 1791 appointed
	Lieutenant 53rd Foot: 11 March 1791 by exchange
	Captain Independent Company: 9 February 1793 appointed
	Captain 53rd Foot: 23 October 1793 by exchange
	Captain 86th Foot: 30 October 1793 appointed[1]
	Major 84th Foot:[2] 31 May 1794 without purchase
	Lieutenant Colonel 84th Foot:[3] 18 September 1794 without purchase
	Lieutenant Colonel Minorca Regiment:[4] c. 8 August 1799 appointed
	Lieutenant Colonel 31st Foot: 19 December 1799 appointed
	Lieutenant Colonel Duke of York's Own (Banffshire) Fencible Infantry:[5] c. 10 April 1801 appointed
	Brevet Colonel: 1 January 1800
	Brigadier General on the Staff: 1804–1808
	Major General: 25 April 1808
	Lieutenant General: 4 June 1813
	General: 22 July 1830
Regimental Colonel:	Sicilian Regiment: 25 January 1809–March 1816[6]
	79th Regiment: 24 March 1828–10 April 1841
Major Commands under Wellington:	Temporarily commanded Brigade: 23 June–7 August 1808
	2nd Brigade: 7 August–5 September 1808[7]
	Second-in-command at Cadiz: 25 May 1810[8]–October 1810
Awards:	AGM: Roliça & Vimeiro
	KCB: 2 January 1815
	GCB: 13 September 1831
Thanks of Parliament:	Vimeiro
Member of Parliament:	Kirkcaldy: 1806–1830
	Nottingham: 1830–1841
Date of Death:	10 April 1841, Bolton-Row, Piccadilly, London

Ronald Ferguson was born in 1773, the second son of William Ferguson of Raith Fifeshire and Jane Craufurd. Sources vary about his place of birth. Some state it was in the family home of Raith House in Fifeshire, while others state it was in Edinburgh. He attended Edinburgh High School from 1778 to 1779.

---

1. *London Gazette*; War Office Announcements dated 16 & 26 November 1793.
2. 2nd Battalion; disbanded 1795.
3. Ibid.
4. Named variously as Minorca Regiment, the Queen's German Regiment, numbered 97th Foot 1803, renumbered 96th Foot 1816, and disbanded 1818.
5. Disbanded 1802.
6. Disbanded March 1816.
7. General Order, 7 August 1808.
8. General Order, 19 September 1810; to date from 25 May.

In 1790, Ronald Ferguson purchased a commission in the 53rd Foot and a year later was promoted to lieutenant in an independent company. Shortly after he joined the independent company it was disbanded and he went on half-pay. He was not on it long, before he exchanged back into the 53rd Foot. About this time Lieutenant Ferguson traveled to Berlin to attend the Berlin Military Academy. He was there for about two years when war with France was declared in February 1793. He returned home and found that he had been appointed captain of an independent company. His company was attached to the 53rd Foot and with the regiment when it joined the British expedition to Flanders. He fought with the regiment at Valenciennes, Dunkirk and Nieuport. On 23 October Captain Ferguson exchanged back into the 53rd Foot and two days later, while leading his company at Furnes, he was seriously wounded in the knee. On 30 October, he was appointed a captain in the 86th Foot, but since he had just re-joined the 53rd Foot, his appointment was given to another officer.

Captain Ferguson stayed in Flanders until May 1794 when he was appointed a major in the 2nd Battalion 84th Foot. In September, he was appointed a lieutenant colonel and commander of the battalion. Both the 1st and 2nd Battalions of the 84th Foot were part of the 1795 expedition to capture the Cape of Good Hope from the Dutch. After the colony fell to the British the 2nd Battalion was disbanded and Lieutenant Colonel Ferguson was without a job. Despite the disbanding of his battalion, he was still carried on the regimental rolls and thus received his full pay. He had no regimental duties. This lasted until 1798 when he was placed on half-pay.[9] Lieutenant Colonel Ferguson remained on half-pay until August 1799 when he was appointed a lieutenant colonel in the Minorca Regiment. There is no evidence that he ever served with them, because four months later he was appointed a lieutenant colonel in the 31st Foot. Shortly after being assigned to the 31st Foot, he was promoted to colonel on 1 January 1800. The summer of 1800 saw Colonel Ferguson and his regiment with General Thomas Maitland's expedition that destroyed the French forts at Quiberon and Belle Island. After the expedition was disbanded, they were sent as reinforcements to join the British forces in the Mediterranean.

In the spring of 1801, Colonel Ferguson returned to England to take command of the Duke of York's Own (Banffshire) Fencible Infantry. In July 1801 he exchanged to half-pay on the rolls of the disbanded 93rd Foot.[10] He would remain on half-pay with the regiment until 1809. While on half-pay, Colonel Ferguson was appointed an Inspecting Field Officer of Yeomanry and Volunteer Corps on 4 October 1803. He was promoted to brigadier general in 1804 and placed on the Home Staff in the York District. On 31 August 1805, he was given command of the Highland Brigade of General David Baird's force that captured the Cape of Good Hope on 18 January 1806. While there, General Ferguson contracted a serious liver disease that forced him to return to England. He spent the next two years recuperating.

In April 1808, General Ferguson was promoted to major general and then placed on the staff of General Brent Spencer's corps. On 14 June he was attached to Wellington's force, and assigned to temporarily command General Rowland Hill's brigade on 23 June. When General Spencer's corps joined Wellington's force in Portugal, Wellington reorganised it and General Ferguson was given command of the 2nd Brigade. He led it at Roliça on

---

9. His biography in the 1889 *Dictionary of National Biography* states that he went to India with his regiment, but this cannot be confirmed by any other sources.

10. *London Gazette*, War Office Announcement dated 28 July 1801.

17 August and at Vimeiro on 21 August. He distinguished himself at both battles, but in particular at Vimeiro where Wellington credited him 'to have most contributed to the completest victory that could be obtained'.[11] When the army was reorganised by General Hew Dalrymple on 5 September, he was given command of a brigade in General John Hope's 2nd Division. However, General Ferguson decided to return home on family business. He sailed with Wellington on 21 September aboard the sloop HMS *Plover* and arrived in England on 4 October.[12]

General Ferguson was appointed to General John Moore's army in Spain on 17 November 1808, however, he was retained in England to testify at the Cintra Inquiry. He did not leave England until late December and arrived at Corunna in January 1809, too late to participate in the campaign and evacuated Spain with the army. He was appointed the regimental colonel of the Sicilian Regiment upon his return. He had no other military duties until the summer of 1810, when he was assigned to the British garrison in Cadiz.[13] He was initially given command of the 2nd Brigade, but due to his seniority he was made the second-in-command of the garrison. By October, his liver problems forced him to resign and return to England.

General Ferguson was promoted to lieutenant general in June 1813. He continued to have no military duties until March 1814, when General Thomas Graham requested him by name to be sent to the British Forces in the Netherlands. After the debacle at Bergen-op-Zoom on 8 and 9 March, General Graham needed replacements for four of his six generals who were killed, captured, or wounded during the battle. He wrote to Lord Bathurst on 11 March: 'if a superior officer sh'd be sent out I would beg leave to suggest Lieutenant Genl. [Sir Ronald] Ferguson an officer of the most try'd gallantry & judgement & of whose cordial cooperation I have had experienced at Cadiz.'[14] General Ferguson arrived in the Netherlands in April 1814 and was given command of the 1st Division. About the time he assumed command, Napoleon abdicated. General Ferguson served as the force's second-in-command and when General Graham was absent, as the force's commander. He returned to England in August 1814.

The six months that he spent in the Netherlands was the last time General Ferguson had an active command. He lost his regimental colonelcy in 1816, when the Sicilian Regiment was disbanded. It was not until 1828 that he was appointed colonel of the 79th Foot, which he would command until he died.

Ronald Ferguson was an MP for thirty-six years. He was initially a Whig, but after losing his seat in Kirkcaldy, he ran as a Liberal in 1830. He was best known for his liberal and reformist views, as well as being one of the 'most strenuous defenders of Scotland'.[15] He rarely voted with the government. Unlike many generals in the MP, he rarely missed sessions, was an active MP, and often spoke from the floor.[16] Twice he voted to ban flogging in the military.[17]

Ronald Ferguson married Jean Munro, the illegitimate daughter of General Sir Hector Munro, on 4 January 1798. Their marriage was short. She died in 1803 at the age of 40. They had a daughter and a son, who was an army officer. When General Munro died in

11. Warre; page 18. Ross-Lewin pages 121–2.
12. Ibid; pages 20 and 23.
13. General Order dated 19 September 1810, with the appointment backdated to 25 May 1810.
14. Bamford, Andrew. *A Bold and Ambitious Enterprise*; page 234.
15. 'Ferguson, Sir Ronald Craufurd (1773–1841), of Muirtown, Fife and 5 Bolton Street, Mdx.'
16. Ibid. During a ten-year period he gave 170 speeches in the House of Commons.
17. Ibid.

1805, he had no living heirs. His estate was passed to his daughter's family and Ronald Ferguson became very wealthy. He died in 1841 in his house at Bolton-Row in Piccadilly.

General Ferguson was well liked and admired by the junior officers under him. When he officers of the 1st Battalion 36th Foot heard that they would be in his brigade, the news was received 'with great delight.'[18] Captain William Warre, General Ferguson's ADC in Portugal, also left some vivid descriptions of him. When rumors reached them in Ireland that the brigade would probably be heading to Spain, Captain Warre was able to obtain maps. He intended 'to offer them to the General, but I fear he will not be prevailed upon to accept them. He [was] always ready to oblige or give anything away himself, but would not take a pen from anyone, if he thought he deprived him of it ... He is not amiable in his manners, but very clever, and though very good friends, we are not likely ever to be very intimate or confidential.'[19] His courage was also well known. At Vimeiro General Ferguson rode a black stallion,[20] and 'his gallantry and conduct it is almost impossible to give an idea ... We could adore Ferguson for his bravery and skill and coolness in a fire like hail about him.'[21]

General Ferguson was a capable commander and a friend of Wellington. However, he took his duties as an MP seriously and this might have impacted his military career. In 1809, when the mistress of the Duke of York was accused of selling commissions in the army, the House of Commons censured the Duke and he resigned as the Commander-in-Chief of the Army. General Ferguson voted for the censure and on 17 March 1809 gave a speech in the House of Commons on the matter. He said that the impression the scandal 'has made on my mind is, that the Duke of York is extremely culpable. Throughout the country a cloud of suspicion has been collecting, and it has settled upon his character; while that cloud remains, until it has been dispelled, my opinion is, that it is not for the honour of the Army that the chief command should remain in the hands of the Duke of York.'[22]

It was bad enough that General Ferguson broke ranks with the other military MPs by voting for censure, but he also publicly called for the Duke of York's resignation on the floor of the House of Commons. The Horse Guards did not forget this betrayal. When a general was needed to replace General Stewart, who was the Second-in-Command of the British forces in Cadiz, Lord Liverpool suggested to Sir David Dundas, the Duke of York's replacement as the Commander-in-Chief of the Army, that General Ferguson be sent, Dundas replied that 'while there were other people to choose he did not think that officer the person to select or appoint to an active situation'.[23] When a replacement for General Stewart could not be found, 'Sir David [Dundas] (I confess to my great astonishment) fixed upon ordering Ferguson, with the *intention of forcing* him to go; and I am persuaded from his manner and from the way in which he spoke of Ferguson that, so far from meaning him a kindness, Sir David really thought that he would not like the service and that he would object to it ...'[24]

General Ferguson went to Cadiz, but three months later resigned due to health reasons. He was not given any further military duties until 1814, when he was sent to the Netherlands to serve as the commander of the 1st Division of the British Forces there. He would never have an active command again.

---

18. Murchison; page 127.
19. Warre; page 6.
20. Murchison; page 128.
21. Warre; pages 18–19.
22. Cobbett; Vol. 13, page 662.
23. Letter from Colonel Henry Torrens to the Duke of York dated 29 May 1810. Ward; page 33.
24. Ibid.

Grant, Colquhoun

Date of Birth:	c. 1763
Date Commissioned:	Ensign 36th Foot: 16 September 1793 by purchase
Promotions:	Lieutenant 36th Foot: 27 May 1795 by purchase
	Lieutenant 25th Light Dragoons:[1] 26 October 1797 by exchange
	Captain 9th Light Dragoons: 29 September 1800 by purchase
	Major 28th Light Dragoons:[2] 21 February 1801 by purchase
	Lieutenant Colonel 72nd Foot: 1 May 1802 by purchase
	Lieutenant Colonel 15th Light Dragoons: 25 August 1808 by exchange[3]
	Brevet Colonel: 4 June 1811
	Major General: 4 June 1814
	Lieutenant General: 22 July 1830
Regimental Colonel:	12th Lancers: 2 June 1825–22 January 1827
	15th Hussars: 22 January 1827–20 December 1835
Major Commands under Wellington:	Temporarily commanded Hussar Brigade: 7 April–2 July 1813
	Cavalry brigade: 6 September–24 November 1813
	5th Cavalry Brigade: 31 May–30 November 1815
	3rd Cavalry Brigade AOOF: 30 November 1815–November 1818
Awards:	AGM with clasp: Sahagun & Vitoria
	KCB: 2 January 1815
	KCH: 1816
	GCH: 1831
	Waterloo Medal
	KSW
	KW 3rd Class
Thanks of Parliament:	Waterloo
Member of Parliament:	Queenborough: 1831–1832
Date of Death:	20 December 1835 at Frampton, Dorsetshire

Little is known about Colquhoun Grant before he became a soldier. His parents were Ludovick Grant of Ardchattan Argyllshire and Margaret Davidson. His father was the minister of the Ardchattan Parish and his brother was Major Alexander Grant of the HEIC Service. His date of birth is unknown, however, it was probably 1763, since his obituary states he was 72 years old when he died in 1835.

Coloquhoun Grant purchased a commission in the 36th Foot in 1793 at the age of 30. He was much older than many of his contemporaries. Upon being commissioned he joined his regiment in India. He purchased his lieutenancy in 1795 and then exchanged into the 25th Light Dragoons. He was with his regiment in the 2nd Madras Cavalry Brigade of General George Harris's army at the siege of Seringapatam from March to May 1799. Lieutenant Grant's commanding officer in the 25th Light Dragoons was Stapleton Cotton, the future Lord Combermere and commander of Wellington's cavalry

---

1. Renamed the 22nd Light Dragoons.
2. Disbanded in 1802.
3. Removed from the regiment as a general officer receiving unattached pay 1816.

n the Peninsula. In 1800, he purchased a captaincy in the 9th Light Dragoons which were stationed in Ireland.

Captain Grant was only in the 9th Light Dragoons until he purchased a majority n the 28th Light Dragoons in 1801 and when the regiment was disbanded in 1802, he purchased a lieutenant colonelcy in the 72nd Foot. On 31 August 1805 Lieutenant Colonel Grant's regiment was assigned to the Highland Brigade, commanded by General Ronald Ferguson of General David Baird's force that was sent to capture the Cape of Good Hope. The Dutch colony surrendered after a battle on 18 January 1806, where Lieutenant Colonel Grant was wounded.

Lieutenant Colonel Grant stayed with the 72nd Foot until August 1808, when he exchanged into the 15th Hussars. In October they were assigned to General John Slade's Brigade in General Baird's force that was sent to reinforce General John Moore's army in Spain. They landed in Corunna on 12 November. The regiment distinguished itself at the Battle of Sahagun on 21 December, where Lieutenant Colonel Grant was wounded again. The regiment was part of the rearguard during the retreat to Corunna in early January 1809. Rather than leave its horses to be taken by the French, the regiment destroyed all but thirty of them prior to embarking on transports to England.

The 15th Hussars embarked for Spain in October 1808 with over 750 horses. It lost 95 per cent of its horses in three months. It would spend the next four years rebuilding itself, but it would never again reach the strength it left England with in 1808.[4] On 8 February 1811, Lieutenant Colonel Grant was appointed an ADC to the Prince Regent and in June he was promoted to colonel.

In January 1813, the 15th Hussars, which formed part of the Hussar Brigade, embarked for Portugal. By February they were joined by the 10th and 18th Hussars. In late March they were still in Lisbon awaiting orders. Compounding the problem was the fact that no general was available to command them. On 7 April Wellington wrote to General Cotton, the army's cavalry commander, discussing the organisation of the cavalry: 'The hussar brigade is vacant, and is at present commanded by Col. Grant of the 15th … I must observe to you, however, that the English hussar brigade having come out as a brigade, I don't think with propriety we can break it up.'[5]

Colonel Grant was never formally appointed the commander of the Hussar Brigade but, as the senior officer, he assumed command. He led it to Morales on 2 June, where they decimated a French cavalry brigade that was acting as the rearguard. Colonel Grant's handling of the brigade was by the book. The 10th Hussars were on the left and the 18th Hussars on the right. The 15th Hussars were in the rear in support. After they broke the enemy brigade and after pursuing them for 4 kilometers, they came upon formed infantry. Colonel Grant was able to halt the 10th Hussars, but the 18th Hussars ignored the command and came running back after being hit by the French reserves. Wellington described the action as a 'gallant affair, which reflects great credit upon Major Robarts and the 10th hussars, and upon Col. Grant, under whose directions they acted.'[6] Among the British wounded was Colonel Grant.

This was a superb start for the Hussar Brigade, however, its actions at Vitoria on 21 June damned it in Wellington's eyes. The brigade was in reserve until late afternoon and in the

---

4. When it arrived in Portugal in February 1813, its strength was only 75 per cent of what it was in October 1808.

5. *WD* (enlarged ed.); Vol. 6, pages 406–7.

6. Ibid; page 516.

general advance against the retreating French, the 10th and 18th Hussars went through Vitoria while the 15th and one squadron of the 18th went around the left side of the town with Colonel Grant. There they came across the French cavalry acting as a rearguard. Colonel Grant immediately ordered a charge but they were badly outnumbered and were beaten back. The 10th and 18th Hussars arrived and captured the French baggage train. Instead of continuing to pursue the French, the 18th Hussars stopped and looted the Baggage. The regiment's junior major, James Hughes, described the chaos in a letter to his brother:

> ... the extraordinary, wild, confused & shocking scenes that took place here. We took all King Joseph's baggage & almost captured him. But the Regiment was utterly broken & fit for nothing. I could only collect a handful of men with which I advanced against the French, when we took some guns.[7]

Wellington was furious at the behavior of the 18th Hussars. He called Colonel Grant and 'expressed himself in strong terms against the 18th and desired him to state his opinion of their conduct to the officers in the plainest manner'.[8] On 26th June, Colonel Grant gathered the officers of the 18th Hussars in a field near Pamplona. He told them:

> his Lordship was very much displeased with the insubordination of the Regiment, particularly of the conduct of the men in Vitoria on the 21st. Numbers of them he saw plundering in the streets; he was likewise very much displeased with several of our officers who was [sic] there likewise, instead of being in the field, and to finish he had to inform us that his Lordship was determined if he heard any complaint against the Regiment he would immediately dismount us, and march the Regiment to the nearest sea port and embark us for England.[9]

Colonel Grant continued to command the Hussar Brigade until 2 July, when news of the latest promotions to major general arrived from England. He was too junior to be promoted and was replaced in command by General Lord Edward Somerset. Rather than staying with his regiment, Colonel Grant left for England on 6 July.[10] He went to Santander and while waiting for a ship he changed his mind. He wrote to Colonel Torrens at the Horse Guards that he wished to remain with the army. Colonel Torrens passed the news on to Wellington. Colonel Grant was appointed a colonel on the staff on 6 September and given command of General Long's brigade in September.[11] Shortly after assuming command Colonel Grant became very ill with a liver problem and word among the senior officers was that he may not live. If he did recover 'it will be necessary for him to go to England.'[12] On 24 November[13] he relinquished his command and sailed for England aboard the packet ship *Catherine*. The ship was taken by a French privateer and Colonel Grant was captured. He was released after the abdication of Napoleon and was in Bordeaux on 17 April.

---

7. Hunt; page 105.
8. Mollo; page 132.
9. Hunt; page 110.
10. Glover, Gareth (ed.); *From Corunna to Waterloo*, page 159.
11. General Order, 6 September 1813, with the appointment backdated to 25 August 1813.
12. Vivian; page 138.
13. General Order, 24 November 1813.

Upon returning to England Colonel Grant was placed on the staff of the Northern District Ireland. In June he was promoted to major general. After Napoleon escaped from Elba in March 1815, the British began to send troops to the Netherlands. Wellington was informed on 15 April 1815 that General Grant was appointed on his staff and coming from Ireland with three cavalry regiments.[14] He was confirmed on the staff on 29 April[15] and assigned to command the 5th Cavalry Brigade on 31 May.[16] On 30 May he was appointed the Groom of the Bedchamber to the Duke of Cumberland.[17]

During the Battle of Waterloo, General Grant and his brigade was stationed on the British right, in the vicinity of Hougomount. He wore the uniform of the 15th Hussars and rode a chestnut horse. The brigade was heavily engaged and took 28 per cent casualties. Of the brigade's seven senior officers, two were killed and four wounded. General Grant was one of the wounded and had five horses shot or killed under him.

After Waterloo, General Grant took part in the British invasion of France. He was retained on the staff of the AOOF on 30 November 1815 and given command of the 3rd Cavalry Brigade. He commanded it until November 1818, when the army was disbanded. In 1820 he was appointed the commander of the Leinster District and remained on the Irish Staff until 1826. He became the regimental colonel of the 12th Lancers in 1825 and then of his old regiment, the 15th Hussars, in 1827.

General Grant ran for Parliament in 1830, but dropped out of the race when it became too expensive. He ran again in 1831 and won as an MP for Queenborough. He was an anti-reformist Tory who said the only reason he ran was 'to express his hostility to reform'.[18] He also voted against an enquiry into corporal punishment in the army. He did not run for re-election in 1832, but ran unsuccessfully for the seat for Poole in 1835.[19]

Colquhoun Grant married Marcia Richards on 7 August 1810. They had two daughters and a son. In 1833 he inherited the estate of his wife's sister's husband, at Frampton in Dorsetshire. He died there in 1835 from dropsy in the chest, better known as pulmonary edema.[20]

Colquhoun Grant was tall and had a black moustache. When he first reported to Wellington at the Army HQ in Freneda, the meeting was in a room with a low ceiling, so low that General Grant 'could hardly stand upright in it.'[21] His brigade major in the Peninsula was Lieutenant Charles Jones, 'a small man with fox-red hair, a red moustache and red whiskers, and he also wore a red shako. It was very funny to see him galloping behind the tall black-whiskered general who wore an enormous three-cornered hat with a long fluttering feather; and from that day those two were never spoken of in the brigade except as the black giant and the red dwarf'.[22]

Colonel Grant's efforts to discipline and train the Hussar Brigade was widely resented by its officers. The diaries and letters home reflected their growing hatred. He was rarely mentioned except in a negative way. After Vitoria, rumors abounded that the brigade

14. *WSD*; Vol. 10, pages 78–9.
15. General Order, 29 April 1815.
16. General Order, 31 May 1815.
17. Prince Ernest Duke of Cumberland, son of King George III and later King Ernest Augustus of Hanover. He was regimental colonel of the 15th Light Dragoons.
18. 'Grant, Sir Colquhoun (1763–1835).'
19. Ibid.
20. Ibid.
21. Hunt; page 80.
22. Ibid; page 81.

was to be disbanded and Colonel Grant fired. One officer wrote that 'Wellington is not at all pleased with Colonel Grant's manoeuvres at the Battle of Vitoria; they all allow this officer to be possessed of courage and resolution, but all say he wants judgement.'[23] When word reached the 18th Hussars that Colonel Grant was being replaced, the same officer wrote, 'Grant went to Lord Wellington … to remonstrate with him and Lord Wellington gave him leave to go back to England immediately, which Grant accepted … God be thanked we have got rid of the Black Giant.'[24] When news of his capture by the French reached the regiment, Major Edwin Griffith, who commanded the 15th Hussars while Colonel Grant commanded the Hussar Brigade, wrote home: 'was ever anything so delightful as the capture of the little *Catherine*! Grant was onboard, & his having been taken prisoner gives us the Commanding officer whom I should have from the world.'[25]

In addition to the less than flattering nickname, which was picked up by officers in other brigades,[26] one particularly nasty piece of gossip also made the rounds. Possibly in an attempt to justify their own looting, word spread that Colonel Grant also received his share of the plunder after Vitoria. Captain William Bragge, of the 3rd Dragoon Guards, wrote home: 'I was amidst all the Carriages the next Morning and made nothing. Lots of Ladies' Jewels Lace Dresses, some of which you will probably see round Mrs. Grant at Weymouth, as I hear the Col was active.'[27]

The speculation by his subordinates on why Colonel Grant was removed from command of the Hussar Brigade was completely wrong. The real reason was simple. On 4 June 1813 there was a general brevet promoting a number of colonels, serving in the Peninsula, to the rank of major general. Unfortunately Colonel Grant was not promoted and he could not be kept in command of the brigade with so many others who were senior to him needing a command. Wellington wrote to Colonel Grant on 2 July 1813, the same day the general order was written, appointing the new general to command of the Hussar Brigade:

> Sir S. Cotton is arrived, and a new division of cavalry into brigades has been made; and I am sorry to tell you that it is not in my power at present to give you command of a brigade. I assure you, however, that I regret these circumstances very particularly, and I hope I shall soon be able to make an arrangement which will place you permanently in a situation which you have already filled with advantage to the public and credit to yourself.[28]

The same day he wrote to Colonel Grant, Wellington wrote to Colonel Torrens at the Horse Guards suggesting the recall of another cavalry brigade commander and put forward Colonel Grant as his replacement: 'this would give Grant of the 15th, a brigade, of which he is deserving.'[29]

Wellington was true to his word and Colonel Grant was given command of General Long's brigade two months later. A further indicator of Wellington's regard for Colonel Grant's abilities was that he gave him command of the 5th Cavalry Brigade at Waterloo and the 3rd Cavalry Brigade in the AOOF.

---

23. Hunt; page 114.
24. Mollo; page 136.
25. Glover, Gareth (ed.); *From Corunna to Waterloo*, page 204.
26. Bragge; page 107.
27. Ibid; page 116.
28. *WD* (enlarged ed.); Vol. 6, page 571.
29. Ibid; page 575.

Halkett, Colin

Date of Birth:	7 September 1774 at Venloo, the Netherlands
Dutch Service:	Cadet Dutch Service: 1792
	Ensign & Lieutenant 2nd Battalion Dutch Foot Guards: 12 March 1792
	Lieutenant & Captain 1st Battalion Dutch Foot Guards: 1792[1]
British Service:	Cornet Lanark & Dumbarton Fencible Cavalry:[2] 1798 without purchase[3]
	Ensign 3rd Foot:[4] 16 January 1799 appointed
	Captain 2nd Dutch Light Infantry:[5] 1800
	Major German Levies:[6] 1803
	Lieutenant Colonel 2nd Light Battalion KGL: 17 November 1803
	Brevet Colonel: 1 January 1812
	Brigadier General on the Staff: 25 March 1814
	Major General: 4 June 1814
	Lieutenant General: 22 July 1830
	General: 9 November 1846
Regimental Colonel:	2nd Light Battalion, KGL: 9 February 1805–1 January 1812[7]
	2nd Light Battalion, KGL: 1 January 1812–24 February 1816
	95th Foot: 1 December 1823–21 September 1829
	71st Foot: 21 September 1829–28 March 1838
	31st Foot: 28 March 1838–12 July 1847
	45th Foot: 12 July 1847–24 September 1856
Major Commands under Wellington:	Temporarily commanded Brigade 7th Division: October 1811–6 December 1812
	Temporarily command Brigade KGL 1st Division: 6 May–30 October 1813
	5th Brigade: 11 April–18 July 1815
Awards:	AGC: Albuera, Salamanca, Vitoria & Nive
	Waterloo Medal
	KCB: 2 January 1815
	GCB: 30 December 1847
	KCH: 1815
	GCH 1820
	KW 3rd Class
	KCMJ
	KTS
Thanks of Parliament:	Waterloo
Date of Death:	24 September 1856 in his residence at the Chelsea Hospital

1. Retired 27 April 1795.
2. Disbanded 1799.
3. *London Gazette*; War Office Announcement dated 4 December 1798.
4. Resigned his commission in the army, c. 14 February 1800.
5. In British pay and disbanded 1802.
6. Became King's German Legion.
7. Depending on his rank, the KGL battalions had either a lieutenant colonel commandant or colonel commandant. Lieutenant Colonel Halkett was the lieutenant colonel commandant until he was promoted to colonel in 1812. He then became the colonel commandant of the battalion.

Colin Halkett was born in 1774 in the Netherlands. His parents were Major General Frederick Halkett of Hall Hill in Fifeshire and Georgina Seton. At the time of his birth, Colin's father was the commander of the Scots Brigade in Dutch service. His younger brother was General Hugh von Halkett of the Hanoverian Service. Colin entered Dutch service as a Cadet in 1792, but was commissioned shortly afterwards in the Dutch Foot Guards. In September 1792 he was promoted to captain and remained in the regiment until 1795, when he retired. He entered the British Army in 1798 as a cornet in the Lanark & Dumbarton Fencible Cavalry. In January 1799 he was appointed an ensign in the 3rd Foot.

It is possible that Ensign Halkett never served with either regiment.[8] In February 1800, Dutch soldiers loyal to the Prince of Orange were taken into British service. Ensign Halkett resigned his British commission and was appointed a captain in the 2nd Dutch Light Infantry Battalion. He served with them until 1802 when the Peace of Amiens was declared and the battalion was disbanded. During the two years he was with the Dutch, he was promoted to major. He was unemployed until August 1803 when he was given permission by the British Government to recruit soldiers from the disbanded Hanoverian Army to form a light battalion. Major Halkett was quite successful. In November they became the 2nd KGL Light Battalion and he, a newly promoted lieutenant colonel, was its commander.

Lieutenant Colonel Halkett led the 2nd KGL Light Battalion for the next eleven years. Their first deployment was with the British Expedition to northern Germany in November 1805, but by February they were back in England. In May they sailed for Ireland, where they were stationed in Middleton. They were there for two years when they received orders to join the expedition to Copenhagen. Lieutenant Colonel Halkett and three companies embarked on the *Northumberland* and on 30 May they were shipwrecked on the Runnell Stone off of Land's End. They were rescued but lost their baggage and weapons. They returned to England in December 1807.

In April 1808, Lieutenant Colonel Halkett and his battalion were in Colonel Charles Alten's brigade of General Edward Paget's 3rd Division of General John Moore's force being formed to help Sweden. After the army arrived in Sweden, the Swedish King declined their assistance and it left Sweden on 4 July. The army was back in Portsmouth by 21 July. It was then decided to send General Moore's force to reinforce the army in Portugal. It arrived on 24 August and landed at Maceira Bay. Lieutenant Colonel Halkett's battalion remained in Colonel Alten's brigade, but when the army commander reorganised his army on 5 September, the brigade was assigned to General Paget's Advance Corps. In October the army in Portugal was divided into a field army under General Moore for service in Spain and a garrison to stay in Portugal. Lieutenant Colonel Halkett's battalion was selected to join the field army and remained assigned to General Alten's brigade in General Paget's division.[9] While at Salamanca, on 1 December 1808 the brigade was removed from General Paget's division and became an independent Flank Brigade. It remained an independent brigade during the retreat to Corunna. However, the brigade, along with Colonel Robert Craufurd's Flank Brigade, was detached to Vigo and evacuated from there, in January 1809. Lieutenant Colonel Halkett temporarily

---

8. *DNB*; Vol. 14, page 50.
9. General Order, 8 October 1808.

commanded General Alten's brigade as General Moore had placed General Alten in command of the two Flank Brigades during the retreat on 31 December.

After landing in England in late January, Lieutenant Colonel Halkett spent the next six months rebuilding his battalion. In July 1809, they were once again placed in General Alten's brigade and they were assigned to General James Lord Rosslyn's Light Corps that was part of the British Expedition to Walcheren. The 2nd KGL Light Battalion saw little action, but were struck heavily by Walcheren Fever. By November it could only muster 45 per cent of its strength. By Christmas they were back in England and would spend the next fifteen months recovering from the debilitating effects of the fever.

In March 1811, Lieutenant Colonel Halkett and his battalion were sent to the Peninsula. Once again it was in General Alten's brigade. Although the brigade was assigned to the 7th Division on 5 March 1811, it did not join it until after the Battle of Albuera in May 1811. At Albuera, General Alten's brigade held the village for much of the battle. In October 1811 Lieutenant Colonel Halkett was given temporary command of General Alten's brigade. In January 1812 he was promoted to colonel. He led the brigade throughout the campaigns of 1812, including at the Battle of Salamanca on 22 July. He distinguished himself on 23 October at Venta del Pozo during the retreat to the Portuguese border. It was the steadfastness of his brigade that prevented the army's rearguard from being destroyed by the pursuing French.

Lieutenant Colonel Halkett was rewarded for his service by being appointed a colonel on the staff on 6 December 1812. However, he was too junior to continue in command of the brigade. It was disbanded and he and both of its battalions were transferred to General Low's brigade in the 1st Division. Although they were assigned to General Low's brigade, the KGL Light Battalions operated as a separate unit under Colonel Halkett within the KGL Brigade of the 1st Division. In early May, Colonel Halkett assumed temporary command of the KGL Brigade, which consisted of three line battalions and two light battalions. He led the brigade at Vitoria on 21 May 1813 and throughout the summer. In October he was replaced in command by General Henry de Hinuber and he reverted back to commanding the light battalions.

Colonel Halkett led the KGL Light Battalions during much of the winter campaign of 1814. In March 1814 he was sent to the British force in the Netherlands as a replacement for many of the generals who were killed or captured at the assault on Bergen-op-Zoom. He was appointed a brigadier on the staff of the Army and commanded the 3rd Brigade of the 2nd Division. After peace was declared in April 1814, he continued to command the 3rd Brigade of the 2nd Division of the Subsidiary Army in the Netherlands. In June he was promoted to major general. When Napoleon escaped from Elba in March 1815, Wellington assumed command of the Anglo-Allied Army in the Netherlands. General Halkett was placed on the staff of Wellington's army and in April he was appointed to command the 5th Brigade in General Alten's 3rd Division.

At Quatre Bras on 16 June, the 5th Brigade was on the right of the army, between the Bois de Bossu and the Charleroi Road. General Halkett was in front of the position when he saw French cuirassiers massing for an attack. He immediately ordered his brigade into square, however, the Prince of Orange[10] countermanded his order to the 69th Foot and

---

10. Prince William, the Hereditary Prince of Orange, later King William II of the Netherlands. He was a general in the British Army.

they were ridden down. The brigade repulsed several cavalry charges and by the end of the battle had taken 346 casualties, about 15 per cent of its strength.

At Waterloo, General Halkett and his brigade were on the right of the British line, about a kilometer behind Hougoumont. They spent most of the day in two large squares and when they were not being charged by French cavalry, they were being shelled by French artillery. By the end of the battle the brigade had taken another 781 casualties, about 40 per cent of its strength at the beginning of the battle. In three days, the brigade had lost 50 per cent of its men.

By 7 p.m. General Halkett was talking with Major Dawson Kelly when a musket ball entered his mouth, breaking his palate and passing out of his cheek. He fell from his horse and had to be evacuated to the rear. It was his fourth wound of the day. He had been shot in the thigh and the heel, and had been bruised on the back of the neck by a spent ball.[11] General Halkett spent the rest of 1815 in Brussels recovering from his wounds. He was replaced in command of his brigade in July and was not given another command when the army was broken up in November 1815.

When the KGL was disbanded and incorporated into the Hanoverian Service in 1816 many of its officers joined the newly formed Hanoverian Army. Unlike most of the Hanoverian officers who had joined the KGL and received only temporary rank in the British Army, General Halkett had been appointed to the KGL with permanent rank in the British Army. He chose to stay in the British Army. However, in 1820 he was carried on the Hanoverian Unemployed List with the rank of lieutenant general.

In 1820, General Halkett was appointed to the Consolidated Board of General Officers and was a member of its five-man Acting Committee that year. He resigned from the Acting Committee the next year, probably because he was appointed the Lieutenant Governor of Jersey on 23 July 1821. He was promoted to lieutenant general in July 1830. He remained in Jersey until 26 November 1830. On 17 July 1831 he was appointed the Commander-in-Chief of the Bombay Presidency in India. He was there from 31 January 1832 until October 1833. Upon returning to England he had no military duties other than a member of the Consolidated Board of General Officers and those of the regimental colonel of the 71st, 31st, and then the 45th Foot. On 18 May 1849, General Halkett was appointed the Lieutenant Governor of the Royal Hospital at Chelsea. On 26 November 1849, upon the death of General Sir George Anson, he became its governor. He held the command until his death.

Colin Halkett married Letitia Tyler, the widow of Captain Tyler (RA) on 12 July 1820 in London. They had three daughters and a son, who became an army officer. General Halkett died on 24 September 1856 at a few minutes before 11 a.m. from complications of a severe attack of the gout. He was buried in the Chelsea Hospital Cemetery.[12]

General Halkett led from the front and inspired his men by personal example. At Quatre Bras, the 33rd Foot began to waiver under intense artillery fire and men were beginning to flee. General Halkett modestly wrote twenty-four years later about the incident:

> The 33rd I rode to the moment I could absent myself from the front, and I recollect I had some difficulty in getting them to the order they ought to have remained in,

---

11. Siborne; page 339. *United Services Magazine*; 1856, Part 3, page 331. Morris; page 81.
12. *United Services Magazine*; 1856, Part 3, page 331.

and I took one of their Colours and advanced to the front with it, which I think had the desired effect, and soon got them into the order they ought *never* to have lost. They then appeared steady and I left them.[13]

At Waterloo, he was in the square formed by the 30th and 73rd Foot when Wellington took shelter in it from the charging French cavalry. Legend has it Wellington said:

Well Halket, [*sic*] how do you get on?' The general replied, 'My Lord, we are dreadfully cut up; can you not relieve us for a little while?' 'Impossible', said the Duke. 'Very well, my Lord', said the general; 'we'll stand till the last man falls!'[14] He then turned to the men in the square and '... made an elegant speech to us in the middle of the action, which was answered, by the reiterated shouts of our brave fellows, 'Let's charge your honour, we'll stick it to them.[15]

Although there is little written evidence of what Wellington thought of General Halkett's abilities, his actions speak volumes. Wellington kept him as a brigade commander for two months in 1811 and for all of 1812, when he was initially only a lieutenant colonel and then one of the most junior colonels in the army. By early December 1812, there were enough senior officers available that Wellington could not keep him in command of a brigade. Wellington's solution was to disband his brigade and assign him and the two battalions to a KGL Brigade in another division. Although not officially a brigade, Colonel Halkett commanded the two light battalions for five months when, at the beginning of the Vitoria Campaign, he was place in temporary command of the KGL Brigade and its five battalions. He would command it for another five months. When replacement brigade commanders were needed in the Netherlands in March 1814, Colonel Halkett, still one of the most junior colonels in Wellington's army, was the one Wellington chose to go. During his many months as a brigade commander, General Halkett never caused Wellington to regret giving him command.

---

13. Siborne; page 324.
14. Morris; page 78.
15. Glover, Gareth; *Waterloo Archive*, Vol. 1, page 163.

Hay, Andrew

Date of Birth:	1762
Date Commissioned:	Ensign 1st Foot: 6 December 1779 without purchase
Promotions:	Lieutenant 1st Foot: 21 July 1781 without purchase
	Captain 88th Foot:[1] 24 January 1783 without purchase
	Captain 1st Foot: 17 April 1784 appointed
	Major 129th Foot:[2] 1 September 1794 without purchase
	Major 93rd Foot:[3] 9 December 1795 appointed
	Major 73rd Foot: 1803 appointed[4]
	Brevet Lieutenant Colonel: 1 January 1800[5]
	Lieutenant Colonel 16th Battalion of Reserve: 1803[6] without purchase
	Lieutenant Colonel 72nd Foot: 1 December 1804[7] appointed
	Lieutenant Colonel 1st Foot: 19 March 1807 by exchange
	Temporary Colonel:[8] 29 December 1798
	Brevet Colonel: 25 April 1808
	Brigadier General on the Staff: 6 August 1810–1811
	Major General: 4 June 1811
Regimental Colonel:	Duke of York's Own Banffshire Fencibles: 29 December 1798–10 May 1802
	York Chasseurs: 5 November 1813–14 April 1814
Major Commands under Wellington:	Brigade 5th Division: 30 September 1810–14 April 1814
	Temporarily commanded 5th Division: c. 15 November–c. 1 December 1811; January–April 1813, September–October 1813, and November 1813–February 1814
Awards:	AGC: Corunna, Vitoria, San Sebastian & Nive
Thanks of Parliament:	Badajoz & San Sebastian
Date of Death:	14 April 1814, Bayonne, France

Andrew Hay was born in 1762, the son of George Hay of Carnousie House, Forglen, Banffshire and Margaret Sinclair. He was commissioned as an ensign in the 1st Foot in 1779. Over the next twenty-five years he would be on half-pay for almost ten years! Ensign Hay was promoted to lieutenant in 1781 and in 1783 was appointed a captain in the 88th Foot. That same year, the 88th Foot was disbanded and he went on half-pay. He remained on half-pay until April 1784, when he was appointed as a captain in the 1st Foot. Captain Hay stayed with the 1st Foot until January 1787 when he exchanged to

1. Disbanded 1783.
2. Disbanded 1796.
3. Disbanded 1796.
4. *London Gazette*; War Office Announcement dated 19 July 1803.
5. Backdated in 1805 to 1 January 1798.
6. *London Gazette*; War Office Announcement dated 13 September 1803. It was renamed the 16th Garrison Battalion on 30 October 1804.
7. *London Gazette*; War Office Announcement on 8 December 1804. Shown in army lists as 1 December 1802. This is clearly an error that was not corrected.
8. Colonel of a Fencible Regiment that was disbanded 1802.

half-pay captain of the disbanded 72nd Foot. He remained on half-pay until 1794, when he was appointed a major in the 129th Foot which had been raised the year before. Major Hay was appointed a major in the 93rd Foot in 1795, which was disbanded the following year. According to the Army List, despite the disbanding of his regiment Major Hay was still carried on the regimental rolls and thus received his full pay. He had no regimental duties. Major Hay remained unemployed until 1798, when he was placed on half-pay.

While on half-pay in 1798, Major Hay raised a regiment of fencible infantry, the Duke of York's Own Banffshire Fencibles. The letter of service was dated 26 July 1798 and Major Hay was promoted to temporary colonel[9] in the army as its regimental colonel in December 1798. The regiment was stationed on Guernsey and fought in Ireland during the Rebellion. In January 1800 he was promoted to brevet lieutenant colonel in the army. In May the regiment volunteered for overseas service in Gibraltar where it remained until it returned home and was disbanded at Gosport on 10 May 1802. Colonel Hay lost his temporary rank of colonel when the regiment was disbanded and again showed in the army lists as a half-pay major, despite being a brevet lieutenant colonel of the disbanded 93rd Foot.

Major Hay remained on half-pay until 1803, when he was appointed a major in the 73rd Foot. The same year he was promoted to lieutenant colonel and appointed the commander of the 16th Battalion of Reserve. In December 1804, he was transferred to the newly raised 2nd Battalion of the 72nd Foot, which was formed from soldiers who were in the army reserve in Scotland. He commanded the battalion until March 1807, when he exchanged into the 1st Foot and became the commander of its 4th Battalion. By March 1808 Lieutenant Colonel Hay commanded the 3rd Battalion and was promoted to colonel in April.

In the summer of 1808, General Hay's 3rd Battalion 1st Foot was selected to join a force under General David Baird being organised to reinforce the British Army in Spain. The battalion was in General John Slade's brigade at Cork in September. Later that month, General Slade was appointed to command a cavalry brigade and General Coote Manningham took command of the brigade. General Baird's force arrived in Corunna on 13 October and began landing on the 26th. In early November it was organised in two temporary divisions for the advance to link up with General John Moore's army. General Manningham commanded the 2nd Division and Colonel Hay took command of his brigade. Colonel Hay resumed command of his battalion when the two divisions united with General Moore and the army was reorganised again. General Manningham's brigade was assigned to the 1st Division on 20 December. The battalion fought at the Battle of Corunna on 16 January 1809 and was evacuated home with the army. Colonel Hay was wounded while in Spain, but where or when is not known.[10]

9. Field officers of the fencibles were listed in the army lists of the period, but they ranked under regular army officers when they served together. Officers of the Fencible Regiments in 1795 were given precedence of the Militia, ranking with the army, according to their commissions except for Embodied militia where they rank according to dates of commission. On 25 July 1795, 'officers of fencibles, militia, yeoman cavalry and volunteer corps shall rank together according to date of their respective commission; the officer of regular corps to take precedence of and command the officer of equal degree of all others. However, fencible officers commissioned on or before 25 July 1798 would continue to rank with officers of the regular army of equal degree according to the dates of their commissions except when acting together.' Scobie; page 4.

10. *Army List*; March 1809, page 105.

Colonel Hay and his battalion were in England for about six months when they were ordered to Portsmouth to join the army being formed for the expedition to the Low Countries.[11] He was given temporary command of General Thomas Graham's brigade in the 1st Division on Walcheren when he was appointed the commander of the 1st Division. Colonel Hay and his brigade were selected to remain as part of the garrison of Walcheren after the evacuation of the army in September. They were among the last troops to leave Walcheren in late December.

After returning to England Colonel Hay and the 1st Foot spent the next two months recruiting back to strength. Colonel Hay was placed on the staff of Wellington's army in Portugal as a brigadier general in September 1810.[12] On 30 September he was appointed the commander of a brigade in the newly formed 5th Division.[13] His brigade included his old battalion, the 3rd Battalion 1st Foot. Two of the brigade's battalions had served on Walcheren and were still too sickly for active campaigning. It was not until the next spring did the brigade find itself close to the enemy. It was at Sabugal on 3 April and at Fuentes de Oñoro on 1–3 May. At both battles, the brigade was in reserve and saw little action. In June he was promoted to major general.

In July 1811, General Hay requested permission to go to England and settle his affairs.[14] His request was denied for the rest of the year. He was at the sieges of Ciudad Rodrigo and Badajoz in 1812, but did not take part in the assaults. His request for leave was finally approved in early June 1812. General Hay did not return to the Peninsula for six months and missed the Battle of Salamanca, the liberation of Madrid, and the retreat back to Portugal. Almost immediately after his return, General Hay was appointed the temporary commander of the 5th Division and commanded them until April. He led his brigade in the Vitoria Campaign during the summer of 1813. Lieutenant Colonel John Cameron, one of General Hay's battalion commanders,[15] wrote in his diary that General Hay was seriously wounded in the attack on Gamarra Mayor[16] during the Battle of Vitoria on 21 May 1813, yet it was never mentioned in Wellington's official dispatch of the battle. If he had been wounded, it did not incapacitate him for long.

By mid-July General Hay was in the trenches around San Sebastian and led his brigade in the failed assault on the city on 25 July. He led them again in the final assault on 31 August. General Hay took temporary commanded of the 5th Division after its commander was seriously wounded in the assault on 31 August. He led it at the crossing of the Bidossoa River on 7 October. In early November, General John Oswald took command of the division and General Hay returned to commanding his brigade, including at Nivelle on 10 November. By early December, he was again in temporary command of the 5th Division and led it at Nive on 9–11 December. Two days later, General Charles Colville took command of the division. Although General Colville was appointed the commander of the 5th Division on 13 December, he was plagued with rheumatism and spent the next two months convalescing in St Jean de Luz. General Hay continued to temporarily command the division while in winter quarters. General Colville assumed active command of the division in late February, just before the crossing of the Adour.[17]

---

11. Modern-day Holland and Belgium.
12. General Order, 20 September 1810, to date from 6 August.
13. General Order, 30 September 1810.
14. *WD* (enlarged ed.); Vol. 5, page 185.
15. He commanded the 1st Battalion 9th Foot.
16. Cameron, James; page 46.
17. Colville; pages 162–7.

In late February 1814, General Hay and his brigade were attached to the 1st Division for the crossing of the Adour River and the investment of the Citadel of Bayonne. They crossed the river on 25 February and would remain on the right bank of the river. On 14 April, General Hay was in charge of all the outposts when the French sortied from the citadel at 3 a.m. and took them by surprised. He was killed rallying his troops.

Andrew Hay married Elizabeth Robinson on 2 April 1784. They had three sons and four daughters. Three days before he was killed at Bayonne, his wife and three of his daughters had arrived at his headquarters, after travelling overland from Lisbon.[18] He was buried in the churchyard of St Etienne, France but re-interred in the Guards Cemetery in Bayonne in 1868. Mrs Hay received a £300 pension and each of his six surviving children received a £100 pension.[19]

General Hay led from the front and paid for it with his life at Bayonne. When the church of St Etienne fell to the French, 'General Hay met the men running back from it, and was stopping and leading them on again, saying he would show them how to defend the church, when he was killed.'[20] Two of his three ADCs were also killed in action: In addition to his son Major George Hay, who was mortally wounded at Vitoria in 1813, he lost Captain James Stewart, 1st Foot, who was killed during the siege of San Sebastian on 31 August 1813.[21]

As a battalion commander, Colonel Hay was a strict disciplinarian. In the spring of 1809 he was the president of a court-martial where the soldier was found guilty of being intoxicated and striking a sergeant in another battalion. The sentence was 800 lashes. 'The man received 775 lashes without so much as asking for a drink of water. He then ordered him to be taken down and addressing the 2 battalions, or the man, he says "Now Sir, I would sooner flog you for giving insolence to a Lance Corporal than for striking an officer, for that is the link in the chain by which the whole army is fastened."'[22] In the following summer, half his battalion was aboard the HMS *Eagle*. The soldiers believed that it was against regulations for them to be flogged with the naval cat-o-nine tails. They soon found out differently:

A Corporal ... having a dispute with one of the Midshipmen, got reported to Captain Rowley of the *Eagle*, who ordered a parade, read a Section of the Articles of War against mutiny and desertion, tied him up to a grating, and served him out with 3 dozen lashes, and the loss of his stripes. The poor Corporal, considering himself not fairly dealt with, wrote to Col Hay in the *Revenge*, stating his grievance and particularly dwelt on being punished with sailors' cats. The Col takes a boat and over the *Eagle* he goes and acquaints the Captain with his errand, when a parade was ordered. The Col taking out the ex-Corporal's letter stated, 'So, Sir ... you have written to me complaining of being punished with sailors' cats and by god, if you do not behave better in future, I will hang you with sailors' ropes.'[23]

18. Gomm; page 336.
19. *Journals of the House of Commons*; Vol. 70, page 547.
20. Larpent; Vol. 3, pages 200–201.
21. Frazer; page 248. Hay; Vol. 2, page 262.
22. Douglas; page 5.
23. Ibid; page 6.

General Hay cared for his men and looked after their health on campaign and often joked with them. During a lull in the Battle of Fuentes de Oñoro he 'gave us a treat by allowing us to take off our accoutrements and clothes for the purpose of de-lousing as the weather was uncommonly warm, and not having had our clothes off for many days and nights, we were pretty well stocked with the grey horse. The general, taking off his shirt and twining [*sic*] it exclaimed "I'll put them a day's march in the rear." 'Twas a regular and standing order that no man was to be seen de-lousing himself within 200 yards of the lines. Thus you see what attention was paid to the cleanliness and comfort of the men.'[24] After Vitoria, his brigade had not been re-supplied with food so some of his soldiers were foraging:

> One house was occupied by the General Officers and their staff. Yet this protection was not proof against hunger. One house was occupied by General Hay … Into this house the prowling wolves entered, and finding some wheat and flour, a light became necessary. But the struggle was so severe as to who would get most that the light was unheeded and, making contact with some rubbish, the house was in flames in a few minutes. The old general, running out, exclaims 'What would I think of it but my own Regiment to set fire to the house over my head.' However, house or no house, the point in question was the belly.[25]

During the siege of San Sebastian he ensured that arrangements were made to take care of casualties prior to the costly assault on 25 July.[26]

Despite being known for looking after the welfare of his troops, the soldiers did not like General Hay, mostly because of his strict discipline. It is difficult to determine what the junior officers thought, since so few of them mentioned him. Lieutenant William Swabey of the Royal Horse Artillery complained that General Hay 'permitted me last year to sleep, wet as I was, in my clothes without offering me a blanket.'[27] A modern author uses the quote to conclude that General Hay was unpopular in the army.[28] Yet the entry in Lieutenant Swabey's diary about the incident has no comment about his dislike of General Hay. 'I went to dine with General Hay and was obliged to sit all the day in my wet things, my saddle-bags, in which I had a change, being quite wet. I had this night neither bed or blanket, and was obliged to lay my head on my wet saddle bags, but still I slept soundly and felt no inconvenience'.[29] In the next entry in his diary Lieutenant Swabey states he had breakfast with the general. Lieutenant Gomm of the 9th Foot described him in a letter as 'the man who had so often commanded us on fortunate occasions, and for whom I had so high a respect and regard'.[30]

Without a doubt General Hay was at odds with some of his fellow generals. Camp gossip told of a heated argument with General Dunlop at Sabugal in April 1811.[31] He was despised by General Frederick Robinson, who wrote to his wife on 22 September 1813

---

24. Ibid; pages 33–4.
25. Ibid; pages 74–5.
26. Frazer; pages 244–5.
27. Swabey; page 179.
28. Glover, Michael; *Wellington as Military Commander*, page 199.
29. Ibid; page 49.
30. Gomm; page 336.
31. For more information see the entry for General James Dunlop.

bout the fall of San Sebastian: 'Genl Hay…is a fool, and I verily believe, with many others n my side, an arrant [*sic*] coward. That he is a paltry plundering old wretch is established eyond doubt. That he is no officer is as clear, and that he wants spirit is firmly believed. rgo he ought not to be a General.'[32] What sparked General Robinson's comments was nost likely a belief that all the credit for the storming of San Sebastian went to General Iay's brigade, even though it was General Robinson's brigade which took 80 per cent nore casualties and were first into the breach. During the assault General Robinson iad been seriously wounded in the face and possibly was still feeling the effects of the vound when he wrote the letter. Others felt differently. General Kenneth Howard, the :ommander of the 1st Division, to which General Hay's brigade was attached at Bayonne n April 1814, wrote, 'In Major-General Hay, who was well known to you, His Majesty's ervice has lost a most zealous and able officer, who has served a considerable time in this army with great distinction.'[33]

Wellington wrote a letter of complaint on 5 February 1814 to General Colville, the :ommander of the 5th Division. He was livid about General Hay's handling of the elegraph network for the division while General Hay temporarily commanded the livision. In it Wellington complained that he was instructed to choose an officer to uperintend the telegraph for the division and yet chose an officer

known to him to be so stupid as to be unfit to be trusted in any way … I shall also be obliged to you if you will inform Major Gen. Hay, that when I call upon a General officer to recommend an officer to fill a station in the public service, I mean that he should recommend one fit to perform some duty, and not one so stupid as to be unable to comprehend that which he is to perform; who is recommended only because he is a favorite with such General officer. We have not yet been able to pass one message from the right to the left of the army, on account of the stupidity of the officer …[34]

Despite the opinions expressed by others and writing this letter, there is no evidence that Wellington wished for General Hay's recall and he remained with the army until his death. Wellington wrote to Lord Liverpool on 18 May 1814, forwarding a letter from Mrs Hay asking for some provision for her family. Wellington added his own support of the request, writing 'of my testimony of Gen. Hay's merits as an officer …'.[35]

---

32. Atkinson; page 168.
33. *WD*; Vol. 11, page 663.
34. *WD* (enlarged ed.); Vol. 7, pages 303–4. Names and division were suppressed in the published letter.
35. Ibid; page 490.

Hinuber, Henry de

Date of Birth:	25 January 1767 in London
Hanover Service:	Cadet Foot Guards Regiment: April 1781
	Ensign 15th Infantry Regiment: 1 July 1781
	Lieutenant 15th Infantry Regiment: 27 November 1781
	Captain 14th Infantry Regiment:[1] 6 April 1788
	Major 6th Infantry Regiment: 26 October 1798
	Major General: 1816[2]
	Lieutenant General: 17 April 1818
British Service:[3]	Major 1st Line Battalion KGL: 17 November 1803
	Lieutenant Colonel 3rd Line Battalion KGL: 16 June 1804
	Colonel: 9 July 1805
	Major General: 4 June 1811[4]
	Lieutenant General: 12 August 1819
Regimental Colonel:	3rd Line Battalion KGL: 9 July 1805–24 February 1816[5]
	5th Hanoverian Infantry Regiment: 1 March 1816–2 December 1833
Major Commands under Wellington:	KGL Brigade 1st Division: 30 October 1813–April 1814
	4th Division: 11 April–28 April 1815
Awards:	AGM: Nive
	KCB (Honourary): 2 January 1815
	KCH: 1815
Thanks of Parliament:	Waterloo
Date of Death:	2 December 1833, Frankfurt am Main

Henry de Hinuber's real name was Eduard Christoph Heinrich von Hinüber. While in British service he went by Henry de Hinuber. His family and friends also called him Harry.

Henry de Hinuber was born in 1767 in London to Carl Heinrich von Hinuber and Margarethe Ludovica von Reiche. His father was the German tutor of the children of King George II. Henry lived in London until he was 10 or 12, when he was sent to live with his uncle in Hanover in order to receive a German education.[6] He was fluent in English.

In April 1781, Henry de Hinuber became a cadet in the Hanoverian Foot Guards. Three months later he was commissioned an ensign in the 15th Infantry Regiment. That same month the regiment received orders that they would be going to India to reinforce the British Army there. After seven months of training in both Hanover and England, they sailed in March 1782 and arrived in Madras in September. While in England, Ensign de Hinuber was promoted to lieutenant in November 1781.[7]

1. The 15th Infantry Regiment was renumbered the 14th Infantry Regiment in 1785.
2. Backdated to 4 June 1811. British Army rank recognised when KGL officers entered the new Hanoverian Army.
3. All ranks were temporary in the British Army until 1812.
4. Permanent rank in the British Army was granted on 18 August 1812.
5. KGL battalions had colonel–commandants instead of regimental colonels.
6. Von Hinüber, Hartmut.
7. Ibid.

Six month after landing in India, Lieutenant de Hinuber was part of the British force that besieged the French garrison in Cuddalore. Both forces were decimated by disease and the siege only ended when word of the Treaty of Paris of 1783 ended the war between France and England. In 1788, Lieutenant de Hinuber was promoted to captain. In July 1792, the Hanoverian forces left India and Captain de Hinuber was one of the last officers to embark.[8]

In February 1793 the War of the 1st Coalition began. Almost immediately upon his return to Hanover, Captain de Hinuber went with his regiment to the Netherlands where he stayed for two years. He returned to Hanover in 1795 and was promoted to major in the 6th Infantry Regiment in 1798. In June 1803, the French invaded Hanover and its army was disbanded in July.

Rather than accept French rule, Major de Hinuber was one of the first officers who chose to go to England to continue the fight against the French. These men formed the King's German Legion. The officers were given temporary rank in the British Army while they served. He was appointed a major in the 1st Line Battalion of the KGL in November 1803 and in July 1804 was promoted to lieutenant colonel and given command of the 3rd Line Battalion. In July 1805 he was promoted to colonel. He led his battalion in the expedition to liberate Hanover in November 1805 and in the expedition to Copenhagen in August 1807. In the spring of 1808, Colonel de Hinuber and his battalion were sent to the Mediterranean as part of the garrison of Sicily. He temporarily commanded a brigade during the British Expedition to Calabria and the Bay of Naples from 11 June to 26 July 1809. In June 1811 he was promoted to major general and placed on the staff of the British forces in Sicily.

General de Hinuber remained in Sicily until he was placed on the staff of Wellington's army on 30 October 1813.[9] He took command of the KGL Brigade in the 1st Division that had been temporarily commanded by Colonel Colin Halkett. The brigade had five battalions and a strength of over 3,000 officers and men, making it the strongest brigade in Wellington's army. He led it in the Battle of Nivelle on 10 November 1813, the investment of Bayonne on 27 February 1814, where he was wounded by a severe contusion, and the sortie from Bayonne on 14 April 1814.

After Napoleon abdicated in April 1814, General de Hinuber took command of the KGL Division in the Subsidiary Army in the Netherlands. In March 1815, in response to Napoleon's escape from Elba, Wellington was sent to the Netherlands to form an Anglo-Allied Army. General de Hinuber was appointed to command the 4th Division on 11 April 1815. However, he was only a major general and he lost command of the division to a senior officer later that month.[10] General de Hinuber objected to being replaced and refused the offer of a brigade. He left the army and most likely returned first to Hanover and then to England. Although he never participated in the Waterloo Campaign, he was included in the list of recipients when the British Parliament gave the army it thanks for the victory on 23 June 1815.

When the KGL was disbanded in early 1816, General de Hinuber joined the newly organised Hanoverian Army. He commanded its 3rd Infantry Brigade from 1 March 1816 until he took command of its 2nd Infantry Brigade on 1 April 1820. He was placed

---

8. Ibid.
9. General Order, 30 October 1813, backdated to 25 June 1813.
10. He was outranked by Charles Colville, who held the local rank of lieutenant general.

on British half-pay on 24 February 1816 until 1827, when he retired from the British army. He was allowed to keep his rank in the British Army, but without pay or progressive promotion. His name was also retained in the army lists. On 18 February 1831 he was appointed the commander of the 2nd Division, X Army Corps of the Federal German Army. He commanded the division until his death in 1833.

Henry de Hinuber married Sophie Marie Lucie Eleonore Fahle on 7 August 1815. She was the daughter of Corporal Johann Heinrich Georg Wilhelm Fahle and sister of Sergeant Wilhelm Fahle, both of the KGL. They were married in St Martin-in-the-Fields Church in London. She was 17 years old. They had a daughter and four sons. Their daughter was born in 1813, when her mother was only 15. One son became a hussar officer in the Austrian Army. Henry de Hinuber died in 1833 in Frankfurt am Main from mastitis[11] possibly cause by an ulcer in his lungs.[12]

General de Hinuber was a competent commander but his relationship with Wellington was strained. After the storming of St Etienne, a suburb of Bayonne on 25 February, he felt his brigade's efforts during the battle were ignored by Wellington when he wrote his official dispatch. Part of the problem was the report General Sir John Hope gave to Wellington on the battle. It completely downplayed the part of General de Hinuber's brigade in the battle, despite it taking over 300 casualties. He never mentioned the brigade by name, writing, 'The troops behaved as well as possible upon this occasion and although the opposition of the enemy was greater than I expected, yet I hope our loss has not been great. I am, however, sorry to say that Major-General Hinuber has been wounded.'[13]

General de Hinuber wrote directly to the Duke of Cambridge[14] about the matter. The Duke responded on 4 April with a short letter. 'I have to acknowledge the receipt of your letter containing the account of the gallant conduct of the battalions under your command before Bayonne, and I request that you will express to all the officers and men, my public approbation of their conduct, and the satisfaction which I feel in being at the head of such a corps.'[15]

General de Hinuber also wrote a rather pointed letter to General Edward Pakenham, the AG of Wellington's army:

> The attention which his excellency the commander of the forces has always been pleased to pay to the conduct of the troops ... whenever it has met with his approval, in his public despatches, led the battalions of the King's German Legion fondly to hope that their conduct and exertions on the 27th of February last, in taking and maintaining the fortified position of St Etienne, close to the enemy's intrenched [sic] camp, and under the guns of the citadel of Bayonne might have obtained for them that most honourable distinction ... Yet we have seen his lordship's despatch on the subject ... but without even naming the corps by whom the position of St. Etienne had been taken, although the battalions of the King's German Legion executed that

11. Inflammation of the breast.
12. Von Hinüber, Hartmut.
13. *WSD*; Vol. 8, page 604.
14. Adolphus Duke of Cambridge was the KGL's Regimental Colonel-in-Chief, as well as the Governor General of Hanover, ruling for both his father King George III and his brother, the Prince Regent of Great Britain.
15. Beamish; Vol. 2, pages 442–3.

service, and not without struggling hard for it, as the return of killed and wounded sufficiently proves … The silence of his lordship in this instance cannot be attributed to casual omission, but must be founded on some particular reason, and the only one which we can at all guess at – however painful to our feelings – is that from some circumstance unknown to us, we have incurred his lordship's displeasure, and that laboring under such, we must necessarily be precluded from the honours which a public notice of our services, would otherwise have bestowed upon us.[16]

The Adjutant General wrote back to General de Hinuber a terse note:

I mentioned to my lord Wellington the sentiments expressed in your letter … am desired to observe that his excellency has ever had the pleasure in being satisfied with the conduct of the legion … I am in no way authorized to enter into further explanation on the subject to which your communication relates, but I should recommend you to subdue any anxiety that may have arisen …[17]

General de Hinuber's tense relationship with Wellington carried over into 1815. In March 1815, he was the commander of all the KGL infantry in the Netherlands. Although he was originally given command of the 4th Division, he was replace seventeen days later by a more senior officer. General de Hinuber protested his supersession in command of the KGL. General de Hinuber argued that he had been specifically appointed to command the KGL Infantry by the Commander-in-Chief. Wellington wrote to General Henry Torrens of the Horse Guards on 2 May asking for clarification of General de Hinuber's status in the new organisation of the army, including whether His Royal Highness 'wishes that the German Legion should serve as a separate division under Major General Hinüber'.[18] General Torrens responded on 5 May that:

though His Royal Highness puts a very high value on the Major-General's services, he could not consider himself justified in authorising that the Legion should be kept together in order that he should command them, when the good of the service requires they should be differently organized. Under those circumstances, should the Major-General's health require his absence at any of the German Spas, your Grace will be pleased to accept the resignation of his Staff appointment.[19]

General de Hinuber did resign and went home. Wellington would have made an arrangement to satisfy him had he remained, probably giving him one of the KGL brigade commands. Ironically, General de Hinuber was senior enough to have commanded a division after Waterloo because of the number of casualties among division commanders. Because of his stubbornness General de Hinuber missed out on the glory attached to the victory at Waterloo.

16. Ibid; pages 444–5.
17. Ibid; page 446.
18. *WD;* Vol. 12, page 341.
19. *WSD;* Vol. 10, page 237.

Hoghton, Daniel

Date of Birth:	27 August 1770
Date Commissioned:	Cornet 11th Light Dragoons: 5 April 1793 by purchase
Promotions:	Lieutenant 11th Light Dragoons: 8 June 1793 without purchase
	Captain Independent Company: 4 October 1793 without purchase[1]
	Captain 82nd Foot: 27 October 1793 appointed[2]
	Major 97th Foot:[3] 8 February 1794 without purchase
	Major 67th Foot: 12 August 1795 by exchange
	Major 88th Foot: 31 January 1799 by purchase?
	Brevet Lieutenant Colonel: 3 May 1796
	Lieutenant Colonel 8th Foot: 23 November 1804 without purchase
	Brevet Colonel: 1 January 1805
	Brigadier General on the Staff: April 1808–25 July 1810
	Major General: 25 July 1810
Major Commands under Wellington:	On Staff at Cadiz: 24 May–25 September 1810
	Brigade 2nd Division 8 October 1810–16 May 1811
Awards:	AGM and clasp: Martinique & Albuera
Date of Death:	16 May 1811 Albuera Spain. Buried in the military cemetery Elvas, Portugal

Name was also spelled as Houghton.

Daniel Hoghton was born in 1770, the second son of Sir Henry Hoghton and his second wife, Fanny. Daniel's father was the 6th Baronet of Hoghton Tower and Walton Hall, Lancashire, and a Member of Parliament. His mother was the eldest daughter of Daniel Booth, a director of the Bank of England. Daniel's family purchased a commission for him in the 11th Light Dragoons in 1793. Two months later he was promoted to lieutenant in the regiment. He was only with them for four months when he was promoted to captain of an independent company. On 7 October, three days after receiving his captaincy, he was placed on half-pay as captain in the disbanded 101st Foot. Captain Hoghton stayed on half-pay for twenty days when he was brought back on full pay in the 82nd Foot. He most likely never served with the 82nd Foot since he was appointed a major in the 97th Foot less than four months later. Major Hoghton exchanged into the 67th Foot in August 1795. In the space of two years he had been assigned to five different units and promoted three times.

Major Hoghton served with the 67th Foot for forty-two months. During that time his commander was Lieutenant Colonel William Stewart, who would be his division commander in 1811. Major Hoghton and his regiment went to the West Indies in February 1796, serving first in Santo Domingo and then in 1798 in Jamaica. Shortly after arriving in the West Indies, Major Hoghton was promoted to brevet lieutenant colonel. He returned to England in late 1798.

In January 1799, Lieutenant Colonel Hoghton transferred to the 88th Foot, which had sailed to India earlier in the month. He followed his regiment to India. His commander

---

1. *London Gazette*; War Office Announcement dated 15 October 1793.
2. *London Gazette*; War Office Announcement dated 1 February 1794.
3. Disbanded 1795.

was Lieutenant Colonel William Beresford, who commanded the British Army at Albuera. While in India, he became friends with Wellington and his brother Richard, Marquess Wellesley. Lieutenant Colonel Hoghton stayed in India when the 88th Foot was sent to Egypt in 1801. In the spring of 1804, he carried dispatches back to England.

In November 1804, Lieutenant Colonel Hoghton was promoted in the 8th Foot and given command of its 2nd Battalion. In January 1805 he was promoted to colonel. He remained with the regiment and commanded the 1st Battalion in General Robert Macfarlane's brigade in the expedition to Copenhagen from August to October 1807. In January 1808, Colonel Hoghton and the 1st Battalion went to Nova Scotia. Shortly after arriving in Canada he was appointed a brigadier on the staff of the garrison.[4] In November 1808 he sailed from Nova Scotia to the West Indies and commanded the 1st Brigade 1st Division at the siege and capture of Martinique in January and February 1809. General Hoghton returned to Nova Scotia in April and left for England later that year.

On 24 May 1810 General Hoghton joined the British garrison in Cadiz Spain. He was appointed a brigadier general on the staff of Cadiz, in a General Order dated 29 June 1810 with the appointment to date from 14 April. He was given command of the 4th Brigade on 29 May. In July he was promoted to major general. On 9 August the garrison was reorganised and he was given command of the 2nd Brigade. With the reorganisation the brigades were renumbered to reflect the seniority of commanding officers. By August, Wellington began to reduce the size of the British garrison in Cadiz.[5] General Hoghton's brigade was reduced by 50 per cent and he wanted to go to Portugal, where the action was. He asked the British Ambassador to Spain, Henry Wellesley, who was Wellington's younger brother, to intercede on his behalf. The ambassador wrote to Wellington on 16 August 1810, stating, 'Houghton [*sic*] is very anxious to join you, and begged me to say so.'[6] His wish was granted and General Hoghton left Cadiz to join Wellington's army in Portugal on 25 September.

General Hoghton was initially assigned to temporarily command General Richard Stewart's brigade in the 2nd Division.[7] General Stewart was sick and recuperating in Lisbon. He retained the brigade after General Stewart fell to his death from a balcony on 19 October. General Hoghton spent the next five months in the vicinity of Lisbon, first behind the Lines of Torres Vedras and then north of Lisbon near Chamusca. On 5 March 1811, General Hoghton was given an independent command to assist in the pursuit of the retreating French. This command consisted of his brigade and Colonel Richard Collins's Portuguese brigade from the 4th Division. When his ad hoc division reached Condeixa in mid-March, General Hoghton received new orders. He was to head south, cross the Tagus River, and re-join the 2nd Division, which was part of Marshal William Beresford's force that was massing to besiege the fortress city of Badajoz. Upon re-joining the 2nd Division, General Hoghton's ad hoc division was disbanded. The 2nd Division did not take an active part in the siege, but was used as the covering force for the troops that were besieging the city.

It was not until 16 May at Albuera did General Hoghton and his brigade see action. At Albuera, the 2nd Division initially was not in the front lines; however, after Lieutenant Colonel John Colborne's brigade was decimated by the French cavalry General Hoghton's

---

4. *Army List*; April 1808.

5. Bamford, Andrew. 'British Forces at Cadiz 1810–1814'.

6. *WSD*; Vol. 6, page 574.

7. General Order, 8 October 1810.

and Lieutenant Colonel Alexander Abercromby's brigades were ordered to the front. General Hoghton's brigade moved up and were behind the Spanish infantry, whom they mistakenly opened fire on. After the mess was sorted out, the brigade replaced the Spanish in the front line, where it came under heavy artillery fire. General Hoghton 'was on horseback in front of the line, in a green frock-coat, which he had put on in the hurry of turning out. Some time afterwards his servant rode up to him with his red uniform coat, and without dismounting he immediately stripped off the green and put on the red one. It may be said that this public display of our national colour and of British coolness actually was done under a salute of French artillery ...'"[8]

The brigade was not in position long, when the French 5th Corps assaulted them. General Hoghton could muster about 1,650 men to oppose the 8,000 French. At a range of 20 yards the brigade stood and fought for thirty minutes in the most violent exchange of fire in the history of the Napoleonic Wars. When the French finally broke, the brigade ceased to exist. The 'brigade went into action led by a major-general, and with its due proportion of field-officers and captains. I saw it at three in the afternoon: – a captain commanded the brigade; the 57th and 48th regiments were commanded by lieutenants; and the junior captain of the 29th regiment was the senior effective officer of his corps.'[9] At the end of the firefight, only 607 men were still with the colors. Over 1,000 men were killed or wounded. Among the wounded was General Hoghton.

According to his servant Thomas Coffin, General Hoghton was taken 'to a Surgeon where the greatest atencion whase paid im by all the surgeons of the Staff But all in vain and at Twenty Minutes Past Thre in the Afternoon expired in my arms and in Presant of Gorge Ramsden.'[10] General Hoghton's body was brought back to the fortress city of Elvas, Portugal for burial. Ensign Robert Bakewell was there when his body arrived at the hospital.

> General Hoghton had been killed, and was brought here for interment. He had received one shot through his left shoulder; but the second was in his right breast, which proved mortal. The officers here were all ordered to attend his funeral, where we saw him before the lid on the coffin was fastened; and he was honoured with the cannon firing the customary salute from the ramparts.[11]

Daniel Hoghton never married and had no children. He was a competent brigade commander in action; however, he was noted for not taking his duties as a senior officer too seriously. Wellington described him as 'the most inattentive regimental Officer that ever was seen; and I should doubt that attention to duty was his style even as a General Officer.'[12] That being said, his brigade performed superbly at Albuera. He was a friend of Wellington, but this friendship did not prevent General Hoghton from getting in trouble.

In January 1811, General Hoghton and his brigade occupied Chamusca and while there he assumed the position of commanding officer of the garrison, resigning the temporary command of his brigade to the senior battalion commander. He did this

8. Leslie; page 224.
9. Sherer; page 215.
10. Panikkar; page 17.
11. Bakewell; page 93.
12. The names were suppressed in the letter published in *WD* (enlarged ed.); Vol. 4, pages 639–40. However, the names were supplied by Michael Glover in a letter of 19 May 1989 and by Rory Muir in an e-mail dated 22 August 2006.

without notifying headquarters. In a letter to Marshal Beresford on 24 January 1811, Wellington disapproved of the arrangement, observing that Chamusca was a cantonment of the army and did not require a garrison commander. He ended by commenting that, in future the troops may continue to be organized, and officers may continue with the commands as ordered by the General Orders.'[13]

General Hoghton also did not get along with his division commander, General William Stewart, in 1811. Even Wellington recognised this. On 28 February he wrote to Marshal Beresford, 'I think however, that I can remove Hoghton. Now that you mention it, I believe I recollect that there was an old breeze between General Stewart and Hoghton when both were in the 82nd ...'[14] In the same letter Wellington places the blame for these difficulties on General Hoghton and his indifferent attitude to performing his duties.[15]

Wellington proposed a solution to the problem in a letter to Marshal Beresford dated 1 April 1811. He would place General Charles Alten's brigade of the 7th Division in the 2nd Division and withdraw General Hoghton's brigade from General Stewart's Division. Wellington never specified what he would do with him but it was most likely he would be sent to the 7th Division.[16] However, the exchange never took place. Marshal Beresford wrote to Wellington on 29 April 1811 stating the problem had gotten worse.

Hoghton is really so importunate to be removed from his situation under Stewart, that, however I dislike pestering you on these subjects I can only say I would be most glad if you could get him from Stewart, as it will save me an[d] therefore division hearing what is in no way amusing. What is very singular he told me he had particularly wished, next to serving directly where you were, to be in Cole's division. I do not know if this is reciprocal, but from the information you had I though[t] one party desiring it was odd enough. He wishes leave to go [text missing] ... personally, but as I did not know how you would like that I have postponed giving it. In fact he has worked himself into misery and he daily visits me with his lamentations tho' I have told him that circumstances have delayed the removal of his brigade. But Dan will be quite satisfied in being able to remove his person.[17]

On 22 May, Wellington wrote to his brother Richard Marquess Wellesley about General Hoghton's death. In many ways it sums up his character in a few lines:

I am convinced that you will feel severely the loss of poor Hoghton, whose last hours must have tended to raise him in the estimation of every body. I understand that it was impossible for anybody to behave better than he did throughout the terrible scene, to him novel, in which he was an actor. He was not only cool and collected, as he ought to have been throughout the action, but animated and anxious to a degree beyond what could have been expected from his former habits, and the indifference with which he always appeared to perform the ordinary duties of his profession; and he actually fell waving his hat and cheering his brigade on to the charge.[18]

---

13. *WD* (enlarged ed.); vol. 4. page 548.
14. Actually in the 67th Foot where Stewart was the lieutenant colonel and Hoghton his major.
15. See Footnote 12.
16. *WD* (enlarged ed.); Vol. 4, page 718.
17. Letter provided by Rory Muir in an e-mail dated 23 August 2006.
18. *WSD*; Vol. 7, page 134.

Hulse, Richard

Date of Birth:	c. 1775
Date Commissioned:	Ensign Coldstream Foot Guards: 24 March 1790 by purchase
Promotions:	Lieutenant & Captain Coldstream Foot Guards: 25 April 1793
	Captain-Lieutenant & Lieutenant Colonel Coldstream Foot Guards: 23 September 1799
	Captain & Lieutenant Colonel Coldstream Foot Guards: 9 May 1800
	Brevet Colonel: 25 October 1809
	Brigadier General on the Staff: 23 July 1811
	Major General in the Peninsula: 26 October 1811
	Major General: 1 January 1812
Major Commands under Wellington:	Temporarily commanded Guards Brigade 1st Division: 8 November–15 December 1809
	Brigade 6th Division: 14 November 1810–31 July 1812
	Temporarily commanded 5th Division: 31 July–7 September 1812
Awards:	AGM with clasp: Talavera & Salamanca
Date of Death:	7 September 1812, Arevalo, Spain

Richard Hulse was the third son of Sir Edward Hulse, 3rd Baronet of Lincoln's-Inn-Fields in Middlesex, and Mary Lethieullier. His family was very wealthy after his mother inherited the estate of her uncle, Smart Lethieullier. The exact date of Richard's birth is unknown, but it was probably in the mid-1770s, since he had two older brothers who were born in the early 1770s. He was the nephew of Field Marshal Sir Samuel Hulse. Richard Hulse never married. He was also the great-great-uncle of Captain Sir Edward Hulse, 7th Baronet, of the Scots Guards, who was involved in the Christmas Truce of 1914.

In March 1790, Richard Hulse purchased a commission as an ensign in the Coldstream Guards. It was the only time that he purchased a promotion in his twenty-two years of service. He spent the next twenty years in the regiment. Ensign Hulse went with his battalion when it was assigned to the British Expedition to Flanders in February 1793. Shortly after arriving there, he was promoted to lieutenant and captain and returned to England to join the 2nd Battalion. He was promoted to captain-lieutenant and lieutenant colonel in 1799 and to captain and lieutenant colonel the next year. He commanded the 1st Battalion's Light Company when they joined General Edward Finch's Guards Brigade during the Hanover expedition from November 1805 to February 1806. He was still in command of the Light Company when the battalion was with General Finch's Guard Brigade during the British Expedition to Copenhagen from August–October 1807.

By December 1808, Lieutenant Colonel Hulse commanded the 1st Battalion and was in the Guards Brigade in General John Sherbrooke's force sent to secure Cadiz. It sailed on 15 January 1809, despite contrary winds and a gale, and the force reached Cadiz on 8 March, but the Spanish government refused to allow it to land. The force sailed to Lisbon and arrived there on 13 March. Lieutenant Colonel Hulse and his battalion joined the garrison of Portugal. They fought in the Oporto Campaign in May and with the reorganisation of the army in June, the Guards Brigade was assigned to the 1st Division. He and his battalion fought at Talavera on 27–28 July, where they took

30 per cent casualties. Most of them occurred when he lost control of his battalion in an attack on the second day and they were decimated by a French counter-attack. He was promoted to colonel in October 1809. Colonel Hulse was given temporary command of the Guards Brigade in November. By mid-December he was back with his battalion, which he led at Busaco on 27 September 1810, but they saw little action.

In October 1810, Wellington decided to form the 6th Division. Colonel Hulse was appointed a colonel on the staff on 14 November[1] and given command of one of its brigades. The division was on the army's left flank at Fuentes de Oñoro on 3–5 May 1811 but was not engaged. Colonel Hulse was appointed a brigadier general on the staff in August.[2] He and his brigade were at Fuente Guinaldo on 26 September, but once again saw no action. He was promoted to major general on 26 October 1811.[3] This promotion was local rank and was only valid while he served in the Peninsula. It was unusual and Wellington wrote to Colonel Henry Torrens of the Horse Guards thanking the Duke of York for permitting it.[4]

General Hulse and his brigade continued to be on the sidelines through the first five months of 1812. They were part of the covering force in Estremadura and missed the sieges of Ciudad Rodrigo and Badajoz. In June they marched with the army into central Spain and its light companies took part in the unsuccessful assault on Fort San Cayetano in Salamanca on 23 June. The brigade finally saw action on 22 July at Salamanca. They were instrumental in stopping the main French attack on the centre of the British line and then leading the counter-attack that ended the battle. Their valor came at a heavy price; 58 per cent of the brigade were casualties and they had more killed and wounded than the other two brigades in their division combined.

After the Battle of Salamanca, General Hulse requested a transfer from the 6th Division. There were apparently conflicts between him and General Henry Clinton, the division commander.[5] Wellington approved his request and General Hulse was appointed to command General Andrew Hay's brigade in the 5th Division until further orders.[6] As he was now the senior brigade commander, he succeeded to the temporary command of the 5th Division in the absence of General James Leith, who had been wounded at Salamanca. Wellington appointed him to command the brigade knowing full well that he would succeed to the temporary command of the division by seniority.

General Hulse did not command the 5th Division for long. Four weeks after being appointed its temporary commander, he contracted typhus.[7] 'He had violent convulsions and twitchings, the almost certain forerunners of death.'[8] General Hulse died at 10 a.m. on 7 September in Arevalo, Spain. His horses and belongings were sold to his fellow officers on 14 September.[9]

---

1. General Order, 14 November 1810.
2. General Order, 6 August 1811, backdated to 23 July.
3. General Order, 2 December 1811, backdated to 26 October 1811.
4. *WD* (enlarged ed.); Vol. 5, page 386.
5. Glover, Gareth; *Wellington's Lieutenant*; pages 140–1.
6. General Order, 31 July 1812.
7. Typhus is usually transmitted to humans via fleas. Many of the accounts left by the British officers of Wellington's army complain about the flea infested buildings they were housed in.
8. Mills; page 220.
9. Glover, Gareth; *Wellington's Lieutenant*; page 147. Mills; pages 222 and 227.

Although his performance as a battalion commander at the Battle of Talavera was not good, General Hulse was one of the heroes of the day at Salamanca three years later. Colonel William de Lancey, the Army's acting Quartermaster General, wrote a few weeks after the battle that 'Hulse is very highly spoken of in the Attack of the 6th Division. I understand he executed it extremely well and had nothing to say to the planning of the attack.'[10] Major Frederick Newman, who assumed command of the 11th Foot[11] after its battalion commander[12] was seriously wounded, was also unsparing in his approbation. 'Hulse's conduct in regard to the whole of the battle was beyond praise.'[13]

General Hulse was well thought of by those who knew him. In a letter to the Duke of York on 7–8 September 1812, Wellington described his death as a 'melancholy event'.[14] Lieutenant Colonel George Bingham, one of his battalion commanders, wrote that:

The officers of the brigade have come to the determination of offering Hulse a sword on leaving us; when it was first mentioned to me, I with great satisfaction acceded to the proposal, as there is no man in the army, or indeed anywhere else beyond our little circle, for whom I have greater respect. I did not, however, expect they would have made it so expensive; Mansel[15] has just put his name down for twenty guineas ...[16]

The junior officers of the Coldstream Guards also had a high opinion of General Hulse. Captain John Fremantle, in a letter to his uncle, wrote:

I am sorry to tell you the army has been deprived of one of its ablest officers by the death of poor General Hulse at Arevalo a few days since, regretted by everyone who knew him, Lord Wellington is very much concerned for he reckoned upon him as his greatest support. I believe if it were possible he never had an enemy.[17]

Ensign John Mills wrote that:

His loss as an individual will be nothing in comparison to that of an officer. There is no-one in this army that stands as high in the estimation of everyone ... It is hard that one who had upon so many occasions distinguished himself should be carried off in that way. He would one day or other been a great man. It would have been comparative happiness had he died in the field.[18]

10. Muir, Rory; *Salamanca*; page 180.
11. The 1st Battalion 11th Foot was one of the battalions in General Hulse's brigade.
12. Lieutenant Colonel George Cuyler.
13. Muir, Rory; *Salamanca*, page 186.
14. *WD* (enlarged ed.); Vol. 6, page 56.
15. Brevet Lieutenant Colonel John Mansel, 53rd Foot.
16. Glover, Gareth; *Wellington's Lieutenant*, page 141.
17. Glover, Gareth; *Wellington's Voice*, page 124.
18. Mills; pages 220 & 222.

Date of Birth:	1764[1] in Edinburgh, Scotland
Date Commissioned:	Ensign 57th Foot: 11 October 1779 by purchase
Promotions:	Lieutenant 57th Foot: 3 May 1782 by purchase
	Captain-Lieutenant 57th Foot: 11 July 1785 by purchase
	Captain 57th Foot: 15 August 1788 by purchase
	Brevet Major: 6 May 1795
	Major 57th Foot: 1 September 1795 without purchase
	Brevet Lieutenant Colonel: 1 January 1800
	Lieutenant Colonel 57th Foot:[2] 16 August 1804 without purchase
	Brevet Colonel: 25 July 1810
	Brigadier General on the Staff: 21 January 1813
	Major General: 4 June 1813
	Lieutenant General: 27 May 1825
Regimental Colonel:	57th Foot: 16 April 1830–29 November 1835
Major Commands under Wellington:	Temporarily commanded Brigade 2nd Division: 13 August–8 October 1810
	Brigade 7th Division: 21 May 1813–April 1814
Awards:	KCB: 7 April 1815.
	AGC: Albuera, Pyrenees, Nivelle & Orthes
Thanks of Parliament:	Peninsula & Orthes
Date of Death:	29 November 1835 at Ramsgate, England. Buried in Canterbury Cathedral

William Inglis was born in Edinburgh in 1764, the third son of Dr William Inglis and Margaret Spens. His name is long associated with the 57th Foot and is credited with shouting the words while lying severely wounded at Albuera that became the regimental nickname (of which more later). William Inglis purchased a commission in the 57th Foot in 1779 and served with it for the next thirty-five years. In the latter years of his life, he was its regimental colonel.

Although he was commissioned in 1779, Ensign Inglis did not join his regiment, which was stationed in New York, until 1781. The following year, he purchased his lieutenancy and in 1783 went with the regiment to Nova Scotia. He would remain there until November 1791 when the regiment returned to England. During those ten years, he was given a two-year leave of absence. While in Nova Scotia he was promoted to captain-lieutenant in 1785 and to captain in 1788.

In June 1793, Captain Inglis went with his regiment to Flanders and was part of the garrison of Nijmegen when it was besieged in the autumn of 1794. He returned to England in May 1795 when the British Army was evacuated from Bremerhaven. Captain Inglis was promoted to brevet major in May 1795 and then to major in October. That autumn the regiment sailed with General Ralph Abercromby to the West Indies and remained there until December 1802. While in Trinidad in 1800, Major Inglis was promoted to brevet lieutenant colonel. Upon arrival in England in the winter of 1803,

---

1. His exact date of birth is unknown. Some also state 1762.
2. Removed from the regiment as a general officer receiving unattached pay, 1814.

Lieutenant Colonel Inglis was tasked with organising the regiment's 2nd Battalion. After it was formed, he returned to the 1st Battalion which was stationed on Guernsey. In August 1804, he was promoted to lieutenant colonel and assumed command of the 1st Battalion. In November 1805, he and the battalion sailed to Gibraltar and arrived there in January 1806. They formed part of its garrison for the next forty-one months.

On 9 July 1809, Lieutenant Colonel Inglis and his battalion sailed for Lisbon. They arrived on 17 July too late to fight in the Talavera Campaign. They were assigned to General Richard Stewart's brigade in the 2nd Division and spent the next year guarding the right flank of the British Army, much of the time along the Guadiana River. In July 1810, Lieutenant Colonel Inglis was promoted to colonel. The next month, Colonel Inglis was given temporary command of his brigade when its commander became sick. He led the brigade at Busaco on 27 September 1810, but it was only engaged by the French artillery. He continued in command of the brigade during the retreat to the Lines of Torres Vedras and relinquished command to General Hoghton on 8 October. In January 1811, General Daniel Hoghton and his brigade occupied Chamusca and he appointed himself the commandant of the city. Colonel Inglis was given temporary command of the brigade. Wellington was less than pleased when he heard of this and ordered General Hoghton to assume command of his brigade.[3]

On 5 March 1811, General Hoghton was given an independent command to assist in the pursuit of the retreating French. This command consisted of his brigade and Colonel Richard Collins's Portuguese brigade from the 4th Division. Since General Hoghton was commanding this ad hoc division, Colonel Inglis commanded his brigade. When the division reached Condeixa in mid-March, General Hoghton received orders to head south, cross the Tagus River and rejoin the 2nd Division which was assigned to Marshal Beresford's force that was guarding the southern approaches to Portugal. Once there, General Hoghton's ad hoc division was disbanded and Colonel Inglis resumed command of his battalion.

In early May 1811, Colonel Inglis and his battalion were part of the covering force that was protecting the troops besieging Badajoz. Word reached the British that the French were marching to relieve the fortress and Marshal William Beresford set out to prevent it. The two armies met at Albuera on 16 May and the French under Marshal Soult attempted to turn the Allies's right flank. About noon the situation had become critical and the 2nd Division was sent forward to halt the French. General Hoghton's brigade was in the centre of the British line and Colonel Inglis and the 57th Foot were in the centre of the brigade. The British had about 1,600 men to stop the 8,000 French infantrymen.

After being ordered forward,

The regiment formed line on its destined position from open columns of companies. Sir William,[4] close to and immediately in front of the colours, was dressing the line on the centre: he had finished with the right wing, and being turned to the left, was coolly scanning the men as they formed, when a shot brought his charger to the ground, leaving his master erect on his feet. At that critical moment, I observed his unchanged countenance, and that while he extricated his feet from the stirrup, he

---

3. For more information on this incident, see the entry for General Hoghton.
4. General William Stewart who commanded the 2nd Division.

never once turned his eyes from the line he was continuing to perfect and not until that was completed did he cast a glance on the remains of his noble steed.[5]

For the next thirty minutes the 57th Foot and the rest of the brigade stood and exchanged fire at close quarters with the French soldiers. General Hoghton was mortally wounded shortly after the firing began and Colonel Inglis assumed command of the brigade. He did not command it long, because he was seriously wounded before the French finally fell back. Colonel Inglis remained on the battlefield until the following day before being evacuated to Valverde and then on to Olivenza, where he was operated on two days after he had been wounded.[6] The surgeon who performed the surgery wrote that,

> The ball ... struck the lower part of his stock & made a deep incision in his neck a little above his collar bone, luckily escaping the artery. I thought it had passed, but on stripping and examining him I found that it had lodged in the back upon the surface of the blade bone – it was immediately extracted and proved to be grape.[7]

The grape shot weighed four ounces and was four inches in circumference.[8]

Upon the recommendation of a medical board, Colonel Inglis was sent back to England to recover in the autumn. He returned to Portugal in January 1812. On 7 February, Wellington wrote to General Rowland Hill that since Colonel Inglis was senior to Colonel John Byng, he had to employ him in command of the brigade which contained the 57th Foot. This would displace Colonel Byng from command of the brigade.[9] However, Colonel Inglis's health was still too fragile for him to take an active command. Instead he served as the president of general court-martials in Lisbon through the rest of 1812. By the end of 1812 his seniority was once again causing problems for Wellington. Colonel Henry Torrens of the Horse Guards wrote to Wellington that Colonel Byng had just been appointed a brigadier and was junior to Colonel Inglis. Colonel Torrens wrote concerning Colonel Inglis, 'but you will let me know whether you wish him to have the Rank.'[10]

In January 1813, Colonel Inglis was promoted a brigadier on the staff of the Army. But as late as 1 May 1813 he had still not been given a brigade to command.[11] On 21 May, he was finally given command of a brigade in the 7th Division. In June he was promoted to major general. Despite being appointed a brigade commander in May, he did not join his new command until July, after orders came out retaining him on the staff of Wellington's army.[12] He led his brigade at the 2nd Battle of Sorauren on 30 July, where his horse was shot out from under him, at Venta de Urroz on 31 July, and at San Marcial on 31 August, where he had another horse killed. All was quiet for him and his brigade until 10 November at the Battle of Nivelle, when he was wounded in the foot. General Inglis and his brigade went into winter quarters after the battle and did not see action again until

5. *United Services Magazine*; Part 2, 1829. Page 107.
6. *Annual Biography and Obituary*; Vol. 21, page 33.
7. Dempsey; page 151.
8. *Annual Biography and Obituary*; Vol. 21, page 33.
9. *WD* (enlarged ed.); Vol. 5, page 505.
10. Unpublished letter dated 26 November 1812 from Colonel Torrens to Wellington.
11. *WD* (enlarged ed.); Vol. 6, page 457.
12. General Order, 2 July 1813.

the next year. They fought at Orthes on 27 February, where General Inglis's horse was wounded, and were part of the force sent to occupy Bordeaux in March.

After Napoleon abdicated in April 1814 and Wellington's army was disbanded in June, General Inglis returned to England. He had no official duties for many years. He was promoted to lieutenant general in 1825 and was appointed the Lieutenant Governor of Charles Fort, Kinsale on 8 March 1827 and the Governor of Cork on 8 January 1829. In April 1830 he became the regimental colonel of his old regiment, the 57th Foot. He served as its colonel until his death on 29 November 1835.

William Inglis married Margaret Raymond, the oldest daughter of General William Raymond, at Bath on 2 May 1822. They had two sons, both of whom joined the army.

General Inglis was a competent brigade commander who led from the front. Between 1811 and 1814, he had been wounded twice and had four horses shot out from under him. A legend still exists today about his efforts to inspire his regiment at the Battle of Albuera. After he had been seriously wounded, he allegedly refused to be evacuated to the rear for treatment. Instead he laid next to the regimental colours and exhorted his men to 'Die hard, 57th. Die hard!' Within a year, the 57th Foot was known as the 'Die Hards' and its successor units carried the nickname throughout the years. Unfortunately there is little documentary evidence that Colonel Inglis actually said those immortal words. The regiment took extremely heavy casualties and the only known account by a survivor from the regiment does not mention the incident.[13]

---

13. A detailed examination of the whole controversy can be found on pages 292–295 in Guy Dempsey's *Albuera 1811* which was published by Frontline Books in 2008.

Johnstone, George

Date of Birth:	Unknown
Date Commissioned:	Ensign 29th Foot: 1 November 1780 without purchase
Promotions:	Lieutenant 29th Foot: 24 September 1787 without purchase
	Captain-Lieutenant 29th Foot: 24 August 1792 without purchase
	Captain 29th Foot: 5 February 1794 without purchase
	Major 29th Foot: 9 August 1799 without purchase
	Lieutenant Colonel New Brunswick Fencibles: 9 July 1803 without purchase
	Lieutenant Colonel 93rd Foot:[1] 3 May 1810 by exchange
	Brevet Colonel: 1 January 1812
	Major General: 4 June 1814
Major Commands under Wellington:	6th Brigade: 11 April–30 November 1815
Awards:	Waterloo Medal
Date of Death:	19 December 1825 in Edinburgh, Scotland

Little is known about George Johnstone. His name is sometimes spelled Johnston and he is often confused with Brevet Lieutenant Colonel George Johnstone, a major in the 102nd Foot,[2] who was court-martialed and cashiered in 1811 for leading a mutiny in New South Wales in 1808. He was the only surviving son of Major William Johnstone of Methantae, a branch of the Johnstone Margintaes of Annandale. George Johnstone was a distant and poor relative of General Sir John Hope and Admiral Sir William Hope Johnstone. Despite having such distinguish relatives, there is no indication that they had any impact on his or his father's career.[3]

George Johnstone was a volunteer[4] with the 29th Foot, which was stationed in Canada, when he was commissioned an ensign in 1780. He remained with the regiment for the next twenty-three years. During those years he would serve as the adjutant, a company commander, and as a major. In September 1787 he was promoted to lieutenant and the following month sailed with it to England. Lieutenant Johnstone was promoted to captain-lieutenant in August 1792 and to captain in 1794. In late December the regiment boarded transports to go to the West Indies. They eventually sailed in February, arriving at Barbados on 31 March. A temporary brigade was formed with General Archibald Campbell as its commander and it was sent to Grenada the next month to put down an insurrection. Captain Johnstone was appointed its brigade major. They stayed in Grenada until July 1796. Only four officers and eighty-eight men returned to England. Before the regiment departed for England 202 men were draughted into other regiments and remained behind in Grenada. Three officers were too sick to board the transports, while the regimental commander stayed as the lieutenant governor of the island. The other 272 officers and men died during the campaign, most through disease.

---

1. Removed from the regiment as a general officer receiving unattached pay, 1814.
2. Formerly the New South Wales Corps.
3. George's father, William, was only promoted to brevet major after thirty-two years of service.
4. A volunteer was a gentleman who served in the ranks but messed with the officers. By serving as a volunteer, the individual hoped to obtain a commission in the army without having to buy it.

The 29th Foot spent the next two years rebuilding its strength. In the spring of 1798 it was ordered to Ireland to help suppress the Rebellion. It arrived in mid-June. They remained in Ireland until July 1799, when the regiment was ordered back to England for service in Flanders. Shortly after landing in England, Captain Johnstone was promoted to major. He stayed with the regimental depot, when the regiment deployed to Flanders. In June 1802 the 29th Foot went to Nova Scotia arriving in Halifax in September. Major Johnstone served with the regiment until July 1803, when he was promoted to lieutenant colonel in the newly raised New Brunswick Fencibles.

Lieutenant Colonel Johnstone commanded the regiment until 1810. While in Canada he served as the temporary governor of New Brunswick from 17 December 1808 to 28 April 1809. North America was far from the action and, hoping to serve with the British army in the Peninsula, he exchanged into the 93rd Foot in May 1810. Unfortunately for his ambitions, instead of going to Portugal he joined his regiment at the Cape of Good Hope. In January 1812 he was promoted to colonel. Two years later, in April 1814, the 93rd Foot was ordered back to Great Britain.

In June 1814, Colonel Johnstone was promoted to major general and in December was ordered to Cork to take command of a Highland Brigade being readied for service in British North America. Contrary winds delayed the brigade's departure and with news of the end of the war of 1812, the brigade was sent to Flanders instead. General Johnstone was placed on the staff of Wellington's Anglo-Allied Army in March 1815. General Henry Torrens of the Horse Guards explained to Wellington on 31 March that,

> Major General Johnston [*sic*] was embarked for some weeks at Cork with a reinforcement for America and when the destination of the chief part of his troops was changed to Brabant it was impossible to withhold employment from him. He is said to be a good officer, and he came home from the Cape of Good Hope with the view of seeking employment in the Peninsula.[5]

General Johnstone was assigned command of the 6th Brigade of the 4th Division on 11 April 1815. His brigade was stationed with the 4th Division at Hal during the Battle of Waterloo on 18 June and missed the battle. He was at the capture of Cambray on 24–25 June. When the army was reorganised into the AOOF on 30 November 1815, General Johnstone was not retained on the staff. Upon his return to England he went to Scotland and had no other military duties. General Johnstone died in Edinburgh on 19 December 1825. It is unknown if he ever married or had children.

---

5. *WSD*; Vol. 10, pages 9–10.

Keane, John

Date of Birth:	6 February 1781 in Waterford, Ireland
Date Commissioned:	Ensign Ward's Regiment: 11 October 1794 without purchase
Promotions:	Lieutenant 122nd Foot: 30 October 1794 without purchase
	Captain 124th Foot:[1] 12 November 1794 by purchase
	Captain 44th Foot: 7 November 1799 by exchange
	Major 60th Foot: 27 May 1802 by purchase
	Lieutenant Colonel 13th Foot: 20 August 1803 by purchase
	Lieutenant Colonel 60th Foot: 25 June 1812 by exchange[2]
	Brevet Colonel: 1 January 1812
	Major General: 4 June 1814
	Lieutenant General: 22 July 1830
Regimental Colonel:	94th Foot: 18 April 1829–13 April 1831
	68th Foot: 13 April 1831–6 April 1838
	46th Foot: 6 April 1838–1 August 1839
	43rd Foot: 1 August 1839–26 August 1844
Major Commands under Wellington:	Temporarily commanded brigade 3rd Division: c. October 1812–25 March 1813
	Brigade 3rd Division: 1 August 1813–April 1814
	8th Brigade: 15 July–30 November 1815
	9th Brigade AOOF: 30 November 1815–25 April 1817
Awards:	AGC with two clasps: Martinique, Vitoria, Pyrenees, Nivelle, Orthes & Toulouse
	KCB: 2 January 1815
	GCH: 1831
	GCB: 12 August 1839
	Medal for Egypt
	Order of the Durrani Empire
Date of Death:	26 August 1844 at Burton Lodge, Hampshire

John Keane was born in 1781, the second son of John and Sarah (*née* Keiley) Keane of Belmont, County Waterford. He was the younger brother of Lieutenant Colonel Sir Richard Keane, 2nd Baronet and older brother of Colonel Edward Keane. His father was created Baronet Keane of Cappoquin House in 1801 and was an MP for Bangor in the Irish Parliament and Youghal in the British Parliament. There are conflicting sources on the exact date John Keane was commissioned in the army and his initial years as an officer.[3] The most compelling evidence states that in October 1794, when he was 13 years old, John was appointed an ensign in Colonel Ward's Regiment. He was an ensign for less

---

1. Disbanded 1795.
2. Removed from the regiment as a general officer receiving unattached pay 1814.
3. There is confusion on his promotions to Ensign and Lieutenant. In Fisher's *Colonial Magazine*, Vol. I 1844, he is listed in Ward's Regiment as Ensign 11 October 1794 and in Stratford's [122nd] Regiment 30 October 1794. These promotions are shown in the *London Gazette* for an officer identified only as Kane. He is shown in Hart's Annual Army List 1844 as an Ensign in 1793 and as a Lieutenant 29 April 1793.

than three weeks when he was appointed a lieutenant in the 122nd Foot. It is doubtful he ever reported for duty with them because his father purchased a captaincy for him in the 124th Foot thirteen days later. The 124th Foot was disbanded in May 1795; however, before it was disbanded Captain Keane exchanged to half-pay of the 73rd Foot, which had been disbanded in 1763. He remained on half-pay for four years.

On 7 November 1799, Captain Keane exchanged into the 44th Foot and joined his regiment at Gibraltar. The regiment was part of the British Expedition to Egypt in October 1800. Captain Keane served as the ADC to General Richard Earl of Cavan while in Egypt. He fought at Mandora on 13 March and Alexandria on 21 March 1801. After the capitulation of the French forces in Egypt, he went to Malta and served on the staff of the British Army in the Mediterranean. While in Malta, in May 1802, Captain Keane purchased a majority in the 60th Foot, but continued to serve on the staff there until March 1803 when he returned to England. In August 1803, he purchased his lieutenant colonelcy in the 13th Foot and joined the regiment in Gibraltar in the winter of 1804. Lieutenant Colonel Keane and his regiment returned to England in January 1806 and spent the next two years both there and in Ireland rebuilding its strength. In January 1808 they were ordered to the West Indies. The regiment was initially stationed in Bermuda but took part in the capture of Martinique in 1809. He remained in Martinique until the summer of 1812, when he exchanged into the 60th Foot. While he was in Martinique he was promoted to colonel.

Colonel Keane arrived in the Peninsula in October 1812. Instead of immediately taking command of the 5th Battalion 60th Foot, he was appointed the temporary commander of a brigade in the 3rd Division. By the time he assumed command of the brigade it was in winter quarters and the command was more of an administrative position than anything else. Colonel Keane led the brigade until 25 March 1813, when General Thomas Brisbane took command. Colonel Keane then assumed command of the 5th Battalion. Many of the companies of the 5th Battalion were attached to other brigades in the army. In the 3rd Division was its battalion headquarters and three companies. They fought at the Battles of Vitoria on 21 June, 1st Sorauren on 28 July, and 2nd Sorauren on 30 July. In early August 1813, Colonel Keane succeeded to the command of a brigade in the 3rd Division as the senior battalion commander in the division. He retained command of it until the end of the war.[4] He led the brigade at Nivelle on 9 November 1813, Orthes on 27 February, Tarbes on 20 March, and Toulouse on 10 April 1814.

With the war ended in Europe, in April 1814 the British Government decided to send a large force to fight in North America against the United States. Most of the officers and men were to be taken from Wellington's army. Colonel Keane was selected to join this force by the Commander-in-Chief. However, when the size of it was reduced and its objectives changed, he was not included in the new force.[5] Shortly after the names of the brigade commanders in it were announced, word was received at Wellington's HQ that Colonel Keane had been promoted to major general on 4 June. In the early autumn of 1814 he was sent to Jamaica with reinforcements. At a stop at Madeira on his way to Jamaica, he learned that General Robert Ross, who commanded the British forces in Maryland, had been killed and his troops – after being rebuffed at Baltimore – had

---

4. In a General Order of 15 May 1814 he was appointed a colonel on the staff backdated to 1 August 1813 for the purpose of receiving allowances for commanding a brigade.
5. *WSD*; Vol. 9, page 136.

Sir Frederick Adam. (*By William Salter.*
© *National Portrait Gallery, London*)

r George Anson. (*Courtesy of Tony Broughton*)

Sir William Anson. (*By John Young.*
© *National Portrait Gallery, London*)

Lieutenant General Lord Aylmer, KCB. I
H.W. Pickersgill. (*Courtesy Anne S.K. Bro*
Military Collection, Brown University Libr

Sir Edward Barnes. (*By William Salter.*
© *National Portrait Gallery, London*)

Sir Thomas Bradford. (*By W. Joseph Edwar*
© *National Portrait Gallery, London*)

Sir Thomas Makdougall Brisbane 1842. (*By Frederick Bromley after Thomas Frain mezzotint Collection: National Portrait Gallery, Canberra. Purchased with funds provided by Ross A. Field 2008*)

John Byng, 1st Earl of Strafford. (*By William Salter.* © *National Portrait Gallery, London*)

Sir Alan Cameron of Erracht KCB. (*Courtesy of the Highlanders Museum (Queens Own Highlanders Collection)*)

James Catlin Craufurd. (*By Lady Anne Barnard. Courtesy of Balcarres Heritage Trust*)

Sir Henry Fane. (*Courtesy of Tony Broughton*)

Sir Ronald Craufurd Ferguson. (*Possibly by William Ward. © National Portrait Gallery, London*)

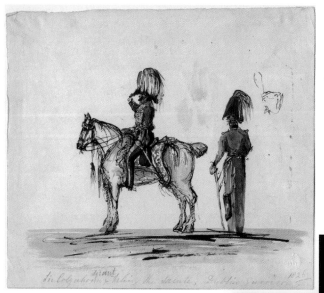

Sir Colquhoun Grant Receiving the Salute in Dublin Square 1826. (*By unknown artist. Courtesy Anne S.K. Brown Military Collection, Brown University Library*)

Sir Colin Halkett. (*By William Salter. © National Portrait Gallery, London*)

Andrew Hay. (*By William Say. © National Portrait Gallery, London*)

r Henry de Hinuber. (*Courtesy of Arbeitskreis annoversche Militärgeschichte*)

General Sir John Keane later Lord Keane of Ghuznee and of Cappoquin. Underneath hangs the sword of the Governor of Ghuznee surrendered after the battle. (*By Martin Archer Shee. By kind permission of Sir Charles Keane Bart of Cappoquin House*)

Sir William Inglis. (*Courtesy of Tony Broughton*)

Sir John Lambert. (*By William Salter. © National Portrait Gallery, London*)

Ernest Baron Langwerth. (*Courtesy of Arbeitskreis Hannoversche Militärgeschichte*)

Major General John Gaspard Le Marchant. (*By J.D. Harding. Courtesy Anne S.K. Brown Military Collection, Brown University Library*)

Robert Ballard Long. (*By Charles Turner. © National Portrait Gallery, London*)

Major General Henry Mackinnon. (*By H.R. Cook. Courtesy Anne S.K. Brown Military Collection, Brown University Library*)

Sir Peregrine Maitland. (*By William Salter. © National Portrait Gallery, London*)

Sir Denis Pack. (*By Char.
Turner. © National Portrai.
Gallery, London*)

Major General the Honourable
Sir William Ponsonby KCB
MP. (*By George Maile. Courtesy
of the Anne S.K. Brown
Military Collection, Brown
University Library*)

Lieutenant General Sir William Pringle. (*By unknown artist. © Staffordshire Regt Museum*)

eneral Francis Slater Rebow of Wivenhoe rk. (*By unknown artist. © Colchester and swich Museum*)

Sir Frederick Robinson. (*Courtesy of Government of Ontario Art Collection, Archives of Ontario*)

Major General Robert Ross of Rostrevor. (© *The Fusilier Museum, Lancashire*)

Lord Robert Edward Somerset.
(*By William Salter. © National
Portrait Gallery, London*)

r John Ormsby Vandeleur.
*By William Salter. © National
rtrait Gallery, London*)

Richard Hussey Vivian, 1st Baron Vivian. (*By William Salter.* © *National Portrait Gallery, London*)

Sir George Townshend Walker, 1st Bt. (*By Thomas Heaphy.* © *National Portrait Gallery, London*)

returned to Jamaica. General Keane assumed command of these troops when he arrived in Jamaica on 25 November. He took them, as well as the reinforcements he brought with him, and sailed to the mouth of the Mississippi River. They landed on 8 December. On 24 December General Keane was superseded in command by General Edward Pakenham. General Keane led the left column during the British attack on the American positions on 8 January 1815, at the Battle of New Orleans. He was seriously wounded in the groin. However, he had been wearing

> pantaloons of a thick worsted stuff which saved his life. The ball took the waistband of these pantaloons a considerable depth into his groin carrying the pantaloons with it. In the waistband of his drawers it made a large hole, and a still larger in his shirt; but such was the elasticity of the worsted, of which the pantaloons were made, that it not only resisted perforation effectually, but actually jerked the ball out uninjured, leaving a very severe wound of great depth.[6]

He would receive a pension of £350 for this wound. By February he had sufficiently recovered to assist in the capture of Fort Bowyer, Alabama on 13 February 1815.

After peace was declared between Great Britain and the United States, General Keane returned to England. He arrived too late to participate in the Waterloo Campaign, however, he was selected as a replacement for the general officers who were casualties. On 24 June 1815, General Torrens of the Horse Guards wrote to Wellington that, 'With regard to Major Generals, it is with an assurance that you will like the appointments that the Duke has named ... Keane ... to join you without delay.'[7] General Keane was placed upon the staff of Wellington's army in a General Order dated 2 July 1815 and given command of the 8th Brigade.[8] He was retained on the staff of the AOOF in November 1815 and was named commander of the newly organised 9th Brigade. Upon reduction of the British contingent in France on 25 April 1817, General Keane lost his brigade and was not given another command.[9]

General Keane remained without any official duties until 19 January 1818 when he was appointed the Governor of St Lucia. He remained in that post for five years. In 1823 he became the commander of the British forces in Jamaica. During his seven years in Jamaica he also served as the lieutenant governor of the island from 1827 to 1829. In April 1829 he was appointed the regimental colonel of the 94th Foot. In July 1830 he was promoted to lieutenant general and he returned to England. While in England he was appointed the regimental colonel of the 68th Foot.

On 14 October 1833 General Keane was selected to be the Commander-in-Chief of the Bombay Presidency in India. He assumed command on 2 July 1834. In the First Afghan War, he joined the Army of the Indus with a detachment of the Bombay Army in December 1838. When General Henry Fane, the army's commander, resigned, General Keane took command of the army for the invasion of Afghanistan and captured the fortress of Ghazni on 23 July 1839. On 6 August the army entered Kabul, the capital of Afghanistan. General Keane left a garrison in Afghanistan and returned home with the

---

6. Codrington; Vol. 1, page 339.
7. *WSD*; Vol. 10, page 573.
8. He replaced General James Kempt, who took command of the 5th Division after General Thomas Picton was killed.
9. General Order, 30 March 1817.

Bombay Force. He remained in Bombay until 18 October 1839, when his tenure as the Commander-in-Chief of the Bombay Presidency ended.

While in India General Keane was appointed the regimental commander of the 46th Foot in April 1838 and then the 43rd Foot sixteen months later. He was also made a GCB the same month and became the 43rd Foot's regimental colonel. When he returned to England in 1840, he received the news that he had been raised to the Peerage on 12 August 1839 with the title of Baron Keane of Ghuznee and of Cappoquin of County Waterford. With these honours came a yearly pension of £2,000.[10]

John Keane married Grace Smith, the second daughter of General Sir John Smith, on 10 August 1806. They had eight children of whom three sons went into the army and one into the Royal Navy. His wife died on 14 January 1838. He married Charlotte Maria Boland, the youngest daughter of Colonel John Boland on 20 August 1840. General Keane died on 26 August 1844 from edema most likely caused by congestive heart failure.

Not much was written about General Keane by his contemporaries. Wellington thought highly of him. He wrote to General Keane on 5 April 1817 to break the news to him that he would be sent home from the AOOF: 'I assure you that it was with the greatest pain that I gave the order to remove you from the Staff of this army. It will always give me the greatest pleasure to have your assistance again ...'[11] In his autobiography, Sir Harry Smith, who served with General Keane at New Orleans, wrote that he was 'as noble a soldier as our country ever produced'.[12] Lieutenant George Gleig, who was also at New Orleans, stated that General Keane,

> Being a young and dashing officer, he had been selected as most fit to serve under General Ross ... Young as he was, however, his arrival produced much satisfaction throughout the armament ... it was felt that a leader of more experience was wanted on the present expedition.[13]

10. *DNB*; Vol. 10, page 1155.
11. *WSD*; Vol. 11, page 663.
12. Smith; page 228.
13. Gleig; *The Campaigns of the British Army*, page 246.

Kemmis, James

Date of Birth:	1 January 1751
Date Commissioned:	Ensign 9th Foot: 1775 by purchase
Promotions:	Lieutenant 9th Foot: 3 June 1777 by purchase
	Captain 9th Foot: 21 January 1784 by purchase
	Captain 40th Foot: 31 March 1790 by exchange
	Brevet Major: 1 March 1794
	Major 40th Foot: 5 August 1799 without purchase
	Brevet Lieutenant Colonel: 1 January 1798
	Lieutenant Colonel 40th Foot:[1] 1 August 1804 without purchase
	Brevet Colonel: 25 April 1808
	Brigadier General on the Staff: 23 January 1811
	Major General: 4 June 1811
Major Commands under Wellington:	Brigade 4th Division: 16 July 1809–April 1812
	Temporarily commanded 4th Division: July–October 1809 & May–July 1811
Awards:	AGM with clasp: Roliça & Vimeiro & Talavera
Thanks of Parliament:	Ciudad Rodrigo
Date of Death:	2 April 1820 at Cheltenham, Gloucestershire

James Kemmis was born on 1 January 1751, the second son of Thomas and Susannah[2] Long Kemmis of Shaen Castle, Queen's County, Ireland.[3] On 15 February 1775 he sold his share of the family home to his older brother for £370 and an annuity of £50.[4] He used this money to purchase a commission as an ensign in the 9th Foot. At the age of 24, he was much older than the typical ensign.

The 9th Foot was stationed in Ireland at the time and in April 1776, Ensign Kemmis sailed with it to Montreal which was being besieged by American rebel forces. They arrived in June after the siege had been lifted. He was promoted to lieutenant in June 1777. He and his regiment took part in the Saratoga Campaign. They were part of General Henry Powell's brigade of General John Burgoyne's army which surrendered at Saratoga on 17 October 1777. Lieutenant Kemmis remained a prisoner of war until he was exchanged in 1781 and returned to England. He purchased a captaincy in the regiment in January 1784, but went on half-pay the same year. He remained on half-pay until 1790, when he exchanged into the 40th Foot.

In March 1794, Captain Kemmis was promoted to brevet major. He went with the regiment to Flanders in June and fought with it until the British Army was evacuated from Bremen in April 1795. Major Kemmis was not in England long when the regiment was ordered to the West Indies. They sailed in July and served there for over forty months. While there Major Kemmis was promoted to brevet lieutenant colonel. In December

---

1. Removed from the regiment as a general officer receiving unattached pay 1814.
2. Some sources give his mother's name as Susan.
3. The modern-day County Laoise.
4. 'Kemmis of Shaen'.

1798 they were ordered home. He was one of the 40th Foot's eighty-one officers and men who survived the West Indies.[5]

Lieutenant Colonel Kemmis went back to Flanders with the 2nd Battalion of his regiment in August 1799, fighting in what was known as the Den Helder Campaign. By November an armistice had been reached and the British force returned to England. The regiment was only home for four months when they were ordered to the Mediterranean. They were part of the British Expedition to Egypt and fought at Aboukir Bay on 8 March and Alexandria on 21 March 1801. After the ejection of the French from Egypt, the 2nd Battalion went to Malta and then to Minorca in November 1801. They left for England in June 1802.[6]

The regiment stayed in England until 1806 when it was ordered to South America. Lieutenant Colonel Kemmis did not go with them. Instead he served on the staff of the Western District of Ireland from 1807 to 1808. In April he was promoted to colonel and assumed command of the 1st Battalion after it returned to Ireland in June. Colonel Kemmis and his battalion formed part of Wellington's corps that was to be sent to serve in Spain or Portugal. On 23 June, the regiment was assigned to the Highland Brigade at Cork. The corps sailed in July and began landing in Portugal on 1 August. It was reorganised on 7 August and the 1st Battalion 40th Foot was assigned to General Ronald Ferguson's 2nd Brigade. Colonel Kemmis saw action at Roliça on 17 August and Vimeiro on 21 August 1808. On 5 September, General Hew Dalrymple, now commanding the army, reorganised it. Colonel Kemmis's battalion was moved to General Miles Nightingall's brigade, which was part of the Reserve commanded by General Brent Spencer. General Spencer and Colonel Kemmis had previously served together in the 40th Foot. In October, the army in Portugal was formed into a field army for service in Spain and a garrison that would be left in Portugal. Colonel Kemmis and his battalion was part of the garrison. They did not stay in Lisbon. By 14 November, they were stationed in Elvas and by 18 March 1809 in Seville, Spain.

On 29 April, Wellington decided to keep Colonel Kemmis and his battalion in Seville. Three days later he ordered them to return to Portugal.[7] They arrived in Lisbon in early June and in July the battalion was assigned to the 4th Division. The same month Colonel Kemmis was appointed a colonel on the staff and given command of a brigade in the 4th Division.[8] Part of his brigade was the 1st Battalion 40th Foot. He led the brigade at Talavera on 27 and 28 July. Due to the wounding of the division commander, Colonel Kemmis was appointed its temporary commander. He remained as its commander until General Lowry Cole arrived in mid-October. In the autumn Colonel Kemmis was at Badajoz and Wellington was considering leaving him and his brigade as its garrison.[9] But Wellington changed his mind. They were ordered north to be with the army in the vicinity of Almeida in late November. In February 1810, Colonel Kemmis was reconfirmed as a colonel on the staff and given command of General Cole's brigade while he commanded the 4th Division.[10] Colonel Kemmis retained command of the brigade during the rest of his time in the Peninsula.

---

5. Smithies; page 75.
6. Ibid; page 96.
7. *WD* (enlarged ed.); Vol. 3, pages 197 and 204–5.
8. General Order, 16 July 1809.
9. *WD* (enlarged ed.); Vol. 3, page 548.
10. General Order, 22 February 1810.

Colonel Kemmis was present at Busaco on 27 September 1810 but being on the left flank of the British line, his brigade was not engaged. They entered the Lines of Torres Vedras in October. While there Colonel Kemmis was promoted to brigadier general in January 1811. The brigade was part of the pursuit of the retreating French Army in March 1811. However, rather than chasing it back to Ciudad Rodrigo, the brigade was sent to the British force being assembled in the vicinity of Badajoz. The city had been captured by the French the previous month. They took part in the siege of Olivença and after it fell besieged Badajoz. When word reached Marshal William Beresford, the commander of the British besieging force, that a French army under Marshal Soult was advancing to relieve Badajoz, he lifted the siege and moved his forces to meet the French. They fought at Albuera on 16 May. General Kemmis missed the battle because his brigade was ordered to remain at Badajoz and protect the siege equipment and supplies. On the day of the battle he was ordered forward but arrived too late. His division commander, General Cole, was wounded at the battle, and General Kemmis assumed command of the 4th Division until he returned in July.

In June 1811, Brigadier General Kemmis was promoted to major general. At 60 years old, he was the oldest British general with Wellington.[11] Active service was beginning to take its toll. On 2 December 1811, Wellington wrote to Lieutenant Colonel Henry Torrens of the Horse Guards that,

> there are two whom we could dispense with advantage Burne and Kemmis. They are both respectable Officers as commanders of regiments, but they are neither of them very fit to take charge of a large body … Kemmis has been very ill lately, and I think might be induced to go. I shall try if I can get them away in this manner, as I would not on any account hurt the feelings of either.[12]

Colonel Torrens replied on 4 January 1812 that, 'The Duke will relieve you from the burthen of Burne and Kemmis, if possible, yet to be recalled without some object might appear harsh to the old veterans who have done their best.'[13] On 28 January Wellington replied that he agreed with the Duke of York that 'It will be very desirable to get rid of Burne and Kemmis, but not in a manner to mortify them.'[14] Wellington was notified by Colonel Torrens on 6 February 1812 that General Kemmis would be recalled. By the end of March, General Kemmis was headed back to England.

Upon his return to Great Britain, General Kemmis was placed on the staff in Ireland. Over the next two years he commanded the Centre District, the Eastern District and then the Western District. In 1814 he took command of the Centre District and commanded it until 1819 when he retired. He died at Cheltenham, Gloucestershire on 2 April 1820. James Kemmis was married. His wife died at Southampton on 24 June 1810 while he was in Portugal. They had no children.

General Kemmis was not well liked by his subordinates. Lieutenant William Coles, 40th Foot, wrote to his brother in 1808 that his battalion commander had 'become effeminate from comfort and indulgence … as much capable of commanding a Regt. In the Field as

---

11. He was eighteen years older than Wellington.
12. *WD* (enlarged ed.); Vol. 5, page 387. The names were suppressed in the published letter but other unpublished correspondence provides evidence that Burne and Kemmis are the two referred to.
13. Unpublished letter from Colonel Torrens to Wellington dated 4 January 1812.
14. *WD* (enlarged ed.); Vol. 5, Page 487. The names were suppressed in the published letter.

a Serjeant of Militia.'[15] He also accused his commander of becoming 'involved with the wife of a common soldier.'[16] Lieutenant Coles was so disgusted with him that within a year he had transferred out of the regiment. Lieutenant Francis Simcoe, 27th Foot, wrote in his journal that General Kemmis was 'very much disliked.'[17] General Kemmis was Anglo–Irish, but in a letter to his brother, he stated that he had a 'deep-rooted antipathy to papist Irish'[18] and in another letter to his brother in 1813 he 'displayed a marked hostility to Irish Catholic officers who managed to obtain commissions.'[19] This had to have caused problems for the officers of the 27th Foot, which was an Irish Regiment and one of the battalions in his brigade. General Kemmis was the regiment's brigade commander for over three years.

15. Letter from William Coles to his brother John dated 19 December 1808, quoted in Kennedy; page 48.
16. Kennedy; page 48.
17. Fryer; page 115.
18. Letter from James Kemmis to his brother Thomas dated 31 July 1800, quoted in Kennedy; page 62.
19. Kennedy; page 62.

Date of Birth:	28 April 1772
Date Commissioned:	Ensign 1st Foot Guards: 27 January 1791 by purchase
Promotions:	Lieutenant & Captain 1st Foot Guards: 9 October 1793 by purchase
	Captain-Lieutenant & Lieutenant Colonel 1st Foot Guards: 14 May 1801 without purchase
	Captain & Lieutenant Colonel 1st Foot Guards:[1] 21 August 1801 without purchase
	Brevet Colonel: 25 July 1810
	Major General: 4 June 1813
	Lieutenant General: 27 May 1825
	General: 23 November 1841
Regimental Colonel:	10th Foot: 18 January 1824–14 September 1847
Major Commands under Wellington:	Brigade on Cadiz: July 1811–September 1812
	Temporarily commanded 1st Guards Brigade 1st Division: March 1813–July 1813
	Brigade 6th Division: 2 July 1813–April 1814
	10th Brigade: 21 May–30 November 1815
	Temporarily commanded 6th Division: 18 June–July 1815
	8th Brigade AOOF: 30 November 1815–30 March 1817
	7th Brigade AOOF: 30 March 1817–24 June 1818
	1st Brigade AOOF: 24 June–November 1818
Awards:	AGC: Nivelle, Nive, Orthes & Toulouse
	KCB: 2 January 1815
	GCB: 19 July 1838
	Waterloo Medal
	KSW 3rd Class
	KCMJ
Thanks of Parliament:	Orthes & Waterloo
Date of Death:	14 September 1847 at Weston House, Thames Ditton

John Lambert was born on 28 April 1772, the son of Captain Robert Lambert RN and Catherine Byndloss.[2] He was the younger brother of Rear Admiral Robert Lambert RN and the older brother of Captain Henry Lambert RN, Major General Samuel Lambert, and Admiral Sir George Lambert RN. He attended the Westminister School. One of his older classmates was General Robert Anstruther. John was commissioned as an ensign in the 1st Foot Guards in January 1791 and spent the next twenty-two years with the Guards.

Ensign Lambert went with the 1st Battalion to Flanders in March 1793 and fought with it at the siege of Valenciennes from 18 May to 25 July, Lincelles on 18 August, and the siege of Dunkirk in September and October. During the siege of Dunkirk he was promoted to lieutenant and captain in October 1793 and left Flanders to join the 3rd Battalion upon receiving notification of this promotion. He was made the adjutant of the 3rd Battalion on 14 May 1794 and served in that position until 1801. He spent

---

1. Removed from the regiment as a general officer receiving unattached pay on 25 July 1814.
2. Catherine Byndloss was a distant relative of the pirate Henry Morgan.

his spare time playing cricket with the Marylebone Cricket Club during the summer. In June 1798, Captain Lambert and the 3rd Battalion were sent to Ireland to fight the Irish Insurrection. They left Ireland in February 1799 and stayed in England until July when they joined General Francis D'Oyly's brigade in the expedition to Den Helder. They returned to England in November. Captain Lambert was promoted to captain lieutenant and lieutenant colonel in May 1801 and then to captain and lieutenant colonel in August 1801. In 1806 he was the commander of one of the two light companies in the 1st Battalion. They joined the British Expedition to Sicily, sailing from Ramsgate in late September. Lieutenant Colonel Lambert and company stayed in Reggio, Sicily until October 1807 and arrived in England in January 1808.

In late 1808 the government decided to reinforce General John Moore's army in Spain. The force under General David Baird included the 1st Battalion 1st Foot Guards which was in the 1st Guards Brigade under General Henry Warde. Lieutenant Colonel Lambert went with the brigade as the commander of an ad hoc flank battalion formed by the brigade's light companies. The force arrived at Corunna on 13 October and landed on 26 October. When General Baird joined General Moore on 20 December 1808, their two forces were reorganised and the Guards Brigade was assigned to General Baird's 1st Division. It remained in the division on the advance into Spain and the retreat to Corunna. It fought at Corunna on 16 January 1809 and afterwards was evacuated home with the army. The summer of 1809 saw Lieutenant Colonel Lambert back in Flanders. He and the 1st Battalion were part of 1st Guards Brigade commanded by General Moore Disney in the British Expedition sent to capture Antwerp. Known as the Walcheren Expedition, it soon became bogged down on Walcheren Island and the mission was aborted in late August. After taking numerous casualties due to disease, the 1st Battalion returned to England in September.

In July 1810, Lieutenant Colonel Lambert was promoted to colonel. He remained in London with the 1st Battalion. He took command of the 3rd Battalion in May 1811 and went with them to Cadiz. They arrived in the besieged city in late June. In early July he assumed command of the British Reserve which consisted primarily of his battalion, and detachments from the 2nd Battalion 95th Rifles and the 2nd KGL Hussars. In October, he commanded the defenses on Isla de Leon. When the Spanish first discussed requesting assistance in garrisoning Cartagena, Wellington chose Colonel Lambert to command the British troops chosen to go there.[4] He was to command until a general officer could be sent. The force sailed in late January 1812. In February he was replaced by General Andrew Ross and he went back to Cadiz and assumed command on Isla de Leon.[5]

In September 1812, Colonel Lambert and the 3rd Battalion were ordered to Lisbon. The initial plan was for them to sail from Cadiz, however, when the French retreated from southern Spain, the 3rd Battalion was part of a force sent to Seville. By late October they joined up with General Rowland Hill in Madrid. On 11 November they were at Salamanca, having marched over 640 miles in two months. There they found the 1st Battalion 1st Foot Guards. Within a month the British Army was back along the Portuguese border and in winter quarters. The two 1st Foot Guards's battalions were

---

3. 'John Lambert'.
4. *WD*; Vol. 8, pages 449 and 599.
5. Nicols; pages 142–4.

ormed as the Guards Brigade 1st Division the same month. While in winter quarters the men became very sick and the brigade was sent to Oporto to recuperate in March 1813.[6]

Before the brigade marched to Oporto, Colonel Lambert became its temporary commander and commanded it during their stay there. Because it was so far from the nearest enemy, the atmosphere was more of garrison duty in England than one of a unit in active service. There were numerous balls and social events that Colonel Lambert had to attend as the senior British officer.[7] In late May rumors began to spread within the 3rd Battalion that Colonel Lambert would be given permanent command of the Guards Brigade, when the brevet promotions to major general were announced. However, by mid-June 'everyone had given up the idea a brevet coming out this year.'[8] The pessimism of the Guards officers was misplaced for on 19 June the mail arrived in Oporto and with it came the news that Colonel Lambert had been promoted. That night in the officer's mess they 'drank General Lambert's health with three times three, which appeared to gratify him very much, & he made us a very pretty speech.'[9] Despite being on what had to be easy duty, their recovery was slow and they missed the opening stages of the 1813 Campaign, including the Battle of Vitoria. The brigade finally marched on 30 June but it took an indirect route and arrived in Vitoria around 9 August.[10]

On 2 July, General Lambert was placed on the staff of Wellington's army and given command of a brigade in the 6th Division.[11] However, when his appointment was announced he was still with the 1st Guards Brigade on their march from Oporto. On 25 July they were at Palencia when word reached him of his appointment. This was unofficial news and General Lambert refused to leave the brigade until he received confirmation from the army headquarters. Two days later, he received new march routes from the QMG. This was most likely when he was officially told of his appointment. He immediately began to make plans to leave the brigade and proceed to his new command.[12] Some histories have him leading his new brigade at 1st Sorauren on 28 July and 2nd Sorauren on 30 July. However, he was still in Palencia on 28 July, which was 400 kilometers from Sorauren. General Lambert assumed command of his brigade in mid-August. He led them at Nivelle on 9 November 1813, Nive on 9 December 1813, and Orthes on 27 February 1814. Except for Nivelle, their casualties were very light. At Toulouse on 10 April 1814, they were in reserve but were thrown into the attack on the Great Redoubt on Mont Rave. Their casualties at Toulouse exceeded the total of the previous three battles.

After Napoleon abdicated in April 1814, regiments were selected from Wellington's army to go to North America to reinforce British troops fighting the United States. General Lambert was not given command initially; however, he was sent out with a brigade in mid-October. They joined the British Army outside of New Orleans on 5 January 1815 and formed the reserve during the assault on the American positions on 8 January. Late in the battle, General Lambert took command of the force upon the death of General Edward

---

6. The 1st and 3rd Battalions of the 1st Foot Guards had 801 men die from fever between 25 January and 25 July. Hamilton; Vol. 3, page 450.
7. For a very good description of their stay in Oporto, see Bridgeman; pages 107–24.
8. Ibid; page 121. Brevet promotions to major general were traditionally announced each year on 4 June, the King's birthday.
9. Ibid; pages 121–2.
10. Ibid; pages 123 and 128.
11. General Order, 2 July 1813.
12. Bridgeman; pages 125–8.

Pakenham. He ordered the withdrawal of the army when it became apparent that another assault would not succeed. After the troops embarked, they sailed for Mobile Bay and captured Fort Bowyer on 13 February 1815. Shortly after it was captured word arrived that a peace treaty had been signed between Great Britain and the United States.

General Lambert left for England on 5 March and arrived to the news that Napoleon had escaped from exile and was back in France. General Lambert was offered a place in the British Army being raised to fight Napoleon and was sent to Flanders for a fourth time. He was appointed to command the 10th Brigade in Wellington's Anglo-Allied Army. His brigade was part of the 6th Division which was supposed to be commanded by General Lowry Cole. However, General Cole was on his honeymoon, so General Lambert commanded it at Waterloo on 18 June. The 10th Brigade was initially in reserve behind Mont Saint Jean, while its other brigade, the 4th Hanoverian Brigade, was to the left and rear of La Haye Sainte. For most of the day General Lambert was with the 4th Brigade, however, about 3 p.m. he was ordered to bring the 10th Brigade forward to stabilise the centre of the line. Its new position was almost directly behind La Haye Sainte. Although most of the brigade was protected by the rising ground between it and the French, the 1st Battalion 27th Foot stood exposed in a square and took the heaviest casualties of any British infantry unit that day. During the battle General Lambert was wounded: 'he had a most violent contusion on his right arm. It was fearfully swelled ... and as black as ebony from the shoulder to the wrist ... An arm in that state, if inflammation succeed, might slough, and ... lose it.'[13]

General Lambert continued to command the 6th Division as it advanced into France and to the outskirts of Paris. Around 7 July, General Cole arrived and took command. When the British Army was reorganised into the AOOF on 30 November 1815, General Lambert remained on the staff. Over the next three years he commanded three different brigades. When the AOOF was disbanded in November 1818, he returned to England but had no military duties. In 1822 he was appointed the commander of the Southern and Munster District in Ireland. In early 1825, he was one of the officers whom Wellington put forward to Charles W. Wynn, the President of the HEIC, to command in India. Wellington thought him 'fit to be employed'.[14] General Lambert was not selected for the position in India. He stayed in command of the district until he was promoted to lieutenant general in May 1825. General Lambert was made the regimental colonel of the 10th Foot in 1824 and served as its colonel until his death in 1847. He was made a GCB in 1838 and promoted to general in 1841. After leaving Ireland in 1825, he had no military duties other than those associated with being the regimental colonel of the 10th Foot.

John Lambert married Jane Morant on 19 October 1816. They had two daughters and two sons, one of whom joined the army. He was an avid cricket player who played for the Marylebone Cricket Club and Lord Beauclerk's XI when he was not on active service.

General Lambert was a competent officer who was careful with the lives of his men. That does not mean he was overly cautious, but he took steps to ensure that they were not needlessly exposed to enemy fire.[15] Yet when he received orders that could cause heavy

---

13. Smith; page 280.

14. *WND*; Vol. 2, page 425. Duke of Buckingham; Vol. 2, page 231.

15. A good example of this was his deployment of his brigade at Waterloo, behind La Haye Sainte. Three out of four of his battalions were placed behind the ridge and avoided much of the French artillery fire. Unfortunately the fourth battalion, the 1st Battalion 27th Foot, was needed to anchor a position that was very exposed and they took extremely heavy casualties.

casualties, such as the assault on the Grand Redoubt at Toulouse, he did not hesitate to obey them. General Lambert also listened to recommendations of his subordinates. After the initial assault at New Orleans failed, he held a council of war. The naval commanders and several of the surviving senior army officers pushed for a second assault. However, the junior officers on the staff who were veterans from the Peninsula stated that it would likely fail and that the army might be destroyed.[16] He took their advice and withdrew the army.

There are very few primary sources that mention General Lambert. He was well liked, with one junior Guards officer writing, with a touch of hero worship, 'I declare he is one of the best creatures in the world & the more I see of him the more I like him, he will be a cruel loss to our battalion when the brevet comes out …'[17] Interestingly the same young officer and Captain Harry Smith, who was his brigade major at Waterloo, both said the same thing about his relationship with his junior officers. Captain Smith wrote that, 'General Lambert has ever treated me as one of his own family.'[18] While Ensign Orlando Bridgeman wrote in a letter home that, 'It is impossible to me to express all the kindness I have received from Colonel Lambert, I am sure his behaviour is like that of a near relation …'[19]

---

16. Smith; pages 238–9. Reilly; page 295.
17. Bridgeman; page 109.
18. Smith; pages 243–4.
19. Bridgeman; page 29.

Langwerth, Ernest Baron

Date of Birth:	20 July 1757
Date Commissioned:	Ensign Foot Guards: 4 May 1773
Hanover Service:	Lieutenant Foot Guards: 16 September 1777
	Captain 8th Regiment: 7 December 1784
	Major 13th Regiment: 26 May 1795
	Lieutenant Colonel Foot Guards: 19 September 1799
British Service:	Lieutenant Colonel 1st Line Battalion KGL: 14 November 1803
	Colonel: 16 December 1804
	Brigadier General on the Staff: 1808–1809
Regimental Colonel:	4th Line Battalion KGL: 16 December 1804–28 July 1809[1]
Major Commands under Wellington:	1st Brigade KGL: 27 April–18 June 1809
	Brigade KGL 1st Division: 18 June–28 July 1809
Awards:	AGM: Talavera
Date of Death:	28 July 1809 at Talavera, Spain

His given name was Ernst Eberhard Kuno Langwerth von Simmern, however, while in British service he went by Ernest Baron Langwerth.

Ernest was born in Hanover in 1757 to George Reinhard Freiherr Langwerth von Simmern and Melusine von Campen. His father was a civil servant. Some sources have him commissioned as an ensign in the Hanoverian Foot Guards in 1769, however, most state it was in 1773 when he was 16 years old. Over the next thirty years he would serve in several regiments but he returned to command the Foot Guards in 1799. During those years he became friends with Sigismund Baron Löw and Johann Baron Bülow, and was the commander of Christian Baron Ompteda, all of whom commanded brigades in the King's German Legion. Despite his thirty years in the Hanoverian Army, Lieutenant Colonel Langwerth never saw combat.

With the disbanding of the Hanoverian Army after the French overran Hanover in 1803, many officers and men went to England to continue the fight. This was possible because the King of Great Britain was also the ruler of Hanover. These men became the nucleus of the newly formed KGL. The Hanoverian officers who joined the KGL were given temporary rank in the British Army. Lieutenant Colonel Langwerth was one of the first to join and was appointed the commander of the 1st Line Battalion when it was raised in November 1803. In July he was appointed the commander of the KGL Line Brigade. With this new responsibility came a promotion to colonel in December 1804. By January 1805 this brigade was reorganised into two brigades and he took command of the 2nd KGL Brigade. He led his brigade in the British expedition to Hanover in November 1805, but was back in England three months later.

In April 1808, Colonel Langwerth was appointed a brigadier general of the staff of General John Moore's army that was being formed for service in Sweden. General Langwerth and his brigade were assigned to the 2nd Division of the army and sailed with it to Sweden in May. After the Swedish Government refused to give the army permission to land they were sent to reinforce the British Army in Portugal on 31 July. Colonel

---

1. KGL battalions had colonel–commandants instead of regimental colonels.

Langwerth landed with his brigade at Maceira Bay on 25 August. On 5 September, the army was reorganised and Langwerth was not listed on the staff nor given a brigade command. It is not clear if he served under General John Murray who commanded four KGL Battalions.

In September it was decided to form a field army for service in Spain under General Moore and a force left to garrison Portugal and supply the field army. In a General Order of 26 September the garrison of Portugal was formed and General Langwerth was assigned to the garrison and given command of a KGL brigade. They were stationed in Lisbon. In March 1809 his brigade was part of the KGL Division which was commanded by General Murray. In April 1809, General Langwerth was retained on the staff of the army when Wellington was appointed its commander.[2] His brigade was kept under General Murray's command and was in the force that Wellington took north to liberate Oporto in May 1809. After the city fell, General Langwerth's brigade was part of the pursuit of the retreating French Army. Once the French were across the border in Spain, General Langwerth and his men returned to Oporto.

On 18 June 1809 the British forces were reorganised and General Langwerth's brigade was assigned to the newly formed 1st Division, commanded by General John Sherbrooke. He led the brigade into Spain that summer. During the first day of the battle of Talavera on 27 July, his brigade saw little action. Things were quiet for most of the next day until 3 p.m., when the 1st Division was attacked by two French divisions. General Sherbrooke ordered his brigades not to fire until the French were 50 yards away. They were to fire one volley and then charge. General Langwerth's brigade executed these orders perfectly. They and the other three brigades in the division fired once and then attacked the French with bayonets. The French fled across the Portina Stream, closely followed by the KGL and British soldiers. The pursuit soon became disorganised and was caught by the French reserves on the far side of the stream. The KGL and British soldiers were brought under heavy fire from the French infantry to their front and the artillery, which fired grapeshot into their flanks. Three of the four brigades in the 1st Division, including General Langwerth's brigade, broke under the tremendous fire and fled back to the British lines.

British casualties were severe and General Langwerth's brigade had lost 50 per cent of its strength in 30 minutes of fighting. Among those killed was General Langwerth, who was hit in the stomach by grapeshot[3] and abandoned on the field. His body was recovered after the battle and he was buried under an acacia tree on the battlefield.[4] The following day, Wellington wrote to Viscount Castlereagh[5] that he had 'particularly to lament the loss of … Brig. Gen. Langwerth, of the King's German Legion …'[6] He also expressed his sorrow in a letter to General John Murray on 10 September 1809, when he wrote, 'You will be sorry for poor Langwerth.'[7]

Ernest Langwerth married Juliane von Ahlefeldt on 28 June 1796. Her father was General Siegfried von Ahlefeldt. They had one son. Upon his death, his wife received an annual pension of £300.

---

2. His appointment was confirmed in a General Order dated 27 April 1809.

3. Other sources state he was shot in the forehead.

4. Langwerth von Simmern; page 530.

5. Robert Stewart Viscount Castlereagh, Secretary of State for War.

6. *WD* (enlarged ed.); Vol. 3, page 374.

7. Ibid; page 491.

Le Marchant, John Gaspard

Date of Birth:	9 February 1766
Date Commissioned:	Ensign Wiltshire Militia: 25 September 1781
Promotions:	Ensign 1st Foot: 18 February 1783
	Cornet 6th Dragoons: 30 May 1787 by purchase
	Lieutenant 2nd Dragoon Guards: 18 November 1789 by purchase
	Captain 2nd Dragoon Guards: 31 December 1791 by purchase
	Major 16th Light Dragoons: 1 March 1794 by purchase
	Lieutenant Colonel[1] Hompesch's Hussars:[2] 6 April 1797 without purchase
	Lieutenant Colonel 29th Light Dragoons:[3] 22 May 1797 by appointment
	Lieutenant Colonel 7th Light Dragoons: 1 June 1797 by appointment
	Lieutenant Colonel 2nd Dragoons Guards: 19 July 1799 by appointment
	Lieutenant Colonel 6th Dragoon Guards: 25 July 1811 by appointment
	Brevet Colonel: 30 October 1805
	Major General: 4 June 1811
Major Commands under Wellington:	Cavalry brigade 30 August 1811–22 July 1812
Awards:	AGM: Salamanca
Date of Death:	22 July 1812 at Salamanca, Spain

John Le Marchant was born in 1766 in Amiens, France to John Le Marchant and Mary Hirzel. His grandfather was Count Hirzel of Saint Gratien, while on his father's side they were the descendants of Normans who settled in Guernsey in 1200. Before he was 10 years old, John was sent to King Edward's School in Bath, where he became good friends with Sidney Smith, who would become an admiral in the Royal Navy. Despite his future reputation as a scholar, the headmaster of King Edward's School stated 'that of all the dunces he had ever known Le Marchant and his friend Smith were the greatest.'[4]

When he was 15, John's father arranged for him to be commissioned in the Wiltshire Militia. He jeopardised his future as a soldier when he challenged his colonel to a duel. Fortunately, the colonel was a family friend and Ensign Le Marchant's punishment was a stern lecture by the colonel.[5] In 1783, he was appointed an ensign in the 1st Foot and served with them in Ireland and Gibraltar. Four years later he was still an ensign with little prospect for advancement, so he purchased a cornetcy in the 6th Dragoons. Cornet Le Marchant was noticed by King George III, when he commanded the King's escort in southern England. The King was so impressed that he promised to see him promoted at the first opportunity. While waiting for his promotion, he caught the eye of Sir George Yonge, the Secretary at War, who became his patron. Through his patronage, Cornet Le Marchant was often invited to attend royal functions. Yonge also arranged for Cornet Le Marchant to be able to purchase a lieutenancy in the 2nd Dragoon Guards in 1789.

1. Permanent rank in the army.
2. Disbanded 1797.
3. Renamed the 25th Light Dragoons in 1802.
4. Le Marchant; page 6.
5. Ibid; page 6. *DNB*; Vol. 33, page 23.

Although Lieutenant Le Marchant was assigned to the regiment, his patron obtained for him a two-year leave of absence to study in Strasburg. While there, Lieutenant Le Marchant became fluent in French. He returned to his regiment in 1791 and purchased his captaincy in December.

In May 1793, Captain Le Marchant and a squadron of the 2nd Dragoon Guards were sent to Flanders. He fought at Kassel on 30 June and in early August was appointed the brigade major of General William Harcourt's cavalry brigade. He fought with them at Lincelles on 17 August and at Le Cateau on 26 April 1794. Shortly after the battle, Captain Le Marchant found out that he was successful in purchasing a majority in the 16th Light Dragoons and he returned to England.

Major Le Marchant joined his new regiment at Weymouth, where the King was in residence. Over the next two years he wrote *Rules and Regulations for the Sword Exercise of the Cavalry*, which was adopted by the British Army in 1796. In April 1796 he was promoted a lieutenant colonel in Hompesch's Hussars, but it is doubtful that he spent any time with them, for the following month he was appointed a lieutenant colonel in the 29th Light Dragoons, and then in the 7th Light Dragoons on 1 June. During his time with the regiment, he used his royal connections to lobby for the establishment of a military school to train junior officers. In May 1799 the Royal Military College was established at High Wycombe. Lieutenant Colonel Le Marchant was appointed its first superintendent.[6]

Lieutenant Colonel Le Marchant spent the next eleven years at the Royal Military College. He was appointed the Lieutenant Governor and Superintendent General of the Royal Military College in July 1801. In February 1803 he exchanged to half-pay in the 15th Light Dragoons. This was not a financial hardship for his annual earnings from his half-pay and the pay he received as the Lieutenant Governor and Superintendent was £2,000.[7] In October 1805 he was promoted to colonel. By January 1809 he had been removed from half-pay and became an unattached lieutenant colonel of cavalry on full pay at the Royal Military College.

While at the Royal Military College, Colonel Le Marchant continued to cultivate friendships with high government officials and not just among the royalty. One patron was William Windham, who served as the Secretary of War from 1806 to 1807. Many of the bills in Parliament that were introduced by Mr Windham were first sent to Colonel Le Marchant for his recommendations. Mr Windham also consulted with the colonel on a variety of subjects, including the length of enlistments for the soldiers.[8]

Upon his promotion to major general in June 1811, John Le Marchant became too senior to continue at the Royal Military College. Wellington wrote to Earl Liverpool on 27 August 1811, 'that we cannot have too much British cavalry ... an augmentation of cavalry therefore, should the season be favorable ... will enable us to relieve those in front occasionally, and thus always to have a body of cavalry in good condition. I am therefore very glad that you have sent Le Marchant's brigade.'[9] General Le Marchant arrived in Portugal on 24 August and he was formally appointed as the brigade commander on 30 August.[10] Within ten days of his arrival in Portugal, he received word that his wife had died giving birth. He was offered the opportunity to relinquish his command and return

---

6. The appointment was backdated to 4 January 1799.
7. If he had stayed with his regiment, his annual pay would have been £404.
8. Le Marchant; pages 125–7.
9. *WD* (enlarged ed.); Vol. 5, page 239.
10. General Order, 30 August 1811.

to England, however, he found that his relatives had already made arrangements to look after his children, so he stayed with the army.

On 8 November, General Le Marchant's brigade was assigned to the 1st Cavalry Division.[11] They spent two months in winter quarters and in January 1812 were part of the covering force during the siege of Ciudad Rodrigo. He was at Wellington's side during the assault on the city on 19 January and after the city fell, the brigade moved south to cover the force that was besieging Badajoz. General Le Marchant's first action in eighteen years came on 11 April at the combat of Villa Garcia. He led his brigade on an all-night march through rugged terrain and fell on the flank of the French cavalry that was about to overwhelm General George Anson's light cavalry brigade. After the battle, General Le Marchant returned to the vicinity of Ciudad Rodrigo. On 13 June, they crossed the Agueda River and entered Spain.

At Salamanca on 22 July 1812, General Le Marchant was on the right of the British Army screening General Edward Pakenham's 3rd Division which was moving to attack the French left. Wellington approached him and 'told him that the success of the movement of the third division would greatly depend on the assistance they received from the cavalry; and that he must therefore be prepared to take advantage of the first favourable opportunity to charge the enemy's infantry.'[12] The commander of the British cavalry, General Stapleton Cotton, ordered him to charge. There was some confusion on where exactly he was supposed to go and General Le Marchant asked General Cotton for clarification. General Cotton lost his temper and replied, 'To the enemy, Sir.'[13] Captain William Bragge wrote:

> Our Brigade literally rode over the Regiments in their Front[14] and dashed through the Wood at a Gallop, the infantry cheering us in all Directions. We quickly came up with the French Columns and charged their Rear. Hundreds threw down their Arms, their Cavalry ran away, and most of the Artillery jumped upon the Horses and followed the Cavalry.[15]

After breaking the first two French lines, General Le Marchant's brigade was disordered but continued to charge the fleeing French. He saw some French in the woods trying to form a square and charged them with a troop of the 4th Dragoons. They were met with heavy fire and he was shot in the groin. He fell unconscious from his horse into the French ranks. 'The bullet, passing through the sash, had lodged deeply in a vital part, and the surgeons upon examining the wound, stated that death must have been instantaneous.'[16] Shortly after they stopped the British charge, the French infantry retreated and General Le Marchant's body was found by some of his dragoons and carried to the rear, where he was put in a stable.[17]

General Le Marchant was buried two days later in an olive grove near where he died. His brigade was no longer near, having continued the pursuit of the defeated French. His funeral was simple and attended only by his son, Lieutenant Carey Le Marchant, Major

---

11. General Order, 8 November 1811.
12. Le Marchant; page 288.
13. Combermere; Vol. 1, page 274.
14. The British 3rd Division.
15. Bragge; page 64.
16. Le Marchant; pages 300–1.
17. Ibid; page 304.

William Onslow of the 4th Dragoons, a doctor, and the general's servant. Major Onslow gave the eulogy. The general was buried wrapped in the cloak he wore on the day he died.[18]

John Le Marchant married Mary Carey on 29 October 1789. She died in childbirth in 1811. They had ten children. His nine surviving children each received a pension on his death.[19] His eldest son, Captain Carey Le Marchant, was severely wounded at the Battle of the Nive on 13 December 1813 and died from the wound on 12 March 1814. Two other sons also joined the army.

In many ways, John Le Marchant was a renaissance man whose impact on the British Army was far greater than one would have assumed for a relatively junior officer. He designed the sword that was adopted by the British light cavalry in the Peninsula, while his treatise, *Rules and Regulations for the Sword Exercise of the Cavalry*, in 1796 became the sword drill that the British cavalry used. It was through his efforts that the Royal Military College at High Wycombe and Great Marlow were established. Over 200 junior officers attended the school while he was its superintendent. Many of these officers would serve on the staff of Wellington's army in the Peninsula and at Waterloo. John Le Marchant's interests, however, were not just confined to the military. He was also an accomplished artist and an amateur musician, as well as a philanthropist. While at the Royal Military College, he funded out of his own pocket a school for poor children.[20]

General Le Marchant was well liked by the officers in his brigade, however, they did voice concerns about his lack of field experience. Captain Bragge, an officer in the 3rd Dragoons, wrote home in October 1811 that 'He is a pleasant Man, highly accomplished and a great Theoretical Warrior, but I greatly fear we shall in him experience how very much Practise exceeds Theory.'[21] The same officer wrote in March 1812 that:

> Genl Le Marchant has his whole Brigade within reach of him and has therefore begun playing Soldiers in order to prove the efficiency of some miserable awkward Manoeuvres which he has himself been coining. I have no doubt they all occurred to Sir David [Dundas][22] but were rejected for others infinitely superior. Be that as it may, our Schoolmaster had the three Regts out yesterday and would I have no doubt treat us with more Field Days should opportunities offer themselves.[23]

It was unlikely General Le Marchant was able to institute any changes on how the brigade would manoeuvre on the battlefield prior to the start of the Salamanca Campaign. Regardless of the drill that they used, his brigade's charge at Salamanca on 22 July was one of the greatest cavalry charges of the Napoleonic Wars. In the space of 40 minutes, his 800 men crushed three French infantry divisions and destroyed the left wing of the French Army. Prior to General Le Marchant's arrival in the Peninsula, Wellington was searching for a commander of his heavy cavalry. He found one in General Le Marchant. Had he not been killed at Salamanca, General Le Marchant would have been destined for greater things.

---

18. Ibid; pages 304–5.
19. The pensions totaled £1,200 per year and included £300 for his son Carey, who was a captain in the army.
20. *DNB*; Vol. 33, page 24.
21. Bragge; page 18.
22. General Dundas was the commander-in-chief of the British Army from 1809 to 1811. He is best known for formalising and instituting the drill used by the British during the Napoleonic Wars.
23. Bragge; page 38.

Lightburne, Stafford

Date of Birth:	Unknown
Date Commissioned:	Ensign 37th Foot: 15 August 1775
Promotions:	Lieutenant 37th Foot: 10 February 1778 without purchase
	Captain-Lieutenant 37th Foot: 18 October 1787 by purchase
	Major 119th Foot: 22 August 1794 without purchase
	Lieutenant Colonel Royal Dublin Regiment of Foot: 3 December 1794 without purchase
	Lieutenant Colonel 53rd Foot:[1] 1 September 1795 appointed
	Brevet Colonel: 1 January 1801
	Brigadier General on the Staff: 1805–1808
	Major General: 25 April 1808
	Lieutenant General: 4 June 1813
Major Commands under Wellington:	Independent Brigade: c. 8 July 1809–2 January 1810
	Brigade 4th Division: 2 January–22 February 1810
	Brigade 3rd Division 22 February–c. 6 October 1810
Date of Death:	27 September 1827 in London

Some sources give his family name as Lightburn and other sources spell his name as Strafford.

Little is known about the personal life of Stafford Lightburne, including his date of birth. He was the son of John Lightburne and Mary Hatton (*née* Tench). Since his father was the mayor of Wexford, he was probably born in Ireland. It is unknown whether Stafford ever married, however, at least one source gives Mary Hatton as his wife, instead of his mother.

Stafford Lightburne was commissioned as an ensign in the 37th Foot in 1775. The following year, the regiment was sent to New York and took part in the Battle of Long Island in August. Over the next five years he fought in many of the major battles and campaigns of the American Revolution, including Brandywine and Germantown in 1777, Stoney Point in 1779, and the siege of Charlestown in 1780. He was appointed a lieutenant in the regiment in 1778. Lieutenant Lightburne was with the British Army at the siege of Yorktown in 1781, where he was wounded. When the army surrendered in October, he gave his parole and went home. After the war was over, Lieutenant Lightburne re-joined his regiment in North America and served in Newfoundland and Nova Scotia. He purchased the rank of captain-lieutenant in 1787 and remained in North America until 1789, when the regiment returned to England.

Captain Lightburne stayed in England until March 1793, when his regiment was sent to Flanders. He fought at the sieges of Valenciennes and Dunkirk. At the Battle of Tournay on 22 May 1794, he distinguished himself during the intense fighting at the village of Pond de Chien. In August Captain Lightburne was appointed a major in the 119th Foot, which was stationed in Ireland. Within four months of his promotion to major, he was promoted to lieutenant colonel in the Royal Dublin Regiment. The

---

1. Removed from the regiment as a general officer receiving unattached pay 1814.

regiment was disbanded the following year and Lieutenant Colonel Lightburne was transferred to the 53rd Foot in September 1795.

Lieutenant Colonel Lightburne joined his new regiment in Southampton, England and sailed with it to the West Indies in November 1795. He was at the capture of St Lucia in May 1796 and fought the insurgents on St Vincent through the rest of the year. In February 1797 he took part in the capture of Trinidad and in April the expedition to Puerto Rico. Lieutenant Colonel Lightburne returned to England because of his poor health in 1798 but went back to the West Indies in 1799. He became the commandant of Fort Morne Fortune on St Lucia and was promoted to colonel in January 1801. Colonel Lightburne and his regiment sailed for England in late autumn 1802.

Colonel Lightburne was appointed a brigadier on the staff of the Eastern District in Ireland in 1805. He remained there for the next four years. In April 1808, he was promoted to major general. On 9 June 1809, General Lightburne was informed that he was to be sent to the Peninsula with reinforcements for Wellington's army.

In late June, General Lightburne sailed for Portugal and disembarked at Lisbon on 4 July. Wellington was with the army in Spain, but received word of their arrival by 8 July.[2] The AG informed General Lightburne on 9 July 1809 that Wellington wanted the regiments under his command to remain near Lisbon in order to bring them to a state of discipline that would render them capable of taking the field when ordered to join the army. He was to regularly report on their progress.[3] By 17 July, General Lightburne and his brigade were placed under Marshal William Beresford's command. However, it was not until 21 August that he was officially appointed on the staff of the army.[4] By early August they had left Lisbon and was headed to Castello Branco. On 26 August Wellington gave Beresford the option to keep General Lightburne's brigade or if he did not want it, he was to order it to go to Abrantes. By September, General Lightburne and his brigade were in Abrantes, however, he was temporarily replaced in command of his brigade because he was absent due to his indisposition.[5] Exactly what was wrong with him is unknown.

In January 1810, General Lightburne and his brigade were assigned to the 4th Division, but seven weeks later were re-assigned to General Thomas Picton's 3rd Division. They would spend the next seven months in northern Portugal in the vicinity of Celorico supporting the Light Division, which was screening the border. In July the French invaded Portugal and began besieging Almeida. It was at this time that Wellington suddenly and vehemently asked for General Lightburne's recall. He wrote to Lieutenant Colonel Torrens at the Horse Guards on 29 August 1810, asking that he be relieved:

Then there is General Lightburne, whose conduct is really scandalous. I am not able to bring him before a court-martial as I should wish, but he is a disgrace to the army which can have such a man as a Major General … However, I pray God and the Horse Guards to deliver me from General Lightburne …[6]

---

2. *WD* (enlarged ed.); Vol. 3, page 346.
3. *WSD*; Vol. 13, page 330.
4. General Order, 21 August 1809. His appointment was backdated to 26 July.
5. General Order, 17 September 1809.
6. *WD*; Vol. 6, page 582. General Lightburne's name was suppressed in the volume.

On 15 September, the French Army crossed the Coa River and started marching towards Lisbon. General Lightburne continued to command his brigade during the British retreat. His brigade was at the Battle of Busaco on 27 September, however, it saw little action. Shortly after the battle, Wellington received a response to his request for the relief of General Lightburne from Lieutenant Colonel Torrens.

> ... by my Official letters of this date that your prayers to The Horse Guards have been complied with. May all your prayers be equally propitious! ... Nothing surprised me more than the original Appointment ... to the Staff of the Army in The Field, and as I have known his Character for several years, not only from report but from my own personal Experience of his unworthiness, I cannot but rejoice that you are relieved of such a burden! Sir David Dundas desires me to tell you that he does not wish to shrink from the responsibility of ordering this Officer Home, but he considers it necessary to apprise you that upon the Major-General's arrival here He may most probably think it his duty to acquaint Him that the representations which have been received of his conduct from you and others will render it impossible for Sir David ever to lay his name before the King for promotion or further employment, and it may possibly be recommended to him to retire from the Service upon the sale of his Lieut Colcy. You are left of course [to] use your discretion as to preparing General Lightburne for this possible reception, but I would recommend you not torment yourself further with the subject.[7]

Wellington never revealed the specific incidents that caused him to insist that General Lightburne be relieved. In a letter to Lieutenant Colonel Torrens, dated 4 October 1810, he wrote:

> I am much obliged to you for relieving me from Major General Lightburne ... I have no public objection to make of the former, but he has been guilty of many little improprieties which render him a discreditable person with the army; and before I had received your letter of the 19th, with the official letter announcing his recall, Major General Picton who commands the division in which his brigade is posted, had urged his recall so strenuously, that I had determined to send him word that he had my leave to quit the army, and go to Lisbon. Sir D. Dundas will be the best judge whether this communication will be sufficient authority to hold the language which he proposes to hold to him. In these times I should prefer avoiding to employ him and give no reason; and I should have acted accordingly, if I had sent him leave of absence, as I intended before I received your letter.[8]

The cause of Wellington's displeasure may have been alcohol related. Rumors had spread through the army after Busaco that General Lightburne had been drunk on the day of the battle and his division commander would not risk them in battle.[9] There may have been some truth in these rumors because he did not receive an Army Gold Medal that was given to senior officers commanding at the battle. By 6 October, General Lightburne

---

7. Unpublished letter dated 19 September 1810.
8. *WD* (enlarged ed.); Vol. 4, pages 314–15. General Lightburne's name was suppressed in the volume.
9. Cameron; page 94.

was relieved of his command and he returned to England. Regardless of the reason for him being sent home, no further action was taken against him. However, he was never given any other military duties. Since the whole matter was kept quiet, he was promoted to lieutenant general in 1813. General Lightburne died in 1827.

Like his personal life, little is known about General Lightburne's personality. He may have been a bit parsimonious. The custom in Wellington's army was for a general to invite officers who were visiting his headquarters to dinner. It soon became known throughout the army who provided the best meal. Wellington once stated that 'Cole[10] gives the best dinners in the army; Hill,[11] the next best. Mine are no great things; and Beresford's and Picton's are very bad indeed.'[12] According to one officer, General Lightburne fell into the same category as Beresford and Picton. He wrote in his diary, 'I dined with General Lightburne, who was here with his brigade, and to do him justice he gave us the worst dinner I ever sat down to.'[13]

---

10. General Lowry Cole.
11. General Rowland Hill.
12. Cole; Vol. 1, page 322.
13. Glover, Gareth; *Wellington's Lieutenant Napoleon's Gaoler*, page 82.

Long, Robert Ballard

Date of Birth:	4 April 1771
Date Commissioned:	Cornet 1st Dragoon Guards: 4 May 1791 by purchase
Promotions:	Lieutenant 1st Dragoon Guards: 25 February 1793 without purchase
	Captain 1st Dragoon Guards: 10 October 1794 by purchase
	Major York Rangers:[1] 26 July 1797 by purchase
	Lieutenant Colonel Hompesch's Mounted Rifles:[2] 8 March 1798 by purchase
	Lieutenant Colonel York Hussars:[3] 30 May 1800 appointed
	Lieutenant Colonel 2nd Dragoon Guards: 3 December 1803 by exchange
	Lieutenant Colonel: 16th Light Dragoons: 22 August 1805 appointed
	Lieutenant Colonel: 15th Light Dragoons: 12 December 1805 by exchange
	Brevet Colonel: 25 April 1808
	Brigadier General on the Staff: 25 January 1811
	Major General: 4 June 1811
	Lieutenant General: 19 July 1821
Major Commands under Wellington:	Brigade 7th Division: 5 March–20 March 1811
	Cavalry with Hill's detached corps: 20 March 1811–16 May 1811
	Cavalry brigade: 13 June 1811–c. August 1813
Awards:	AGM: Vitoria
Thanks of Parliament:	Albuera
Date of Death:	2 March 1825 at Berkeley Square, London

Robert Long was born in 1771 at Chichester. He was the second son of Edward Long of Aldermaston House in Berkshire and Mary Palmer (*née* Beckford). The family was very wealthy and owned numerous plantations in Jamaica. Robert had a twin brother and when they were 9 years old he and his twin were sent to Harrow, where they remained until 1789. The following year Robert was sent to Orbe in Switzerland to study French, but transferred to the University of Göttingen. In May 1791, Robert Long's family purchased him a cornetcy in the 1st Dragoon Guards.[4]

It is unknown when Cornet Long quit his studies on the continent, however, by 1792 he was with his regiment just north of London. When war with France was declared in 1793, the regiment was expanded by 25 per cent and Cornet Long was appointed a lieutenant. He went to Flanders later in the year and fought at Beaumont on 26 April and Tournay on 22 May 1794. Lieutenant Long was appointed the brigade major that spring and purchased his captaincy in October 1794. He continued to serve in Flanders and was appointed a DAG in 1795. When the British Army was evacuated from the continent in late 1796, he was among the last to leave and only boarded his ship in January 1797.

---

1. Disbanded in December 1797.
2. Disbanded in 1802.
3. Disbanded in 1802.
4. McGuffie; page 20.

Upon returning to England Captain Long was appointed a brigade major on the Home Staff and then an ADC to General William Augustus Pitt, the commander of the Southwestern District. In July 1797, Captain Long purchased his majority in the York Rangers. He was not with them long, because the regiment was disbanded in December. Technically, Major Long was on half-pay, but he was still carried on the regimental rolls and received full pay. He had no regimental duties. In March he purchased his lieutenant colonelcy in the Hompesch Mounted Rifles. He went with the regiment to Ireland in 1798, but not as its commander. While with the regiment, he became close friends with John Le Marchant.

In May 1800, Lieutenant Colonel Long was appointed a lieutenant colonel in the York Hussars. The regiment was disbanded in 1802 after the Peace of Amiens, which forced him on half-pay. Instead of retiring to the family estates, he took the opportunity to become a student at the Royal Military College. He was the only general officer in Wellington's Peninsular Army who studied there. One of his instructors was his friend, John Le Marchant. In December 1803, Lieutenant Colonel Long exchanged into the 2nd Dragoon Guards. He served with the regiment in Ireland for two years. In August 1805 he transferred to the 16th Light Dragoons, which were also stationed in Ireland. He commanded them for only four months, when he exchanged into the 15th Light Dragoons.

Lieutenant Colonel Long joined his new regiment in southern England. He spent the next three years training and instilling discipline in the officers and men. He took an interest in anything that could affect his regiment, whether it was the cleanliness of the barracks and the maintenance of trooper's uniforms and equipment, to the professional education of his officers and NCOs. During this time he oversaw the conversion of the regiment from light dragoons to hussars. Unfortunately for Lieutenant Colonel Long, his methods often conflicted with the regimental colonel, the Duke of Cumberland.[5] In April 1808, he was promoted to colonel.

Colonel Long did not go to Spain with the 15th Hussars when they were sent there in October 1808. Instead, he was appointed a colonel on the staff of General John Moore's army the same month. Colonel Long arrived in Vigo, Spain in mid-December. He sailed with the transports for Corunna on 14 January, arriving there the next day. He was present at the Battle of Corunna but had no official duties. He was at General Moore's deathbed when he died that night. Colonel Long returned to England with the army and in the late spring was appointed the AG of the ill-fated Walcheren Expedition. When the bulk of the Walcheren Army was evacuated back to England in September 1809, Colonel Long went with it. He would spend much of the next five months assisting the army commander in testifying before Parliament. Colonel Long had no official duties after the Parliamentary Inquiry was finished and was not employed on the staff for the rest of 1810.

In January 1811 Colonel Long was offered a position as a brigadier general on the staff of Wellington's army. He arrived in Lisbon on 3 March. Two days later he was appointed the commander of an infantry brigade in the 7th Division. He only commanded it for fifteen days, for on 20 March he was assigned to command the cavalry with General Rowland Hill's detached corps, which was temporarily commanded by Marshal William

---

5. Prince Ernest, Duke of Cumberland. Son of King George III. Later King Ernest Augustus I of Hanover.

Beresford.[6] His command consisted of three British and two Portuguese cavalry regiments. Five days after assuming command of the cavalry, General Long was at Campo Mayor where he ordered a charge by his British light dragoons and the two Portuguese regiments on a retreating French column, which included numerous artillery pieces and their caissons. After breaking the French cavalry, General Long lost control of his regiments and they began a vigorous 10-kilometre pursuit to the gates of Badajoz. He was about to order a charge by his remaining British dragoons on several French infantry squares, when Marshal Beresford countermanded the order. By the end of the battle, the French escaped with about 200 casualties, but General Long lost over 150 men.

Unfortunately for General Long, a more senior general, William Erskine, applied for the command of Marshal Beresford's cavalry in late April and Wellington could not ignore his claim. General Erskine was appointed commander on 11 May.[7] Wellington wrote General Long a long letter the same day he gave General Erskine the command explaining why he was superseded, noting that General Madden[8] would probably be joining Marshal Beresford's force and would have taken command as the senior officer regardless of Wellington having given the command to General Long. He informed General Long that General Erskine had applied for the command of the cavalry and that since he was senior, Wellington gave the command to him. Wellington wrote that he had intended to appoint General Long to

> the command a good brigade of light dragoons with this army, only that I yesterday received the notification of the appointment, by command of the Prince Regent, of Major Gen. V. Alten to command the hussars of the Legion. This appointment, and his expected early arrival, must alter that arrangement; and I have not yet determined in what manner it will be most advantageous to the service to employ you. I request you, therefore, to remain with the troops under Sir W. Beresford till you shall hear further from me.[9]

It took a while for the news to reach Marshal Beresford that General Long was being replaced, so General Long continued to command the cavalry until the Battle of Albuera on 16 May. The British and Portuguese force had combined with a Spanish army for the battle. General Long was junior to the Spanish cavalry generals and General William Lumley was appointed the overall commander of the British cavalry in his place. Suddenly General Long was without a command. With what is possibly one of the worse pieces of staff work made in Wellington's army, Marshal Beresford did not announce the decision until the day of the battle and there is considerable doubt about who actually commanded the cavalry. Fortunately for the British, there was not much need for them during the battle.

A month later, Wellington appointed General Long to command a cavalry brigade.[10] When Wellington decided to create two cavalry divisions, General Long's brigade was assigned to the 2nd Cavalry Division on 19 June.[11] This division was attached to the

---

6. General Order, 20 March 1811.
7. General Order, 11 May 1811.
8. General George Madden was a British officer commanding a Portuguese cavalry brigade.
9. *WD* (enlarged ed.); Vol. 5, pages 3–4.
10. General Order, 13 June 1811.
11. General Order, 19 June 1811.

corps that had been under Marshal Beresford, but was now commanded by General Hill. General Long remained in the 2nd Division until the whole of the cavalry was formed into one division in April 1813. For most of the next year, he and his brigade were in the vicinity of Badajoz and fought in numerous combats and actions, including Usarge on 25 May, Arroyo dos Molinos on 28 October, and the raid on Almaraz in May 1812. General Long and his brigade did not arrive in time for the Battle of Salamanca, but was part of the covering force during the retreat back to the Portuguese border in the autumn of 1812.

In March 1813, one of the regiments in General Long's brigade was sent home because it was understrength. It was not replaced and for the next four months his brigade consisted of one light dragoon regiment that had less than 400 men. They were at Vitoria on 21 June, but saw little action. In early July, another regiment was added to his brigade. At this time, Wellington's army was spread out guarding the passes that led through the Pyrenees from Spain to France. General Long's brigade had the mission of maintaining communications between the wings of the army. On 11 August he received notification of his recall to England.

General Long arrived in England on 1 September 1813. He was offered a command in Scotland, but declined it. He never had active military employment again. In many ways the army deliberately forgot him and his service; and the slights were many. Although he received the Thanks of Parliament for his contributions at Albuera, he did not receive the AGM given to the senior commanders at the battle. Despite serving thirty months in the Peninsula, his name was conspicuously left off the list of officers who were made KCBs on 2 January 1815. He was promoted to lieutenant general in 1821, but that was due to seniority rather than any recognition of merit. General Long was one of the few generals who was not made a regimental colonel.

Robert Long never married. He was fluent both in French and German. Although he died in London, he was buried in the family crypt in St Laurence's Church in Seale, Surrey.

As a regimental commander, Robert Long was well thought of by his subordinates. When the York Hussars were disbanded, the regimental officers gave him a presentation sword to show their appreciation for what he did for the regiment. In the 15th Hussars he was affectionately referred to as 'Bobby Long' by the enlisted soldiers.[12] One trooper in the regiment wrote:

Coincident with my joining the regiment was the appointment of a new commanding officer, for the purpose, as reported, of reforming both the morals and discipline of the corps; and in this undertaking, no one could labour more, both physically and mentally, than the talented Colonel L—g. To an untiring zeal, activity, and perseverance, he added a thorough knowledge for perfecting the hussar in every branch of his duty, from his entrance into the barrack-room, to his completion and fitness for the field. Nothing came amiss to this highly gifted officer; and he possessed the ability and tact of rendering obedience to his instructions as much a pleasure as a duty. It is my belief he never penned a regimental order merely for form's sake.[13]

---

12. Tale; page 42.
13. Ibid; pages 26–7.

Although he was well liked by his subordinates, Robert Long was outspoken and this caused him many problems with his superiors. While he commanded the 15th Hussars he was at odds almost from the very beginning with his regimental colonel, the Duke of Cumberland. The regimental colonel was a sinecure and the better colonels took an active interest in the administrative matters of the regiment. Traditionally they did not command the regiment in the field or became involved in its daily operations. Yet the Duke of Cumberland often took command of the regiment during manoeuvres. One of the issues was that the Duke was a proponent of picqueting as a punishment. Picqueting involved suspending a soldier by his wrists overhead and making him stand on a picquet stake. This was considered inhumane, even for the early nineteenth century. Lieutenant Colonel Long opposed this, although he would flog a soldier when necessary. After he was promoted to colonel in 1808, the Duke of Cumberland arranged for Lieutenant Colonel Colquhoun Grant to exchange into the regiment. He was one of the Duke's favourites and was the Duke's Groom of the Bedchamber.[14] Although Colonel Long was the senior lieutenant colonel and commanded the regiment, if he was serving on a staff outside the regiment, then Lieutenant Colonel Grant would command. Within two months of him exchanging into the regiment, Colonel Long was serving on the staff and the Duke had his man in command.

The Duke of Cumberland was not the only high official Robert Long alienated. After he returned from the disastrous Walcheren Expedition, he was quite vocal in his defense of the army command and blamed the government for what went wrong. He felt that the poor planning and their ignorance of a place that was less than 150 kilometers from England was inexcusable and led to the destruction of the army from disease.

Robert Long's outspokenness continued to cause him problems. When he was summoned to London to discuss a possible position in Wellington's army, he told his family that he did not want to have 'anything to do with Marshal Beresford and his Portuguese Heroes.'[15] Whether he expressed this to the Horse Guards is unknown, however, that sort of attitude would be difficult to hide, especially if he was assigned to a command under the marshal. Unfortunately for him, General Long was assigned to Marshal Beresford's command shortly after he arrived in Portugal. Their relationship soured after Campo Mayor and continued to worsen over the next year. General Long believed that the marshal took every opportunity to undermine him and blamed his own failures on his subordinate. In November 1811, Marshal Beresford wrote to Wellington accusing Long of the misuse of Portuguese officers as his ADCs. General Long vigorously defended himself and got General Hill involved. General Long was very bitter that Wellington took Marshal Beresford's side in the dispute. The feud continued for years after General Long left the Peninsula and did not end at his death. After William Napier published his *History of the War in the Peninsula and the South of France* in the 1820s, General Long's nephew took up his cause in a series of pamphlets that pitted William Napier and him against Marshal Beresford and his supporters.

General Long's relationship with Wellington started off well. On 21 January 1811, Lieutenant Colonel Henry Torrens of the Horse Guards wrote to Wellington with the news that General Long was being sent out to Portugal. He described General Long as

---

14. McGuffie; pages 31–6. Mollo; page 41.
15. McGuffie; pages 44–5.

'active, able, and intelligent'.[16] Initially Wellington had high hopes for General Long and gave him the equivalent of a cavalry division to command. But after the Battle of Campo Mayor, he quickly became disillusioned. On 30 March 1811, he wrote to Marshal Beresford of his displeasure:

> I wish you would call together the officers of the dragoons, and point out to them the mischiefs that must result from the disorder of the troops in action. This undisciplined ardour of the 13th dragoons, and 1st regiment of Portuguese cavalry, is not of the description of the determined bravery and steadiness of soldiers confident in their discipline and in their officers. Their conduct was that of a rabble galloping as fast as their horses would carry them over a plain, after an enemy to whom they could do no mischief when they were broken, and the pursuit had continued a limited distance; and sacrificing substantial advantages, and all the objects of your operation, by their want of discipline. To this description of their conduct I add my entire conviction, that if the enemy could have thrown out of Badajos only 100 men, regularly formed, they would have driven back these two regiments in equal haste and disorder, and would probably have taken many whose horses had been knocked up. If the 13th dragoons are again guilty of this conduct, I shall take their horses from them, and send the offices and men to do duty at Lisbon.[17]

Wellington considered replacing General Long and wrote to Marshal Beresford on 13 April 1811: 'I intended General Long should command the cavalry on the left of the Tagus, conceiving him to be the best we have. He does not appear, however, to have conducted matters much better than others would; and if you think proper to employ Madden with that force, he, as senior must take the command of the whole.'[18] The situation was resolved when the 2nd Cavalry Division was formed and General Erskine was given command of it.

General Long was able to rehabilitate himself in Wellington's eyes through much of 1811 and 1812. However, by late 1812, Wellington wished to rid himself of a number of cavalry generals including Long. He wrote to Colonel Torrens on 2 December 1812 that, 'I should wish, if possible, to get rid of Sir Wm. Erskine, General Slade & General Long, particularly the first and the last'.[19] Colonel Torrens replied on 30 December, 'You will see by the Duke's official Letter that H.R.H. has decided upon recalling ... Long ...'[20] Although Wellington no longer wanted the generals in his army, he wanted to ensure they were taken care of. He responded to Colonel Torrens on 22 January 1813: 'I have perused the copy of my letters to you of the 2nd and 6th Dec., and I observe that I did not recommend that the General officers mentioned should be otherwise provided for if removed. I therefore proposed to suspend till further orders the execution of His Royal Highness' orders in regard to all these General Officers ...'[21]

Colonel Torrens wrote back on 16 February that the Duke of York's original official recall letter contained an offer of eventual employment but the Duke could not guarantee

---

16. Fortescue; Vol. 8, Part 2, page 26.

17. *WD*; Vol. 4, page 710.

18. *WD* (enlarged ed.); Vol. 4, page 745. General Long's name was suppressed in the book.

19. *WSD*; Vol. 7, page 485. General Long's name was suppressed in the book.

20. Unpublished letter dated 30 December 1812.

21. *WD* (enlarged ed.); Vol. 6, pages 243–4.

it would occur: 'And as you state that you do not wish them removed unless to other employment, HRH can have no objection to your retaining them if you should not think the communication of His favourable intentions towards them as stated in the accompanying Official Letter, sufficient to meet the difficulty.'[22]

In April 1813 Wellington sought General Stapleton Cotton's opinion on reorganising the cavalry. In a letter of 7 April he told him:

> I have received discretionary orders to send to England Slade, Alten and Long ... I have not sent home any of these officers, because I am not quite certain what your wishes and opinions are, and because I doubt whether you would mend matters very materially by their removal ... One of the Generals above mentioned must go at all events, as I conclude that you will wish to put the 13th light dragoons in the brigade with the 12th and 16th ... I beg to know which of the three you wish should go.[23]

Despite asking General Cotton's opinion about the three generals, it is obvious that Wellington wanted General Long sent home, since the 13th Light Dragoons were in General Long's brigade.

Despite Wellington's feelings about General Long, he was not recalled. No decision was made for four months and he was kept in command of his brigade during the 1813 Campaign. One of the reasons why he was not removed was because Wellington did not wish to send him back to England with no position lined up for him. Wellington wrote to Colonel Torrens on 2 July 1813, 'It would likewise be very advisable to appoint Major General Long to the Home Staff, as he is not very useful here, and I believe would be very much so at home ... But I do not wish to remove Long unless he can be provided for at home.'[24] It was too late. Wellington got his wish on 22 July, when Colonel Torrens responded, 'I have the Commander-in-Chief's commands to acquaint your Lordship that the Prince Regent has been pleased to remove M. General Long from the Staff of the Peninsula to that of Great Britain, and your Lordship will therefore be pleased to cause that officer to return to this country with his earliest convenience.'[25]

By early July General Long saw the writing on the wall and let his family know he was about to be recalled. On 5 August, Colonel Torrens wrote to alert Wellington to his feelings on commanding a cavalry brigade with Wellington's army:

> I have seen a letter from General Long to his brother, wherein he expresses high satisfaction with his present command, having, through your kindness, got the brigade which of all others in the world he prefers, and that nothing will ever induce him to think of England in the shape of a wish to return while a British soldier remains in Spain! As near as I can recollect these are his words; and I determined to lose no time in apprising you of them, as being likely to create embarrassments upon the subject of his removal to the home staff.[26]

---

22. Unpublished letter dated 16 February 1813.
23. *WD* (enlarged ed.); Vol. 6, pages 406–7.
24. *WD* (enlarged ed.); Vol. 6, pages 574–5. General Long's name was suppressed in the book.
25. McGuffie; page 288.
26. *WSD*; Vol. 8, page 172.

Colonel Torrens was correct that General Long would not go quietly. In response to the news of his recall Long wrote to Colonel Torrens and implied he would be asking for a court of inquiry on how he was treated. The same day he wrote to his brother that he had

> ... thrown down the gauntlet of defiance to them, and shown my determination not to be 'Sladed'[27] in silent passiveness ... The conviction of this step having been taken to give Col. Grant[28] a Brigade at my expense ... no military man can be removed from active to home service, unless at his own request, without feeling it a slur upon him. I wish the practice to be discontinued, and that they should find out a way to provide for their favorites without offending those whom they determine to supersede. They dare not be honest, and they have not sense enough to be civil ... They possess not the delicate sense of Honor which should be a soldier's breastplate.[29]

Except for his initial handling of the cavalry at Campo Mayor in March 1811, General Long was a competent brigade commander and took care of his men. His main fault was that he tended to be cautious when manoeuvring his brigade; not a trait one would wish to have in a light cavalry commander. His problems in the Peninsula, however, stemmed from his outspokenness about things he observed or perceived slights. His letters to his family were filled with criticism of Marshal Beresford and to some extent Wellington. The contents of these letters were not kept private and his feelings were known at the highest levels of the British Government. It is probable that had he kept quiet he would not have been recalled and would have received the honours his contemporaries did at the end of the war. But his recall, combined with his refusal to take any other employment upon his return from Spain, was enough to ensure he was ignored when the honours were awarded.

Unfortunately for General Long, his disputes with Wellington and Marshal Beresford overshadowed his achievements. Future historians would judge him harshly. One noted historian confused General Long's caution with a lack of courage, when he wrote that General Long was one of several generals 'of whose gallantry the army seem ever to have had any doubt ...'[30]

---

27. General John Slade, another cavalry general, was recalled from the Peninsula in April 1813.
28. Colquhoun Grant, who was brought into the 15th Hussars by the Duke of Cumberland to replace Robert Long.
29. McGuffie; page 289.
30. Glover, Michael; *Wellington as Military Commander*, page 199.

Low, Sigismund Baron

Date of Birth:	7 November 1757 in Staden in the Wetterau Region of Hesse Kassel
Date Commissioned:	Ensign Foot Guards: 1 April 1774
Hanover Service:	Lieutenant Foot Guards: 5 October 1778
	Captain Foot Guards: 8 December 1787
	Major Foot Guards: 15 August 1794
	Brevet Lieutenant Colonel Foot Guards: 8 December 1802
	Major General: 1816[1]
	Lieutenant General: 11 February 1817
	General: 1838
British Service:[2]	Lieutenant Colonel 7th Line Battalion KGL: 21 January 1806
	Colonel: 20 December 1804
	Brigadier General on the Staff: 18 June 1809
	Major General: 25 July 1810 [3]
Regimental Colonel:	4th Line Battalion KGL: 17 August 1809–24 February 1816[4]
Major Commands	
under Wellington:	KGL Brigade 1st Division: 18 June 1809–6 May 1813
Awards:	AGM with clasp: Talavera & Salamanca
	KCB (Honourary): 2 January 1815
	KCH: 1815
Thanks of Parliament:	Ciudad Rodrigo & Salamanca
Date of Death:	16 July 1846 in Offenbach, in Hesse

His German name was Freiherr Sigismund Christoph Gustav von Löw von und zu Steinfurth, but it was sometimes spelled Steinfurt. While in Hanoverian service he was known as Sigismund von Löw. While in British service he was called Sigismund Baron Low, but the British Army Lists gave his name as Siegesmund Baron Low. In official British correspondence, his name was occasionally spelled Lowe.

Sigismund Low was born in 1757, the youngest child of Johann Freiherr von Low von und zu Steinfurth, the Hanoverian Lord Chamberlain, and Sophie Freiin Marie Margarethe Diede zu Fürstenstein. Sigismund Low was commissioned as an ensign in the Hanoverian Foot Guards in 1774. He would spend the next twenty-eight years with the regiment.

Ensign Low was on garrison duty in Hanover for many years. In 1787 he was promoted to captain and six years later went with his regiment to Flanders. He fought at Famars on 23 May 1793 and was part of the force that captured Valenciennes on 28 July 1793. Captain Low was in Flanders through the next year and in August 1794 he was promoted to major. After the Peace of Basel in the spring of 1795, Major Low returned to Hanover with his regiment. The next seven years were quiet and he was promoted to brevet lieutenant colonel in December 1802.

---

1. Backdated to 25 July 1810. British Army rank was recognised when KGL officers entered new Hanoverian Army.
2. All ranks were temporary in the British Army until 1812.
3. Permanent rank in British Army dated 18 August 1812.
4. KGL battalions had colonel-commandants instead of regimental colonels.

With the disbanding of the Hanoverian Army after the French overran Hanover in July 1803, many officers and men went to England to continue the fight. These men formed the King's German Legion. Lieutenant Colonel Low joined the KGL in January 1806 and was appointed the commander of the 7th Line Battalion. Shortly after joining the KGL, he was promoted to colonel with his date of rank being backdated to 20 December 1804.[5] Colonel Low and his battalion were in Colonel Peter Du Plat's brigade during the expedition to Copenhagen from August to October 1807. In 1808, it was in Colonel George de Drieberg's brigade of the 2nd Division of General John Moore's army that was sent to Sweden in April. The expedition was not allowed to land in Sweden, so it returned to the British Isles in July.

Colonel Low and the 7th Battalion accompanied General Moore's corps that was sent to reinforce the British Army in Portugal on 31 July. They landed at Maceira Bay on 25 August, too late to participate in either the Battles of Roliça or Vimeiro. On 5 September, the army was reorganised and his battalion was placed under General John Murray, who commanded four KGL Battalions in the 3rd Division. In September a decision was made to form a field army for service in Spain under General Moore. A force would be left to garrison Portugal and supply the field army. Colonel Low's battalion was selected to join the garrison in Lisbon.[6] Once again he was in General de Drieberg's brigade. By 6 January 1809, Colonel Low and his battalion were in Santarem. In March 1809 they were part of a small KGL Division commanded by General Murray. They participated in the Oporto Campaign in May, but did not fight at Oporto on 12 May.

On 18 June 1809, Colonel Low was appointed a brigadier general on the staff to command General de Drieberg's brigade.[7] Wellington explained his reasons for promoting him in a letter to Lieutenant Colonel Henry Torrens of the Horse Guards on 1 July 1809: 'I appointed Col. Baron Low to be a Brig. General, as he was the senior Colonel of the Legion present; Brig. Gen. Drieberg was gone to England for the recovery of his health, and Col. Baron Low was senior as a Colonel to many officers who are Brigadiers in this army.'[8]

General Low led his brigade at Talavera on 27–28 July 1809. He lost control of his men in an ill-timed charge across the Portina Stream. They took heavy casualties from the French counter-attack, which broke the brigade, causing it to flee in disorder behind the British lines. In August, General Low was given command of a newly formed brigade that combined the two KGL brigades of the 1st Division.[9] This consolidation was caused by the death of General Langwerth on 28 July. His brigade was the largest in Wellington's army. General Low commanded the brigade at Busaco on 27 September 1810 and Fuentes de Oñoro on 3–5 May 1811, but saw little action at either battle. It was part of the covering force during the siege of Ciudad Rodrigo in January 1812 and fought at Salamanca on 22 July 1812. The brigade distinguished itself at the siege of Burgos from 19 September–18 October, where it took heavy casualties in two of the failed assaults.

After the retreat back to the Portuguese border in the autumn of 1812, General Low was in poor health. This came to Wellington's attention and in a letter to Colonel Torrens on 6 December he requested that General Low be recalled to England: 'I have a word or two to say respecting those of infantry. There is a German General Lowe, [*sic*] a very

---

5. *London Gazette*; War Office Announcement dated 21 January 1806.
6. General Order, 26 September 1808.
7. General Order, 18 June 1809.
8. *WD* (enlarged ed.); Vol. 3, page 388.
9. General Order, 23 August 1809.

respectable man, but who is by no means fit for service in this country ...'[10] In addition to concerns about General Low's health, Wellington was worried that when the commander of the 1st Division, General William Stewart, returned to England, he would have to give General Low command of the division because he was the senior brigade commander. In the same dispatch he wrote that General Low 'will command the 1st Division when General Stewart will quit it, for which situation he is quite unfit.'[11]

General Low's poor health was already known at the highest level. When Colonel Torrens wrote to Wellington on 14 January 1813 informing him that General Low had been recalled, he stated that 'I believe [he] is worn out ...'[12] Wellington was worried that he had asked for General Low's recall without asking for assurances that he would be taken care of. He wrote to Colonel Torrens on 22 January 1813: 'I have perused the copy of my letters to you of the 2d and 6th Dec., and I observe that I did not recommend that the General officers mentioned should be otherwise provided for if removed. I therefore proposed to suspend till further orders the execution of His Royal Highness' orders in regard to all these General Officers ...'[13]

Colonel Torrens wrote back on 16 February that the Duke of York's original official recall letter contained an offer of eventual employment which the Duke could not guarantee would occur. However, "... as you state that you do not wish ... removed unless to other employment, HRH can have no objection to your retaining ... if you should not think the communication of His favourable intentions ... as stated in the accompanying Official Letter, sufficient to meet the difficulty."[14]

Wellington wrote to General Low to break the news to him on 23 April 1813:

It has been some time since His Royal Highness, the Commander in Chief, made known to me that he had ordered another officer of the Legion to come to this army in order to replace you; and I believe that he will arrive shortly. Under these circumstances and being on the eve of the opening of the campaign in this country, and seeing that the affairs in your own country advance in such a manner that your service, if your health still permits your giving them or at least your counsel would strongly be desired, I have believed my obligations to you to announce this disposition, so that you may take in hand the measures you will find convenient. In the meantime, I wish you to believe that I am very sensible, and that I will always remember with pleasure your services that you have rendered to this army; and that wherever you may go, you will have my wishes for your success and good health.[15]

On 6 May 1813, General Low relinquished command of his brigade. He returned to England shortly afterwards and was not employed by the British Army again. General Low was placed on half-pay from the British Army on 24 February 1816 and remained on it until his death. He was pensioned from the Hanoverian Army in 1817. He married a widow, Wilhelmine von Linsingen (*née* von dem Busch).

10. *WSD*; Vol. 7, pages 494–5. General Low's name was suppressed in this edition.
11. Ibid.
12. Ibid; page 527.
13. *WD* (enlarged ed.); Vol. 6, pages 243–4.
14. Unpublished letter dated 16 February 1812.
15. *WD* (enlarged ed.); Vol. 6, page 443. The original letter was in French. Our translation was done by Howie Muir.

Lumley, Hon. William

Date of Birth:	28 August 1769
Date Commissioned:	Cornet 10th Light Dragoons: 24 October 1787 by purchase
Promotions:	Lieutenant 10th Light Dragoons: 19 May 1790 by purchase
	Captain 10th Light Dragoons: 4 December 1793 by purchase
	Major in Lieutenant Colonel Ward's Regiment of Foot: 10 March 1795[1] without purchase
	Lieutenant Colonel 22nd Light Dragoons:[2] 25 May 1795[3] without purchase
	Brevet Colonel: 29 April 1802
	Brigadier General on the Staff: 1804–1809
	Major General: 25 October 1809
	Lieutenant General: 4 June 1814
	General: 10 January 1837
Regimental Colonel:	3rd Reserve Battalion:[4] 9 July 1803–24 February 1805
	Royal West India Rangers:[5] 7 November 1812–June 1819
	6th Dragoons: 3 November 1827–30 April 1840
	1st Dragoon Guards: 30 April 1840–15 December 1850
Major Commands under Wellington:	Brigade 2nd Division: 30 September 1810–16 May 1811
	Cavalry with Hill's detached corps: 16 May–c. 30 May 1811
	Brigade 2nd Division: c. 30 May 1811–4 August 1811
Awards:	Awarded the Freedom of the City of London and £100 Sword: 15 September 1807[6]
	AGM: Albuera
	KCB: 2 January 1815
	GCB: 13 September 1831
	MGSM with clasp for Egypt
Thanks of Parliament:	Monte Video & Albuera
Date of Death:	15 December 1850 at home on Green Street, Grosvenor Square, London

William Lumley was born on 28 August 1769 at Lumley Castle, the seventh son of Richard Lumley, the 4th Earl of Scarborough, and Barbara Savile. His was a military family and his brothers included Captain Richard Lumley-Savile, Captain Frederick Lumley, Lieutenant Colonel Savile-Henry Lumley, and Captain Thomas Lumley RN. William attended Eton and at the age of 18 was commissioned as a cornet in the 10th

---

1. Lieutenant Colonel Ward's Regiment of Foot was disbanded in 1795.
2. The 22nd Light Dragoons were disbanded in 1802.
3. He was promoted to lieutenant colonel on 27 February 1796, his date of rank was backdated to 25 May 1795.
4. The 3rd Reserve Battalion was renamed as 3rd Garrison Battalion 30 October 1804 and disbanded in February 1805.
5. The Royal West India Rangers were disbanded in June 1819.
6. For service in South America.

Light Dragoons in 1787.[7] Eight years later he was a lieutenant colonel in the 22nd Light Dragoons.

Lieutenant Colonel Lumley fought with his regiment during the Irish Rebellion and was gravely wounded in the ankle at the Battle of Antrim on 7 June 1798. The seriousness of his wound forced him to return to England in January 1799 and he did not go back to Ireland until August 1800. In 1801, he took command of the regiment and went to Egypt with them. While in Egypt he oversaw the evacuation of the French from Cairo and participated in the siege of Alexandria. His regiment returned to England in December 1801, but he took several months leave of absence to travel home via Malta, Italy, and France.[8]

William Lumley was promoted to colonel in 1802 and in 1804 he was appointed a brigadier general on the staff of the London District. He was there for two years and then went to the Cape Colony in 1806. In 1807, he went with General Samuel Auchmuty's expeditionary force to South America as the second-in-command of the British ground forces.[9] He was at the capture of Montevideo and led a brigade in the disastrous attempt to capture Buenos Aires under General John Whitelocke. His brigade took heavy casualties in the assault on the city. General Lumley returned to England in November 1807 and nine months later he took a position on the staff in Sicily. He commanded a light brigade during the capture of the island of Istria in June 1809. Poor health forced General Lumley to return to England in November 1809.[10]

William Lumley had the misfortune of being placed on half-pay three times in a seventeen-year period. The first occurred when his regiment, Lieutenant Colonel Ward's Regiment of Foot, was disbanded on 24 June 1795.[11] He remained on half-pay until 27 February 1796, when he became a lieutenant colonel in the 22nd Light Dragoons. Six years later he was placed on half-pay a second time when his regiment was disbanded. In 1803, he was appointed as Colonel of the 3rd Reserve Battalion. His run of bad luck continued when, in 1805, it too was disbanded and he was placed on half-pay a third time. He remained on half-pay until November 1812, when he was appointed the Colonel of the Royal West India Rangers. Although he was on half-pay it was in his regimental rank. By the time he went on half-pay the third time he was brigadier general on the staff and continued to receive the pay and privileges of the rank.[12]

General Lumley arrived in the Peninsula on 17 September 1810.[13] He came without an appointment to a specific command but was appointed to the staff three days later. The appointment was to date from 6 August 1810.[14] General Lumley was fortuitous

---

7. *DNB*; Vol. 12, page 276.
8. *RMC*; Vol. 2, pages 352–3.
9. The commander of the ground forces was Brigadier General Samuel Auchmuty, whom General Lumley had served with in Egypt.
10. *RMC*; Vol. 2, page 354.
11. According to the Army Lists for the following year, despite the disbanding of his regiment, Major Lumley was still carried on the regimental rolls and receiving his full pay. He claims to have been on half-pay, but he may have meant that he had no regimental duties. He was not the only officer this happened to. Lowry Cole was also in the regiment and was in the same situation in regards to being on half-pay, but still receiving his pay.
12. *RMC*; Vol. 2, pages 352–3.
13. Fortescue; Vol. 7, page 418.
14. *General Orders*, Vol. 1, Page 167.

vith his timing. Although he had mostly cavalry service until 1802, he also had recent experience commanding infantry brigades. With no vacancy in the cavalry, his only chance at command was of an infantry brigade. Shortly after his arrival General Catlin Craufurd died from malaria. General Lumley assumed command of Craufurd's brigade in the 2nd Division on 30 September 1810. He was the senior brigade commander in the division. The 2nd Division was part of Marshal William Beresford's Anglo-Portuguese force conducting the siege of Badajoz and covering the southern approach into Portugal. During the approach to Badajoz, General Lumley became so ill that he had to be evacuated to Elvas in a wagon.[15] He recovered in time and during the siege of Badajoz, he commanded the forces that covered the northern side of the city, including Fort Christoval. General Lumley's British and Portuguese soldiers were the work parties and covering force that built the siege lines.[16]

On 12 May, Marshal Beresford received word that a strong French force was marching to relieve the city. He ordered the siege to be abandoned and marched his divisions to Albuera. At this point General Lumley was still in command of his infantry. However, on 15 May 1811, on the eve of the Battle of Albuera, Marshal Beresford decided to appoint him commander of all cavalry assigned to the allied army. This unusual move supposedly was because the British cavalry commander, General Robert Long, was junior to the Spanish cavalry commanders. There were two reasons why General Lumley was chosen for the command. The first was that he was the senior major general in Marshal Beresford's force who was not commanding a division. The second was that he was an experienced cavalry officer. Marshal Beresford did not announce the change of command until the battle had begun the next day. General Lumley immediately took command but there was not much he could do to impact the battle since the cavalry was already deployed and in some instances engaged with the enemy.[17] General Long, who was rather bitter at being superseded by General Lumley, wrote a few days after the battle that:

> The only difference in what afterwards happened between what General Lumley did and what I should have done, was his not availing himself of a favorable opportunity to attack the Enemy's Cavalry during their retreat, and at a time when their Infantry was flying in all directions. By shaking their covering force at such a moment we should have been put in a situation to cut off a great part of the runaways.[18]

General Lumley's cavalry began a tepid pursuit of the retreating French Army but they appeared to have slipped away. However, the French commander wanted to know what the British were doing, so he had four brigades of French cavalry under General Latour-Maubourg turn about and head back to Albuera. More by chance than any design on his part, General Lumley caught up with the French at the village of Usagre. The British were in a better position on the far side of the Usagre River with much of their force hidden by a ridge. The resulting clash saw the most one-sided cavalry action between the British and the French since Sabugal in 1808. At the cost of twenty men killed and wounded, the British inflicted over 200 casualties on the French and captured seventy-two men. Among those captured was Colonel Pierre Farine, the commander of the 4th

15. Dickson; Vol. I, page 377.
16. Jones; Vol. 1, pages 19–24.
17. McGuffie; page 104.
18. Ibid; page 106.

Dragoons.[19] General Lumley actually under-reported the extent of the damage inflicted on the French. His official dispatch of the battle stated:

> ... it is difficult, therefore, to decide upon the enemy's loss; many severely wounded escaped through the town, others threw themselves off their horses, and escaped over the brook and through the gardens; but besides 78 prisoners, 29 lay dead on the spot, many were also observed lying dead on the bridge and in the first street; and a peasant reports that from 30 to 50 were sent off wounded to their rear on horses and cars.[20]

General Lumley's health began to decline and during the summer of 1811 he requested that he be allowed to return to England.[21] On 4 August 1811, Wellington made arrangements for his passage to England.[22]

Upon his return to England, General Lumley did not go overseas for many years. In 1812, he was appointed a Groom-in-Waiting to King George III and held the same position with King George IV, King William IV, and Queen Victoria. In 1842 he became an Extra Groom-in-waiting to Queen Victoria. His military promotions continued and he was promoted to lieutenant general on 4 June 1814 and general on 10 January 1837.[23]

On 1 July 1819, General Lumley was appointed the Governor and Commander-in-Chief of Bermuda and served there until 15 September 1825. Upon his return to England his only military duties was as the colonel of the 6th Dragoons, which he was appointed on 3 November 1827. He remained as their colonel until 30 April 1840, when he was appointed the colonel of the 1st Dragoon Guards. He held that appointment until his death on 15 December 1850.

William Lumley was married twice. He married Mary Sutherland on 3 October 1804, but she died in July 1807 while he was in South America.[24] He remarried ten years later and his second wife, Louisa Cotton, who was Stapleton Cotton's sister-in-law, would survive him. He had no children.[25]

Initially, General Lumley was not highly thought of by Wellington or those in the Horse Guards. Wellington was not happy when he received word that General Lumley was being sent out. On 29 August 1810 he wrote to Lieutenant Colonel Henry Torrens, Military Secretary at the Horse Guards, that he thought that he had said that General Lumley was not very wise. Wellington then went on to say that he would be happy to get rid of him.[26] On 19 September 1810, Lieutenant Colonel Torrens replied that:

> I certainly never thought General Lumley a clever man! But He is zealous, active, obedient and as Brave as a Lion. He is not intended by nature to conduct any

19. Oman; *History of the Peninsular War*; Vol. 4, page 414. Burnham; *Charging against Wellington*; pages 245–7.
20. *WSD*; Vol. 13, page 655.
21. In 1809 Lumley 'suffered repeated violent and dangerous attacks of a liver complaint', *RMC*; Vol. 2, page 354. Could this have been a relapse?
22. *WSD*; Vol. 8, page 162.
23. *DNB*; Vol. 13, pages 276–7.
24. Milner; page 281.
25. Ibid; page 277.
26. *WSD*; Vol. 6, page 582.

command more Extensive than a Brigade, but it is generally thought that he will do that well. Colonel Bunbury[27] the present under Secy in the War Department who has lately served with Lumley gives an excellent account of him. In short I hope you will have reason to change your mind in regard to him ...[28]

After meeting Lumley and giving him a brigade command in the 2nd Division, Wellington wrote back to Lieutenant Colonel Torrens on 4 October 1810 that, 'I have seen Erskine[29] and I think he will do very well; and I dare say so will Lumley.'[30]

General Lumley did meet Wellington's later expectations with his performances at Albuera and Usarge, but still does not seem to garner anything more than faint praise. Future historians also offered mixed praise. One hundred years later, John Fortescue stated that, 'Lumley, who, though no genius with pen, ink, and paper, was capable enough in action.'[31] In 1973, Michael Glover's opinion was that General Lumley 'turned out successfully'.[32] Sir Charles Oman was quite complimentary of him:

Of the cavalry generals who took part in the great campaigns, after Paget the most successful was Lumley, who has two very fine achievements to his credit – the containing of Soult's superior cavalry during the crisis of the battle of Albuera, and the combat of Usagre of 25th May 1811.[33]

27. Henry Bunbury.
28. Unpublished letter.
29. General William Erskine.
30. *WD*; Vol. 6, page 458.
31. Fortescue; Vol. 8, page 220.
32. Glover, Michael; *Wellington as a Military Commander*, page 194.
33. Oman; *Wellington's Army*; pages 106–7.

Mackenzie, John Randoll

Date of Birth:	c. 1763
Date Commissioned:	2nd Lieutenant Marine Forces:[1] July 1778
Promotions:	1st Lieutenant Marine Forces:[2] 3 November 1780
	Lieutenant 7th Foot: 1793[3] without purchase
	Captain 78th Foot: 13 March 1793 without purchase
	Major 78th Foot: 10 February 1794 without purchase
	Lieutenant Colonel 78th Foot:[4] 15 November 1794 without purchase
	Lieutenant Colonel 78th Foot:[5] 27 February 1796 appointed
	Brevet Colonel: 1 January 1801
	Brigadier General on the Staff: 1804–1808
	Major General: 25 April 1808
Major Commands under Wellington:	2nd Brigade: 27 April–18 June 1809
	Brigade 3rd Division: 18 June–28 July 1809
	Temporarily commanded 3rd Division: 18 June–28 July 1809
Awards:	AGM: Talavera
Member of Parliament:	Tain Burghs 1806–1808, Sutherland 1808–1809
Date of Death:	28 July 1809 at Talavera, Spain

Name also spelled as M'Kenzie. Styled as Mackenzie of Suddie.

Little is known about the early life of John Mackenzie. His exact date of birth is unknown, but it is probably 1763. He was the second and only surviving son of William Mackenzie of Suddie Black Isle, Ross-shire, and Margaret Mackenzie. In 1790 his father died and he inherited the family estate. His uncle, John Mackenzie, was a colonel commandant in the Marine Forces and arranged for him to be commissioned as a 2nd lieutenant in the Marine Forces in 1778. He was promoted to 1st lieutenant in 1780.

Little is known about John Mackenzie's time in the Marine Forces except that he served as the Adjutant of the Chatham Division and was in India in 1787. By 1792, 1st Lieutenant Mackenzie was back in the British Isles. Even though his uncle was a senior officer in the Marine Forces, promotion was slow and he was still a 1st lieutenant thirteen years after he was commissioned. Lieutenant Mackenzie resigned his commission in the Marine Forces and was appointed a lieutenant in the 7th Foot in early 1793. It is unlikely he ever served in the regiment. In March 1793 he was appointed a captain in the 78th Foot, which was being raised by his relative, Francis Mackenzie, Lord Seaforth. A year later he was appointed a major in the 2nd Battalion of the regiment. He was appointed the lieutenant colonel of the 2nd Battalion in November 1794 and went with it to the Cape of Good Hope in June 1795.

Shortly after its arrival in Africa, the 2nd Battalion was disbanded and the men were absorbed into the 1st Battalion. Lieutenant Colonel Mackenzie was unemployed, but still carried on the regimental rolls and thus received his full pay. He had no regimental

---

1. Became the Royal Marines in 1802.
2. Resigned the Marine Forces c. 1791.
3. *London Gazette*; War Office Announcement dated 30 April 1793.
4. His appointment was in the 2nd Battalion.
5. This appointment was in the 1st Battalion.

uties. In February 1796, he was appointed the lieutenant colonel of the 1st Battalion and
ent with it to India, where they were on garrison duty for the next five years. Lieutenant
Colonel Mackenzie remained in India until 1801, when he returned to England 'in the
ope of finding more active employment in Europe'.[6] By the time he arrived in the
British Isles peace had been declared. He was, however, promoted to colonel the same
ear. In 1804 he was placed on the staff of the Northern District as a brigadier general.
He commanded the militia of the five northern counties of Scotland. From August to
October 1806, General Mackenzie was the governor and commandant of Alderney. In
April 1808, he was promoted to major general.

On 26 September 1808 General Mackenzie was placed upon the staff of the British
army at Lisbon. This appointment came as a surprise to him and he was not pleased
with it. He wrote in his diary on 10 October that it was 'a circumstance which distressed
me beyond description and for which I was altogether unprepared by any former hint
of communication.'[7] Instead of proceeding straight to Portugal, General Mackenzie was
given temporary command of a brigade with General David Baird's corps destined to
join General John Moore's army in Spain. He landed at Corunna in early November. By
9 November he was ordered to Lisbon to command there after the departure of General
Harry Burrard. He arrived by 29 November and commanded until the arrival of the new
commander, General John Cradock, in December. On 6 January 1809 he was in Sacavem
and on 14 January a brigade, probably under General Mackenzie, was ordered to go to
Vigo and reinforce General Moore. As they were about to sail, word of General Moore's
retreat arrived and their orders were cancelled. In February, General Mackenzie and his
brigade were ordered to Cadiz. He was refused permission by the Spanish to land there
and arrived back in Lisbon on 11 March.

After Wellington took command of the British forces in Portugal, General Mackenzie
was retained on the staff of the army on 27 April 1809. During the Oporto Campaign,
he was chosen to command a semi-independent force covering Wellington's flank at
Abrantes. The force was to watch the Eastern frontier and guard the passages over the
Tagus River between Abrantes and Santarem. This independent command was the
equivalent of a corps with over 11,500 soldiers. It consisted of his own reinforced brigade,
a brigade of British heavy cavalry under General Henry Fane, a Royal Artillery battery,
ten battalions of Portuguese infantry, two Portuguese cavalry regiments, three Portuguese
militia regiments, and three Portuguese artillery batteries.

Despite the size of the force, General Mackenzie was disappointed in not being allowed
to serve with the main army in the Oporto Campaign. He wrote in his diary on 29 April:

This movement has disappointed and distressed me. I dare say it will be accompanied
by all those expressions that can gild the Pill. But being the first act of Sir Arthur
Wellesley's Command, I do not bade much of the fortunate kind from it. I dare
say I shall be told of the importance of the Post entrusted to my Charge and that
the selection is honourable to me. This is sort of reasoning easily applied and most
fallacious. I would be sorry to suppose my political connexions have occasioned any
of the [text here is indecipherable] in line of my profession. Time will shew.[8]

---

6. 'Mackenzie, John Randoll'.
7. 'Extracts from General Mackenzie's Diary'.
8. Ibid.

In addition to not being permitted to serve directly under Wellington, General Mackenzie was not happy about having to command Portuguese troops. On 1 May he wrote in his diary:

> The command is represented of great importance, and undoubtedly may become so. I do not like having any thing to do with the Command of Portuguese troops, and I wish I was with the main Army, at the head of my Brigade, instead of this important, but certainly troublesome Command in which there is much Reputation to be lost, little to be acquired.[9]

General Mackenzie did not keep his disappointment to himself and word of it reached Wellington of his concerns. On 21 May, Wellington wrote to him: 'You are in an error in supposing that the Portuguese soldiers will not fight. One battalion has behaved remarkably well with me; and I know of no troops that could have behaved better than the Lusitanian Legion did at Alcantara.'[10] Wellington also wrote John Villiers the same day, passing on, 'Mackenzie has no confidence in the Portuguese troops ...'[11] Because of General Mackenzie's lack of faith in the Portuguese, Wellington saw no reason to increase their numbers with him and deployed them elsewhere to secure Lisbon.

General Mackenzie's friends sympathised with his situation. General Richard Stewart wrote to him after the Oporto Campaign on 14 June that he 'felt and condoled with you most sincerely upon the mortification you must have suffered from not being present with us, as well as the critical situation in which you were placed by our movement so far to the north, but I am now look [*sic*] forward again with an almost certainty of our being together and well employed.'[12] Though General Mackenzie was indiscreet with his comments, Wellington was satisfied with his conduct. He wrote on 28 May 1809, 'All that you have done is perfectly correct in every part.'[13]

When Wellington formed his army into divisions in a General Order dated 18 June 1809, General Mackenzie took temporary command of the 3rd Division as he was the senior brigade commander in the division. No source mentions an interim commander for his brigade. He probably held simultaneous command of both the division and the brigade. General Mackenzie led them in the Talavera Campaign during that summer. It was his division that was responsible for screening the army in the vicinity of Casa de Salinas on 27 July. His troops were careless and the French were able to slip past his men and nearly captured Wellington, who was reconnoitring the area.

The next day, General Mackenzie and his division were deployed just south of the Cerro de Medllin Heights in the centre of the British lines at the Battle of Talavera. After the 1st Division fell back in disorder across the Portina Creek, around 3 p.m., it was his brigade that stood fast and took the brunt of the French counter-attack. After a twenty-minute musketry duel between his three battalions and the French division commanded by General Sebastiani, the British forced the French to retreat. If General Mackenzie and his men had not held, the British line would have collapsed and they would likely have lost the battle. The cost to his brigade was terrible. In those twenty

---

9. Ibid.
10. *WD* (enlarged ed.); Vol. 3, page 245.
11. Ibid; page 246.
12. Unpublished letter from General Richard Stewart to General John Mackenzie, dated 14 June 1809.
13. *WD* (enlarged ed.); Vol. 3, page 257.

minutes, they took 25 per cent casualties. Among the fallen was General Mackenzie. Because he died, he never wrote an after-action report to Wellington and the critical role played by his brigade was not mentioned in Wellington's dispatch on the battle. The army knew though. In a letter home to his father, Captain Edward Cocks stated, 'The gallant General Mackenzie, the man who did more than anyone towards our victory, is killed … everybody deeply regrets Mackenzie.'[14]

Had General Mackenzie survived the battle he mostly likely would have been given permanent command of the 3rd Division because of his seniority. His early death ended a career of much promise. Wellington wrote after Talavera that, 'I have particularly to lament the loss of Major General Mackenzie, who had distinguished himself on the 27th …'[15] There are very few primary sources that mention anything about his character, however, in his obituary he was described as 'a zealous, steady, cool soldier; a mild and most friendly man. The Service loses in him a most excellent officer; his friends an estimable and amiable man. The 78th adored him, and will long lament him.'[16]

John Mackenzie never married and upon his death his estate passed to his youngest sister, Henrietta Wharton. He was an MP from 1806 to 1809. His military duties kept him from attending sessions very often. He was a Whig, but did occasionally vote with government. He did vote against the government over the Copenhagen Expedition. There is no record of him giving a speech before the House.[17]

---

14. Page; page 37.
15. *WD*; Vol. 4, page 536.
16. *Gentleman's Magazine*; 1809, Part II, page 780.
17. 'Mackenzie, John Randoll'.

Mackenzie, Kenneth

Date of Birth:	1768
Date Commissioned:	Ensign 83rd Foot:[1] 13 June 1781
Promotions:	Lieutenant 83rd Foot: 13 December 1782
	Lieutenant 19th Foot: 25 September 1787 appointed
	Lieutenant 14th Foot: 14 May 1788 by exchange
	Captain-Lieutenant 90th Foot: 1794[2]
	Major 90th Foot: 13 May 1794
	Brevet Lieutenant Colonel: 19 October 1798
	Lieutenant Colonel 44th Foot: 5 April 1801 appointed
	Lieutenant Colonel 52nd Foot: 24 February 1803 by exchange
	Lieutenant Colonel 91st Foot: 18 February 1808 by exchange
	Brevet Colonel: 25 April 1808
	Major General: 4 June 1811
	Lieutenant General: 19 July 1821
Regimental Colonel:	58th Foot: 1 March 1828–22 November 1833
Major Commands under Wellington:	On staff at Cadiz: August 1810–March 1811
	7th Brigade: 11 April–30 November 1815
Date of Death:	22 November 1833 in London

Name was also spelled as M'Kenzie.

Kenneth Mackenzie was born in 1768, the oldest son and heir of Kenneth Mackenzie of Kilcoy, Ross County and Janet Douglas. His grandfather was Sir Robert Douglas the author of the *Peerage of Scotland*. His mother was the heiress of her brother, Sir Alexander Douglas, the 7th Baronet of Glenbervie.

Kenneth Mackenzie was commissioned as an ensign in the 83rd Foot at the age of 13. Despite his young age, he joined his regiment in Guernsey. He was promoted to lieutenant eighteen months later, but went on half-pay when the regiment was disbanded in 1783. He was appointed a lieutenant in the 19th Foot in 1787, but went on half-pay shortly thereafter and continued to remain on half-pay until he exchanged into the 14th Foot in 1788, which were part of the garrison in Jamaica. He remained with the regiment in the West Indies until it returned to England in 1791. Lieutenant Mackenzie went to Holland with his regiment in March 1793. While there he was in its light company and was seriously wounded in the shoulder by grapeshot at the siege of Dunkirk.

Lieutenant Mackenzie was appointed a captain-lieutenant in the 90th Foot in 1794. Shortly after joining the regiment in Scotland he was promoted to major. His regiment was heavy with future general officers, including its commander, Sir Thomas Graham, whom Major Mackenzie would serve under in Holland in 1813 and 1814. The regiment's lieutenant colonel was Rowland Hill, who would be the commander-in-chief of the British Army in the 1820s, while its other major was Robert Ross, who was killed at the Battle of North Point during the war of 1812. Major Mackenzie fought with his regiment at the capture of Isle de Dieu in 1795 and went with it to Gibraltar in April 1796.

---

1. Disbanded in 1783.
2. *London Gazette*; War Office Announcement dated 27 May 1794.

Major Mackenzie remained in Gibraltar for about six months. In the autumn of 1796 he was appointed to the staff of General Charles Stuart, who commanded an expeditionary force to Portugal. He was promoted to local lieutenant colonel in October and given command of the flank battalion, which consisted of the grenadier and light companies of the force's regiments. Since his promotion was only local rank, he reverted back to being a major when the force was disbanded. General Stuart was impressed with his service and appointed him DAG. With this position came a promotion to brevet lieutenant colonel.[3] Lieutenant Colonel Mackenzie served with his regiment during the Egypt Campaign in 1801 and 1802. He commanded the advance guard of the army until the Battle of Aboukir on 8 March 1801, when the 90th Foot's commander, Lieutenant Colonel Rowland Hill, was seriously wounded and he assumed command. Lieutenant Colonel Mackenzie led the 90th Foot at the Battle of Alexandria on 21 March 1801. In April, he was appointed a lieutenant colonel in the 44th Foot and returned with the regiment to the British Isles in December 1802.

In January 1803, the 52nd Foot was reorganised as a light regiment. Its regimental colonel, Lieutenant General John Moore, did not believe its lieutenant colonels were capable of making the transition to light infantry and specifically asked that Lieutenant Colonel Mackenzie be brought into the regiment.[4] The following month, General Moore's request was approved and Lieutenant Colonel Mackenzie exchanged into the regiment. Over the next two years he and the 52nd Foot spent most of their time at the Shorncliffe Camp. While there he was the primary factor in converting the regiment to light infantry and training them to the high standard that they were known for during the Peninsular War.

Towards the end of the Shorncliffe Camp, Lieutenant Colonel Mackenzie fell from his horse and suffered from a severe concussion. He was slow in recovering and continued to have relapses after he returned to his regiment. In late 1804, his health continued to decline and he went on half-pay. On 9 April 1808, he exchanged to half-pay into the 15th Foot.[5] Despite being on half-pay for four years, he was promoted to colonel in 1808. On 15 August 1810, Colonel Mackenzie joined the British garrison of Cadiz as a colonel on the staff. He was assigned to command the Reserve on 16 August. In a reorganisation in September, Colonel Mackenzie was replaced in command of the Reserve. It is not clear what command he then held. While in Cadiz, Colonel Mackenzie continued to be plagued by poor health and he had returned to England by March 1811.

In June 1811, Colonel Mackenzie was promoted to major general and was assigned to the Home Staff in the Kent District. In November 1813, he was chosen for the staff of General Thomas Graham's force sent to assist the Allies in the Netherlands. He was originally assigned a brigade command. In December the force landed in the Netherlands and General Mackenzie commanded the Light Brigade. When more reinforcements arrived in January 1814, the force was organised into divisions and he was given command of the 2nd Division. On 1 February, he fell from his horse when it slipped on ice and took another blow to his head, which knocked him unconscious. His horse fell on him and it was some time before he was found.[6] His injuries were so severe that he was temporarily replaced in command of the division and missed the second attack on Merxem on 2 February. He returned to duty in early March but was not at the failed assault on Bergen-

---

3. *London Gazette*; War Office Announcement dated 4 June 1799.

4. Moore; Vol. 2, page 68.

5. *London Gazette*; War Office Announcement dated 9 April 1808. In 1814, he was removed from half-pay of the regiment as a general officer receiving unattached pay.

6. Bamford; *A Bold and Ambitious Enterprise*, page 131.

op-Zoom on the night of 8 March. In a final reorganisation of the army on 15 April 1814, General Mackenzie was assigned to command the Reserve.

General Mackenzie remained in the Netherlands after Napoleon abdicated in April 1814. He commanded the 2nd Brigade 1st Division of the Subsidiary Army in the Netherlands from 1814 to 1815 and was stationed in Antwerp. On 28 March 1815 he was appointed to the staff of Wellington's Anglo-Allied Army. General Mackenzie was given command of the 7th Brigade on 11 April and kept as the commander of the garrison of Antwerp.[7] He was not present at Waterloo nor the advance into France. He remained in Antwerp until December when his brigade was disbanded and was not retained on the staff of the AOOF. Upon his return to England in December 1815, General Mackenzie had no other military duties. He was promoted to lieutenant general in 1821 and appointed the regimental colonel of the 58th Foot in 1828. He commanded it until his death in 1833.

Kenneth Mackenzie married Rachel Andrews of Hythe on 18 December 1804. They had six sons and one daughter. Four of their sons became army officers. He was a Jurat of Hythe, a traditional municipal official of one of the Cinque Ports. When his uncle, Sir Alexander Douglas, the 7th Baronet of Glenbervie, died in 1812, the Baronetcy went dormant. On 30 September 1831 General Mackenzie was created the 1st Baronet of Glenbervie and on 19 October 1831 he changed his name to Douglas. He died on Holles Street, Cavendish Square, London on 22 November 1833. He was interred in the Hythe churchyard.

Kenneth Mackenzie was best known as a commander of light infantry. General Moore recognised his talent and wrote on 31 August 1804, 'The officers owe it to their own good conduct and to the attention they have paid to their duty, but above all to the zeal which they have followed the instructions of Lieutenant-Colonel M'Kenzie [*sic*], to whose talents and to whose example the regiment is indebted for its discipline and the character it has so justly acquired.'[8] General George Napier, who served under him in the 52nd Foot, wrote that, 'General Mackenzie was an old, experienced, and skilful [*sic*] officer, and had served a great deal, and particularly distinguished himself in Egypt in command of the 90th Regiment, and indeed was generally considered the best commanding officer in the army, Sir John Moore was fully justified in his choice of such an officer to command his regiment ...'[9]

General Mackenzie's limitation as a general officer was caused solely by his poor health. He suffered brain injuries when he fell from his horse in 1804 and 1814. It affected his ability to command at Cadiz and in the Netherlands. General Graham was so concerned about his health that two months after his accident on 1 February, he wrote to Earl Bathurst, the Secretary of State, on 11 April: 'Were M. Gl. Mackenzie's health quite what it was, I sh'd wish these two officers to retain the two Div'ns, but perhaps in the state he is still in from his accident it may not be considered advisable to leave him 2d in the Command of this Corps.'[10] When it came time to appoint brigade commanders in 1815, Wellington had to consider General Mackenzie's poor health when he assigned him to command the garrison of Antwerp.

Most sources give Kenneth Mackenzie's date of birth as 1754. This is based on a typo in the 1820 *Royal Military Calendar* (RMC) which states he was commissioned as an ensign in the 33rd Foot at the age of 13 in 1767. He never served in the 33rd Foot and was commissioned as an ensign in the 83rd Foot in 1781. Other data in his *RMC* entry concerning his length of service and duty locations as a lieutenant supports this.

---

7. *WD* (enlarged ed.); Vol. 8, page 50.
8. Moore; Vol. 2, page 84.
9. Napier; page 14.
10. Bamford; *A Bold and Ambitious Enterprise*, page 235.

Mackinnon, Henry

Date of Birth:	August 1773
Date Commissioned:	Ensign 43rd Foot: 31 May 1790 without purchase
Promotions:	Lieutenant 43rd Foot: 30 November 1792 without purchase
	Captain Independent Company: 11 April 1793 without purchase
	Lieutenant & Captain Coldstream Foot Guards: 9 October 1793 by exchange
	Captain & Lieutenant Colonel Coldstream Foot Guards: 18 October 1799 purchase
	Brevet Colonel: 25 October 1809
	Brigadier General on the Staff: 23 July 1811
	Major General Spain 26 October: 1811
	Major General: 1 January 1812
Major Commands under Wellington:	Brigade 3rd Division: 29 November 1809–19 January 1812
Awards:	AGM with two clasps: Busaco, Fuentes de Oñoro & Ciudad Rodrigo
Date of Death:	19 January 1812, killed in the assault on Ciudad Rodrigo

The family name was also spelled as M'Kinnon.

Henry Mackinnon was born in August 1773 the third son of William Mackinnon of Mackinnon and Louisa Vernon. His father was the 32nd Chief of Clan Mackinnon. His family were supporters of Bonnie Prince Charlie and sheltered him after the battle of Culloden in 1746. This cost the family many of their ancestral lands. Despite the loss of their estates on the Isles of Skye and Mull, the family had a plantation on Antigua which yielded an annual profit of £8,000 in 1793. Although they lost much of their land in Scotland, they were not destitute. Henry was born at Longwood House, the estate of the Earl of Northesk, which is near Winchester. When Henry was 12, the family moved to France and he attended the Military College of Tournon in Languedoc. Henry's nephew was Colonel Daniel Mackinnon, the author of *Origin and Services of the Coldstream Guards*.[1]

Henry Mackinnon was commissioned as an ensign in the 43rd Foot in 1790 and joined the regiment in Ireland. He was promoted to lieutenant in 1792 and five months later became the captain of an independent company. He stayed with his company for six months but then exchanged into the Coldstream Guards. Captain Mackinnon was in Ireland during the Rebellion of 1798, however, he did not serve with his regiment. He was the brigade major to General George Nugent commanding the Northern District of Ireland. He fought at Antrim on 7 June and Ballynahinch on 12 June.

In the summer of 1799, the Coldstream Guards received word that they would be part of the British Expedition to Den Helder. Captain Mackinnon resigned his staff appointment and rejoined the regiment. He fought at Bergen on 19 September 1799 and at Alkmaar on 2 October 1799. A few weeks after the Battle of Alkmaar, the British withdrew to Great Britain. During the final days of the campaign, Captain Mackinnon was promoted to captain and lieutenant colonel. In August 1800, the Coldstream Guards sailed to Egypt as part of the expedition to oust the French. Lieutenant Colonel

---

1. Mackinnon, Donald; pages 76–91. Burke, Bernard; Vol. 2, page 856.

Mackinnon fought at Aboukir on 8 March and at Alexandria on 21 March 1801, wher he was in temporary command of his battalion. He remained in Egypt until October an arrived in England in December 1801.

Lieutenant Colonel Mackinnon remained with the 1st Battalion of the Coldstream Guards for the next eight years. After the Peace of Amiens in March 1802, he took th opportunity to travel to Prussia, where he was well received by the Prussian Royal Family By October 1805, he was the commander of the 1st Battalion's Grenadier Company an led them in General Edward Finch's Guards Brigade during the expedition to Hanove from November 1805 to February 1806 and the expedition to Copenhagen from Augus to October 1807.

In December 1808, Lieutenant Colonel Mackinnon was the acting major of th 1st Battalion Coldstream Guards. The battalion was part of the Guards Brigade i General John Sherbrooke's force sent to secure Cadiz. They sailed on 15 January 1809 and reached Cadiz on 8 March. The Spanish Government refused to give the Britis permission to land, so the force sailed to Lisbon, arriving there on 13 March 1809. Th brigade joined the garrison of Portugal and participated in the Oporto Campaign in Ma 1809. Lieutenant Colonel Mackinnon fought with his battalion at Talavera on 27 and 2 July 1809. According to his family history, he had two horses shot out from him and fiv bullet holes in his cloak.[2]

After the Battle of Talavera, Lieutenant Colonel Mackinnon was placed in charge o the city of Talavera and the British hospital located there. On 2 August he received wor that the French were advancing towards Talavera and would be there in a few days. H quickly organised the evacuation of the wounded and sick soldiers from the hospital Because he had only forty wagons and carts, he had to leave many of those unable t travel on their own to the mercy of the French. By 18 August his convoy arrived at Elvas Portugal, having travelled 300 kilometers in two weeks. His efforts saved over 2,00 British soldiers.[3] He was promoted colonel in October 1809.

On 1 November 1809, Colonel Mackinnon received permission to return to England On his ship was Mr John Villiers, the British Envoy to Portugal. Their ship had just saile from Lisbon when it met a ship from England with news that required Mr Villiers t return to Lisbon. Colonel Mackinnon decided to cancel his leave in England and sailed with Mr Villiers back to Lisbon. He rejoined his battalion in Badajoz.[4] On 29 Novembe he was appointed a colonel on the staff to command a brigade in the 3rd Division.[5] In February 1810, General Thomas Picton arrived in Portugal to take command of Colonel Mackinnon's brigade. Wellington, however, appointed him the commander of the 3rd Division and Colonel Mackinnon kept the brigade.[6] He commanded it until his death in 1812.

Colonel Mackinnon's brigade consisted of three of the hardest fighting battalions[7] in Wellington's army. He led them at Busaco on 27 September 1810, Redinha on 12 March 1811 and at Fuentes de Oñoro on 3–5 May 1811. In July 1811, he was promoted to

---

2. Mackinnon, Donald; page 96.
3. Mackinnon, Henry; pages 35–8.
4. Ibid; pages 41–2.
5. General Order, 29 November 1809.
6. General Order, 22 February 1810.
7. They were the 1st Battalions of the 45th, 74th, and 88th Foot. They were part of the reason the 3rd Division was nicknamed the 'Fighting Division'.

rigadier on the staff in Wellington's army. However, he fell sick and obtained permission o return to England. General Mackinnon was in England for only a short time and ⸜as back in Lisbon by 21 October.[8] Towards the end of the year, there were questions bout his seniority and whether he should be commanding a brigade when there were fficers senior to him without a command. Wellington solved this problem by promoting im to local major general in the Peninsula.[9] Wellington's manoeuvre to ensure General ⸜Jackinnon kept his brigade by promoting him locally was done with the permission f the Duke of York, for he wrote to Lieutenant Colonel Henry Torrens at the Horse ⸜uards, asking him to thank the Duke of York for permitting him to do so.[10] Wellington's fforts were a bit early, for General Mackinnon was promoted to major general in the rmy on 1 January 1812. However, he could not have known that when he applied for ⸜eneral Mackinnon's local promotion.

General Mackinnon and his brigade were part of the assault on the main breach of the ⸜alls of Ciudad Rodrigo on 18 January 1812:

> The head of the column had scarcely gained the top, when a discharge of grape cleared the ranks of the three leading battalions and caused a momentary wavering; at the same instant a frightful explosion near the gun to the left of the breach, which shook the bastion to its foundation, completed the disorder. Mackinnon at the head of his brigade was blown into the air. His aide-de-camp, Lieutenant Beresford[11] of the 88th, shared the same fate, and every man on the breach at the moment of the explosion perished.[12]

Although this eyewitness implies the explosion was caused by a mine in the breach, it was ⸜ot. General Mackinnon actually made it over the breach and was leading his brigade eft along the ramparts when a powder magazine exploded. An officer from the Light ⸜Division wrote:

> I saw General Mackinnon lying dead. He was on his back just under the rampart on the inside, that is on the town side. He had, I think, rushed forward and fallen down the perpendicular wall before spoken of, probably at the moment of receiving his mortal wound. He was stripped of everything, except his shirt and blue pantaloons; even his boots were taken off. He was a tall thin man ... It is said that he was blown up. I should say decidedly not. There was no appearance indicating that such had been his fate. Neither his skin nor the posture in which he was lying led me to think it. When a man is blown up, his hands and face I should think could not escape. I never saw any whose face was not scorched. MacKinnon's [*sic*] was pale and free from marks of fire.[13]

---

8. Mackinnon, Henry; page 87.
9. General Order, 2 December 1811. His promotion was to date from 26 October 1811.
10. *WD* (enlarged ed.); Vol. 5, page 386.
11. Lieutenant John Beresford.
12. Grattan; page 152.
13. Cooke; pages 108–9.

General Mackinnon was initially buried in the breach where he died, but shortl afterwards the officers of the Coldstream Guards had him disinterred and buried wit full military honours at Espeja, Spain.

Henry Mackinnon was fluent in French, could speak German, some Spanish, an some Portuguese.[14] He married Catherine Call on 10 April 1804. They had three sons, tw of whom joined the army. Catherine was the sister of General Matthew Lord Aylmer' wife. Catherine planted in their garden 'a laurel for every action in which her husban was engaged; and when in his last visit she took him into the walk where they wer flourishing, he said to her that she would one day have to plant a cypress at the end.' After his death, she received an annual pension of £300 and his sons received £100 each

As a commander, General Mackinnon never asked his men to do something he wa not willing to do himself. When the village of Fuentes de Oñoro needed to be cleare of the French on the final day of the battle, he personally led the bayonet attack of th 74th and 88th Foot that ejected the enemy. When the attack on the breach at Ciudac Rodrigo began to falter he was one of the first to make it over the wall. His courage wa unquestionable and he paid for it with his life.

One officer who served in General Mackinnon's brigade described him as a 'stric disciplinarian, but a man of an extremely mild temper.'[16] Yet when he believed that hi men had been wronged by a superior, he would stand up for them. This at times pu him at odds with his division commander, General Picton, who did not like the poorl disciplined Irish soldiers in the 88th Foot. In 1798, Lady Londonderry perhaps summe up his character best when she wrote, 'Major Mackinnon[17] is indeed admired in Irelan for his person and courage, but he is adored for his humanity.'[18]

Family legend has Henry Mackinnon and Napoleon Bonaparte as close friends Supposedly, while Henry attended the Military College of Tournon, Napoleon was frequent visitor to his home and had proposed to Henry's sister Eliza. After Henry wa killed at Ciudad Rodrigo, his brother Charles claimed that Napoleon had offered hin a marshal's baton.[19] How much truth there is to these anecdotes is unknown, however Robert Southey, one of the first historians of the Peninsular War, believed it. He wrot that:

> It is one of the redeeming points of Buonaparte's character that he never forgot his attachment to the MacKinnon family, that during the peace of Amiens, he invited them to France where they might receive proofs of it, and that when he heard of General Henry MacKinnon's death at Ciudad Rodrigo he manifested some emotion.[20]

---

14. Mackinnon, Donald; pages 111–12.
15. Southey; Vol. 5, page 426. The cypress tree is a traditional symbol of mourning and can be found in many cemeteries.
16. Grattan; page 18.
17. Henry Mackinnon was never a major, brevet or substantive, in the army. However, officers holding a staff appointment as a Brigade Major were sometimes referred to as 'Major' as long as they held the appointment.
18. Mackinnon, Donald; page 94.
19. Mackinnon, Donald; pages 91–2.
20. Southey; Vol. 5, pages 425–6.

Maitland, Peregrine

Date of Birth:	6 July 1777 at Longparish House, Hampshire
Date Commissioned:	Ensign 1st Foot Guards: 25 June 1792 by purchase
Promotions:	Lieutenant & Captain 1st Foot Guards: 30 April 1794 without purchase
	Captain & Lieutenant Colonel 1st Foot Guards:[1] 25 June 1803
	Brevet Colonel: 1 January 1812
	Major General: 4 June 1814
	Lieutenant General North America: 21 August 1828
	Lieutenant General: 22 July 1830
	General: 9 November 1846
Regimental Colonel:	1st West India Regiment: 22 February 1830–19 July 1834
	76th Foot: 19 July 1834–2 January 1843
	17th Foot: 2 January 1843–30 May 1854
Major Commands under Wellington:	Temporarily commanded 1st Guards Brigade: July 1813–April 1814
	1st Guards Brigade: 11 April–30 November 1815
	Temporarily commanded 1st Division: 18 June 1815–July and 2 October–30 November 1815
	1st Guards Brigade AOOF: 30 November 1815–8 January 1818
Awards:	KCB: 22 June 1815
	GCB: 6 April 1852
	AGM: Nive
	MGSM with clasp: Corunna
	Waterloo Medal
	KW
	KSW
Thanks of Parliament:	Waterloo
Date of Death:	30 May 1854 in Eaton Place, London

Peregrine Maitland was born in 1777, the oldest son of Thomas Maitland and Jane Mathew, the daughter of General Edward Mathew.[2] His younger brothers were Lieutenant Edward Maitland RN and Captain Charles Maitland RA.

Peregrine Maitland's family purchased him an ensigncy in the 1st Foot Guards in 1792 and he served with the regiment for the next twenty-three years. He went with the regiment to Flanders in 1793, but after being promoted to lieutenant and captain in the spring of 1794, he returned to England and joined the 2nd Battalion's Light Company. He went back to Flanders with the Light Company in late 1794. He was only there for six months when the army was evacuated to England. By May he was performing guard duty at Windsor Castle. Captain Maitland served with the flank companies of the 1st Foot Guards in the unsuccessful raid on the Bruges Canal at Ostend in May 1798. These companies were unable to land and avoided captivity, unlike others in the force who had. When he was not tied up with his military duties, Peregrine was an avid cricket player who played for the Marylebone Cricket Club.

---

1. Removed from the regiment as a general officer receiving unattached pay, 25 July 1814.
2. Some sources incorrectly state that he was the son of Thomas Maitland and a Miss Dewar.

Captain Maitland was promoted to captain and lieutenant colonel in the 1st Foot Guards in 1803. He continued to serve on garrison duty. By 1808 he was the commander of the Grenadier Company 3rd Battalion of the 1st Foot Guards in the 1st Guards Brigade under General Henry Warde. In September 1808, the brigade was selected to join a force under General David Baird being sent to Spain to reinforce General Moore's army. It landed at Corunna on 28 and 29 October. It joined General John Moore's army on the advance into Spain and was with it during the subsequent retreat to Corunna. Lieutenant Colonel Maitland served at the Battle of Corunna on 16 January 1809 and returned with the army to England after it was evacuated from Spain. They were not home long. In July they sailed to the Low Countries and participated in the Walcheren Campaign. They were recalled within a month of landing and were back in England by early September.

In July 1811, Lieutenant Colonel Maitland was in Cadiz, Spain with the 3rd Battalion. He was promoted to colonel in January 1812. In August he was second-in-command of Colonel John Skerrett's expedition to force the French from Seville. In addition to those duties he was also the commander of the six companies that the 3rd Battalion provided to the expedition. After the French departed Seville, the British continued north and linked up with the British Army in mid-October. Colonel Maitland and his 3rd Battalion joined the 1st Battalion of the 1st Foot Guards in the newly formed 1st Guards Brigade of the 1st Division. He was given temporary command of the 1st Guards Brigade in July 1813. He led it at the crossing of the Bidassoa on 7 October, at Nivelle on 10 November, and at Nive on 11–12 December. Colonel Maitland continued in command of the 1st Guards Brigade in 1814 and led them at the passage of the Adour on 23 February and at Bayonne on 14 April. After Napoleon abdicated, Wellington's army was disbanded in June and the 1st Guards Brigade returned to England.

Although Colonel Maitland commanded the 1st Guards Brigade for a year in the Peninsula, he was never given permanent command of it. This was due to the tradition that only a Guards officer could command the Guards. Colonel Maitland was the senior 1st Foot Guards officer in the Peninsula, who was not already commanding a brigade or a division. However, Wellington could not give him permanent command because those Guards officers commanding other brigades would have a right to command it because of their seniority. Colonel Maitland was able to command it because General Kenneth Howard, the actual brigade commander, was temporarily commanding the 1st Division. He was in command of the division because Generals Thomas Graham and then John Hope, who were the 1st Division commanders, commanded the corps in 1813–1814.

Colonel Maitland was promoted to major general in June 1814 and was given command of the Guards Brigade in the Subsidiary Army in the Netherlands in January 1815. When Wellington arrived in Brussels in the spring of 1815, General Maitland was retained on the staff of the Anglo-Allied Army on 28 March 1815. Wellington had confidence in his abilities and assigned General Maitland to the command of the 1st Guards Brigade on 11 April. In doing so he anticipated the commander-in-chief's wishes regarding who would command the Guards Brigades in the 1st Division. He was correct in his assumptions for on 16 April 1815, General Henry Torrens of the Horse Guards wrote to Wellington that it was, 'His Royal Highness's wish that the division of Guards now in Flanders should be commanded as follows … 1st Regiment, 2nd and 3rd Battalions, Major-General P. Maitland …'[3]

---

3. *WSD*; Vol. 10, page 85.

General Maitland commanded the 1st Guards Brigade at Quatre Bras on 16 June and at Waterloo on 18 June. His brigade was one of the two brigades that were instrumental in defeating the assault by Napoleon's Imperial Guard in the final stages of the battle. During the battle, the commanders of both the 1st Division and the 1st Corps were wounded. When General George Cooke was wounded, General John Byng, the 2nd Guards Brigade commander, assumed command of the division. He then took command of the corps when its commander, the Prince of Orange,[4] was wounded late in the battle. After the battle, General Maitland became the temporary commander of the 1st Division.

General Maitland led the 1st Division during the advance on Paris and at the capture of Péronne on 26 June. Once in Paris, he was too junior to continue commanding the 1st Division so General Howard was sent from England to take command. By 23 July, General Maitland had returned to his brigade. General Howard was given command of the 1st Corps in late August and General Byng was made the 1st Division commander. General Byng went on leave in early October and once again General Maitland took temporary command of the 1st Division. He commanded it until the end of November when the British Army was reorganised into the AOOF. General Maitland was retained on the staff of the AOOF and given command of the Guards Brigade on 30 November 1815.

General Maitland commanded the Guards Brigade in France until January 1818, when he was appointed the Lieutenant Governor and Commander of the Forces of Upper Canada.[5] He took office on 12 August 1818 and governed until 1828. His tenure was not easy, for there were powerful reformists who attempted to undermine his rule by opposing him at almost every turn. In August 1828 he was promoted to local lieutenant general. He was recalled on 4 November 1828 but was immediately appointed Lieutenant Governor of Nova Scotia on 29 November. His service there was much quieter and he returned to England in 1832 because of poor health. He never went back to Nova Scotia, but continued to govern through correspondence. He was replaced in July 1834. While in Nova Scotia he was promoted to lieutenant general in the British Army.[6]

On 17 April 1836, General Maitland was appointed the Commander-in-Chief of the Madras Presidency in India. He assumed command on 11 October 1836 and served there until 21 December 1838. When he returned to England he had no official military duties other than as the regimental colonel of the 76th Foot until January 1843, when he was appointed the regimental colonel of the 17th Foot. Later that year, General Maitland was thrust back into colonial administration and was appointed the Governor and Commander-in-Chief of the Cape of Good Hope on 9 December 1843. Less than three years after he arrived in the colony, war broke out with the Xhosa, in what became known as the 7th Kaffir War. The British forces were caught by surprise during the early stages of the war and the Xhosa poured into the colony. After a local commander negotiated a peace treaty with the Xhosa, General Maitland rejected it as too lenient and the war continued for another year. This caused him to be recalled to London on 1 October 1846.

General Maitland's recall did not affect his standing in the army. Less than a month after being recalled he was promoted to general. He was 69 years old and had no further military duties other than as the 17th Foot's Regimental Colonel.

---

4. Prince William, the Hereditary Prince of Orange, later King William II of the Netherlands was a general in the British Army.
5. He was appointed on 8 January 1818. *London Gazette*, dated 10 January 1818.
6. Bowsfield.

Peregrine married Hon. Louisa Crofton, daughter of Baroness Crofton, on 8 June 1803. They had one son who was an army officer and served as his father's military secretary when he was the Commander-in-Chief of the Madras Presidency. Louisa died in 1805. Peregrine was the occasional target of matchmakers and by 1815 was being pursued by Lady Mountnorris in hopes he would marry her daughter Juliana.[7] While in Belgium in 1815, Peregrine began to court Lady Sarah Lennox, daughter of General Charles Lennox, 4th Duke of Richmond. She was nineteen years younger than him. Her father opposed their relationship and the couple decided to elope in October 1815. They approached Reverend George Stonestreet, the chaplain of the Guards Division. He wrote:

> She was sobbing loud, 'Here we are' said the general. 'We have just run away from the Duke's, we shall be pursued, will you marry us instantly?' ... 'What', I said (to myself), 'steal a young lady out of a duke's family; the ex viceroy of Ireland; the friend of Wellington; the offender too a good staid widower of near 40; this is a most terrible piece of larceny ... I told him and there was only one course to be pursued. He *must* get me the Ambassador's or Wellington's licence (not that the civilians think that more than waste paper). He said they would both refuse. The Duke by this time had warned them that if I did not marry them 'blood would be spilt'. He could refuse the Duke of R[ichmond's] challenge as a son in law, but not otherwise. The Duke might call him villain and only one consequence could ensue. I said I should greatly regret such consequences, that it was independent of my duty; into the course of which I might never to be terrified, by such improper considerations; the mention of which I hinted only, served to distress the lady at his side.[8]

General Maitland went to Wellington, who patched things up with the bride's father. On 9 October 1815, Wellington called in Reverend Stonestreet and ordered him to prepare the papers so that General Maitland could be married. While he was doing that, Peregrine and Sarah were married by Wellington's personal chaplain.[9] They had three sons and seven daughters, of whom one son was an army officer while another was an officer in the Royal Navy.

Peregrine Maitland is best remembered for his command of the 1st Guards Brigade at Waterloo. One of the legends that arose from the climax of the battle was Wellington calling, 'Now Maitland. Now's your time,' which triggered the Guards to stand up and fire a murderous volley into the advancing French Imperial Guard. Surprising little is known about what his subordinates or contemporaries thought of him, for very few memoirs and diaries of the period mention him. Wellington thought highly enough of him to keep him in temporary command of the 1st Guards Brigade in the Peninsula for almost a year and then appoint him again to command it in 1815. General Byng, who was senior to him, and took command of the 1st Division at Waterloo after its commander was wounded, wrote to the Duke of York the day after Waterloo that General Maitland's 'judgement and gallantry directed everything was necessary. I cannot say too much in his praise ...'[10]

---

7. Glover, Gareth; *Waterloo Archive*, Vol. 4, page 20.
8. Stonestreet; pages 55–6.
9. Ibid; page 56.
10. Glover, Gareth; *Waterloo Archive*, Vol. 4, page 144.

Nightingall, Miles

Date of Birth:	25 December 1768
Date Commissioned:	Ensign 52nd Foot: 4 April 1787 without purchase
Promotions:	Lieutenant 52nd Foot: 12 November 1788 without purchase
	Captain 125th Foot: 5 September 1794 by purchase
	Major 121st Foot: 28 February 1795 by purchase
	Lieutenant Colonel 115th Foot: 9 September 1795 by purchase
	Lieutenant Colonel 92nd Foot: c. September 1795 appointed[1]
	Lieutenant Colonel 38th Foot: 28 October 1795 by exchange
	Lieutenant Colonel 51st Foot: 23 July 1802 by exchange
	Lieutenant Colonel 69th Foot: 8 May 1806 by exchange[2]
	Brevet Colonel: 25 September 1803
	Brigadier General on the Staff: c. February 1808
	Major General: 25 July 1810
	Lieutenant General: 4 June 1814
Regimental Colonel:	6th West India Regiment:[3] 20 March 1815–1817
	49th Foot: 19 February 1820–19 September 1829
Major Commands under Wellington:	3rd Brigade: 7 August–5 September 1808.
	Brigade 1st Division: 23 January–June 1811
	Temporarily commanded 1st Division: May–June 1811
Awards:	KCB: 2 January 1815
	AGM: Roliça & Vimeiro
Member of Parliament:	MP for Borough of Eye, Suffolk: 1820–1829
Date of Death:	19 September 1829 in Gloucester

Sometimes his name is spelled Nightingale.

Little is known about Miles Nightingall's early life. It is likely that he was the illegitimate son of General Charles 1st Marquess Cornwallis, who surrendered his army to the American-French Army at Yorktown, Virginia on 19 October 1781. His mother was Ann Nightingall. Miles's life and career were closely associated with the Cornwallis family.

Miles was commissioned as an ensign in the 52nd Foot in 1787. His regiment was stationed in India and he sailed there in December. By the summer of 1788 Ensign Nightingall was in India, where his father, General Cornwallis, was the Commander-in-Chief. By the end of the year he was promoted to lieutenant. He was not in India long before the 3rd Mysore War broke out. Lieutenant Nightingall fought in numerous battles and sieges over the next two years. In 1790, he was appointed the brigade major of the 1st Brigade and fought with it at Seringapatam on 15 May 1791 and the capture of Pondicherry in August 1793. After four years of campaigning, his health began to decline and he was permitted to return to England in 1794.

While Lieutenant Nightingall was en route to England his family purchased him a captaincy in the 125th Foot in October. Captain Nightingall arrived in England in

---

1. *London Gazette*; War Office Announcement dated 29 September 1795.
2. Removed from the regiment as a general officer receiving unattached pay in 1814.
3. Disbanded 1817.

January 1795 and was appointed an ADC to his father, who commanded the Eastern District. In February he was able to purchase a majority in the 121st Foot. Shortly after being promoted to major, he was appointed the Brigade Major of the Eastern District. In September 1795 he purchased a lieutenant colonelcy in the 115th Foot and volunteered to join the expedition to the West Indies, which was being formed by General Ralph Abercromby. He was part of the 115th Foot for less than a month when the regiment was disbanded and he was appointed to the 92nd Foot. Within a month after his appointment to the 92nd Foot, it too was disbanded and he exchanged into the 38th Foot.

Lieutenant Colonel Nightingall went to the West Indies with his regiment and led them at the capture of Trinidad in February 1797. He served as an extra ADC to General Abercromby during the expedition to Puerto Rico in April, but was forced to return to England due to poor health. In December he was appointed the DAG for Santo Domingo and returned there in the winter of 1798. He help negotiate the evacuation of Port-au-Prince and in July was sent back to England with dispatches. While Lieutenant Colonel Nightingall was in England, his father, who was now the Lord-Lieutenant of Ireland, appointed him his ADC and then gave him command of the 4th Battalion of Light Infantry that was formed under General John Moore to help suppress the Irish Rebellion. In 1799, Lieutenant Colonel Nightingall accompanied General Thomas Maitland back to the West Indies, but returned to the British Isles in July.

After his arrival in England, Lieutenant Colonel Nightingall was appointed the AAG on the staff of the British force being sent to Den Helder. He fought in the Battle of Bergen on 19 September and at Alkmaar on 2 October. His health began to decline and he returned to England in November. The following January he was the DAG in the force that was sent to Quiberon Bay to raid the French coast. He was sent back to England in July. In June 1801 Lieutenant Colonel Nightingall was appointed the AQMG in the Eastern District, but was only in the job for three months. In October 1801, after his father was appointed the British Ambassador to France, he joined him as his secretary, and served with him during the peace negotiations at Amiens in March 1802.

Lieutenant Colonel Nightingall went back to India in 1803 and served as the QMG of General Gerard Lake's army during the Second Anglo–Maratha War. In September he was promoted to colonel. In July 1805, his father was appointed the Commander-in-Chief in India, and he became his military secretary. His father died in October 1805 and Colonel Nightingall was appointed the QMG of the British Forces in India. He returned to England in September 1807.

In February 1808, Colonel Nightingall was appointed a brigadier on the staff to command a brigade in General Brent Spencer's corps, which was stationed in Falmouth but destined for the Mediterranean. It sailed for Gibraltar and on 14 June it was ordered to join Wellington in Portugal. It landed on 6 August and the two corps were merged. The next day General Nightingall was assigned to command the 3rd Brigade.[4] He led the brigade at the Battles of Roliça on 17 August and Vimeiro on 21 August 1808. On 5 September, General Hew Dalrymple reorganised the army and General Nightingall was assigned a brigade in the Reserve. When it was decided to form both an army to operate in Spain and a garrison for Portugal, he was not initially assigned to either. No reason was given. General Nightingall was later assigned to General John Moore's army in Spain but he never joined it. Instead he left on a leave of absence in October 1808. His departure did

---

4. General Order, 7 August 1808.

not come as a surprise to Wellington, who was in Ireland. He wrote to General Spencer on 22 October that 'I conclude that Nightingall is on his way home'[5] and then to General Nightingall on 31 October welcoming him back.[6] General Nightingall's assignment to General Moore's army was confirmed in a General Order dated 17 November. However, he was not under orders to return to Spain until after the Convention of Cintra Inquiry was finished.[7]

General Nightingall never rejoined General Moore's army. By the time the Convention of Cintra Inquiry was over, the army was in full retreat back to Corunna, where it would be evacuated on 16 January 1809. While he was waiting to return to Spain, General Nightingall was offered the position of governor of New South Wales. After accepting the appointment, General Nightingall suffered a severe rheumatic attack which delayed his departure as late as April 1809. By then he had had second thoughts about going and declined the appointment.[8] He was eventually placed upon the staff in the Kent District[9] and was promoted to major general in July 1810.

On 21 December 1809, Wellington wrote to the Earl of Liverpool about generals he 'should like to have'[10] for his army. In the list were such notable generals as James Leith and Thomas Picton. He also requested Miles Nightingall, but in the same letter, he wrote, 'I fear that ... Nightingall would not like to come.'[11] No action was taken on his request for many months. However, in September 1810, Lieutenant Colonel Henry Torrens wrote to General Nightingall to enquire on the state of his health. He asked as he wanted to know if he was healthy enough to serve in Wellington's army in the field. He also noted that, 'Lord Wellington would be glad to receive you on the Staff of His Army.'[12]

General Nightingall accepted Wellington's offer and left England on 29 December 1810, arriving in the Peninsula on 9 January 1811. He was placed on the staff of Wellington's army on 22 January 1811[13] and assigned to command a brigade in the 1st Division on 23 January. He led his brigade in the pursuit of the French as they retreated from Portugal and temporarily commanded the 1st Division during the Battle of Fuentes de Onoro on 3–5 May, because General Spencer was commanding a corps at the time. During the battle he was wounded by grapeshot 'which fortunately struck the stirrup iron first. This turned the ball and saved my leg as it merely grazed the foot near the instep, but it struck me so hard, I really thought all the small bones of the foot had been broken'.[14] He likely continued to temporarily command the division in May and June 1811, as General Spencer was in command of the army while Wellington went south to confer with Marshal William Beresford after the Battle of Albuera.

General Nightingall was not happy about serving in the Peninsula and within a few weeks was politicking to be sent to India. On 8 April he wrote to General Alexander

5. *WD* (enlarged ed.); Vol. 3, page 131.
6. *WSD*; Vol. 6, page 182.
7. The Parliamentary Inquiry into the Convention of Cintra ended around 22 December 1808.
8. Parker; pages 126–7.
9. Muir et al.; *IWPA*, page 54.
10. *WD*; Vol. 5, page 385.
11. Ibid.
12. Unpublished letter dated 18 September 1810.
13. The appointment was backdated to 25 October 1810.
14. Glover, Michael (ed.); 'The Nightingall Letters', page 149.

Ross[15] that, 'I expect to hear soon from Torrens on the subject of India as I should be particularly anxious to go to Bengal now that Nugent[16] has got the command, as we are very great friends and he would, I am sure, give me any command I wished in that country.'[17]

On 28 June 1811, General Nightingall was appointed to the staff in India. He wasted no time in leaving the Peninsula, for Wellington wrote to Lieutenant Colonel Torrens on 25 July that he had already left the Peninsula.[18] He arrived in India in November, where he served on the staff of the Bengal Presidency and was sent to the frontier to command a division. In the late summer of 1813, he was appointed the Commander-in-Chief of Java[19] and arrived there in October 1813. While there he was promoted to lieutenant general in June 1814. General Nightingall was appointed the Commander-in-Chief of the Bombay Presidency on 10 January 1815, but stayed in Java until the following November. He assumed the office on 24 February 1816 and served until 9 January 1819. He and his wife decided to take the overland route home by sailing from Bombay to Suez and then travelling through Egypt and Europe. They trip went well until they were shipwrecked off the coast of Yemen. They eventually made it home by the end of the year.

After returning to England, General Nightingall had no further military duties other than as the regimental colonel of the 49th Foot. He was elected an MP for the Borough of Eye in 1820. His seat was a pocket borough controlled by the Cornwallis family. He was a Tory and consistently voted against Catholic relief, Irish franchise, and parliamentary reform. He was not known for having given any speeches before the House and only one before a committee. He held his seat until his death.[20]

Miles married Florentia Elizabeth Darrell on 13 August 1800. His wife was born in India in 1777. Her maternal grandfather was Timothy Tullie, the Chairman of the Honourable East India Company. They had no children. Miles died in 1829 at a spa in Gloucester.

Wellington asking for General Nightingall to serve in the Peninsula was a mistake. His health up until 1811 was always an issue and it influenced his decisions on where he served. Several times he returned early from overseas service because of it. When he reported to Wellington's HQ in January 1811 he was offered what he called a 'very good'[21] brigade in the 1st Division.[22] Instead he took a brigade that he thought was not as good because 'I have a very good house over my head, an object of the first importance during the heavy rains with which we are deluged at this season ... I was the more inclined to adopt this measure from the dread of a return of my rheumatic complaint, which the present weather is likely to bring on ... it will be a miracle if I am not laid up.'[23] General

15. General Ross was a family friend having served as ADC to Lord Cornwallis during the American Revolution and as Cornwallis's AG in India.
16. Lieutenant General George Nugent.
17. Glover, Michael (ed.); 'The Nightingall Letters', page 143.
18. *WD* (enlarged ed.); Vol. 5, page 185.
19. The British had captured the Dutch colony in September 1811.
20. 'Nightingall'.
21. Glover, Michael (ed.); 'The Nightingall Letters', page 131.
22. He turned down the offer to command General William Erskine's brigade, which consisted of the 1st Battalions of the 50th, 71st, and 92nd Foot.
23. Glover, Michael (ed.); 'The Nightingall Letters', page 131.

Nightingall continued to complain about his health in the rest of his letters from Portugal, especially in regards to how the weather affected his rheumatism and his inability to walk.

In addition to his medical complaints, General Nightingall had the reputation for being negative on a wide range of issues about the British Army in Portugal. Within a month of arriving in Portugal he felt that the British Army was trapped and their only hope was that the government would make peace with the French.[24] A month later he was still pessimistic and wrote that:

> I do not think it would not be possible to withdraw our army, even if we wished it, without the most enormous sacrifice or the alternative of a convention, neither of which would go down well in England. It therefore appears to me that this machine has been worked up to too large a size for we cannot get rid of it and it is not sufficiently large to drive the enemy out of the country. The error appears to be the idea that was entertained by many that the enemy would be obliged to retreat in a few weeks after he came before the Lines for want of provisions, but all these sanguine ideas must now vanish for he has now been four months near us and has not the smallest intention of retreating.[25]

Despite being wrong about whether the French could be forced to retreat, General Nightingall continued to complain. He felt that the cost of maintaining both the British and Portuguese armies too high and could not be continued by the British Government. He was also opposed to any operations to eject the French from Spain for the same reasons. His criticisms may have been influenced by a perceived slight by Wellington. General Nightingall was unhappy when Wellington gave division commands to two officers[26] who were junior to him, while he only commanded a small brigade.[27]

Although General Nightingall was a competent commander, he should not have returned to the Peninsula in 1811. It was very obvious from his letters home that he would rather have been in India. Considering that Wellington had little patience for those who complained or those who wrote negative letters home about the military situation, he was probably happy when General Nightingall was recalled from the Peninsula so that he could take an appointment in India.

---

24. Ibid; page 133.
25. Ibid; page 137.
26. They were Alexander Campbell, who was a personal friend of Wellington, and Robert Craufurd, who was the preferred light commander. Both had their divisions since 1810 (October and February respectively).
27. Glover, Michael (ed); 'The Nightingall Letters', pages 143–4.

O'Callaghan, Hon. Robert William

Date of Birth:	October 1777
Date Commissioned:	Ensign 128th Foot: 29 November 1794 without purchase
Promotions:	Lieutenant 30th Light Dragoons:[1] 6 December 1794 without purchase
	Captain 30th Light Dragoons: 31 January 1795 without purchase
	Captain 22nd Light Dragoons:[2] 19 April 1796 appointed
	Captain 18th Light Dragoons: 3 December 1802 by exchange
	Major 40th Foot: 17 February 1803 by purchase
	Lieutenant Colonel 39th Foot: 16 July 1803 by purchase[3]
	Brevet Colonel: 1 January 1812
	Major General: 4 June 1814
	Lieutenant General: 22 July 1830
Regimental Colonel:	97th Foot: 7 September 1829–4 March 1833
	39th Foot: 4 March 1833–9 June 1840
Major Commands under Wellington:	Temporarily commanded brigade 2nd Division: 5 January–23 July 1813 and 15 February–April 1814
	13th Brigade: 24 August–30 November 1815
	3rd Brigade AOOF: 30 November 1815–30 March 1817
	7th Brigade AOOF: 24 June–November 1818
Awards:	KCB: 2 January 1815
	GCB: 19 July 1838
	AGC with two clasps: Maida, Vitoria, Pyrenees, Nivelle, Nive & Orthes
Member of Parliament:	Irish Parliament for Bandon-Bridge, Cork: 1797–1800
Date of Death:	9 June 1840, Clarges Street, London

Sometimes referred to as William O'Callaghan.

Robert O'Callaghan was the second son of Cornelius O'Callaghan, 1st Baron Lismore, and Frances Ponsonby. His mother was an aunt of Major General Sir William Ponsonby. His younger brother George was in the army. Robert grew up in Ireland, where his father was an MP in the Irish Parliament. He was quite athletic in his youth. He was an accomplished equestrian and loved the chase.

In November 1794, Robert O'Callaghan was appointed an ensign in the 128th Foot. He was only assigned to the regiment for eight days when he was appointed a lieutenant in the 30th Light Dragoons. His tenure as a lieutenant was short, for less than two months later he was promoted to captain. It is doubtful that he ever served with either regiment as he was ADC to Earl Fitzwilliam, the Lord Lieutenant of Ireland, and then to 1st Marquess Camden, who replaced Earl Fitzwilliam as the Lord Lieutenant in 1795. When the 30th Light Dragoons were disbanded in 1796, Captain O'Callaghan was appointed a captain in the 22nd Light Dragoons. He saw service in suppressing the Irish Rebellion of 1798 and the same year he was became a Member of the Irish Parliament from his family seat of the Borough of Fethard.

---

1. Disbanded in 1796.
2. Disbanded in 1802.
3. Removed from the regiment as a general officer receiving unattached pay in 1814.

Captain O'Callaghan led his troop in the Egyptian Campaign of 1801. When the regiment returned to England in 1802, it was disbanded and he went on half-pay on 23 June. He remained on half-pay until 3 December 1802, when he exchanged into the 18th Light Dragoons. Two months after exchanging into the regiment, Captain O'Callaghan purchased a majority in the 40th Foot. Once again he was only with his new regiment for a short time, for in July 1803 he purchased a lieutenant colonelcy in the 39th Foot. Unlike his time with his previous regiments, Lieutenant Colonel O'Callaghan would serve with the 39th Foot for the next eleven years.

After war with France broke out in 1803, Lieutenant Colonel O'Callaghan and the 1st Battalion of the 39th Foot were stationed along the coast of Sussex in anticipation of a French invasion. He sailed with them to Malta on 25 March 1805, where they joined its garrison. In October he was court-martialled on allegations of misuse of regimental funds, but was found not guilty. The next month, the Grenadier and Light Companies of the 1st Battalion were sent to Naples. Rather than staying in Malta, Lieutenant Colonel O'Callaghan went with them. In January 1806, the British evacuated their force from Naples and sent it to Sicily. On 27 June, a British Expedition sailed back to the Italian mainland and Lieutenant Colonel O'Callaghan was given command of a Grenadier Battalion, which consisted of the Grenadier Companies of the ten British battalions in Sicily. He led the battalion at the Battle of Maida on 4 July, but rejoined the 1st Battalion 39th Foot in Malta after the British returned to Sicily later in the month.

Lieutenant Colonel O'Callaghan sailed for Portugal with the 1st Battalion on 20 August 1811. They arrived in Lisbon in October. On 25 December the regiment's 2nd Battalion, which had been in Portugal since July 1809, transferred its rank and file that were still capable of campaigning to the 1st Battalion. This gave his battalion over 1,000 effectives and made it one of the strongest battalions in Wellington's army. Lieutenant Colonel O'Callaghan was promoted to colonel on 1 January. They were assigned to the 2nd Division and were part of the covering force during the siege of Badajoz in April 1812. After the city fell, they spent the rest of the year marching through central Spain and saw little action. By 1 December they were back in winter quarters in Coria, Portugal.

On 5 January 1813, Colonel George Wilson, the commander of the brigade in which the 39th Foot was assigned, died of a fever. Because he was the senior officer in the brigade, Colonel O'Callaghan became its temporary commander. He led it at Vitoria on 21 June and was mentioned in dispatches for its defense of the 'village of Subijana de Alava against all the efforts of the enemy to regain possession of it.'[4] Colonel O'Callaghan continued to command the brigade until General William Pringle arrived in Spain and was given it on 23 July. He led his battalion at Maya on 25 July, the Nivelle on 10 November, and at Nive on 9 December. At the Battle of Garris on 15 February,

His horse was shot, and he was leading his regiment on foot, when he was attacked by three French officers. The gallant colonel, being an old dragoon, was an excellent swordsman, and a fine powerful fellow. He cut down one at the first blow, and taking his sword in his left hand, attacked the other two. By a back blow he houghed[5] the second, and the third was an easy victory.[6]

Despite his heroics, he did not come out of the fight unscathed. He 'received one French bayonet at the breast, and another at the shin, at the same time.'[7] Once again he was

---

4. *WD*; Vol. 6, page 541.

5. Hough is an old term that means to hamstring.

6. Cadell; pages 209–10.

7. *United Service Journal*; 1839, Part 3, page 168.

mentioned in dispatches. Wellington wrote: 'The enemy made repeated attempts to regain the position, particularly in two attacks, which were most gallantly repulsed by the 39th Regiment, under the command of the Hon. Colonel O'Callaghan.'[8] Despite being wounded twice, he was able to assume command of the brigade when its commander was also wounded. He led it at Orthes on 27 February and at Toulouse on 10 April 1814.

With the war ended in Europe in April 1814, the British Government decided to send a large force to fight in North America against the United States. Most of the officers and men were to be taken from Wellington's army. Colonel O'Callaghan was selected to command a brigade in this force by the Commander-in-Chief. When the number of brigades were reduced, he was not senior enough to be given command of one of the remaining brigades and he did not go with it.[9] On 14 June 1814, Colonel O'Callaghan was appointed a colonel on the staff to date from 1 August 1813. This was so he would receive pay and allowances for commanding a brigade.[10] Unbeknownst to him, he was also promoted to major general ten days before the General Order was published.

General O'Callaghan returned to England and had no official duties. Upon learning of Napoleon's escape from Elba, he volunteered for service with the British Army in the Netherlands, but his offer was not accepted. Because of the casualties among general officers at Waterloo, Wellington requested that additional generals be sent to the army. On 24 June 1815, General Henry Torrens informed Wellington that 'it is with an assurance that you will like the appointments that the Duke has named Major-Generals … O'Callaghan to join you without delay'.[11] He was placed on the staff on 2 July[12] and was assigned to command the 13th Brigade 7th Division on 24 August.[13] General O'Callaghan was retained on the staff of the AOOF when it was organised on 30 November 1815, but when the British contingent of the AOOF was reduced in March 1817, he returned to England. In June 1818, he was reappointed to the staff of the AOOF.

After the AOOF was disbanded in November 1818, General O'Callaghan returned to England. He had no military duties for seven years until he was appointed the Commander-in-Chief of the military forces in Scotland. In 1829 he became the regimental colonel of the 97th Foot. He was promoted to lieutenant general in July 1830 and appointed the Commander-in-Chief of the Madras Presidency in India on 17 October 1830. He assumed command there on 11 May 1831. While in India, he was appointed the regimental colonel of his old regiment, the 39th Foot. In 1834, the Raja of Coorg led his kingdom in a bid for independence, after being a protectorate of the British East India Company. General O'Callaghan led the forces that put down the rebellion. On 11 October 1836, he returned to England. He never married and died in London in 1840. He was buried in the family vault in Lismore, Ireland.

Robert O'Callaghan had very little practical command experience prior to assuming command of the 1st Battalion 39th Foot in 1803. Yet he excelled at both battalion and brigade command. Although he was never given a permanent brigade command in the Peninsula because he was too junior, Wellington kept him as a temporary commander for nine months in 1813 and 1814. Wellington thought highly enough of him to ensure he remained as a brigade commander in the AOOF for several years.

---

8. *WD*; Vol. 11, page 522.
9. *WSD*; Vol. 9, page 136.
10. General Order, 14 June 1814.
11. *WSD*; Vol. 10, page 573.
12. General Order, 2 July 1815.
13. General Order, 24 August 1815.

O'Loghlin, Terence O'Bryan

Date of Birth:	c. 1764
Date Commissioned:	Ensign 45th Foot: 6 November 1782 without purchase
Promotions:	Ensign 27th Foot: 30 April 1787 by exchange
	Lieutenant 27th Foot: 31 October 1789 without purchase
	Cornet & Sub-Lieutenant 1st Life Guards: 14 December 1792 without purchase
	Lieutenant 1st Life Guards: 13 March 1793 without purchase
	Lieutenant 7th Light Dragoons: 24 December 1793 by exchange
	Captain-Lieutenant 7th Light Dragoons: 1 April 1795 without purchase
	Major 14th Light Dragoons: 19 February 1799 without purchase
	Major & Lieutenant Colonel[1] 1st Life Guards: 14 August 1801 appointed
	Lieutenant Colonel & Colonel[2] 1st Life Guards: 1 September 1808 by purchase
	Lieutenant Colonel 90th Foot 17 July 1821 by exchange
	Major General: 1 January 1812
	Lieutenant General: 27 May 1825
Major Commands under Wellington:	Household Cavalry Brigade: 15 September 1813–April 1814
Date of Death:	15 August 1843 Bentinck Street, Manchester Square, London

Family name was sometimes spelled O'Loughlin. He was occasionally referred to as Terence O'Brien O'Loghlin.

The exact date of Terence O'Loghlin's birth is unknown, however, it was probably 1764. His parents were Terence O'Loghlin of Burren, County Clare, Ireland and Henrietta O'Brien. His mother was a niece of the 4th Earl of Inchiquin and sister to the 5th Earl of Inchiquin. His father was Chief of the O'Loghlin Clan. Little is known about his childhood.

Terence was commissioned as an ensign in 1782 in the 45th Foot, but exchanged as an ensign to half-pay in the 103rd Foot on 27 August 1785. Two years later he went back on active duty when he exchanged into the 27th Foot. He was finally promoted to lieutenant in 1789, after languishing as an ensign for seven years. Lieutenant O'Loghlin resigned his commission and left the army on 31 May 1790. He was a civilian for less than two years when he was appointed a cornet in the 1st Life Guards. Three months after joining the regiment, he was appointed a lieutenant, but nine months later he exchanged into the 7th Light Dragoons.

Lieutenant O'Loghlin joined his new regiment in Flanders and distinguished himself at the Battle of Beaumont on 26 April 1794 and was wounded at Tournay of 10 May. The following year he was promoted to captain. Upon his return to England in 1795 he was appointed the ADC to General John Egerton,[3] who was on the staff in Ireland. Captain O'Loghlin accompanied the general when he was appointed on the staff of the

---

1. Originally announced on 5 September 1801. He exchanged as Major from the 14th Light Dragoons to Second Major 1st Life Guards (with a date of 14 August 1801). However, in a War Office Memorandum of 17 August 1802, this was changed to appointed Major and Lieutenant Colonel 1st Life Guards and not Second Major.
2. This was dual rank in the regiment and the army. He was not the regimental colonel of the regiment.
3. He became the Earl of Bridgewater in 1803.

Eastern District in May 1796. General Egerton was a lieutenant colonel in the 7th Light Dragoons and in 1797 became the regimental colonel of the 14th Light Dragoons. In 1799, Captain O'Loghlin was appointed a major in his regiment.

Major O'Loghlin exchanged into the 1st Life Guards in August 1801. He would be part of the regiment for the next twenty years. In 1808 he purchased a lieutenant colonelcy and with the promotion he became its commander. In January 1812 he was promoted to major general and appointed the commander of the Centre District in Ireland, but by May he was on the staff of the Eastern District in Dublin. General O'Loghlin was appointed the commander of the Household Cavalry Brigade on the staff of Wellington's army in October 1812, but never took command. He resigned the appointment on 25 October due to ill health.

The Household Cavalry Brigade consisted of the 1st and 2nd Life Guards, and the Royal Horse Guards. The Life Guards had not seen active service since the Battle of Fontenoy in 1745, while the Royal Horse Guards had last served in Flanders from 1793 to 1796. In the autumn of 1812, the Prince Regent finally consented to allow them to go to the Peninsula. The three regiments were ordered to send two squadrons each. They arrived in Lisbon in late November and were still in Lisbon in February. It was initially commanded by General Francis Rebow, who went on a leave of absence by mid-January 1813. This left no general officer to command the brigade.[4] Wellington, however, knew by early April 1813 that General O'Loghlin was coming out to take command of it.[5] He was placed upon the staff of the army on 17 June[6] but he did not join the brigade until mid-September 1813.

By the time General O'Loghlin took command, the Household Brigade was in poor shape. In October 1813, General Stapleton Cotton inspected the Household Brigade and made a number of observations as to its condition. He noted in particular that the Life Guards were in bad order and that,

> there are in the two regiments of Life Guards a great many man who ought to be sent home, being much too old for this country, or indeed for active service in any country. The remounts which arrived in June ... there are not many strong enough for that service ... There are many of the officers of the Life Guards who wish to resign, and the service would be benefited thereby; but until officers are sent from England to replace them, I have desired the General will not forward their resignations.[7]

General Cotton did not spare General O'Loghlin criticism. He found that General O'Loghlin had too many field days.[8] He instructed him to have the brigade out occasionally in marching order and discontinue the field days. General Cotton, however, was pleased with the messing arrangements that General O'Loghlin had established, especially that of breakfast.[9] Wellington apparently took General Cotton's observations to heart and the Household Brigade was kept in the rear until the Battle of Toulouse on 10 April 1814, but even then it was in reserve and saw no action. After Napoleon abdicated, the Household Brigade returned to England in June 1814.

---

4. It was temporarily commanded by Robert Hill, the senior lieutenant colonel in the brigade.
5. *WD* (enlarged ed.); Vol. 6, page 407.
6. General Order, 17 June 1813, to date from 6 March.
7. *WSD*; Vol. 8, page 324.
8. A field day was when a regiment held parade ground manoeuvres for an audience.
9. *WSD*; Vol. 8, page 324.

After Napoleon escaped from Elba and Wellington began assembling an army in Flanders, General O'Loghlin petitioned the Horse Guards for a staff appointment with the army. Rather than waiting for a reply, he also wrote a letter to Wellington on 10 April 1815, discussing the circumstances of his not going to the Peninsula when the Household Cavalry Brigade was sent in the autumn of 1812,

> When I was first appointed to the staff of the army, then in the Peninsula, my health was in a very bad state; and before I could proceed to join it, I was seized with a dangerous complaint, which prevented the possibility of my doing so at the time. Immediately upon my recovering sufficiently to undertake a sea voyage, I solicited and obtained my reappointment long before my state of health justified it in a prudential point of view.[10]

He then went on to point out that Wellington had known him for twenty-five years, since serving in Flanders together. He requested that Wellington name him the Commander-in-Chief for a staff appointment with his army. Wellington wrote a note in reply, 'I am very sorry that the army is very small and the staff very numerous, and there are no means of employing him.'[11]

Unbeknownst to either Wellington or General O'Loghlin, plans were being made to send the Household Cavalry to Flanders. General O'Loghlin was to command it. On 16 April, General Henry Torrens of the Horse Guards wrote to Wellington with the news and passed on to him that General O'Loghlin 'says he is a great favourite of yours.'[12] However, two days later, on 18 April, General Torrens again wrote to Wellington that it was proposed that another officer command the Household Brigade instead of General O'Loghlin. No reason was given.[13] He was on the staff in Ireland from 1815 to 1820 commanding in the Eastern and South East Districts and then the Lower Shannon and the Connaught Districts. He was promoted to lieutenant general in 1825.

In 1814, General O'Loghlin had the option of leaving the 1st Life Guards and be assigned as a general officer receiving unattached pay. He chose to stay with the regiment. In July 1821 he exchanged into the 90th Foot and on 9 August 1821 exchanged onto half-pay of the 27th Foot. He disposed of his half-pay by taking a lump sum payment on 15 August 1826 and was retired from the army by February 1827. He was specially allowed to retain his rank in the army and be listed in the army lists, but without pay or progressive promotion.

Terence O'Loghlin married Charlotte Dupre on 26 October 1799. They do not appear to have had any children. He died on 15 August 1843 in London.

General O'Loghlin was a hard luck officer. He missed out serving in the important battles of the Peninsular War and only arrived when the terrain limited the use of cavalry. He did not qualify to receive the AGM for any actions. In 1815, when it appeared that he would be placed upon the staff of Wellington's army, the brigade command was given to General Henry Fane by order of the Prince Regent. When General Fane declined the brigade command, it was not offered to General O'Loghlin. Thus he also missed out on the glory of Waterloo.

---

10. *WSD*; Vol. 10, pages 59–60.
11. Ibid.
12. *WSD*; Vol. 10, page 84.
13. Unpublished letter dated 18 April 1815.

Pack, Denis

Date of Birth:	7 October 1775
Date Commissioned:	Cornet 14th Light Dragoons: 30 November 1791 without purchase
Promotions:	Lieutenant 14th Light Dragoons: 12 March 1795 by purchase
	Captain 5th Dragoon Guards: 27 February 1796 by purchase
	Major 4th Dragoon Guards: 25 August 1798 by purchase
	Lieutenant Colonel 71st Foot:[1] 6 December 1800 by purchase
	Brevet Colonel: 25 July 1810
	Major General: 4 June 1813
Portuguese Promotions:	Brigadier General: 7 July 1810–2 July 1813
Regimental Colonel:	York Chasseurs: 8 January 1816–1819[2]
	84th Foot: 9 September 1822–24 July 1823
Major Commands under Wellington:	Independent Brigade[3] Portuguese Army: 7 July 1810–1 July 1813
	Brigade 6th Division: 2 July 1813–April 1814
	Temporarily commanded 6th Division: 22 July–28 July 1813
	9th Brigade: 21 May–30 November 1815
	4th Brigade AOOF: 30 November 1815–November 1818
Awards:	KCB: 2 January 1815
	AGC with seven clasps: Roliça & Vimeiro, Corunna, Busaco, Ciudad Rodrigo, Salamanca, Vitoria, Pyrenees, Nivelle, Nive, Orthes & Toulouse
	Waterloo Medal
	CTS
	KMT
	KSW 2nd Class
Thanks of Parliament:	Ciudad Rodrigo, Salamanca, the Peninsula, Orthes & Waterloo
Date of Death:	24 July 1823, Wimpole Street, London

Denis Pack was born in 1775, the son of the Very Reverend Thomas Pack, Dean of the Diocese of Ossory, Ireland and Catherine Sullivan. He was commissioned as a cornet in the 14th Light Dragoons in late 1791. The regiment, like his home, was located in County Kilkenny. In 1793 Cornet Pack was convicted of assaulting his troop commander, but instead of being cashiered he was suspended without rank and seniority. Officers who were junior to him were promoted over him during the next two years.[4] After his conviction, he joined the expedition to Flanders as a volunteer in the spring of 1794. He carried a dispatch into the besieged city of Nieuport in July 1794 and helped 200 French emigré troops to escape being captured and executed. For his actions, he was reinstated as a cornet in his regiment. Cornet Pack continued to serve with the army in Flanders

---

1. Removed from the regiment as a general officer receiving unattached pay in 1814.
2. The regiment was disbanded in 1819.
3. Numbered as the 1st Brigade in a General Order dated 13 August 1813.
4. The verdict and sentence of the court-martial were not recorded in the *London Gazette* nor the *Army Lists*. Most biographies of Denis Pack either ignore this episode of his career or make vague references to it.

until it was evacuated to England in the winter of 1795. Upon returning to England, he purchased a lieutenancy in the regiment.

Lieutenant Pack was only in England a short while when he took command of a detachment of eighty light dragoons and joined the British force heading to Quiberon Bay in Brittany. After the attempt by the French emigré troops failed to cause a general uprising in July, the force was withdrawn and occupied Ilse Dieu off the French coast. Lieutenant Pack stayed as part of the garrison until early 1796, when he purchased his captaincy in the 5th Dragoon Guards. He went with the regiment to Ireland and led his troop during the Irish Rebellion. In August 1798 he purchased his majority in the 4th Dragoon Guards and went with the regiment to England in 1799.

In December 1800, Major Pack purchased his lieutenant colonelcy in the 71st Foot. He would be closely associated with the regiment for the rest of his life. He took command of the regiment on 24 April 1801 and spent the next four years with it in Ireland. In August 1805, Lieutenant Colonel Pack and the 1st Battalion of the regiment sailed from Cork in General Ronald Ferguson's brigade as part of the expedition to capture the Cape Colony. On 6 January 1806, he was severely wounded during the landing at Cape Town. His wound did not keep him from commanding his battalion at the Battle of Blueberg[5] on 8 January. In April 1806, they sailed for South America and were part of the force that captured Buenos Aires on 27 June. The ground forces were commanded by General William Beresford, his future brother-in-law. On 10 August the garrison was surrounded and forced to surrender. Lieutenant Colonel Pack and the 1st Battalion became prisoners. After the Spanish authorities refused to honour an agreement that the prisoners would be exchanged for Spanish prisoners captured by the British, he and General Beresford escaped to Montevideo and joined the British forces there. He was given command of all the light companies and fought in the 2nd Battle of Buenos Aires in July 1807, where he was wounded three times and captured a second time. Word reached the people of the city and a mob formed demanding he be turned over to them. He escaped the city by disguising himself as a priest.[6] After an armistice was signed, the British evacuated the city and Lieutenant Colonel Pack was back in England by the end of the year.

Part of the armistice agreement was the return of British soldiers to Great Britain. The 1st Battalion 71st Foot landed in Ireland on 27 December and Lieutenant Colonel Pack spent the next six months rebuilding it. On 14 June, they were selected to join Wellington's force for service in either Spain or Portugal. On 23 June it was assigned to General Catlin Craufurd's Highland Brigade. It landed in Mondego Bay, Portugal on 6 August and was transferred to General Ferguson's 2nd Brigade the next day. Lieutenant Colonel Pack led his battalion at Roliça on 17 August and Vimeiro on 21 August. In the 5 September reorganisation of the army in Portugal it remained in General Ferguson's brigade of the 2nd Division. When it was decided to form a force to serve in Spain, the regiment was selected to serve in the force and on 8 October was placed in General Catlin Craufurd's brigade of General John Hope's Division. It went with the army into Spain and fought at Corunna on 16 January 1809. They returned to England in late January after the army was evacuated from Spain.

The 71st Foot returned to England in poor condition. For the second time in a year Lieutenant Colonel Pack had to rebuild it. Six months later, on 15 July 1809, the 71st Foot embarked on ships as part of the Light Brigade of the British Expedition to Walcheren.

---

5. Also known as Blaauwberg.
6. Fletcher; pages 118–19.

They landed on 30 July and were at the capture of Middleburg on 1 August and Flushing on 17 August. After the fall of Flushing, the 71st Foot was pulled back to Middleburg and he became the garrison commander. Like many other soldiers who were stricken with Walcheren Fever, Lieutenant Colonel Pack also became sick by 31 August 1809.[7] Despite this illness, he stayed with his regiment and formed the rearguard, when the rest of the expedition evacuated to England during the autumn. They finally boarded ships on 23 December and landed in England on Christmas Day.

Lieutenant Colonel Pack spent the next several months rebuilding the 71st Foot for a third time in two years and fighting to retain their distinction of being a Highland Regiment. His lobbying was successful and the regiment was allowed to have a piper in full Highland regalia and the men could wear a Highland bonnet.[8] Lieutenant Colonel Pack requested the regiment be allowed to go back on active service, but the Horse Guards felt it was not fully recovered from the effects of Walcheren Fever. He was, however, given permission to join the British Army in Portugal if he could find a position. Lieutenant Colonel Pack wrote to Wellington requesting a position and he was offered one in the Portuguese Army.

By early July 1810, Lieutenant Colonel Pack was in Portugal and on 7 July was appointed a brigadier general in the Portuguese Army. The same day, he was given command of an independent infantry brigade. He commanded the brigade for the next three years. That same month he was made an ADC to the King and promoted to colonel in the British Army. General Pack's brigade was blooded at Busaco and in the rearguard during the retreat to the Lines of Torres Vedras. In the spring of 1811, his brigade was part of the force that blockaded Almeida and after the French escaped, he was one of the few commanders who received any recognition for doing his job. The following January, General Pack and his brigade participated in the siege of Ciudad Rodrigo. On the night of the assault on the walls, he was given the mission of making a feint on the walls opposite of where the main attack was to be made. His feint was so successful, his troops were among the first to enter the town.

When the 71st Foot returned to Portugal in late September 1810, General Pack wrote to Wellington asking permission for him to return to his regiment. Wellington denied his request, believing that he would best serve as a commander of the Portuguese brigade. Wellington did not forget his desire and wrote to Lieutenant Colonel Henry Torrens at the Horse Guards on 28 January 1812 that 'Pack has long wished to return to the British service, but I doubt whether it would come to his turn to have a British brigade ... As soon as it shall come to his turn, I will remove him to the British service, and apply to have him made a Brigadier General.'[9] Wellington could have used General Pack due to the casualties among general officers during the assault on Ciudad Rodrigo, but he was too junior to be given command of a British infantry brigade.

General Pack led his brigade at Salamanca on 22 July. It was at the centre of the Anglo-Allied line and was given the mission of seizing the hill known as the Greater Arapiles. It was defended by three battalions of French and despite their best efforts, his brigade was unable to take it. General Pack wrote in his journal that:

---

7. Gavin; page 71.
8. This was later changed to a stovepipe shako with red and white checks along the bottom edge.
9. *WD* (enlarged ed.); Vol. 5, page 487.

My cacadores stood well at Busaco and Ciudad Rodrigo, much to my wonderment, but my mind misgave me somewhat when I received the order to attack the hill at Hermanito, the strongest part of the enemy's position; it is the duty of a soldier to obey and not to question, hence we advanced up the hill and were within thirty paces of the top when the hidden French reserves leaped on us from the rocks on our front and flank. I did what in me lay, but the Lisbon Volunteers disappeared sooner than smoke ... No one admires Lord Wellington more than myself, but I fear he expected overmuch from my Hidalgos, whose courage is of a vastly changeable nature.[10]

By the end of the battle the brigade had taken about 20 per cent casualties.

During the siege of Burgos in the late summer of 1812, General Pack's brigade was part of the assault on the Horn Work on 19 September. The initial attack faltered but the Anglo-Allied troops succeeded in capturing the position. General Pack wrote that, 'It was a very murderous conflict, but on this occasion my troops did not fail me and with the noble help of Major Cocks,[11] we gained the fort ...'[12] The siege failed and soon the army retreated to the Portuguese border. General Pack's brigade was in the rearguard for much of the retreat.

After his brigade was settled in Portugal, General Pack returned to England on leave. While he was there he received an offer to command a force, with local rank of major general, to operate on the Atlantic Coast of the United States. He declined the offer and returned to Portugal. Upon arriving in Lisbon, General Pack wrote to Wellington about this offer on 26 April 1813.[13] Wellington wrote back to him on 29 April 1813 that he was 'highly flattered by your preference of the service in this country to that which has been proposed to you by the Sec. of State. I think you were right; but, at all events, I am very sensible of the kindness of your motives in refusing to accept the offer.'[14] Two days later, Wellington took the time to write and explain to General Pack that he had not forgotten his wish to join the British service. He outlined that there were only two vacancies in brigade commands and how they had to be filled by senior officers, one of whom temporarily commanded a division and might lose that command. However, he ended by stating that 'if no General Officer should be sent out, you shall be removed to the British army as you desire.'[15]

By early June the army was on the move and General Pack was with his Portuguese brigade as they marched into Spain. He led them at Vitoria on 21 June, where they were on the left flank of the army under General Thomas Graham. His brigade was part of the pursuit of the defeated French and fought at Villafranca on 24 June and Tolosa on 25 June. In late June, General Pack received word that he had been promoted to major general in the British Army. He got his wish and was transferred to British service and given command of a brigade in the 6th Division on 2 July.[16]

---

10. Carew; page 394.
11. Major Edward Cocks 79th Foot was killed at Burgos on 8 October 1812.
12. Carew; page 394.
13. *WSD*; Vol. 7, page 611.
14. *WD* (enlarged ed.); Vol. 5, page 455.
15. Ibid; page 456.
16. General Order, 2 July 1813.

General Pack's new brigade was known as the Highland Brigade and consisted of three Highland battalions.[17] Twenty days after assuming command of his brigade, he was appointed temporary commander of the 6th Division. There was a dispute regarding the command of the 6th Division by him over General George Madden, who commanded the Portuguese brigade in the division. General Madden was General Pack's senior in the Portuguese Army but not in the British Army. He had been promoted a major general in the Portuguese Army the same date that General Pack was promoted in the British service. Wellington ruled in General Pack's favour. General Madden was relieved from his command and sent to Lisbon to await orders.

General Pack led the 6th Division at the Battle of 1st Sorauren on 28 July. He was seriously wounded in the head and was evacuated to Renteria to recover. General Pack was back with his brigade for the invasion of France in the autumn and led them at Nivelle on 10 November, Nive on 9–13 December, and Orthes on 27 February 1814. In the final battle of the Peninsular War, General Pack and his brigade fought at Toulouse on 10 April, where they assaulted the French redoubts on Mont Rave. The brigade took redoubts but with heavy casualties[18] and once again General Pack was seriously wounded.

After Napoleon abdicated in April 1814 and thus ending the war in Europe, the British Government planned to send a large force to fight in North America in the war of 1812. Most of the officers and regiments were to be taken from Wellington's army. General Pack was initially chosen to accompany the expedition by the Commander-in-Chief on 14 April 1814.[19] However, the size of the expedition was reduced. On 14 May, Wellington wrote to General Pack offering him a brigade in the reduced force and requested a reply.[20] Pack accepted the offer in a letter dated 16 May, but it was slow to reach Wellington. Wellington wrote back to him on 26 May: 'I understood that you had not recovered from your wound, and that you had gone to Bordeaux with the intention of returning to England for your recovery. Under these circumstances, as it was necessary to settle the expedition before I should quit France, I made the arrangements for the command of the brigades without you.'[21] General Pack returned to England and was given the command of the Kent District on the Home Staff in September.

After Napoleon escaped from Elba in March 1815, the British Army sent Wellington to the Netherlands to take command of the Allied forces there. He was informed on 16 April that General Pack was being sent to his army along with reinforcements.[22] Wellington wrote to General Torrens on 21 April that, 'I shall be very happy to have Kempt and Pack, and will do the best I can for them.'[23] On 20 May General Pack was placed on the staff of Wellington's Anglo-Allied Army. His appointment was backdated to 25 April.[24] On 21 May, he was given command of the 9th British Brigade in General Thomas Picton's 5th

---

17. The 1st Battalions of the 42nd Foot (the Black Watch), the 79th Foot (Cameron Highlanders), and the 91st Foot (the Argyllshire Highlanders). The brigade also had one company of the 5th Battalion 60th Foot.
18. The brigade had 739 men killed and wounded – which was 35 per cent of all British casualties of the battle.
19. *WSD*; Vol. 9, page 83.
20. *WD* (enlarged ed.); Vol. 7, page 479.
21. *WD*; Vol. 12, pages 28–9.
22. *WSD*; Vol. 10, page 84.
23. *WD* (enlarged ed.); Vol. 8, page 38.
24. General Order, 20 May 1815.

Division.[25] He led them at Quatre Bras on 16 June where they were caught in the open by French cavalry and took 35 per cent casualties. At Waterloo, the brigade was in the left centre of the British line and in the mid-afternoon he ordered the 92nd Highlanders to attack the advancing French columns of General D'Erlon's Corps. They joined with the 2nd Dragoons in the charge that broke the French Corps, inflicting over 2,000 casualties and capturing two eagles. By the end of the battle, his brigade had loss 52 per cent of its strength in three days. Of the brigade's 145 officers, 65 per cent of them were casualties. General Pack was wounded, while his ADC and Brigade Major were both killed. Two of his battalion commanders were killed, while the other two were wounded.

Despite his wound, General Pack led his brigade during the advance into France. In October 1815, General Pack was offered a command in the West Indies. However, he was concerned about the expenses he would incur while serving there. He and Wellington discussed it and he would only accept the command if 'it was lucrative enough'[26] to cover them. On 30 November 1815 General Pack was retained on the staff of the AOOF and given command of the 4th Brigade. The following January, he supervised the embarkation of British Troops not serving with the AOOF from France. That same month, he was appointed the regimental colonel of the York Chasseurs. He commanded the 4th Brigade until the disbanding of the AOOF in November 1818. On 12 August 1819 he was appointed the commander of the Western District of the Home Staff and the Lieutenant Governor of Plymouth. While serving there, General Pack became the regimental colonel of the 84th Foot in 1822.

Denis Pack married Lady Elisabeth Beresford on 10 July 1816. She was the daughter of the 1st Marquess of Waterford and sister of General Lord George Beresford, and half-sister of General William Viscount Beresford and Admiral John Beresford. They had four children; both of their sons joined the army. The children received a pension on the English Civil List upon the death of their father. In the summer of 1823 General Pack suffered from a ruptured blood vessel which led to edema and probable congested heart failure. He died in his brother-in-law's house on 24 July 1823.[27] He was interred in the family vault in St Canice's Cathedral, Kilkenny on 9 August. At the funeral were Lord Combermere[28] and General Colquhoun Grant.[29]

General Pack earned the AGC with seven clasps during the fifty-two months he served in the Peninsula.[30] This made him the most decorated British soldier of the Peninsular War other than Wellington, who had the AGC with nine clasps.[31] The award was given to senior officers who came under fire in any of the eighteen different battles of the Peninsular War.[32] General Pack's AGC with seven clasps meant he had received the award for eleven different battles.

---

25. General Order, 21 May 1815.
26. *WD* (enlarged ed.); Vol. 8, page 285.
27. Lord Henry Beresford.
28. Also known as General Stapleton Cotton, who commanded Wellington's cavalry in the Peninsula.
29. Graves; page 339.
30. The actual award was the AGM. Subsequent awards was a clasp to go on the original medal's ribbon. If an officer received four awards he would be given the AGC, with additional awards being clasps on the Cross's ribbon.
31. General William Beresford also had the AGC with seven clasps.
32. The award was also given for six other battles outside the Peninsula.

As a commander, General Pack was a superb tactician who would adjust his plans as the situation dictated. At the assault of Ciudad Rodrigo, his orders were to make a feint on the Saint Jago Gate. The attack was virtually unopposed. He quickly ordered his troops over the wall and they were among the first into the city. At the Nive in 1813 the proposed route of advance would have 'led us into such a brake of furze, thorns, and brambles, that it would have been impossible to have taken our bare thighed regiment through its impenetrable meshes. The general, observing our painful but ineffectual struggling, withdrew us from that spot, and pointed to another place by which we should have advanced, and which would have been practicable ...'[33]

As both a battalion and brigade commander, Denis Pack led from the front. At the siege of Flushing in August 1809, his battalion received orders to spike a French battery: 'Towards midnight, when the tide was ebb, Colonel Pack made a sally into one of the enemy's batteries. We crossed the cut in silence; Colonel Pack entered first, and struck off the sentinel's head at one blow. We spiked their guns, after a severe brush.'[34] While at Quatre Bras and Waterloo he was always in the thick of the fighting, encouraging his men. Unlike some commanders, General Pack was noted for displaying a calm demeanor in battle. At Toulouse he 'sat on horseback in the middle of the road, showing an example of the most undaunted bravery to the troops. I think I see him now, as he then appeared, perfectly calm and unmoved; and with a placid smile upon his face amidst a perfect storm of shot and shells.'[35] A sergeant of the 42nd Highlanders noted at Quatre Bras he was in their square waiting to be charged by French cuirassiers:

> General Pack was on the right angle of the front face of the square, and he lifted his hat towards the French officer, as he was wont to do when returning a salute. I suppose our assailants construed our forbearance as an indication of surrendering; a false idea: not a blow had been struck nor a musket levelled; but when the general raised his hat, it served as a signal though not a preconcerted [*sic*] one, but entirely accidental; for we were doubtful whether our officer commanding was protracting the order, waiting for the general's command, as he was present. Be this as it may, a most destructive fire was opened ...[36]

Not surprisingly, General Pack paid the price for exposing himself as often as he did. He was severely wounded eight times, but it did not seem to slow him down. At Sorauren on 28 July 1813 he was wounded in the head. A month later, a family friend wrote: 'I am happy to have the pleasure of saying that my good friend Genl. Pack has quite recovered from his wound. He says now that if the ball had struck any other but an Irish head, it would certainly have broken it.'[37] At Toulouse in April 1814, he was wounded a seventh time:

> His aid-de camp [*sic*], Le Strange, who was afterwrads [*sic*] killed at Waterloo, had his horse shot under him, and both came down together. A few minutes afterwards, I observed General Pack suddenly turn pale, and seem as if going to faint. This was

33. Anton; page 96.
34. Sinclair; page 44.
35. Malcolm; page 295.
36. Anton; page 195.
37. Vandeleur; page 112.

occasioned by a ball which had passed through his leg. He rode slowly to the rear, where he had his wound dressed, and in a few minutes returned again.[38]

An early biographer wrote that General Pack 'was scarred with wounds, and covered with glory. But he had a very restless, uneven temper, which led him to interfere so much with the minor details of duty, that his popularity was less than his high military qualities deserved.'[39] Although there is evidence to support his interference in the minor details of duty, there is little to support that he was unpopular at any level. Colonel Benjamin D'Urban, a British officer serving in the Portuguese Army, wrote in 1810 upon receiving word that General Pack would be given command of a Portuguese brigade: 'This is a great acquisition, – an Officer of tried service, sound judgement, and proved intrepidity.'[40] General Charles Colville, who was a brigade commander with him in the spring of 1811, wrote that he 'has the character of a more than ordinarily zealous and alert officer.'[41] General Pack was also immensely popular among the junior officers and they often wrote of him with a touch of hero worship.

The enlisted soldiers also thought highly of General Pack. They left numerous accounts of how his attention to detail made their life better, especially when it came to rations and quarters. If the circumstances warranted it, he was known to have countermanded Wellington's prohibition of foraging. A good example of this was during the advance into France after Waterloo. The commissary trains were not able to keep up with the rapidly moving army and the soldiers were hungry:

> A few of our men had made free to enter the gardens, along the fences of which our tents were pitched, and were returning with vegetables for their respective messes, when they were met by our officer commanding, who ordered them off to the rear-guard; fortunately for them, General Pack was passing, and he, after hearing the case, gave great satisfaction to all, no doubt to the very officer who had ordered the arrest, by releasing the prisoners, and setting the matter at rest regarding the supplying the wants of the camp from the enemy's fields.[42]

The men appreciated his concern for their welfare and took care of him when necessary. During the retreat to Corunna in January 1809, one of his soldiers found a bullock and,

> shortly after he received a humble message from Colonel Pack, begging a present of the heart, which request was not only complied with, but the kidneys were given in addition. This was not the only instance of officers being obliged to solicit a meal from privates: just at this very time several of them came and begged a few potatoes from us: those offices who were well liked received a supply with the greatest alacrity on our part, while the tyrannical ones were served with a grudge.[43]

Denis Pack was possibly the best battalion and brigade commander in the British Army. His death at the age of 47 cut short a career of much promise.

---

38. Malcolm; page 295.
39. Cole; Vol. 1, page 183.
40. D'Urban; page 124.
41. Colville; page 55.
42. Anton; page 224.
43. Anonymous; *With Wellington in the Peninsula*; page 50.

Peacocke, Warren Marmaduke

Date of Birth:	21 September 1766
Date Commissioned:	Ensign 88th Foot:[1] 12 December 1780
Promotions:	Lieutenant 88th Foot: 22 May 1782
	Captain-Lieutenant 88th Foot: 14 April 1783
	Captain 17th Foot: 1 December 1786 appointed
	Captain 59th Foot: 1792 by exchange[2]
	Captain Independent Company 1793 by exchange[3]
	Lieutenant & Captain Coldstream Foot Guards: 6 November 1793 by exchange
	Brevet Major: 1 March 1794
	Brevet Lieutenant Colonel: 1 January 1798
	Captain-Lieutenant & Lieutenant Colonel Coldstream Foot Guards: 9 May 1800
	Captain & Lieutenant Colonel Coldstream Foot Guards:[4] 19 November 1800
	Brevet Colonel: 25 April 1808
	Brigadier General on the Staff: 23 January 1811
	Major General: 4 June 1811
	Lieutenant General: 19 July 1821
	General: 28 June 1838
Regimental Colonel:	19th Foot: 31 May 1843–31 August 1849
Major Commands under Wellington:	4th Brigade: 14 June–18 June 1809
	Brigade 4th Division: 18 June–22 June 1809
	Commandant of Lisbon: 22 June 1809–April 1814
Awards:	Kt: 27 July 1815
	KCH: 1832
	KC
	CTS: 17 December 1814
Date of Death:	22 August 1849, London. Buried in Kensal Green Cemetery

Some sources give his name as Marmaduke Warren Peacocke.

Warren Peacocke was born in 1765, the oldest son of Marmaduke Peacocke, who married his cousin Mary Peacocke. His father was from London and his mother was from County Clare, Ireland. He was a brother of Vice Admiral Richard Peacocke, Lieutenant Colonel Stephen Peacocke, General Thomas Peacocke, and Ensign John Peacocke.

Warren Peacocke was commissioned as an ensign in the 88th Foot in 1780. At the time of his commissioning, the regiment was stationed in the West Indies and there is no evidence that he ever joined it there. He was promoted to lieutenant in 1782, but went on half-pay when the regiment was disbanded in 1783. He remained on half-pay until 1786 when he was appointed a captain in the 17th Foot. In 1789 the 17th Foot received orders

---

1. Disbanded 1783.
2. *London Gazette*; War Office Announcement dated 3 April 1792.
3. *London Gazette*; War Office Announcement dated 22 October 1793.
4. Removed from the regiment as a general officer receiving unattached pay 25 July 1814.

o provide soldiers to serve as marines in the Royal Navy. Captain Peacocke served for six months on HMS *Colossus*. He stayed with the 17th Foot until 1792 when he exchanged into the 59th Foot, and in October 1793 he exchanged into an independent company. He never served with the independent company and used it to exchange into the Coldstream Guards in November 1793. He would be part of the Coldstream Guards until July 1814. Unlike most of his contemporaries, he never purchased any of his ranks: every promotion was by appointment.

In 1794, Captain Peacocke was promoted to brevet major and in May 1796 he was appointed on the staff of the army in Ireland as the ADC to General George Nugent. He was promoted to brevet lieutenant colonel in January 1798 and continued to serve as General Nugent's ADC during the Irish Rebellion that year. He went to Flanders in 1799, but arrived after the fighting had ended and the British had agreed to evacuate their forces. In May 1800, Lieutenant Colonel Peacocke was promoted to captain-lieutenant and lieutenant colonel in the 1st Battalion and given command of a company. He led his company during the campaign in Egypt and by the end of 1801 he was back in England. During the campaign he was promoted to captain and lieutenant colonel in the regiment. Lieutenant Colonel Peacocke commanded his company in the 1st Battalion which was assigned to General Edward Finch's Guards Brigade in the expedition to Hanover in November 1805, but they saw no action and returned to England in February 1806. They remained on garrison duty until August 1807, when the 1st Battalion was again assigned to General Finch's Guards Brigade, this time as part of the force sent to Copenhagen to capture or destroy the Danish fleet. After the Danes surrendered, Lieutenant Colonel Peacocke and his company returned to England.

In April 1808, Lieutenant Colonel Peacocke was promoted to colonel. Despite this promotion he continued to serve in the 1st Battalion of the Coldstream Foot Guards in General Henry Campbell's brigade of General John Sherbrooke's force sent to secure Cadiz. They sailed on 15 January 1809 and upon arrival the Spanish Government refused to allow them to disembark. They sailed to Lisbon, arriving on 13 March, and joined the British garrison in Portugal. Colonel Peacocke participated in the Oporto Campaign and was at the capture of Oporto on 12 May. The rigors of the campaign was too much for his health and he returned to Lisbon to recover. While there, Wellington made him temporary commander of the Lisbon garrison.

In May, Colonel Peacocke requested that he be placed on the staff of the army as a colonel instead of continuing to serve as a company commander in his battalion.[5] His request was initially denied because there were other colonels with the army who were senior to him and who were not placed on the staff. By mid-June he became the second senior colonel with the army. On 14 June, Colonel Peacocke was placed on the staff of the army and given command of the 4th Brigade.[6] Four days later, this brigade was assigned to the 4th Division. He never assumed command of either brigade.

Wellington realised that he needed a senior officer in Lisbon to manage the day-to-day operations there in support of the army in the field. Colonel Peacocke was named the Commandant of Lisbon on 22 June 1809.[7] Wellington recognised his talents and he was appointed a brigadier general on the staff on 9 May 1811 with the promotion backdated

---

5. *WD* (enlarged ed.); Vol. 3, page 262.

6. General Order, 14 June 1809.

7. General Order, 22 June 1809.

to 23 January 1811.[8] Twenty-six days later, General Peacocke was promoted to major general in the army and on 26 June was retained on the staff of Wellington's army.[9]

As Commandant of the British garrison in Lisbon, General Peacocke had a wide variety of duties. He was responsible for maintaining discipline among the numerous soldiers assigned to the garrison, as well as passing through on their way to and from Wellington's army. He also arranged billeting for these officers and men. All new units arriving in Portugal were inspected by him and were only allowed to join the army when he deemed them to be ready. Occasionally units were sent back to Lisbon to rebuild their strength. Like newly arrived units, these units were also inspected by General Peacocke and were only sent forward when they passed his inspection. Wellington had complete confidence in him and would use his reports when he complained to the Horse Guards about the poor quality of troops being sent out. For example, in 1811 he wrote to Earl Bathurst the Secretary of State for War and the Colonies, 'I have the honour to transmit a letter from Colonel Peacocke[10] with its enclosures reporting the imperfect state in which some Detachments have been sent from England and I shall be much obliged to your Lordship if you give such directions as may prevent the recurrence of such irregularities.'[11]

Other duties included arranging transportation for units and individuals returning to England, overseeing the hospitals and the officers who came from the army to recover from their wounds, and working with the Portuguese Government. Because Lisbon was relatively close to the British Isles, a large number of civilians came to the city to visit. Some came as battlefield tourists, while others came to visit relatives serving in the army. Many were members of the upper levels of society and expected to be received by the senior officer in the city, preferably Wellington, but since he was rarely there, it was usually General Peacocke.

A Guards officer left a vivid description of General Peacocke's duties and how he handled them:

> While at Lisbon, his duties were arduous in the extreme. He had to reconcile the Portuguese Government and authorities to a military occupation, which they always looked upon with suspicion; and he had to control and direct all the transport service of the navy: but his most onerous labours were in connexion with the many questions arising with regard to the army. Lisbon at the period to which I refer, was a sort of hospital for the army of the Peninsula, whilst it was at the same time the basis of those glorious operation the effect of which was to drive the French out of Spain, and General Peacocke was referred to on all occasions by the Portuguese and English ... Whilst tormented with these petty annoyances, he was constantly engaged in the most important correspondence with the British Government, the Duke of Wellington, and the Portuguese officials. Many of the services he rendered his country at that time were such as cannot be transferred to the pages of history, being of the most delicate and confidential character. Throughout all, Sir Warren was remarkable for his urbanity of manner, his untiring business habits, and a keen judgment, which made him alike an accomplished statesman and an intelligent soldier.[12]

---

8. General Order, 9 May 1811.
9. General Order, 26 June 1811.
10. This letter was written prior to his promotion to general in June.
11. Bamford; *Sickness, Suffering, and the Sword*, page 114.
12. Gronow, Rees; *Captain Gronow's Last Recollections*, pages 11–14.

With the movement of so many officers and soldiers through Lisbon, their billeting was always a source of complaint. A commissary officer wrote in 1812:

As I expected to remain many months in Lisbon, I thought it would be economical to be billeted at a private house, and I therefore went to the town major. Had I previously been acquainted with General Peacocke, the Commandant at Lisbon, I would have spared myself the pains of having to run about for hours in the company of a Portuguese military policeman while my pack mules and my horse stood starving in the street. First this house had no stable; then we found a stable and no house; anon we came to a place which already had people billeted in it, or to the abode of a conde or marques who was exempted from supplying quarters. This April fool system of organising the billeting was the work of General Peacocke, who, incapable of taking command in the field, had been specially sent here by Lord Wellington, who knew his eccentric and harsh character, in order, by means of every kind of interference, to make the life of English officers in Lisbon as difficult and unhappy as possible.[13]

General Peacocke had little patience when it came to the complainers:

On one occasion an assistant-surgeon complained, in no measured terms, of the quarters allotted to him stating that he was obliged to sleep in a pigsty; upon which Sir Warren inquired of one of his subalterns if he knew anything of the said pigsty. The answer was, that the quarters which the surgeon complained of were very good, in fact, better than the majority of the officers occupied. 'Oh, then, sir,' said Peacocke, turning to the injured medico, 'if you are a prince in disguise, declare yourself; but if you are only what your diploma states you to be, I consider the quarters you have quite good enough.[14]

One of the thankless duties General Peacocke had was handling requests and

… dealing with the friends and relations of officers in our army, a crowd of whom came over from England, each with a special object in view. Some wanted a prolongation of leave for a son or brother, others that their friends or relations might be permitted to return to England on account of urgent domestic affairs; while with the rest the excuse was, that ill health, owing to change of climate, ought to influence the Governor to permit some stalwart soldier to visit his native land. To all these importunities Sir Warren was wont to reply, that 'he could not, on any account, permit domestic affairs to interfere with the duties of the service.[15]

In Belem, a suburb of Lisbon, was the largest military hospital in Wellington's army. Although General Peacocke did not oversee the day-to-day running of the hospital, he did have responsibility for assuring officers and men who were in Lisbon receiving treatment for their wounds or illnesses returned to their units after they were recovered.

13. Schaumann; pages 341–2.
14. Gronow, Rees; *Captain Gronow's Last Recollections*, pages 13–14.
15. Ibid; pages 12–13.

Many who came to convalesce took the opportunity to extend their time there, long after they should have gone back to their regiment. They were known as Belem Rangers.

> Whilst the Duke was insisting on Sir Warren Peacocke's acting with severity against the skulkers from the army, these gentlemen were complaining bitterly of the Governor for not allowing them to shirk their duties, alleging that on account of 'ill health,' (unfortunately a common excuse in the service), they ought to be allowed to remain at Lisbon to recruit it: this 'recruiting of health,' be it understood, generally consisting of a minimum of work, combined with a maximum of dissipation.[16]

Eventually General Peacocke became 'so disgusted with the amount of extra work and anxiety entailed upon him by these useless officers, that he several times requested the Duke to find some one to supply his place as Governor; but the answer he generally received was, "You are too valuable here to be replaced by anyone. I cannot possibly spare you."'[17] He remained as the Commandant of Lisbon until the end of the Peninsular War in April 1814.

The Portuguese Regency Council recognised the difficulty that General Peacocke's job entailed and wrote to Wellington on 2 August 1813 expressing their satisfaction with him. Wellington replied on 16 August 1813 that,

> I experience great satisfaction in hearing that the conduct of Major Gen. Peacocke, in the discharge of his command at Lisbon, has been always regulated in a manner satisfactory to their Excellencies the Governors of the Kingdom … and I shall take the earliest opportunity to make this known to Peacocke's superior officers.[18]

In addition to letting Wellington know how well he thought General Peacocke did his duties, the Portuguese Regent appointed him a Knight Commander of the Tower and the Sword in 1814. The British Government belatedly recognised his service when they made him a Knight Bachelor on 27 July 1815. Unlike most of his contemporaries who served under Wellington in the Peninsula, General Peacocke was not made a KCB when the awards were announced in 1815. It is likely that the only reason he was made a Knight Bachelor was because the Portuguese Government had knighted him the year before.

After he returned from the Peninsula in 1814, General Peacocke had no military duties for many years. He was promoted to lieutenant general in 1821 and became the Governor of Kinsale, Ireland on 3 August 1830. This position was a sinecure and had no official duties. It did, however, come with an annual salary of £319 5s 4d. He was promoted to general in 1838 and appointed the regimental colonel of the 19th Foot in 1843.

General Peacocke spent much of his time at the family estate, Rivers Hall in Boxted, Essex. He died at the age of 82 on 22 August 1849 in the Coulson Hotel at 49 Brook Street, London. He never married and left his estate to his nephew.

---

16. Ibid; pages 16–17.
17. Ibid; pages 16–17.
18. *WD* (enlarged ed.); Vol. 6, page 686.

Ponsonby, Hon. William

Date of Birth:	1772
Date Commissioned:	Ensign Independent Company: 1794 without purchase[1]
Promotions:	Lieutenant Independent Company: 30 November 1794 without purchase
	Captain 83rd Foot: 1794
	Major[2] Loyal Irish Fencible Infantry: 15 December 1794 without purchase
	Major 5th Dragoon Guards: 1 March 1798 by exchange
	Brevet Lieutenant Colonel: 1 January 1800
	Lieutenant Colonel 5th Dragoon Guards: 24 February 1803 by purchase
	Brevet Colonel: 25 July 1810
	Brigadier General on the Staff: 1 October 1812
	Major General: 4 June 1813
Major Commands under Wellington:	Cavalry brigade: 22 July 1812–April 1814
	Cavalry brigade: 5 May–31 May 1815
	2nd Cavalry Brigade: 31 May–18 June 1815[3]
Awards:	AGM with clasp: Salamanca & Vitoria
	KCB: 2 January 1815
	Waterloo Medal
Member of Parliament:	MP Irish Parliament: Bandon-Bridge Cork 1796–1798, Fethard Borough Tipperary 1798–1800; MP Londonderry 1812–1815
Date of Death:	18 June 1815 at Waterloo, Belgium

From 13 March 1806 he was known as Hon. William Ponsonby, when his father was created a Peer of the Realm.

William Ponsonby's exact date of birth is unknown. All sources agree that it was in 1772. Some sources do not give a day, while others have it as 13 October. To confuse matters other sources give that date as his wife's date of birth. He was the second son of William Brabazon Ponsonby, 1st Baron Ponsonby of Imokilly, and Louisa Molesworth, daughter of the 3rd Viscount Molesworth. Little is known about his youth except that he lived in County Cork, Ireland.

In the autumn of 1794, William Ponsonby was commissioned as an ensign in an independent company and by the end of November was promoted to lieutenant. Several sources state that he was promoted to captain in the 83rd Foot. The only documentary evidence to support this is his promotion notice in the *London Gazette* to Major in the Fencibles, which refers to him as a captain in the 2nd Battalion 83rd Foot. However, by the end of December he was a major in the Loyal Irish Fencible Infantry. Within three months the 22 year old went from ensign to major without purchasing any of his ranks.

---

1. *London Gazette*; War Office Announcement dated 1 November 1794.
2. This promotion was permanent substantive rank in the army and not rank only in the fencibles. Rank just in the fencibles was held only while serving with or until disbanding of the regiment.
3. The cavalry in the Allied Army in Flanders was reorganised on 31 May 1815 and the brigades were numbered.

Major Ponsonby stayed with the Loyal Irish Fencible Infantry until March 1798, when he exchanged into the 5th Dragoon Guards. He was in the regiment for the next sixteen years.

In Major Ponsonby's new regiment was Captain Denis Pack, whose infantry brigade was in line in front of his brigade at Waterloo. Major Ponsonby help suppress the Irish Rebellion of 1798 and fought at Ballinamuck on 8 September which defeated the French force that had come to Ireland to aid the rebels. In 1799 the 5th Dragoon Guards embarked for Den Helder in the expedition commanded by the Duke of York. Their orders were cancelled at the last minute and they went to England instead. The regiment remained in England until June 1805, when it returned to Ireland. While in England Major Ponsonby was promoted to brevet lieutenant colonel in 1800 and purchased his lieutenant colonelcy in 1803. Lieutenant Colonel Ponsonby and his regiment stayed in Ireland until September 1808, when they were ordered back to England. He was promoted to colonel in July 1810.

In the summer of 1811, Colonel Ponsonby received orders to prepare his regiment for service in the Peninsula. They sailed on 12 August and landed in Lisbon on 4 September. They spent six weeks in Lisbon acclimatising themselves to the country before joining General John Le Marchant's brigade. They were part of the screen that covered the British force that besieged Badajoz in April 1812. He led the regiment at Villagarcia on 11 April. At Salamanca on 22 July, Colonel Ponsonby assumed temporary command of the brigade after General Le Marchant was killed. The next day he was appointed a colonel on the staff and officially assigned command of it.[4] He led it at Majalahonda on 11 August and it served as Wellington's escort when he entered Madrid the next day. In September and October the brigade screened the British forces that were besieging Burgos. They were part of the rearguard during the initial stages of the retreat to Portugal in late October. During the latter half of the retreat they were ordered to take a secondary road by mistake and were separated from the main body of the army until they reached the safety of the Portuguese border.

Wellington wished to keep Colonel Ponsonby in command of the brigade and wrote to the Horse Guards requesting his appointment as a brigadier general. Colonel Henry Torrens replied on 4 October, 'As you have given Ponsonby a Brigade he will be a Brigr according to your desire'.[5] He was promoted to brigadier general on 4 November.[6] In the late spring of 1813, General Ponsonby and his brigade were part of General Thomas Graham's flanking movement that forced the French out of central Spain. He led them at Vitoria on 21 June 1813 and after the battle was part of the pursuit of the retreating French Army. Once the French were on the other side of the Pyrenees Mountains there was little need for cavalry, so the brigade went into cantonments for the rest of 1813. On 24 December, General Ponsonby applied for leave to go home. Wellington's Military Secretary responded on 28 December that Wellington would grant a short leave despite the government wanting to keep officers from going home over the winter. Wellington allowed his leave because his brigade would be remaining in its cantonments for several months.[7] General Ponsonby left on 25 January and was gone until April. He returned in time to lead it at Toulouse on 10 April.

After Napoleon abdicated in April 1814, General Ponsonby and his brigade remained in southern France until 1 June when they began a 1,000-kilometer march to Boulogne. They

---

4. General Order, 23 July 1812.
5. Unpublished letter dated 4 October 1812.
6. General Order, 4 November. The promotion was backdated to 1 October 1812.
7. *WSD*; Vol. 8, page 448.

arrived in the port city in mid-July and the brigade was disbanded. The regiments embarked for England on 19 July. After he returned to England, General Ponsonby had no official military duties, but assumed his seat in Parliament. He had been a Member of the Irish Parliament from 1796 until it was dissolved in 1800. He was not a Member of the British Parliament until he was elected in 1812, while he was serving in the Peninsula. It was unlikely he attended Parliament until February 1815. He was a Whig and the only two times he voted was with the opposition against transferring Genoa on 21 February and against maintaining the militia on 28 February. He was not known to have given any speeches.[8]

When Napoleon escaped from exile in March 1815, a British Army under Wellington was formed in Flanders. General Torrens wrote to him on 9 April that General Ponsonby was being sent out to command the heavy cavalry brigade being assigned to his army.[9] He was placed on the staff of the army on 4 May.[10] The next day he was given command of a cavalry brigade.

On 31 May, the cavalry was reorganised and General Ponsonby received command of the 2nd Cavalry Brigade. His brigade was also known as the Union Brigade as it consisted of dragoon regiments from England, Scotland and Ireland.[11] He was quite pleased with his brigade and wrote to his friend, General Henry Fane, 'the Greys and Inniskillings are very fine regiments and in excellent order. The Royals ... only came up the night before ... and I am told they also are in very fine trim; so I have reason to be very satisfied with my brigade.'[12] On 9 June he held manoeuvres with his brigade and afterwards told them, 'They are the finest body of men and horses I ever saw'.[13]

General Ponsonby was at the Duchess of Richmond's Ball in Brussels on the evening of 15th June, but left when word was received that the French had crossed the border into Belgium. He sent his ADC to Lieutenant Colonel Alexander Hamilton, the commander of the 30th Foot, who 'had a powerful and beautiful charger, which he wished to dispose of ... being aware (having had many horses killed under him during his service) that he would only get £25 allowed him in case of a casualty, whereas his charger was worth £100 ... General Ponsonby's ADC came to Colonel Hamilton to treat for the horse, but nothing decisive took place, and from not hearing anything more upon the subject, Colonel Hamilton concluded that the General considered the animal was overvalued ...'[14]

General Ponsonby and his brigade arrived at Quatre Bras too late the next day to take part in the battle, but was part of the rearguard as Wellington's army retreated to Waterloo on 17 June. At Waterloo, they were in the centre of the army in a hollow behind Generals James Kempt's and Denis Pack's brigades. About 2 p.m. the French Corps commanded by General D'Erlon was advancing on the British positions. The commander of Wellington's cavalry, Henry Paget the Earl of Uxbridge, rode up to General Ponsonby and ordered him to charge. The charge of the Union Brigade would be one of the greatest charges of the British Army. In the space of thirty minutes they broke the French Corps, captured 2,000 prisoners, and a French Eagle. But it was at a huge cost. The brigade had

---

8. 'Ponsonby'.
9. *WSD*; Vol. 10, page 49.
10. General Order, 4 May 1815. The appointment was backdated to 3 April.
11. They were the 1st Royal Dragoons, the 2nd Scots Greys Dragoons, and the 6th Inniskilling Dragoons.
12. Glover, Gareth; *Waterloo Archive*, Vol. 6, page 51.
13. Glover, Gareth; *Waterloo Archive*, Vol. 1, page 44.
14. *United Services Journal*; 1838, Part III, page 432.

234 Wellington's Brigade Commanders

a strength of 933 officers and men on the day of the battle and by the end of the day over 50 per cent of them were casualties. This included fifteen officers killed and twenty-three wounded. Among the dead were General Ponsonby.

There is some controversy about the fate of General Ponsonby. He was initially thought captured but his body was found the next day. There are several stories about how he died, the accepted one revolves around his horse. According to his extra ADC, Major De Lacy Evans,

> The General was mounted on a secondary untrained horse, and some round shot frightened the horse, and his cloak, being loose flew off ... Poor Sir William Ponsonby might perhaps have been spared to his country had he been better mounted. He rode a small bay hack.[15] He had a handsome chestnut charger, which he meant to mount when real business began, but the groom or Orderly who had charge of the chestnut was not forthcoming or within call at the moment the General wanted his horse.[16]

At the end of the charge he and his brigade major were trying to rally the scattered survivors of the brigade when they were attacked by Polish Lancers[17] of the Imperial Guard. They tried to escape, but their horses became bogged down in the wet muddy fields and they were ridden down by the lancers and killed. His body was found the next day and depending on the source, he had been stabbed either three or eight times.

Legend has it that when he realised that he could not escape, 'He took a picture and watch out of his pocket and was just delivering them to his A.D.C. to give his wife when the lancers were on him.'[18] This is supported by Corporal Dickson of the Scots Greys:

> We were returning past the edge of the ploughed field, and then I saw a spectacle I shall never forget. There lay brave old Ponsonby, the General of our Union Brigade, beside his little bay, both dead. His long, fur-lined coat had blown aside, and at his hand I noticed a miniature of a lady and his watch; beyond him, our Brigade-Major, Reignolds[19] of the Greys. They had both been pierced by the Lancers a few moments before we came up.[20]

A correlation of this story is that General Ponsonby had surrendered to the lancers, but was killed by them when they thought the retreating British cavalry would try to rescue him. Despite the poignancy of the tale of him being ridden down by the lancers, there are numerous accounts that contradict it. Most of the eyewitness accounts from Waterloo all say the same thing: that he was shot. Lieutenant George Gunning of the 1st Dragoons wrote:

> General Ponsonby rode up to me by himself, and said, 'For God's sake, Sir, collect your men, and retire on the brigade.' At this moment the French infantry on our left advanced rapidly, and fired a volley of musketry among the scattered cavalry. By this

---

15. A hack is a horse that is meant for riding at regular speed on roads and trails.
16. Siborne; *Waterloo Letters*, pages 64–5.
17. Most accounts state that it was Polish Lancers. However, other accounts specifically state the lancers wore red uniforms. These were the Dutch Lancers of the Imperial Guard. Their red uniforms were very similar to the Polish Lancers, which wore blue uniforms.
18. Dalton; page 19.
19. Major Thomas Reignolds.
20. Robertson; page 146.

volley General Ponsonby was killed, within twenty yards of me. I saw him fall from his horse at the bottom of the hollow way, to the left of General Picton's Division. The ridiculous story about the general's horse being unmanageable was all a farce to please the lovers of the marvelous.[21]

William Ponsonby married Georgiana Fitzroy, the daughter of 1st Baron Southampton, on 20 January 1807. They had five children. Their only son was born eight months after his father's death. Lady Ponsonby and her four daughters each received a pension.

It is difficult to assess General Ponsonby's performance as a brigade commander. The great historians who wrote about Wellington's army in the early twentieth century, Sir John Fortescue and Sir Charles Oman, do not help the matter. They often confused him with his cousin, Lieutenant Colonel Frederick Ponsonby, and at times it is difficult to determine which of the two they were writing about. While General Ponsonby commanded in the Peninsula, his brigade saw little action during the two major battles he commanded them in.[22] Most of the time they served as a screen for the army. The little action they did see were mostly skirmishes between outposts. Compounding the problem is the lack of letters, diaries, and memoirs from officers who served under him in the Peninsula. The only known primary source from his brigade in Spain was that of Captain William Bragge, an officer in the 3rd Dragoons. He wrote to his father on 25 September 1812 a very unflattering portrayal of him:

Our present Leader (Colonel Ponsonby) is no great Genl. He was ordered the other day to advance until he was stopped, which he did by moving our Regt down an Avenue with a Front of Threes and no advanced Guard until the Enemy thought proper to Fire a Gun, which enfiladed the Road and might have killed 30 Men had it been pointed properly. Another shot took two Light Dragoons Heads off and the next passed under my Mare's legs and the covering Sergts horses without doing either any Injury.[23]

General Ponsonby is best known for the charge of his brigade at Waterloo. In addition to the circumstances of the death of General Ponsonby, there is much controversy on how he handled his brigade during the charge. Although it achieved spectacular results it did so at a heavy cost. There is little disagreement that once the charge was launched, he lost control of his brigade. The individual regiments did not respond to the recall and charged on until their horses were spent and they were counter-attacked by fresh French cavalry. What started as a glorious charge turned into a rout as they fled back to the British lines.

The second issue with the charge was whether he ordered the 2nd Dragoons to stay in support. Cavalry doctrine called for charging with only part of the force, while leaving the other part to stay back in support. The supporting element would be there to cover the charging force in the event they had to fall back. The controversy is whether General Ponsonby left a regiment in reserve. Some sources state that all three regiments charged simultaneously, while others say that the 2nd Dragoons ignored the order to stay in support and charged on their own initiative. Thus when the French counter-attacked the scattered and disordered troops of his brigade, there was no regiment to protect them as they fled back to the safety of their own lines. The death of General Ponsonby saw the issue being downplayed lest it sullied a fallen hero.

---

21. Glover, Gareth; *Waterloo Archive*, Vol. 6, page 57.
22. Vitoria and Toulouse.
23. Bragge; page 76.

Power, Manley

Date of Birth:	1773
Date Commissioned:	Ensign 20th Foot 27 August 1785 without purchase
Promotions:	Lieutenant 20th Foot: 4 May 1789 without purchase
	Captain Independent Company: 28 June 1793 without purchase
	Captain 20th Foot: 16 January 1794 by exchange
	Major 20th Foot: 7 October 1799 without purchase
	Lieutenant Colonel 20th Foot :20 June 1801 by purchase
	Lieutenant Colonel 32nd Foot: 6 June 1805 by exchange[1]
	Brevet Colonel: 25 July 1810
	Major General: 4 June 1813
	Lieutenant General: 27 May 1825
Portuguese Promotions:	Brigadier General: 5 August 1811
	Major General: 4 June 1813
Major Commands under Wellington:	Portuguese Infantry Brigade: 12 August 1811–July 1812[2]
	Portuguese Infantry Brigade: July 1812–April 1814[3]
	Temporarily commanded 3rd Division: September?–October 1813
	11th Brigade: 6 July–30 November 1815
	2nd Brigade AOOF: 30 November 1815–November 1818
Awards:	KCB: 2 January 1815
	AGC with clasp : Salamanca, Vitoria, Nivelle, Orthes & Toulouse
	KTS
Thanks of Parliament:	Badajoz & Salamanca
Date of Death:	7 July 1826, Berne, Switzerland

Some sources give his name as Manly Power.

The exact date of birth for Manley Power is unknown other than he was born in 1773, most likely in England. His parents were Thomas Bolton Power of Killmurray, Ireland and Ann Corney. His father was a captain in the 20th Foot and fought in the American Revolution. Little is known about Manley Power's childhood but it is possible that he grew up in Ireland, as one individual noted in his memoirs that he was from there.[4]

In 1785, at the age 12, Manley Power was commissioned as an ensign in the 20th Foot, his father's regiment, which was stationed in Ireland. He was promoted to lieutenant in May 1789 and went with the 20th Foot to Nova Scotia a month later. His regiment was sent to the West Indies in 1792, but he did not go with it. In 1793 he was promoted to captain of an independent company and in January 1794 he exchanged back into the 20th Foot. Although his regiment was stationed in the West Indies, Captain Power never joined it there.

When the 20th Foot returned to England in 1796, it could muster only seventy-six officers and men. Captain Power joined them the same year and served with it for the next three years in England. Most of the time was spent recruiting the regiment

---

1. Removed from the regiment as a general officer receiving unattached pay in 1814.
2. This brigade was an independent brigade serving in Elvas and was not numbered in 1813.
3. This brigade would be named the 8th Brigade on 13 August 1813.
4. Hill; Vol. 1, pages 84.

back to strength. The recruiting was very successful and in August 1799 the regiment was expanded into two battalions. Although the 2nd Battalion had just been formed, both battalions were sent to Flanders on 25 August. During their ten weeks there, they were involved in six different battles. At Egmont-op-Zee on 6 October, his battalion's commander was killed. As the senior captain in the battalion, Captain Power took command and the next day was promoted to major due to the death of a senior officer killed in action there.

The expedition to Flanders returned to England in November and in early 1800 the regiment was sent to Cork, Ireland. In June, both battalions were ordered to the Mediterranean and garrisoned in Minorca. While on the island, Major Power purchased his lieutenant colonelcy in the regiment in June 1800. They were part of the British expedition to Egypt in 1801 and Power was at the siege of Alexandria in August and September. After the capitulation of the French, the battalions were sent to Malta in December. The 2nd Battalion was disbanded in September 1802 and Lieutenant Colonel Power went on half-pay. He was appointed the Inspecting Field Officer of Yeomanry and Volunteer Corps in October 1803 and by 1805 was an AAG on the Home Staff in the Severn District.

In June 1805, Lieutenant Colonel Power exchanged into the 32nd Foot and by June 1807 was the commander of its 2nd Battalion. In July 1810 he was promoted to colonel. At this time the British Government allowed British officers to serve in the Portuguese Army, usually in at least one rank higher than their rank in the British Army. Colonel Power volunteered and was accepted by the Portuguese Government in the spring of 1811. Exactly when he arrived in Portugal is unknown, but most likely he came with the 1st Battalion of his regiment in early July. He was assigned to the Portuguese Army on 21 July 1811.[5]

Colonel Power was promoted to brigadier general in the Portuguese Army on 5 August 1811 and given command of a Portuguese infantry brigade stationed in Elvas. His new brigade served as the garrison of this key border fortress until April 1812, when it was part of the force besieging Badajoz. During the main assault on the breaches on the night of 6 April, the brigade had the mission of making a feint against the bridgehead on the right bank of the Guadiana River.

After the city was captured in the early morning of 7 April, the British and Portuguese soldiers began to sack it. In hope of preventing the complete destruction of the city by the marauding soldiers, Wellington ordered General Power's brigade into the city to restore order. Once they were in the city, General Power's soldiers ignored their orders and joined the looters. That night Wellington had had enough and sent in the Provost Marshal with orders to execute any soldier caught plundering. The next day, Wellington reprimanded General Power and his troops:

Brigadier General Power is ordered and held responsible, that no British or Portuguese soldiers, excepting those belonging to the place, or having a passport from a Field Officer, shall go into Badajoz, till further orders. The Commander of the Forces is sorry to learn that the Brigade in Badajoz, instead of being a protection to the people, plunder them more than those who stormed the town. Brigadier General Power's Brigade are to be put under arms to-morrow morning, at day-light,

---

5. General Order, 21 July 1811.

and to continue under arms till further orders. The Brigadier General is to send a State to Head Quarters every six hours, of the number of men under arms, in the form of the daily morning State.[6]

Despite the public reprimand for losing control of his troops at Badajoz, General Power received no other punishment. When Wellington moved the bulk of his army north in late April, he left General Power and his brigade as the temporary garrison of the city. In July 1812 he was transferred from his command and appointed the commander of the Portuguese brigade assigned to the 3rd Division. He commanded the brigade at Salamanca on 22 July and during the retreat back to the Portuguese border in the autumn.

General Power led his brigade into Spain in May 1813 and was promoted to major general in both the British and Portuguese Armies on 4 June. He was retained on the staff of the Portuguese Army on 2 July and continued to command his brigade until the end of the war. He led them at Vitoria on 21 June and after the defeat of the French, was part of the force that blockaded the French garrison in Pamplona. His brigade was renamed the 8th Brigade in August.

In September 1813, General Thomas Picton, the commander of the 3rd Division, returned to England due to ill health. This caused a problem about who would temporarily command the division in his absence. General Power took command of the division as the senior brigade commander. He did so as he held superior rank in the Portuguese Army over General Thomas Brisbane, who was General Power's senior in British Army rank. General Brisbane objected to not being placed in command, believing that his British date of rank made him senior to General Power. The AG responded on 18 October on behalf of Wellington, who had decided in General Power's favour.[7] He commanded the division until General Charles Colville took temporary command in late October. After he returned to his brigade, General Power led them at the Nivelle on 10 November 1813, at Orthes on 27 February 1814, and Toulouse on 10 April 1814.

With the war won in Europe, in April 1814 the British Government decided to send a large force to fight in North America against the United States. Most of the officers and men were to be taken from Wellington's army. General Power was initially selected to command a brigade in the force by the Commander-in-Chief.[8] When the size of the force was reduced and the objectives of the force changed, General Power was selected to command a brigade destined for Canada, but only if General Frederick Robinson failed to arrive before the force sailed.[9] In the end he, along with General Robinson, went to Canada in command of brigades.[10] He commanded the brigade in the Plattsburg Campaign in September 1814. He was sent from Canada with reinforcements to join the British force at New Orleans. They arrived at Bermuda on 24 January 1815, too late to serve at the attack on New Orleans.

In late March, word was received that peace had been declared between Great Britain and the United States. On 3 April General Power and General John Keane sailed for England. While en route, on 2 May a passing ship passed the news that Napoleon was

6. General Order, 8 April 1812.
7. *WD* (enlarged ed.); Vol. 7, page 72.
8. *WSD*; Vol. 9, page 82.
9. Ibid; page 88.
10. Ibid; page 135.

back in Paris. General Power landed in England on 30 May, but was too late to obtain a command in Wellington's army in Flanders.[11]

However, in late June, General Power was selected to join Wellington's army. He was placed on the staff of the army on 4 July 1815[12] and assigned command of the newly formed 11th Brigade 6th Division on 6 July.[13] When the army was reorganised on 30 November 1815, General Power was kept on the staff and given command of the 2nd Brigade of the AOOF. On 7 December 1815, he was ordered to Boulogne to oversee the embarkation of British regiments that were returning to England.[14] General Power continued to serve in France for the next three years. In anticipation of the disbanding of the AOOF on 30 November 1818, General Power was selected by Wellington in October to reside at Calais in order to supervise the embarkation of the British Army leaving the country.

General Power returned to England by the end of 1818. In 1819, he was appointed the Commander of British troops and Lieutenant Governor of Malta. He held the position until 1825. While in Malta he was promoted to lieutenant general in May 1825. In early 1825, he was one of the general officers whom Wellington put forward to Charles W. Wynn, the President of the HEIC, to command in India. Wellington thought he was 'very good'.[15] On his way home to England, General Power died from a sudden illness in Berne, Switzerland on 7 July 1826.

Manley Power was married twice. His first wife was Sarah Coulson, whom he married on 5 June 1802. They had three sons, of whom the surviving son joined the army. On 7 May 1818 he married Anne Evans, daughter of Colonel Kingsmill Evans. They had two sons, one of whom joined the army.

Because he served with the Portuguese troops during the Peninsular War, General Power was rarely mentioned in the diaries and memoirs of the British officers who served there. Wellington thought highly enough of him to keep him in temporary command of the 3rd Division in 1813 and to select him to go to Canada in 1814. Wellington praised him and the other generals sent to Canada to serve in the war of 1812 in a letter to Earl Bathurst on 30 October 1814, 'the general officers I sent him, which are certainly the best of their rank in the army'.[16] General Power was also well thought of by the Horse Guards. In June 1813, Colonel Henry Torrens wrote to Wellington, 'I look upon Skerrett, Ross, and Power to be three of the best officers in the service.'[17]

11. Hill; Vol. 1, pages 84, 97–9.
12. General Order, 4 July 1815.
13. General Order, 6 July 1815.
14. *WSD*; Vol. 14, page 610.
15. *WND*; Vol. 2, page 425. Duke of Buckingham; Vol. 2, page 231.
16. Hitsman; page 267. Wellington was referring to Generals Power, Kempt, Brisbane, and Robinson.
17. *WSD*; Vol. 7, page 627.

Pringle, William Henry

Date of Birth:	c. 1771
Date Commissioned:	Cornet 16th Light Dragoons: 6 July 1792
Promotions:	Lieutenant 16th Light Dragoons: 24 February 1793
	Captain Independent Company: 15 October 1794
	Major 111th Foot:[1] 19 September 1794
	Major 4th Foot: 6 August 1799
	Lieutenant Colonel 4th Foot: 5 December 1799
	Captain & Lieutenant Colonel Coldstream Foot Guards: 17 September 1802 by exchange
	Lieutenant Colonel 1st Foot: 1 December 1808 by exchange
	Lieutenant Colonel unattached:[2] 15 December 1808 by exchange
	Brevet Colonel: 25 October 1809
	Major General: 1 January 1812[3]
	Lieutenant General: 27 May 1825
Regimental Colonel:	Royal Newfoundland Fencible Infantry: 12 May 1814–1 April 1816
	64th Foot: 1 April 1816–29 November 1837
	45th Foot: 29 November 1837–23 December 1840
Major Commands under Wellington:	Brigade 5th Division: 28 June 1812–9 March 1813
	Temporarily commanded 5th Division: 22–31 July 1812 and 7 September–25 October 1812
	Brigade 2nd Division: 23 July 1813–April 1814
	Temporarily commanded 2nd Division: 30 July–c. 4 August 1813
Awards:	KCB: 2 January 1815
	GCB: 19 December 1834
	AGC: Salamanca, Pyrenees, Nivelle & Nive
Thanks of Parliament:	Salamanca, the Peninsula, & Orthes
Member of Parliament:	St Germans, Cornwall: 1812–1818 and Liskeard Cornwall: 1818–1832
Date of Death:	23 December 1840 at Stratford Place, Marylebone, London

The exact date of birth of William Pringle is unknown, but it is probably 1771. He was the only son of Major General Henry Pringle and Mary Godley. His place of birth is unknown, but his family was from County Tyrone in Northern Ireland. He was educated at the Drogheda Grammar School until 1789.

William Pringle was commissioned a cornet in the 16th Light Dragoons in 1792. Like all future promotions, he was appointed to the rank and did not purchase it. He was promoted to lieutenant the following year and went with the regiment to Flanders in April. He fought in numerous battles and skirmishes over the next eighteen months. He returned to England when he was promoted to major in the 111th Foot in September

---

1. Disbanded 1795.
2. Not holding a regimental commission while serving as an Inspecting Field Officer of Militia in Canada.
3. Upon being promoted to major general, he was placed on half-pay of the staff. In 1814, he left half-pay when he was appointed Regimental Colonel of Royal Newfoundland Fencible Infantry on 12 May 1814.

1794. There was a mix up with his promotions for the following month he was promoted to captain of an independent company.[4] Major Pringle stayed with the 111th Foot in Ireland until it was disbanded in late 1795. Despite the disbanding of his regiment, he was still carried on the regimental rolls and received full pay. He had no regimental duties. Major Pringle remained unemployed until he was appointed a major in the 4th Foot in August 1799. He went with its 1st Battalion to Flanders in September and was taken prisoner at the Battle of Beverwyck on 6 October. He was held until November when a prisoner exchange was made as part of the agreement that saw the British force evacuate from Flanders.

Major Pringle returned to England and in December was promoted to lieutenant colonel. On 1 January 1800 he was promoted to brevet lieutenant colonel in the army. Like his promotion to major in 1794, there was some confusion on his promotions to lieutenant colonel. His promotion to brevet lieutenant colonel in the army was announced in the *London Gazette* on 1 January 1800, while his promotion to lieutenant colonel in his regiment was announced in the *London Gazette* on 18 January 1800. He stayed with the regiment until September 1802, when he exchanged into the Coldstream Guards. Lieutenant Colonel Pringle commanded a company in the 1st Battalion in General Edward Finch's Guards Brigade in the expedition to Hanover from November 1805 to February 1806 and during the expedition to Copenhagen from August to October 1807. In December 1808 he exchanged into the 1st Foot. Two weeks later, he exchanged to become an unattached lieutenant colonel and went to Canada as the Inspecting Field Officer of Militia British North America. While in Canada, he was promoted to colonel.

Colonel Pringle returned to England in early 1812 and found that he had been promoted to major general. He was selected by the Horse Guards to join Wellington's army as a replacement for generals killed in action in early 1812. He was selected before Colonel Henry Torrens received Wellington's letter stating that he had a sufficient number of generals and required no more. Colonel Torrens wrote to Wellington on 21 February informing him that General Pringle was appointed to his staff that he was 'now sorry for ... selecting him per Wellington's letter.'[5] Had Colonel Torrens been aware of Wellington's wishes, General Pringle might not have been sent out to serve in Spain, which proved to be the high point of his military career.

General Pringle was placed on the staff of Wellington's army on 2 May 1812.[6] On 28 June he was appointed the commander of a brigade in the 5th Division. He led it at Salamanca on 22 July and was given temporary command of the division after its commander was wounded during the battle. He led the division until 31 July when General Richard Hulse took over. However, General Pringle was back in temporary command of the division on 7 September when General Hulse died from typhus. He led the division as part of the covering forces besieging Burgos in September and during the retreat to the Portuguese border in October. On 25 October, General Pringle returned to his brigade and led them at Villa Muriel the same day.

After his brigade was settled in winter quarters in Portugal, General Pringle went to England in January 1813. The exact reason why he returned home is unknown, however, he had been elected a MP the previous year and may have wished to attend a session. He

---

4. Dates are correct. He was promoted a major with a seniority date before that of being made a captain. *London Gazette*; War Office Announcements dated 21 October 1794 and 21 February 1795.
5. Unpublished letter dated 21 February 1812.
6. General Order, 2 May 1813. His appointment was backdated to 25 February 1812.

voted in the House of Commons on 10 February and 2 March. While he was in England another officer was given command of his brigade. General Pringle returned to Portugal in June and on 23 July assumed command of a brigade in the 2nd Division. He led the brigade at the Battle of Maya on 25 July and because the division commander, William Stewart was in the rear, General Pringle commanded the division until he arrived later in the day. Five days later, General Stewart was wounded at Beunza and General Pringle took command of the division through the rest of the battle. He commanded it until General Stewart returned in early August.

General Pringle led his brigade through the autumn of 1813 and at the Battles of Nivelle on 10 November and at St Pierre[7] on 13 December, where his brigade defeated a French division that outnumbered them by 2.5 to 1. General Pringle was shot through the body at the Battle of Garris on 15 February 1814.[8] The exact nature of his wound is unknown, however, it was serious enough that he was not able to command his brigade through the rest of the war. He did receive the Thanks of Parliament for Orthes, even though he was still recovering from his wound and not at the battle. In early May, he was healthy enough to assume command of the 2nd Division on 7 May, when General Stewart returned to England. General Pringle commanded it until General William Anson took over on 25 May.

After he returned to England, General Pringle had few military duties but was appointed the regimental colonel of the Royal Newfoundland Fencible Infantry. After it was disbanded in 1816, he was appointed the colonel of the 64th Foot. In addition to being a regimental colonel, General Pringle was appointed to the Consolidated Board of General Officers in 1817 and served on it until his death. In February 1825 he was considered for command of the British Army in India, but not selected for the job. Three months later he was promoted to lieutenant general. In 1837 he became the colonel of the 45th Foot and held the position until his death in 1840.

William Pringle was a Tory MP from 1812 to 1832. His seat was in Cornwall and was the family seat long held by his wife's uncles, the 1st and 2nd Earls of St Germans. His attendance at Parliamentary Sessions was 'occasional' but when he was there he usually voted with the government on most bills. He voted for Catholic Relief in 1813, but against it in 1821, and for the Irish Insurrection Bill in 1824. In his twenty years as an MP he only gave one speech, when on 29 July 1831 he 'bore testimony to the intelligent character of the constituency of Liskeard [the borough of his seat]'. He chose to retire in 1832 rather than running for re-election.[9]

William Pringle inherited Cornacrew Estate, Armagh, Northern Ireland from his uncle in 1799. On 20 May 1806 he married Hester-Harriet Pitt Eliot. His wife was the granddaughter of both William Pitt the Elder and Lord Eliot Edward Craggs-Eliot, 1st Baron Eliot. She was also the niece of William Pitt the Younger. William and Hester had five children, of whom one joined the army. William died from a heart attack in 1840.[10] He is interred in Kensal Green Cemetery in London.

William Pringle was a competent brigade commander who has not been remembered well by history. As the temporary commander of the 5th Division during the siege of

---

7. St Pierre was one of the smaller combats that are grouped together under the Battle of Nive, which was fought from 9–13 December 1813.
8. Cadell; page 210.
9. 'Pringle'.
10. Ibid.

Burgos in September 1812 he is often blamed for the British Army not catching the remnants of the retreating French Army in the vicinity of Valladolid on 7 September. A Guards Officer in the 1st Division wrote the failure of his division was caused by

> Maj.-Gen. Pringle, who commanded the 5th Division ... in not sending explicit orders and a guide to the Artillery attached to it. We bivouacked on the 5th in a wood near the Fresma and shame be it said we were delayed nearly 3 hours in the morning from ignorance or neglect in the QMG's department – nobody could conduct the columns to the proper road – and it was most ludicrous and melancholy to see three different Divisions attempting to get out of the wood – their leaders becoming so confused – changing the direction of march and returning to whence they had set out from ...[11]

General Pringle was also strongly condemned by Lieutenant Colonel William Gomm, the AQMG assigned to his division. He wrote in October 1812 'we are commanded by a man who is liked by all the world in private life, and respected by no one in public.'[12]

This dislike of General Pringle also extended to his time as an MP. When he was being considered for the command of the British Forces in India, Charles W. Wynn, the President of the East India Board, wrote to the Duke of Buckingham on 23 February 1825 that, 'Pringle appears a very dull man, and has never been in any situation which enabled him to exhibit the sort of ability which is required. His connexion is wholly with the Pitts and Elliots.[13]

Yet this disdain was not reflected in the memoirs of an officer who served in General Pringle's brigade. A company commander in the 28th Foot noted General Pringle's 'coolness' while he commanded the 2nd Division at Maya on 25 July 1813. He also went on to describe him as 'gallant' at the Battle of Garris on 15 February 1814.[14]

---

11. Aitchison; pages 197–8.
12. Gomm; page 287.
13. Duke of Buckingham; Vol. 2, page 215.
14. Cadell; pages 165 and 210.

Rebow, Francis Slater

Date of Birth:	1770
Date Commissioned:	Ensign 60th Foot: 14 November 1787 without purchase
Promotions:	Lieutenant 60th Foot: 14 October 1789 by purchase
	Captain 60th Foot: 18 September 1792 by purchase
	Major 60th Foot: 20 February 1796 by purchase
	Supernumerary Major 2nd Life Guards: 16 February 1797 by exchange
	Major & Lieutenant Colonel 2nd Life Guards: 25 September 1799 appointed
	Supernumerary Lieutenant Colonel 1st Life Guards:[1] 20 August 1807 by purchase
	Brevet Colonel: 25 October 1809
	Major General: 1 January 1812
	Lieutenant General: 27 May 1825
	General: 23 November 1841
Major Commands under Wellington:	Household Cavalry Brigade: 28 November 1812–January 1813
Date of Death:	7 October 1845 at Wivenhoe Park, near Colchester, Essex

Name was initially Francis Slater.

Francis Slater was born in 1770. He was the son of Richard Slater of Chesterfield, Derbyshire, and Catherine Heaton. His brother was Midshipman Gill Slater. Francis married Mary Hester Rebow, daughter of Colonel Isaac Rebow of Wivenhoe Park, on 22 March 1796. They had two children. His wife was her father's only heir and upon marrying her, Francis added the name of Rebow.[2]

Francis Slater was appointed an ensign in the 4th Battalion 60th Foot in 1787 and served in the regiment for the next ten years. He went with his battalion to the West Indies in the autumn of 1788 and was there until late 1795. He purchased his lieutenancy in the regiment in 1789 and his captaincy in 1792. He was the commander of the Grenadier Company of the 4th Battalion and led them in the expedition to capture the French possessions of Martinique, St Lucia, and Guadeloupe in 1794. During the campaign to subdue Guadeloupe in April, he was severely wounded through both thighs. By the winter of 1796 he was back in England, where he purchased his majority in the regiment, got married, and changed his name to Rebow.

In March 1797, Major Rebow exchanged into the 2nd Life Guards as a supernumerary major. Two years later he was appointed major and lieutenant colonel in the regiment. His appointment was originally announced on 1 October 1799 that he was promoted to the second major in the 2nd Life Guards, bearing the date of 25 September 1799. However, this mistake was not caught for three years, when a War Office Memorandum of 25 September 1802 changed his promotion to major and lieutenant colonel. Because of this mix up Major Rebow had been promoted brevet lieutenant colonel in the army on 29 April 1802. Lieutenant Colonel Rebow stayed with the 2nd Life Guards until 1807,

---

1. He was removed from the regiment as a general officer receiving unattached pay c. 1818.
2. *London Gazette*; 12 April 1796.

when he purchased a lieutenant colonelcy in the 1st Life Guards. In October 1809, he was promoted to colonel. He served with his regiment until he was promoted to major general in January 1812. In April he was appointed on the Home Staff of the Inland District.

In 1812, the Household Cavalry Brigade consisted of the 1st and 2nd Life Guards, and the Royal Horse Guards. The Life Guards had not seen active service since the Battle of Fontenoy in 1745, while the Royal Horse Guards had last served in Flanders from 1793 to 1796. In the autumn of 1812, the Prince Regent finally allowed them to join Wellington's army in the Peninsula. General Terence O'Loghlin was supposed to command the brigade but resigned the appointment on 25 October due to ill health. General Rebow was selected to go in his stead. He was placed on the staff of Wellington's army to command the Household Cavalry Brigade on 28 November 1812.[3] He arrived in Portugal by the end of the year but by mid-January had requested and received a leave of absence to return to England.

Why General Rebow left Portugal after spending such a short time there is unknown. After arriving in England he was given no further military duties and he retired to the family estate of Wivenhoe Park. He was appointed a Magistrate and Deputy Lieutenant for the County of Essex. He was promoted to lieutenant general in 1825 and general in 1841. These promotions, however, were based on longevity and not on merit. He died at his home in 1845.

General Rebow had an unremarkable career. He had the chance to make a name for himself as the commander of the Household Brigade in the Peninsula, but he resigned from the position at the first opportunity. His tenure as a brigade commander in Wellington's army was the shortest of any general. Unlike his contemporaries, he was never awarded any medals or a knighthood. He is best remembered not as a military officer, but as a patron of noted British artist John Constable.

---

3. General Order, 28 November 1812.

Robinson, Frederick Philipse

Date of Birth:	September 1763 near New York City
Date Commissioned:	Ensign Loyal American Regiment:[1] February 1777 without purchase
Promotions:	Ensign 17th Foot: 11 September 1778 without purchase
	Lieutenant 60th Foot: 1 September 1779 without purchase
	Lieutenant 38th Foot: 4 November 1780 appointed
	Captain-Lieutenant 38th Foot: 24 March 1794 without purchase
	Captain 38th Foot: 3 July 1794 without purchase
	Major 127th Foot: 1 September 1794 appointed
	Major 32nd Foot: 1 September 1795 appointed
	Major 134th Foot:[2] 29 July 1796 by exchange
	Major 86th Foot: 19 February 1807 appointed
	Major 28th Foot: 26 March 1807 by exchange
	Major 18th Foot: 16 April 1807 by exchange
	Brevet Lieutenant Colonel: 1 January 1800
	Brevet Colonel: 25 July 1810
	Brigadier General on the Staff: 7 October 1812
	Major General: 4 June 1813
	Lieutenant General: 27 May 1825
	General: 23 November 1841
Regimental Colonel:	2nd Garrison Battalion: 14 January 1814–5 December 1814[3]
	59th Foot: 1 December 1827–15 June 1840
	39th Foot: 15 June 1840–1 January 1852
Major Commands under Wellington:	Brigade 5th Division: 9 March 1813–April 1814
	Temporarily commanded 5th Division: 14 April–? April 1814
Awards:	AGM with two clasps: Vitoria, San Sebastian & Nive
	KCB: 2 January 1815
	GCB: 20 April 1838
Thanks of Parliament:	Vitoria & San Sebastian
Date of Death:	1 January 1852 in Brighton, Sussex

Frederick Robinson was born in 1763 to Colonel Beverley Robinson and Susannah Philipse. His paternal grandfather was John Robinson, the Speaker of the House of Burgesses in Virginia, while his mother's family owned a large tract of land north of New York City in what is now Westchester and Putnam Counties, New York. The exact location and date of Frederick's birth is unknown, however, it was in September 1763 and somewhere on the family estates. He was the brother of Lieutenant Colonel Beverley Robinson (Jr), Lieutenant Colonel Morris Robinson, Lieutenant John Robinson, and Commissary-General Sir William Robinson.

With the outbreak of the American Revolution, Frederick's father used his own money to raise the Loyal American Regiment in the fall of 1776. Frederick was commissioned as an ensign in the new regiment. Eighteen months after joining the regiment, Ensign Robinson

---

1. A Loyalist Provincial Regiment raised in 1776.
2. Disbanded in 1796.
3. Disbanded on 5 December 1814.

was appointed an ensign in the 17th Foot and in 1779 was promoted to lieutenant in the 60th Foot. The following year he was appointed a lieutenant in the 38th Foot. Despite moving from regiment to regiment, Lieutenant Robinson saw much action. He fought at Horseneck Landing, Connecticut on 26 February 1779 and was wounded in the shoulder and captured at Stony Point, New York on 26 July 1779. He was held prisoner in Lancaster, Pennsylvania until November 1780, when George Washington, who was a friend of his father before the war, ordered his release. His final action of the war was the raid on New London, Connecticut on 6 September 1781. After the war ended his family lost their holdings in New York and Lieutenant Robinson went to England with his regiment.

On 24 November 1793, the Grenadier and Light Companies of the 38th Foot were sent to the West Indies as part of General Charles Grey's expedition to capture French possessions there. Lieutenant Robinson was part of the force that besieged Fort Bourbon on Martinique and two days after it surrendered, he was promoted to captain-lieutenant on 24 March 1794. Captain Robinson was at the capture of St Lucia and Guadeloupe in April. Soon after the fall of Guadeloupe, he became ill and had to return to England to recover his health. He was promoted to captain in the regiment in July and appointed a major in the 127th Foot. He stayed with the regiment in Ireland for a year but left it when he was appointed a major in the 32nd Foot. His new regiment was ordered to the West Indies in the spring of 1795, but Major Robinson did not go with it. In July he exchanged into the 134th Foot.

Major Robinson's 134th Foot was disbanded within six months of his joining it. However, according to the *Army List* despite the disbanding of his regiment, he was still carried on the regimental rolls and received full pay until 1798. He had no regimental duties. He was placed upon half-pay and would remain on regimental half-pay of the 134th Foot until 19 February 1807, when he exchanged into the 86th Foot. He was only in the regiment for a month when he exchanged into the 28th Foot on 26 March. He did not stay with them long, for on 16 April 1807 he exchanged into the 18th Foot and finally he exchanged to half-pay of the disbanded 91st Foot on 30 April 1807. He remained on half-pay of the 91st Foot until 1814, when he was appointed the regimental colonel of the 2nd Garrison Battalion.[4]

In May 1796 Major Robinson was appointed the Inspecting Field Officer of the Bedford Recruiting District. While there he was promoted to brevet lieutenant colonel in January 1800. He continued to serve in Bedford until 1802, when he became the Inspecting Field Officer of the London Recruiting District. Lieutenant Colonel Robinson was quite outspoken about some of the recruiting practices that he saw and tried to reform the system. Among the things he suggested was abolishing regimental recruiting and have all recruiting done for general service. The recruits would then be assigned to the regiments that needed them the most. He also suggested lowering the minimum height standard from 5 foot 5 inches to 5 foot 2 inches; raising the maximum age of a recruit from 30 to 40 years; and the minimum age for boys to 12 years. The boys were to be kept at the regimental depot, where they would be taught to read and write, and a trade, such as a tailor or a shoemaker.[5] Lieutenant Colonel Robinson was promoted to colonel in 1810 and continued to serve in the London Recruiting District until 1812.

---

4. When the 2nd Garrison Battalion was disbanded on 1 December 1814, General Robinson had no regimental affiliation and was listed as a major general with unattached pay.

5. *RMC*; Vol.3, pages 212–20.

In the summer of 1812, Colonel Robinson was selected to join Wellington's army in the Peninsula. In a letter dated 6 August 1812, Wellington was informed that the Duke of York had proposed that Colonel Robinson be sent out to him.[6] Colonel Henry Torrens of the Horse Guards also wrote to Wellington on the same day telling him that, 'Ever since the lesson I have had in the case of Long,[7] I never speak to any Man's military character without some personal experience of it, therefore I am silent upon the qualifications of these Brigadiers. They are spoken of as sensible men ...'[8] Colonel Robinson was placed on the staff of Wellington's army on 7 October 1812 as a brigadier general[9] and was in the Peninsula by 21 October 1812. Wellington did not initially want him on his staff and wrote back to Colonel Torrens on 6 December to inform him, 'General Robinson might as well be ordered home, as he is not to be employed. Indeed I don't believe he would be of any use.'[10] Wellington never wrote why he objected to having him on his staff, however, the fact that General Robinson had never commanded a unit larger than a company in combat, had never commanded a battalion, and had not been on active service in eighteen years had to have been factors in shaping his opinion. Colonel Torrens's refusal to provide an assessment of his abilities did not help.

General Robinson was kept in limbo for five months and not assigned to a brigade until 9 March 1813, when he was appointed the commander of General William Pringle's brigade in the 5th Division.[11] Like many of his contemporaries, General Robinson had a large retinue. It consisted of his brigade major, an ADC, six servants, five horses, seven mules, and a donkey.[12] Six months later it had expanded to '12 men employed in various ways – Four horses, Ten mules, Five Sheep, Two goats & a large Dog'.[13] plus his brigade major and ADC. General Robinson led his brigade at Vitoria on 21 June 1813, where he was ordered to seize the village of Gamarra Mayer, which was defended by two French regiments. The fighting was fierce and after initially taking the village, the brigade had to defend it against three counter-attacks. By the end of the day, the brigade had over 350 casualties; among them was their commander. General Robinson wrote to his sister that he 'had some very narrow escapes – one ball through my Hat, another through my clothes & grazing my Ribs on my right side, and my horse shot in two places ...'[14]

General Robinson's brigade was part of the force that besieged San Sebastian in July and August 1813. It was his brigade that led the assault that took the city on 31 August. Twelve hundred men from the brigade were in the assault and they had over 860 casualties – 72 per cent of its strength – including General Robinson, who had been seriously wounded in the face while he was climbing the breach in the city's walls. Two days later he wrote to his wife with the news that he had been wounded and assured her that he had 'been laid sprawling in the mud by a Ball through my beautiful face ... Fortunately my teeth and jawbone are safe ... but I shall have a nice little scar ...'[15]

---

6. *WSD*; Vol. 7, page 375.
7. General Robert Long.
8. Unpublished letter from Colonel Henry Torrens to Wellington dated 6 August 1812.
9. General Order, October 1812.
10. Name is suppressed *WSD*; Vol. 7, page 495.
11. General Order, 9 March 1813.
12. Atkinson; page 154.
13. Ibid; page 163.
14. Ibid; page 161.
15. Ibid; page 166.

He wrote to his sister on 11 September how close to dying he had come, for 'had the Ball gone a hair breath closer to my neck I should have slept with my fathers ...'[16] He described his wound further to his wife in a letter on 22 September: 'the Ball entered at the corner of the mouth and the other at the point of the jaw.'[17]

Among the casualties of the assault was General James Leith, General Robinson's division commander. General Andrew Hay was placed in temporary command of the division and wrote the division report to Wellington after the assault. This report caused a feud between General Hay and General Robinson, who felt that General Hay gave much of the credit for the success of the assault to his own brigade rather than to General Robinson's brigade, which had 50 per cent more casualties and were the ones who took the breach. General Robinson was furious and wrote home to his wife that 'Genl Hay… is a fool, and I verily believe, with many others on my side, an arrant [*sic*] coward. That he is a paltry plundering old wretch is established beyond doubt. That he is no officer is as clear, and that he wants spirit is firmly believed. Ergo he ought not to be a General.'[18]

General Robinson recovered from his wounds by early October and led his men in the crossing of the Bidassoa River into France on 7 October. He fought at Nivelle on 10 November and was seriously wounded at Nive on 9 December. The extent of his wound is unknown, but he had to be carried from the field to the rear for medical treatment.[19] General Robinson spent many months convalescing, but he was never officially replaced in command of his brigade. It spent the rest of the war as part of the blockading force around Bayonne and saw little or no action. General Robinson was given temporary command of the 5th Division on 14 April, when General Charles Colville took command of General John Hope's corps after he was wounded and captured during the French sortie that day. Normally General Hay, the senior brigade commander, would have taken command, but he was killed during the sortie. General Robinson's command of the division was not long and since hostilities had ceased the command mostly entailed administrative duties.

When the war ended in Europe in April 1814, the British Government decided to send a large force to fight in North America during the war of 1812. Most of the officers and men were to be taken from Wellington's army. General Robinson was initially selected to command a brigade in the force by the Commander-in-Chief. When the size of the force was reduced and the objectives of the force changed, General Robinson let it be known that he wanted to serve with it. He was selected to command the 4th Brigade destined for Canada but only if he arrived before the force sailed. General Robinson made it to Bordeaux where the force was assembling and took command of his brigade.[20]

The force arrived Pot à l'Eau-de-Vie, Quebec on 8 August 1814 and within a month was participating in the Plattsburg Campaign. General Robinson was supposed to lead the main attack against the Americans's left flank at the Battle of Plattsburg on 11 September. However, the attack was called off after the Royal Navy's flotilla was defeated. The force retreated back to Canada and went into winter quarters. In November he was appointed the Commander-in-Chief and Provisional Lieutenant Governor of Upper Canada. He was confirmed in his position of Lieutenant Governor on 10 June 1815. He served until

16. Ibid; page 168.
17. Ibid; page 168.
18. Ibid; page 168.
19. Frazer; page 361.
20. *WSD*; Vol. 9, pages 82, 88 and 136.

29 September. General Robinson returned to England in 1816 and on 13 November was appointed the Commander of the Troops and Governor of Tobago. His tenure on the island was stormy and eventually the House of Assembly of Tobago made numerous accusations and charges against him. He left the island in 1828.

After General Robinson returned to England in 1828, he had no further military duties other than as a regimental colonel. He was appointed the regimental colonel of the 2nd Garrison Battalion in 1814, but when it was disbanded at the end of the year he did not receive another regiment for thirteen years. In 1827, he became the colonel of the 59th Foot, one of the regiments that were part of his brigade in the Peninsula. In 1840, he was appointed the colonel of 39th Foot, a regiment under his command in the Plattsburg Campaign. On his death in 1852, his seventy-five years as an officer made him the longest serving soldier in the British Army![21]

Frederick Robinson was married twice. His first wife was Grace Boles. They had four children. Their oldest son, Ensign Frederick Philipse Robinson, served as his father's ADC in 1814. Grace died in 1806. Frederick remarried in 1811 to Anne Fernyhaugh of Stafford. She died in Tobago.[22] General Robinson was cared for in his old age by his daughter and niece. He lived in Brighton for the last seven years of his life. He was in 'good health and in the exercise of all his mental faculties'[23] until his death. He died of a sudden illness on 1 January 1852 and was buried in the Hove churchyard on 7 January.

General Robinson was a competent brigade commander whose men were always in the thick of the action. Under his command it fought in five battles and sieges and took over 66 per cent casualties. He led them from the front on his horse and he paid for his bravery by being wounded three times in seven months. He was seriously wounded on the breach at San Sebastian. At the crossing of the Bidassoa River on 7 October 1813, he led the way through the chin-high water. Although he demanded the most from his men, he always looked out for them. His letters are filled with descriptions of the fights he had with the army's commissary officers to ensure his men received the freshest provisions available and the pressure he put on the local officials to provide cattle to feed his men.

Despite being relatively unknown prior to his service in the Peninsula, General Robinson's actions convinced his doubters that he was a capable commander. Colonel Torrens wrote to Wellington in August 1813: 'I am a little proud... whom I selected for your staff, and...General Robinson formed part of the batch of Generals that alarmed you so much.'[24] Even Wellington changed his opinion and praised General Robinson along with the other generals sent to Canada to serve in the war of 1812 in a letter to Earl Bathurst on 30 October 1814: 'the general officers I sent him, which are certainly the best of their rank in the army ...'[25]

---

21. Upon his death in 1859, General John Slade had surpassed General Robinson's time in service record by four years.
22. Some sources spell her family name as Fernehough. Many sources has her given name as Ann, however, in his letters home in 1813, he calls her Anne.
23. *Gentleman's Magazine*; Vol. 191, page 190.
24. Unpublished letter dated 19 August 1813.
25. Hitsman; page 267. Wellington was referring to Generals Power, Kempt, Brisbane, and Robinson.

Ross, Robert

Date of Birth:	1766
Date Commissioned:	Ensign 25th Foot: 1 August 1789 purchase
Promotions:	Lieutenant 7th Foot: 13 July 1791 without purchase
	Captain 7th Foot: 19 April 1795 without purchase
	Major 90th Foot: 23 December 1795 purchase
	Major 20th Foot: 6 August 1799 appointed
	Brevet Lieutenant Colonel: 1 January 1801
	Lieutenant Colonel 20th Foot: 21 January 1808 without purchase
	Brevet Colonel: 25 July 1810
	Major General: 4 June 1813
Major Commands	
under Wellington:	Brigade 4th Division: 2 July 1813–April 1814
Awards:	AGC with one clasp: Maida, Corunna, Vitoria, Pyrenees & Orthes
Thanks of Parliament:	Peninsula & Orthes
Date of Death:	12 September 1814 North Point, Maryland, USA

Robert Ross was born in 1766. Neither his exact date of birth nor his birthplace is known. Most sources give his place of birth as either Dublin or Rostrevor, County Down in Northern Ireland. He was the second son of Major David Ross of Rostrevor[1] and Elizabeth Adderley, the half-sister of the Earl of Charlemont. His brother was Lieutenant James Ross RN. In 1784, Robert attended Trinity College in Dublin and finished his studies in 1789. Upon leaving Trinity College, he was commissioned as an ensign in the 25th Foot.

Ensign Ross joined his regiment in Gibraltar. While there he became friends with Prince Edward Augustus,[2] the regimental colonel of the 7th Foot, and sailed with him to Quebec in May 1791. They arrived in August and while he was en route, Ensign Ross was appointed a lieutenant in the 7th Foot. In 1795, his father died and he was given permission to return home. While there, Prince Edward appointed him a captain in the regiment's 2nd Battalion. Eight months after he joined the 2nd Battalion he used his inheritance to purchase his majority in the 2nd Battalion of the 90th Foot.[3] Major Ross was only in his new battalion a short time when it was disbanded. According to the *Army List*, despite the disbanding of the 2nd Battalion of the 90th Foot he was still carried on its regimental rolls and received full pay. He had no regimental duties. In early 1798 he was placed on half-pay of the disbanded 2nd Battalion 90th Foot.

In May 1798, Major Ross, although still on half-pay, was appointed a brigade major on the Home Staff in the Sussex District. He served as a brigade major until August 1799, when he was appointed a major in the 1st Battalion 20th Foot. He joined the regiment just in time to sail with them to Den Helder in late August. He was seriously wounded at the Battle of Krabbendam on 10 September, which kept him from participating in the rest of the campaign. In October the regiment returned to England and went to Ireland in January 1800. In June, Major Ross went with the 1st Battalion to Minorca and was

---

1. Also spelled Rosstrevor.
2. Prince Edward Augustus was the Duke of Kent, a son of King George III.
3. McCavitt; pages 11–12.

given command of the garrison's flank battalion. On 1 January 1801, he was promoted to brevet lieutenant colonel. Six months after his promotion they sailed to Egypt and were part of the siege of Alexandria in August. They stayed in Egypt until December and then went to Malta.

The 20th Foot remained in Malta for the next four years. After the Treaty of Amiens was signed in March 1802, Lieutenant Colonel Ross took a leave of absence, toured Italy, and went back to Ireland. He returned to Malta the following spring and in September 1803 assumed command of the 1st Battalion. He spent the next three years drilling the battalion and conducting field exercises. One officer stated that Lieutenant Colonel Ross would march the battalion

> out into the country at five in the morning, and not bring us home till one p.m ...
> We were repeatedly out for eight hours during the hot weather; frequently crossing
> the country, scouring the fields over the stone walls, the whole regiment acting as
> light infantry; and the best of the joke was, that no other corps in the island was
> similarly indulged.[4]

In November 1805, the regiment sailed for Naples, but after a few months withdrew to Sicily. In July 1806 they were back in southern Italy and on 4 July fought the French at Maida. Lieutenant Colonel Ross was mentioned in dispatches by the force commander, who wrote, 'The most brilliant parts on this stage were acted by Colonels Kempt[5] and Ross; to them the glory of the fight at Maida is chiefly due.'[6] By the end of the month they had returned to Sicily and remained there until October 1807.

By early January 1808, Lieutenant Colonel Ross and the regiment were in England and spent the next five months rebuilding its strength. After being a brevet lieutenant colonel for seven years, he was appointed a lieutenant colonel. In June 1808, the regiment was at Harwich in a brigade commanded by General Wroth Acland. This brigade was assigned to Wellington's Corps for service in Portugal on 15 July. It landed in Portugal on 20 August and was numbered the 8th Brigade. On 5 September the army was reorganised and the 20th Foot remained in General Acland's brigade in the 2nd Division. When it was decided to form a force to operate in Spain under General John Moore and leave a garrison in Portugal, the 20th Foot was selected to serve in the force for Spain. It was assigned to General Robert Anstruther's brigade in General Edward Paget's division.[7] Lieutenant Colonel Ross temporarily commanded the brigade in the absence of General Anstruther, who was in northern Portugal coordinating supplies and billets for the movement of the army into Spain. He commanded the brigade on the advance into Spain until the middle of December when General Anstruther rejoined it. When General Anstruther died on 14 January, Lieutenant Colonel Ross again succeeded to the command of the brigade. The retreat was strenuous and one officer wrote that Lieutenant Colonel Ross 'frequently fell fast asleep and nearly fell of his horse, being almost worn out.'[8] He led it at the Battle of Corunna on 16 January 1809 and was evacuated with the army. During the campaign, he rode a chestnut Arab that was quite valuable (he had been offered 150 guineas for it

---

4. Steevens; page 38.
5. James Kempt.
6. Smyth; page 120.
7. General Order, 8 October 1808.
8. Steevens; page 69.

the previous year). It was among the horses that could not be evacuated to England after Corunna and it was killed rather than leaving it to the French.[9]

The regiment returned to England in late January and once again Lieutenant Colonel Ross spent many months rebuilding its strength. In July it sailed with the British force that was sent to Walcheren. It was part of General William Erskine's brigade of the Reserve Division. The regiment saw no action but was struck hard by Walcheren Fever and by early September it was sent back to England. The regiment had sailed for the Low Lands with close to 1,000 men, but by the time it returned to England, over 600 had been hospitalised. They spent a year in England rebuilding its strength for a third time. In July 1810 the regiment was sent to Ireland, where they stayed for two years while recovering from the effects of Walcheren Fever. Shortly after arriving in Ireland Lieutenant Colonel Ross was promoted to colonel and made an ADC to the King.

In the autumn of 1812, the 20th Foot received orders to join Wellington's army. They sailed on 13 October and initially landed in Corunna, but re-embarked the next day and landed in Lisbon on 15 November. They were assigned to General John Skerrett's brigade in the 4th Division. This brigade was also known as the Fusilier Brigade. They linked up with their brigade just in time to go into winter quarters. Colonel Ross applied for a brigade command in a letter to Wellington on 29 April 1813. Wellington replied on 1 May that, 'I shall be very happy to appoint you to the command of a brigade in the army when it shall be in my power.'[10] He then went on to explain why certain colonels commanded brigades in which their regiments served and listed colonels and brigadier generals without brigade commands all senior to Colonel Ross. He ended by stating that,

It has been the practice not to move senior officers from the command of their regiment to command brigades until it was quite certain that, by the arrival of other officers with the army, they would not be obliged to return to the command of their regiments; and it is very desirable not to depart from this practice.[11]

Colonel Ross led his regiment at Vitoria on 21 June 1813, where they were only lightly engaged. Soon after the battle he was notified that he had been promoted to major general on 4 June. Wellington kept his word to General Ross. On 2 July, he transferred General Skerrett to the Light Division and appointed General Ross the commander of the Fusilier Brigade.[12] He led his brigade at Roncesvalles on 25 July and at Sorauren on 27 and 28 July, where he had two horses shot out from under him. They were lightly engaged at Nivelle on 10 November and were in the reserve at Nive on 10 December. At the end of the day, General Ross's brigade was tasked with assisting the two battalions of the 2nd Nassau Regiment and the Frankfurt Battalion in crossing into the British lines. These three battalions had received orders from their governments to defect to the Allies at the first opportunity.

After the battle, the brigade went into winter quarters. They fought at Orthes on 27 February 1814, where it was ordered to dislodge the French from the village of St Boes and take the hill on the other side. Five times they tried to take the hill but were repulsed with heavy casualties. Among the wounded was General Ross who was shot in the face

---

9. Ibid; page 75.
10. *WD* (enlarged ed.); Vol. 6, page 457.
11. Ibid; page 457.
12. General Order, 2 July 1813.

early in the day. He wound was so serious that he was sent to St. Jean de Lux. He wrote on 12 March, 'the hit I got in the chops is likely to prove of mere temporary inconvenience. I am doing remarkably well, and trust in two or three weeks to be again equal to the fight.'[13] General Ross was a bit optimistic, for he spent the next several months recuperating and fought no more in the Peninsula.

After the war ended in Europe, in April 1814 the British Government decided to send a large force to fight in North America during the war of 1812. Most of the officers and men were to be taken from Wellington's army. General Ross was initially selected to command a brigade in the force.[14] Soon after his selection, the size of the force was reduced and the objectives of the force were changed. On 18 May, Earl Bathurst stated that a brigade would be chosen for independent duty to work with Admiral Cochrane[15] along the Atlantic Coast of the United States. Wellington was left with the decision as to who would command it, either General Edward Barnes or General Ross. On 29 May, General Ross was appointed.[16] There is some speculation on why General Ross was selected to command the force. One theory described him as 'even-tempered but energetic, and having had some experience of cooperation with the navy, he could be relied upon to work in partnership with Cochrane.'[17]

General Ross and his force arrived in Chesapeake Bay in mid-August and by 22 August were marching on Washington. He defeated the American Army at Bladensburg, Maryland on 24 August, where he had a horse shot out from under him. The British Army occupied Washington that night and proceeded to burn the public buildings, including the Capitol and the White House. The following day he withdrew his force and marched back to Chesapeake Bay. He embarked his army and sailed north towards Baltimore on 30 August.

On 11 September, General Ross and his army landed at North Point, Maryland and began marching on Baltimore. He was with the lead brigade when it came under fire from American riflemen. He rode forward to see what was happening when he was shot through the arm and the bullet penetrated his chest.[18] An officer in the 85th Foot wrote that as his battalion was moving up,

> another officer came at full speed towards us, with horror and dismay in his countenance, and calling loudly for a surgeon. Every man felt within himself that all was not right, though none was willing to believe the whispers of his own terror. But what at first we would not guess at, because we dreaded it so much, was soon realized; for the aide-de-camp had scarcely passed, when the general's horse without its rider, and with the saddle and housings stained with blood, came plunging onwards. Nor was much time given for fearful surmise, as to the extent of our misfortune. In a few moments we reached the ground where the skirmishing had taken place, and beheld General Ross laid, by the side of the road, under a canopy of blankets, and apparently in the agonies of death. As soon as the firing began, he had ridden to the front, that he might ascertain from whence it originated, and, mingling with the

13. *United Services Magazine*; 1829, Part I, page 413.
14. *WSD*; Vol. 9, pages 82–4.
15. Admiral Alexander Cochrane commanding the North American Station.
16. *WSD*; Vol. 9, pages 82–4, 117–19, and 135.
17. Reilly; page 140.
18. Smyth; page 347.

skirmishers, was shot in the side by a rifleman. The wound was mortal: he fell into the arms of his aide-de-camp, and lived only long enough to name his wife, and to commend his family to the protection of his country. He was removed towards the fleet, but expired before his bearers could reach the boats ...[19]

The surgeon who treated him found that the bullet

was found deeply embedded in ... the last dorsal vertebra.' The ball passed through the general's right arm just above the elbow and entered his torso, fractured the fifth and sixth ribs, passed through the Diaphragm, and wounded the right lobe of the Liver, passing deep and dividing the vena porta, which may have thrown its blood into the right cavity of the Thorax which was found filled with Blood.[20]

General Ross's body was preserved in 129 gallons of rum and brought back to Halifax. He was interred in St Paul's graveyard in Halifax, Nova Scotia on 29 September, 1814.[21] A monument was raised to him on the family estate at Rostrevor and a memorial was placed in St Paul's Cathedral at government expense. The Prince Regent conferred an honourary distinction on the family by adding 'of-Bladensburg' to their name and thus they would be known as Ross-of-Bladensburg.[22]

Robert Ross was a talented artist and musician. He was fluent in French and spoke passable Portuguese.[23] He married Elizabeth Glascock on 9 December 1802 at St George's Church in London. They had seven children, but only three survived infancy. She and her children received pensions after his death. In letters he referred to her as Ly.[24] She was not one for sitting at home while her husband was on campaign. Shortly after they were married, she sailed with him to Malta and was in northern Spain in the winter of 1814 when he was seriously wounded. When she heard the news she

mounted her mule, and in the midst of rain, hail, wind, and all the et ceteras of bad weather, set off from Bilboa [*sic*] for this place which she reached early on the fifth day, a distance between eighty and ninety miles, over snowy mountains and bad roads. Her anxiety and spirit carried her through, enabling her to bear the fatigue without suffering from cold or bad weather ...[25]

Rather than risking the life of their young son, she left him with his nurse in Bilbao. She did not accompany him to America in 1814 and legend has it that Robert Ross promised his wife before his departure for America in 1814 that it would be his last campaign.

Robert Ross was well thought of by both his subordinates and those above him. In a letter dated 3 June 1813 in which he passed on the news of the latest promotions to major general, Colonel Henry Torrens of the Horse Guards told Wellington that, 'I look upon

19. Gleig, George; *The Campaigns of the British Army at Washington and New Orleans*, pages 177–8.
20. McCavitt; page 185.
21. Ibid; pages 187 and 192.
22. *London Gazette*; 9 September 1815.
23. Steevens; page 56.
24. McCavitt; page 17.
25. *United Service Magazine*; 1829, page 414.

Skerrett, Ross, and Power to be three of the best officers in the service.'[26] A junior officer who served under him in the Washington Campaign wrote on his death,

> By the courteousness and condescension of his manners, General Ross has secured the absolute love of all who served under him, from the highest to the lowest; and his success on a former occasion, as well as his judicious arrangements on the present, had inspired every one with the most perfect confidence in his abilities.[27]

Major Harry Smith, who was General Ross's Brigade Major, was very fond of him. However, he was quite candid when he wrote,

> I cannot say my dear friend general Ross inspired me with the opinion he was the officer Colborne[28] regarded him as being. He was very cautious in responsibility – awfully so, and lacked that dashing enterprise so essential to carry a place by a *coup de main*. He died the death of a gallant soldier, as he was, and friendship for man must honour the manes of the brave.[29]

Robert Ross was an officer who demanded the most from his men. Like many of his contemporaries, he led from the front, being wounded several times, having many horses killed in battle, and eventually being killed himself. He looked after his men, but also ensured his officers looked after them too. One officer wrote that during the retreat to Corunna in 1809,

> Our Colonel (poor Ross) gave orders, that whenever we did happen to get into a town, the officers were not to go to their billets, but to remain with their men; the consequence was that we were always a check upon our men, and prevented them from drinking ... also, if we had been called upon in the night, we were then always ready to turn out with our different companies.[30]

The same officer also observed his humanity during the retreat to Corunna. During one of the worse days, when soldiers and their wives were falling by the roadside unable to keep up, he saw Colonel Ross with a small boy whose parents had died from the hardship of the march. He was carrying the boy in front of him on his saddle.[31]

---

26. *WSD*; Vol. 9, page 627.
27. Gleig, George; *The Campaigns of the British Army at Washington and New Orleans*, page 178.
28. Colborne was John Colborne, later Lord Seaton. He served in the 20th Foot from 1794 until 1809.
29. Smith; page 197.
30. Steevens; page 70.
31. Ibid; page 73.

Skerrett, John Byne

Date of Birth:	c. 1778
Date Commissioned:	Ensign 99th Foot: 1783 without purchase[1]
Promotions:	Lieutenant 79th Foot:[2] 25 October 1783
	Lieutenant 19th Foot: 1791 appointed[3]
	Lieutenant 48th Foot: 6 January 1792 by exchange
	Captain 123rd Foot: 27 August 1794 without purchase
	Captain 69th Foot: 23 March 1795 appointed
	Major 83rd Foot: 29 March 1798 purchase
	Lieutenant Colonel 83rd Foot: 23 October 1800 purchase
	Lieutenant Colonel 10th Battalion of Reserve: 9 July 1803 appointed
	Lieutenant Colonel 47th Foot: 16 January 1804 appointed
	Brevet Colonel: 25 July 1810
	Major General: 4 June 1813
Major Commands under Wellington:	On staff of Cadiz: 4 May 1811–September 1812
	Brigade with Hill's Corps: September–October 1812
	Brigade 4th Division: 17 October 1812–2 July 1813
	Brigade Light Division: 2 July–September 1813
Awards:	AGM: Vitoria
Date of Death:	10 March 1814

The exact date of birth of John Skerrett is unknown. His obituary states he was 36 years old when he was killed in 1814, which makes his year of birth either 1777 or 1778. He was the only child of Lieutenant General John Nicholas Skerrett of Nantwich Cheshire and Anne Byne of Surrey. Little is known about his younger years except that he enrolled in the Rugby School in 1785. He never married.

John Skerrett was commissioned as an ensign at the age of 5 in the 99th Foot in 1783. A month later he was a lieutenant in the 79th Foot. His regiment was disbanded in 1784 and he went on half-pay. He remained on half-pay until 1791 when he was appointed a lieutenant in the 19th Foot at the age of 13. He exchanged into his father's regiment, the 48th Foot, in 1792 and stayed on the regimental rolls until 1794, when he was appointed a captain in the 123rd Foot. Seven months after joining the 123rd Foot he was appointed a captain in the 69th Foot. It is unknown when John Skerrett actually reported to duty with his regiment. Because of his youth, it was probably not before 1792 when he exchanged into his father's regiment.

John Skerrett's rapid rise through the ranks at such an early age was not unusual for the time. However, in 1795 there had been so much abuse of the system that it was reformed. An officer had to have two years as a subaltern before he could be promoted to captain and had to have at least six years of service before being promoted to major. Captain Skerrett purchased his majority in the 83rd Foot in 1798 and joined the regiment in Jamaica, where he spent the next five years. While there, he purchased his lieutenant colonelcy

---

1. *London Gazette*; dated 20 September 1783.
2. Disbanded 1784.
3. *London Gazette*; dated 17 September 1791.

in the regiment. They returned to England in 1802 and were stationed in Chelmsford. The regiment quickly developed a reputation for bad behaviour in the local community and the Commander-in-Chief received numerous complaints from its magistrates. As a punishment, on 18 March 1803 Lieutenant Colonel Skerrett was removed from the regiment and placed on half-pay of the 62nd Foot. He successfully appealed the decision and was appointed the commander of the 10th Reserve Battalion in July 1803.

Lieutenant Colonel Skerrett was transferred to the 47th Foot in January 1804 and took command of its 2nd Battalion in Ireland. In 1807 it was sent to Chelmsford and then to Jersey. By January 1809, Lieutenant Colonel Skerrett was the commander of the 1st Battalion, which was stationed in India. There is no evidence that he ever joined it there. In July 1810, he was promoted to colonel.

By the spring of 1811, Colonel Skerrett was in Cadiz and in May was given command of the 2nd Brigade of the British forces in Cadiz. Although in command, he was not officially appointed its commander. The next month, he and the 2nd Battalion 47th Foot were sent to aid the beleaguered Spanish garrison at Tarragona. After arriving there, he considered the situation hopeless and refused to land his troops. By August, they were back in Cadiz and Colonel Skerrett resumed command of the 2nd Brigade. Colonel Skerrett was finally appointed a colonel on the staff in a General Order dated August 1811, backdated to 4 May 1811. On 10 October 1811, he was detached from his command and sent to take command of the British force defending Tarifa. He returned to Cadiz in February 1812, after successfully defending Tarifa, and again commanded the 2nd Brigade which was on the Isla de Leon.

The summer of 1812 saw the French Army besieging Cadiz withdraw north towards Madrid. As the French retreated, Colonel Skerrett was sent with an ad hoc force to help the Spanish liberate Seville, which they accomplished on 28 August. On 8 September 1812, Wellington ordered Colonel Skerrett to bring reinforcements from Cadiz to his army operating in central Spain. He was given the option of sailing to Lisbon or marching overland. He chose to march and by October had linked up with the army. His force was disbanded and the various battalions were sent to different divisions. On 12 October Colonel Skerrett was given command of the Fusilier Brigade in the 4th Division.

Colonel Skerrett commanded the brigade in the retreat back to the Portuguese border and in December they went into winter quarters. In May 1813, he was part of the advance into Spain and led his brigade at Vitoria on 21 June. By early July word had reached the army that he had been promoted to major general on 4 June. Wellington decided to give him command of a brigade in the Light Division on 2 July. By the end of August his brigade was on the heights overlooking a bridge across the Bidassoa River at the village of Vera. His brigade was between the retreating French and their safety on the other side of the river. The only way to cross the river was over the bridge. General Skerrett gave orders to the 2nd Battalion 95th Rifles to provide a picket in Vera on 31 August. Captain Daniel Cadoux and his company of about 100 riflemen were sent into the village. The French attacked in overwhelming numbers the next day trying to force their way across the river, but were continually beaten back by Captain Cadoux's Company. General Skerrett refused to reinforce the isolated company despite the urging of his brigade major. Instead he ordered them to retreat. Up to this time, the riflemen had only taken two casualties and were in no danger of being overrun. As they pulled back, they were decimated by the French fire. Captain Cadoux and seventeen riflemen were killed and another forty-five wounded.

The officers of his brigade never forgave General Skerrett for what they perceived as his unnecessary sacrifice of Captain Cadoux and his men. Later in the month, he received word that his father had died on 18 August. He requested permission to return to England to settle the estate, which was quite large – camp gossip said it had an annual income of £7,000.[4] He did not return to the Peninsula.

In late November 1813, General Skerrett was selected for the British expedition that was being formed under General Thomas Graham to go to Holland. He was chosen because he was available, although Earl Bathurst assured General Graham that he was very good.[5] In early January, on the advance to Bergen-op-Zoom, General Skerrett fell off his horse and was seriously injured. Legend has it that he broke his leg. However, by late January he had returned to duty. In early March they began the siege of Bergen-op-Zoom and he was in command of the attack on the north side of the city on the night of 9 March. During the assault, General Skerrett used a crutch as he led the forward most elements of the assault on the walls.[6] He was wounded in the hand and then the thigh. Rather than falling back to have his wounds treated, he stayed with his men. He stood up to get a better view and was shot in the head. Although this wound did not kill him initially, it proved to be mortal. General Skerrett was captured and died the next day.[7]

John Skerrett is not well known because he only served briefly with Wellington's army. He did have supporters at the Horse Guards. In a letter dated 3 June 1813 in which he passed on the news of the latest promotions to major general, Colonel Henry Torrens told Wellington that, 'I look upon Skerrett, Ross, and Power to be three of the best officers in the service.'[8] Wellington is silent on his abilities, possibly because General Skerrett only served under him for a short time. When he was promoted to major general in 1813, Wellington had the option to ask for General Skerrett's recall. Instead, Wellington appointed him to command of a brigade in the Light Division. After he returned to England in September 1813, Wellington kept the brigade command vacant for his return as it was still called Skerrett's in January 1814. This may have been deliberate, since it allowed Wellington to leave deserving junior colonels in command of it in his absence.

General Skerrett's subordinates were quite vocal about him. He was describe as fidgety by a staff officer who served under him during the siege of Tarifa,[9] and bilious[10] by his brigade major in 1813.[11] Yet it was not his personality that they disliked – it was his inability to make a decision. One wrote that during the siege of Tarifa he

> was wanting in the bold decision, which, in military practice, must often take the lead of science, and established rules. The quality was wanting, as shown in the opinion by this officer on the untenable condition of the town. He saw no further than its mouldering [*sic*] walls, and imperfect fortifications, whereas a perspicuous moral view would have discerned strength where weakness was perceptible, and the triumph of boldness, aided by valour, over a timid adherence to the rules of art.

---

4. Smith; page 128.
5. Bamford, Andrew; *A Bold and Ambitious Enterprise*, page 64.
6. Anonymous; *Letters from Germany and Holland*; page 165.
7. Ibid; page 207.
8. *WSD*; Vol. 9, page 627.
9. Bunbury; Vol. 1, page 123.
10. Irritable or cranky.
11. Smith; page 125.

The preservation of the fortress was therefore mainly attributable to the Engineer officer, Captain Smith,[12] who by a more skillful and enlarged view of the application of its resources, over-ruled objections that tended to its evacuation ...[13]

Another officer who served under him at Tarifa also noted the same failings in General Skerrett, when he wrote, 'At the head of troops he was the most undecided, timid, and vacillating creature I ever met with.'[14]

Although none of those who wrote of him thought much of his leadership, they all commented on General Skerrett's courage, which bordered on suicidal. Captain Harry Smith, his brigade major when he was in the Light Division, wrote that he

was by nature, a gallant Grenadier and no Light Troop officer, which requires the eye of a hawk and the power of anticipating the enemy's intention – who was always to be found off his horse standing in the most exposed spot under the enemy's fire while our Riflemen were well concealed, as stupidly composed for himself as inactive for the welfare of his command.[15]

Lieutenant Thomas Bunbury observed that 'Skerrett, as an individual, was brave to rashness; but I should have doubted it had I not so frequently witnessed proofs of his cool intrepidity and contempt of danger.'[16] While a third described him as 'unimpeachable in the courageous bearing of a soldier'.[17]

It was this disregard for his own safety that got General Skerrett killed in the end.

---

12. Captain Charles Felix Smith, Royal Engineers.
13. Henegan; Vol. 1, pages 127–8.
14. Bunbury; Vol. 1, page 116.
15. Smith; page 118.
16. Bunbury; Vol. 1, page 116.
17. Henegan; Vol. 1, page 127.

Slade, John

Date of Birth:	30 December 1762
Date Commissioned:	Cornet 10th Dragoons: 11 May 1780 without purchase
Promotions:	Lieutenant 10th Dragoons: 28 April 1783 without purchase[1]
	Captain 10th Light Dragoons: 24 October 1787 without purchase
	Major 10th Light Dragoons: 1 March 1794 without purchase
	Lieutenant Colonel 10th Light Dragoons: 29 April 1795 purchase
	Lieutenant Colonel 1st Dragoons:[2] 18 October 1798 by exchange
	Brevet Colonel: 29 April 1802
	Brigadier General on the Staff: June 1804–1809
	Major General: 25 October 1809
	Lieutenant General: 4 June 1814
	General: 10 January 1837
Regimental Colonel:	5th Dragoon Guards: 20 July 1831–13 August 1859
Major Commands	
under Wellington:	Cavalry brigade: 7 October 1809–April 1813
	Temporarily commanded the Cavalry: January–11 April 1811
	Temporarily commanded 2nd Cavalry Division: March–April 1813
Awards:	GCH: 1835
	AGM with one clasp: Corunna & Fuentes d'Onor
	MGSM with two clasps: Sahagun & Benevente & Busaco
Thanks of Parliament:	Corunna
Date of Death:	13 August 1859 at Monty's Court, Somerset

His friends called him Jack. He was also known as Black Jack Slade.[3]

John Slade was born in 1762, the only son of John Slade of Maunsel House Bridgewater, Somersetshire, and Charlotte Portal. He was commissioned in the 10th Dragoons in 1780 and served with the regiment for eighteen years. Although initially stationed in Scotland, in 1781 it returned to England where it spent much of its time in the south. During his time with the regiment, John Slade was promoted through the ranks until he was its lieutenant colonel. In 1798, he had a dispute with Colonel William Cartwright, who was senior to him in the regiment and an ADC to the King. What the problem was is unknown, however, it was serious enough to reach the attention of the Duke of York and the King. To resolve the problem, the Prince of Wales, the 10th Light Dragoons's Regimental Colonel, arranged to have Lieutenant Colonel Slade exchange into the 1st Dragoons.[4] In 1800, Lieutenant Colonel Slade was appointed an Equerry to the Duke of Cumberland[5] and in 1802 was promoted to colonel. In June 1804 he was appointed a brigadier general on the staff of the South-West District. The following year he commanded a brigade of cavalry during field exercises at a camp of instruction in the vicinity of Radipole. In May 1806, he was transferred to Ireland, where he commanded the cavalry in Dublin.

In late 1808, the government decided to reinforce the army which was to operate in Spain. A force was organised in September 1808 to be commanded by General David

---

1. The 10th Dragoons were converted to Light Dragoons on 29 September 1783.
2. Removed from the regiment as a general officer receiving unattached pay 1814.
3. Bragge; page 53.
4. Mollo; page 27.
5. Ernest Duke of Cumberland, son of King George III. He became King Ernest Augustus I of Hanover.

Baird. At Cork, General Slade was selected to command an infantry brigade with the force on 12 September. However, on 22 September he was transferred to the command of a cavalry brigade. He joined his brigade in England where it was preparing for embarkation. While it was boarding the ships, the Prince of Wales removed his own sword, pelisse and jacket, and presented them to General Slade.[6] The brigade sailed on 31 October and arrived at Corunna on 10 November. He commanded the brigade on the advance into Spain and the retreat to Corunna.

General Slade was directly under General Henry Lord Paget who commanded the army's cavalry. The two men did not get along. On 7 December his brigade was delayed due to a mix-up on where they were supposed to go. Lord Paget

> rode along the flank of the column giving directions respecting the order of the march and precautions to be attended to, which he desired the General to repeat to the squadron officers of the Tenth [Hussars]; but no sooner had Slade left him than his lordship called one of his aides-de-camp whom he ordered to 'ride after that damned stupid fellow' and take care that he committed no blunder. This speech – which, to say the least of it, was very ill-timed – was made within hearing of a number of officers and soldiers, and was calculated to deprive the Brigadier even of the slight degree of respect previously entertained for him by the troops.[7]

General Slade's relationship with General Paget continued to deteriorate and the latter began to ride with his brigade. At Sahagun on 21 December, General Paget took command of the brigade's 15th Hussars and ordered them to charge a French chasseur brigade. Meanwhile, General Slade was with his other regiment, the 10th Hussars, and arrived too late to participate in the battle. General Paget continued to ride with his brigade and at Mayorga on 26 December, he ordered General Slade to charge two squadrons of French chasseurs with the 15th Hussars:

> The General moved off at a trot, but had not advanced far when he halted to have some alteration made in the length of his stirrups. An aide-de-camp was sent to inquire the cause of this delay, and the squadron again put in motion; but the General's stirrups were not yet adjusted to his mind, and he halted again before they had advanced a hundred yards. Lord Paget, whose patience was by this time quite exhausted, then ordered Colonel Leigh[8] to take the lead. The Tenth charged gallantly, routed the enemy, and took between forty and fifty prisoners.[9]

General Paget lost confidence in General Slade and at Benevente on 1 January 1809 he personally directed the placement of the 10th Hussars rather than going through General Slade. On 3 January Generals Paget and Charles Stewart were both incapacitated with ophthalmia and General Slade assumed command of the army's cavalry.[10] By 10 January they were within a day's march of Corunna and General Slade received permission from the army's commander to ride to Corunna because he was ill. He 'established himself in comfortable quarters, took a dose of cadomel, and retired to bed. When Lord Paget ... was informed of the General's arrival, he sent him a peremptory order to return to his

---

6. Liddell; page 81.
7. Gordon; page 66.
8. Colonel George Leigh, 10th Light Dragoons.
9. Gordon; page 134.
10. Mollo; page 73.

brigade without a moment's delay; and forced him to set out at night, in a soaking rain, regardless of his pathetic remonstrances and intestinal commotions!'[11]

General Slade oversaw the loading of his brigade onto troop transports on 15 January and volunteered his services to General John Moore the next day. He was present at the Battle of Corunna on 16 January 1809 and with General Baird when the general was wounded in the arm and had to turn over command to General John Hope. General Slade remained on the battlefield until the army was evacuated. General Hope wrote in his official dispatch that, 'I was indebted to Brigadier-General Slade during the action for a zealous offer of his personal services, although the cavalry was embarked.'[12]

After returning to England, General Slade was assigned to the South East District in Ireland on 25 February. He commanded there until August, when he was notified he was going back to the Peninsula. General Slade was placed on the staff of Wellington's army as a brigadier general on 29 September 1809.[13] On 7 October he was given command of a cavalry brigade, which he led for the next four years. They first saw action in July 1810 in the vicinity of Almeida and formed part of the rearguard during the long retreat towards Lisbon in the autumn. After the French began to withdraw back to Spain in January 1811, General Slade commanded the army's cavalry due to the absence of General Stapleton Cotton, who was on leave in England. His direction of the pursuit was half-hearted and he tended to micro-manage his regiments. General Slade continued to command the cavalry until 11 April, when General Cotton arrived. Wellington was not happy with General Slade and expressed his feelings to Marshal William Beresford in a letter dated 13 April 1811. The marshal was temporarily commanding General Rowland Hill's corps and Wellington was looking for an officer to command its cavalry. 'I have no General Officer to send there, excepting Slade, whose presence would not be of much use'.[14]

General Slade commanded his brigade at Sabugal on 3 April and Fuentes de Oñoro on 3–5 May 1811, where they were on the right flank of the army. They participated in numerous charges to help the Light Division when it was surrounded by a large force of French cavalry and had to retreat for several kilometers across open fields. During the battle General Slade had his horse shot out from under him and he had to ride a trooper's horse. In June the brigade was ordered south to operate with General Hill's corps in Estremadura. The following spring they were screening the British Army as it laid siege to Badajoz. When General Hill made his raid to destroy the bridge at Almaraz in mid-May, General Slade's brigade was left behind to screen their movement.

Unfortunately for his reputation, General Slade is best remembered for his mishandling of his brigade at Maguilla on 11 June 1812. There he had the opportunity to destroy a French dragoon brigade. His troops initially broke the French, but he quickly lost control of his regiments and they pursued them for many kilometers until their horses were spent. They were taken in the flank by French reinforcements and driven back with heavy loss.[15] This prompted Wellington to write a letter to General Hill on 18 June 1812:

I have never been more annoyed than by General Slade's affair, and I entirely concur with you in the necessity of inquiring into it. It is occasioned entirely by the trick

---

11. Gordon; page 194.
12. Liddell; page 178.
13. General Order, 29 September 1809. His appointment was backdated to 17 August 1809.
14. *WD* (enlarged ed.); Vol 4, page 745. General Slade's name was suppressed in the published *Dispatches*.
15. The brigade saw twenty-two men killed, twenty-six wounded, 118 taken prisoner, and 200 horses killed or captured.

our officers of cavalry have acquired of galloping at every thing and their galloping back as fast as they gallop on the enemy. They never consider their situation, never think of manoeuvring before an enemy – so little that one would think they cannot manoeuvre, excepting on Wimbledon Common ...[16]

General Slade and his brigade spent much of the summer in Estremadura. After the French Army evacuated the region in late July they marched north and by August were in the vicinity of Madrid. In early November, the army began its retreat to Portugal and by the end of the year were in winter quarters at Alcantara.

By the end of 1812, Wellington was tired of dealing with some of his cavalry brigadiers. He wanted them gone. He wrote to Colonel Henry Torrens of the Horse Guards on 2 December that, 'I should wish, if possible, to get rid of Sir Wm. Erskine, General Slade & General Long, particularly the first and the last.'[17] Colonel Torrens replied on 30 December, 'You will see by the Duke's official Letter that H. R. H. has decided upon recalling ... Slade'.[18] However, even with all the problems he had with General Slade, Wellington was reluctant to have him recalled if he could not be employed elsewhere. Wellington responded to Colonel Torrens on 22 January 1813: 'I have perused the copy of my letters to you of the 2nd and 6th Dec., and I observe that I did not recommend that the General officers mentioned should be otherwise provided for if removed. I therefore proposed to suspend till further orders the execution of His Royal Highness's orders in regard to all these General Officers ...'[19]

Colonel Torrens wrote back on 16 February that the Duke of York's original official recall letter contained an offer of eventual employment which, however, the Duke could not guarantee would occur. However, 'And as you state that you do not wish them removed unless to other employment, HRH can have no objection to your retaining them if you should not think the communication of His favourable intentions towards them as stated in the accompanying Official Letter, sufficient to meet the difficulty.'[20] Colonel Torrens then went on to caution Wellington that should circumstance 'prevent Sir Stapleton Cotton from returning, General Slade would be the senior Officer of Cavalry. This would never do, & therefore an order for his recall would be immediately sent out.'[21]

By late April 1813 General Slade had still not been recalled. Wellington sought General Cotton's advice on reorganising the cavalry and in a letter dated 7 April he told him, 'I have received discretionary orders to send to England Slade, Alten and Long ... I have not sent home any of these officers, because I am not quite certain what your wishes and opinions are, and because I doubt whether you would mend matters very materially by their removal.'[22] Wellington also asked him which of the three generals he wished to have recalled in order to make room for General Henry Fane who was coming out. General Slade was selected and Wellington used the excuse that he had been recalled because he was about to promote a general who was junior to him in order to give him a division.[23]

16. *WD* (enlarged ed.); Vol. 5, page 712. General Slade's name was suppressed in the published *Dispatches*.
17. *WSD*; Vol. 7, page 485. General Slade's name was suppressed in the published *Dispatches*.
18. Unpublished letter dated 30 December 1812.
19. *WD* (enlarged ed.); Vol. 6, pages 243–4.
20. Unpublished letter dated 16 February 1813.
21. Ibid.
22. *WD* (enlarged ed.); Vol. 6, page 406.
23. 'General Slade has been recalled in consequence of General Henry Clinton having been made a Lieutenant General in the peninsula.' *WD* (enlarged ed.); Vol. 6. page 442; to General Cotton 23 April 1813.

As the senior cavalry general in Wellington's army, General Slade was in temporary command of the 2nd Cavalry Division in March and April 1813. While he served in this position, he had no idea that Wellington was pushing for his recall. His friend, General Robert Long, wrote home on 14 March that something was amiss for 'Slade has naturally succeeded to the Command of this Division of the Cavalry, his appointment has not been confirmed in General Orders, which looks very suspicious!'[24] However, a week later word had gotten out and General Slade wrote to General Long that 'Erskine, Slade and Long are the General Officers said to be relieved by Stewart,[25] Fane and another whose name I cannot recollect …'[26] Surprisingly, camp gossip had it that General Slade's recall was the work of the Horse Guards and that Wellington 'disclaims any participation in the act that recalled Slade.'[27]

By the end of April 1813, General Slade had left his command. He was fairly closed mouth about being sent home, but confided in General Long 'that he has been scandalously treated by the Horse Guards.'[28] Despite his feelings about what happened, General Slade was happy to return home, having been gone for four years. His main disappointment was that his son, Cornet John Henry Slade, of the 1st Royal Dragoons, had arrived in the country the year before and he was planning to make him his ADC.[29]

General Slade spent a day at Wellington's HQ in Freneda, Portugal on 1 May and then went to Lisbon. After his return to England General Slade was placed on the Home Staff in the Centre District in Ireland. Upon his promotion to lieutenant general in June 1814, he was removed from the staff and given no further military duties. In 1831, he was appointed the regimental colonel of the 5th Dragoon Guards. The same year, King William IV was crowned and a large of number of individuals were created baronets, including John Slade, who became the 1st Baronet Slade of Maunsel House on 20 September.[30]

John Slade married Anne Dawson on 20 September 1792. They had nine children. She died on 24 December 1819. On 17 June 1822, he married his sister-in-law, Matilda Dawson. They had four children. Of his eleven sons, six went into the army and two went into the Royal Navy. General Slade ran for Parliament at least three times. In 1812 he was a candidate for Old Sarum, a rotten borough in Wiltshire. He was never elected or appointed an MP.[31] John Slade died on 13 August 1859 at his family home in Somerset at the age of 96. He was the second oldest soldier in Great Britain. At the time of his death he had served seventy-nine years as an officer, of which fifty-five of those years were as a general. He was buried at Norton Fitzwarren, Somerset.

As a brigade commander, General Slade was indecisive, often came across as nervous, and had an incompetent staff. One officer wrote after the Battle of Sabugal that General Slade

let no possible opportunity of inaction pass him – pretending not to comprehend orders, which the events passing before him would have made comprehensible to a trumpeter – Complaining that his hands were tied, and letting the opportunity slip – a curse to the cause, and a disgrace to the service. Had he acted with common spirit on the 3rd April at the Coa, we must inevitably have taken a Division of Regnier's

---

24. Long; page 257.
25. Charles Stewart was the Army's AG.
26. Long; page 261.
27. Ibid; page 268.
28. Ibid; page 268.
29. Ibid; page 266.
30. Generals William Anson and Kenneth Mackenzie were also created baronets that day.
31. Long; page 180.

Corps ... He heard the skirmishing begin, thicken, grow more distant, the Guns open, The Lines Volley, and the Cheers of Charging, – and not one foot did he stir, because he had no orders. Staff Officers were in all directions in full Gallop. Who has seen the six Squadrons of Cavalry? Was the question, nobody imagining he had not moved from his original ground.[32]

General Slade was heartily disliked by his junior officers and they resented his micromanaging. During the pursuit of the French as they retreated from Portugal in 1811, he

'ordered picquets of officers and thirty men where half would have done. I supposed he thought we had not enough to do. Every one talked loudly of his conduct through the day.'[33] The officers of the 1st Dragoons kept a Regimental Mess Journal that they recorded the daily events of their regiment. This Journal was for the junior officers only and was quite candid in their assessments of their superior officers. In early June 1811 they described General Slade's reaction when a French cavalry patrol surprised the brigade as it was about to leave its encampments: "Well, well! Bridges"[34] cried our Slade, "What news? Where are the French?" "Why, Sir, they are there." "There! In God's name, what do you mean?" "There, Sir." Calls out Bridges, pointing to some undulating ground a few hundred yards away.'[35]

As word spread through the army that General Slade had gone home, it was greeted with a sigh of relief among the cavalry officers. One troop commander wrote of the news, 'The change I consider a good one, and so do most others.'[36]

Despite his tendency for micro-managing, General Slade's operations often had problems due to his own or his staff's inattention to detail. Movements were delayed because orders were not sent on time, coordination was not made with higher HQ wrong routes were chosen for the brigade to travel on, and occasionally they got lost. This shoddy staff work was not just while they were on campaign but extended to the administration of his brigade. He was often in trouble with Wellington's HQ because of his inability to get required reports on the state of his brigade to them on time. It finally reached a point that he received a letter from the AG on 26 October 1810 in which 'I am to call your very serious attention, by direction of the Commander of the Forces, to the irregularity and incorrectness with which the returns of your brigade are made out'.[37] The letter included General Slade's Brigade Major, whom Wellington threatened to relieve of his duties if the returns were not sent in on time in the future. A year later, things had not improved and the AG had to rebuke him again.[38]

Although General Slade was unpopular due to what many officers considered his incompetence, there is no record of anyone questioning his courage. One officer wrote home that 'no one stands Shot and Shell with greater Phlegm than General Slade and I hear he was in conversation with Col. Hervey[39] when a spent Shot struck the latter's Sabretache, which together with the Shot and a Volume of 'Tristram Shandy' lodged in the Horse's side'.[40]

---

32. *Pakenham Letters*; page 88.
33. Tomkinson; pages 87–8.
34. Cornet Charles Bridges 1st Dragoons.
35. Clark-Kennedy; page 43.
36. Tomkinson; page 235.
37. *WD* (enlarged ed.); Vol. 4, page 359.
38. *WSD*; Vol. 13, page 720.
39. Felton Hervey 14th Light Dragoons.
40. Bragge; page 10.

Somerset, Lord Robert Edward Henry

Date of Birth:	19 December 1776
Date Commissioned:	Cornet 10th Light Dragoons: 4 February 1793 purchase
Promotions:	Lieutenant 10th Light Dragoons: 4 December 1793 purchase
	Captain 10th Light Dragoons: 28 August 1794 purchase
	Major 20th Light Dragoons: 21 November 1799[1] without purchase
	Major 12th Light Dragoons: 21 November 1799 appointed
	Major 28th Light Dragoons: 1800 by exchange[2]
	Lieutenant Colonel 5th Foot: 25 December 1800 purchase
	Lieutenant Colonel 4th Dragoons:[3] 3 September 1801 by exchange
	Brevet Colonel: 25 July 1810
	Major General: 4 June 1813
	Lieutenant General: 27 May 1825
	General: 23 November 1841
Regimental Colonel:	21st Light Dragoons: 15 January 1818–1820[4]
	17th Light Dragoons:[5] 9 September 1822–23 November 1829
	1st Dragoons: 23 November 1829–31 March 1836
	4th Light Dragoons: 31 March 1836–1 September 1842
Major Commands under Wellington:	Hussar Brigade: 2 July 1813–April 1814
	Cavalry brigade: 9 May–31 May 1815
	1st Cavalry Brigade:[6] 31 May–30 November 1815
	1st Cavalry Brigade AOOF: 30 November 1815–November 1818
Awards:	AGC with one clasp: Talavera, Salamanca, Vitoria, Orthes & Toulouse
	Waterloo Medal
	KCB 2 January 1815
	GCB 17 October 1834
	KMT 3rd Class
	KTS
	KSW
Thanks of Parliament:	Orthes & Waterloo
Member of Parliament:	Monmouth: 1799–1802, Gloucestershire: 1803–1831, Cirencester: 1834–1837
Date of Death:	1 September 1842

Although his full name is Robert Edward Henry Somerset, many sources refer to him as Edward Somerset.[7] He was the third son of Henry Somerset, 5th Duke of Beaufort, and Elizabeth Boscawen, daughter of Admiral Edward Boscawen. An older brother

---

1. According to the Army Lists the date for his promotion in the 20th Light Dragoons is the same as for his promotion in the 12th Light Dragoons. He was promoted major in the 20th Light Dragoons in *London Gazette*; War Office Announcement dated 26 November 1799.
2. *London Gazette*; War Office Announcement dated 22 November 1800.
3. Removed from the regiment as a general officer receiving unattached pay 1816.
4. Disbanded in 1820.
5. Became Lancers in 1823.
6. His cavalry brigade was numbered in a General Order dated 31 May 1815.
7. Some sources refer to him as Lord Somerset. This is incorrect. He was not a lord in his own right, however, because his father was a duke, and he was not the heir, he was given the courtesy title of Lord Edward Somerset. If he had been the heir he would then have been known as Lord Somerset.

was General Lord Charles Somerset and his four younger brothers were Captain Lord Arthur Somerset, Major Lord William Somerset, Colonel Lord John Somerset, and Field Marshal Fitzroy Somerset, 1st Baron Raglan.

In 1793, Lord Edward's family purchased him a commission in the 10th Light Dragoons, one of the fashionable regiments which many young men from upper-class families became officers in. His regimental commander was Lieutenant Colonel John Slade, while the regimental colonel was the Prince of Wales. This connection to the future King would put him in good standing in later years. Within eighteen months Lord Edward had purchased his lieutenancy and captaincy in the regiment. In 1798 he was the ADC to General James Rooke, the commanding officer of the Severn District. The following year he was appointed the ADC to the Duke of York and went with him to Holland during the Den Helder Campaign. He fought at Bergen on 19 September and at Egmont-on-Zee on 2 October. An armistice was declared in early November and Captain Somerset returned to England.

Shortly after he arrived in England, Captain Somerset was promoted simultaneously to major in both the 12th and the 20th Light Dragoons. He most likely never joined the 20th Light Dragoons except on paper. Instead he went to Lisbon where the 12th Light Dragoons were stationed. He was there for less than a year when he exchanged into the 28th Light Dragoons. It is unlikely that he ever served with that regiment either for on 25 December he purchased his lieutenant colonelcy in the 5th Foot. He stayed with his new regiment until September 1801 when he exchanged into the 4th Dragoons. Initially, the regiment was on garrison duty in northern England, but in 1802 it was sent to southern England. It remained in the south until April 1809 when it went to Portugal. He led his regiment at Talavera on 27–28 July 1809. In July 1810, he was promoted to colonel and made an ADC to the King. The regiment saw little action after Talavera and by October 1810 was in the Lines of Torres Vedras. Colonel Somerset went on home leave in January 1811 and did not return to the Peninsula until May. He joined the regiment too late to lead it at Albuera on 16 May, but was with them at Usagre on 25 May. In February 1812, they were assigned to General John Le Marchant's brigade and participated in the cavalry charge that broke the French centre at Salamanca on 22 July. During the charge one of Colonel Somerset's stirrups was hit by a shell splinter and he rode with only one stirrup.[8] After Salamanca the regiment performed screening operations while Wellington besieged Burgos.

By late 1812, Wellington was aware that Colonel Somerset was one of the senior colonels in the Peninsula. Furthermore, Wellington felt that Colonel Somerset was more capable of commanding a brigade than several general officers already serving in the Peninsula or who would be sent out from Britain. Wellington wrote to Colonel Henry Torrens at the Horse Guards on 2 December 1812 that he wished 'if possible, to get rid of Sir Wm. Erskine, General Slade & General Long, particularly the first and the last … I do not desire any General officers from England'.[9] His intention was to assign Colonel Somerset to command the cavalry brigade of whomever was recalled. On 7 April 1813 Wellington wrote to General Stapleton Cotton concerning the reorganisation of the cavalry. He informed General Cotton that he had received discretionary orders to send home Generals Alten, Long and Slade, and that General George Anson had requested

8. Luard; page 58.
9. *WSD*; Vol. 7, page 485. General Slade's name was suppressed in the published *Dispatches*.

to be assigned to the Home Staff. He noted that the next to senior colonel[10] was Lord Edward Somerset. He also pointed out that the only way he could give him a cavalry brigade was by sending home those three generals and by not giving one to General John Vandeleur, who had requested transfer from the infantry.[11]

Colonel Somerset was still in command of the 4th Dragoons in mid-May when the army began its move into Spain. He commanded the regiment in battle one last time at Vitoria on 21 June 1813. In early July word reached the army that he had been promoted to major general on 4 June. Wellington immediately placed him on the staff and gave him command of the Hussar Brigade on 2 July 1813.[12] General Somerset took command of his new brigade by 9 July and his assumption of command was initially met with some trepidation by his subordinates. However, he quickly won them over and one of his senior officers wrote that 'our new Brigadier, is a perfect gentleman, and it is wonderful how completely reconciled I am to the change.'[13]

General Somerset's command was plagued with problems. They had been in the Peninsula for less than six months and had already acquired a reputation for being undisciplined. Like most hussar regiments, they considered themselves elite because their officers were from the cream of society, above everyone. The brigade's performance at Vitoria on 21 June was so bad that Wellington threatened that 'if he heard any complaint against the Regiment he would immediately dismount us, and march the Regiment to the nearest sea port and embark us for England.'[14] This regiment (the 18th Hussars) was not sent home, but was removed from the brigade. When he received word that he was appointed to command the brigade, General Somerset was probably relieved with not having the 18th Hussars in his brigade. He wrote that the other two regiments (the 10th and 15th Hussars) were 'infinitely superior in every respect to the 18th.'[15]

General Somerset took to being a hussar general enthusiastically. By mid-August he wrote that he had grown a moustache and that he was acquiring 'all the other costume of an Hussar General, the dress of which is very handsome & splendid.'[16] His nephew, who was an extra-ADC to Wellington, commented that his uncle 'made a good Hussar ... and must be perfect now his mutton-chops are grown.'[17] The Hussar Brigade spent much of the summer and autumn blockading the French in Pamplona. They finally moved into France in early December, but went into winter quarters almost immediately after arriving. The brigade fought at Orthes on 27 February 1814, but were only lightly engaged until the end of the battle where they pursued the retreating French. He wrote that the 'country being enclosed, they had nothing to do but to dash down the lanes, & charge their infantry as it was retiring in confusion.'[18] The Hussar Brigade was also present at Toulouse on 10 April, but like Orthes they saw little action.

10. The senior colonel of cavalry in the army not commanding a brigade at the time was Granby Calcraft of the 3rd Dragoon Guards.
11. *WD* (enlarged ed.); Vol. 6, pages 406–7.
12. General Order, 2 July 1813.
13. Glover, Gareth (ed.); *From Corunna to Waterloo*, page 162.
14. Hunt; page 110.
15. Mollo; page 136.
16. Ibid; page 142.
17. Ibid; page 142.
18. Ibid; page 162.

After Napoleon abdicated in April 1814, Wellington's army was disbanded. The cavalry was ordered to march from southern France to Boulogne where it would be transported to England. General Somerset's brigade left Bordeaux on 2 June. They arrived in Boulogne and on 16 July returned to England. Except for four months in 1811, General Somerset had been in the Peninsula for five years. When Napoleon escaped from Elba in March 1815, the British Government decided to form an army in the Netherlands. General Torrens wrote to Wellington on 25 April 1815 that General Somerset was chosen by the Prince Regent to command the Household Brigade in place of General Henry Fane, who did not want to command just a brigade.[19] General Somerset was placed on the staff of Wellington's Anglo-Allied Army by a General Order dated 29 April 1815. The appointment was backdated to 24 April. The first elements of his brigade landed in Ostend on 3 May and General Somerset was confirmed in command of the Household Brigade on 9 May.

General Somerset commanded the brigade during the Waterloo Campaign. They arrived too late in the evening to fight at Quatre Bras on 16 June, but were part of the rearguard the next day. At Waterloo, they were stationed in the vicinity of La Haye Sainte and by the end of the battle had taken so many casualties it was combined with General William Ponsonby's brigade and 'our 19 squadrons were at that time reduced to one.'[20] During the battle, General Somerset's favourite mare 'was killed by a cannon shot, that went through her flank, and carried off part of the skirt of my great coat'.[21]

After Waterloo, General Somerset and his brigade were part of the advance into France and paraded through Paris on 7 July. When the army was reorganised as the AOOF on 30 November he was given command of its 1st Cavalry Brigade. He commanded it until the AOOF was disbanded in November 1818. While in France he was appointed the regimental colonel of the 21st Light Dragoons. General Somerset's tenure as its regimental colonel did not last long, for in 1820 the regiment was disband. In 1819, General Somerset was appointed the Inspecting General of the Cavalry and held the position until 1825, when he was promoted to lieutenant general. He was appointed the regimental colonel of the 17th Light Dragoons in 1822 and served as its colonel until 1829. In early 1825, he was one of the general officers whom Wellington put forward to Charles W. Wynn, the President of the HEIC, to command in India. Wellington thought he was the third best candidate.[22] He did not get the job.

From 1825 until 1829, General Somerset had no military duties other than that of the regimental colonel of the 17th Light Dragoons. In 1829, he became the regimental colonel of the 1st Dragoons. The same year, he was appointed the Lieutenant General of the Ordnance, which was the deputy to the Master General of the Ordnance Board. As the Deputy, General Somerset was the second-in-command of the artillery and engineers. He was appointed by Wellington and after the Tories lost power in 1834, he became the Surveyor General of the Ordnance on 30 December 1834. This was a temporary appointment and he was replaced by General Rufane Donkin on 25 April 1835. As the Surveyor General, his primary responsibility was the inspection of the supplies that the military received.[23] In 1836, he was appointed the regimental colonel of

19. Unpublished letter dated 25 April 1815.
20. Glover, Gareth (ed.); *Waterloo Archive*; Vol. VI, page 20.
21. Ibid; page 16.
22. *WND*; Vol. 2, page 425. Duke of Buckingham; Vol. 2, page 231.
23. *Journals of the House of Commons*; Vol. 40, page 126.

the 4th Light Dragoons and held the post until his death. He was promoted to general in November 1841 and the next year he expressed an interest in becoming the governor of either Gibraltar or Malta. He died before he was appointed to either post.

Lord Edward was a Tory MP for thirty-eight years. He was first elected to the family seat in Monmouth in 1799 and held it for three years but stepped down so his brother could hold the seat. Starting in 1803, he represented Gloucestershire until he was defeated in the election of 1832. Two years later he ran again and was elected as the MP for Cirencester. He did not run in 1837. The Somerset family was considered a friend of the Pitt government. Lord Edward was conservative and when present, usually voted with the government. Unlike many of his military peers who were also MPs, he was quite active in Parliament. He voted against Catholic Relief in 1817 and over the years he presented numerous anti-Catholic petitions. He did vote for the Catholic Relief Act in 1829 and consistently voted against slavery.[24]

On 17 October 1805, Lord Edward Somerset married Louisa Courtenay, the daughter of the 2nd Viscount Courtenay and sister of the wife of his brother, Lord Charles Somerset. They had eight children, of whom two went into the army. He died in 1842 in London and is buried in St Peter's Church, of St George's parish in Hanover Square, London.

Lord Edward Somerset was a competent and brave commander who was liked by his subordinates. Yet nothing in his service as a commander of cavalry regiment was so outstanding that would have caught the attention of Wellington. However, he had several things in his favour. Like Wellington, he was the son of a peer, and they both moved in the upper levels of society. Additionally there was a family connection between Wellington and the Somersets. At the time of his appointment as the commander of the Hussar Brigade, General Somerset's brother, Lieutenant Colonel Lord Fitzroy Somerset, was Wellington's Military Secretary, while his nephew, Lieutenant Henry Marquess of Worcester, was Wellington's ADC. General Somerset's royal connections also did not hurt his career. Although Wellington chose him to command the Hussar Brigade in 1813, it was the Prince Regent who picked him to lead the Household Brigade during the Waterloo Campaign.

---

24. 'Somerset'.

Sontag, John

Date of Birth:	27 October 1747 in Den Hague, the Netherlands
Date Commissioned:	Cornet 12th Light Dragoons: 8 September 1780
Promotions:	Lieutenant 12th Light Dragoons: 19 November 1781 without purchase
	Captain-Lieutenant 8th Light Dragoons: 16 September 1786 without purchase
	Captain Guides:[1] 2 July 1793
	Brevet Major: 1 March 1795
	Brevet Lieutenant Colonel: 5 October 1795
	Brevet Colonel: 25 September 1803
	Brigadier General on the Staff: 1808–1810
	Major General: 25 July 1810
	Lieutenant General: 4 June 1814
Major Commands under Wellington:	4th Brigade: 27 April–14 June 1809
	On staff of Cadiz: c. May–c. August 1810
	Commanded at Torres Vedras: 6 October 1810–31 March 1811
	Brigade 7th Division: 31 March–October 1811
	Temporarily commanded 7th Division: 1 August–October 1811
Date of Death:	4 May 1816, Earl's Court, Old Brompton, Kensington

His full name was John Salomon Balthasar Sontag.

Little is known about the early life of John Sontag other than he was born in Den Hague, the Netherlands in 1747. Who his parents were and why they were in the Netherlands is unknown. He was a Dutch merchant who was naturalised as a British citizen on 11 February 1780.[2] Seven months after he became a British citizen, John was commissioned as a cornet in the 12th Light Dragoons at the age of 32. He joined the regiment in Ireland and stayed with them until 1789, when he was sent to Brussels by the Foreign Office. His mission was to keep them informed of what was going on during the rebellion of the Austrian Netherlands, the future Belgium.[3] In 1792, he sold his commissioned and became a civilian. By the following year he was in the Netherlands. In July he was appointed a captain in the Guides of the British Army in the Netherlands and served as a DQMG on the Army Staff. He was with the army at the siege of Valenciennes in July, Lincelles on 17 August 1793, and the siege of Dunkirk in late August and early September. In March 1795, Captain Sontag was promoted to brevet major and appointed the Commandant of the British Military Hospitals in the Netherlands.[4]

Major Sontag went with the British Army when it was evacuated from Holland in the spring of 1795. On 5 October he was promoted to brevet lieutenant colonel and placed on the staff as a DQMG of the expedition that was being formed under General Ralph Abercromby to go to the West Indies.[5] He participated in the taking of the islands of

---

1. This unit was not in the *Army Lists*.
2. *Journal of the House of Lords*; Vol. 36, page 33.
3. Hutton; pages 137–9.
4. *The London Gazette*; War Office Announcement dated 7 April 1795.
5. Ibid; 6 October 1795.

St Lucia and St Vincent in the spring of 1796. After he came back to England in 1797 he became the Military Superintendent of Hospitals in South Britain.[6] He held the position until 3 June 1800. In 1799, Lieutenant Colonel Sontag was appointed an extra ADC to General Ralph Abercromby and was with him during the Den Helder Expedition in Holland. He was wounded at Alkmaar on 2 October 1799.[7] An armistice was reached in early November and the British Army returned to England.

While he was in Holland, on 15 October 1799, Lieutenant Colonel Sontag became the British Military Commissary[8] to Dutch troops in British service that were raised under the Hereditary Prince of Orange.[9] When the Dutch units in England were disbanded in 1802, Lieutenant Colonel Sontag was still kept on as the Military Commissary to the Dutch troops. He was promoted to colonel in 1803 and in May 1804 the Treasury appointed him the Paymaster to the Dutch Officers receiving allowances from the British Government. Two years later, in June 1806, he became the Inspector General of Reduced Foreign Officers. These were mostly Dutch officers formerly in British pay receiving allowances and were allowed to reside on the continent. He held this position until 1814. Surprisingly, in 1804, he moved to Hamburg and resided there until August 1807.[10]

When war broke out between Prussia and France in October 1806, Colonel Sontag joined Lord Hutchinson, the British Minister Extraordinary to the Prussian Court. On 9 December he arrived in Wehlau, East Prussia with dispatches from London and then went on to the Russian Army HQ at Ortelsburg.[11] He arrived there on 21 December and tried to join them as an observer, but its commander refused to allow him to stay with them without permission from the Russian Government. On 1 January 1807 he arrived at Königsberg, where the remnants of the Prussian Army had gather.[12] He attached himself to them as an observer and was at Eylau on 8 February 1807 when it and the Russian Army were defeated.[13] Colonel Sontag returned to London in August 1807.

In May 1808, Colonel Sontag was appointed a brigadier general on the staff of General John Moore's force that was going to Sweden in the summer. His duties were not specified in his appointment. When General Moore's force returned to England in July, General Sontag was given a political assignment in Portugal. Once again he had no specific duties, but served as an investigating / liaison officer for Viscount Castlereagh[14] and to report on affairs in Portugal. Because he was available, he was made the Commandant of Lisbon on 18 October 1808. As Commandant he looked after the sick who were left behind by General Moore's army and forwarded supplies to the army as it advanced into Spain. By 14 December he was on the staff of the garrison in Portugal. He was stationed in Lisbon and on 18 March 1809 he was commanding a brigade.

---

6. Ibid; 7 October 1797.
7. This battle is also known as the Second Battle of Bergen.
8. Some sources state his title was Inspector of the Dutch Troops.
9. *The London Gazette*; War Office Announcement dated 15 October 1799.
10. *Seventh Report*; pages 19–23.
11. Ortelsburg is now known as Szczytno, Poland.
12. The Prussian Army was virtually destroyed by Napoleon's Army at the twin battles of Jena and Auerstadt on 14 October and the subsequent pursuit. Only a small corps under General Lestocq escaped into eastern Prussia.
13. Wilson; page v. Jackson; pages 66–71.
14. Robert Stewart Viscount Castlereagh was Secretary of State for War.

In April 1809, when Wellington returned to Lisbon and took command of the forces, General Sontag was commanding the 4th Brigade. General Sontag was not originally placed upon the staff of Wellington's army in April, but was finally confirmed on the staff and officially given command of the brigade on 6 May.[15] He commanded the brigade for five weeks. By 14 June General Sontag had left Portugal and returned to England. He was probably recalled by the Horse Guards to serve in the Walcheren Expedition because he was born in Holland and had extensive service with Dutch troops. General Sontag was appointed a brigadier general on the staff of the Walcheren Expedition in June 1809. After Middleburg was captured in August 1809, he became the commandant of the city and served in that capacity until the British Army was evacuated to England in the late autumn.

General Sontag remained in England for only a few months. By late April he was back in the Peninsula and by May was commanding the 3rd Brigade of the British garrison in Cadiz. General Sontag was not confirmed on the staff at Cadiz until 29 June.[16] He was promoted to major general in late July and when word of his promotion reached Cadiz he was not retained on the staff.[17]

General Sontag went to Lisbon and Wellington wrote to him on 6 October 1810 that he wanted him to go 'to Torres Vedras … to take command of the troops destined for the defence of the redoubts constructed at and in the neighbourhood of Torres Vedras'.[18] After the French had retreated from the Lines of Torres Vedras, General Sontag wrote to Wellington asking for an active command, however, he was not in good health. Wellington replied on 8 March that he had appointed him to 'the most important point in our position; and I have detained you there contrary to your inclination, because I conceived the public service still required your stay.'[19] Wellington also wrote that 'the enemy have retired, and the war is now likely to assume a new shape, it is but justice to you to remove you to a situation of more activity, according to your desire.'[20] Wellington placed a caveat on his promise, that he would only do it when General Sontag had recovered his health.[21]

Wellington kept his word and gave General Sontag command of a brigade in the 7th Division by the end of the month.[22] He led his brigade at Fuentes de Oñoro on 3–5 May 1811, where it was on the right flank of the army. One of its battalions occupied Pozo Bello but was forced out of the village and the brigade had to retreat under the threat of being charged by French cavalry. After the battle General Sontag and his brigade were sent south to assist in the siege of Badajoz and elements of it was involved in the failed assault on San Cristobal on 6 June. The siege was abandoned on 10 June and the brigade spent the summer in the Caya River Valley. Like the Guadiana River, the Caya River was disease ridden. On 1 August, General Sontag was given temporary command of the 7th Division when its commander, General William Houston, was invalided home.

15. General Order, 6 May 1809.
16. General Order, 29 June 1810. His appointment was backdated to 16 March 1810.
17. General Order, 12 September 1810, but his removal from the staff was backdated to 11 August 1810.
18. *WSD* (enlarged ed.); Vol. 4, pages 318–19.
19. *WD* (enlarged ed.); Vol. 4, page 657.
20. Ibid.
21. Ibid.
22. General Order, 31 March 1811.

The 7th Division suffered heavily from Guadiana Fever and fortunately for them, they received orders in mid-September to head north to a safer climate. By the beginning of October, General Sontag's health began to fail and he went home to recover. Wellington wrote to Lieutenant Colonel Henry Torrens of the Horse Guards on 16 October 1811 that 'General Sontag is so ill as to be obliged to go away, and I imagine will never again be fit for service.'[23] On 28 April 1812, Colonel Torrens wrote to Wellington that 'Old Sontag has reported Himself quite recovered and looks upon his rejoining the Army as a matter of course! He must be a burthen to you, and I shall prevent him from going if I can.'[24]

General Sontag had no further military duties upon reaching England, but was promoted to lieutenant general in 1814. He died in 1816 at Earl's Court, Old Brompton, Kensington. Little is known about his personal life except that he was married at least twice. He married Susanna Hatfield of Doncaster in 1777, but she died three years later. They had no children. He was also married to Joanna Sontag who died in 1817. He was likely a native speaker of Dutch. One source mistook his Dutch accent for something else, for he claimed that John Sontag spoke English with a heavy German accent.[25] During the Den Helder Campaign the soldiers gave him the nickname of 'General Ney' because he had a long nose.[26]

General Sontag's military career was unlike any of Wellington's other brigade commanders. He had limited troop time and most of his staff experience was not at the tactical level. Three times during his career he worked for the Foreign Minister, while he spent ten years working for the Treasury. Although he was a brigade commander three different times, his first two brigades were more a garrison command than a field command. It was not until 1811 did he command a brigade in the field. At Fuentes de Oñoro his brigade had problems, including the commander of the 51st Foot panicking and ordering the battalion colours be burned when he thought they might be captured. General Sontag was not censured for his performance during the battle nor was he kept from assuming command of the 7th Division four months later. However, unlike his contemporaries, he did not receive an AGM for leading his brigade at the battle nor was he ever invested in the Order of the Bath.

---

23. *WSD* (enlarged ed.); Vol. 5, page 324.
24. Unpublished letter from Colonel Torrens to Wellington, dated 28 April 1812.
25. Hutton; page 139.
26. Smith, George; page 11.

Stewart, Richard

Date of Birth:	1756
Date Commissioned:	Ensign 51st Foot: 6 December 1775 purchase
Promotions:	Lieutenant 51st Foot: 23 December 1778 without purchase[1]
	Captain-Lieutenant 51st Foot: 29 October 1793 purchase
	Captain 51st Foot: c. 12 November 1794[2] without purchase[3]
	Brevet Major: 12 September 1794
	Major 72nd Foot: 11 October 1798 without purchase
	Major 32nd Foot: c. 11 September 1800 by exchange[4]
	Brevet Lieutenant Colonel: 30 November 1796
	Lieutenant Colonel 43rd Foot: 5 November 1800 without purchase
	Brevet Colonel: 25 September 1803
	Brigadier General on the Staff: 1807–1810
	Major General: 25 July 1810
Major Commands **under Wellington:**	6th Brigade: 27 April–18 June 1809
	Brigade 2nd Division: 18 June 1809 –19 October 1810
Awards:	AGM: Talavera
Thanks of Parliament:	Talavera
Date of Death:	19 October 1810, Lisbon

Although the correct spelling of his family name is Stewart, it was also shown in the early *Army Lists*, *London Gazette*, and even the General Orders published by Wellington's HQ as Richard Stuart.

Little is known about Richard Stewart's early life. He was born in 1756 in Kingarth, Bute, Scotland. His family were neighbours of John Stuart, 3rd Earl of Bute. Richard would serve under the Earl's son, General Charles Stuart, several times. He was commissioned an ensign in the 51st Foot in 1775 and then promoted to lieutenant three years later. He then waited fifteen years for his promotion to captain-lieutenant.

The 51st Foot was stationed on the island of Minorca when Richard Stewart was commissioned in 1775 and was still there when he was promoted to lieutenant in 1778. Besieged there in July 1781, the regiment surrendered to French and Spanish Forces in February 1782 and went back to Britain in May. The regiment was stationed in northern England and Scotland until 1784 when it was sent to Ireland. Whether he was with the regiment during this period is unknown. He probably joined the regiment in Ireland and served there for several years. On 31 August 1790 he was appointed the regiment's adjutant, a position that was usually given to a very experienced junior officer. He was the adjutant until he was promoted to captain on 12 November 1794.

---

1. It is unclear from the announcement in the *London Gazette* whether he purchased the promotion.
2. The exact date of his promotion is unknown. The promotion created vacancies below him. The 12 November date was the date the officers below him were promoted. This was probably the date Captain Stewart was promoted, since the officers were usually promoted on the same date.
3. *London Gazette*; War Office Announcement dated 9 January 1795.
4. Ibid; 4 November 1800. The exact date of his appointment was not listed. The date given is for the officer who exchanged with Major Stewart. His date was not listed.

In March 1792, the 51st Foot was sent to Gibraltar and in late 1793 went to Toulon to reinforce the British garrison there. Prior to their arrival in Toulon, they learned that the French had taken the city, so the regiment joined the expedition to capture Corsica. They landed in January 1794 and remained on the island until November 1796, when they were evacuated and sent to Elba. While he was on Corsica, Captain Stewart was promoted to brevet major in September 1794. In November 1796 he was appointed DAG with the rank of lieutenant colonel in the army with the forces in Portugal under General Charles Stuart.[5] This promotion was a brevet promotion. He was the DAG for two years when he was appointed the AG to the forces in Portugal in July 1798.[6] In October 1798 he was promoted to major in the 72nd Foot. He never joined the regiment because at the time of his promotion he was still serving as the AG to the force under General Charles Stuart that captured Minorca in December 1798. He continued to serve under General Stuart in Minorca and while there he exchanged into the 32nd Foot in September 1800. Three months later he was promoted to lieutenant colonel in the 43rd Foot.

Lieutenant Colonel Stewart most likely did not join his new regiment in England until after General Stuart died in March 1801. In 1803, he was sent to Portugal to prepare a report on its plans and resources.[7] On 25 September 1803 he was promoted to colonel and also made an ADC to the King. In June 1804, Colonel Stewart was court-martialed when the commander of the Light Company of the 1st Battalion 43rd Foot pressed charges against him for conduct unbecoming of an officer by making a false report to General Hew Dalrymple and the disrespectful and degrading treatment of the Light Company Commander which undermined his ability to discipline his company. Colonel Stewart was found not guilty of both charges.[8]

Colonel Stewart's 1st Battalion 43rd Foot served during the Copenhagen Campaign of 1807 from August to October. While his battalion was in Wellington's Reserve Brigade, he was assigned as Wellington's second-in-command with the rank of brigadier general. This was an unusual arrangement, but Wellington described it as follows:

When the Horse Guards are obliged to employ one of those fellows like me in whom they have no confidence, they give him what is called a second in command – one in whom they have confidence – a kind of dry nurse. When I went to Zealand they gave me General Stewart as second in command, that is in reality intended for first in command, though I was the first in name. Well, during the embarkation, the voyage out, and the disembarkation, General Stewart did everything. I saw no kind of objection to anything he suggested, and went *à merville*.[9] At last, however, we came up to the enemy. Stewart, as usual, was beginning his suggestions and arrangements, but I stopped him short with 'Come, come. 'tis my turn now.' I immediately made my own dispositions, assigned him the command of one of the wings, gave him his orders, attacked the enemy, and beat them. Stewart, like a man of sense, saw in a moment that I understood my business, and subsided with (as far as I saw) good humour into his proper place.[10]

---

5. Ibid; 3 December 1796.
6. Ibid; 14 July 1798.
7. When Wellington went to Portugal in 1808 he took this report with him.
8. Jekyll; page 41.
9. *à merville* is French for wonderfully.
10. Coker; Vol. 1, page 343.

General Stewart served as Wellington's second-in-command at the Battle of Kioge on 29 August. When Wellington went home on 18 September, General Stewart commanded the brigade until the expedition returned to England in October. Since his rank during the Copenhagen Expedition was only temporary while serving, his rank reverted back to colonel upon that force disbanding. Colonel Stewart was not happy about this and approached Wellington about the matter. In January 1808, Wellington wrote to him that he had brought the matter up with the Duke of York several times, but was not able to get his rank restored.[11]

In the spring of 1808, Colonel Stewart was appointed the AG to General John Moore's force that was being formed for service in Sweden. This appointment also made him a brigadier general on the staff. After being refused permission to land by the Swedish Government, the force returned to Britain in July. Before it could be disbanded, it was ordered to reinforce the British Army in Portugal and sailed there on 31 July. It arrived in Portugal on 24 August and landed the next day. It was too late to participate in the Battles of Roliça on 17 August and Vimeiro on 21 August. On 5 September, General Hew Dalrymple reorganised the army and General Stewart was assigned to command a brigade in the 1st Division. When it was decided to split the army to form a force to campaign in Spain and a garrison for Portugal, General Stewart was selected to serve in the garrison. For a time in November he commanded the garrison in Portugal as the senior officers had either been recalled or had not yet arrived.

In late December 1808, General Stewart commanded a force sent to reinforce General Moore in Spain. It advanced to Castello Branco and on 8 January 1809, failing to get through to the British Army in northern Spain, retired to Abrantes. By the end of the month it had pulled back to Santarem. When Wellington arrived in Portugal in April to take command of the army, General Stewart was kept on the staff and given command of the 6th Brigade.[12] On 18 June, Wellington reorganised his army into divisions and General Stewart and his brigade were placed in General Rowland Hill's 2nd Division.

General Stewart led his brigade during the Oporto Campaign in May 1809 and then into Spain two months later. At Talavera on 27 July the brigade was in the centre of the British line on the south side of the large hill that anchored the left of the line, called the Cerro de Medellin. That evening it was about to be overrun by the French when General Hill ordered the brigade to attack up the hill to keep the French from turning the flank of the British line. After a vicious fight, the brigade held the hill. The next morning they moved off the hill and took a position between it and the French line. After repulsing the first French attack of the day, they charged across the Portina Creek, chasing the retreating French. General Stewart was able to keep them in hand and stop them before they became disordered and vulnerable to a French counter-attack. By the end of battle the brigade had taken 30 per cent casualties.

After the battle Wellington's army began a slow retreat back to the Portuguese border. By mid-December 1809, General Stewart's brigade was back in Portugal and went into winter quarters. The campaigning over the past six months had taken a toll on the brigade. Two of its three battalions were hovering at 50 per cent strength. At the beginning of 1810, General Stewart was afflicted with an eye infection that affected his ability to command his brigade. The brigade spent the first eight months of 1810

---

11. Unpublished letter from Wellington to Colonel Richard Stewart dated 8 January 1808.
12. General Order, 27 April 1809.

guarding the Portuguese border and rebuilding its strength. On 13 August 1810 General Stewart became so ill he was unable to command his brigade. Word soon reached the army that he had been promoted to major general in late July. Despite his inability to command his brigade due to his poor health, Wellington kept him on the staff of the army instead of sending him home.[13]

General Stewart's illness caused him to miss the Battle of Busaco on 27 September. Wellington finally realised that he needed to find a replacement for him and on 8 October he was temporarily replaced in command of his brigade by General Daniel Hoghton.[14] General Stewart went to Lisbon to recover but his health continued to decline. On 19 October he fell off a balcony and was killed. For some reason the bannister had been removed from the balcony and it is believed that General Stewart wandered out on to the balcony in his delirium.

It is unknown if General Stewart ever married. Some of his correspondence survives and from the tone of the letters he was good friends with Charles Stuart, 1st Baron Stuart de Rothesay, who was the British Ambassador to Portugal, and his brother Captain John James Stuart, RN. The two brothers were the sons of General Charles Stuart, whose staff General Stewart was on ten years before. This friendship may have been based on being neighbours in Scotland

Nothing in the early career of Richard Stewart indicated that he was a future general. However, Stewart had some powerful friends who looked after his career. Initially it may have been General Charles Stuart who selected him to be his DAG and the AG for his command in the late 1790s. This patronage should have ended upon the death of General Stuart in 1801, yet it did not. Whoever his patron was, he continued looking after his protégé, for in 1803 Richard Stewart was one of only four officers who were selected to be an ADC to the King. In 1807, in a move that was unusual for the time, he was made the second-in-command of a brigade and promoted to brigadier general.

Despite not being allowed to keep his rank as a brigadier general after the Copenhagen Campaign in 1807, this was not a reflection of Richard Stewart losing his patron. The Duke of York was a stickler for seniority and doing things in a proper manner. He had turned down Wellington, who had written on behalf of Stewart. The Duke even refused his brother, the Prince of Wales's request to promote an officer outside of his turn. He was also never awarded the rank of brevet colonel for merit. The fact that Richard Stewart was made a brigadier on the staff under General Moore, retained it in Portugal, and then under Wellington would suggest the Duke of York was mindful of Wellington's request perhaps in addition to that of his patron.

General Stewart's early death ended a career where his seniority might have placed him in a position to receive command of a division in Wellington's army. Had he served further he no doubt would have earned a KCB, AGC, Foreign Orders, a Waterloo Medal, and an obituary in the *Gentleman's Magazine*.

---

13. General Order, 8 September 1810.
14. General Order, 8 October 1810.

Stopford, Hon. Edward

Date of Birth:	28 September 1766
Date Commissioned:	Ensign 3rd Foot Guards: 20 October 1784 purchase
Promotions:	Lieutenant & Captain 3rd Foot Guards: 25 April 1792 purchase
	Captain-Lieutenant & Lieutenant Colonel 3rd Foot Guards: 28 May 1798 without purchase
	Captain & Lieutenant Colonel[1] 3rd Foot Guards: 25 October 1798 without purchase
	Brevet Colonel: 25 April 1808
	Brigadier General on the Staff: 23 January 1811
	Major General: 4 June 1811
	Lieutenant General: 19 July 1821
Regimental Colonel:	Royal African Corps: 21 September 1818–14 June 1819
	41st Foot: 14 June 1819–14 September 1837
Major Commands under Wellington:	Temporarily commanded Guards Brigade 1st Division: 28 July 1809–18 June 1811
	Temporarily commanded 1st Division: June 1811
	Brigade 4th Division: 18 June–28 July 1811
	Brigade 1st Division: 28 July 1811–7 May 1812
	Guards Brigade 1st Division: 15 March 1813–April 1814
Awards:	Equerry to Queen Charlotte 1795–1818
	AGM with two clasps: Talavera, Vitoria & Nive
	KCB: 2 January 1815
	GCB: 28 March 1835
	KTS
Member of Parliament:	Marlborough: 1810–1818
Date of Death:	14 September 1837, Leamington Spa, Warwickshire

Edward Stopford was born in 1766, the son of James Stopford, 2nd Earl of Courtown, and Mary Powys. He was the younger brother of Lieutenant Colonel James Stopford, 3rd Earl of Courtown, and the older brother of Admiral Sir Robert Stopford. His uncle was Lieutenant General Edward Stopford. He entered Eton in 1779 and left in 1783. The year after he left Eton, Edward's family purchased him his commission in the 3rd Foot Guards. He would be with the regiment in one capacity or another for the next twenty-eight years. He was on garrison duty for the first nine years of his service with the regiment. In 1792, he purchased his lieutenant and captaincy in the regiment and in May 1793 he went to Flanders with the 1st Battalion. He was in Flanders until late November 1794, when the British Army retreated to Bremen. They were evacuated back to England in April 1795.

In May 1798, Captain Stopford was promoted to captain-lieutenant and lieutenant colonel. Only one officer in the regiment held this rank and his duty was to serve as the senior lieutenant in the company whose captaincy was maintained by the regimental colonel. When the regimental colonel was not available to command the company, he

---

1. Removed from the regiment as a general officer receiving unattached pay on 25 July 1814.

would command it. The 3rd Foot Guards Regimental Colonel was John Campbell, 5th Duke of Argyll, who was 75 years old in 1798. It is unlikely that the Duke ever took command during the time Edward Stopford was its captain-lieutenant. In October 1798, Captain-Lieutenant Stopford was promoted to captain and lieutenant colonel. It would be his last promotion within the regiment. By 1805, Lieutenant Colonel Stopford was one of the senior captain and lieutenant colonels in the regiment and commanded a company in the 1st Battalion. They were in General Edward Finch's Guards Brigade in the expedition that was sent to Hanover in November 1805, but due to Napoleon's defeat of the Austrians and Russians at Austerlitz, it returned to England in February 1806.

In the summer of 1807, an expedition was formed to capture the Danish fleet. Although Lieutenant Colonel Stopford was not the senior lieutenant colonel in the regiment, he was the only one who was available to command the 1st Battalion when it was selected to join the expedition. They were part of General Finch's Guards Brigade at Copenhagen from August to October, when they returned home. Lieutenant Colonel Stopford relinquished command to Colonel William Dilkes upon his arrival in England.

In April 1808, Lieutenant Colonel Stopford was promoted to colonel and by the end of the year was in command of the 1st Battalion. It was part of the Guards Brigade that was assigned to General John Sherbrooke's force to secure Cadiz. They sailed on 15 January 1809 and reached Cadiz on 8 March. The Spanish Government refused to allow them to land. The force then sailed to Lisbon, arriving on 13 March, and joined the garrison of Portugal. Lieutenant Colonel Stopford led his battalion during the Oporto Campaign in May and the Talavera Campaign in the summer. On 28 July, the second day of the Battle of Talavera, the Guards Brigade was in the centre of the British line. After stopping the initial French assault on their line, the Guards charged across the Portina Creek in pursuit of the fleeing French. Colonel Stopford lost control of his battalion and they continued chasing the French until they were counter-charged by the French reserves and fled as a disorganised mob back towards the British lines. Colonel Stopford was finally able to rally his troops, but only after they lost 30 per cent of their men, including five officers killed and six wounded.

Among the serious wounded was the Guards Brigade Commander, General Henry Campbell. As the senior colonel in the brigade, Colonel Stopford was appointed a colonel on the staff of the army and given command of the Guards Brigade on 1 August 1809.[2] Once his brigade was back in Portugal, Colonel Stopford took the time to visit Cadiz later in the month and returned to his brigade in late September. He commanded the Guards Brigade for the next two years, including at Busaco on 27 September 1810 and Fuentes de Oñoro on 1–3 May 1811. After the Battle of Fuentes de Oñoro, Colonel Stopford was appointed a brigadier general on the staff.[3] General Stopford commanded the 1st Division for a short time in June. The division commander, General Brent Spencer, had taken temporary command of the army when Wellington went south to confer with Marshal William Beresford after the Battle of Albuera.

On 5 June General Stopford and his brigade began marching south to reinforce the British Army in the vicinity of Badajoz. By mid-June General Campbell returned to command the Guards Brigade. Since General Stopford was too senior to return to battalion command, Wellington transferred him to the 4th Division and gave him

---

2. General Order, 1 August 1809.
3. General Order, 9 May 1811. The promotion was backdated to 23 January 1811.

command of the Fusilier Brigade.[4] About this time, word reached Army HQ that General Stopford had been promoted to major general and Wellington decided to retain him on the staff.[5] General Stopford was not with the Fusilier Brigade long when he was ordered north on 28 July to take command of a British line brigade in the 1st Division.[6] He commanded the brigade until April 1812, when he returned to England.

General Stopford's health may have been poor as he was on leave of absence a number of times between 1809 and 1813. While he was gone in 1812, General William Wheatley took command of General Stopford's brigade.[7] By September he still had not returned and Colonel James Stirling was in command of the brigade.[8] This brigade was transferred to the 6th Division in November and General Stopford never resumed command of it. Wellington inquired about his status in a letter to the Duke of York on 7 September 1812. In it he discussed the generals selected to command the 1st Division and the two Guards Brigades.[9] He noted that General Stopford was absent in England. Wellington intended to give General Stopford command of one of the Guards Brigades when he returned, however, he needed to know if the Duke of York approved of it or whether he had made arrangements for someone else to command it.[10]

By mid-January 1813, General Stopford was back in Lisbon.[11] However, he was in no hurry to give up the luxuries of Lisbon and join the army in its winter quarters. An officer in the 1st Foot Guards wrote on 23 January that, 'I breakfasted this morning with General Stopford, he has as yet settled nothing about going, except that he means to send his baggage off three days before he starts as that cannot go in less than ten days & he means to go in seven, my baggage will of course go with his; he says he will carry a few things for me in his saddle bags; but he is to let me know as soon as anything is settled.'[12]

Two months later, General Stopford was appointed the commander of the Guards Brigade that he had temporarily commanded from 1809 to 1811.[13] He arrived at the brigade's winter quarters about a week later.[14] He led them at the Battle of Vitoria on 21 June, the siege of San Sebastian from July to September, the crossing of the Bidassoa River on 6 October, Nivelle on 13 November, and Nive on 10 December. Despite being at numerous battles from June to December, General Stopford's brigade was only lightly engaged in them. On 23 February 1814, General Stopford's brigade crossed the Adour River in boats to secure a foothold on the river's right bank, so that a bridge could be built across it. The brigade would spend the rest of the war investing Bayonne. On 14 April, the French garrison sortied from the city and caught the British by surprise. The brigade

---

4. General Order, 18 June 1811.
5. General Order, 26 June 1811.
6. General Order, 28 July 1811.
7. General Order, 7 May 1812.
8. General Order, 11 September 1812.
9. The plan was to create another brigade of Guards with the 1st Battalion and 3rd Battalions of the 1st Foot Guards. The 1st Battalion was still in England at the time, while the 3rd Battalion was in Cadiz. The new brigade was not formed until November.
10. *WD* (enlarged ed.); Vol. 6, page 56.
11. Lionel Challis states that he was back in Lisbon in November.
12. Bridgeman; page 71.
13. General Order, 15 March 1813.
14. Blackman; page 53.

took heavy casualties before the French withdrew. Among the wounded was General Stopford. How serious the wound was is unknown.

Peace was declared in April 1814 and the British Army began to withdraw in June. It was not until late July that General Stopford's brigade was disbanded and returned home. He chose not to accompany them back to England, and instead spent several months touring France. General Stopford was not offered a command in the Waterloo Campaign and had no further military duties until 1818, when he was appointed the regimental colonel of the Royal African Corps. He held the position until June 1819 when he became the colonel of the 41st Foot. He was promoted to lieutenant general in 1821.

Edward Stopford was elected to Parliament in 1810, however, there is no record of him having attended a session prior to 1815. He was a Tory who rarely voted, but when he did it was always with the government. He was not known to have ever given a speech and when his seat in Marlborough was dissolved in 1818, he did not run again. General Stopford never received the Thanks of Parliament for his service in the Peninsula. The Speaker of Parliament refused to thank him 'because he stayed abroad for several months for his own private amusement after the war was over'[15] and neglected his duties as an MP.

Little is known about General Stopford's personal life. He was a Freemason.[16] He never married. While he was in Lisbon, he became infatuated with an unnamed married woman. He wrote from France in December 1813 to Sir Charles Stuart, the British Ambassador to Lisbon 'you may suppose I am a little anxious to know how my little friend is, & where she is, & I have nobody at Lisbon to whom I can write about her – Will you therefore excuse my troubling you & requesting you to let me know whether you have seen her lately, & whether the Spouse?'[17] Three months later he was still writing to Sir Charles Stuart asking him to forward a letter to her.[18] General Stopford eventually gave up on the woman and found a mistress. She was Anaïs Pauline Nathalie Aubert, a French actress who was born in 1802. Their son, Edward Stopford Claremont, was born in 1818, and like his father became a general in the British Army. General Stopford died on 14 September 1837 at Leamington Spa, Warwickshire and was interred in the parish church of Leamington on 19 September.

During the Peninsular War, General Stopford participated in eleven battles, sieges and actions. An AGM was awarded for seven of them, yet he only received an AGM for three.[19] This was not a reflection of his performance during the battle, but a requirement that the recipient had to be a commander or a staff officer who came under musket fire sometime during the battle. Although his brigade took casualties in the other four battles,[20] he did not come under fire, and thus was not eligible to receive the medal.

15. 'Stopford, Hon. Edward.'
16. Blackman; page 80.
17. Unpublished letter to Sir Charles Stuart, dated 18 December 1813.
18. Unpublished letter to Sir Charles Stuart, dated 7 March 1814.
19. The battles of Talavera, Vitoria and Nive.
20. The battles of Busaco, Fuentes de Oñoro and Nivelle; and the siege of San Sebastian.

Vandeleur, John Ormsby

Date of Birth:	1763
Date Commissioned:	Ensign 5th Foot: 20 December 1781 purchase
Promotions:	Lieutenant 67th Foot: 21 July 1783 purchase?
	Lieutenant 9th Foot: 6 July 1788 by exchange
	Captain 9th Foot: 7 March 1792 purchase
	Captain-Lieutenant 8th Light Dragoons: 30 November 1792 by exchange
	Captain 8th Light Dragoons: 21 December 1793 without purchase
	Major 8th Light Dragoons: 1 March 1794 purchase
	Brevet Lieutenant Colonel: 1 January 1798
	Lieutenant Colonel 8th Light Dragoons: 1 November 1803 without purchase
	Lieutenant Colonel[1] 19th Light Dragoons: 16 April 1807 by exchange
	Brevet Colonel: 25 April 1808
	Major General: 4 June 1811
	Lieutenant General: 19 July 1821
	General: 28 June 1838
Regimental Colonel:	19th Light Dragoons: 12 January 1815–10 November 1821[2]
	14th Light Dragoons: 28 October 1823–18 June 1830
	16th Lancers: 18 June1830–1 November 1849
Major Commands under Wellington:	Brigade Light Division: 30 September 1811–2 July 1813
	Temporarily commanded Light Division: c. 15 April–c. 2 May 1812
	Cavalry Brigade: 2 July 1813–April 1814
	2nd Cavalry Brigade: 11 April–31 May 1815
	4th Cavalry Brigade: 31 May–30 November 1815[3]
	Temporarily commanded the Cavalry: 18 June–c. 14 July 1815
Awards:	AGC: Ciudad Rodrigo, Salamanca, Vitoria & Nive
	Waterloo Medal
	KCB: 2 January 1815
	GCB: 29 July 1833
	Kt: 8 August 1833
	KSW
	KCMJ
Thanks of Parliament:	Ciudad Rodrigo, Salamanca, Vitoria & Waterloo
Date of Death:	1 November 1849, Merrion Square, Dublin

The Vandeleurs were a large Irish family from Kilrush, County Clare, many of whom were cavalry officers in the British Army. In the mid-1700s there were four John Ormsby Vandeleurs all related to each other. General John Ormsby Vandeleur, who served under Wellington in the Peninsula and at Waterloo, is sometimes confused with his cousin, Colonel John Ormsby Vandeleur of the 5th Dragoon Guards.

---

1. Removed from the regiment as a general officer receiving unattached pay 1814.
2. The regiment became lancers in 1817 and was disbanded on 10 November 1821.
3. The cavalry brigades were reorganised and renumbered by a General Order, dated 31 May 1815.

John Vandeleur was born in 1763, the son of Captain Richard Vandeleur and Elinor Firman. He was commissioned in 1781 as an ensign in the 5th Foot in 1781 which was stationed in Ireland. Two years later he became a lieutenant in the 67th Foot, another regiment also in Ireland. It is unknown whether he purchased his lieutenancy. In 1785, the 67th Foot was sent to the West Indies, however, Lieutenant Vandeleur chose to go on half-pay rather than accompany the regiment. He stayed on half-pay until July 1788 when he exchanged into the 9th Foot, which had left Ireland the previous January and was part of the garrison at Saint Kitts in the West Indies. Lieutenant Vandeleur served with his regiment in the West Indies and in 1792 purchased his captaincy in it.

Captain Vandeleur stayed with the 9th Foot for another eight months until he exchanged into the 8th Light Dragoons, which were stationed in Ireland. The 8th Light Dragoons was an Irish Regiment and its commander was Captain Vandeleur's cousin, Lieutenant Colonel Thomas Pakenham Vandeleur. Captain Vandeleur's rank in his new regiment was captain-lieutenant, which meant he commanded the regimental colonel's troop when he was absent. A year later he had his own troop and in March 1794 purchased his majority. The regiment was sent to Flanders in May 1794, but for some reason Major Vandeleur did not go with them. He eventually joined the regiment and fought with it in several engagements until October 1795, when it returned to England. The regiment stayed in England for the next ten months rebuilding its strength.

In August 1796, Major Vandeleur and the 8th Light Dragoons sailed for the Cape of Good Hope. While in the Cape Colony he was promoted to brevet lieutenant colonel. He and the 8th Light Dragoons stayed in the colony until February 1803, when it was returned to the Dutch. The 8th Light Dragoons were sent to the Bengal Presidency in India, rather than back to Ireland. The next three years were spent on campaign in the Second Anglo-Maratha War. In November 1803, he assumed command of the regiment when his cousin, Major General Thomas Pakenham Vandeleur, was killed. Through much of the war he held local rank of colonel and commanded a cavalry brigade. He distinguished himself at Laswari on 1 November 1803 and Futty Ghur[4] on 17 November 1804. In 1806, Colonel Vandeleur decided to return home. He could not leave his regiment without permission, so he arranged to exchange into the 19th Light Dragoons which had been recalled to England. This exchange was not formalised until the regiment arrived in England in 1807.

Upon leaving India, Colonel Vandeleur reverted back to lieutenant colonel, since his promotion to colonel was only valid while in India. He was promoted to colonel in 1808 and continued to command the 19th Light Dragoons in England until 1810, when he was appointed on the staff as an AAG in Limerick, Ireland. In June 1811 he was promoted to major general and placed on the staff of Wellington's army.[5] It is unknown when he arrived in the Peninsula. However, because there were no cavalry commands available when he did show up, he was given command of a brigade in the Light Division.[6] He led his brigade on the assault on Ciudad Rodrigo on 19 January 1812 and after the Light Division commander was mortally wounded, he temporarily took command of the division. He was to the right of the 2nd Battalion 52nd Foot as it stormed the lesser breach of the walls when the defenders fired a volley into the flank of the battalion.

---

4. Also called Farrukhabad.
5. General Order, 29 June 1811.
6. General Order, 30 September 1811.

Among those wounded was General Vandeleur.[7] He was shot in the shoulder, but the musket ball went under the collarbone.[8] He went to Portalegre to recover. Although no bones were broken he was plagued by rheumatism in the shoulder for the rest of his life.[9]

General Vandeleur spent several months recovering from his wound and missed the siege of Badajoz in April 1812. By early summer he was back with his brigade and led them into Spain. They were at Salamanca on 22 July but were not heavily engaged. The brigade spent much of the summer in the vicinity of Madrid but was in the rearguard during the retreat back to the Portuguese border in the autumn. General Vandeleur commanded the brigade when the army moved into Spain in May 1813 and at Vitoria on 21 June 1813. After the battle they marched to Pamplona and was part of the force that invested the city.

Despite commanding one of the elite brigades in the army, General Vandeleur was not happy. He was a cavalry officer and in late 1812, he asked Wellington for command of a cavalry brigade. Wellington had no objection to him receiving a cavalry brigade, provided there was a vacancy. This was a problem, for there were none available. Wellington wrote to Colonel Henry Torrens at the Horse Guards on 2 December 1812 that he wished the recall of certain cavalry brigade commanders and that he 'would recommend that General Vandeleur should have one brigade of cavalry, of which he is very desirous'.[10] Nothing happened for several months and on 7 April 1813 Wellington wrote to General Stapleton Cotton, the commander of his cavalry, asking for his views on transferring General Vandeleur to the cavalry. 'You will recollect that Gen. Vandeleur has long had a claim to a command in the cavalry; and if he is to have one, you must fix upon ... who is to go ... shall General Vandeleur be removed to the cavalry?'[11] Three weeks later, on 23 April, Wellington wrote again to General Cotton because General John Slade had been recalled to England and a position was available. 'It now rests with you whether you will make another vacancy, and if you should, whether you will appoint to it General Vandeleur ...'.[12]

By this time General Vandeleur had become impatient about the apparent lack of response to the request he had made four months before. Wellington replied on 26 April, 'I assure you I should be very happy to appoint you to command a brigade of cavalry if I could; but, notwithstanding that General Slade is ordered home, there is no brigade vacant.'[13] Wellington explained that he had orders to send four cavalry regiments home and although two cavalry brigades were being sent out there were also two general officers of cavalry coming out:

> Unless I remove General Long[14] from his command, or some other General Officer of the cavalry, I do not see how I can give you the command of a brigade of cavalry ... I have written 2 letters to Sir S. Cotton on the subject ... and I sincerely wish that he may be able to suggest an arrangement which may give you a situation in

---

7. Dobbs; page 33.
8. Pakenham; page 143.
9. Smith, Harry; pages 63 and 111.
10. *WSD*; Vol. 7, page 485.
11. *WD* (enlarged ed.); Vol. 6, page 407.
12. Ibid; page 442.
13. Ibid; page 450. General Slade's name was suppressed in the volume.
14. Robert Ballard Long.

the cavalry, which I acknowledge I cannot, without sending home some officer or other.[15]

Wellington concluded the letter by stating that the matter was out of his hands and advised him 'to settle this matter in England. I have nothing to do with the choice of General Officers sent out here or with their numbers, or the army with which they are to serve; and when they do come I must employ them as I am ordered.'[16]

General Vandeleur was not happy with Wellington's response and immediately wrote back to him with ideas on how to reorganise the cavalry so that he could have a command. These suggestions were so radical that Wellington wrote back to him on 28 April 1813 that he was

> convinced that you are not in earnest in wishing me to adopt the plan you have proposed to open the door for your removal to the cavalry. If General Long were [*sic*] not already in the cavalry, I might have it in my power, with justice, to make the selection between you and him; but as it is I have it not.[17]

Wellington then explained again that he had orders to send home four cavalry regiments and while receiving five more in exchange he also had two general officers coming with them. He ended by telling General Vandeleur, again, that he had 'written to Sir S. Cotton on the cavalry arrangements, and I assure you that I shall be very happy to do what you wish.'[18] Unfortunately what General Vandeleur proposed is unknown. It was likely that he asked to be given General Long's brigade. Even though Wellington had asked for General Long's recall, he was not prepared to arbitrarily remove him, if for no other reason than because he wanted to involve General Cotton in the decision.

On 2 July 1813, Wellington wrote to General Vandeleur that he had appointed him to command General George Anson's Light Dragoon brigade.[19] He wasted no time turning over his light infantry brigade to his replacement and rode to San Sebastian, where his new brigade was part of the force besieging the city. His cousin, Lieutenant John Vandeleur who was in the 12th Light Dragoons, wrote that 'I was told to my great astonishment that Genl. Vandeleur was appointed to the brigade, and that Anson was going home, all which was realised on the 6th by his riding in with a servant and a pair of saddle-bags, without bag or baggage, all which has since come up.'[20]

The brigade stayed as part of the covering force until San Sebastian fell on 8 September. General Vandeleur and his brigade were at the crossing of the Bidassoa on 7 October. The brigade was heavily engaged at Nive on 10 and 11 December. During the battle he and his staff were trying to rally the infantry skirmishers, who had fallen back in disorder, when they came under fire. His orderly was shot through the neck, his two ADC's horses were killed, while his horse was wounded. After the battle, the brigade went into winter quarters. In late February they were part of the force that crossed the Adour River on the

---

15. *WD* (enlarged ed.); Vol. 6, page 450. General Long's name was suppressed in the volume.
16. Ibid; pages 450–1.
17. Ibid; page 453. General Long's name was suppressed in the volume.
18. Ibid; page 453.
19. Ibid; page 571. This appointment was announced in the General Orders on the same day.
20. Vandeleur; page 95.

bridge of boats in an effort to surround Bayonne. They remained attached to the corps that invested the city until Napoleon abdicated in April 1814.

In June 1814, General Vandeleur was given command of several cavalry brigades and ordered to march them 1,000 kilometers to Calais, where they were embarked on ships and returned to Great Britain. He was not in England long when he was placed on the staff of the Subsidiary Army in the Netherlands. At first he was given command of a brigade and then command of the 2nd Infantry Division in October 1814. When Napoleon escaped from Elba in March 1815 and Wellington was given command of the Anglo-Allied Army in the Netherlands, General Vandeleur was confirmed on the army's staff on 28 March 1815. General Torrens wrote to Wellington on 31 March 1815 explaining the appointment of certain generals to his army. In regards to General Vandeleur, he informed Wellington that the Duke of York was obliged by actual necessity and a sense of justice to appoint him to command a light cavalry brigade: 'This officer was originally appointed to the command of a brigade in Brabant, by the request of Sir H. Clinton; and the Duke thought it fair, as he was on the spot, that he should have the first brigade of cavalry sent over.'[21] General Vandeleur was assigned to command the 2nd Cavalry Brigade on 11 April.[22] On 31 May the brigade was re-numbered the 4th Cavalry Brigade.

At Waterloo on 18 June, General Vandeleur and his brigade were located about 300 metres north of La Haye Sainte and to the left of General Thomas Picton's 5th Division. The brigade was in reserve until General Vandeleur ordered it to charge in an effort to cover General William Ponsonby's Union Brigade which had ridden down a French infantry corps, but in the process was so disordered it was in danger of being destroyed by French cavalry. General Vandeleur left one regiment in reserve and charged at the head of his brigade. It was his initiative in ordering the charge which saved the remnants of General Ponsonby's brigade. The rest of the day they sat in reserve, but were part of the force that initially pursued the retreating French that night. They captured an artillery battery before they were recalled. During the battle, General Vandeleur was grazed on the wrist by a musket ball, but it did not break the skin or leave a bruise.[23] His baggage was sent to the rear before the battle began and he lost 'a cart with his wine and all his maps, which was very valuable.'[24]

As the senior cavalry commander who was not seriously wounded or killed at Waterloo, General Vandeleur led Wellington's cavalry into France after the battle. He stayed in command until 14 July, when General Lord Combermere[25] arrived. When Wellington's army was reorganised into the AOOF on 30 November, General Vandeleur was not kept on the staff and he returned to Great Britain. He had no further military duties other than as the regimental colonel of the 19th Light Dragoons. The following year he was still unemployed and requested an appointment on the staff of the AOOF. General Torrens wrote to Wellington on 29 November 1816 that it would be difficult to place him on the staff of the AOOF as he was senior to George Murray, who held superior local rank of lieutenant general in France.[26]

---

21. *WSD*; Vol. 10, page 9.
22. General Order, 11 April 1815.
23. Vandeleur; page 151.
24. Ibid; page 168.
25. General Lord Combermere was General Stapleton Cotton raised in the peerage.
26. *WSD*; Vol. 14, page 656.

By November 1819, General Vandeleur had major financial problems. Although his yearly income as a regimental colonel was £599 he had moved to the Continent to reduce his expenses. He had been talking of moving his family to Bordeaux as early as April 1814, because 'the society is good, and the country is beautiful, and cheap'.[27] His cousin, Lieutenant John Vandeleur, who served as his ADC in the Peninsula and the Waterloo Campaign, wrote that 'the poor general has met with a disappointment in some money speculations. He does not even keep a saddle-horse, and is living the most economical manner possible. He was always dabbling in French funds and I fear he has burnt his fingers.'[28] His financial problems worsened in November 1821, when his regiment, the 19th Light Dragoons, was disbanded and he lost his annual salary as a regimental colonel. However, because he had been promoted to lieutenant general the previous July he was placed on half-pay of a lieutenant general, which was £596 per year, a loss of £3 per year. General Vandeleur found it difficult to live on his salary. He wrote several letters to Wellington asking him for assistance in receiving another regimental colonelcy. Wellington forwarded one of the letters to the Duke of York, however, he was concerned with the tone that General Vandeleur used in them and warned him that 'it is quite impossible for me to be the channel of conveying to the Commander-in-Chief the kind of reproaches which your letters contain.'[29]

Wellington wrote to General Sir Herbert Taylor, the Military Secretary to the Duke of York,[30] about General Vandeleur. It was not a very enthusiastic endorsement:

General Vandeleur was a very old officer of cavalry, as his Royal Highness knows. He commanded a brigade of cavalry during part of the war in Spain, and in the battle of Waterloo. The command of the whole cavalry devolved upon him on the march to Paris; and he was afterwards put off the Staff because he had a regiment, which he has since lost.[31]

In January 1823, General Vandeleur was living in Karlsruhe, Germany and again wrote to Wellington for help. He stated that he had little money and that his family had to give up most of their comforts because he could not afford them. He was concerned because he was barely able to provide housing, clothing and education for his children. Furthermore, because he was getting old and had young children, he was worried that he would not be able to leave them anything when he died.[32] In October 1823 he was appointed the regimental colonel of the 14th Light Dragoons. This raised his salary back to £596, however, by 1827, the government had reduced the annual salary of a cavalry regimental colonel to £456.

By January 1825, General Vandeleur had moved to Mannheim, Germany and wrote to Wellington once again requesting assistance in having him appointed the Commander of Forces in Ireland. He pointed out that at Waterloo, not only was he the senior major general in Wellington's army, but was not offered employment in the AOOF, and was

---

27. Vandeleur; page 138.
28. Ibid; page 168.
29. *WND*; Vol. 1, page 342.
30. General Taylor replaced Major General Henry Torrens in 1820.
31. *WND*; Vol. 1, page 342.
32. Unpublished letter from John Vandeleur to Wellington dated 13 January 1823. In the Wellington Papers Database, Southampton University. (#Docref=WP1/754/22).

one of the few generals who did not receive a peacetime position. General Vandeleur hoped that Wellington would recommend him as Lord Combermere's replacement as the Commander of Forces in Ireland.[33] Wellington wrote back that he could not recommend him for the position since he had no right to interfere in the appointment of officers in Ireland.[34]

On 27 July 1825, General Vandeleur wrote from Neuchatel, Switzerland to Wellington again asking for his help in obtaining further employment. This time he accused Wellington of forgetting the service of those officers who served under him in the Peninsula and at Waterloo. He continued to complain about how badly he had been treated since the Waterloo Campaign, by not being offered a position in the AOOF and then having to wait for two years to receive another regimental colonelcy after the 19th Light Dragoons were disbanded.[35] Wellington replied on 14 August that he could not understand General Vandeleur's accusation and stated that he spends most of his time assisting officers by making recommendations for them. He did not deny that he refused to recommend him for the position in Ireland. He justified his decision by telling General Vandeleur that he could not recommend everyone for a position they wanted and had to take into consideration whether the officer had the chance of getting the job.[36]

After receiving this last letter General Vandeleur seemed to have accepted that he would not receive any further assistance from Wellington. In 1830, General Vandeleur requested that he be appointed the regimental colonel of the 16th Lancers. This was an unusual request, for it was rare for a regimental colonel to request a colonelcy in a regiment that was junior to the regiment he currently commanded. It is unknown why he requested the move. It might be because the regiment had served under him in the Peninsula and at Waterloo, and he felt loyal to it. Whether Wellington was involved with him receiving the appointment is not known, however, General Vandeleur wrote to Wellington, thanking him. By 1835, the government had again changed the pay for regimental colonels. His annual salary was raised to £900, however, with the emoluments for clothing his annual pay was £1,501. He also received a wound pension of £350.[37] He was promoted to general in June 1838, but this would not affect his pay.

John Vandeleur married Catharine Glasse at Bath on 27 February 1809. They had two children. He died in Dublin, Ireland in 1849 and was buried in the Mount Jerome cemetery in Dublin.

General Vandeleur was a competent brigade commander who, although he was a cavalry officer, was just as comfortable commanding infantry. He was the consummate professional who was a stickler for detail and looked after the development of his officers. In 1801 he wrote *Duty of Officers Commanding Detachments in the Field*, a book to train junior light cavalry officers on their duties while on campaign. His brigade orders during the 1815 Campaign were the equivalent to a modern army's standard operation

---

33. Unpublished letter from John Vandeleur to Wellington dated 1 January 1825. In the Wellington Papers Database, Southampton University. (#Docref=WP1/810/3).
34. Unpublished letter from Wellington to John Vandeleur dated 16 January 1825. In the Wellington Papers Database, Southampton University. (#Docref=WP1/811/12).
35. Unpublished letter from John Vandeleur to Wellington dated 27 July 1825. In the Wellington Papers Database, Southampton University. (#Docref=WP1/823/12).
36. Unpublished letter from Wellington to John Vandeleur dated 14 August 1825. In the Wellington Papers Database, Southampton University. (#Docref=WP1/826/6).
37. *Black Book*; page 581.

procedures.[38] When he arrived in the Peninsula, he brought a large stable of horses with him and he was quite generous with them. He often loaned a horse to his brigade major when he needed one. Several officers reported he kept a good table and that he liked to drink. He did not speak Spanish.[39]

His cousin, Lieutenant John Vandeleur, who served as his ADC in the Peninsula and at Waterloo, left a vivid description of him in the field:

> He always gets up at 4 or 5 o'clock; rides 4 leagues, and comes home to breakfast, which is two eggs, tea and dry toast. He always writes letters, etc., in the heat of the day, dines at 3 o'clock, drinks very little wine, eats some soup and plain beef or mutton, never meddles with made dishes, stews, etc. he keeps a very neat and gentlemanlike table, always sits down eight. He mounts his horse after dinner, rides till half-past 7 or 8, returns, takes his coffee, smokes a cigar, and goes to bed at 9 ... Now that we are again on outpost duty, the Genl. has quite a new and regular method of living. He gets up every morning at 4 o'clock, mounts his horse, and rides up to the picquets, which he generally reaches a little before daylight; he visits all the chain of outposts, and gets home about 8 o'clock. We breakfast then, and after breakfast he mounts again and takes a ride to get an appetite for his dinner. He generally canters about 5 or 6 leagues. He dines at 7; he generally has two friends, or officers of the brigade, to dine with him, so that he sits down about 6 people every day. He smokes his pipe after dinner, takes his coffee, and goes to bed about ½ past 8 or 9 o'clock.[40]

General Vandeleur was not well thought of by Wellington. It was unlikely anything to do with his competence, but stemmed from General Vandeleur's insistence that he deserved better than what he had. Although he was a cavalry officer, in order to give him command Wellington gave him a brigade in the army's most famous unit – the Light Division. But this was not enough for General Vandeleur. Within a year of taking command he was writing to Wellington asking for command of a cavalry brigade. At that time there were none available, but he continued to bother Wellington with his requests until a brigade finally opened up in July 1813. Wellington did not forget how he was pestered by General Vandeleur and was not inclined to do him any other favours. In August 1813, he asked permission from Wellington for him to appoint his cousin, Lieutenant John Vandeleur, as his extra ADC:

> Wellington refused and said 'he could not comply with a request so irregular', altho' only a few days before he granted the same request to M. Genl. Ponsonby, a junior officer who commanded a brigade that never was or is intended to be on outpost duty, and another thing, the very officer who the Genl. succeeded (Anson) was allowed an extra ...[41]

Despite his excellent service at Waterloo, Wellington refused to help General Vandeleur in personal matters. He wrote to Wellington on 26 September 1815 complaining that

---

38. Vandeleur; pages 102, 191–3.
39. Smith, Harry; pages 80, 93 and 127.
40. Vandeleur; pages 106 and 120.
41. Ibid; page 108.

General James Kempt, who was junior to him, received the GCB on 22 June 1815, yet he did not. General Vandeleur pressed his claim to receive the Grand Cross as being both the commander of the cavalry after General Lord Uxbridge was wounded at Waterloo and the senior KCB with the army. He was quite upset with this perceived slight and wrote that it:

> cannot fail to be as injurious to my reputation as it is mortifying to my feelings ... The wound which it has inflicted can never be healed, but it may still be palliated by the kind interposition of your Grace; otherwise the having been present at the most important of your many glorious achievements, instead of being to me a circumstance of pride and exultation, will become a source of shame and regret never to be obliterated. To obviate this calamity I appeal to your Grace's well known kindness, and once more implore your generous protection.[42]

Wellington wrote a short reply to General Vandeleur on 28 September 1815 sympathising with him, but made no commitment to help him other than to forward his complaint. He stated that he was

> much concerned that the recent appointment ... have made any unpleasant impression on your feelings ... I have never had any say to the nominations ... I am inclined to believe that the arrangement was made without adverting to seniority, and from respect to the fifth division, which had been so severely engaged during the two days. I am certain that I have never found in any quarter any wish but to do what was most agreeable to you.[43]

General Vandeleur would not be made a GCB until 1833.

By this time Wellington had had enough of General Vandeleur's whining. Two months later, his name was conspicuously absent from the list of officers who were given commands in the AOOF and General Vandeleur went home. However, he continued to write to Wellington over the next ten years requesting assistance on a variety of matters. The more he wrote, the less Wellington did for him, until General Vandeleur stopped writing.

Although General Vandeleur's relationship with Wellington was strained at times, he was well thought of by his subordinates. Major George Napier, who was with him during the assault on Ciudad Rodrigo, described him as 'a fine, honourable, kind-hearted, gallant soldier, and an excellent man. I never knew him say or do a harsh thing to any human being. No man can or ought to be more respected than he is.'[44] His Brigade Major, Captain Harry Smith, called him 'a fine, gentleman-like old Irish hero'.[45]

---

42. *WSD*; Vol. 11, pages 173–4.
43. *WD* (enlarged ed.); Vol. 8, pages 273–4. The names were suppressed in this edition.
44. Napier, George; page 183.
45. Smith, Harry; page 51.

Vivian, Richard Hussey

Date of Birth:	28 July 1775
Date Commissioned:	Ensign 20th Foot: 31 July 1793 without purchase
Promotions:	Lieutenant Independent Company: 20 October 1793 purchase
	Lieutenant 54th Foot: 30 October 1793 by exchange
	Captain 28th Foot: 7 May 1794 purchase
	Captain 7th Light Dragoons: 8 August 1798 by exchange
	Major 7th Light Dragoons: 9 March 1803 purchase
	Lieutenant Colonel 25th Light Dragoons: 28 September 1804 purchase
	Lieutenant Colonel 7th Light Dragoons: 1 December 1804[1] by exchange
	Brevet Colonel: 20 February 1812
	Major General: 4 June 1814
	Lieutenant General: 22 July 1830
Regimental Colonel:	12th Lancers: 22 January 1827–20 January 1837
	1st Dragoons: 20 January 1837–20 August 1842
Major Commands under Wellington:	Temporarily commanded cavalry brigades: 24 November 1813–April 1814
	1st Cavalry Brigade: 28 April–31 May 1815
	6th Cavalry Brigade: 31 May–30 November 1815[2]
	2nd Cavalry Brigade AOOF: 30 November 1815–November 1818
Awards:	Equerry to the Prince Regent: 10 March 1812
	AGM with clasp: Benevente[3] & Orthes
	Waterloo Medal
	Equerry to Prince Regent: 10 March 1812
	KCB: 2 January 1815
	GCB: 30 May 1837
	KCH: 1816
	KMT
	KSW
	GCH: 1831
	Groom of the Bedchamber to King William IV: 24 July 1830
Thanks of Parliament:	Waterloo
Member of Parliament:	Truro: 1820–1826, New Windsor: 1826–1831, Truro: 1832–1834, Cornwall East: 1837–1841
Date of Death:	20 August 1842, Baden-Baden, Germany

Was also known as Hussey Vivian and Sir Hussey. The name Hussey came from his maternal great-uncle.

Richard Vivian was born on 28 July 1775 in Truro, Cornwall. His parents were John Vivian of Truro and Betsey Crunch. His younger brother was Major John Vivian. His

---

1. Removed from the regiment as a general officer receiving unattached pay 1814.
2. The British cavalry brigades were reorganised and renumbered on 31 May 1815.
3. His entry in the 1820 edition of the *Royal Military Calendar* (Vol. 3, page 390), states that he received the Army Gold Medal for Sahagun, Benevente, and Orthes. We could find no record of his receiving the Sahagun & Benevente AGM which was awarded to those who served at both battles. Commanding officers who served at either of the battle received only the AGM for the one they were at. His regiment was not at Sahagun nor does he mention being there in his *Memoir*.

family was very wealthy, having made their fortune in the Cornish copper industry. Richard was well educated for his time, studying at Harrow and entering Exeter College at Oxford in 1790. He left Oxford after two terms and went to Montreuil, France to complete his education. Upon his return to England he studied law for a while, but found he would rather be a soldier.[4]

In July 1793, Richard Vivian was commissioned as an ensign in the 20th Foot which was stationed in Jamaica. He did not go to the West Indies and instead purchased a lieutenancy in an independent company in October. Ten days later he exchanged into the 54th Foot. Lieutenant Vivian's timing did not appear to be fortuitous, for within a week the regiment was ordered to the West Indies. He was aboard the transport when word was received cancelling the orders. In May 1794, Lieutenant Vivian convinced his father to purchase him a captaincy in the 28th Foot. The following month the regiment was ordered to Flanders and Captain Vivian was in Ostend by 26 June. He was at the siege of Nijmegen in November and at the combat of Geldermalsen on 4 January 1795. In June, Captain Vivian and his regiment returned to England.

Captain Vivian spent most of the year in southern England and rumors abound that the regiment was going to the West Indies. He had no desire to go there and tried to convince his father to help him exchange into either another infantry regiment or a dragoon regiment, but he would need £1,200 if he was to become a cavalry officer.[5] His regiment sailed to the West Indies in the late summer of 1795 but after spending almost fourteen weeks on board the ship, they were forced to return to England due to bad weather. Their orders for the West Indies were cancelled in early February and in August they sailed for Gibraltar. He served as part of its garrison until July 1798 when he exchanged into the 7th Light Dragoons. He went with his regiment to Holland in August 1799. He fought at the Battle of Bergen on 19 September. By the end of November the government decided the expedition had failed to achieve its objectives and was withdrawn. Captain Vivian was back in England in December.

While Captain Vivian was in the 7th Hussars, he became close friends with its commander, Colonel Henry Lord Paget, the future Earl of Uxbridge and 1st Marquess of Anglesey. He would serve under Lord Paget many times in the next thirty years. Captain Vivian purchased his majority in the 7th Hussars in 1803 and eighteen months later purchased his lieutenant colonelcy in the 25th Light Dragoons. Within three months of joining that regiment, he exchanged back in to the 7th Light Dragoons. On 4 April 1805, he was the senior lieutenant colonel in the regiment and thus its commander. He would command it for the next seven years. The year after he assumed command, the 7th Light Dragoons were redesignated as the 7th Hussars.

In late summer of 1808, the government decided to reinforce the British Army which was to operate in Spain. A force was organised in September 1808 that would be commanded by General David Baird. On 23 September, Lieutenant Colonel Vivian received orders to prepare his regiment for service in it. By 2 October the regiment was aboard transports and they initially sailed for Spain on 6 October. However, contrary winds kept them from leaving British waters for eighteen days. Lieutenant Colonel Vivian brought with him five horses for his own use. The regiment arrived at Corunna on

---

4. Vivian, Claud; pages 1–3.

5. The actual cost of the exchange would have been £3,000, however, Captain Vivian would have been able to get £1,800 for his captaincy in the 28th Foot.

8 November.[6] He led the 7th Hussars on the advance in to Spain and during the retreat to Corunna he was part of the rearguard that was commanded by his friend, General Lord Paget. He fought at Benevente on 1 January 1809, but did not see action at the Battle of Corunna on 16 January 1809 because they were already aboard transports. He and the regiment were evacuated from Spain and returned home with the army.

By the time the 7th Hussars arrived in England it was a cavalry regiment in name only. It had embarked for Spain with 746 horses but by mid-January it was had less than 300 horses left. There was a shortage of transports and the Army Commander, General John Moore, ordered the regiments to only embark their officers's horses and thirty troop horses. All other horses were to be killed to prevent them from falling into French hands. The regiment's poor luck did not end in Corunna. On the way back to England one of the transports was shipwrecked off Cornwall and three officers, fifty-six men, and thirty-two horses drowned.[7]

Lieutenant Colonel Vivian spent the next four years rebuilding his regiment. On 30 May 1809, he served as a second to General Lord Paget, who was challenged to a duel by Captain George Cadogan of the Royal Navy.[8] In May 1810, the regiment was sent to Ireland. While there, Lieutenant Colonel Vivian was appointed an ADC to the Prince Regent in March 1811, promoted to colonel in February 1812, and the following month appointed an Equerry to the Prince Regent. By 1813, the regiment was back up to strength and in London. They replaced the Household Cavalry which was sent to Portugal and served as escorts to the King.

In the summer of 1813, the 7th Hussars received orders to join the Hussar Brigade in Wellington's army in Spain. They sailed on 15 August and arrived at Bilbao two weeks later. The regiment was at the crossing of the Bidassoa River on 7 October but then was sent back to be part of the covering force blockading the French in Pamplona. On 24 November Colonel Vivian was appointed a colonel on the staff and given temporary command of Colonel Colquhoun Grant's Cavalry Brigade.[9] He led the brigade at Nive on 11 December but they saw little action. On 28 December, Colonel Vivian was transferred to the command of General Victor Alten's brigade, who was on leave.[10] This too was supposed to be a temporary command until General Alten returned. The next two months the brigade was in winter quarters and on 27 February 1814 was at the Battle of Orthes. There they were under intense artillery fire for much of the battle, but took few casualties. On 8 April, Colonel Vivian's brigade was part of the forward element of the army when it came under fire by dismounted French cavalry near Croix d'Orade. General Vivian was shot in the right arm. The wound was so serious that he was unable to command for the rest of war and would receive a £350 pension because of it.

After Napoleon abdicated in April 1814 and peace was declared, Wellington's army began to disband. General Vivian was promoted to major general on 4 June and returned to England the same month. He was placed on the Home Staff and commanded the Sussex District. When Napoleon returned to France in March 1815, the British began to expand its forces in the Netherlands and Wellington was given command. He was

6. Vivian, Claud; pages 64–6.
7. Mollo; pages 80–1.
8. Captain Cadogan, the future Earl of Cadogan, challenged Lord Paget to the duel because he had an affair with his sister, who was Wellington's sister-in-law.
9. General Order, 24 November 1813.
10. General Order, 28 December 1813.

informed in a letter dated 28 March that General Vivian had been appointed to his army. General Henry Torrens of the Horse Guards wrote to him on 31 March explaining how this appointment and others were made. 'The Duke of York ... was obliged to make appointments, some of which have arisen in the actual necessity and others in the justice due to individuals. Among the former are ... Major-General Vivian, commanding the Hussar brigade ...'[11] Although he was ordered on active service, General Vivian had not fully recovered from the wound he received the year before. During the Waterloo Campaign his right arm was in a sling.[12]

General Vivian left England with his brigade on 16 April and arrived in Ostend the next day. It was not until 28 April was he officially placed on the staff of Wellington's army and given command of a cavalry brigade.[13] On 15 June, General Vivian rode to Brussels and had dinner with General Lord Uxbridge. After dinner he went to the Duchess of Richmond's ball. It was there that Wellington learned that Napoleon had crossed the border and was advancing on Brussels. General Vivian hurried back to his brigade and had them underway early the next morning. Despite his efforts, he arrived at Quatre Bras too late to take part in the battle on 16 June. The next day, he and his brigade were part of the rearguard as Wellington's army retreated towards Waterloo.

General Vivian's brigade initially was on the left flank of the army at Waterloo on 18 June. During the battle he rode a white horse that belonged to the 10th Hussars.[14] Around 6 p.m. he realised that there was little possibility of them being needed where they were and took the initiative to move his brigade to the center without receiving orders first. On his way there, he met General Lord Uxbridge who ordered him to a position that was to the right and behind La Haye Sainte. They continued to remain in reserve. After the Imperial Guard's attack had been repulsed, Wellington ordered General John Vandeleur's and his brigades to pursue the retreating French. It was during this pursuit his brigade took most of its casualties.

After Waterloo, General Vivian and his brigade formed the advance guard on the march to Paris. It was joined by the 7th Cavalry Brigade and General Vivian in reality had command of a cavalry division. When the Anglo-Allied Army was disbanded in November 1815, he was retained on the staff of the AOOF when it was formed on 30 November and given command of the 2nd Cavalry Brigade.[15] General Vivian went on leave in the summer of 1816 and there was some discussion as to whether or not he would return to the AOOF. General Torrens wrote to Wellington on 29 November 1816:

> I have been on the watch for any movement on the part of Sir Hussey Vivian to show his intention of not returning to your army; but he has neither said nor written anything of it, directly or indirectly, to me; and on the contrary, in the only interview I had with him, he talked of returning as a matter of course.[16]

General Vivian did return to France and stayed with his command until the AOOF was disbanded in November 1818. Upon his return to England he was initially without any

---

11. *WSD*; Vol. 10, page 9.
12. Vivian, Claud; page 315.
13. General Order, 28 April 1815. The appointment was backdated to 25 March.
14. Vivian, Claud; page 334.
15. General Order, 30 November 1815.
16. *WSD*; Vol. 14, page 656.

military duties. In 1819, he was placed on the Home Staff in Newcastle-on-Tyne and was responsible for helping to quell civil disturbances in Glasgow in 1820. By the mid-1820s, General Vivian began to have financial problems. They were serious enough that he could not pay his bill with his army agent. His brother implied most of it was due to him being a gambling addict. He denied this allegation, but admitted he was 'a careless fellow about money … I have spent very much more than I ought to have done … I could sell Beechwood [the family home in Hampshire] and take a small house in town and live no doubt on £2,000 a year … could live at Beechwood on a somewhat reduced establishment, but it would be out of the question to live in the county and give up its amusements.'[17] His financial problems continued until 1827, when his father died and left half of the family estate to him.[18]

In an effort to improve his financial situation he wrote to Sir William Knighton, the private secretary to King George IV, on 11 August 1824 asking for help for him to be appointed the Governor of the Royal Military College:

> I would not through you (and I do it with the utmost reluctance) thus presume to intrude myself on His Majesty … did not the state of my finances make it absolutely necessary that I should take some steps in order to releive [*sic*] myself from difficulties which will otherwise oppress and inconvenience me during my life. And had I not daily opportunities of seeing that unless a man makes known his wishes (even when the kindest intentions are entertained towards him), he is constantly passed over under the impression that he desires to remain unemployed.[19]

General Vivian was not appointed the Governor of the Royal Military College but on 1 February 1825 he became the Inspecting General of the Cavalry. In 1827 he was appointed the regimental colonel of the 12th Lancers, which gave him an additional £456 per year. On 19 January 1828, he was created a Baronet of Truro, Cornwall. General Vivian remained as the Inspecting General of the Cavalry until 20 July 1830, when he was promoted to lieutenant general and became too senior to hold the position. With this promotion, he was appointed a Groom of the Bedchamber to King William IV on 24 July 1830.

Unfortunately for General Vivian, with his promotion to lieutenant general he became unemployed again. However, in November 1830 his friend, the Marquess of Anglesey, became the Lord Lieutenant of Ireland. General Vivian was appointed the Commander-in-Chief of Ireland on 1 July 1831. This position came with an annual income of £3,600. He held this command until 5 May 1835 when he was appointed the Master General of the Ordnance. On 31 August 1841 he was created Baron Vivian of Glynn and of Truro, Cornwall. He stepped down from the position of Master General of the Ordnance on 9 September 1841. He had no further military duties except as the regimental colonel of the 1st Dragoons, which he assumed in 1837.[20]

In 1818, General Vivian ran for Parliament from the Corporation Borough of Truro, but was defeated. He ran again in 1820 and was elected. He held the seat for six years and

---

17. 'Vivian, Sir Richard Hussey'.

18. Ibid.

19. Aspinall; Vol. 3, pages 87–8.

20. Due to a change in the pay structure in 1835, the regimental colonelcy of the 1st Dragoons paid him £900 per year plus emoluments of £200.

then was selected to represent the Royal Seat of New Windsor in 1826. He resigned his seat in 1831 when he was appointed the Commander-in-Chief of Ireland. Despite being in Ireland, he successfully ran for the Truro seat in 1832. He was voted out of office in early 1835, but two years later he was elected from Cornwall East. He represented the district until 1841 when he chose not to run. Richard Vivian was an active supporter of the army in the Parliament. He consistently voted against tax reduction and Catholic relief, but in 1829 voted for Catholic Emancipation. Not surprisingly, he was very protective of the Cornish copper interests.[21]

Richard Vivian married twice. First he married Eliza Champion de Crespigny on 14 September 1804. They had five children. Both of his sons joined the army. Eliza was described by her daughter's future mother-in-law as 'a very pretty woman, a great coquette, & practices her art with great success upon my eldest brother who is a great admirer of hers. I don't like her at all, for she is the most complete Mrs. Candour I have ever met with, and an amazing gossip.'[22] Richard himself described Eliza as 'violent, jealous and touchy, but she has a good heart at bottom and is open and honourable to an extreme'.[23] She died in 1831. Two years later Richard married Letitia Webster on 10 October 1833. They had one child. Richard Vivian also had an illegitimate son who was born in 1802, whom he raised as a member of the family.[24]

In August 1842, General Vivian was visiting Baden-Baden, Germany when he felt a pain in his chest and arms and had trouble breathing. He realised that something was wrong and wrote in his diary, 'I hope when the time comes I shall meet my end as becomes a man and a soldier, and that God, in their distress, will support my dear wife, my children, and my funeral.'[25] General Vivian died shortly afterwards from an aortic aneurysm on 20 August 1842. His body was brought back to Truro and he was buried in a quiet ceremony in St Mary's churchyard.[26]

Richard Vivian was an officer of some competence and ability. The destruction of his regiment during the Corunna Campaign kept him from returning to the Peninsula until late in the war, when there was not much need for cavalry. This prevented him from distinguishing himself further during the war. Due to his brigade being in reserve at Waterloo, he had little opportunity to gain distinction for himself until the battle was almost over. His performance during the pursuit of the retreating French was almost flawless. Initially, because there was still a large amount of French cavalry covering the retreat, he placed two of his regiments in line and kept the third behind them in support in the unlikely event they encountered too large of a force and had to retreat. As they were forming up, General Vivian saw that,

> The leading half-Squadron ... on approaching some of our Guns wheeled to the right instead of to the left, and was consequently moving to the rear. I was on the flank of the Squadron. I immediately (I recollect perfectly well), with a considerable degree of emphasis, etc., and a good hearty damn, galloped to the flank of the second half-Squadron, and said that it was towards the Enemy and not from the Enemy

21. 'Vivian, Sir Richard Hussey'.
22. Arbuthnot; Vol. 1, page 417.
23. 'Vivian, Sir Richard Hussey'.
24. Sir Robert John Hussey Vivian became a well-known general in the HEIC service.
25. Vivian, Claud; page 342.
26. Ibid; page 342.

they were to wheel. I then took the flank Officer's place and I led the Column down the hill in the direction I wished it to move until the leading half-Squadron was brought back into its place, when I went to the flank of that half-Squadron, and in this way conducted the Column some little distance.[27]

The one major mistake General Vivian made during the pursuit was that he led the 10th Hussars against a square of French infantry. He thought they were unsteady and would flee at the approach at his cavalry. Unfortunately for his hussars, the square consisted of the 2nd Battalion of the 3rd Regiment of the Imperial Guard Grenadiers. They did not break and the regiment took heavy casualties.

---

27. Siborne; page 163.

Walker, George Townshend

Date of Birth:	25 May 1764
Date Commissioned:	Ensign 95th Foot: 4 March 1782 without purchase[1]
Promotions:	Lieutenant 95th Foot: 13 March 1783 without purchase
	Lieutenant 73rd Foot:[2] 22 June 1783 appointed
	Lieutenant 36th Foot: 15 March 1785 appointed
	Lieutenant 35th Foot: 25 July 1787 appointed
	Captain-Lieutenant: 14th Foot 13 March 1789 without purchase
	Captain 60th Foot: 4 May 1791 without purchase
	Major 60th Foot: 28 August 1794 without purchase
	Lieutenant Colonel 50th Foot: 6 September 1798 without purchase
	Brevet Colonel: 25 April 1808
	Brigadier General: December 1810
	Major General: 4 June 1811
	Lieutenant General: 19 July 1821
	General: 28 June 1838
Regimental Colonel:	De Meuron's Regiment: 24 October 1812–21 May 1816
	3rd Battalion Rifle Brigade:[3] 21 May 1816–2 July 1818
	2nd Battalion Rifle Brigade: 2 July 1818–13 May 1820
	84th Foot: 13 May 1820–9 September 1822
	52nd Foot: 9 September 1822–23 December 1839
	50th Foot: 23 December 1839–14 November 1842
Major Commands under Wellington:	Brigade 5th Division: 3 October 1811–28 June 1812
	Temporarily commanded 5th Division: c. 3 October–c. 15 November 18?
	Brigade 2nd Division: 25 March–18 November 1813
	Temporarily commanded 2nd Division: c. 4 August–c. September 1813
	Temporarily commanded 7th Division: 18 November 1813–27 February 18?
Awards:	AGM with two clasps: Vimeiro, Badajoz & Orthes
	KCB: 2 January 1815
	GCB: 11 March 1817
	CTS: 17 December 1814
	Groom of the Bedchamber to the Duke of Sussex: 1817
Thanks of Parliament:	Badajoz & Orthes
Date of Death:	14 November 1842 in residence on the grounds of the Chelsea Royal Hospital

George Walker was born in 1764, the son of Major Nathaniel Walker and Henrietta Bagster, who was the daughter of Captain John Bagster, RN. George was the older

---

1. Sources differ as to whether he was an ensign or a 2nd lieutenant. He was listed as an ensign with a date of rank of 4 March 1781 in the 1782 *Army List* and as a 2nd lieutenant with a date of rank of 4 March 1782 in Hart's *New Annual Army List* for 1842. The War Office Announcement of his promotion to Ensign 95th Foot in the *London Gazette* is dated 16 March 1782. The entry in the *Army List* giving the date of 1781 is probably a typo. The reason for the confusion about whether he was a ensign or a 2nd lieutenant stems from when the 95th Foot was reformed in 1800. Its newly commissioned officers were 2nd lieutenants rather than ensigns.
2. Renumbered as the 71st Foot in 1786.
3. The rifle battalions had a colonel commandant in addition to the Brigade's Colonel-in-Chief.

brother of General Frederick Walker and Captain Charles Walker, RN. He attended Rugby School beginning in 1773.

George Walker was appointed an ensign in the 95th Foot in 1782 and was promoted to lieutenant a year later. His regiment was not the 95th Foot that was armed with Baker rifles and made a name for itself during the Peninsular War. It was raised by John Reid in 1779 and disbanded on 31 May 1783. Lieutenant Walker went on half-pay for three weeks until he was appointed a lieutenant in the 2nd Battalion of the 73rd Foot. He had not been in his new battalion long when it too was disbanded and he went on half-pay again. In March 1785, Lieutenant Walker was appointed a lieutenant in the 36th Foot which was stationed in India. After arriving there he was appointed the DQMG to the King's troops in the Madras Presidency. In February 1786, he served in that position in a force under Colonel Henry Cosby in the action against the Polygars in Tinnevelli District in southern India. In 1787, he returned to England due to poor health and was appointed a lieutenant in the 35th Foot.

Lieutenant Walker was with his new regiment for about a year when he was appointed an ADC to General Thomas Bruce, who was on the staff in Ireland. He was with the general for less than a year when he was promoted to captain-lieutenant in the 14th Foot and given command of its colonel's company in March 1789. The 14th Foot was stationed in Jamaica at the time and rather than going there, he took a leave of absence to go to Germany to study tactics and German. When his regiment returned to England in 1790, Captain-Lieutenant Walker joined them at Hilsea and took command of his company. He was promoted to captain in the 60th Foot in 1791, but since all of the regiment's battalions were stationed in North America, he stayed at the regimental depot. In 1793, he led a group of volunteers to Flanders where they joined the British Army that had deployed there in late winter. He fought at Tournay on 10 May 1793 and then was attached to the QMG of the army. While he was in Flanders, he was promoted to major. He was sent on several confidential missions to Den Hague, Rotterdam, and Amsterdam. In 1795 he was appointed Inspector of Foreign Corps on the Continent. After the British Army returned to England, Major Walker remained in Germany and went to the Black Forest, where he supervised the raising of De Roll's Regiment.

Major Walker returned to England in August 1796. In March 1797 he was appointed the ADC to General Simon Fraser, who commanded the British forces in Portugal. Shortly after his arrival, Major Walker was appointed the British ADC to Prince Christian of Waldeck, the commander of the joint British-Portuguese Army. He began to have problems with his health and returned to England in late 1797. Instead of joining his regiment, Major Walker became the Inspecting Field Officer of a Recruiting District in Manchester in February 1798. While he was in Manchester he was appointed a lieutenant colonel in the 50th Foot. He continued as the Inspecting Field Officer until March 1799, when he joined his regiment in Portugal. In October 1799, he was ordered to join the British Expedition in Flanders, where he became the British Commissioner to the Russian Army. After the expedition was withdrawn, the Russians went to the Channel Islands and Lieutenant Colonel Walker remained with them until they returned to Russia in October 1800.

While Lieutenant Colonel Walker was serving with the Russians, his regiment was part of the expedition to Egypt and sailed there in November 1800. After the French were defeated, the 50th Foot were sent to Malta in October 1801. He joined them in Malta and went with it to Belfast in May 1802. While in Belfast, they helped suppress the Irish Rebellion of 1803. Lieutenant Colonel Walker spent the next four years with his regiment. He commanded it during the 1807 expedition to Copenhagen, where they were part of General Brent Spencer's brigade in the 2nd Division. They returned to England in November but within a month they sailed to the Mediterranean Sea, still under the command of General Spencer. Lieutenant Colonel Walker, his headquarters, and the flank companies were on one ship, while the rest of the battalion were on another. His ship was separated from the convoy during a heavy storm and was driven far into the Mediterranean Sea. It eventually made Sicily, where he waited until word reached him several weeks later that the rest of the convoy had been forced to land at Gibraltar. Lieutenant Colonel Walker joined them there.[4] While in Gibraltar, he was promoted to colonel. General Spencer received word in June that his force was placed under Wellington's command and were to join him in Portugal. They landed at Mondego Bay on 6 August 1808.

After they joined Wellington's army, Colonel Walker and the 50th Foot were initially assigned to General Catlin Craufurd's 5th Brigade.[5] Although they were at Roliça on 17 August, they were part of the reserve and saw no action. The next day, the army was reorganised and they were transferred to General Henry Fane's 6th Light Brigade. Colonel Walker and his regiment fought at Vimeiro on 21 August. During the battle they were in the centre of the British line on what was known as Vimeiro Hill. Their brigade was the focus of the French main attack. Colonel Walker received permission to deploy his regiment on the flank of the approaching French column. Their fire into the column halted the French and caused them to retreat.

In September, the British Government decided to split the British Army in Portugal into two forces. The main part would march into Spain under General John Moore to fight the French, while the rest would form a garrison in Portugal. The Duke of York directed that the 50th Foot would be part of the garrison. Since his regiment would not be participating in the forthcoming campaign into Spain, Colonel Walker decided to take personal leave and return to England. Despite the orders he received from England about leaving the 50th Foot as part of the garrison, in late October, General Moore ordered them to join his army in a brigade commanded by General Moore Disney. Colonel Walker left Portugal for England by the end of October. He was there for about six weeks when he was sent back to the army with dispatches from Lord Castlereagh,[6] the Secretary of State for War and the Colonies. He arrived at Corunna with them on 18 January 1809, two days after the battle. Instead of returning to England with the army, he sailed to Lisbon to give the dispatches to General John Cradock, the commander of the British garrison there. After delivering them, he returned home and rejoined his regiment.

In July 1809, the 50th Foot was assigned to General William Dyott's brigade as part of the expedition to Walcheren. Colonel Walker was later appointed a colonel on the staff to command a brigade in the garrison after the majority of the expedition returned to England. He also served as one of the commissioners that decided on how revenue received from the sale of seized government property and military material would be distributed as prize money. He returned to England when the British expedition was withdrawn in December 1809. Colonel Walker was sent to Spain in August 1810 to serve as the British Liaison Officer with the Spanish Army in Galicia. Lieutenant Colonel Henry Torrens of the Horse Guards wrote to Wellington that Colonel Walker had been made a brigadier

4. Patterson, John; *The Adventures of Captain John Patterson*, page 19.
5. General Order, 7 August 1808.
6. Robert Stewart, Viscount Castlereagh.

general[7] in Spain and although placed under his orders, for communication purposes, was not considered attached to his army.[8] By March 1811 he was assigned to Cadiz as a brigadier general, but his duties were not specified.

General Walker remained as the British Government's liaison officer to the Spanish Army until the late spring. On 3 June 1811, Lieutenant Colonel Torrens wrote to Wellington that General Walker 'has been ordered to your army.'[9] The day after he wrote the letter, General Walker was promoted to major general. On 29 June, he was placed on the staff of Wellington's army as a major general.[10] When he joined the army is unknown, however, he was appointed to command a brigade in the 5th Division on 3 October.[11] Upon his arrival at the division HQ, General Walker was given temporary command of it until its new commander arrived in mid-November. They remained in winter quarters along the Spanish border for several months. Although his brigade was within a day's march of Ciudad Rodrigo when the city fell on 16 January 1812, they did not take part in the siege.[12]

General Walker led his brigade during the siege of Badajoz in March and April 1812. During the assault on the city on the night of 6 April, his brigade was given the mission of making a diversionary attack on the San Vicente Bastion on the opposite side of the city where the main assault took place. They initially came under intense fire, but successfully scaled the walls after taking heavy casualties. His soldiers were clearing the walls and two other bastions to their right when they saw smoke. Thinking it was a mine that was about to explode, they panicked and fled back to the San Vincente Bastian. General Walker was rallying his men when he was shot in the upper body by a French soldier less than 2 metres away. The bullet was deflected by his watch but still penetrated his chest. As he lay on the ramparts, another French soldier bayonetted him four times. The soldier ripped off his epaulettes and was about to kill him when General Walker made a Mason sign to another French soldier, who protected him.[13]

General Walker lost a lot of blood and the surgeon's initial prognosis was that he would die. Several of his ribs were broken, one being shattered, and his surgeon at first thought his lung was also damaged. For some reason his surgeon did not immediately close his wound. Because of its severity it became a bit of a medical curiosity and his surgeon even made a drawing of it.[14] General Walker was too injured to move and spent four months recovering in Badajoz. Wellington wrote to Lord Liverpool on 20 May updating him on the officers who were wounded at Badajoz and specifically mentioned him. 'Gen. Walker has been doing better the last 3 days; but he is much weakened by repeated hemorrhage, and he is not out of danger, although the hemorrhage has stopped. He was badly wounded, and was very imprudent, both in exerting himself improperly, and in his food, during the first day after he was wounded, which brought on hemorrhage.'[15]

---

7. The exact date of his promotion to brigadier general is unknown.
8. Unpublished letter dated 1 January 1811.
9. Unpublished letter dated 3 June 1811.
10. General Order, 29 June 1811.
11. Ibid; 3 October 1811.
12. Bowlby; page 29.
13. Legend has it that the French soldier who saved him was sent as a prisoner to Edinburgh. After he recovered, General Walker tracked him down, thanked him for saving his life, and ensured that he was well taken care of while he was a prisoner.
14. Henry, Gomm; page 48; Gomm, pages 56 and 59.
15. *WD* (enlarged ed.); Vol. 5, page 660.

By June, it became apparent that General Walker would not recover for several months and he was replaced in command of his brigade.[16] He never resumed command of it. In late August, General Walker returned to England. Prior to his departure, Wellington wrote to him on 18 August, 'I hope that you will soon be able again to join us.'[17] For the next seven months his status was unknown, however, Wellington gave him command of a brigade in the 2nd Division, despite his absence.[18] By May 1813, General Walker had still not returned. On 1 May Wellington wrote to General Denis Pack, who had asked to command a British brigade, that, 'I think it probable that … Gen. Walker will not come out.'[19]

By the summer of 1813, General Walker had still not fully recovered from his wounds but returned to the Peninsula in August to assume command of his brigade, which included his old regiment the 50th Foot. He may have temporarily commanded the 2nd Division for a short time after his return until its commander, General William Stewart, recovered from wounds he received on 31 July. General Walker was in command of his brigade by mid-September. They were at the Battle of Nivelle on 13 November, but saw no action. Eight days after the battle, General Walker was appointed the temporary commander of the 7th Division.[20] Instead of having the senior colonel in his brigade take command of it while he was gone, Wellington placed General Edward Barnes in temporarily command of it.[21]

On 17 December 1813, the AG wrote to General Walker that General Thomas Picton was returning to Spain to resume command of the 3rd Division. This would displace General Charles Colville, who was in temporary command of the 3rd Division. General Colville had been promised a division and Wellington intended to give him the 7th Division. The AG then stated that, 'I am directed to ask, under these circumstances, and the arrangements in consequence proposed, how you wish your further services to be disposed of, as his Excellency is willing, as far as possible, to meet your inclination on this point.'[22] What General Walker's preference was is unknown. However, when General Colville was given command of the 5th Division instead, General Walker continued in temporary command of the 7th Division. In February 1814, word was received that the 7th Division Commander, General George Ramsay Lord Dalhousie, was returning and General Walker informed Wellington on 10 February that he wished to resume command of his old brigade in the 2nd Division. The AG acknowledged the letter on 12 February and informed him that he would resume command of his brigade in the 2nd Division when the 7th Division's commander arrived.[23]

General Walker led the 7th Division at the Battle of Orthes on 27 February 1814, where he was slightly wounded.[24] Shortly after the battle he received word that his wife had died and he returned to England in the middle of March. On 5 April 1815 he was appointed the lieutenant governor of Grenada and served there until 17 February 1816. Upon his return to England, he found that De Meuron's Regiment, of which he had been the regimental

16. General Order, 28 June 1812.
17. *WD* (enlarged ed.); Vol. 6, page 32.
18. General Order, 25 March 1813.
19. *WD* (enlarged ed.); Vol. 6, pages 456–7.
20. General Order, 18 November 1813.
21. Ibid; 20 November 1813.
22. *WD* (enlarged ed.); Vol. 7, page 206.
23. Ibid; page 318.
24. *London Gazette*; 20 March 1814, page 620.

colonel for the past four years, had been disbanded. On 21 May, General Walker was appointed the colonel commandant of the 3rd Battalion of the Rifle Brigade. The following year he received recognition for his service in the Peninsula. He was awarded the GCB and made a Groom of the Bedchamber of the Duke of Sussex. He was also appointed to the Consolidated Board of General Officers. By 1818 he was on its Acting Committee and served on the Committee for several years.[25] When the 3rd Battalion of the Rifle Brigade was disbanded on 2 July 1818, he was appointed the colonel commandant of the 2nd Battalion the same day. He served as their colonel commandant until 1820, when he was appointed the regimental colonel of the 84th Foot. In 1821 he was promoted to lieutenant general and late in 1824 he became the regimental colonel of the 52nd Foot.

In February 1825, General Walker's name was suggested by Wellington to Charles W. Wynn, the President of the HEIC, to command in India.[26] Unfortunately for him, he was not known to the Board of the HEIC. President Wynn did some checking on General Walker and wrote that he 'is spoken of in the highest imaginable terms, but, I fear has a very bad temper.'[27] On 7 March Wellington sent him a list of eight officers to choose from, with the caveat that General Walker was one of the two best on the list.[28] He was appointed the Commander-in-Chief of the Madras Presidency on 11 May 1825 and arrived in India on 3 March 1826. In 1827, General Walker requested that he be appointed to the command of the Bengal Presidency which would become vacant in December 1828. If he received this appointment, he would be the Commander-in-Chief of India. In February 1828, General Walker had not heard from Wellington in regards to his request and wrote again. Wellington finally responded on 24 September 1828 that the position was to be filled in 1830 by Lord Dalhousie.[29] General Walker continued to serve in Madras until 11 May 1831.

Upon his returned to England, General Walker had no further military duties except as the regimental colonel of the 52nd Foot. He continued to serve on the Consolidated Board of General Officers, but as an inactive member. On 28 March 1835 he was created a Baronet of the United Kingdom for his Peninsula service. At the same time he received a grant for a coat-of-arms, which included the words Vimiera, Badajoz and Orthes, and a representation of the colours of the 50th Foot.[30]

General Walker was appointed the Lieutenant Governor of the Royal Hospital Chelsea on 24 May 1837 and promoted to general the next year. In 1839 he became the regimental colonel of his old regiment, the 50th Foot. He would hold both positions until his death on 14 November 1842. He died at home in his residence on the grounds of the Royal Hospital Chelsea and was buried in Kensal Green cemetery, London. He was re-interred at Marylebone Church, London in December 1859.[31]

Unlike many of his contemporaries, George Walker had little outside income and was dependent on his pay as a soldier. He never purchased any of his promotions. His pay as a general officer during the Peninsular War was dependent on him serving in a

---

25. An appointment to the Consolidated Board of General Officers involved little work, unless the individual was on the Acting Committee, which oversaw the duties of the clerks, inspectors, etc.
26. Duke of Buckingham; Vol. 4, page 214.
27. Ibid; page 218.
28. *WND*; Vol. 2, page 425.
29. Ibid; Vol. 4, pages 82–3 and Vol. 5, page 79.
30. *Gentleman's Magazine*; January 1843, page 89.
31. Bromley; Vol. 2, page 388.

general officer's position. Despite not being fully recovered from the wound he received at Badajoz, he returned to Spain in the summer of 1813 in order that he would continue to receive a general's pay. If he had not returned and was not placed in another general's billet, his pay would have reverted back to that of his regimental rank of lieutenant colonel. His financial problems were known at the highest levels and it was a factor in his being appointed as the Commander-in-Chief of the Madras Presidency in 1825. When he was being considered for the job, Charles Wynn, the President of the HEIC, noted that for General Walker, 'It would be very desirable to him, as he has a family, and is poor.'[32] Ten years later, when he was created a baronet, it was without a place name because he had no estate to name it after.[33] By the time of his death in 1842, General Walker had achieved some financial stability. His annual income was £1,350, which included a £350 wound pension, £600 (plus emoluments) for serving as the Regimental Colonel of the 50th Foot, £400 for being the Lieutenant Governor of the Chelsea Royal Hospital, plus allowances and a house on the grounds of the hospital.

George Walker married Anna Allen of Bury, Lancashire in July 1789. They had two daughters. Anna died on 15 February 1814. He was very close to Anna and after he had been wounded at Badajoz, his ADC thought that 'it extremely probable Mrs. Walker would leave England the moment she heard of his situation, and not rest till she reached him.'[34] George married Helen Caldcleugh of Croydon Surrey on 15 August 1820. They had four sons and two daughters. His last son was born in 1834, when George was 70 years old. All four sons went into the army.

George Walker spent much of his time as a junior officer in various capacities on the staff and thus had little time commanding soldiers in either garrison or in combat. This lack of experience, however, did not hamper him as a battalion commander. His handling of his battalion at Vimeiro in 1808 was brilliant and he was noted for his courage. That being said, his day-to-day activities of his battalion while not in combat was not considered good by those above him. He also had a reputation for being a strict disciplinarian.[35] Wellington found no fault with his command of a brigade and kept him in temporary command of a division several times in the Peninsula. A junior officer who served under him in the 50th Foot described him as

[a] man endued with extraordinary coolness and intrepidity of mind, knew right well how to go about his work; he also knew the stubborn elements of which his regiment was composed. He was of the middle stature, well proportioned, and of a pale complexion; with a remarkably handsome set of features, animated by keen expressive eyes, that were full of intelligence and fire.[36]

One of the curious incidents in George Walker's career occurred in the autumn of 1808. After his regiment was assigned to the force that would garrison Lisbon while the rest of the army marched into Spain, he decided to go on home leave. After he made his decision, but while he was still in Portugal, General Moore decided to allow his regiment to participate in the upcoming campaign. Colonel Walker could have changed his mind

32. Duke of Buckingham; Vol. 4, page 218.
33. General Richard Vivian was created the Baronet of Truro, Cornwall, which was his family estate.
34. Gomm; page 258.
35. Napier, Charles; Vol. 1, pages 93, 111–12.
36. Patterson, John; *Camps and Quarters*, Vol. 1, pages 216–17.

about going on leave, but did not. Why he chose to leave his regiment is unknown. It might have had to do with his relationship with General Moore. Major Charles Stanhope, who was in his regiment, wrote a letter home that General Moore sent for General Walker,

> and gave him a dressing [down] about the state of the regiment and then told him he expected them to be much better now they were commanded by another person, and he had just spoke to him before he went that he might know what to expect when he returned if he did not pay more attention, in short he spoke in such a way I do not think we should see the fellow again.[37]

Major Charles Napier, who commanded the battalion after Colonel Walker, believed it was because General Moore was angered by the harsh discipline he imposed.[38] How much truth there is in these allegations is unknown, however, in the end Colonel Walker did not stay with his regiment.

Regardless of the reasons for his return to England in 1808, Colonel Walker's absence from command of his battalion during the campaign in Spain had no impact on his future career. A close examination of it both before and after the incident reveals he might have had a patron who looked after him. There are several clues that indicate that the patron may have been a member of the royal family. Several sources state that his father had been given an apartment in Hampton Court Palace after he retired. When George was appointed an ensign in the 95th Foot in 1782, it was because Queen Charlotte intervened on his behalf. There is nothing to suggest that his promotions over the next sixteen years were unusual, except that he never purchased one of them. Each was by appointment which was very rare for the time. Additionally at that time, it was quite common for an officer to move from one regiment to another to increase his chances for promotion. It was usually done by exchanging regiments with another officer. George Walker served in seven different regiments in sixteen years. Each time he moved to a new regiment it was by appointment, rather than exchanging with another officer.

There are some indications that even after he was promoted to general officer someone continue to look after George Walker's career. A general could usually expect to be made a regimental colonel by the time he was a senior major general or junior lieutenant general. A few would be appointed a regimental colonel within three years of being promoted to major general.[39] General Walker received his colonelcy fifteen months after becoming a major general. The initial appointment as a regimental colonel was to the most junior regiment in the army. After the end of the Napoleonic Wars, the British Army began to downsize by disbanding junior high numbered[40] and foreign regiments first. If a regiment was disbanded, the regimental colonel position disappeared. Often it would be several years before a general was offered another colonelcy. Twice General Walker's regimental colonelcy was in danger of disappearing. De Meuron's Regiment was disbanded in 1816 and the 3rd Battalion the Rifle Brigade in 1818. Yet both times, unlike many of his contemporaries, he was appointed to another colonelcy the same day.

---

37. Stanhope; page 220.
38. Napier, Charles; Vol. 1, page 93.
39. One exception was General Ronald Ferguson who became the regimental colonel of the Sicilian Regiment nine months after becoming a major general. However, he had been a brigadier general for four years prior to being promoted to major general.
40. Beginning in 1816, the 94th to 104th Foot were disbanded with the 95th taken out of the line and named the Rifle Brigade.

Wheatley, William

Date of Birth:	14 August 1771
Date Commissioned:	Ensign 1st Foot Guards: 23 June 1790 purchase?
Promotions:	Lieutenant & Captain 1st Foot Guards: 14 August 1793 without purchase
	Captain-Lieutenant & Lieutenant Colonel 1st Foot Guards: 25 November 1799 without purchase
	Captain & Lieutenant Colonel 1st Foot Guards: 12 January 1800 without purchase
	Brevet Colonel: 25 October 1809
	Major General: 1 January 1812
Major Commands under Wellington:	On staff of Cadiz: c. August 1810–c. May 1811
	Brigade 1st Division: 7 May–1 September 1812
Awards:	AGM with one clasp: Barrosa & Salamanca
Date of Death:	1 September 1812 of typhus at San Lorenzo de El Escorial, Spain

William Wheatley was born in 1771, the son of William Wheatley of Lesney House, Kent, and Margaret Randall. His younger brother was Sir Henry Wheatley, Baronet, a major general in the Hanoverian Service. William was commissioned as an ensign in the 1st Foot Guards. Whether he purchased his commission or was appointed is not known. William served in the regiment for twenty-two years until he was promoted to major general in 1812. Unlike most of his contemporaries, he never served as a staff officer outside of the regiment.

Ensign Wheatley was assigned to the 1st Battalion when it was part of General Gerard Lake's Guards Brigade that was sent to Flanders on 27 February 1793. He was promoted to lieutenant and captain on 14 August and fought at the Battle of Lincelles on 18 August. After word of his promotion was received, Captain Wheatley returned to England. By July 1794, he was the adjutant of the Guards Light Infantry Battalion that was formed for service in Flanders. Captain Wheatley was wounded in the fighting on 14 January 1795 at Rhenen along the Waal River. He returned to England when the British Army was evacuated from Bremen in late April 1795. Four years later, Captain Wheatley was still with the light companies of the 1st Foot Guards and participated in the raid on the Ostend-Bruges Canal on 19 May 1798. After they successfully destroyed the canal's locks, they were unable to retreat back to their transports due to the high surf and he and his men were captured. Captain Wheatley remained as a prisoner-of-war in Lille until he was released in November 1798.

In November 1799, Captain Wheatley was promoted to captain-lieutenant and lieutenant colonel in the 1st Battalion. He was the only officer in the regiment to hold this rank at the time. He was assigned to the Colonel's Company of the Regiment and commanded it when the regimental colonel was absent.[1] Two months later he was promoted to captain and lieutenant colonel. As the junior captain and lieutenant colonel

---

1. The 1st Foot Guards Regimental Colonel in 1799 was Prince William, the Duke of Gloucester and Edinburgh. It is highly unlikely that he ever took command of the Colonel's Company while Lieutenant Colonel Wheatley was in it.

he was assigned to the regiment's 3rd Battalion. By 1806, Lieutenant Colonel Wheatley had enough seniority that he was assigned to the 2nd Battalion and did not go with the regiment when the 1st and 3rd Battalions were sent to Sicily. By November 1807, he was the commander of the 2nd Battalion.

By the summer of 1808, Lieutenant Colonel Wheatley was serving in the 3rd Battalion. It was assigned to General Henry Warde's Guards Brigade that was under orders to join General David Baird's force being sent to reinforce General John Moore's army in Spain. It arrived off Corunna on 13 October but the 3rd Battalion did not land until 28 October. General Baird formed his force into temporary divisions on 19 November and Colonel Robert Cheney commanding the 3rd Battalion was assigned to the temporary command of a line brigade in the absence of its commander. Lieutenant Colonel Wheatley then succeeded to the command of the battalion. It advanced into Spain and joined General Moore's army on 20 December. The two forces were combined and General Warde's brigade was placed in General Baird's 1st Division. On 20 December, Colonel Cheney resumed command of the 3rd Battalion. Lieutenant Colonel Wheatley stayed with the battalion and fought with it at the Battle of Corunna on 16 January 1809. They returned home when the army evacuated from Spain. In the summer of 1809, Lieutenant Colonel Wheatley again commanded the 2nd Battalion at home while the 1st and 3rd Battalions went on campaign to Walcheren. He was promoted to colonel in October.

In early March 1810, Colonel Wheatley and six companies of the 2nd Battalion of the 1st Foot Guards were sent to Cadiz as part of General William Dilkes's Guards Brigade. They arrived there in late March and served as part of the garrison under General Thomas Graham that was defending the city. On 11 August, Colonel Wheatley was given command of the garrison's 3rd Brigade. He was not, however, placed on the staff until 12 September, when he was transferred to the command of the Reserve Brigade.[2] He was not its commander long, for on 24 September the garrison was ordered to send two of its battalions to Wellington's army in Portugal. This forced General Graham to re-organise the garrison and both the 3rd and Reserve Brigades were disbanded. Eight days later a new battalion arrived and Colonel Wheatley became the commander of the 2nd Brigade. Colonel Wheatley commanded his brigade at Barrosa on 5 March 1811, where they were on the left of the British line. General Graham ordered them to attack the French Division commanded by General Leval. Although his brigade was outnumbered by 3–2, its attack routed the French and it was the first British unit to capture a French eagle in the Peninsular War. Because of its heavy losses at Barrosa, Colonel Wheatley's 2nd Battalion of the 1st Foot Guards was ordered home. They left Cadiz on 4 May and were back in England in June.

Colonel Wheatley was promoted to major general on 1 January 1812 and was selected by the Horse Guards to join Wellington's army in Spain. Colonel Henry Torrens notified Wellington on 6 February 1812 that General Wheatley, whom he noted was an excellent officer, was among those selected to replace general officers killed at the siege of Ciudad Rodrigo.[3] General Wheatley was placed on the staff of Wellington's army as a major general on 2 May 1812, but the appointment was backdated to 25 February.[4]

---

2. General Order, 12 August 1810. His appointment to the command of the 3rd Brigade was backdated to 11 August.
3. Unpublished letter from Colonel Henry Torrens to Wellington dated 6 February 1812.
4. General Order, 2 May 1812. His appointment to the command of major general was backdated to 25 February.

General Wheatley sailed from Portsmouth on 30 March aboard the *Lalona* and arrived in Lisbon within two weeks. By 23 April he was on the road to join Wellington at Fuenteguinaldo, just over the Portuguese border in Spain. General Wheatley, like many other British generals of the era, did not travel light. His retinue consisted of 'nearly thirty animals and a heterogeneous mixture of British, Portuguese and Spaniards to the number of about 22.'[5] They included a French deserter as his cook, who 'is no great catch, but is a willing dirty dog; to-day I have had an offer from a lady and to-morrow she is to be added to the establishment, so between the two cooks I hope to be pretty well served.'[6] By 4 May, General Wheatley was at Wellington's HQ.

Although he knew he would be assigned as a brigade commander, General Wheatley did not know which one until he was interviewed by Wellington. He wanted to be in the 1st Division, which contained a small Guards Brigade. General Henry Campbell, who commanded the Guards Brigade, 'spoke to Sir T. Graham[7] on the subject and it was only in consequence of the early application made to Lord Wellington that I can impute my success, as General Hope[8] was exceedingly desirous of having the Brigade and is likewise an old friend and fellow-countryman of General Graham's.'[9] General Wheatley got his wish and was given command of General Edward Stopford's brigade. General Stopford had gone to England the previous month but was expected to return. The General Order appointing General Wheatley to the command of the brigade had the stipulation 'until the return of Hon. Major General Stopford to his duty.'[10]

General Wheatley was quite pleased with his new brigade. He wrote to his brother, Lieutenant Colonel Henry Wheatley,

a very pretty one it is. The 1st Battalion of the 42nd is just arrived from England and the second is to be drafted into it which will complete it to 1200 men. The 79th is likewise a very smart regiment ... The 24th is also very good, though weak. The 58th the less said about the better. It is certainly one of the best in the army, in numbers superior to all; I can bring 2700 or 2800 firelocks into the field – above 200 more than the Guards, which is the next strongest.[11]

Although General Wheatley was very enthusiastic about commanding his brigade, he was disillusioned with the war. He wrote to his brother, 'My opinion of this damn war has never varied since my campaign with Sir John Moore; he saw the whole in its true light, ambition has blinded the eyes of the other.'[12] He was even critical of Wellington in a letter to his wife. 'It is a dashing game that His Lordship is playing; the courage, good-will and discipline of the Army will, I trust, ensure us success, but it may be purchased at vastly too dear a rate.'[13]

---

5. Wheatley; page 435.
6. Ibid; page 439.
7. Lieutenant General Sir Thomas Graham, the commander of the 1st Division.
8. General John Hope was given command of the 7th Division instead.
9. Wheatley; pages 437–8.
10. General Order, 7 May 1812.
11. Wheatley; pages 438 and 440.
12. Ibid; page 345.
13. Ibid; page 446.

On 20 May the 1st Division was ordered south to Albuquerque in anticipation of a French thrust against Wellington's forces in the vicinity of Badajoz. A week later they were heading back north and by 18 June were in Salamanca. General Wheatley and his brigade were on the left flank of the army at Salamanca on 22 July, but were not engaged. On 14 August they were part of the force that liberated Madrid. He wrote to his wife the next day: 'Little did my mother imagine at the time I was born that on the very day 41 years later I should enter the Spanish capital in triumph, dine in the palace of His Catholic Majesty and accompany our Commander-in-Chief to the play in the evening!'[14]

General Wheatley and his brigade were sent to the El Escorial Royal Monastery about 45 kilometers north-west of Madrid later in the month. While there, he became sick and died of typhus on 1 September. He was buried in the Garden of the Friars in the El Escorial. Shortly after his death, rumor spread through the Foot Guards that General Wheatley had been appointed the commander of the 1st Guards Brigade and his friend General Richard Hulse, who died from typhus six days after him, had been appointed the commander of the 2nd Guards Brigade. Both officers died before they received news of their appointment.[15] This rumor, however, cannot be substantiated.

William Wheatley married Jane Williams on 20 January 1796. Her sister married General Henry Campbell. He was quite close to his wife, writing to her often while on campaign. He sometimes called her Janny in his letters. Upon his death, she received a pension of £150. They had four children, one of whom joined the Royal Navy.

William Wheatley's many years in the 1st Foot Guards allowed him to become friends with the Duke of York. He was comfortable enough to considering requesting that Captain George Fitzclarence, the illegitimate son of the Duke of Clarence,[16] be sent out to serve as his ADC.[17] He was also close friends with Generals William Anson and Richard Hulse. His career closely paralleled that of General Hulse's. Both were commissioned in the Guards the same year and were promoted through the ranks in the same years. They each died from typhus the same week and legend has it that the two generals were buried together in the El Escorial.[18]

It is strange how fate sometimes works. General Wheatley was selected to join Wellington's army as a replacement for generals killed in action in early 1812. The selection was made before Colonel Torrens received Wellington's letter stating that he did not need any additional generals at that time. If Colonel Torrens had been aware that Wellington did not need any more generals, General Wheatley might not have been sent out and died in Spain. Who knows how his career might have gone?

---

14. Ibid; page 450.
15. Mills; pages 218–19.
16. The Duke of Clarence was the future King William IV.
17. Wheatley; page 544.
18. Wheatley; page 452.

Appendix

Wellington's Brigade Commanders in Portugal: June–September 1808

Acland, Wroth Palmer
Anstruther, Robert
Bowes, Barnard
Craufurd, James Catlin
Fane, Henry
Ferguson, Ronald
Nightingall, Miles

Wellington's Brigade Commanders in Portugal, Spain and France: 1809–1814

Alten, Victor
Anson, George
Anson, William
Aylmer, Matthew
Barnes, Edward
Bayly, Henry
de Bernewitz, John
Bock, George
Bowes, Barnard
Bradford, Thomas
Brisbane, Thomas
Brooke, William
Burne, Robert
Byng, John
Cameron, Alan
Campbell, Henry
Craufurd, James Catlin
de Grey, George
de Drieberg, George
Drummond, George
Dunlop, James
Erskine, James
Fane, Henry
Grant, Colquhoun
Halkett, Colin
Hay, Andrew
de Hinuber, Henry
Hoghton, Daniel
Hulse, Richard
Inglis, William
Keane, John
Kemmis, James
Lambert, John
Langwerth, Ernest
Le Marchant, John
Lightburne, Stafford
Long, Robert
Low, Sigismund
Lumley, William
Mackenzie, John Randoll
Mackinnon, Henry
Maitland, Peregrine
Nightingall, Miles
O'Callaghan, Robert
O'Loghlin, Terence
Pack, Denis
Peacocke, Warren
Ponsonby, William
Power, Manley
Pringle, William
Rebow, Francis Slater
Robinson, Frederick
Ross, Robert
Skerrett, John
Slade, John
Somerset, Lord Edward
Sontag, John
Stewart, Richard
Stopford, Edward
Vandeleur, John
Vivian, Richard
Walker, George
Wheatley, William

Wellington's Brigade Commanders Flanders and France: April 1815–November 1815

Adam, Frederick
Beresford, Lord George
Bradford, Thomas
Brisbane, Thomas

Byng, John
de Dornberg, William
Grant, Colquhoun
Halkett, Colin
Johnstone, George
Keane, John
Lambert, John
Mackenzie, Kenneth

Maitland, Peregrine
O'Callaghan, Robert
Pack, Denis
Ponsonby, William
Power, Manley
Somerset, Lord Edward
Vandeleur, John
Vivian, Richard

Wellington's Brigade Commanders in the Army of Occupation France: November 1815–November 1818

Bradford, Thomas
Brisbane, Thomas
Grant, Colquhoun
Keane, John
Lambert, John
Maitland, Peregrine

O'Callaghan, Robert
Pack, Denis
Power, Manley
Somerset, Lord Edward
Vivian, Richard

Bibliography

'Adam, William (1751–1839), of Woodstone, Kincardine, and Blair-Adam, Kinross.' *The History of Parliament Online*. 15 November 2014.

Adams's Parliamentary Handbook. London: Henry Adams, 1854.

Aitchison, John. *An Ensign in the Peninsular War: the Letters of John Aitchison*. London: Michael Joseph; 1981.

Anderson, William. *The Scottish Nation: Or the Surnames, Families, Literature, Honours, and Biographical History of the People of Scotland*. 3 vols. Edinburgh: Fullerton, 1867.

Annual Biography and Obituary. Multiple volumes.

Anonymous. *Letters from Germany and Holland, During the Years 1813–14; with a Detailed Account of the Operations of the British Army in Those Countries, and of the Attacks Upon Antwerp and Bergen-Op-Zoom, by the Troops Under the Command of Gen. Sir. T. Graham*. London: 1820.

Anonymous. *With Wellington in the Peninsula: the Adventures of a Highland Soldier, 1808–1814*. Barnsley: Frontline, 2015.

'Anson, Sir George (1769–1849), of Rushal Hall, Staffs. and 5 Bulstrode Street, Mdx.' *The History of Parliament Online*. 5 December 2014.

Anstruther, Robert. 'Extracts from Journal'. *London Quarterly Review*. Vol. *LVI, April & June 1836*. Pages 105–18; 241–54.

Anton, James. *Retrospect of a Military Life*. Cambridge: Ken Trotman, 1991.

Arbuthnot, Harriet. *The Journal of Mrs. Arbuthnot, 1820–1832*. 2 vols. London: MacMillan, 1950.

Aspinall, A. (ed.). *The Letters of King George IV 1812–1830*. 3 vols. Cambridge: University Press, 1938.

Atkinson, C.T. 'A Peninsular Brigadier: Letters of Major-General Sir F.P. Robinson, K.C.B. Dealing with the Campaign of 1813'. *Journal of the Society for Army Historical Research*. Vol. 30, pages 153–70.

Bakewell, Robert. *The Exploits of Ensign Bakewell: with the Inniskillings in the Peninsula, 1810–1811; and in Paris, 1815*. Ian Robertson (ed.). London: Frontline, 2012.

Bamford, Andrew. *A Bold and Ambitious Enterprise: the British Army in the Low Countries, 1813–1814*. London: Frontline, 2013.

Bamford, Andrew. 'British Army Individual Unit Strengths: 1808–1815'. *The Napoleon Series*. 1 October 2014.

Bamford, Andrew. 'British Forces at Cadiz 1810–1814'. *The Napoleon Series*. 9 June 2015.

Bamford, Andrew. *Sickness, Suffering, and the Sword: The British Regiment on Campaign, 1808–1815*. Norman: University of Oklahoma, 2013.

Bamford, Andrew. 'The Guadiana Fever Epidemic'. *The Napoleon Series*. 1 October 2014.

Barnard, Anne L. T*he Cape Diaries of Lady Anne Barnard, 1799–1800*. Vol. 1. Goodwood: Van Riebeeck Society, 1999.

Beamish, N. Ludlow. *History of the King's German Legion*. 2 vols. London: Buckland & Brown, 1993.

'Beresford, Lord George Thomas (1781–1839), of Bovah, co. Londonderry'. *The History of Parliament Online*. 15 January 2015.

'Bernewitz, Johann Heinrich Karl'. *Deutsche Biographie Online*. 18 January 2015.

Black Book: An Exposition of Abuses in Church and State, Courts of Law, Municipal Corporations and Public Companies; with a Precis of the House of Commons. London: Effingham Wilson, 1836.

Blackwell, Thomas. 'Diary of a Subaltern of the 36th: 1804–1809'. *Firm: the Journal of the Worcestershire Regiment.* July 1933–April 1934.

Blakeney, Robert. *A Boy in the Peninsular War.* London: Greenhill, 1989.

Bowlby, Peter. *Walcheren, Spain, America and Waterloo: the Memoir of Captain Peter Bowlby 4th Foot (1791–1877).* Godmanchester: Ken Trotman, 2016.

Bowsfield, Hartwell. 'Maitland, Sir Peregrine'. *Dictionary of Canadian Biography Online.* 29 November 2015.

Bragge, William. *Peninsular Portrait 1811–1814: The Letters of Captain William Bragge.* London: Oxford University Press, 1963.

Bridgeman, Orlando. *A Young Gentleman at War: The Letters of Captain Orlando Bridgeman 1st Foot Guards in the Peninsula and at Waterloo 1812–15.* Gareth Glover (ed.). Godmanchester: Ken Trotman, 2008.

Brisbane, Thomas. *Reminiscences of General Sir Thomas Makdougall Brisbane.* Edinburgh: Privately Printed, 1860.

'Brisbane Observatory'. *Secret Scotland.* Online. 14 February 2015.

Bromley, Janet and David. *Wellington's Men Remembered: A Register of Memorials to Soldiers who Fought in the Peninsular War and at Waterloo.* 2 vols. Barnsley: Praetorian Press, 2012.

Brown, Steve. 'All Bound for Lisbon: British Army Movements to and from the Peninsula, 1808 to 1814'. *The Napoleon Series.* Multiple dates.

Brown, Steve. 'British Regiments and the Men Who Led Them 1793–1815'. *The Napoleon Series.* 29 September 2014.

Buckley, Roger N. (ed.). *The Napoleonic War Journal of Captain Thomas Henry Browne 1807–1815.* London: Army Records Society, 1987.

Buckner, Phillip. 'Whitworth-Aylmer, Matthew, 5th Baron Aylmer'. *Dictionary of Canadian Biography Online.* 30 December 2014.

Bunbury, Thomas. *Reminiscences of a Veteran.* 3 vols. Uckfield: Naval and Military Press, 2009.

Burke, Bernard. *Genealogical and Heraldic History of the Landed Gentry of Great Britain & Ireland.* 2 vols. London: Harrison, 1871.

Burke, John. *A Genealogical and Heraldic History of the Commoners of Great Britain and Ireland, Enjoying Territorial Possessions or High Official Rank.* London: H. Colburn, 1835.

Burke, John. *Burke's Genealogical and Heraldic History of the Landed Gentry.* 2 vols. London: Harrison, 1882.

Burnham, Robert. 'The British Expeditionary Force to Walcheren: 1809'. *The Napoleon Series.* 13 November 2014.

Burnham, Robert. *Charging against Wellington: The French Cavalry in the Peninsular War 1807–1814.* Barnsley: Frontline, 2011.

Burnham, Robert and Ron McGuigan. *The British Army against Napoleon.* Barnsley: Frontline, 2010.

'Byng, Sir John (1772–1860), of 6 Portman Square, Mdx. and Bellaghy, co. Londonderry'. *The History of Parliament Online.* 3 March 2015.

Cadell, Charles. *Narrative of the Campaigns of the Twenty-eighth Regiment, since Their Return from Egypt in 1802.* London: Whittaker, 1835.

Cameron, John. *The Letters of Lt. Colonel Sir John Cameron.* Godmanchester: Ken Trotman, 2013.

'Campbell, Henry Frederick (1769–1856)'. *The History of Parliament Online.* 17 March 2015.

Campbell, James. *A British Army, as It Was, – Is – and Ought to Be.* London: T&W Boone, 1840.

Cannon, Richard. *Historical Records of the British Army: The Sixth or Royal First Warwickshire Regiment.* London: Adjutant General's Office, 1837.

Cannon, Richard. *Historical record of the Thirty-Sixth, or the Herefordshire Regiment of Foot.* London: Parker, Furnivall and Parker, 1853.

Cannon, Richard. *Historical Record of the Sixty-First or, the South Gloucestershire Regiment of Foot.* London: Parker, Furnivall and Parker, 1844.

Cannon, Richard. *Historical record of the Thirty-Sixth, or the Herefordshire Regiment of Foot.* London: Parker, Furnivall and Parker, 1853.

Carew, Peter. 'A Gallant Pack'. *Blackwood's Magazine.* Vol. 260, 1946. Pages 391–401.

Challis, Lionel. 'The Peninsula Roll Call''. *The Napoleon Series Website.*

Celtic Magazine. Vol. I, November 1875–October 1876.

Clark-Kennedy, A.E. *Attack the Colour! The Royal Dragoons in the Peninsula and at Waterloo.* London: Research Publishing, 1975.

Cobbett, William. *Parliamentary Debates from the Year 1803 to the Present Time.* Vol. 12 & 13, 1812.

Codrington, Edward. *Memoir of the Life of Admiral Sir Edward Codrington.* 2 vols. Jane Bourchier (ed.). London: Longmans, Green, 1873.

Cole, John W. *Memoirs of British Generals Distinguished during the Peninsular War.* 2 vols. London: Richard Bentley, 1856.

Colville, John. *Portrait of a General.* Salisbury: Michael Russell, 1980.

Cotton, Edward. *A Voice from Waterloo.* East Ardsley: EP, 1974.

Dalrymple, Hew W. *Memoir, Written by General Sir Hew Dalrymple, Bart. Of His Proceedings as Connected with the Affairs of Spain, and the Commencement of the Peninsular War,* London: Thomas and William Boone, 1830.

de Ainslie, Charles. *Historical Record of the First or the Royal Regiment of Dragoons.* London: Chapman & Hall, 1887.

Delavoye, Alexander, M. *Life of Thomas Graham, Lord Lynedoch.* London: Richardson, 1880.

Dempsey, Guy. *Albuera 1811.* Barnsley: Frontline, 2008.

Dickson, Alexander. *The Dickson Manuscripts: Being Diaries, Letters, Maps, Account Books, with Various Other Papers of the Late Major-General Sir Alexander Dickson.* Leslie, John H. (ed.). 5 vols.; Cambridge: Ken Trotman; 1987.

Dictionary of National Biography. 22 vols. Oxford: Oxford University, 1886. [Referenced as *DNB.*]

Dobbs, John. *Recollections of an Old 52nd Man.* Staplehurst: Spellmount, 2000.

Douglas, John. *Tale of the Peninsula & Waterloo: 1808–1815.* Stanley Monick (ed.). Barnsley: Pen & Sword, 1997.

Duke of Buckingham. *Memoirs of the Court of George IV. 1820–1830.* 2 vols. London: Hurst and Blackett, 1859.

'Dunlop, James (1759–1832), of Dunlop, Ayr and Southwick, Kirkcudbright'. *The History of Parliament Online.* 17 April 2015.

D'Urban, Benjamin. *The Peninsular Journal, 1808–1817.* London: Greenhill, 1989.

'Ernst Georg Von Drieberg'. *FamilySearch Online.* 6 April 2015.

Estimate and Accounts: Army; Navy; Civil List; Pensions. 1817.

Estrela, Paulo J. *Ordens e Condecorações Portuguesas: 1793–1824.* Lisbon: Tribuna da História, 2009.

'Extracts from General Mackenzie's Diary'. Email from John Brewster to Rory Muir dated 3 December 2002.

Fane, Henry Edward. *Five Years in India.* 2 vols. London: Henry Colburn, 1842.

'Fane, Sir Henry (1778–1840), of Fulbeck, nr. Grantham, Lincs. and Avon Tyrell, Hants.' *The History of Parliament Online.* 27 April 2015.

'Ferguson, Sir Ronald Craufurd (1773–1841), of Muirtown, Fife and 5 Bolton Street, Mdx.' *The History of Parliament Online.* 13 May 2015.

Fisher, Herbert. *Studies in Napoleonic Statesmanship Germany.* New York: Haskell, 1982.

Fletcher, Ian. *The Waters of Oblivion: The British Invasion of the Rio de la Plata 1806–1807.* Barnsley: Pen & Sword, 2006.

Fortescue, John W. *A History of the British Army.* 13 vols. Uckfield: Naval & Military Press, 2004.

Frazer, Augustus S. *Letters of Colonel Sir Augustus Simon Frazer Commanding the Royal Horse Artillery in Army under the Duke of Wellington.* Uckfield: Naval and Military Press, 2001.

Fremantle, John. *Wellington's Voice: the Candid Letters of Lieutenant Colonel John Fremantle, Coldstream Guards, 1808–1837.* Glover, Gareth (ed.). Barnsley: Frontline, 2012.

French, Henry and Mark Rothery. *Man's Estate: Landed Gentry Masculinities, 1660–1900.* Oxford: University Press, 2012.

Fryer, Mary B. *Our Young Soldier: Lieutenant Francis Simcoe 6 June 1791–6 April 1812.* Toronto: Dundurn, 1996.

Gavin, William. *The Diary of William Gavin, Ensign and Quartermaster 71st Highland Regiment, 1806–1815.* Gareth Glover (ed.). Godmanchester: Ken Trotman, 2012.

General Orders, Portugal, Spain & France, 1809–1815. 7 vols. London: T. Egerton. 1811–1816.

Gentleman's Magazine. Various issues.

Gleig, George. *The Campaigns of the British Army at Washington and New Orleans, in the Years 1814–1815.* London: John Murray, 1836.

Gleig, George. *The Life of Major General Sir Thomas Munro.* London: Henry Colburn and Richard Bentley, 1831.

Glover, Gareth (ed.). *An Eloquent Soldier: The Peninsular War Journals of Lieutenant Charles Crowe of the Inniskillings, 1812–1814.* Barnsley: Frontline, 2011.

Glover, Gareth (ed.). *From Corunna to Waterloo: The Letters and Journals of Two Napoleonic Hussars, 1801–1816.* London: Greenhill, 2007.

Glover, Gareth (ed.). *Letters from the Battle of Waterloo: Unpublished Correspondence by Allied Officers from the Siborne Papers.* London: Greenhill, 2004.

Glover, Gareth (ed.). *The Waterloo Archive.* 6 vols. Barnsley: Frontline, 2010–2014.

Glover, Gareth. *Wellington's Lieutenant Napoleon's Gaoler: The Peninsular Letters & St Helena Diaries of Sir George Ridout Bingham.* Barnsley: Pen & Sword, 2005.

Glover, Gareth. *Waterloo: The defeat of Napoleon's Imperial Guard.* Barnsley: Frontline, 2015.

Glover, Michael (ed.). 'The Nightingall Letters'. *Journal of the Society for Army Historical Research,* Vol. 51, 1973. Pages 129–54.

Glover, Michael. *Wellington as Military Commander.* London: First Sphere Books, 1973.

Goff, Gerald. *Historical Records of the 91st Argyllshire Highlanders.* Argyllshire: R. Bentley & Son, 1891.

Gomm, William M. *Letters and Journals of Field-Marshal Sir William Maynard Gomm from 1799 to Waterloo 1815.* London: John Murray, 1881.

Gordon, Alexander. *A Cavalry Officer in the Corunna Campaign: 1808–1809.* Tyne & Wear: Worley Productions, 1990.

'Grant, Sir Colquhoun (c.1763–1835).' *The History of Parliament Online.* 18 May 2015.

Grattan, William. *Adventures with the Connaught Rangers: 1809–1814.* London: Greenhill, 1989.

Graves, James. *History, Architecture, and Antiquities of the Cathedral Church of St. Canice, Kilkenny.* Dublin: Hodges, Smith, & Co., 1857.

Gronow, Rees. *Captain Gronow's Last Recollections: Being the Fourth and Final Series of His Reminiscences and Anecdotes.* London: Smith, Elder, 1866.

Gronow, Rees. *Reminiscences of Captain Gronow.* London: Smith, Elder, 1862.

Hall, John A. *A History of the Peninsular War: The Biographical Dictionary of British Officers Killed and Wounded, 1808–1814.* London: Greenhill, 1998.

Hamilton, Frederick W. *The Origin and History of the First or Grenadier Guards.* 3 vols. London: John Murray, 1874.

Hannoverscher und Churfürstlich-Braunschweigisch-Lüneburgischer Staatskalender. 1819.

Harris, John. *The Recollection of Rifleman Harris*. Hibbert, Christopher (ed.). London: Leo Cooper, 1970.

Hay, Andrew Leith. *A Narrative of the Peninsular War*. 2 vols. Godmanchester: Ken Trotman, 2008.

Henegan, Richard. *Seven Years Campaigning in the Peninsula and the Netherlands, from 1808–1815*. 2 vols. Stroud: Nonsuch, 2005.

Henry, Walter. *Surgeon Henry's Trifles: Events of a Military Life*. London: Chatto & Windus, 1970.

Heydon, J.D. 'Brisbane, Sir Thomas Makdougall (1773–1860)'. *Australian Dictionary of Biography Online*. 2 February 2015.

Hill, Benson E. *Recollections of an Artillery Officer*. 2 vols. London: Richard Bentley, 1836.

Hitsman, J. Mackay. *The Incredible War of 1812*. Toronto: Robin Brass Studio, 2005.

Hunter, Archie. *Wellington's Scapegoat: The Tragedy of Lieutenant-Colonel Charles Bevan*. Barnsley: Pen & Sword, 2003.

Hurl-Eamon, Jennine. *Marriage and the British Army in the Long Eighteenth Century: 'The Girl I Left Behind Me'*. Oxford: Oxford University, 2014.

Hunt, Eric (ed.). *Charging against Napoleon: Diaries & Letters of Three Hussars*. Barnsley: Leo Cooper, 2001.

Hutton, James (ed.). *Selections from the Letters and Correspondence of Sir James Bland Burges*. London: J. Murray, 1885.

Jackson, George. *The Diaries and Letters of Sir George Jackson, K.C.H*. 2 vols. London: Richard Bentley, 1872.

Jennings, Louis J. (ed.). *The Croker Papers: The Correspondence and Diaries of the Late Right Honourable John Wilson Croker*. 3 vols. London: John Murray, 1885.

'John Lambert'. *Cricket Archive Online*. 14 August 2015.

Johnson, William T. 'Alan Cameron, a Scotch Loyalist in the American Revolution.' *Pennsylvania History*. Vol. 8, No. 1, January 1941. Pages 29–46.

Jones, John. *Journal of the Sieges Carried on by the Army under the Duke of Wellington in Spain*. 3 vols. Cambridge: Ken Trotman, 1998.

Jourdain, H.F. and Edward Fraser. *The Connaught Rangers*. 3 vols. London: Royal United Service Institution, 1924.

Journals of the House of Commons. Multiple volumes.

Journals of the House of Lords. Multiple volumes.

Jekyll, Nathaniel. *The Case of Nathaniel Jekyll, Esquire, Late a Captain in the Forty-Third Regiment of Foot …* London: Self-published, 1810.

'Kemmis of Shaen'. *The Family of Kemmis*. 7 August 2015.

Kennedy, Catriona. *Narratives of the Revolutionary and Napoleonic Wars: Military and Civilian Experience in Britain and Ireland*. New York: Palgrave Macmillan, 2013.

Kingsley, Nicholas. '(16) Palmer-Acland (later Fuller-Palmer-Acland) of Fairfield, baronets'. *Landed Families of Britain and Ireland*, 13 November 2014.

Kortzfleisch, Gustav von. *Geschichte des Herzoglich Braunschweigischen Infanterie–Regiments und seiner Stammtruppen 1809–1867*. Braunschweig: Limbach, 1896.

Landmann, George. *Recollections of My Military Life*. 2 vols. London: Hurst and Blackett, 1854.

Langwerth von Simmern, Heinrich. *Aus Krieg Und Frieden: Kulturhistorische Bilder Aus Einem Familienarchiv*. Wiesbaden: A. Deffner, 1906.

Larpent, Francis. *The Private Journal of F.S. Larpent, Judge Advocate General of the British Forces in the Peninsula Attached to the Head-quarters of Lord Wellington During the Peninsular War from 1812 to its Close*. 3 vols. London: Richard Bentley, 1853.

Leach, Jonathan *Rough Sketches of the Life of an Old Soldier*. Cambridge: Ken Trotman, 1986.

Le Marchant, Denis. *Memoirs of the Late Major General Le Marchant*. Staplehurst: Spellmount, 1997.

Leslie, Charles. *Military Journal of Colonel Leslie, K.H., of Balquhain whilst Serving with the 29th Regt. in the Peninsula, and the 60th Rifles in Canada, &c., 1807–1832*. Godmanchester: Ken Trotman, 2010.

L'Estrange, George. *Recollections of Sir George B. L'Estrange*. London: Sampson Low, 1874.

Liddell, R.S. *The Memoirs of the Tenth Royal Hussars*. London: Longmans Green, 1891.

MacKenzie, Alexander. *History of the Camerons*. Inverness: A. & W. MacKenzie, 1884.

'Mackenzie, John Randoll (c.1763–1809), of Suddie, Black Isle, Ross'. *The History of Parliament Online*. 19 April 2015.

Mackenzie, Morell. *A Manual of Diseases of the Throat and Nose*. New York: William Wood, 1880.

MacKenzie, Thomas. *Historical Records of the 79th Queens Own Cameron Highlanders*. London: Hamilton & Adams, 1887.

Mackinnon, Daniel. *Origin and Services of the Coldstream Guards*. 2 vols. London: Richard Bentley, 1833.

Mackinnon, Donald. *Memoirs of Clan Fingon*. London: Lewis Hepworth, 1894.

MacKinnon, Henry. *A Journal of the Campaign in Portugal and Spain, containing Remarks on the Inhabitants, Customs, Trade, and Cultivation, of Those Countries, from the Year 1809 to 1812*. This journal was published along with John Malcolm's *in Two Peninsular War Journals*. Cambridge: Ken Trotman, 1999.

Malcolm, John. *Reminiscences of a Campaign in the Pyrenees and South of France in 1814*. This journal was published along with Henry MacKinnon's in *Two Peninsular War Journals*. Cambridge: Ken Trotman, 1999.

Maclean, Loraine. *Indomitable Colonel*. London: Shepheard-Walwyn, 1986.

Massue, Melville Henry. *The Plantagenet Roll of the Blood Royal Being A Complete Table of All the Descendents Now Living of Edward III, King of England*. 5 vols. London: T.C. & E. C. Jack, 1905–1911.

McCavitt, John and Christopher T. George. *The Man Who Captured Washington: Major General Robert Ross and the War of 1812*. Norman: University of Oklahoma, 2016.

McGuffie, T.H. (ed.). *Peninsular Cavalry General: the Correspondence of Lieutenant-General Robert Ballard Long*. London: George G. Harrap, 1952.

Mikaberidze, Alexander (ed.). *Russian Eyewitness Accounts of the Campaign of 1807*. London: Frontline, 2015.

Mills, John. *For God and Country: The Letters and Diaries of John Mills, Coldstream Guards 1811–1814*. Staplehurst: Spellmount, 1995.

Milner, Edith. *Records of the Lumleys of Lumley Castle*. London: George Bell, 1904.

Mollo, John. *The Prince's Dolls: Scandals, Skirmishes and Splendours of the Hussars, 1739–1815*. Barnsley: Pen & Sword, 1997.

Moore, John. *The Diary of Sir John Moore*. J.F. Maurice (ed.). 2 vols. London: E. Arnold, 1904.

Moorsom, William. *Historical Record of the Fifty-second Regiment (Oxfordshire Light Infantry)*. London: Richard Bentley, 1860.

Morning Chronicle. 25 October 1810.

Morris, Thomas. *The Napoleonic Wars: Thomas Morris*. Hamden: Archon Books; 1968.

Mosse, R. *The Parliamentary Guide: A Concise Biography of the Members of Both Houses of Parliament*. London: A.H. Baily, 1837.

Mühlhan, Bernhard. 'Dörnberg, Wilhelm Kaspar Ferdinand Freiherr von'. *Deutsche Biographie Online*. 26 March 2015.

Muir, Rory et al. *Inside Wellington's Peninsular Army*. Barnsley: Pen and Sword, 2006.

Muir, Rory. *Salamanca: 1812*. New Haven: Yale, 2001.

Muir, Rory. *Wellington: The Path to Victory, 1769–1814*. New Haven: Yale, 2013.

Murchison, Arthur. *War before Science: Sir Roderick Impey Murchison's Youth, Army Service and Military Associates during the Napoleonic Wars*. Bethesda: Academica Press, 2014.

Nafziger, George. *Napoleon's German Enemies: The Armies of Hanover, Brunswick, Hesse-Cassel and the Hanseatic Cities (1792–1815)*. Privately published, 1990.

Namier, Lewis and John Brooke. *The House of Commons 1754–1790*. London: Boydell & Brewer, 1964. Pages 268–272.

Napier, Charles J. *Life and Opinions of General Sir Charles James Napier*. William Napier (ed.) 4 vols. London: James Murray, 1854.

Napier, George. *The Early Military Life of General Sir George T. Napier*. London: John Murray, 1886.

Napier, William F. *History of the War in the Peninsula and the South of France: From the Year 1807 to the Year 1814*. 6 vols. London: Constable, 1993.

Neale, Adam. *Letters from Portugal and Spain*. London: Richard Phillips, 1809.

New Companion to the Kalendar, a Guide to the Public Establishments of the United Kingdom. London: Suttaby, Evance, and Fox, 1820.

Nicols, Alistair. *Wellington's Switzers: The Watteville Regiment in Egypt, the Mediterranean, Spain and Canada*. Godmanchester: Ken Trotman, 2015.

'Nightingall, Sir Miles (1768–1829), of Redgrave Hall, Botesdale, Suff. and 29 York Place, Portman Square, Mdx.' *The History of Parliament Online*. 3 December 2015.

Oman, Charles. 'A Dragoon of the Legion'. *Blackwood's Magazine*. March 1913. Pages 293–309.

Oman, Charles. *A History of the Peninsular War*. 7 vols. Oxford: AMS, 1980.

Oman, Charles. *Wellington's Army, 1809–1814*. London: Greenhill Books, 1993.

Page, Julia. *Intelligence Officer in the Peninsula: Letters and Diaries of Major the Hon Edward Charles Cocks 1786–1812*. Tunbridge Wells: Spellmount, 1986.

Pakenham Letters 1800 to 1815. Godmanchester: Ken Trotman, 2009.

Panikkar, Margaret. *A Short Biography of Major General Daniel Hoghton: hero of Albuera*. Blackburn: Mararet Panikkar, 1993.

Parker, Derek. *Governor Macquarie: His Life, Times and Revolutionary Vision for Australia*. Warriewood: Woodslane Press, 2010.

Parliamentary Papers, House of Commons and Command, Relating to Courts of Justice; Prisons; Police; Magistracy; Constabulary. 8 vols. 1830–1831.

Parliamentary Papers, House of Commons and Command, Relating to Courts of Justice; Prisons; Police; Magistracy; Constabulary. 20 vols. 1846.

Parliamentary Papers, House of Commons and Command, Relating to Churches; First Fruits; Civil and Military Officers … 1830–1831.

Patterson, John. *Camps and Quarters; Scenes and Impressions of Military Life, Interspersed with Anecdotes of Various Well-known Characters Who Flourished in the War*. 2 vols. London: Saunders, 1843.

Patterson, John. *The Adventures of Captain John Patterson with Notices of the Officer, etc. of the 50th, or Queen's Own Regiment, from 1807 to 1821*. London: T. and W. Boone, 1837.

Pickles, Tim. *New Orleans 1815: Andrew Jackson Crushes the British*. London: Osprey Military, 1993.

Pearson, Andrew. *The Soldier Who Walked Away: The Autobiography of Andrew Pearson a Peninsular War Veteran*. Haley, Arthur H. (ed.). Liverpool: Bullfinch, c. 1991.

'Pleurel Effusion.' *WebMD*. 1 May 2015.

'Ponsonby, Hon. William (1772–1815), of the Manor of Goldsmith's Hall, co. Londonderry.' *The History of Parliament Online*. 29 January 2016.

'Pringle, Sir William Henry (?1771–1840), of 17 Stratford Place, Mdx.' *The History of Parliament Online*. 15 February 2016.

Reid, Stuart. *Wellington's Officers*. 3 vol. Leigh-on-Sea: Partizan Press, 2008.

Reilly, Robin. *The British at the Gates: The New Orleans Campaign in the War of 1812*. New York: Putnam, 1974.

Robertson, Duncan. *With Napoleon at Waterloo: And Other Unpublished Documents of the Waterloo and Peninsular Campaigns, Also Papers on Waterloo by the Late Edward Bruce Low*. London: Francis Griffiths, 1911.

Royal Military Calendar or Army Service and Commission Book. 5 vols. London, 1820. [Referenced as *RMC*.]

Royal Military Calendar or Army Service and Commission Book. London, 1815. [Referenced as *RMC 1815*.]

Royal Military Panorama or Officers' Companion. 4 vols. London: Barrington, 1811. [Referenced as *RMP* 1811.]

Royal Military Panorama or Officers' Companion. 4 vols. London: Barrington, 1814. [Referenced as *RMP* 1814.]

Ross-Lewin, Harry. *With the Thirty-Second in the Peninsular and other Campaigns*. Cambridge: Ken Trotman, 2000.

Sarginson, Diane. 'General Barnard Foord Bowes (?–1812)'. *Genforum*. 30 January 2015.

Schaumann, August L. *On the Road with Wellington: The Diary of a War Commissary in the Peninsular Campaigns*. London: Greenhill, 1999.

Scobie, I.H. Mackay. *An Old Highland Fencible Corps*. Edinburgh: Blackwood & Sons, 1914.

Scots Magazine; various volumes.

Seventh Report of the Commissioners of Military Enquiry. Office of the Secretary at War; 20 January 1809.

Sherer, Moyle. *Recollections of the Peninsula*. Staplehurst: Spellmount, 1996.

Siborne, Herbert. *Waterloo Letters*. London: Greenhill, 1993.

Sinclair, Joseph. *A Soldier of the Seventy-First: The Journal of a Soldier of the Highland Light Infantry 1806–1815*. Hibbert, Christopher (ed.). Warren: Squadron/Signal Publications, 1976.

Smith, George. *The Life of John Colborne, Field-Marshal Lord Seaton*. London: John Murray, 1903.

Smith, Harry. *The Autobiography of Sir Harry Smith 1787–1819: A Classic Story of Love and War*. London: Constable, 1999.

Smithies, Raymond. *Historical Records of the 40*th *(2nd Somersetshire) Regiment*. Privately published. 1894.

Smyth, B. *History of the XX Regiment: 1688–1888*. London: Simpkin, Marshall, 1889.

'Somerset, Lord Robert Edward Henry (1776–1842).' *The History of Parliament Online*. 21 March 2016.

Southey, Robert. *History of the Peninsular War*. 6 vols. London: John Murray, 1837.

Stanhope. James H. *Eyewitness to the Peninsular War and the Battle of Waterloo: the Letters and Journals of Lieutenant Colonel the Honourable James Stanhope 1803 to 1825*. Gareth Glover (ed.). Barnsley: Pen and Sword, 2010.

Steevens, Charles. *Reminiscences of My Military Life from 1795 to 1818*. Winchester: Warren & Son, 1878.

Stonestreet, George. *Recollections of the Scenes of which I was Witness in the Low Countries & France in the Campaigns of 1814 and 1815 and the Subsequent Occupation of French Flanders. The Journal and Letters of the Reverend George Griffin Stonestreet 1814–16*. Godmanchester: Ken Trotman, 2009.

'Stopford, Hon. Edward (1766–1837).' *The History of Parliament Online*. 4 April 2016.

Swabey, William. *Diary of Campaigns in the Peninsula for the Years 1811, 12 and 13*. London: Ken Trotman, 1984.

Thanks Voted by both Houses of Parliament to the Army and Navy ... 1803–1843. London: James & Luke James Hansard, 1843.

'The Fanes'. *The Ancestor*. Oswald Barron (ed.). Issue 12, January 1905.

'The Torrie Collection'. *University of Edinburgh Collections Online*. 23 April 2015.

Tomkinson, William. *The Diary of a Cavalry Officer: 1809–1815*. London: Frederick Muller, 1971.

'Trench Mouth'. *Healthline Online*. 12 April 2015.

United Service Journal. Various dates.

United Services Magazine. Various dates.

Universal Magazine, Volume XI, January–June 1809; pages 81–4, pages 349–51.

Vandeleur, John. *With Wellington's Outposts: The Peninsular and Waterloo Letters of John Vandeleur*. Andrew Bamford (ed.). Barnsley: Frontline, 2015.

Vivian, Claud. *Richard Hussey Vivian First Baron Vivian, a Memoir*. Cambridge: Ken Trotman, 2003.

'Vivian, Sir Richard Hussey (1775–1842), of Beechwood House, nr. Lyndhurst, Hants.' *The History of Parliament Online*. 4 May 2016.

Von Hinüber, Hartmut. Sir Henry (Heinrich) v. Hinüber. *Von Hinüber Familien Zeitung*. Number 79, December 1988.

Von Reumont, Alfred. *General the Right Honourable Sir Frederick Adam: a Sketch of Modern Times*. Privately printed, 1855.

Ward, S.G.P. *Wellington's Headquarters: A Study of the Administrative Problems in the Peninsula 1809–1814*. Oxford: Oxford University, 1957.

Warre, William. *Letters from the Peninsula: 1808–1812*. Staplehurst: Spellmount, 1999.

Wellington, Duke of. *The Dispatches of Field Marshal the Duke of Wellington, During his Various Campaigns in India Denmark, Portugal, Spain, the Low Countries, and France, from 1799 to 1818*. Edited by Lt.-Col. John Gurwood. 13 vols. London: John Murray; 1834–9. [Referenced as '*WD*']

——. Despatches, Correspondence, and Memoranda of Field Marshal Arthur, Duke of Wellington, K.G.: Edited by his son, the Duke of Wellington. 'in continuation of the former series' 8 vols. London: J. Murray, 1857–80. [Referenced as WND or Wellington's New Despatches]

——. *Dispatches of Field Marshal the Duke of Wellington, During his Various Campaigns in India Denmark, Portugal, Spain, the Low Countries, and France*. Edited by Lt.-Col. John Gurwood. 8 vols. London: Parker, Furnivall and Parker, 1844–1847. [Referenced as '*WD* (enlarged ed.)']

——. *Supplementary Dispatches, Correspondence, and Memoranda of Field Marshal Arthur Duke of Wellington, K.G.* Edited by the 2nd Duke of Wellington. Vols vi-xiv. London: John Murray, 1860–1871. [Referenced as '*WSD*'.]

Wheatley, William. 'Letters from the Front, 1812'. G.E. Hubbard (ed.). *United Services Magazine*; Vol. 58, 1919. Pages 432–51.

Whittingham, Ferdinand (ed.). *A Memoir of the Services of Sir Samuel Ford Whittingham*. London: Longmans, 1868.

'Wilhelm von Dörnberg'. German Wikipedia. 26 March 2015.

Williams, William R. *The Parliamentary History of the Principality of Wales, from the Earliest Times to the Present Day, 1541–1895*. Privately printed. 1895.

Wilson, Robert. *Brief Remarks on the Character and Composition of the Russian Army and a Sketch of the Campaigns in Poland in the Years 1806 and 1807*. London: Egerton, 1810.